LAND IS
ALL THAT
MATTERS

ALSO BY MYLES DUNGAN

*Four Killings: Land Hunger, Murder and
a Family in the Irish Revolution*

LAND IS ALL THAT MATTERS

THE STRUGGLE THAT SHAPED IRISH HISTORY

MYLES DUNGAN

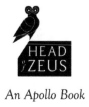

HEAD
ZEUS

An Apollo Book

First published in the UK in 2024 by Head of Zeus Ltd,
part of Bloomsbury Publishing Plc

9 7 5 3 1 2 4 6 8

A catalogue record for this book is available from the British Library.

ISBN (HB): 9781801108140
ISBN (XTPB): 9781035906499
ISBN (E): 9781801108164

Printed and bound in Great Britain by
CPI Group (UK) Ltd, Croydon CR0 4YY

Head of Zeus Ltd
First Floor East
5–8 Hardwick Street
London EC1R 4RG

WWW.HEADOFZEUS.COM

For Nerys

'And God said, "Let the water under the sky be gathered to one place, and let dry ground appear." And it was so. God called the dry ground "land" …'

(Genesis 1:9–10)

'When the Devil upon the mount did show Christ all the kingdoms of the earth and the glory of them, he did not doubt but the Devil left out Ireland, and kept it for himself.'

(Spanish commander Don Juan del Águila, after the Battle of Kinsale, 1601)

'Nothing irritates a quick-witted race (the Irish) like being governed by a slow-witted one.'

(The Spectator, 22 January, 1881)

Contents

Timeline

1608   The O'Neill and O'Donnell lands, as well as those of Sir Cahir O'Doherty, are confiscated and the Ulster Plantation begins during the reign of James I.

1653   The Cromwellian Plantation begins and Cromwellian soldiers are given Irish land.

1656   William Petty starts the process of surveying Irish land for redistribution in the Down Survey.

1703   The Gavelkind Act/Popery Act legalises the traditional Gaelic practice of subdividing lands among male descendants, but only for Catholic families. The English practice of primogeniture is maintained for Protestants. A Catholic eldest son can, however, inherit the entirety of his father's estate if he converts to Protestantism.

1711   The 'Houghers of Connacht' begin a violent campaign against the growth of pasture farming in the province. The agitation continues for two years.

1735   The Irish parliament exempts grasslands from tithe payments.

1741   An exceptionally harsh winter leads to a major famine, in which up to 400,000 people die (15–20 per cent of the population). This is a higher percentage than the morbidity rate caused by the Great Famine of the 1840s.

1756   The Seven Years' War begins between England and France, forcing up agricultural prices and the value of agricultural land.

1761   A major outbreak of Whiteboy violence erupts in Munster (mainly in Tipperary) over the activities of 'tithe farmers' and the enclosure of common land. Military intervention temporarily quells the disturbances.

A similar outbreak in Ulster is laid at the door of the secret society known as the Hearts of Oak/Oakboys.

1762 The Whiteboys march past barracks in Cappoquin, Co. Waterford in military fashion, with their pipers playing the Jacobite marching song 'The Lad with the White Cockade', prompting accusations of Jacobitism. Three men are executed in Cork and seven in Waterford for Whiteboy activities (mostly related to arson).

1763 A pitched battle takes place near Newtownstewart between members of the Hearts of Oak (Oakboys) secret society and three companies of the 68th regiment of foot. In August, a government proclamation grants amnesty to all Oakboys who quit the movement.

1764 Two soldiers and at least fourteen Whiteboy supporters are killed in the so-called 'Battle of Newmarket' after an attempt is made to free nine Whiteboys being escorted to Kilkenny gaol by a small detachment of dragoons.

1765 The 'Whiteboy' Act becomes law, decreeing the death penalty for a number of Whiteboy-type activities and conferring additional powers on local magistrates. In April, six of those found guilty of murder arising out of the events of the 'Battle of Newmarket' are publicly hanged in Kilkenny.

1766 Fr Nicholas Sheehy, parish priest of Clogheen in Co. Tipperary, is hanged for sedition arising out of the Whiteboy campaign.

1769 An agrarian secret society called the Hearts of Steel agitates against rent increases and evictions in Co. Antrim; when the agitation spreads to Armagh, the Steelboys (a Protestant secret society) ally with the Oakboys.

1770 On 23–4 December, hundreds of Steelboys threaten to burn the city of Belfast unless one of their members, David Douglas, is released from prison.

1772 The Battle of Gilford (Co. Down) begins with a protest by c.1,000 Steelboys against local landlord Richard

Johnston and ends in a gun battle in which Rev. Samuel
Morrell, an ally of Johnston, is killed.

1775 In a resurgence of Whiteboy violence, a Tipperary
landlord and magistrate, Ambrose Power, is murdered.
The Tumultuous Risings Act is introduced to deal with
agrarian crime. It is amended and extended in 1777.

1777 A Protestant agrarian secret society, the Peep O'Day
Boys, begins to agitate against tithes in parts of Ulster.
Members raid the homes of Roman Catholics on the
pretext of searching for illegal weapons.

1778 The Penal Law ban on Catholics holding a lease of more
than thirty-one years is repealed.

1779 Bishop Troy of Ossory pronounces a sentence of
excommunication against the membership of the
Whiteboys, some of whom are campaigning for a
reduction in dues owed to Catholic priests.

1780 Arthur Young's *A Tour in Ireland* is published.

1784 Foster's Corn Law introduces bounties on the export of
corn to Britain. This has the effect of increasing the land
area devoted to tillage. Revenues from tithes increase as a
consequence.
Clashes take place between members of the Peep O'Day
Boys and Co. Armagh Catholics.

1785 A Catholic agrarian secret society, the Defenders, is
formed to combat the activity of the Protestant Peep
O'Day Boys.
The Rightboys emerge as a new agrarian threat, with
notices posted near the town of Mallow warning locals
not to pay their tithes. Their campaign continues for three
years.

1786 In August, four Rightboys die after a skirmish with the
military at Rowe's Green near Cashel, Co. Tipperary.
A number of confrontations take place in Ulster between
the Peep O'Day Boys and Defenders.

1787 A Riot Act is introduced which, *inter alia*, makes many
of the symbolic but sinister activities of the Rightboys
(erecting gallows, digging graves) illegal.

In August, a force of 2,000 troops under Lord Luttrell is sent to Munster to quell the Rightboy insurgency.

1788 More clashes follow between the Peep O'Day Boys and Defenders, the former often backed up by members of the Volunteers.

1790 The Prophecies of Pastorini (pen name of the Roman Catholic Bishop Charles Walmsley) predicts the extirpation of Protestantism in Ireland in the 1820s.

1795 In the Battle of the Diamond, a force of Protestant Peep O'Day Boys defeats a force of Roman Catholic Defenders, killing up to thirty Defenders. Out of this confrontation, the Orange Order is formed.

1796 An Insurrection Act is passed to quell civil unrest.

1798 The rebellion of the United Irishmen organisation begins. It ends with the deaths of thousands of rebels, British military, Irish militia and civilians. The United Irishmen incorporate in their ranks many Defenders and other agrarian activists, often with their own localised agendas.

1800 Maria Edgeworth's *Castle Rackrent* is published.

1801 The Act of Union comes into effect, dissolving the Irish parliament in Dublin and sending 100 Irish MPs to the House of Commons in London.

1802 The Tipperary Whiteboy-type organisation the Moyle Rangers emerges in Munster. Its animosity is directed towards larger farmers, particularly graziers.

1806 A vigilante rival to the Moyle Rangers emerges in the form of a group that comes to be known as the Shanavests. This is composed of larger farmers, graziers, shopkeepers and middlemen.
The leader of the Moyle Rangers, Nicholas Hanley, is hanged in Clonmel. Arising out of Hanley's habit of wearing a cravat, the Moyle Rangers come to be known as the Caravats.
The Threshers of Connaught seek regulation of tithes and Roman Catholic priestly dues.

1807 The 1796 Insurrection Act is renewed to deal with the

activities of the Threshers in Connacht, Longford and Cavan.

1811   A Special Commission Grand Jury imposes severe sentences (execution and transportation) on a number of Caravats. This, allied to determined military intervention, brings the Caravat-Shanavest enmity to a temporary end.

1814   Chief secretary Robert Peel's Peace Preservation Act establishes a Peace Preservation Force, a mobile police force to be funded from local rates wherever it is deployed.

1815   Napoleon Bonaparte is defeated at the Battle of Waterloo, bringing an end to a period of almost unprecedented agricultural prosperity in Ireland.

1816   The distribution of volcanic ash from the eruption of Mount Tambora in Indonesia leads to the 'year without a summer'; this will have consequential effects for Irish agriculture, as there is a severe harvest failure.
An agrarian mob attacks Wildgoose Lodge in Co. Louth, and all the inhabitants (eight people, including a young child) are burned to death. Eighteen executions follow.

1817   Weather conditions, related in part to the 'year without a summer', lead to renewed famine conditions in Ireland; between 1817 and 1819, an estimated 65,000 people die of starvation and typhus.

1819   Four people die in anti-tithe riots in Co. Antrim.

1821   The rebellion of the Rockites (the followers of 'Captain Rock') begins on the Courtenay estate in Newcastlewest in Co. Limerick.
On 19 November, Rockites burn the house of well-to-do farmer Edmund Shea, killing sixteen people.

1822   In January, organised Rockite attacks take place in Millstreet and Macroom, Co. Cork and Newmarket, Co. Limerick. British military forces report a number of engagements with organised Rockite detachments.
In February, as many as nine women, members of a travelling party of a dozen wives of members of the 1st Rifle Brigade, are gang-raped by Rockites after being

stopped on the road near Kildorrery, Co. Cork.

Thirty-six Rockite executions take place in the month of February alone.

An Insurrection Act is introduced, bringing a sunset-to-sunrise curfew to parts of Munster and summary justice (non-jury trials) for those found in breach of the coercion legislation. Eight counties are proclaimed, 1,500 are arrested and brought to trial, and 200 are jailed or transported.

The Irish Constabulary Act establishes a police force in each of the four provinces.

The country experiences another major subsistence crisis.

1823   The passage of the first of three Tithe Composition Acts (also 1824 and 1827) restores the levying of tithes on pasture land. Graziers are brought into the tithe net for the first time since 1735.

Thirteen protestors and three policemen die at a tithe riot in Castlehaven, Co. Cork in July after an attempt to distrain cattle for the payment of tithe arrears to Rev. Morritt of Skibbereen.

1824   Some Protestants take the Pastorini-inspired threat of a bloody Catholic revolt so seriously that they remain awake all night on 24 December, prepared for murderous attacks.

The Rockite unrest dwindles as a result of military intervention and improved harvests.

1825   The Ordnance Survey begins to map Ireland. Its work is completed in 1846.

1827   Richard Griffith is appointed Commissioner of Valuation for Ireland. He holds the position until 1868.

1828   The agrarian secret society the Terry Alts is established in Corofin, Co. Clare.

1829   The passage of the Roman Catholic Relief Act (Catholic Emancipation) clears a path for Catholics into public office, including parliament.

Bishop James Doyle, bishop of Kildare and Leighlin (JKL), issues the first of three pastoral letters against

Whiteboy/Whitefeet activities in November.

The Sub-Letting Act makes it, in theory at least, impossible for tenants to sub-let without a landlord or agent's permission.

1830 The potato crop partially fails, leading to a subsistence crisis.

Anti-tithe agitation in Graiguenamanagh, led by Fr Martin Doyle, signals the beginning of the Tithe War. It quickly spreads to other parts of the county and neighbouring Tipperary.

The Griffith valuation process begins.

1831 Captain William Blood, land agent of Lord Stradbrooke, is murdered by the Terry Alts on 21 January. Terry Alt violence reaches its peak, with over 1,000 recorded incidents in April.

In the Newtownbarry massacre (Co. Wexford), Irish constabulary kill twelve people attempting to prevent the seizure of cattle (18 June).

In the Carrigshock massacre (Co. Kilkenny), at least twelve constables are killed by an angry crowd (14 December).

The Irish Board of Works is established; it spends £49 million on public works projects up to 1914.

1833 The Report of the Royal Commission on the Poorer Classes in Ireland ultimately leads to the passage of the Irish Poor Law Act in 1838.

The Church Temporalities Act reduces the number of Church of Ireland bishops and abolishes an additional levy, the 'parish cess' tax.

1834 A pitched battle/faction fight takes place between the Lawlors/Mulvihills and the Cooleens on Ballyveigh Strand in Kerry in June, and is reported to have left up to 200 people dead.

Twelve anti-tithe protestors are killed in Rathcormac (Co. Cork) by members of the constabulary, reinforced by the British Army (18 December).

1835 Alexis de Tocqueville and Gustave de Beaumont tour

Ireland during the summer; both leave important accounts of their journeys.

Thomas Drummond is appointed Irish under-secretary and ends the practice of police escorts for tithe distraint or collection.

1836   A further subsistence crisis, verging on famine, afflicts the country.

The Constabulary Act establishes the paramilitary rural-based Irish Constabulary and the unarmed Dublin Metropolitan Police.

In the last serious affray of the Tithe War, two people are killed in Dunkerrin, King's County, on 21 October.

1837   Queen Victoria succeeds her uncle William IV to the English throne, and the Victorian era begins.

1838   The Tithe Rent-charge Act reduces the level of tithe payments and leaves the bulk to be paid by landlords, who then pass it on to the tenants in the form of increased rent.

The Irish Poor Law Act establishes local Poor Law Unions and creates a system of poor relief in Ireland. The building of workhouses begins. Almost all are completed in time to be overwhelmed by the Great Famine.

1839   On 6 January – 'The Night of the Big Wind' – a gale/ hurricane ravages rural Ireland.

The building of the country's workhouses gets underway.

1841   The population of Ireland is 8,175,000.

1843   The first railway in Ireland from Dublin to Kingstown opens; the railway network will later expand through rural Ireland.

1845   The Devon Commission reports on the operation of leases in Ireland and deems tenants to be lacking basic protections.

The presence of *Phytophthora infestans* (potato blight) is detected in Ireland, and there is a partial failure of the potato crop. The Peel administration takes some corrective action by importing Indian corn from the USA.

1846   There is a catastrophic failure of the potato crop and a widespread subsistence crisis.

'Outdoor relief' in the form of public works employs more than 100,000 people.

The Repeal of the Corn Laws by the Peel administration leads, ultimately, to the installation of a Whig government under Lord John Russell.

The public works policy of the Tory government is at first continued by the new Whig administration but is then abandoned in favour of soup kitchens.

1847   There is no recurrence of potato blight, but the acreage of potatoes planted is extremely small and famine conditions continue.

The Poor Law Amendment Act passes into law, reasserting the principle that 'Irish property must pay for Irish poverty'. The 'Gregory clause' ensures that the new Poor Law Act gives landlords licence to clear their estates of indigent tenants.

The Destitute Poor Act is passed, under which soup kitchens are opened in March and close by the end of September, after feeding up to 3 million people a day.

On 2 November, Strokestown estate landlord Major Denis Mahon is murdered in Roscommon.

1848   Potato blight returns and devastates the (relatively small) potato crop.

The Ulster Tenant Right Association is founded by journalist James MacKnight and the radical MP from Co. Down, William Sharman Crawford. The aim of the association is to secure the formal legalisation of the Ulster Custom.

1849   Ireland experiences a major cholera epidemic.

The Encumbered Estates Act is passed to enable the purchase of bankrupt Irish estates. An Estates Court is established to expedite the sale of the holdings of insolvent landlords, reckoned to be up to 25 per cent of the landed aristocracy.

The sectarian skirmish/battle at Dolly's Brae pitches Orangemen against Catholic Ribbonmen, resulting in up to thirty deaths.

1850　The Tenant Right League (or the Tenant League) is formed by Charles Gavan Duffy and Frederick Lucas. Its aim is to secure the '3Fs' for Irish tenant farmers.

1851　The population of Ireland falls to 6,552,000.

1852　Members of the Orange Order attack and disrupt Tenant League election meetings.

Forty-eight 'pledged' Tenant League/Irish Independent Party (IIP) MPs are returned to parliament in the general election, but only one is from Ulster.

The IIP, holding the balance of power, engineers the defeat of the incumbent Tory government of Lord Derby. Two members of the IIP, William Keogh and John Sadleir, despite prior pledges, accept positions in the incoming Whig/Peelite administration of Lord Aberdeen.

1853　The Great Munster Fair in Limerick proves to be a triumph for cattle breeders and jobbers, as the country moves inexorably from tillage to pasture.

1854　The Catholic Defence Association (whose members are nicknamed 'The Pope's Brass Band') abandons the Tenant League at the behest of the Archbishop of Dublin, Paul Cullen.

Agricultural prices rise with the onset of the Crimean War. This challenges the relevance of the Tenant League, which goes into a rapid decline.

1861　Landlord John George Adair evicts forty-seven families in order to clear 12,000 acres of mountain land on his estate near Glenveagh, Co. Donegal, earning himself the nickname 'Black Jack Adair'.

1867　The second Reform Act increases the size of the franchise for parliamentary elections.

1869　The Church Disestablishment Act abolishes tithes and sells off some Church of Ireland land to tenants.

1870　Gladstone's first Land Act becomes law. A clause inserted at the instigation of the radical MP John Bright offers tenants the opportunity to buy out their landlords. The terms are not sufficiently attractive to tempt many tenants.

1871　The Protection of Life and Property (Ireland) (the

'Westmeath' Act), a new piece of coercion legislation, becomes law in response to agitation in the midland counties of Westmeath, Meath and King's County (Offaly).

1872   The Ballot Act ensures the secrecy of individual votes in future elections and greatly weakens the grip of landlords on the electoral process.

1873   Charles Kickham's popular novel *Knocknagow* or *The Homes of Tipperary* is published.
John Mitchel's polemic *The Last Conquest of Ireland (Perhaps)* is published.
The 'Panic of '73' leads to a serious economic recession in the USA. The resultant fall in agricultural prices there eventually seeps into the UK economy.

1875   Charles Stewart Parnell is elected MP for Meath in a by-election.

1877   There are the beginnings of renewed agricultural crisis in Ireland, which is especially evident in the west of the country, Mayo in particular.

1878   On 2 April, Lord Leitrim is murdered in Donegal after a threat to evict twenty families.

1879   The threat of famine in the west of Ireland spurs former Fenian Michael Davitt to organise a Land League in Mayo; by October, this has become the Irish National Land League.
An increase in agrarian crime across parts of the country – a response to falling prices and an increased eviction rate – signals the beginning of the Land War.
A large public meeting takes place at Irishtown, Co. Mayo on 20 April, designed to secure rent abatements from a local landlord.

1880   The new leader of the Irish Parliamentary Party, Charles Stewart Parnell, declares in a speech in Ennis, Co. Clare on 19 September that if a tenant is evicted and somebody else takes over their land land, that person (a so-called 'land grabber') is to be ostracised by his neighbours and local merchants.
One of the first people subjected to this treatment

(though not himself a 'land grabber') is the agent of Lord Erne, Captain Charles Boycott. A new verb enters the English language, 'to boycott'.

On 25 September, Lord Mountmorres is murdered near his home in Clonbur, Co. Galway.

1881 A Royal Commission under Lord Bessborough reports that the 1870 Land Act has fallen short when it comes to rectifying land tenancy issues. This paves the way for new legislation to be introduced by the Liberal government of William E. Gladstone.

The Property Defence Association (also known as the Emergency Committee or the Orange Emergency Committee) is established in January to provide assistance to landlords wishing to evict tenants. Led by Norris Goddard, its employees become known as 'emergency men'.

The Protection of Persons and Property (Ireland) Act introduces coercion measures to deal with agrarian crime.

Gladstone's second Land Act becomes law, granting the 3Fs but with little satisfaction for tenants in arrears or on long-term leases. Another purchase clause is included in land legislation, but once again the terms are not sufficiently attractive to entice many tenants to buy.

The leadership of the Land League is arrested and the league itself is proscribed. The Ladies Land League assumes leadership of the ongoing land agitation.

The No Rent Manifesto is the response of the Land League to the arrests.

Land Courts/Arbitration Courts begin to assess rents on estates around the country and reduce rents by up to 20 per cent.

1882 The so-called 'Kilmainham Treaty' ends agrarian agitation with the promise of an Arrears Act.

Five members of the Joyce family of Maamtrasna are murdered. Maolra Seoighe is one of three men hanged for the murders.

Lord Frederick Cavendish and Thomas H. Burke are murdered in Phoenix Park.

A new Crimes Act for Ireland is enacted.

The Arrears of Rent (Ireland) Act rectifies one of the failings of the 1881 Land Act by ensuring that those in arrears of rent can benefit from rent arbitration.

1885　The Ashbourne Act, named after the Tory Irish Lord Chancellor, becomes the first piece of land purchase legislation to persuade a significant number of Irish tenants to purchase their farms from their landlords.

1886　The Plan of Campaign begins after an article by Irish National League secretary Timothy Harrington in *United Ireland*.

1887　Arthur Balfour becomes chief secretary for Ireland. To combat agrarian unrest and the Plan of Campaign, he introduces a new Crimes Act.

The 1887 Land Act, also brought in by Balfour, contains more tenant purchase clauses.

On 9 September, a public demonstration in Mitchelstown in support of the Plan of Campaign turns violent, and the Royal Irish Constabulary (RIC) are responsible for the deaths of three demonstrators.

The Bodyke evictions on the Co. Clare estate of Colonel John O'Callaghan begin in late May.

1888　In April, a papal rescript condemns the Plan of Campaign and deprecates the practice of boycotting.

1889　Evictions begin on the Galway estate of the Earl of Clanricarde.

1890　The Parnellite split occurs in the wake of the O'Shea divorce trial.

1891　Parnell dies. The IPP split continues despite his death.

The 1891 Land Purchase Act is introduced by Arthur Balfour. It improves the purchase terms for tenants over those of the Ashbourne Act and makes the Land Commission permanent.

The Congested Districts Board is established as a means of alleviating poverty in 'congested' areas of the country, mainly in the west and north-west.

1894　The Irish Land and Labour Association (ILLA), led by

D. D. Sheehan and James O'Shee, is formed to agitate on
behalf of labourers and smallholders.

The Irish Agricultural Organisation Society is founded by
Sir Horace Plunkett and spearheads the new co-operative
movement.

1896   Amendments to the 1891 Land Act, introduced by
chief secretary Gerald Balfour, allow for further tenant
purchase. The Land Courts are permitted to sell 1,500
bankrupt estates.

1898   The Local Government Act brings an end to the Grand
Jury system and further reduces aristocratic influence.
William O'Brien forms the agrarian organisation the
United Irish League (UIL) in response to a renewal
of adverse economic conditions west of the Shannon.
The new organisation grows rapidly and becomes more
politicised as it does so.

1900   The Irish Parliamentary Party reunites under the auspices
of the United Irish League and on account of the serious
political threat posed by O'Brien's organisation. John
Redmond becomes party leader.

1901   T. W. Russell MP resigns from the South Tyrone
Unionist association and forms the Ulster Farmers' and
Labourers' Union and Compulsory Sale Association to
lobby for the compulsory purchase of landed estates.

1902   A 3 September letter to a number of newspapers, from
Galway landlord Captain John Shawe-Taylor, advocates
a conference of tenants and landlords to resolve ongoing
tensions.

The Land Conference is chaired by Lord Dunraven and
includes representatives of landlords and tenants. The two
sides agree on a new plan for tenant purchase.

1903   The Wyndham Land Purchase Act is shepherded through
parliament by Chief Secretary George Wyndham. It is
based on the agreement reached at the Land Conference.

1906   The Labourers (Ireland) Act is the first of three pieces of
legislation that provides for the building of accommodation
for agricultural labourers on an acre of land.

The so-called 'Ranch War' begins, a conflict between wealthy graziers and small farmers and/or landless labourers. It is characterised by the tactic of 'cattle driving'.

1909   The Birrell Land Purchase Act extends the scope of the 1903 legislation by allowing for the compulsory acquisition of farmland in a greater number of instances. The legislation, however, also introduces landlord disincentives to sell.

The new land purchase legislation leads to a (temporary) halt of cattle driving, and the Ranch War comes to an end.

1914   The era of tenant purchase under the Union effectively comes to an end with the beginning of World War I and the suppression of budgetary largesse.

1915   A rise in agricultural prices brings a measure of prosperity to many large Irish farmers but also raises the costs of agricultural land for small farmers and landless labourers.

1916   More than 1,000 British soldiers – assisted by more than 100 police constables – are deployed on the Roscommon and Galway border to bring an end to a renewed spate of cattle driving.

1917   Anti-grazier activity, including land seizures and cattle driving, begins once again. The new campaign has the full support of the Sinn Féin party.

1918   In December, just over a month after the Great War armistice, Sinn Féin sweeps most of the Irish constituencies in the UK general election, winning seventy-three seats to the IPP's six.

The incidence of land seizure increases in the west of Ireland.

1919   In January, Dáil Éireann convenes in the Mansion House. Only Sinn Féin members attend. On the same day, the first shots of the War of Independence are fired at Soloheadbeg in Co. Tipperary.

1920   Frank Shawe-Taylor from Ardrahan, Co. Galway, a land agent and relative of Lady Gregory, is murdered in an attack related to local animosities over grazing land.

IRA Volunteer Mark Clinton is murdered by an agrarian

gang in Meath in a local land dispute; his killer is later executed by the IRA.

A number of loyalist landowners in West Cork have their land seized by local agrarian activists.

In June, Dáil Éireann issues an order against illegal land seizures.

1921   RIC crime statistics establish that 1920 was the worst year for agrarian crime since 1882.

On 11 July, a truce between the IRA and the Crown forces comes into effect.

On 6 December, the Anglo-Irish Treaty is signed in London, clearing the way for the establishment of an Irish Free State.

1922   In December, with the Civil War continuing, Agriculture Minister Patrick Hogan sends a memo ('Seizures of land') to cabinet, warning about the frequency of the illegal occupation of land around the country.

1923   The Land Law (Commission) Act becomes the first land legislation passed by the Irish Free State government. Money owed to the British government under previous land purchase schemes will be paid as 'land annuities' from a Land Purchase Fund. The Congested Districts Board is abolished and its employees move to a reconstituted Land Commission.

1925   The Land Bond Act is passed. The British Treasury underwrites £30 million in Free State land purchase bonds.

1926   Éamon de Valera abandons Sinn Féin and forms the Fianna Fáil party.

The Ultimate Financial Settlement between the Irish Free State and Britain provides for the collection of annuities by the Irish government and their remission to Britain. Decrees for annuity payment arrears are issued to a number of farmers by the Free State government.

An Poblacht, the IRA newspaper, edited by socialist and republican journalist Peadar O'Donnell, begins a campaign against the further payment of land annuities to the British government.

1927   A new land law outlaws the subdivision or sub-letting, without permission, of Land Commission-allocated holdings. Measures are also introduced to provide for the recovery of land annuities and arrears by the commission.

1932   Fianna Fáil becomes the largest party in Dáil Éireann and takes power with support from the Labour Party.

1933   A Land Act introduced by the new Fianna Fáil government allows the annuity sum, previously paid to the British government, to be diverted to local government funding. This sparks the 'Economic War' between Ireland and the UK.
        The Land Act also gives the government greater powers to acquire agricultural land for redistribution.

1935   Gaeltacht colony #1 is established with the relocation of a number of families from the west of Ireland to land in Rathcairn, Co. Meath.

1936   The Fianna Fáil government introduces a new Land Act, further extending the remit of the Land Commission.

1937   Gaeltacht colony #2 is established with the relocation of a number of families from the west of Ireland to land in Gibbstown, Co. Meath.

1938   An agreement between Ireland and the UK ends the Economic War and the land annuities issue is finally settled with a one-off payment of £10 million.

Preface

We are where we were!

ON THE AFTERNOON of Sunday, 28 November 2010, this writer should have been getting ready for the weekly broadcast of *The History Show* on RTÉ Radio 1. Instead, because of the calamitous ramifications of Ireland's obsession with land/property, I was forced to abandon the script for that night's programme and instead prepare to present an improvised broadcast of indeterminate length – it turned into a three-hour marathon – timed to coincide with the announcement of the details of the financial bailout agreed between the ill-starred Fianna Fáil/Green Party coalition government and the process-servers of the International Monetary Fund (IMF). The agreement to be announced after the humiliating 'take it or leave it' negotiations was designed to stave off bankruptcy and forestall Ireland's descent into an economic netherworld where we would buddy up with Argentina.

On that night in 2010, when the obligatory press conference finally got underway and we could stop filling dead air with speculation, Ireland became familiar with the softly accented vowels of the IMF's Ajai Chopra. He would soon become a mysteriously popular, if relentlessly nerdy, celebrity on Irish media, but that night he was Nemesis in a well-cut suit. Chopra dispassionately outlined how Ireland would be required to lavish upon our zombie banks three-quarters of the pot of money lodged in one of the few fiscally imaginative legacies of the Celtic Tiger – the National Pension Reserve Fund. This amounted to a heart-stopping €17.5 billion. Chopra could afford to be dispassionate, as it wasn't his money. It was our 'rainy day' fund, now being deployed in the face of an economic tsunami. It was also but a small fraction of the gobsmacking €85 billion reckoning now owed by a small country that had been mainlining property for more than a decade and was about to go cold turkey.

Just to labour the fowl metaphor, offstage could clearly be heard the clucking of chickens coming home to roost.

It would be fair to say that the Irish have something of a commitment to the ownership of property: 'commitment' being a euphemism for obsession. Our affinity for bricks, mortar, grass and hedges enticed us towards the craggy cliffs of the worst economic crisis (2008–15) since the Great Depression of the 1930s, when, among many other consequences, property values imploded, declining by half. In Ireland, however, that represented a 50 per cent discount on the cost of a modest Irish suburban home, which previously had been priced at Fifth Avenue or Knightsbridge levels.

One of the most grating clichés of those far-from-halcyon days was the faux philosophical 'We are where we are'. It was a dismissive but distressed *moue* on the part of the disenchanted. It was the last refuge of a beleaguered government minister ignoring his handler's advice about grace under pressure when faced with a barrage of snippy questions from journalists. Far more galling than this neo-Gallic shrug, however, was the rather obvious question running alongside, namely: 'How did we get to where we are?' Surely we could just as easily have binged on gold and got our fingers burned in precious metals. We could have placed our faith and our savings in tulips, as the Dutch had done centuries before. A few years on and we could have lost our shirts on cryptocurrencies. But we had to steer the good ship *Hibernia* onto the rocks of real estate procurement. Could anything have been more Irish?

The urbanisation of Ireland cannot alter the fact that most town-dwellers are but a generation or two removed from the land. Dubliners have a word for it. Anyone whose grandparents were not born and bred within a metropolis defined by two random canals is labelled a 'culchie'. The word is intended by metropolitans as a provocative insult. Most 'culchies', however, see it as a badge of honour. We might not actually know one end of a cow from the other, but we like to pretend that we do and that somehow, despite a familial absence from the land of a century or more, we are still, at heart, sons and daughters of the soil.

From the early 1800s to the 1960s, our fixation was largely with the acquisition and ownership of agricultural land. Anything to escape those 'pastures poor with greedy weeds', in the words of the Meath poet Francis Ledwidge, who never managed to acquire any of his own before his death in 1917 at the Third Battle of Ypres. Such was the passion for acquisition that it could take precedence over husbandry: 'the desire to accumulate more acres often overrode the desire to farm productively'.[1] Then came a sudden gush of economic growth; membership of the European Economic Community (now the European Union); and a spurt of urban sprawl like an unattractive middle-aged paunch. Our focus shifted from a few extra acres of arable land to the three-bed semi with a footprint that, to our 'culchie' grandparents, would have been smaller than a kitchen garden. But make no mistake, we took our land fixation with us from rural Ireland to the growing cities around our coast. We just stopped calling it 'land' and renamed it 'property'. We even jettisoned the wisdom implied in the mantra 'location, location, location'. By the late 1990s, we were flocking to the launch at a Dublin hotel of luxury apartments in Auckland (yes, the one in New Zealand) and allowing the travelling Antipodean PR team to abandon the rest of their projected European sales tour because they had nothing left to offload. Dubliners had snapped up every studio and penthouse in an urban village 19,000 kilometres away.

The frenzy of the Celtic Tiger also convinced far too many of us that it was possible – our persuasive lenders went as far as to suggest that it was desirable – to own that three- or four-bed suburban 'semi' while simultaneously joining the *rentier* class by purchasing an apartment, perhaps two, or maybe even three, and renting them out. Where, one wonders, did we hit upon the idea that property values were no longer governed by the laws of economic gravity? It was as if we were a nation of archers who loosed arrows into the sky, watched them rise towards the sunlight, and then turned our backs to rearm just before they reached their apex and fell to the ground. We seemed to be culpably and idyllically unaware of that most instructive of proverbs, 'what goes up, must come down'. Granted, economic gravity does not always operate precisely according to a Newtonian script – sometimes the financial arrows don't fall all the way back to earth as the real ones tend to. But, from time to time, they do just that. In the world of economics, it leads to a 'global financial crisis' and is related to something called 'illiquidity'. The journalistic terms 'crash' or 'panic' somehow seem more apt and accessible. That is what happened in 2008, when our backs were turned as we reloaded our quivers. For two years, we swallowed assurances about something called a 'soft landing' until the arrows finally returned to earth, points facing downwards.

Just before the Celtic Tiger began to roar, buy overpriced champagne in Lillie's Bordello or do whatever that mythical creature did, in 1990 writer/director Jim Sheridan put together an excellent cast and made a film of John B. Keane's stage drama *The Field*. You probably know it. It's a story set in the 1930s about the murderous rivalry caused by the sale of a few acres of land in Keane's native Kerry. In retrospect, the film was like a bridge between two worlds. In the first of these – the regressive, peasant society we liked to think that we had long since abandoned – the returning 'Yank', Peter, played by Tom Berenger, was a legitimate target for the unwavering fury of the Bull McCabe (perfectly captured in a towering performance by Richard Harris). In that world, no one, not even God himself, had the right to intervene between the Bull and his dream of acquiring *his* field from the Widow (Frances Tomelty) at whatever price he was prepared to pay, given that he had frightened off all the other potential purchasers. The land being bought by the gazumping Yank, in all justice, belonged to the Bull. Had he not rented and improved it like a tenant farmer of the nineteenth century? To be outbid for his few meagre acres would be an insufferable wrench.

But that was in another country. Ireland had moved on. From the other side of the bridge the scenario being played out in *The Field* was atavism at its worst. We were now in the 1990s, had been members of the modernising European Union for nearly two decades and had almost reached the soccer World Cup semi-finals. We could afford to admire the writing, direction and performances in *The Field* without bothering too much about the themes and tropes. It was an excellent and thoroughly entertaining period piece – a throwback.

Except that it was no such thing. The Yank in *The Field* was now that chancer with cash who arrived just before you and nabbed the last apartment on sale in the new development far removed from anywhere you actually *wanted* to live. The only thing that had fundamentally changed was that, when it came to 'land' or 'property', we stopped shooting each other in the face and started shooting ourselves in the foot. To say that it all went pear-shaped in 2008 is to transfer our own irresponsibility onto an inoffensive fruit.

Because when it comes to real estate, the Irish have a long, chequered and often tragic history. It divides us to this day. Issues of inheritance and land transfer ensured that the first tentative efforts to introduce divorce in Ireland in 1986 came to naught. Developers and local authorities are denounced for their failure to exploit banks of land in their possession, the former retaining these parcels for their own greater profit, the latter because of a lack of the funds required to build reasonably priced houses on the land. As recently as 13 April 2022, former Justice Minister Michael McDowell, hardly a bloodthirsty radical, warned in his weekly *Irish Times* column about 'a large and growing transformation of property ownership in Ireland – investment in Irish farmland by wealthy people as part of their personal asset portfolios'. This, McDowell pointed out, might cause 'Irish agriculture to revert after a century and a half to a landlord/tenant sector where the rich and powerful own the land and farmers toil to pay them rent. It's not just our urban homeowners who are being shunted into tenant status.'

We are where we were!

Should this phenomenon continue, the country awaits a new Michael Davitt – although the original may have wanted to rise from the dead in 2017 to smite the leadership of the so-called 'New Land League' as it made common cause with the repossessed owners of a modest €9.5 million mansion on Vico Road in Dalkey in south Co. Dublin, which Bank of Ireland had acquired in part settlement of a €71 million debt.[2]

On a more visceral level, in Co. Cork in 2020, three members of the O'Sullivan family of Assolas, near Kanturk, died in a murder-suicide dispute related to land.[3] In June 2023, three men were jailed for fifteen years each for an attack of 'calculated cruelty'[4] (in Strokestown, Co. Roscommon, in 2018) that was a twenty-first-century echo of Land League attempts to repossess evicted farms from 'caretaker' bailiffs in the 1880s. Violent frenzy over Irish property did not suddenly subside after an appalled nation was forced to engage with the horrors of the Carrigshock killings of 1831 (Chapter 7) or the Maamtrasna massacre of 1882 (Chapter 12).

The final painful popping of the bubble in 2010 was supposed to teach us all a lesson. Property prices would never again return to the levels of 2007 (they have, and shoe boxes are fetching a king's ransom again). Young couples would never again struggle to raise enough money for a deposit on an overpriced house (they do, and many of them are emigrating to countries where two respectable salaries are enough to buy a home). The *rentier* – Thomas Piketty's *mot du jour* – would disappear, and 'owner occupation' of houses and apartments would return to pre-Tiger levels of more than 90 per cent (they haven't: the numbers in rented accommodation have doubled in the last two decades). The distinguished *Irish Times* columnist and historian Fintan O'Toole highlighted this last statistic as recently as July 2022, in a column in which he reminded his readers of an anti-landlord couplet from the nineteenth century:

Like Egypt's king he'll not relint
The gintleman that takes the rint.

O'Toole observed that 'the end of tenancy was, at the level of ordinary families, the equivalent of the achievement of statehood – both were declarations of independence',[5] before acknowledging the irony that a nation that had spent decades attempting to rid itself of landlords had now reinstated the 'The gintleman that takes the rint' with transfers from tenant to property-owner now becoming an urban phenomenon.

What follows is a narrative that fills in some of the gaps on the Bull McCabe side of that hypothetical bridge. It might be of some interest in the context of the real estate obsession of the Irish and may offer some insights into the answer to that question that haunted us in 2010: 'How did we get here?'

Introduction

'History is not the past – it is the method we have
evolved of organising our ignorance of the past.'

(Hilary Mantel, *Guardian*, 3 June 2017)

'"Land is the only thing in the world that amounts to
anything," he shouted, his thick, short arms making wide
gestures of indignation. "For 'tis the only thing in this world
that lasts, and don't you be forgetting it! 'Tis the only thing
worth working for, worth fighting for, worth dying for.'"[1]

(Gerald O'Hara to his daughter Scarlett in *Gone with the Wind*)

THERE IS OUR history. Then there are the tales we tell about
ourselves.

'Held in fee simple' – it's a phrase whose roots lie in feudal
times, well-known in the legal profession, and perhaps vaguely
familiar to anyone who has ever bought a house or a farm. But that
modest legal concept encapsulated the aspirations of generations
of Irish peasants. They killed, burned, slashed, scalded, carded,
boycotted and were hanged, beaten and jailed for the entitlement
to 'fee simple', the right to possess, enjoy and bestow their own
real estate. In so doing, they turned on their equally penniless
neighbours in envious rage far more often than they ever tweaked
the noses of their overlords.

Landlord and tenant relations in Ireland were never entirely
unproblematic, though perhaps they were not always as fraught
as those between the fourteenth-century magnate John de
Bermingham (conqueror of Edward Bruce at Faughart in 1318) and

8

his Louth tenantry. In what has become known as the Braganstown massacre, in 1329 they attacked him within the curtilage of his own manor, 'not wishing that he should rule over them', and hacked to death more than 150 members of the de Bermingham family and his retinue of, clearly, not very effective mercenary defenders. The body count of subsequent landlord/tenants disputes was mercifully lower, though the animosity and the disinclination to submit to authority was often of a similar magnitude.[2]

The struggle for the ownership of Ireland's land encompassed two major famines; a host of minor subsistence crises (one estimate puts this at more than twenty); and a plethora of localised and nationwide insurrections. The invocation of mythical figures of resistance (Queen Sive, Captains Right, Rock and Moonlight, Rory of the Hills), a consequence of the enforced anonymity of a covert command structure, gradually gave way to the emergence of overt and often inspired leaders such as Michael Davitt and William O'Brien. Violent and localised splinter groups with exotic names (Houghers, Threshers, Terry Alts, Molly Maguires) and a sadistic *modus operandi* gave way to nationwide political movements with less aggressive and more mundane titles like the Tenant League and the Land League, employing imaginative forms of passive resistance such as the boycott.

The arc of opposition to the dominance of an elite over the ownership and management of Irish land moved from simmering acquiescence to subsequent phases of piecemeal and localised mayhem (Whiteboys and Ribbonmen); wider collective and quasi-constitutional conflict (the Tithe War); faltering centralised political action (the Tenant League); and effectual parliamentary and communal protest (the Land League); before culminating in a final phase of accommodation and negotiation (land purchase). It was a long revolution that sought and engaged the attention, if not the endorsement, of two increasingly divergent British political parties. In the mordantly incisive truism of Barbara Solow – one of the key researchers whose work opened up and 'disrupted' the study of Irish agrarian history in the 1970s – 'Liberals could be got to care but not to spend, while Tories could be got to spend but not to care'.[3]

It would be naïve to suggest that during the last phases of the conflict, the twilight warriors – given to homicide, the cropping of human ears or the cutting of bovine hamstrings – merely doffed their white smocks, returned their ribbons to the sewing basket and cheered on their political leaders from the nearest *shebeen*. On the contrary, agrarian violence persisted throughout the period covered by this volume, and consistently reinforced the '*après moi le deluge*' message of 'slightly constitutional' figures like Charles Stewart Parnell who were, when it suited them, happy to exploit lawlessness and *anomie*, while tut-tutting in qualified disapproval as they did so.

Over the course of the journey from the ascendancy dominance of the eighteenth century to the establishment of peasant proprietorship in the early 1900s, there were frequent deviations (the religious sectarianism of the Defenders and the Peep O'Day Boys); unavoidable distractions (opposition to the tithe); and a critical process of political liberalisation within the British establishment. The last involved the jettisoning of the utterly repressive (hanging, flogging, transportation) in favour of milder sanctions and, ultimately, a measure of political engagement. This, despite its flaws and occasional return journeys to an era of repression, permitted forms of discourse and accommodation designed to render violent peasant subversion redundant. The gradual process of political modernisation and democratisation in the United Kingdom from the 1830s meant that the constitutional approach to land agitation matured into viability, and then became a *sine qua non*. The complexion of agrarian dissent changed, albeit through rural violence and state repression never entirely disappeared until the process was completed. And, arguably, not even then.

Between the 1600s and the 1900s, the narrative of Irish land tenure developed in a number of clearly discernible chapters, from forced dispossession to democratic repossession. These periods, which often overlap, can be broadly categorised as (1) punishment, (2) insurrection, (3) activism, (4) reclamation and (5) redistribution.

The first punitive, or 'To Hell or to Connaught', phase of the seventeenth and early eighteenth centuries was marked by a newly created Protestant Ascendancy securing and beginning to enjoy the land acquired after the Elizabethan, Stuart, Cromwellian and Williamite seizures. This is not to suggest that the land of Ireland was gradually appropriated by a Protestant colonial elite from the country's indigenous population. The transfer of land was far more complex and, in essence, involved a series of often violent transitions from one elite to another. Ironically, some of the earliest planters and settlers themselves fell victim to subsequent waves of enforced resettlement. To many Irish peasants, however, the entire process of dispossession involved merely a change of overlord. They became an integral part of what American agrarian historian Jo Guldi, in *The Long Land War*, has characterised as 'indigenous labor colonies'.[4]

After a quiescent period of adjustment in the early 1700s, the late eighteenth century witnessed the first glimmer of recalcitrance, an insurrectionary period dating from the 1760s and continuing up to and including the Tithe War of the 1830s. A host of agrarian secret societies (Whiteboys, Rightboys, Oakboys) emerged – with a multiplicity of localised and specific grievances and objectives – to defy the authority of landlords; the Established Church; graziers and wealthy tillage farmers; the Ascendancy-dominated Irish parliament; and the Dublin Castle Executive (delete as appropriate). Denied any credible route of amelioration through peaceful political agitation, or measured guidance from a cohesive national political leadership, these localised secret societies took matters into their own hands and staged a series of what were in effect minor uprisings, with disparate motives and diverse objectives. As political debate was not an option, they had little choice other than to have recourse to violence. As we shall see, not all those conflicts were fought out between landlord and tenant. Other forces, sectarian or class-based, were also at work, pitching peasant against peasant. While the impenetrable 'Irish Question' can be readily boiled down to the issue of political independence, according to University of Galway historian Gearóid Ó Tuathaigh, 'there never was a single "Irish land question", but a dense matrix of interlocking issues and questions relating to the story of land in Ireland'.[5]

Outside of academia – where, despite subtle disagreements, consensus has largely been achieved on most of the knottier conundrums of the land struggle – the old binary template still holds sway. Generations of schoolchildren have been taught that Irish tenant farmers waged an unequal struggle against the forces of landlordism, a David versus Goliath contest that ended with a stirring victory in the three-hundred-year war for the little guy with the slingshot. And therein lies more than a grain of truth.

However, like most Irish historical narratives – which makes the study of the country's history so endlessly fascinating – the ones and zeros of the binary system are unequal to the task of answering simple questions such as, 'Why did that happen?' Or the even more nuanced, 'And why exactly did it happen when it happened?' Yes, tenants often defied their landlords, and yes, the landlords ultimately folded their tents and abandoned the field of battle. But it was not a case of *post hoc ergo propter hoc*. The multiple conflicts over Irish land tenure cannot be boiled down to a convenient syllogism, A=B=C – as in A (tenants coalesced and rebelled), B (landlords conceded and departed) and C (therefore the coalition and rebellion of the tenants brought about the concession and departure of the landlords). This is far from the full, complex and fascinating story.

There were in fact a multitude of overlapping, consecutive, interlinked and discrete Land Wars between 1760 and 1921. Neither were the brakes applied at the moment of independence. While the overarching conflict was between tenant farmers and the members of the dominant and cosseted Irish aristocracy, both sides also picked fights with the Church, and the tenantry often engaged in a murderous dialogue with itself.

Even the description 'tenant' signally fails to cover the range of disparate interests and social sub-categories in rural Ireland during the nineteenth and early twentieth centuries. When turned upside down and thoroughly shaken, the term 'tenant' splits into a number of distinct chunks. It entirely excluded an important and populous category, that of the landless farm labourer. Had the Great Famine not caused the near extinction of this class, the activist phase of the land struggle might have looked quite different. Pre-Famine history had amply demonstrated that, before tackling their 'betters', tenant farmers needed to ensure that their subordinates had been squared off.

With a gradualist high-political reform agenda in place from the middle of the nineteenth century, more or less coinciding with the Victorian period, legitimate organised agrarian agitation became a real possibility. This marked the activist or 'tenant rights' phase of the struggle, one that has many parallels with the early trade union movement. It was characterised by a series of peaceful(ish) constitutional struggles for improved 'conditions' ('fair rent', 'free sale', 'fixity of tenure'), often reinforced by the muscular remnants of the insurrectionary phase, in the form of 'ribbonmen' or 'moonlighters'. These were the shadowy types whose menacing activities were thoroughly deprecated by constitutional agrarian activists. Mostly.

During this chapter of the narrative, the Tenant League of the 1850s was a precursor of the more effective Land League, the Plan of Campaign of the 1880s and ideas of shared ownership. Towards the end of this phase of the struggle, however, the mood began to change. Collectivist objectives moved beyond demands for mere palliative measures and there was a gradual but perceptible shift towards the notion of a 'peasant proprietary'. The impetus towards 'merger' metamorphosed into a drive for 'acquisition'.

This penultimate chapter of the struggle, one of 'reclamation', was characterised by an acceptance in official circles, and among the more astute (or desperate) members of the landowning class, that the democratisation of Irish land ownership was both inevitable and beneficial to both sides. It was just a matter of coming up with the right terms and conditions. While political agitation still had a role to play during this process, negotiation was equally important. This was exemplified by the land purchase legislation of the Tory chief secretary George Wyndham in 1903, following a template devised by the Dunraven Conference, which brought the landlord and tenant leadership together to agree the 'terms and conditions' for a handover.

The final phase, some of which took place after the creation of the Irish Free State, was redistributive. While many of the landlords had cashed in their chips and made their exit before the end of the Union in 1922, the shape of land ownership in an independent Ireland had not yet been formalised. The 'reclamation' period had seen a number of disputes and extra-judicial land seizures as the disparate elements of rural Ireland vied for a share in the land being vacated by the aristocracy. It was left to the government of the Irish Free State to finalise the redistribution of Irish land that had not already been conveyed. The manner in which this was achieved did not please all those disparate interests.

Of course, the above categorisations are defined and explicit, where the reality was more vague and fluid. These five assigned phases often overlapped or presented common characteristics. The Tithe War, for example, while it preceded the (slightly) constitutional political struggle for tenant rights of the 1880s by half a century, bore many of its hallmarks (peaceful agitation, public meetings, ostracisation). The redistribution of tenancies, whether conducted legally under the auspices of Westminster land purchase acts, or illicitly in the activities of conspiracies like that of the Black Hand Gang of north Co. Meath, coincided with the 'reclamation' period of the early twentieth century. Historic truth (insofar as it exists) is neither linear nor uncomplicated. If it were otherwise, many historians would be out of a job.

To return briefly to the systematic debunking of the binary 'holy writ' of the land struggle by a generation of 'revisionist' historians since the 1970s, the old orthodoxy was of the brutal oppression of the Irish tenant farmer by a leech-like class of aristocrats. The new orthodoxy, based on the research in the 1970s and 1980s of academics like Joseph Lee, Barbara Lewis Solow, William Vaughan, Samuel Clark and, perhaps the 'first among equals', James Donnelly Jr,*

---

* Enhanced in recent years by the work of the likes of Terence Dooley, Cormac Ó Gráda, Fergus Campbell and Tony Varley.

is a great deal more nuanced. Oppressed tenants and aristocratic leeches there certainly were, but they were the exception rather than the rule. Evictions, other than at times of extreme crisis – famine, economic depression – were a relatively rare occurrence on Irish estates. The actual evidence, diligently ferreted out by a generation of professional historians, does not support the thesis of Charles Kickham's novel *Knocknagow*, the thrust of a thousand anonymous letters to landlords, agents and 'land grabbers', or the teaching of a thousand and one Irish Christian Brothers.

It would also be a mistake to assume that all the raw and bloody land confrontations between the middle of the eighteenth century and the eve of World War II involved conflict between perfumed earls and earthy peasants. The insurgency of the Rightboys in 1785, for example, was actively encouraged by many members of the duelling classes and was targeted at the Church. When the almost prehistoric Houghers of Connacht – that primordial agrarian secret society of the early 1700s – took their knives to the hamstrings of cattle, they were intent on destroying the livelihoods of their fellow (wealthier) peasants, not of their landlords. When the faction fighters of the Caravats laid into their 'betters', the more prosperous Shanavests, during melees at fairs or patterns in the early nineteenth century, there wasn't a landlord, agent or 'Peeler' in sight. They had no need to burn their supposed oppressors in effigy as long as they had each other. In Marxist terms, their struggle was one of proletarian forces against an assertive rural 'bourgeois' overclass. In Irish argot, it was 'tuppence halfpenny' contending with 'tuppence' by means of targeted assassinations and impromptu faction fights. As if that wasn't sufficiently rancorous, just add kidnapping, rape and forced marriage into the mix, and then stir vigorously.

As the wealthy Irish Catholic early twentieth-century 'grazier' or 'rancher' brought a renewed emphasis on pastoralism to the agricultural economy, as well as a new ruthlessness in the acquisition and repurposing of all available arable land, the agrarian underclasses began to feel as if they had lost out in the dispersal of the spoils after the long war for peasant proprietorship. Their response was to revert to the old familiar ancestral ways of violent ribbonism and 'moonlighting' in the tussle with their new antagonists. As Fintan O'Toole pointed out in an *Irish Times* article (2 August 2022), in one of Michael Collins's last speeches, 'he foresaw a radical reduction in the scale and number of cattle farms … it was a common demand of Irish nationalists that cattle ranches should be broken up. As terms of political abuse, "ranchers", "graziers" and "grabbers" were pretty much interchangeable.' Of course, we shall never know if Collins would have delivered on this programme; his successors in government in the 1920s certainly did not.

This is not to say that there was a total absence of solidarity among the ranks of the Irish peasantry in the battle for tenant ownership – there was plenty of fellow-feeling and commonality – but there were also barely concealed rivalries and violently conflicting interests. When William Carleton wrote his two great books of short fiction in 1830 and 1834, both entitled *Traits and Stories of the Irish Peasantry*, it was not his intention to depict only soulful paragons of virtuous Irish rural life. It was Carleton who gave us the savagery of 'Wildgoose Lodge', a story that largely wrote itself, based as it was on the actual burning to death by an agrarian wolfpack of a comparatively prosperous Co. Louth family. This was followed by the hanging of dozens of men who had made up the numbers in that murderous mob and, doubtless, many who hadn't.

Each of the agrarian revolts, uprisings, insurgencies or protest movements, from the emergence of the Whiteboys in 1761 to the neutralisation of the Allenstown Gaeltacht in the 1940s, was unique and distinct. Granted, they often shared common characteristics, methods and objectives, but they should never be conflated. Sometimes it was a bareknuckle fight between tenants of all classes and their landlords. Occasionally, tenants and landowners found themselves on the same side, especially when the tithe proctor* came calling. At other times, the lowest

---

* An agent who established crop valuations and collected tithe contributions on behalf of a Church of Ireland rector for a commission of around 10 per cent.

of the low – landless labourers and cottiers – combined to take on all comers, or set themselves up to confront the wealthier tenant farmers who exploited them to a far greater extent than did any landlord. It all depended on the circumstances.

It would be well worth the reader's while to bear in mind, as they read this volume, the compelling, quasi-dialectical thesis put forward by James Donnelly Jr in much of his voluminous work on this subject, but neatly summarised in his introduction to his 2009 publication, *Captain Rock: The Irish Agrarian Rebellion of 1821–1824*. Donnelly, in seeking explanations for the occurrence and the timing of the various agrarian 'rebellions' of the eighteenth and nineteenth centuries, especially those that took place before the Great Famine, detected a pattern. First, he recognised the importance of class in these periodic eruptions. Ireland, pre- and post-Famine, was a highly stratified society, the only difference being the size of each class cohort before and after the 1845–50 subsistence crisis. By the eve of the Great Famine, the agrarian population, just under 2 million households, was divided thus:

1.   Landowners: 10,000
2.   Wealthy farmers (80 acres +): 50,000
3.   Comfortable farmers (50 acres +): 100,000
4.   Family farmers (c.20 acres): 250,000
5.   Cottiers (c.5 acres): 300,000
6.   Labourers (*c.*1 acre): 1 million[6]

Leaving out the landlords entirely, there was ample room for mutual animosity evident in this list. It should be apparent that those in row 2 (wealthy farmers) had little or nothing in common with anyone unfortunate enough to live, move and have their being in rows 4–6. Neither did the comfortable farmers of row 3 (Donnelly describes them as 'snug') have many shared interests with those in the categories beneath. So, plenty of scope for envy, frustration, resentment and mischief.

Donnelly goes on to offer an explanation as to why, in particular circumstances and at certain times, the occupants of rows 2–5 succeeded in shelving their obvious class differences and uniting against the marquesses, earls, viscounts and cavalry officers of row 1. He also manages to elucidate the reasons (to the satisfaction of this writer at least) as to why, at other times and in different circumstances, the peasantry were at one another's throats. It all depended on the prevailing economic climate. Was the Irish agricultural economy trending upwards, bringing prosperity to some, or was it in a downward spiral, bringing hard times or utter misery to all? 'A simplified version of the argument,' according to Donnelly, 'would run as follows. Movements that arose in periods of prosperity, when farm prices were buoyant and land values were rising sharply, were usually dominated by the landless and the land-poor, whose fortunes were adversely affected by the prevailing economic winds.' Conversely, agrarian upheavals 'that were fuelled by a drastic decline in agricultural prices were generally marked by a distinct widening in the social composition of the rebellious groups ... Conditions of acute depression did indeed create more fertile ground for the forging of alliances of various kinds across the traditional lines of social division.'[7]

Hence the murderous feuding of the Caravats (agricultural labourers, cottiers and small farmers) and the Shanavests (prosperous farmers) from 1806 to 1811, during the Napoleonic Wars, at a time when Irish agriculture was at the crest of an economic wave from which a select few were benefiting. Contrast that with the emergence of the broader coalition of the Rockite movement in the 1820s, at a time when the agricultural prosperity of the heyday of Bonaparte was a distant memory. If we move further into the nineteenth century, we can see that Donnelly's thesis holds good for the Land War (1879–82), when a number of heterogenous social classes were yoked together in (short-term) opposition to the country's landowners at a time of profound economic crisis.

In eighteenth- and nineteenth-century Europe, everyone lived 'off the land' in one way or another, insofar as agricultural activity provided the essential food supplies nourishing the continent's increasingly industrialised and service-oriented population. Ireland, however, was an outlier, because almost everyone lived 'on the land' as well. They were either tenant farmers beholden to the small privileged landowning class for their rented holdings; members of a quasi-communal tenantry, also paying rent but operating under the 'rundale' system (described later); penurious cottiers living on the borders of starvation; or landless labourers hugely dependent on a tillage economy to keep them in the employment that warded off destitution.

As a consequence, in Ireland the struggle for 'peasant proprietorship' was every bit as important as the fight for independence, and usually far more so. *Terroir* generally trumped *patrie*. 'Passion on the land issue gave vigour to Irish nationalism,' writes Paul Bew.[8] In an early section of the culturally significant but politically toxic novel *Gone with the Wind*, Gerald O'Hara, the fictional slave-owning Meath man who fled Ireland after killing a landlord's agent, berates his spoiled daughter, Scarlett. The sixteen-year-old Southern belle has spoken disparagingly of their plantation, named Tara by her nostalgic parent. Her father indignantly informs the petulant Scarlett that land is the only commodity 'worth working for, worth fighting for, worth dying for'. When she accuses him of 'talking like an Irishman', he responds, 'To anyone with a drop of Irish blood in them the land they live on is like their mother.'[9]

By comparison, the cause of Repeal (1840s), Home Government (1870s) or Home Rule (1880–1918) was a 'petty parish question' when weighed against the issue of land tenure, at least according to the mid-nineteenth-century agitator, journalist and revolutionary guru James Fintan Lalor – although he himself lived only to witness the unsuccessful Repeal campaign. Would the constitutional struggle for political sovereignty have even gained traction in the nineteenth century had a contented Irish peasantry enjoyed the fruits of their labour on farms they owned themselves? Would the far more lethal struggle in the early twentieth century have been possible had the ground not been prepared by thousands of individual declarations of independence, as tenants rid themselves of their landlords?

While the wider national struggle provoked patriotic emotions and occasionally cost lives among the *engagés*, tenurial issues were a more frequent life-or-death matter for the average ideologically detached Irish peasant farmer. At times when the independence battle might have dominated, to the exclusion of all other considerations, the land issue had a habit of interposing itself. After the 1880s, for example, it was deployed by the ruling British Tories in an overarching exercise in misdirection designed to divert Irish nationalists from their pursuit of the perilously realisable holy grail of Home Rule. During the Anglo-Irish War of 1919–21, it became an incipient distraction when disgruntled elements exploited the lawlessness of those times to push their own agrarian agenda.

The Industrial Revolution largely bypassed Ireland, leaving a growing nineteenth-century population overwhelmingly dependent for survival on the ground upon which they lived. In 1871, Dublin, Belfast, Cork, Limerick and Galway accounted for barely 10 per cent of the Irish population – hence the aspiration to possess property 'held in fee simple'. If you were one of that tiny minority whose farm belonged to you, then you were entitled to develop it as you saw fit, without fear of a landlord malevolently possessing himself of the results of your hard work – your 'improvements' – after finding a spurious reason to evict you. While this didn't happen nearly as often as received wisdom suggests, perception is all. The tenant farmer's fear of expulsion from his holding was often very real, and as pervasive was the notion that eviction itself was commonplace. In fact, the 'readmission' of excluded tenants was almost as frequent as dispossession itself, except in times of crisis. However, there were more than enough of those sorts of upheavals to perpetuate the dismal image of the immiserated peasant – deposited at the side of road with his large family and few belongings, tearfully viewing the ruins of their thatched cottage or *bothán* – as being the rule rather than the exception. When assessing the credentials of the Irish landlord class, the tenant farmer could also take note of examples from beyond Ireland's shores of the avaricious capitalism of the eighteenth-century English enclosure movement, and the grim revolutionary capitalism of the early nineteenth-century Scottish highland clearances.

The folkloric corollary was the grasping landlord who considered his day to have been wasted without the expulsion of half-a-dozen tenants before a hearty breakfast. Perhaps, for reasons of balance, it is incumbent upon chroniclers of the land struggle to introduce some sort of gauge to assess the levels of perfidy of individual members of the Irish aristocracy from the 1660s to the 1900s. A Graduated Landlord Malignity Scale (GLMS), if you will. This would be a simple standardised yardstick for measuring the malevolence of members of the landlord class. Our GLMS would offer a reading of 1 in the case of Charles Stewart Parnell as a landowner (the accompanying report card might read 'singularly benign in his interaction with tenants to the point of incipient bankruptcy'); rise meteorically to a maximum 10 in the presence of the execrable Hubert de Burgh-Canning, 2nd Marquess of Clanricarde ('absentee, barely saw his Irish estates and fortunate not to have been garrotted by his tenants'); with the Marquess of Lansdowne hovering somewhere in the middle ('an improving landlord who often displaced indigent tenants but also funded assisted emigration'). The reality was that most Irish late nineteenth-century landlords, at a time when agrarian agitation was at peak intensity, merited no more than a reading of 3 or 4 on our putative GLMS. That, however, was not the received wisdom. Myth trumped reality. Expedient fiction trumped inconvenient fact. Look no further than the invaluable National Folklore collection for verification of the primacy of 'memory' over verifiable historical fact.

Centuries of bloody conflict spurred by the proxies of Queen Elizabeth I, King James I, Oliver Cromwell and King William III had left the bulk of the land of Ireland in the hands of some 10–12,000 'Ascendancy' – mostly Protestant – families. Barely a tenth of that number, however, were of any serious political, social or economic consequence. These were the Beresfords, Lansdownes, Fosters *et al.* In the eighteenth century, a small number traded on the misery of their latter-day vassals and kept their tenants in penury, while also relying for a portion of their wealth on plantations worked by slaves in far-flung British colonies. They have not been remembered affectionately by history for either transgression.* By the 1870s, half a century before their aristocratic

---

* In the case of the latter offence, witness the recent effacement of the name of George Berkeley, Bishop of Cloyne (1734–53), from the eponymous library in Trinity College, Dublin.

dominance ceased almost entirely, a typical Irish landlord owned about 2,000 acres, but fewer than 800 members of that class had managed to possess themselves of 50 per cent of the entire country's land area, around 10 million acres. Half of that exceptionally fortunate clutch lived abroad, mostly on manicured British demesnes. More than half of the largest estates were also in the hands of Protestants and Non-Conformists (far more of the former than the latter), in a nation that was overwhelmingly Roman Catholic – another major point of contention.

Enduring acrimony over issues of land tenure brought with it most of the coercive legislation of the 1800s and a disproportionate share of the century's homicides; it consequently had a lopsided impact on more than 100 years of capital punishment statistics as well as the national psyche. It also schooled generations of peasants in political activism, some of which was actually legal. You could even argue that it was the perennial issue of the ownership of Irish land that created tribal Irish-America, just as the Highland clearances informed the outlook of much of the Scots-Canadian population of British North America (which finally matured into Canada). In a triumph of circularity, post-Fenian emigrant involvement in Irish politics forcefully reasserted itself in American support of the Land League in the 1880s.

A less arrogant colonial government, with more timely and sympathetic policies, might have expected to retain the loyalty of the traditionally conservative peasant element of Irish society. However, when the Age of Agrarian Enlightenment finally dawned in the 1880s, the tempered altruism of British prime minister William Gladstone, followed by the useful cynicism of his successor, the Marquess of Salisbury, came too late to overcome decades of hostility, condescension and neglect.

In 1870, before Gladstone began his 'mission to pacify Ireland' by introducing a landmark but largely ineffective piece of agrarian legislation, only 3 per cent of Irish farmers owned their own land, while 97 per cent were tenants. Sixty years later, those figures had been reversed, but not without a struggle that in the intervening period pitched an omnipotent Ascendancy class – often abetted

by a highly partisan government – against the peasantry and their
petit bourgeois mercantile allies.

The desire of the Irish ascendancy class to retain its landed
wealth and its ancient privileges is easy to understand. Less
comprehensible perhaps is the full-blooded support of most
British administrations from the early 1800s for their lordships
and ladyships – until, that is, the political and social engineering
of the last two decades of the century turned the tide against the
gentry. However, given the number of British luminaries with
extensive Irish holdings of their own (prime ministers Lord John
Russell and Lord Palmerston, to name but two); considering the
influence of members of the Anglo-Irish Ascendancy on the
British body politic; taking into account the contribution that
Irish rents made to British economic prosperity – as well as the
fear that any systemic concessions to the Irish peasantry would
invite similar demands from their British counterparts – it should
hardly be surprising that the Westminster establishment sought
to protect the interests of the Irish Ascendancy until it became
inconvenient and injudicious to do so any longer.

That point was reached when devolution for Ireland became
a live and threatening issue, when the ineffectual campaign for
'Repeal' of the Act of Union gave way to the pursuit of the more
ominous 'Home Rule'. From then on, the imperative among
British potentates opposed to any form of Irish separatism
(mainly in the Tory party) became that of 'killing Home Rule
with kindness'. This sudden spirit of self-interested generosity
among the conservative element of the British ruling class
came primarily at the expense of the Anglo-Irish Ascendancy, a
political and economic establishment rapidly being overtaken in
power, influence and even wealth by a 'native' Roman Catholic
haute bourgeoisie. Once the issue of land became a bargaining chip
in the wider struggle for legislative independence, time began to
run out for the country's tiny battalion of affluent landlords.

Accordingly, when it comes to the land struggle, we can largely
dispense with the mythic misconception of immiserated peasants
triumphing in dynamic combination over their improvident

overlords. Granted, there was no shortage of impoverished tenants in the ranks of the Irish Land League (1879–82), but there were far fewer of them among the organisation's *petit bourgeois* officer corps. Numbered among the league's elite, for example, was the ubiquitous *sagart aroon* (beloved priest). At the outset of the conflict, this was often a Roman Catholic curate taking an executive role in a local branch or at least offering his tacit support. However, when the bandwagon became unstoppable, the parish priest himself often hopped on board, although the bishop could be more standoffish.

Even more prominent were local merchants with interests of their own. The grocer, publican and hardware storekeeper – often one and the same – had less of a stake in an end to rack-renting and the propagation of peasant proprietorship than in persuading tenant farmers to spend their rent money on a variety of consumer goods and to clear off debts built up in previous purchases. These debts were being incurred in a newly progressive economy, where goods and services were increasingly obtained 'on tick'. Merchants and farmers alike had discovered the joys of 'credit'.

The merchants' argument from 1879 to 1882, a time of severe agricultural depression, was blessedly unambiguous. Things had been getting better for all. Irish farmers had entered the cash economy and discovered the usefulness of credit. Now that times had suddenly become harder – courtesy of yet another in a long line of American financial panics, this one in 1873 – the merchants pointed out to the farmers that they obviously did not have enough cash to pay both their rent *and* their domestic debts. So why, urged the grocer and the publican, encourage the leeches of the Ascendancy – stereotypically Protestant and profligate to a man – by remitting their rent? Tenant farmers were exhorted instead to campaign vigorously for significant abatements and to settle up their commercial obligations to the shopkeepers with their freed-up cash. The fact that the merchant making this argument might also be chair of the local Land League branch, with sufficient clout to cause untold mischief for any indebted farmer who irked him, was but another inducement to defy the landlord rather than antagonise the grocer.

This is why the Land War has been characterised by some historians as a 'revolution of rising expectations', rather than a stripped-down pitched battle between Big House and Thatched Cottage. After the catastrophic 1845–50 Famine, the inevitable structural changes that followed (the extirpation of bankrupt landlords; the ending of the subdivision of farms; the modernisation of agriculture) were beginning to pay dividends. Irish tenant farmers, of whom there were now considerably fewer than before 1845 (*c.*600,000 as opposed to 800,000 – this figure would decline to 360,000 by 1916 and stands at 135,000 today),[10] had seen the Promised Land; they'd eaten manna on borrowed funds, and they liked the flavour and texture. When you take something desirable away from a person, they will fight harder to regain it than they would ever have done to acquire it in the first place.

However, as may already have become apparent, while fully accepting of the latter-day analysis that challenges the traditional narrative of an oppressive aristocracy and a hounded tenantry, this book will simultaneously argue for the primacy of perception over reality in agrarian conflict. Statistical evidence of a significant increase in post-Famine levels of frugal comfort, of static rents and rising incomes, and of a low incidence of eviction, is incontrovertible. By the midpoint of this account, the late 1860s, it is indisputable that Irish tenant farmers were not nearly as badly off as they had once been, or, perhaps, as they liked to think they still were – the anguished complaints of the 'poor poor farmer' are not a uniquely twentieth- or twenty-first-century phenomenon.

During the turmoil of the 1880s, there were many establishment propagandists who were happy to bang that particular drum and highlight the reluctance on the part of landlords to increase rents, as well as the rarity of evictions. However, those who made a habit of it – Tory and loyalist newspapers; the activists of the Property Defence Association; the apologists of Irish Loyal and Patriotic Union – were not voices to which the average Irish tenant farmer was accustomed to pay much attention. Their commentary was perceived as being entirely partisan.* Other voices, the ones to which our archetypal tenant farmer did listen, were telling him otherwise. These were advising him that he was worse off than he had ever been and that it was high time 'his lordship' shared in the pain; insisting that there should be no recurrence of the abject passivity that had led to the Famine clearances; while exhorting him to 'keep a firm grip on your homestead(s)'. The evidence immediately before the Irish tenant farmer's eyes in 1879 was of incipient famine in the west of Ireland and a return to the clearances of the 1840s and 1850s, prompted by economic turmoil. The underlying truth, the statistics, the long term-trends were buried in RIC data and concealed in parliamentary Blue Books, to be retrieved in 'the bliss of solitude' by diligent twentieth-century historians.

Furthermore, with a highly capable and committed national agrarian leadership cadre – the first of its kind – devising mischievous strategies (the boycott, stopping the hunt) for a united peasantry, who could resist the received wisdom that times were bad, rents were too high and tenurial insecurity was rife? After all, everyone knew, or had at least heard about, someone who had been evicted. In the circumstances, it was easy to ignore the fact that the *poor crathur* had probably been three years behind in his rent before landlord or agent chose to take action.

And alongside all that, the narrative had 'changed utterly'.

The 'forty-shilling freehold' revolt leading to 'Catholic Relief' in 1829; the confident defiance of Daniel O'Connell, whether in court, the House of Commons or a public platform; the spirit of the 'monster' meetings of the repeal movement; the bitter lessons of the Famine; the romantic nationalist journalism of *The Nation*; the explosion in literacy (and English language skills) since the establishment of the National School system in 1831; as well as the much-flagged rise in prosperity that many were now slow to acknowledge – all had combined to undermine the aura of permanency, legitimacy and credibility that had long surrounded

---

* They were also, when advanced in times of economic crisis with evictions on the increase, no longer true.

Dublin Castle and its aristocratic eyes and ears. By the last two decades of the nineteenth century, Irish landlords and their henchmen were no longer the objects of the deference, reverence and fear of the 'long' eighteenth century. They were increasingly seen as the vanguard of an unwelcome colonial power whose ancestors had benefited from a series of sectarian land seizures. Not that these sentiments were particularly new, but growing self-assurance, exceptional leadership and an enhanced sense of popular solidarity meant that they were finally being translated into concerted and meaningful action. On the debit side, but equally important as a motivating factor, was the fear of moral or physical sanction for any deviation from communal cohesion. That was between you and your neighbours. Transgression meant having to deal with the 'midnight legislators'.[11]

By the 1880s, it didn't much matter that rents had, in real terms, hardly increased in the previous forty years. Neither did it signify that evictions, outside of the context of chronic default, were almost as rare as hen's teeth. Nor did remedial British 1880s legislation giving tenants a greater functional and moral interest in their farms make a critical difference. The era of the landlord was passing. Land League and Plan of Campaign tenants did, in truth, not simply bridle at levels of rent. They now took umbrage at the transfer of a portion of their hard-earned income to someone whose entitlement to their patrimony was based entirely on his or her lineage.

'Land' and 'nation' fed off each other, just as James Fintan Lalor had advocated. Agrarianism became infected with the virus of Irish separatism and vice versa. Because of the continued presence of an overweening landowning class, the natural conservatism of the Irish farmer was artificially suppressed, leaving him more susceptible to an unexpected degree of radicalisation. So, whether the rural activism of the late nineteenth and early twentieth centuries was ever really based on legitimate social grievances or sound economic principles is not strictly relevant.

In regard to sources, a volume of this nature must, inevitably, be largely based on the work and original research of others. In previous published and unpublished research of my own, I have navigated some of these waters, but in attempting to cover two centuries of conflict and development I have been heavily reliant on the work of a couple of generations of distinguished Irish historians. The citations and bibliography will clearly identify those to whom I am most heavily in debt.

In seeking to advance the importance of ideas of communal perception and collective 'memory' over statistical reality, I have also tried to incorporate relevant statements from the National Folklore Collection, a vital reservoir of myth as well as of oral history. To illustrate contemporary attitudes – uncontaminated by the invaluable historical research of the 1970s and beyond – I have included extracts from a number of interesting eighteenth- and nineteenth-century texts, from the celebrated accounts of Arthur Young (1776) and Alexis de Tocqueville (1835) to the less well-known work of economists such as Thomas Newenham (1809) and Edward Wakefield (1812), while being conscious of the level of special pleading on both sides of the argument contained within such contemporary accounts. Young, although an agri-economist and often a valuable and neutral source, also got much of his information, as well as access and hospitality, from one side of the agrarian political divide. Equally, memoirists and polemicists like Michael Davitt and Isaac Butt had agendas of their own. Even nineteenth-century journalists like Bernard Becker, Finlay Dun, Henry George, James Redpath and William Henry Hurlbert, who all feature in this narrative, fell well short of any modern notions of impartiality.

From the Down Survey to the Ordnance Survey; the Whiteboys of the eighteenth century to the Black Hand Gang of the 1920s; the debilitating famine of 1741 to its unspeakable counterpart a century later; the murder of Captain William Blood in 1831 to the killing of Mark Clinton in 1920; the socialist journalism of Henry George to the reactionary reportage of William Henry Hurlbert; the incendiary terror of Wildgoose Lodge to the horrors of Maamtrasna; the gibbeting of Patrick Devane in 1816 to the hanging of Poff and Barret in 1882; the Tithe War to the Ranch War; the Diamond to Dolly's Brae, this volume will examine the events and the personalities of centuries of Irish agrarian upheaval that commenced in annexation (the 'planting' of British settlers on Irish soil) and culminated in pragmatic default (the refusal of an independent Irish government to continue the payment of land annuities incurred in the protracted purge of the landlord class).

The narrative of *Land is All That Matters* leans heavily on the story of a social revolution whose peasant and bourgeois parameters defined the limits of the upheaval that culminated in political independence in 1922. When it came to the latter, while the land was not *all* that mattered, once you got beyond the largely symbolic shibboleths of identity and allegiance, it might just as well have been.

1

Topographica Hibernica

'To judge of Ireland by the conversation one sometimes
hears in England, it would be supposed that one half of it
was covered with bogs, and the other with mountains filled
with Irish ready to fly at the sight of a civilised being.'[1]

(Arthur Young, *Tour in Ireland*)

NOVELIST MARIA EDGEWORTH described Arthur Young's 1780
publication, *Tour in Ireland*, as 'the first faithful portrait of its
inhabitants'.[2] By affording Young the honour of primacy she clearly
did not set much store by the earlier splenetic discourse of Gerald
of Wales (Giraldus Cambrensis), who had covered similar ground
six centuries earlier ('The Irish are a rude people, subsisting on the
produce of their cattle only, and living themselves like beasts').[3]

But, while Young's paean to Irish husbandry lionises the
aristocratic social class of which he and the author of *Castle
Rackrent* were both honorary members, it treats of the Irish
peasantry not as individuals, but as elements of a (downtrodden)
lumpen class. So, while it may well be 'the first faithful portrait'
of the Irish ruling elite, it also offers an interesting parallel
snapshot of the country's topography and land use approaching
the halfway point between two catastrophic famines. The
landscape itself had, after all, not changed that much since the
days of the bilious Giraldus Cambrensis, Ireland's least favourite
Welshman. The land mass, for example, was still 21 million acres
(English measure), with inland waters comprising *c.*700,000

acres. The soil – though probably not the local manners – was 'more cultivated than England', despite being 'the most stoney [*sic*] in Europe'.[4]

The classic version of the topography of Ireland in the schoolbooks of the mid-twentieth century was to think of it as a saucer – 'a patchwork of rich pasture lands and immense turf bogs, drained by sluggish rivers while the seaboard is mostly fringed by ranges of hills and mountains'.[5] The reality is that, bar the granite hills of Dublin and Wicklow, the saucer has a large chip missing on its eastern extremity, and it is probably more productive to think of it as a leaky C-shaped container than a viable receptacle. The landscape also lacks the emphatic continental divide of the United States of America, which means that the country's rivers, of which there are many, have minds of their own and drift or flow in any direction they find most appealing. Young was a great admirer of Ireland's waterways: 'Few countries can be better watered by large and beautiful rivers.' The country's mountains were, he wrote, sufficient in number to give the landscape added character, but 'not in such number as to confer the usual character of poverty which attends them'.[6]

When it comes to the country's geology, limestone is plentiful, of sandy or chalky soil there is precious little, and bogland was far more extensive in the eighteenth century than it is today, thanks mainly to the land reclamation efforts of (some) landlords and (mostly) tenant farmers. The Bog of Allen, however, still ranges across nine counties in the heart of the island and takes up 300,000 of those 21 million acres, more than three times the size of the largest lake, Lough Neagh. Much of the country's peat deposits, however, have long since been harvested.

The ubiquity of lakes and rivers has much to do with Ireland's almost legendary levels of rainfall. This can be a boon which precludes parched summers, or a curse which lays waste to over-irrigated fields. It is also the subject, like San Francisco's fogs, of much mythology and exaggeration. Arthur Young, who left little to chance when it came to informing himself, offered his own observations in support of his claim that Ireland was considerably wetter than its larger neighbour to the east. In all, he spent 122 days in the country – from midsummer (19 June) to mid-October – in the course of his 1776 tour. It rained for seventy-five of those days, much of the rainfall being 'incessant and heavy'. Conducting similar experiments in England, Young never encountered comparable volumes of precipitation. His measurements must have been very precise, because average annual rainfall in Ireland at the time was around forty inches. That of England and Wales was a not dissimilar thirty-two inches.

Young later returned as a resident in 1777, when he briefly worked for Lord Kingsborough as a land agent. He spent the winter and early spring of that year in Mitchelstown, Co. Cork, and also lived in Munster in the summer of 1778. He found the winter months 'much more soft and mild than ever I experienced one in England'. His summer was as pleasant as any he had spent in his native country, without being quite as warm. Snow was only in evidence at the summit of the Galtee mountains (at around 1,000 metres above sea level) and frosts he found to be 'slight and rare'. To Young, the worst aspect of the Irish climate was 'the constant moisture without rain'. 'Wet a piece of leather,' he wrote, 'and lay it in a room, where there is neither sun nor fire and it will not, in summer even, be dry in a month.'[7]

When Young first visited the country in 1776, he was struck by the absence of trees, as compared with levels of afforestation in England. The dense forests of early Christian Ireland had long since disappeared. Later, his own experience of living in rural Cork, on the 100,000-acre Kingsborough estate, was that 'you must take a breathing gallop to find a stick large enough to beat a dog'. He recalled how, when questioned about this, his aristocratic hosts blamed their thieving tenants for cutting down mature trees to make walking sticks, spade handles and car shafts and, possibly, even to administer punishment to their dogs. Young dismissed this narrative as absurd. He had no doubt that the blame lay with the 'worthless landowner [who] cuts down his acres, and leaves them unfenced against cattle' and who then imposed punitive fines on tenants gathering scraps of wood for their own use. 'If,' he asserted, 'you would hang up all the landlords who cut woods without fencing, and destroy trees without planting, you would lay your axe to the root of the evil and rid the kingdom of some of the greatest pests in it.'[8]

In a pamphlet originally compiled for a Royal Commission of Inquiry into the operation of the nineteenth- and early twentieth-century land acts – at a time when the country was still divided into 32 counties, 320 baronies, 2,445 parishes and 62,205 townlands (previously known as tates, polls or ballyboes) – the estates commissioner, William Frederick Bailey, separated the country's agricultural land into 'four classes, characteristic of the different provinces'. Ulster was, at the time of the revision of the pamphlet for publication, 'a province of comparatively small tillage holdings, the grass on which is usually produced in the course of a rotation of crops'. Leinster, with the exception of the mountainous county of Wicklow, was 'mainly pastoral, used for the grazing and fattening of cattle'. Munster was a hybrid, with 'pastoral dairying in the richer parts of Tipperary, Limerick, Waterford and Cork' and mixed tillage and dairying in the poorer parts of the province. Connacht was, in the main, 'a province of poor holdings, with small and struggling peasants, living on the margin of subsistence'.[9]

While it was not always thus – the popularity and viability of rearing livestock waxed and waned over the course of the two centuries covered by this volume – Bailey's analysis holds up well for much of the 200 years from the devastating famine of 1741 to the eve of World War II.

It also conceals as much as it reveals. No crude summary of the state of Irish land use written in the second decade of the twentieth century can convey the narrative of struggle, acrimony and mutual loathing that had marked the previous two centuries.

I

Punishment

2

From petty kings to Petty

'The land belonged to the clan, and on the death of a
clansman his share was re-apportioned according to the
number and wants of his family.'[1]

(Thomas Davis, *Literary and Historical Essays*, 1846)

The Rí and the daer-fudir

The *Book of Invasions*, a twelfth-century manuscript that offers
fetching accounts of the 'history' of Ireland – apparently the Irish
are descended either from Noah or from a race of one-armed,
one-legged giants – tentatively, but rather precisely, tells us
that the first people to arrive on the island were three Spanish
fishermen named Capa, Laighne and Luasat. The alternative fate
of these early tourists, it appears, was a wet and salty death. They
were 'drove upon the coast by a storm'. However, the book lacks
the courage of its own citations, noting that 'this landing of the
fishermen is deemed fabulous'.[2] Sadly, we must look elsewhere
to identify the first tillers of Irish land, and unlike these three
Iberian fishermen, they will always remain nameless.

The first hunter-gatherers who reached Ireland around eight
thousand BC made little impact on the landscape. They tended
to confine their activities to the less densely forested coastal
areas, occasionally venturing up the many rivers that fed into the
Atlantic Ocean to the west and the Irish Sea to the east. Gradually,
as they were replaced by visitors better acquainted with animal

husbandry and tillage, more settled communities began to pop up in the previously mysterious interior. Land, however, had no scarcity value. The island was vast in proportion to the numbers of those who wished to settle there.

By the time the impressive stone monument at Newgrange was built, around five thousand years ago, a degree of cultural and technical refinement was evident and the cultivation of crops, implying a significant degree of deforestation, was more general. This was particularly the case in the fertile Boyne Valley, where the megalithic structures at Newgrange, Knowth and Dowth are located.

At around the time of the arrival of the missionary bishop Patrick the Briton in the early fifth century – he came with instructions to convert both the pagan and the heretic because there was already a small extant Irish Christian community, predictably misbehaving – the entire island was populated, albeit thinly in places. Almost 200 small political units called *tuatha* prospered, festered or skirmished. Within these tribal groupings, wealth was measured not so much in holdings of land but in terms of livestock ownership. Possession of an impressive herd of cattle, however – one worthy of the attention of the ubiquitous rustler – was largely contingent upon access to good grazing land. By the time the stringently codified legal system, known as the Brehon laws, had developed (more concerned with civil than with criminal legalities), a small aristocratic class had emerged, retaining land on a stable and personalised basis. Their holdings, however, represented a relatively small slice of the total area covered by the *tuath*. The tenurial priority was an emphasis 'on the survival and well-being of society as a whole' rather than the corrosive 'forces of individualism'.[3]

Beneath these dignitaries in social status, a larger underclass of freemen rented land on which they reared most of their livestock. These were equivalent to the 'churls' (*ceorl*) of Anglo-Saxon England, or a Germanic *karl*. Thanks to the etymological peregrinations of the word 'churlish', that designation has taken on a pejorative meaning in modern times. But a churl was a non-servile peasant, a freeman entitled to hold land.

Further down the pecking order were the 'non free', who were generally members of a subaltern class that did not enjoy the rights and privileges of the more exalted inhabitants of the *tuath*. They were not necessarily serfs, though serfdom did exist in early Christian Ireland. Some of the resident slaves in pre-Viking times were even imported from England, where children were often sold into slavery by their own families. Others were simply kidnapped by Irish raiders and conscripted into a life of servitude.

One of the boons denied to the 'non free' involved access to *tuath* lands that were collectively owned by the members of the tribe or sept. This was a concept similar to the Anglo-Saxon notion of *folc*, i.e. land vested in the community. The bulk of *tuath* land was allocated, without the obligation to pay rent, to freemen, but this prerogative was time-limited. They were entitled, while working this land, to partition it off with earthworks. If, after occupying a farm for a period of time, a freeman was required for some reason to vacate, he would be compensated with land in another part of the *tuath*. Elements of this system remained intact in the remoter parts of Ireland up to the nineteenth century in the practice of rundale (covered later).

Any unprofitable or waste land in the *tuath* was also owned in common by the freemen of the tribe. Livestock could be grazed there without restriction, so the land could not be subdivided or fenced off in any way.[4]

The typical farm settlement up to the dawn of the second millennium was the *rath*. Sometimes called a 'ringfort' – which spuriously suggests a defensive function or capability – this was a farmstead of between 30 and 110 square metres encircled by dry stone or earthen walls of about two metres in height. Sixty thousand of these structures have been identified to date.

The arrival of Christianity and the growth of the Roman church resulted in some transfers of land to local monastic communities. This often gave rise to small urban settlements. However, the urbanisation of the country did not begin in earnest until the Vikings, tired of commuting from the Hebrides, or even Scandinavia itself, to carry out their depredations, established permanent settlements (*longphorts*) along the east and south coasts. The early marauding Vikings of the ninth century, however, had little interest in Irish land. Their preoccupation was mostly with the precious objects that had originated, in raw form, underneath it.

And so it was, before the arrival of the Norman invaders from Wales towards the end of the twelfth century, that an extended family-based, quasi-democratic but tiered social system had emerged. While it permitted an overclass to thrive, it was still cognisant of the needs of a much wider community. It was, in the immortal phrase of the great historian of early Ireland, Professor Daniel Binchy, 'tribal, rural, hierarchical, familiar'.[5] It was 'paradoxically complex, yet simple; stratified, yet egalitarian'.[6] While the concept of rent was not an entirely alien one, it was possible for most pre-Norman Irish peasants to work modest farms without being compelled to transfer wealth to their social superiors. Collectively owned land, or waste land commonage, was, in theory at least, sufficient for the needs of the non-acquisitive early medieval peasant.

However, as was often the case with Irish historiography, some magical thinking prevailed about the true nature of this early Christian social system, until twentieth-century revisionism introduced an element of realism. In the nineteenth-century Irish imagination, for example, pre-Norman society became a pure and almost utopian 'Celtic' paradise. This idyllic landscape was 'adopted as a poster image for a new nation'. Irish cultural exceptionalism created a legendary and largely specious Golden Age in which the reality of a pyramidal society was conveniently ignored. Even the relatively rigorous Marxist James Connolly became dewy-eyed when he invoked early Christian Irish society as 'a kind of primitive socialist utopia, with the Irish people knowing nothing of absolute property in land'. This was, of course, then cruelly obliterated by 'individualistic English feudalism'.[7]

The spirited Protestant nationalist crusader Alice Stopford Green was a one-woman 'Celtic twilight' propaganda machine in her day (that day being the turn of the nineteenth and twentieth centuries). Her object in writing works like *The Making of Ireland and its Undoing* was, she insisted, 'to help in recovering from centuries of obloquy the memory of noble men, Irish and Anglo-Irish, who built up the civilisation who once adorned their country'. The 'civilisation' to which she referred was pre-Tudor Irish society. Her intention is made clear in her preface. Stopford Green's objective was to present an alternative view of Irish history, one that would counter the image of 'unrelieved barbarism' depicted by early modern English scribes that had justified the 'English extirpation of Irish society'. Even the annalists, those doughty champions of Irish uniqueness, were not above her criticism. Their efforts to spice their narratives with sensational and sanguinary interludes, like a Hollywood thriller writer, meant that they were often 'quoted by historians as telling merely the tale of a corrupted land – feuds and battles, murderings and plunderings'.[8]

While her goal was undoubtedly a worthy one, Stopford Green overcompensated by depicting an idyllic Gaelic Ireland of enlightened chieftains, inconsequential rents (where such were even imposed), absolute security of tenure and extensive communal lands where livestock roamed freely. This semi-classless culture, she concluded, posed a threat to the profoundly hierarchical English Tudor dynasty and its successors:

> The propertied classes evidently feared the Irish land system as expressing what might be called the Socialism of the time … the hostility of the Tudor adventurer sprang from the sense that the occupying farmer on the lands he proposed to appropriate had not too little security but too much … The chief could not evict him and take his land … If an Irish chief exceeded the law he might forfeit his estate.

It was a system rather 'of tenant-at-*tenant's*-will than one of tenant-at-*landlord's*-will'[9] (my italics) and a consummation devoutly to be wished by her avid readers. Whether or not it ever existed as depicted is neither here nor there. It reflected a strain of doctrinal nationalist thinking, or self-delusion, that existed long before Stopford Green put pen to paper. The central tenet of this belief system was that if the land had been taken by main force from ancestors who presided over a caring and egalitarian society, then their descendants were entitled to use all means available to have both the land and the compassionate culture restored.

After independence, in the 1920s, this primitive but wholesome society was depicted as a Shangri-La. In a 'tedious nineteenth-century misconception',[10] it was touted as a utopian society, mercifully free of tiered social structures, an idyll snatched from the native Irish by a raft of colonisers from Strongbow to Cromwell. This purportedly egalitarian society was then cruelly replaced by the imposition of an entitled but undeserving elite who had no inherent right to the land they 'owned' or the privileges they enjoyed. It was an interpretation that added spice to the determinism of the dialectic, a philosophical dimension to the struggle for ownership of Ireland's land which raised it above the level of mere class conflict. It fed into the bitter resentment at the incursions of the *Gallaibh* (the Irish equivalent of that delightfully dismissive and rasping Scottish term *Sassenach*) which informed Irish tenants' attitudes to their landholding overlords. There was never any resigned Irish acceptance of the wave of colonial plantation and indigenous dispossession during the Elizabethan, Stuart and Cromwellian eras.

The fact that no such pastoral Eden ever existed was largely irrelevant. In the twenty-first century we have learned never to underestimate the power of myth, illusion, misdirection, special pleading and even fabrication in the prosecution of a political objective. Medieval annalists, Gaelic poets, *Nation* journalists, revolutionary polemicists and romantic historians like Alice Stopford Green collectively provided the philosophical underpinning for three nineteenth- and twentieth-century 'land wars' by harking back to a distant society purportedly based on sound humanitarian principles. As we will see, much havoc was wreaked in indiscriminate fashion in the attempted restoration of this utopia.

Before getting carried away with the idea that early medieval Irish society was infinitely less dynastic than the social and economic model imposed by the ethnic cleansing of Cromwell, it is worth considering the plight of the *fudir* class (ancestors of the cottier and the labourer), impoverished unfree 'tenants at will', or more accurately 'tenants at whim', who could be removed by a Gaelic chieftain or nobleman from whatever land the lowly tenant had managed to acquire. He was also 'generally rackrented ... so as to leave barely enough for subsistence'.[11] A *saer-fudir* at least held his land for a year at a time and had to be offered some compensation for any improvements made to the property he occupied (so this was not originally a Gladstonian concept), but he still resembled the tenant farmer of the eighteenth and nineteenth centuries, rather than the owner-occupier of the 1930s. A *daer-fudir* had even fewer rights and also owed war service to his chieftain. At least tenants on the post-Famine estates of Anglo-Irish grandees were not obliged to follow their 'betters' into imperial wars as mobile cannon fodder. Although, it has to be said, the obligation to go to war in the army of a ninth-century Irish chieftain might well have been preferable to at least one of the alternative Gaelic gestures of fealty, sucking the nipples of his master![12]

Gaelic chieftains might have lacked the political or military power of your average monarch, but they wielded considerable economic clout in their own territory and monopolised a significant portion of the land of the *tuath*. Irish landed elites were not, as it happens, entirely a product of the eighteenth century, albeit the medieval aristocrat was Gaelic speaking, could not guarantee a transfer of power and wealth to his eldest son, and owed at least some duty of care to his immediate neighbours, whether or not the latter were disposed to suck his nipples.

The rose-tinted spectacles of Stopford Green *et al.* were not shared by all. The Unionist/landlord organisation, the Irish Land Committee, in one of its attempts to sow dissension among the ranks of agrarian agitators in 1880 – it disingenuously purported to side with the '444,729 agricultural labourers with their families who are at the mercy of the farmers' – rubbished claims that the Brehon system had constituted some sort of egalitarian Nirvana. On the contrary, in a pamphlet entitled *The Land Question, Ireland: Confiscation or Contract?*, the authors claimed: 'In the old Celtic times the Celtic tenant was in reality a serf.' The pamphlet went even further, insisting that we must look to the Brehon laws 'for the origin of the deplorable relations between landlord and tenant'.[13] However, the agrarian agitators of the 1880s were not enthusiastic readers – nor indeed the target audience – of the writings of the Irish Land Committee.

Whatever the reality, it was materially altered by the entrepreneurial incursion of the small but effective Norman force under Richard de Clare, Earl of Pembroke (aka Strongbow) in 1169–70, followed in 1171 by the full-scale invasion of King Henry II – one of the few pre-nineteenth-century royal visits. The latter excursion was intended to remind Strongbow who was boss, as much as to overawe the Irish. It might well have led to the comprehensive supplanting of the more loosely tiered Gaelic template of land tenure by the ossified feudal system. But because the invaders were never quite able to subdue entirely the resident Irish 'barbarians', the two systems coexisted. As the invaders and the Irish fought (with each other and amongst themselves) and integrated during the Middle Ages, many of the former grew a shade too enamoured of the Gaelic world – in the words of the cliché, they became 'more Irish than the Irish themselves'. This implied some acceptance of the ancient Irish system of land holding, especially since it cost them nothing to accommodate an Old Irish template less radically different from the feudal variant than Alice Stopford Green chose to believe. However, the nationalist journalist and politician Charles Gavan Duffy was not far from the truth when he described this transition as 'the substitution of the feudal for the patriarchal system'.[14]

When this coexistence began to fray and then finally crumble, the primary cause of the disintegration was, inevitably, religion. A process of what can euphemistically be called ecclesiastical reform commenced with Henry VIII's uncontrollable desire for a younger wife. This reform was carried on by two of his three children before being firmly secured by the first Stuart monarch, James I. It was on the latter's watch that a new term of abuse became widespread in Ireland, that of 'planter'.

Tudors, Stuarts and planters

The inability of the post-Norman 'Lordship' to complete the conquest of Ireland contributed to the conditionality, and to the binary nature, of Irish land tenure. During the Middle Ages, this Lordship could be more notional than real. It often fitted neatly within the confines of the Pale, the area of Anglo-Norman control around Dublin that bulged, like a pot-bellied patrician, into Meath or Kildare. Equally, there were times when its remit stretched across much of the island, while never quite managing to reach into every corner. The agricultural economist Raymond Crotty was of the view that 'there is no doubt that the old Gaelic, or Brehon, land system continued substantially to survive'. Its endurance, up to the time of the Elizabethan conquest, was quite 'remarkable'. The predominance of pastoralism in Ireland, according to Crotty, 'greatly facilitated the system'.[15]

The seventeenth century, and the efforts of James I, Oliver Cromwell and William III to complete the colonisation of Ireland, eliminated any vestigial twinning of the Gaelic and feudal systems. What followed the final death throes of the *ancien régime* was the unwelcome arrival of thousands of new faces, strange tongues and unfamiliar accents.

The disappearance of Gaelic influence had less to do with the elimination of a competing system of land tenure than with the importation of these so-called 'New English' colonisers. Land ownership in Ireland would rapidly become the prerogative of a corps of 'settlers' or 'planters'. These men (and they were all male) were in the vanguard of a drive on the part of Ireland's frustrated neighbours to anglicise the country and to create a Protestant *samurai* class that would suppress dissent, because it was in its financial interest to do so. They would not be circumscribed in any way by the sort of traditional constraints that might have inhibited their Gaelic predecessors. They spoke English; they were the beneficiaries of a system of primogeniture which allowed *them* to pass on their land to their eldest sons; and, notwithstanding disingenuous notions of chivalric obligation, they owed no duty of care to anyone other than their families. In case any members of that elite neglected their duties, 'New English' dominance would be underpinned by the presence in their immediate neighbourhood of a bevy of co-religionists. At least that was the theory.

The future of Ireland – and that included the management of its land – after the upheavals of the seventeenth century was to be Protestant.

The Tudor dynasty had made a decent stab at solving their version of the Irish Question, the ubiquity of rebellious minor potentates. The Laois/Offaly plantation of the Catholic Queen Mary – punishment for the constant raids on the Pale by O'Moores and O'Connors – which created Queen's and King's Counties is a case in point. The Munster plantation of the Protestant Queen Elizabeth, which allowed Sir Walter Raleigh to harvest southern forests for the manufacture of tobacco pipes and wine casks, was another. But it was the first Stuart king, James I, who, after a triumphant Nine Years' War waged by his predecessor and followed by the effective collapse of Gaelic resistance with the Flight of the Earls, really began to settle scores. He achieved this by settling hundreds of English and Scottish adventurers on the forfeited O'Neill and O'Donnell lands in Ulster. The plight of the native Irish there was further exacerbated by the ill-judged and futile gesture in 1608 of Sir Cahir O'Doherty – previously known, with supreme irony, as 'The Queen's O'Doherty' – in rebelling and burning the city of Derry. While he suffered the indignity of having his severed head displayed on a spike in Dublin, O'Doherty's egotistical and pointless insurrection rebounded on the occupants of his lands, which were duly confiscated.

The first Stuart administration was determined to avoid the mistakes made by the Tudors in Laois, Offaly and Munster. One of those had been the fatal decision to leave resentful and recalcitrant Gaels *in situ*. Far better, it was thought, to opt for a major ethnic cleansing in Ulster and rid the fields, forests, lakes and drumlins of their previous owners. The beneficiaries of the plantation – who would, in the main, be paying for their newly acquired privileges – would be staunch British Protestants. An exception was made for a few 'deserving Irish' who had assisted in the campaign against O'Neill and O'Donnell. Accordingly, one-fifth of the land subject to plantation was reserved for the precursors of that much-reviled beast, soon to be dubbed the 'Castle Catholic'. The rest went to corporate investors, high-worth individuals, former military men and the representatives of the Established Church. Or, as they are often designated in current historical accounts, 'London companies', 'undertakers', 'servitors' and Anglicans. Were it to happen today, a grateful British government would describe the process as a private finance initiative, an arrangement known in Irish administrative circles as a public private partnership.

While the 'servitors' (the relatively impecunious military types) and the 'deserving Irish' were allowed to retain native Irish tenants, the London investors and the wealthy 'undertakers' – so-called because of their 'undertakings' to the government rather than a penchant for funeral arrangements – were obliged to recruit British settlers at a rate of twenty-four per 1,000 acres. While the lands of Hugh O'Neill, Rory O'Donnell and Cahir O'Doherty were being planted by the Stuart administration, a parallel operation was being carried on by private Scottish adventurers on an incremental basis in Antrim and Down. Here the immigrant settlers were largely Presbyterian, which would later cause entirely novel headaches. The two enterprises brought upwards of 40,000 British non-Catholic settlers to Ulster over the three decades after 1610.

What happened, of course, after those first three decades had elapsed, was a reaction comparable to that of the Powhatans against the adherents of the Virginia Company in 1622. Back then, hundreds of migrants associated with the Jamestown settlement were reminded by their Native American neighbours that they were present on sufferance, and were despatched from the New World to the next world. Over the first thirty years of the Stuart demographic experiment, native Irish resistance had come, sporadically, from isolated attacks by the so-called 'woodkernes', dispossessed Ulstermen who used the extensive forests of the region as shelter for their murderous acts of revenge. This would ultimately lead to increased deforestation by security-conscious planters.

Not entirely unexpectedly, however, many of the new Ulster *samurai* reneged on pledges made to the administration of James I.

For example, in the same year that Opechancanough led the attacks on the English settlements of Virginia, the 'undertakers' of Tyrone could proudly boast of having placed almost 900 British families on their land. They were probably less inclined to point to the fact that they also retained in place almost 1,200 native Irish tenants in absolute defiance of guarantees (their 'undertakings') made in order to secure the land in the first place. The London Ironmongers' Company was formally obliged to enforce a clause in its purchase agreement that did not permit of the letting of land to 'any person or persons whatsoever natives from within the Kingdom of Ireland'. More than 90 per cent of their tenants would have failed that nationality test, had anyone bothered to check. Across Ulster as a whole it appears that between 1610 and 1640, 'ownership changed but not occupancy'.[16]

But even that reality was not sufficient to avoid a hideous day of reckoning.

'We are for our lives and liberties … we desire no blood to be shed, but if you mean to shed our blood be sure we will be as ready as you for the purpose.'[17] So pledged Sir Con Magennis as he marched at the head of a column of Catholic rebels into Co. Down in October 1641. He may well have been sincere in his assertion that he wanted no blood to be shed, but that was far from the outcome of the Ulster insurrection of that fateful year. It was an eruption of violence that would spread beyond the confines of the northern province, though without quite the same visceral quality elsewhere. It was an uprising entwined within the larger conflict between king (Charles I) and parliament. One of its first leaders, Sir Phelim O'Neill, claimed to be acting on the authority of Charles I. The outcome in Ulster was a series of appalling and vengeful sectarian massacres of thousands of Ulster Protestants (up to 30 per cent of the settler population in the province), described in bitter and gory detail in the famous 1641 Depositions. These documents – running to around 20,000 pages and stored in Trinity College, Dublin – recorded the testimonies of some of the survivors of the insurrection, an event that scarred Ulster Protestant memory for generations.

While it is dangerous to oversimplify such events, the 1641 uprising in Ulster can be seen as having been motivated by two primeval and related elements: an overwhelming desire for revenge and frustrated land hunger. Granted, there was an overarching sectarian backdrop and high politics would subsume the baser motives as the English Civil War was mirrored on Irish battlefields, but the first phase of the 1641 uprising in Ulster can be seen as an exceptionally lethal land war conducted for restitution of the seizures of the Ulster plantation. While agrarian issues were never far from the surface of future Irish nationalist rebellions (1641 does not fit comfortably into this category), the outbreak of murderous rage in Ulster was as much about 'thy neighbour's goods' as it was about his form of worship. That frenzy met its match in the revenge of the Puritan Oliver Cromwell on the Irish people.

Which, in turn, would give rise to the most comprehensive 'land grab' in early modern Irish history.

The Down Survey, 1656–8

'Your petitioner now humbly conceives it neither unseasonable nor unreasonable to make the ensuing remonstrance unto your honours of the said grievance, nor doeth he doubt of your tender and conscionable consideration thereof.'[18]

(Sir William Petty to the Lord Protector's Council for the Affairs of Ireland, 1656)

The 'Doctor of Physicke' had had enough. He had spent sufficient of his own funds on this project without reimbursement and was applying to the governing council 'for reliefe'. William Petty wanted his money back. His 'zeale to promote the service' was at a low ebb. He was aware that his predecessor had chronically overspent and that 'their honours' – the members of the Lord Protector's Council for the Affairs of Ireland – were reluctant to throw good money after bad. However, they must now accept that, in attempting to carry out his appointed task, he had been 'exceedingly damnifyed'. Ireland was, after all, a blighted land where unexpected contingencies were the rule rather than the exception. And then there was the damp and wild weather. As he put it himself, 'through the extreame [*sic*] wetness and windiness ... the whole work had miscarried or been retarded'.

If the Council demurred, Dr Petty could always resume his former position as Professor of Anatomy at Brasenose College, Oxford, where he had once denied his students a corpse for dissection by resuscitating a hanged man after he had been taken down from the gallows. Now it looked as if he would have to perform a comparable feat in his new avocation. He must have wondered why he had abandoned the dreaming spires of Oxford for the discomforts of a ravaged country still reeling from the military attentions of 'their honours' and of the Lord Protector himself. Why continue to work at such 'extraordinary charge and hazard' when he could be instructing undergraduate doctors of 'physicke' in the comfortable surroundings of Brasenose, or in London's Gresham College, where Christopher Wren would soon become Professor of Astronomy. Back in Oxford, Petty was unlikely to be required to risk life and limb, as he certainly was while mapping rural Ireland under the resentful gaze of dispossessed Catholics while 'naked of ... guards'.

Enough was enough. Dr Petty was determined to make the Council sit up and take notice. His enterprise was of paramount importance and the payment of hundreds of Cromwellian soldiers depended on it. So 'their honours' – the more he used the phrase, the more it reeked of irony – must be forced 'to relieve him of the aforementioned grievances'.[19]

When the word 'arrears' is used in the context of land, it generally refers to an amount of money outstanding between tenant and landowner. In the middle of the seventeenth century, however, this was not necessarily the case. Back then, it could have an entirely different connotation. 'Arrears' was just as likely to refer to the payment owed to a soldier who had put his life on the line while cutting a swathe through Ireland at the behest of the Lord Protector. Oliver Cromwell, in order to extirpate popery and make Ireland safe for the worship of an implacable Protestant God, had made promises of prompt payment to many of his soldiers. There were up to 35,000 of these eagerly awaiting remuneration, mostly in the form of the land of their luckless opponents.

Cromwell came to 'maintain the lustre and glory of English liberty', and departed prematurely – although not before the demise of up to 20,000 rebels and 8,000 members of his own New Model Army – but well content with his labours. He left behind, however, a troop of grumbling combatants who had not been paid. Also on the debit side was the imminent repayment of the contributions to the war of reconquest by the Merchant Adventurers of Britain, early capitalists who loaned money to the parliamentary forces on a promise of prime Irish land.

There was really only one way to settle these particular arrears – hence the legislation entitled the Act of Settlement (1652) specifying who would forfeit land in Ireland. This was quickly followed in 1653 with the order to transplant Catholic landowners to Connacht, as an alternative to Hell. The final deadline for removal was March 1655.

Unfortunately for many of the victorious veterans of the regrettable (but apparently essential) massacres of Drogheda and Wexford, before they were legally secure in their new holdings, the followers of the restored monarch, Charles II, were on the verge of exhuming the late Lord Protector and beheading his corpse. This was despite the elegantly named Act of Satisfaction of September 1653 that had begun the process of allotting the land of Catholic landowners to the members of this new, ready-made ascendancy class. The survey, which was supposed to map the Irish land that was being gifted to deserving Roundheads – the so-called Down Survey – was not completed until the year of Cromwell's death, 1658.

It was actually the third attempt on the part of the architects of the Cromwellian settlement to quantify their gains. The Grosse Survey of 1653 and the Civill [sic] Survey of the following year – which assigned a monetary value to the land of each Irish townland as of 23 October 1641 – were its precursors, and led to 'wholesale confiscation on a basis of incomplete knowledge and conjectural calculations of measurement'.[20] Much of the management of both exercises had been left to a man named Benjamin Worsley (sometimes spelled Worsly or Worseley), who appears to have been less than puritanical in his devotion to duty, or indeed to budgetary parsimony, and was 'admonished of … miscarriages'[21] by his successor.

Accordingly, the task of carrying out the most efficient and detailed assessment of the value of Irish land was handed to the English army's surgeon general, William Petty. He was a man accustomed to amputation without anaesthetic and was, therefore, unlikely to be too perturbed by the lamentations of Catholics being shorn of their property. The 'Down' Survey was so-called 'to mark its distinction from those former surveys, by its topographical details being all laid down by admeasurement on maps'[22] – which suggests that Worsley, by contrast, was, in modern parlance, something of a 'back of the envelope' operator. However, his services must have been of some value, because they were retained by Petty. The Down Survey used the Civill Survey as a template and created maps on a scale of 40 perches* to an inch. Although the primary object of this vastly ambitious project was to study and record townland boundaries, the resulting maps also included natural features such as rivers and forests, as well as much of the built environment of the time (roads, churches, castles and houses). There were certainly fewer people to gaze in wonder at, or interfere with, the work of the topographers than there had been at the time of the arrival of the Parliamentary soldiers and settlers. Petty himself calculated that the population of Ireland declined from almost 1.5 million people in the mid-1640s to just over 850,000 a decade later, after the ferocious Cromwellian wars.

With the restoration of the monarchy in 1660, the gains of Cromwellian soldiers, and of the English investors in his Irish adventure, could have been threatened. The work of William Petty

---

* A perch is approximately 5.5 yards or 5.03 metres. The unit was abolished in the UK by the 1963 Weights and Measures Act but still survives in the USA; 40 perches to an inch is a scale of around 1:8,000.

and his military surveyors might well have been an elegant waste of energy. The restored king could have negated the concessions of land awarded to the enemies of monarchy and the murderers of his father. However, regrettably – for the former Catholic owners of the redistributed Irish land at least – that was not part of the Grand Plan. Instead, in his 'Gracious Declaration' of November 1660, King Charles II – who owed a debt to Irish Protestants instrumental in the restoration of the monarchy – confirmed the Cromwellian settlement in Ireland a few short months before his followers disinterred and abused the corpse of his father's executioner. The plantation proved to be a dual-purpose vehicle. The widespread transfer of land in the 1650s was not designed merely as payment to loyal Cromwellian soldiers in lieu of cash. It was also intended 'to establish such a strong population of English protestants as would ensure the future loyalty and tranquillity of Ireland'.[23] Of course, it signally failed to achieve either of those objectives, in the longer term at least.

Those whose land had been expropriated, assuming they had not played an active role in the massacres of 1641, or had figured prominently on the losing side of the Cromwellian war – in such cases their lives as well as their lands were forfeit – were transplanted west of the Shannon. This corralling, according to historian Roy Foster, could have been worse, as the land of Ulster was actually considered to be of poorer quality than that of Connacht.[24] The vast majority of Irish Catholic landowners were resettled on smaller holdings in the west of Ireland, although some were able to plead their case before a Restoration-era Court of Claims and regain some or all of their lands in Munster and Leinster. Assuming, of course, that the Cromwellian settlers already in possession were prepared to vacate and move elsewhere. As the Duke of Ormond, future Lord Lieutenant, observed tartly, 'There must be discoveries made of a new Ireland, for the old will not serve to satisfy these engagements.'[25] Conversely, because there was not enough land in the ten eastern and southern counties originally surveyed to satisfy the claims of Cromwell's troops, some of the 'Catholic land' west of the Shannon was also allocated to Protestant settlers.

When the 1641 rebellion began, Catholics still owned nearly 60 per cent of Irish land. After the Cromwellian settlement, that figure had declined by two-thirds. By the middle of the eighteenth century, Irish land in Catholic ownership amounted to around 3 per cent of the total. Cromwell, with unexpected co-operation from King Charles II, had been instrumental in a radical and comprehensive conveyance of Irish property. The activities of the Lord Protector would not be forgotten, nor would the assumption on the part of the Irish peasantry of the eighteenth and nineteenth centuries that their ancestors had been the victims of an illicit land seizure, the fruits of which were now being enjoyed by the Protestant descendants of the Cromwellian era, their current landlords.

Ironically, around two-thirds of those who had originally been granted Irish land never even took possession of it. Instead, they sold on their newly acquired properties. One of the beneficiaries was Thomas Taylor from Sussex, employed by Petty on the Down Survey. Eyeing an extensive piece of land in Co. Meath, he purchased it from its original Cromwellian recipient. His successors would become the Earls of Bective and the Marquesses of Headfort and would acquire an additional vowel in their surname to become the much grander 'Taylour' in the early 1800s. Petty himself was also a beneficiary. He received 3,500 acres of Kerry land for his work on the Down Survey but quickly began adding to this portfolio by snapping up more acres from settlers anxious to be elsewhere. Altogether, he acquired 18,000 acres, mostly around Kenmare in Co. Kerry, but stretching over five counties. By the time of his death in 1687, he was reckoned to be the richest commoner in Ireland (he steadfastly declined all offers of a peerage), with a rent roll of between £5,000 and £6,000 per annum.[26] His descendants, the Petty-Fitzmaurices, would retain the land (they still hold much of the original grant) as the Marquesses of Lansdowne.

Three decades after William Petty became an agent in this unprecedented reassignment of landed wealth, further restitution would be required of the vanquished by the victors in the Williamite wars of the early 1690s. The passage of the Gavelkind

Act in 1703 changed the nature of inheritance and hastened the decline in the size of Catholic landholdings. Inherited Catholic land, rather than going to the eldest male, thus maintaining the integrity of the holding, was now to be divided amongst the surviving male heirs.[27] But by then the die had already been cast. Cromwell, his lieutenants (who included his son, Henry, and son-in-law, Henry Ireton) and able bureaucrats like Petty ensured that a few thousand Protestant landowners would put down roots and enjoy largely unfettered privileges, while Catholics, whether or not their families had ever actually been dispossessed of a significant acreage of land, would seethe for the next two and a half centuries over the great Cromwellian conveyance, ensuring that Irish 'loyalty and tranquillity' would remain elusive. The land, from now on, was all that mattered.

II

Insurrection

3

Na buachaillí bána

'Their first rise was in October last and they have ever since been increasing … They always assembled in the night with their shirts over their clothes which caused them to be called Whiteboys.'[1]

(a Youghal gentleman writing to his son,
The Gentleman's Magazine, April 1762)

Irish Whiteboys – illustration for The Pictorial History of England, *W & R Chambers, 1858*

Cork, 1763

The three convicts had each been escorted to their respective gallows by a platoon of infantry and cavalry. The authorities in Cork were taking no chances. There had been numerous attempts to rescue convicted prisoners. When the three men ascended the gallows' steps on their way to meet their maker, in the towns of Glanworth, Fermoy and Mitchelstown, respectively, they were dressed in the 'uniform' of their secret agrarian society. They were forced to wear their white linen shirts over their outer clothing as a reminder to the spectators, not that one was required, of the nature of the crimes for which the hangman was about to snuff out their lives. The three condemned men were Whiteboys, agrarian activists also known as 'Levellers' or, in the Irish language, *buachaillí bána*, members of an oath-bound movement pledged to end the enclosure of thousands of acres of Munster that had heretofore been treated as common land or 'commonage', available to all for growing a small crop of potatoes or grazing a few head of livestock.

These three Whiteboys, as well as the twenty or so others who were to die on the gallows in the 1760s, would have been puzzled by the accusation – brought by landowners intent on engaging the attention of the authorities in Dublin – that they were the vanguard of a covert Catholic militia devoted to the restoration of the Stuart pretenders to the throne of England, and allied to Catholic France. That line of argument flew in the face of logic. While they might have cheered lustily at the prospect of a Catholic King of England, they were not about to lift a finger on behalf of the moribund Stuart cause.

The demands of the Levellers had more to do with preventing the erection of walls and ditches around common land and thwarting the demands of local 'gombeen men' who had bought out the right to collect clerical tithes. Their allegiance to 'Queen Sive' was more important to them than the Jacobite claims to the British monarchy, claims that had evaporated on the bloody battlefield of Culloden in 1746. To the Whiteboys, even a mythical Celtic princess, 'Sive' or 'Sieve', was a more corporeal presence than Bonnie Prince Charlie.

The three men, who had been convicted together in Cork but met their deaths on separate scaffolds in order to maximise the warning to others who might be hoping to emulate them, were among the first Whiteboy fatalities. They died horribly, probably from strangulation after twisting for some minutes at the end of a noose. The humane 'Haughton knot' – devised by the Carlow-born Trinity College fellow Samuel Haughton – which would have ended their agonies far more quickly by breaking their necks, was more than a century in the future.

Houghers, Whiteboys, Rightboys, Rackavallas, Lady Clares, Black Hens, Terry Alts, Thrashers ...

'It is frequently of late years, in different parts of this kingdom, that several persons calling themselves Whiteboys and others, as well by night and in daytime, have in a riotous, disorderly, and tumultuous manner, assembled together, and have abused and injured the persons, habitations, and properties of many of his Majesty's loyal and faithful subjects ...'²

(Preamble to the 'Whiteboy Act', 1775)

It is a truth universally acknowledged – with apologies to Jane Austen – that Irish insurgencies are a function of political nationalism. The militants of 1798, 1848, 1867 and 1916 who rose against British rule are generally treated as the authentic Irish rebels, as if such insurrections were the be all and end all of Irish defiance. What is often ignored in the hagiography of militant nationalism is that rural Ireland generated numerous insurrections other than those undertaken by the United Irishmen, Young Irelanders or Irish Republican Brotherhood. These localised uprisings were the responsibility of diverse peasant secret societies, often bearing exotic names. They occurred in every decade between 1760 and the Great Famine of the 1840s. Most were more coherent and better organised – though perhaps less as psychologically or spiritually meaningful – than, for example, the hapless *coup d'état* attempts of the Young Irelanders of 1848, or the Fenians of 1867. These agrarian uprisings also generated more fatalities than any nationalist insurrection other than the exceptionally bloody 1798 rebellion.

Many of these disturbances took place in an era during which recourse to peaceful protest was impracticable or inadvisable. The establishment response to public dissent (aka illegal assembly) was rarely serene and restrained. It was more likely to involve a spirited reading of the Riot Act, followed by a cavalry charge that often included the unsheathing of swords. When broken heads, cutlass wounds, incarceration or death were occupational hazards of peaceful dissent, violent reaction to any unacceptable deterioration in economic or social conditions was inevitable. As the leader of the Home Rule League of the 1870s, Isaac Butt, put it, in acknowledging the savagery of the Whiteboy response to oppression, 'The truculence of every servile insurrection is proportioned to the cruelties with which the slaves have been treated.'3

The militancy of the Whiteboys, the Rightboys, the Hearts of Oak and the Hearts of Steel, however, had more to do with liberation from various forms of what amounted to agrarian servitude than with the glorification of the figurative Caitlín ní hUallacháin (Cathleen ní Houlihán). Hence the historiographical tendency to breeze past them, as if they were mere character actors, and pursue the real stars of eighteenth-century Irish history – Wolfe Tone, Henry Joy McCracken, the Sheares brothers, and the unfortunate and romanticised Lord Edward Fitzgerald.

But the agrarian secret societies of the late eighteenth century somehow managed to make a major nuisance of themselves without a Tone, Emmet, Davis or Mitchel at the helm, either leading the charge or articulating the philosophy behind the crusade. Occasionally, agrarian rebels did make common cause with the forces of political nationalism; at other times their interests were antithetical. There were marriages of convenience along the way but, just as often, both these anti-establishment manifestations kept their distance from each other.

Some of these agrarian uprisings were short-lived, arriving with the dandelions and departing with the early frosts. The

Oakboy revolt did not last that long. It has even been suggested that some were mere recreational escapades, amplifications of the rather more innocent Mayboys, Wrenboys and Strawboys – harmless seasonal recreational traditions, some of which persist to this day – or extensions of the somewhat less innocent pursuits of smuggling, poaching and illicit distillation.[4] Some secret societies were so parochial in their reach, and limited in their objectives, that their fame barely spread beyond the boundary of parish or barony. Others, however, were so potent that it took more armed men in red coats to put down their insurgencies than the number of constables who accounted for the Young Irelanders at 'Widow McCormick's cabbage patch' in 1848, or the Fenians at the 'Tallaght Races' of 1867.

If you like your Irish rebels to be lethally effective, the Whiteboys and their rhyming heirs the Rightboys, although they were regional and extemporised militias with constrained aspirations, deserve a place in the pantheon of Irish mischief-makers, situated, in terms of efficacy, somewhere between the 1916 Volunteers and the United Irishmen of 1798, albeit walking on the darker side of the alley of conspiracy, while operating their own 'frontier-type law'.[5]

1741, *Bliain an áir – the year of the slaughter*

To commemorate the centenary of the attempted ethnic cleansing of Ulster Protestants by their Roman Catholic neighbours in 1641, nature took its own revenge.

The 'Year of the Great Frost', the exceptionally harsh winter of 1740–41 – during which a hurling match took place on the river Shannon – was followed by an unusually dry spring, and up to 400,000 people (the lowest estimate is 300,000) out of an already weakened population of around 2.6 million died of starvation, hypothermia or disease. This was *bliain an áir* – the year of the slaughter.[6] In terms of morbidity it was the worst catastrophe since the campaigns of Oliver Cromwell (1650–51), when 'Colonel Hunger and Major Sickness' accounted for between 200,000 and

600,000 excess deaths. Proportionally, it had a more detrimental effect on the population than the Great Famine of the 1840s, with an estimated fatality rate of 13–20 per cent, as against 12 per cent between 1845 and 1850. However, its political impact – because of the urgency of the charitable response and an embargo on most food exports – was less socially and psychologically profound than the mid-nineteenth-century subsistence crisis. Furthermore, unlike the Great Famine, its long-term demographic impact was mitigated by a century of rapid population increase.

By the 1740s, the growing population of Ireland, which had numbered just under 2 million in 1687, had already begun to turn for its nourishment to the increasingly ubiquitous and wholesome potato. However, unlike the later Great Famine, in the 1740s the potato did not dominate the diet of the Irish peasant. Also, unlike the blight (*Phytophthora infestans*) of the Great Famine, the 'super crisis' of 1741 did not attack the humble potato directly. But it hugely reduced the available stores of tubers and grains, increased food prices dramatically – the price of potatoes more than trebled – and led to catastrophic shortages.

What the Great Frost also achieved was to reinforce lessons learned in the 1720s, another decade of famine (1720–21 and 1726–9), about the precarious nature of Irish agrarian life and the vulnerability of agricultural communities to the vagaries of the always uncertain Irish weather. That the Great Frost of the winter of 1740–41 came at the tail end of what we now call the Little Ice Age was not a meteorological fact to which the general population was privy at the time. Neither, despite the general increase in global temperatures from the early 1800s, was it to be the last occasion on which climatic conditions would play havoc with the rural economy.

The 1741 crisis had its origins in extreme weather conditions that began in the autumn and winter of 1739–40. This included seven weeks of 'the black frost', concerning which Jonathan Swift, fearing a Siberian winter, observed that 'our kingdom is turned to be a Muscovy, or worse'.[7] A contributing environmental factor may have been a series of volcanic eruptions in eastern Russia. Most of the deaths in early 1740 came from hypothermia rather than hunger. The crisis was initially less acute in rural Ireland than in Dublin. Poverty and hunger, however, were desperate enough in rural Kildare, for example, to persuade the Conollys of Castletown House in Leixlip to spend £300–400 on a public works scheme that resulted in the building of a distinctive obelisk, which still stands on the estate today.

The crisis, however, quickly overtook the countryside as well. Famine conditions prevailed throughout but were especially severe in Munster, where the potato and wheat crops suffered. Conditions were so bad on the Kerry-Limerick border that there were instances of cattle raids – the practice had not suddenly ended with the arrival of the *Gallaibh* – in a desperate search for food. The emergency was exacerbated by the fact that in the mid-1700s, 'famine in Ireland was caused not simply by the fact that the Irish harvest had failed but that harvests had failed elsewhere as well'.[8] The adverse weather conditions of 1739–41 were felt just as keenly in other parts of Europe. Shrunken agricultural production inhibited supply and elevated prices across the entire continent.

In a pamphlet, *The Groans of Ireland*, published in Dublin in 1741, the author speculated that between 200,000 and 400,000 people died in the subsistence crisis. He described: 'The roads spread with dead and dying bodies … of the colour of the docks and nettles which they fed on; two or three, sometimes more, on a car going to the grave for want of bearers to carry them, and many buried only in the fields and ditches where they perished.'[9]

Emigration to pre-industrial Britain was not an option because similar meteorological conditions prevailed there. Some of those who attempted to seek relief on the neighbouring island were simply deported back to Ireland. Others were publicly whipped for the sin of failing in their attempt to become a drain on scarce English resources. Emigration beyond the borders of what would become the United Kingdom of Great Britain and Ireland in 1801 was possible but prohibitively expensive for all but the affluent. Transportation for food theft was one of the riskier ways of gaining access to North America (where British penal colonies still existed). Most Irish migration during the 1740–41 crisis, however, was internal.[10]

September deluges, followed by October snow, presaged a crisis to follow that of the autumn of 1740, and so it proved. In contrast to the widespread estate clearances of the Great Famine of the 1840s, however, landlords in mid-eighteenth-century Ireland tended more towards forbearance, and most accepted the inevitability of a temporary build-up of rent arrears. However, as the crisis of 1740 became the crisis of 1741, direct charitable intervention by landowners declined on account of 'a growing realisation that they were never going to receive all of what was owed to them because of default as well as death'.[11] Middlemen, who leased from landlords and sub-let to under-tenants, were less tolerant. However, most landowners appear to have taken a longer view than did some of their nineteenth-century counterparts.

'Bucks, bloods, land-jobbers, and little drunken country gentlemen'

Although no longer 'tribal' (notwithstanding the popular leisure pursuit of faction fighting), Irish society in the eighteenth century was still overwhelmingly rural. (It also remained, *qua* historian Daniel Binchy (see Chapter 2), 'familiar' and 'hierarchical', although the nature of that hierarchal structure had radically altered.) In 1725, only about 300,000 people out of a population of up to 2.5 million lived in the country's eight largest towns (six of which were ports – Kilkenny and Lisburn being the most populous inland centres). To put Irish urban life in perspective, Ennis, the Clare county seat, boasted only 120 houses in 1725. Fewer than a thousand people lived in the town. Today, when the population of a more urbanised island of Ireland is barely three times larger than it was in the third decade of the eighteenth century, the inhabitants of Ennis number over 25,000.

While many of those who lived in the larger urban centres were indirectly dependent on agriculture, upwards of three-quarters of the country's population was involved in, or dependent upon, the land. The vast majority were tenants of the 10,000 or so members of the (largely Protestant) Irish landed class. Most of the members of the Irish peasantry were heavily involved in tillage farming. Pastoral land was the preserve of tenants with larger holdings.

The anti-Catholic Penal Laws of the post-Williamite period were never quite as effective or as oppressive as contemporary and subsequent accounts suggest. This was especially true in the case of the restriction placed on the duration of leases for Roman Catholic tenants. Until remedial legislation was passed in 1778, these could be no longer than thirty-one years. In practice, a lease of this duration was usually more than adequate and many such leases were taken up in the eighteenth century by Catholic middlemen (*na tiarnaí beaga* – or 'little landlords'),[12] many of whom were members of former Catholic landholding dynasties, who then sub-let to under-tenants at a higher rent and kept the difference for themselves. By the time the Penal Law restriction was removed, many 'improving' landlords were already offering leases considerably shorter in duration than thirty-one years to Protestant and Catholic tenants alike. This was part of a drive to remove the middleman from the equation and grant leases directly to occupying tenants. Many absentee landed proprietors in particular, whose families had casually drifted into the abrogation of responsibility for their estates to these middlemen – and had, in effect, created a class of rural Catholic 'squireens' (literally 'little squires') – now sought greater involvement in the management of their own estates. The middlemen, in some instances at least, had become 'obnoxious to improvers because of their hard-drinking idle ways',[13] although many Irish landowners – the short-lived Thomas 'Buck' Whaley,* whose estates were worth £7,000 a year, was merely the most egregious – were hardly saintly paragons themselves. Thus did a dollop of snobbery, a tincture of prurience, a hint of hypocrisy and a bushel of self-interest herald the beginning of the end for an often parasitical class of agrarian wholesalers. The middleman had not quite had his day yet, but it was approaching rapidly.

---

* Whaley, by the age of sixteen, was so dissipated that his family was forced to send him abroad to curb his spending. He claimed to have gone through £400,000 during his short life (he died at thirty-four) in drinking and gambling.

In the novel *Castle Rackrent*, Maria Edgeworth, through her narrator 'Honest' Thady Quirk, refers to middlemen as those 'who grind the face of the poor, and can never bear a man with a hat upon his head'.[14] The class was unlikely to be missed by their under-tenants, since, in addition to their many other failings, the ramifications of a middleman's default were often visited upon the conscientious tenant who had paid his rent. Landlords unable to extract rent due from a middleman were apt to instruct their agent to seize livestock or crops from under-tenants, who might well have already remitted their own rent to the middleman.

These *über*-tenants often saw themselves as being of equal status with some of the less affluent landholding squires. Charging their under-tenants up to twice the rent that they were sending to the landlord helped keep them in the manner to which they had become accustomed. Many of the most infamous eighteenth-century Irish rakes, duellists and profligates – the country was noted for the abundance of its patrician reprobates – came from this semi-aristocratic class, or, as Arthur Young characterised them, 'the bucks, bloods, land-jobbers, and little drunken country gentlemen'.[15]

The extent to which the middlemen were enmeshed in pre-Famine rural Ireland can be deduced from an 1843 survey conducted into the extensive land holdings of Trinity College, Dublin. This found that Trinity had more than 12,000 tenants on its various estates. However, only 1 per cent of those, around 120, held their land directly from the college itself. Just under half rented from a college lessee, while a little over half rented from a middleman who was himself renting from another middleman. The success of landowners in curtailing the ubiquity of the middleman can be determined by reference to the same Trinity estates in 1880. In a representative sample of thirty-six townlands, 'the proportion of tenants holding directly either from the College or from a College lessee rose from 22 per cent to 60 per cent. The number of tenants at one remove from the lessors had declined from 78 per cent to 40 per cent.'[16]

In his *Tour in Ireland*, the late eighteenth-century traveller Arthur Young regularly excoriated Irish middlemen who, he observed, 'have flourished almost to the destruction of the kingdom'.[17] Roy Foster, however, believes middlemen to have suffered from a 'bad press', in part due to Young's oft-expressed distaste for the species. Foster has observed that 'the middleman structure was a necessary means of capitalizing the tenants, as middlemen provided stock for the farms they relet', although his observation that 'they were not parasites pure and simple'[18] and economic historian L. M. Cullen's contention that 'middlemen were not always drones'[19] are hardly ringing endorsements of the class.

A *de facto* caste system existed in Irish eighteenth-century rural society. At the apex of the hierarchical structure was the landowner himself (or occasionally herself). The next level down was the middleman or the substantial 'gentleman' farmer. What in England would probably have been described as 'husbandmen' came next in the pecking order. These were modest tenant farmers who might rent anything from 20 to 100 acres. In areas where agriculture was predominantly pastoral, their farms tended to be larger than those in tillage-heavy regions.

Below them – tuppence to the tuppence halfpenny of the 'comfortable' farmer – was the smallholder. Generally working a farm of less than 20 acres – other than in areas of poor land quality where more space was required even to qualify as a smallholder – this was agricultural activity at a level barely above subsistence. A smallholder might have enough acres for one or two cattle and would also be likely to keep a couple of pigs. But to provide for the immediate needs of his own family he was almost invariably a tillage farmer, growing grain crops to pay the rent and potatoes to feed himself, his wife and his children. The smallholder was a fully paid-up member of an eighteenth-century Irish version of the latter-day 'precariat'.

There was, however, a level of hell below that of even the smallholder. The real 'untouchables' of the Irish land system of the eighteenth, and indeed the nineteenth and early twentieth centuries, were the members of that often ill-defined group known as 'cottiers' (sometimes 'cottars'). These were labourers who rented a tiny holding from a tenant farmer, usually based on the 'conacre' system, the rent on the tiny parcel of land – generally around an acre – being paid by the labour of the cottier. According to the economic historian L. M. Cullen, 'The cottier afforded a sharp contrast with the tenant farmer. The latter knew real want only in the worst years of the century; the former lived permanently at the subsistence line.'[20]

The subdivision of farms, rampant in the first half of the nineteenth century, was less of a feature in eighteenth-century Ireland. The arithmetical logic of the population statistics of the 1700s ensured that this was the case. The estimated population of the country in 1749, after the crippling 1741 famine, was between 2 and 2.3 million. However, by 1841, precisely the same area of land was supporting four times as many people. This was largely as a consequence of the constant and detrimental division of farms into ever smaller units. Primogeniture (inheritance by the first-born male) applied only to Ireland's wealthier classes, who had alternative options for their 'spare' children.

In some areas, subdivision, even where it did exist, was not such an ongoing threat to economic stability. In counties like Armagh, whose rural prosperity was based on the linen industry rather than on agricultural production, farms were heavily subdivided in the eighteenth century. But this was because Armagh farmers – who arguably did not even merit the title 'farmer' – were far less dependent on the soil for their income, which came from using locally grown flax to generate their products.

In areas where the traditional rundale system applied, farms were also, in effect, subdivided, in that a group of peasants took a lease and worked their land in partnership. Mayo was a case in point, with much of the county operating under the rundale system, a template whose origins may have stretched as far back as the Iron Age. In Mayo, entire townlands, with a 'nucleated group of farmhouses'[21] or a *clachan* at the centre, were frequently 'divided into two or three categories distinguished by quality'.[22] Parcels of land were then distributed at the behest of the community.

In his evidence in 1845 to the Devon Commission – a parliamentary body investigating a system of land tenure that, unbeknownst to the participants, was on the verge of catastrophe – the Dean of Killala, the Very Rev. John Patrick Lyons, described the rundale system to the commissioners:

A man got a ridge of good, a ridge of middling, and a ridge of bad land, in different parts of the field in proportion to his rent … four men are the parties who are generally responsible to the landlord. They are the persons who determine the … quantity of tillage land to which each of the tenants is entitled in proportion to the rent to which he is liable.[23]

The four headsmen (as they were also called) were, or quickly became, community leaders and dispute arbitrators of the quasi-collective. Rundale was not dissimilar to the traditional British 'infield-outfield' system, which often prevailed in areas where land was plentiful but of poor quality.

While rundale might sound like a highly desirable commune-type system of land usage, it was fraught with predictable difficulties. An early nineteenth-century English visitor, Edward Wakefield, pointed out some of its disadvantages in a book published during the Napoleonic wars, which was actually one of the more prosperous interludes for Irish farmers who operated above mere subsistence levels, i.e. in a cash economy:

As long as this system exists, there can be no emulation for draining, enclosing, limeing [*sic*], or carrying into execution any permanent plan for rendering the land more productive, since none of the party [has] any division which may properly be called their own.[24]

Rundale persisted in Mayo long after it had died out in other parts of the country – 63 per cent of the total area of the county was still held under the rundale system during the period of the Great Famine, while countrywide the figure was by then less than 10 per cent – but this owed more to landscape and land hunger than fraternal amity. The last adherents of the rundale system were pragmatists, not nineteenth-century hippies. It was 'a functional adaptation to the specific ecological circumstances of the Irish Western Seaboard'.[25] The co-operative nature of the system provided a means by which the best pastures in a townland could be shared. It also mitigated some of the more destructive effects of the subdivision of holdings. But, as everyone from Joseph Stalin to the Manson family has discovered, communes in their various guises have a habit of eventually becoming less than communal. With rundale, what began in a spirit of co-operation often concluded, if the headsmen proved ineffectual, in a welter of recrimination or litigation as allegations of encroachment and favouritism superseded fellowship and collaboration.

'The meridian of Barbary'[26]

'... the man of wealth and pride
Takes up a space that many poor supplied;
Space for his lake, his park's extended bounds,
Space for his horses, equipage, and hound.'

(Oliver Goldsmith, *The Deserted Village*, 1770)

'They then, and all along, pretended that their assembling was to do justice to the poor, by restoring the ancient commons and redressing other grievances ... Their number in the county of Waterford is computed at 600 or 700. They have done infinite damage in the county, levelling ditches and stone-walls, rooting up orchards.'[27]

(letter from a property owner in Youghal to his son in London, *The Gentleman's Magazine*, April 1762)

In the wake of the Williamite wars of the 1690s and attempts (not always successful) by the new monarch to gift large tracts of Irish land to his friends and loyalists, the dissenting voice of the dispossessed tended to be represented by the *toraidhe*, or 'tories', of the open road. These were highwaymen who relieved travellers of their wealth or offered 'protection' to the more sedentary. They were seen (often erroneously) as the victims of Williamite confiscation. They have tended to assume a similar status in Ireland as the James

Gang in the post-Civil War American southern states, or as Robin Hood and his Merrie Men in early Plantagenet Nottinghamshire. They were, however, not part of some larger collectivist agrarian movement. While in some cases their chosen profession might have been forced upon them by the dispossessions of the seventeenth century, they were essentially sole traders with a penchant for robbing from the 'rich' to give to themselves.

Although the more dynamic and well-organised covert agrarian organisations mostly date from the period after *Bliain an áir* (1741), there were some collective responses to land-related grievances before the more noteworthy upsurge in agrarian violence from the 1760s onwards. An interesting example is that of the Houghers of Connacht, who flowered briefly in the early 1700s (1711–12) and, in some respects, were violent trailblazers when it came to their particular grievance. Whereas the late eighteenth-century secret societies were generally concerned with issues such as the disappearance of common land; the payment of tithes to the clergy of the Established Church; the levying of local 'cess' taxes; and even excessive levels of financial support to Roman Catholic clergy, the Houghers' campaign was fought over an issue that recurred with a vengeance during the so-called Ranch War of the early 1900s, namely the encroachment of large livestock herds onto land previously used for tillage, and the acquisition of large tracts for grazing by wealthy breeders. The Houghers – the name derived from the cruel practice of maiming animals by cutting their hamstrings – first appeared in west Co. Galway. They objected to the proliferation of stock rearing and demanded an end to dairy farming or, as they styled it, the 'selling of milk, like huxters'.[28] They also created a template for their successors by adopting disguises as they went about their nocturnal activities, and issued threatening letters and published notices in the name of a mythical leader. The Captain Moonlight of the Houghers went by the ubiquitous Connacht name of Joyce ('Ever Joyce').

There then followed half a century of relative, if occasionally simmering, peace, although there was enough communal mischief abroad in the 1750s for the government to introduce legislation outlawing combinations against tithes. But after the Houghers returned, albeit by a different name and in an unexpected part of the country, there would be no further extended periods of concord. From the time those successors, the Whiteboys, donned their linen robes in the 1760s, agrarian unrest was rampant in Ireland. It also became identified with the term Whiteboy. It was many decades into the nineteenth century before the word 'Whiteboyism' was gradually replaced by 'Ribbonism' to describe the depredations of members of agrarian secret societies, but the nomenclature overlapped and is less relevant than the clear continuity of purpose.

Why did the Munster countryside suddenly become unsafe for landlords, middlemen and substantial farmers in the 1760s? While not entirely accurate in his summation, there is a certain legitimacy about the assertion in 1867 of barrister, writer and future leader of the Home Rule League Isaac Butt that, 'previous to this period we find in Irish histories no notice of agrarian outrages. It may be that they existed, but were not of magnitude enough to attract notice.' Butt, who wrote extensively in the mid-Victorian era about land issues, contemporary and historical, speculated as to the reason why land agitation – which would persist in various guises into the 1920s – first erupted in Co. Tipperary in 1762.

> The spirit of the oppressed people may have only then begun to rise in a reaction against the cruelty of the Penal Laws; or possibly when the last hope of political relief appeared to expire with the downfall of the cause of the Stuarts, the despair of the peasantry prompted the wildness of these desultory attempts.[29]

Wider political considerations, such as those Butt suggests, may well have given context to the first serious insurrection of the Irish peasant farmer, but the proximate causes were not nearly as esoteric as the restoration of the Stuarts to the throne.

So what was it that prompted the tenant farmers of Tipperary and the neighbouring counties to don white linen shirts, go abroad under cover of darkness, arm themselves as best they could – this rarely rose above the pitifully inadequate – wield scythes, pitchforks, stones and sods of burning turf, dig simulated graves outside the homes of their antagonists, build mock coffins and gallows, cut off the ears of their adversaries, unleash general mayhem, and then, unlike the vagrant tories and rapparees of the seventeenth century, retire to their beds?

One of the contributory factors was that old Irish chestnut, the weather. In the years up to the renewal of the seemingly perpetual war between England and France in 1756, there had been a series of bad harvests due to adverse weather conditions. Memories of the 1741 famine were still starkly fresh, and there were fears of a recurrence. Then, almost coinciding with the outbreak of war – generally a bountiful period for farmers if not for soldiers – came a series of excellent harvests. Despite this superfluity, food prices rose, thanks to the needs of the British military during the Seven Years' War. The initial upsurge of agrarian crime in Munster in 1762 was not a function of extreme economic hardship: the Seven Years' War ended in February 1763, and the resurgence of the agitation in the summer of that year was influenced by the first of a new series of bad harvests and by the signing of the Treaty of Paris, which halted the run of good agricultural prices for Irish farmers.

The Whiteboy uprising, once underway, gathered grievances like moss on a rolling stone. Poor wage rates for labourers; high food prices (a boon for the comfortable farmer, a scourge for the landless); and the exactions of the Established Church all became bones of contention. However, the opening phase of a movement that in one guise or another arguably lasted for more than a century and a half was primarily a response to changes in agrarian methods and culture championed by 'improving' landlords and amplified by some of their more comfortable tenants. The inverted commas around what should signify progressive changes in agricultural practices are designed to denote the scepticism with which the majority of Irish tenant farmers of the eighteenth and nineteenth centuries viewed the 'improvements' proposed by their landlords. It was not just that most Irish tenant farmers of the two centuries before independence were intensely conservative, but that the changes sought by their landlords often meant serious disruption and/or dispossession. Irish tenants tended to prefer landlords who adhered to the status quo and had no truck with agricultural modernity of any kind. The truth was that 'there were many in the expanding ranks of smallholders who were actively hostile to improvement because it collided with traditional ways'.[30] As with the Houghers of the early eighteenth century, where these improvements involved the introduction of herds of cattle or sheep – or the expansion of aristocratic deer parks – accompanied by the inevitable reduction in land available for tillage, the collision was on a grander scale. The move towards pasture had initially been prompted by the relaxation in 1759 of restrictions originally imposed on the importation of Irish cattle to England in the late seventeenth century. A 1728 law obliging farmers or landlords to devote five acres in every hundred to tillage had proved unenforceable and had done little to prevent a shift to pasture, with negative consequences for surplus agricultural labourers and the land-poor.

What happened in Munster in the 1760s was an inevitable sequel to revolutionary changes in British agriculture and land tenure over the previous half-century in which the British 'open field' agricultural system died the death of a thousand cuts. Geriatric feudalism was finally giving way to adolescent capitalism. Hundreds of thousands of acres of common land were fenced off and became private property. A rural population that had previously enjoyed tillage or grazing rights in the old 'open field' system were suddenly bereft. They were obliged to shift for themselves.

Fortune generally favoured the brazen as this movement took hold. With parliamentary approval and connivance, British farming land, previously accessible to all, was legally seized and appropriated by powerful improving landholders who enriched and aggrandised themselves in the process. For Britain's burgeoning entrepreneurial fellowship, enclosure created a timely and useful underclass of dispossessed peasants who had few options other than migration to large towns and industrial employment – on the factory owners' terms, of course. The dispossessed who remained on the land did so as labourers for hire.

A series of enclosure acts passed through the House of Commons in the eighteenth century, accelerating in frequency as the century progressed. There were fifteen separate pieces of enclosure legislation between 1717 and 1727 and almost fifteen hundred (1,482) between 1761 and 1796.[31] Collusion between regional grandees and their fraternal allies in Parliament guaranteed that there were winners and losers as British rural society changed radically.

The confiscations and plantations of the sixteenth and seventeenth centuries ensured that there were far fewer commonages to be enclosed in Ireland than was the case in rural England. But some common land did exist. Most was already in the ownership of the nation's landlords, so Acts of Parliament were not required to alter its usage. It was often not of the highest quality, but in certain parts of the country, Munster in particular, it was a significant factor in the diurnal existence of Irish tenant farmers, and one that was worth fighting for. The writer and traveller Arthur Young, whose first journey through Ireland took place during a hiatus between the two major Whiteboy uprisings in the 1760s and 1780s, described the status of Irish commonage in the second volume of his *Tour in Ireland*: 'Although the proportion of waste territory is not, I apprehend, so great in Ireland as it is in England … yet are the tracts of desart [*sic*] mountains and bogs very considerable.'[32]

'Waste territory' the land may have been, but the onset of war between Britain and France in 1756 pushed up agricultural prices, raised the value of land and made the seizure of commonages an attractive proposition for landlords. This was especially true in Co. Tipperary, where one of the consequences of enclosure, according to Isaac Butt, was the creation of 'the monster farms in that county'.[33] The erosion of traditional rights and privileges in relation to this land – mirroring the enclosure movement in England and described by Michael Davitt as a 'genteel grabbing of the nation's inheritance'[34] – led to a series of violent agrarian eruptions, mostly in the south-east of the country, beginning in the mid-eighteenth century. There was, however, an added dimension to the campaign. The insurrectionists were not simply aggrieved at the disappearance of grazing and turbary (turf-cutting) rights. Where common land existed on estates, its use by tenants was long factored into the rents they paid. One of the consequences of enclosure which most angered tenants was that when commonage disappeared behind hedges, walls and fences, their rents were not proportionately reduced.

The insurrection of the Whiteboys of Munster, however, did not just come about because of the sudden spate of enclosures. They also sought to curtail the activities of an emerging breed of rural leeches, the so-called 'tithe-farmers'. These were often Roman Catholic impropriators, local gombeen men – the leader of the Irish 'Patriot' parliament of the late eighteenth century, Henry Grattan, described them as adventurers – who had purchased the right to collect the annual tax due to the Established Church, the Church of Ireland. They turned a profit by wringing the maximum reckonable amount from local tenant farmers. It is hardly necessary to point out that tithe farmers were tremendously unpopular. One of their number, for example, one Timothy Loughnan of the parish of Newcastle, was conveyed on horseback for half a mile to a newly dug grave by the Whiteboys and threatened with burial, while still alive, if he did not return the tithe collection lease to the local Church of Ireland rector.

Augmenting the sense of grievance of the smallholder tillage farmers of the Whiteboy movement was the fact that the relatively wealthy owners of the new pasture lands being created by enclosure were not themselves obliged to pay tithes on their earnings. The church-levied tax on pasture land, the tithe of agistment, had been abandoned by the Irish parliament in 1735 at the behest of landed interests, 'an event', according to nineteenth-century economist Thomas Newenham, 'which may be considered as tantamount to giving a premium to the grazier', or constituted a 'bounty on pasturage'.[35] Furthermore, while potatoes were not tithable throughout the country, they were liable to the tax in Munster. The Whiteboys never demanded the abolition of tithes. Instead, they often sought to regulate the rate at which the tax would be levied, while simultaneously imposing a scale of modified charges for the services of their own Roman Catholic clergy.

However, it was the anti-enclosure campaign that gave the Whiteboys their first impetus and their alternative and more evocative name, that of 'Levellers'. They earned this nickname through the systematic destruction of fences and ditches on newly enclosed land. When the movement emerged in the 1760s, although it did so in some of the most prosperous agricultural regions of the country, it was dominated by smallholders, cottiers and landless labourers ('the scum and some of the rabble of three or four counties'),[36] all of whom had much to lose from the enclosure of common land.

Because many of their landlords either did not live on their estates or were safely inaccessible, the focus of the militancy of the Whiteboys was on some of the larger tenants in their immediate vicinity, graziers in particular, and local, much-loathed tithe-farmers.

The movement that would become known as Whiteboyism* emerged first in Co. Tipperary with a local priest as midwife. As with many radical movements, it began life as a response to a specific issue and acquired at least some of its rationale on the hoof. In early 1762, a tithe-farmer named Dobbyn, whose main source of income was an inn in Ballyporeen (in which village the ancestors of future US President Ronald Reagan were still residents at the time), came up with an innovative scheme for increasing his personal wealth. He insisted, without any obvious justification other than invoking his status as the local beneficiary of the payment of tithes, that Ballyporeen couples should pay him a fee of five shillings when they were married by a Roman Catholic priest. This aroused the ire of local cleric Fr Nicholas Sheehy and sent him on a journey that would end with his ascent of the gallows four years later.

In addition to his gripe with the avariciously enterprising Dobbyn, Sheehy also gave vent to an earlier grievance, shared

---

* The name 'Whiteboy' still survived intact a century after its mid-eighteenth-century origins, as is attested to by mid-twentieth-century submissions to the National Folklore Collection.

by his parishioners, at the enclosure of common pasture land in nearby Drumlummin by two Catholic middlemen, the Ross brothers, William and James. The Ross family held land owned by Lord Cahir, a Tipperary Catholic landlord. Sheehy may even have accompanied a nocturnal mob, clad in distinctive white linen shirts, that destroyed fences the Ross brothers had erected around the former commonage.

With Tipperary issues resonating elsewhere in Munster, the Ballyporeen Whiteboy outbreaks quickly spread to Limerick and from there to Waterford. The *modus operandi* developed as the movement spread. The white shirts were retained and, as the protestors went about the business of pulling down fences and filling in ditches, the theatrical blowing of horns was added in case the appearance of a claque of angry tenant farmers dressed in white was not sufficiently menacing. From those humble beginnings, *na buachaillí bána* would develop into an oath-bound movement – albeit one without a central command structure – which would establish a formidable code of 'Whiteboy law' across half-a-dozen counties.

A penchant for display was also in evidence at the first serious act of collective defiance organised by the Whiteboys. This took place in Cappoquin, Co. Waterford, in March 1762, when agrarian militants marched past the local barracks and made no secret of their presence by firing several shots and parading behind a piper playing the Jacobite marching tune 'The Lad with the White Cockade'. A few days later, a force of around 400 Whiteboys gathered in the village of Ferrybank and fired shots across the river Blackwater into the town of Youghal, Co. Cork.

If the Waterford demonstration was intended as a mobilising hint to the tenant farmers of Cork, the challenge was taken up quickly. The movement spread to the north of that county, where large groups assembled at nightly protests, describing themselves ironically or self-deprecatingly as 'fairies'. This terminology, however, did not connote a softer, gentler aspect to the movement, for, after an assembly near Fermoy in late March 1762, attended by upwards of 500 Whiteboys, a stolen horse belonging to a local magistrate, James Grove of Ballyhimock, was put on 'trial' and found guilty. The luckless animal was then tortured and shot as a vicarious warning to Grove. Subsequently, two of the participants in this equestrian 'trial' were identified, captured, put on trial themselves and executed.

Attempting to curtail the activities of the Whiteboys by traditional means proved futile. Their support was too broadly based, whether it derived from genuine sympathy or was prompted by threats and intimidation. Magistrates were powerless to identify the members of the leadership cadre, and where they managed to do so, had difficulty in obtaining witnesses prepared to testify against those charged with assault or criminal damage (in this first period of their operations, the Whiteboys tended to avoid murdering their victims). The primary phase of Whiteboy engagement was severely curtailed by the summer of 1762, after the passage of legislation that made Whiteboy activity a capital offence, followed by a suitably vigorous and repressive military response. A regiment of dragoons and a light cavalry regiment were despatched to deal with the conspiracy. This, and an element of landlord vigilantism – the most egregious enforcer being the Earl of Carrick, owner of the Mount Juliet estate in Kilkenny – had the desired effect, and the agitation subsided.

However, by the spring of 1763, the men in linen shirts returned with a vengeance. The founder of Methodism, John Wesley, on a visit to Ireland, took a personal interest in the uprising and was told that the Whiteboys 'compelled everyone they met to take an oath to be true to Queen Sive ... Those who refused to swear, they threatened to bury alive.'[37] The name of the mythical Celtic Goddess Queen Sive was often appended to threatening letters, although these were also signed by a bizarre array of fictional entities such as Calfskin, Cropper, Echo, Madcap Setfire, Slasher and Thumper.

The Whiteboys could be very persuasive when it came to recruitment. In their efforts to enlist one James Cunningham of Kilbaha on the Limerick-Kerry border, for example, they were especially determined. Cunningham worked a farm five miles from Abbeyfeale with his brother Myles. He had to hide from them several times. One night, when they came for him they couldn't find him and for revenge began jumping their horses over his potato pits till they levelled them to the ground. They put Myles on his knees and made him swear that he was not James. James had to leave his house altogether and did not return till the days of the Whiteboys were over.[38]

Oath-swearing, ordinarily a legal or religious practice, was used by the Whiteboys as a counterintuitive form of moral suasion, 'fusing local activists into the wider network of a regional movement'.[39] The text of a written oath, found on a captured Tipperary Whiteboy, included the mandatory blood-curdling imprecations against informing, before concluding with the more surprising pledge, 'that I will not drink of any liquor whatsoever whilst on duty, without the consent of any one or other of the officers, serjeants [sic], or corporals'.[40] In spite of this apparent abstemiousness, there is considerable contrary anecdotal evidence suggesting that 'ardent spirits' played a substantial role in nocturnal Whiteboy activities.

Some of the punishments meted out by the organisation were harsh and sadistically inventive. One tenant farmer in Waterford, who had displeased the local section of the Levellers, was instructed to mend his ways 'upon pain of having his tongue drawn through his under-jaw, and fastened with a skewer'.[41] In Queen's County (Laois) in December 1774, a Protestant farmer, William Abraham, described (in an affidavit compiled by his solicitor) how he was kidnapped by Whiteboys, beaten, then placed on a horse.

> They beat, battered, and abused him with their guns, and the man behind whom he rode wounded him severely in the legs, with long nails in his heels, commonly called heel spurs. They carried him ten miles off, to a place near Ballyconra, where they held a consultation whether they should cut out his tongue, or pull out his eyes; and at last agreed to cut off his ears, which they did with circumstances of great barbarity.[42]

Abraham was then buried up to his chin in a grave lined with furze.

As with any organisation committed to a violent response to the redress of grievances, the inclusion in the ranks of the Whiteboys of a thuggish element, intent on personal gain rather than social change, was almost inevitable. Arthur Young, although hardly an unimpeachable source given the probability that his information emanated from some of his many affluent landed hosts, wrote of Kilkenny and Tipperary that, during the initial phase of Whiteboy activity, '[They] carried off the daughters of rich farmers, ravished them into marriages, of which four instances happened in a fortnight.'[43] This assertion tallies with accounts of subsequent agrarian uprisings in that region in the early nineteenth century. Rape was used not just as a form of revenge or intimidation, but for male self-aggrandisement. A woman who was raped had little option but to agree to a marriage with her assailant. Thus sexual violence could be used by the rapist to elevate his social status. Kidnapping and 'defiling' the daughter of a landlord or a wealthy farmer could be a means, albeit sadistic and criminal, to a 'good' (i.e. advantageous) marriage. In his 1836 survey *On Local Disturbances and the Irish Church Question*, the Poor Law commissioner, Cornewall Lewis – later Home Secretary and Chancellor of the Exchequer in the Palmerston administration – cited eleven such cases in Munster in 1833 alone.

According to Arthur Young, the mercenary *thuggee* of the Whiteboy movement also 'levied sums of money on the middling and lower farmers, in order to support their cause ... Sometimes they committed several considerable robberies, breaking into houses and taking the money, under pretence of redressing grievances.'[44]

What then of the establishment reaction to this sudden and spontaneous uprising by the previously quiescent peasants of Munster and south Leinster?

The response of the landed classes of the region, in an effort to force the hand of the authorities in Dublin, was to misrepresent the genesis of the eruption. Although the grievances and the objectives of the Whiteboy movement were clear and unambiguous (reverse enclosures and consign tithe-farmers to history or, preferably, perdition), the grandees of Tipperary and Kilkenny chose to see the hands of the Papist French and the 'Young Pretender', Bonnie Prince Charlie, in the agitation. The Whiteboys marched to the tune of 'The Lad with the White Cockade'. This was a Jacobite air. These agitators were Roman Catholic to the last linen shirt. Some had (anecdotally) been found with French coinage about their person. Ergo, the Whiteboy movement was the vanguard of a resurgence of the Jacobite cause. Militant popery was on the march again, and hard-working, God-fearing Protestants would be murdered in their beds.

While it was a thesis that had little appeal in Dublin Castle, it gained wide currency in the propertied bastions of Tipperary, Waterford, Limerick, Cork and Kilkenny. Cornewall Lewis wrote in 1836 that: 'The government ... were unable to restrain the local and subordinate authorities from raising the alarm of a popish rebellion'.[45] Sixty years earlier, Arthur Young had been equally scathing. 'No foreign money appeared,' he wrote, 'no arms of foreign construction, no presumptive proof whatever of such a connection.'[46]

Some of the more insouciant members of the Munster aristocracy, gentlemen grounded in reality and dismissive of hysteria, adopted a radically different approach to the insurrection. They sought opportunity in emergency and quietly reached an accommodation with the insurrectionists. Fastening on the issue of tithe farming, they creatively sought to widen the scope of the conflict, exploit the resentment of Catholics towards their enforced financial support of the clergy of the Church of Ireland and turn the local Whiteboy movement against the tithe itself. After all, they too were liable for this irksome tax. Cornewall Lewis, more than half a century after the events of the 1760s, but ensconced in a decade where the campaign against the payment of tithes had come to a head, wrote of how some landlords and middlemen, originally targeted by the Whiteboys, were skilfully able to change the order of battle: 'Finding it easier to divert than to suppress the newly awakened spirit of resistance, [they] encouraged or connived at the attempts which were soon made by the Whiteboys to withhold the payment of tithe; a payment to which they themselves were equally liable.'[47]

A 1787 pamphlet written by the Church of Ireland Bishop of Cloyne, Dr Richard Woodward, testified to the efficacy of this perplexing coalition, when he wrote that: 'These enemies to the public peace and the Protestant clergy, though [themselves] nominal Protestants, suggested to the farmers to enter into a combination, under the sanction of an oath, not to take their tithes or to assist any clergyman in drawing them.' Woodward went on to list a number of clergy in his own diocese who had been brutalised or intimidated by the Cork Whiteboys, including a 'dignitary in my cathedral' who was 'forced to come out of his house at midnight, by a band of 150 ruffians, to swear that he would give up his legal rights; a gun being pointed close to his head whilst the oath was tendered, and a horse produced with a saddle full of spikes, on which he was to be mounted if he refused to swear'.[48]

Although the Whiteboys were responsible for relatively few murders in their first iteration in the 1760s, one of the exceptions to this generalisation cost more than a dozen members or 'fellow travellers' of the organisation their lives in Kilkenny in 1764. In September of that year, nine Whiteboys were being escorted from Clonmel, Co. Tipperary to Kilkenny city by a small force of fourteen dragoons. At a strategically vulnerable location, where the road narrowed between the villages of Newmarket and Sheepstown, a mob of Whiteboy sympathisers, armed with cudgels and *sleáns* (implements used for the harvesting of turf) attacked the dragoons with a barrage of stones, freed the prisoners and killed two of the soldiers. However, a lethal volley unleashed by the surviving dragoons, fighting for their lives, killed at least eight of their assailants. A number of the alleged attackers were later identified and eight were condemned to death at the Kilkenny Spring Assizes in 1765. Six of those convicted of capital crimes were executed in the most grisly fashion in St James's Green on the outskirts of the city in April. After being left to hang for a brief period, their bodies were cut down, their breasts were 'scored' and they were then beheaded.

Turbulent priests

The ordinary Roman Catholic clergy of the southern counties subject to Whiteboy violence were divided as to the correct response to the uprising. They were encouraged by their bishops to condemn from the pulpit the activities of the Whiteboys. When he became Bishop of Ossory (Kilkenny) in 1776, the future Roman Catholic Archbishop of Dublin, John Troy, delivered a pastoral in which he denied the rites of the Church to any member of the Whiteboys. This included a Catholic burial. The pastoral – not unlike marriage banns – was to be read at three consecutive Sunday masses by Kilkenny priests, accompanied by an explanation in the Irish language. A similar pastoral was issued by the Roman Catholic Bishop of Cloyne (east Cork).

Clerical opposition was galvanised when an element of the Whiteboy movement began to attach the issue of the financial support of Roman Catholic clergy by their parishioners to their list of grievances. They complained that contributing to the upkeep of their priests at current rates, on top of tithes and rent, was a luxury they could not afford. A number of Catholic priests were actually assaulted by Whiteboys, although this may have had as much to do with their support for episcopal opposition to the movement as with excessive priestly dues for the celebration of masses, marriages or baptisms.

Some clerics, most notably Fr Nicholas Sheehy, defied his superiors and sided with the insurgents. Others, such as Fr Alexander Cahill, the parish priest of the Kilkenny village of Ballyragget, adopted a stance diametrically opposed to Sheehy's during the resurgence of the dormant Whiteboys in the mid-1770s. Cahill offered moral and physical support to the local landed opponents of the movement, the Butler family. The Ballyragget Butlers were a Catholic branch of the famous Kilkenny family, the Dukes and Marquesses of Ormonde, dominant in city and county – and often Dublin Castle – affairs for generations. The Butlers had made themselves useful to the authorities in the identification and pursuit of agrarian activists and were, therefore, a threat to the Whiteboys. One of the consequences of this anti-Whiteboy activity was that the local Ballyragget landlord, Robert Butler – who was also responsible for a number of land enclosures – was forced to flee to England for fear of his life. Fully certain that the village of Ballyragget would be targeted by the Whiteboys, Fr Alexander Cahill, with the co-operation of a member of the Butler family, the Roman Catholic Archbishop of Cashel, Dr James Butler, organised to have as many inhabitants as possible sympathetic to the Butlers, armed and ready for a siege. Cahill went as far as to mimic the Whiteboys themselves by having an oath administered to the Catholic supporters of the Butlers in the Ballyragget church. This small oath-bound Anti-Whiteboy League, drawn from among the more affluent inhabitants of Ballyragget and its hinterland, then received basic military training from a former army officer, Captain Christopher Hewetson. Emboldened by the arrival of weapons paid for, at Hewetson's insistence, by Dublin Castle, the Ballyragget Anti-Whiteboy League became highly proactive and even ventured out on patrol in the hope of encountering Whiteboys engaged in their nocturnal revels. On 8 February 1775, they got what they wished for, routing a small detachment of members of the secret society in a night-time raid. Intent on revenge, the Kilkenny Whiteboys began to plot their retaliation. They decided to attack Ballyragget in numbers on 25 February 1775.

The Ballyragget loyalists had been forewarned of the Whiteboys' plan by a local female informant named Kitty Kearney, and were well prepared. A group of fourteen defenders gathered in the house of Robert Butler under the command of a former naval officer, Larry Power, later known as 'Captain Fire-low', based on the orders he issued loudly to his troops in the subsequent siege.

The force of 200–300 Whiteboys bound for Ballyragget, mounted and on foot, was recruited from the nearby towns of Freshford, Durrow, Callan and Gowran. When Whiteboy cavalry and infantry descended on the village at around 3 a.m., they were, according to the *Leinster Journal*, 'all dressed in white uniforms … some with lighted sods of turf threatened fire and devastation to the whole town'. They challenged the Butlers and their supporters, sequestered in the house of the reluctant emigré, Robert Butler, to come out and fight them, calling the defenders of the Butler household a 'pack of cowardly scoundrels'.

Wisely, the Butlers and their allies chose to remain behind cover and responded to three shots being fired into the house by the lightly armed Whiteboys with a lethal volley of their own. This had the effect of dampening the enthusiasm of the Whiteboys, who quickly dispersed, but not before their leader, a man called Moore from Higginstown, swore to return within a fortnight and burn the entire town. The threat was never carried out. The Whiteboys withdrew, taking an unknown number of dead and wounded with them, and leaving the bodies of two men (one of whom, ironically, bore the name of Patrick Butler) behind them. The spectacularly unsuccessful siege subsequently gave rise to the writing of an anonymous 'poetical lamentation', a line of which – 'Cursed Ballyragget, that never gave man relief' – became a local aphorism.[49] In his *Tour in Ireland*, Arthur Young put the Whiteboy fatalities at between forty and fifty. The more credible *Leinster Journal* confirmed three Whiteboy deaths from bullet wounds. Young, though clearly not a fan of the secret society, does point out in his own recounting of the brief siege that the withdrawal of the Whiteboys was solely attributable to the fact that 'they had but very few arms, those in bad order, and no cartridges'.[50]

The most notorious and controversial of almost thirty Whiteboy executions in the 1760s was that of the parish priest of Clogheen, Co. Tipperary, Fr Nicholas Sheehy. Sheehy, as we have already seen, was a Whiteboy sympathiser from the outset. He was voluble in his criticism of the enclosures of commons that sparked the agrarian uprising in 1761–2. Sheehy, described by the eighteenth-century historian John Curry as 'giddy and officious, but not ill-meaning, with somewhat of a quixotic cast of mind',[51] quickly became a marked man because of his activities in support of the uprising, and a reward was offered for his arrest. When he turned himself in to the authorities, he was charged with Whiteboy recruitment. He was brought to Dublin to be tried. This was a condition of his surrender to the authorities, one he imposed himself because he was not sanguine of a fair hearing in a Tipperary court. Sheehy was acquitted when the principal witness against him, John Bridge, failed to show up to testify. Bridge was a well-known informer who had given evidence in a number of Whiteboy trials.

Sheehy, however, was not at liberty for long and was immediately re-indicted, now accused of having murdered Bridge, the missing Crown witness. Although the alleged victim's body was never produced, Sheehy was returned from Dublin to Clonmel for trial, his feet being pinioned under the stomach of the horse on which he was placed for the journey. In Clonmel, a local Protestant jury, alarmed by the prevailing anti-Jacobite hysteria, found the priest guilty. His execution in 1766 was, and is to this day, viewed as a form of judicial murder. The supposed victim of Sheehy's 'crime', John Bridge, was allegedly seen in Cork after his 'death' and, it was claimed, emigrated to Canada to save himself from Whiteboy retribution.

On 15 March 1766, Sheehy was hanged, drawn and quartered in Clonmel. His head was placed on a spike and displayed over the gate of Clonmel gaol. A number of others accused as his co-conspirators, including one of the priest's own cousins, were hanged six weeks later.

Sheehy, however, had the final word, his trial leaving a trail of human devastation in its wake. In a bloody footnote to the legalised assassination of the Tipperary priest, in 1780 his executioner was stoned to death by a vengeful mob. The bizarre fates of the members of his jury are also well documented. Only one appears to have died of what can credibly be described as natural causes. Two were thrown from their horses and killed, one died of a fit while defecating, one choked to death, one died of disease after a period spent begging, one drowned 'in a shallow stream', one went mad and another cut his own throat. One of a number of dubious witnesses against Sheehy, a man named Toohey, later contracted leprosy and was subsequently hanged as a horse thief. Another of his accusers, one Moll Dunlea, aka Mary Brady, to whom Sheehy had wished a long life in court – he may have intended this to be ironic – was fatally injured in a fall into the cellar of a public house. The official who impanelled the jury, Thomas Maude, 'contracted a disease that caused his eyes to fall from their sockets and his body to give off a disgusting smell. After he died, screaming that the priest was dragging him down to hell, he was entombed in his room because nobody could bear to go near his body.'[52]

Sheehy had been indicted for illegal recruitment and sedition, and then for being an accessory to murder, but the legislature in Dublin sought and found other legal means of curtailing the activities of *na buchaillí bána*. In 1765, the old Irish parliament – before its brief flowering as the 'Patriot Parliament' of Henry Grattan and Henry Flood – passed the Whiteboy Act and ten years later the first Tumultuous Risings Act. In its original iteration in 1775, this introduced fines, imprisonment and the 'pillory, whipping or other corporal punishment' for anyone caught with an offensive weapon, 'or wearing any particular badge, dress, or uniform not usually worn by him, her, or them upon his, her, or their lawful occasions [and] shall rise, assemble, or appear by day or by night to the terror of his Majesty's subjects'.[53]

James Donnelly Jr, the acknowledged chronicler of the Whiteboy movement, has logged a total of twenty-six executions of members of the movement, with just over forty lesser punishments, including transportation. Most of the convictions were secured with informer evidence, much of which came from fellow-accused ('approvers' in the legal vernacular of the time) who offered to testify in return for some form of amnesty.

Despite his association with many members of the Irish landed gentry, Arthur Young was sufficiently liberal and open-minded, while pointing out the mote in the eye of the agitators, to highlight the beam in that of some of his erstwhile hosts. In the second volume of his *Tour in Ireland*, he took aim at the authorities for passing vindictively punitive anti-Whiteboy legislation 'which seemed calculated for the meridian of Barbary'. This included one fiat that would have permitted hanging 'without the common formalities of a trial'. His own observations forced him to conclude that: 'It is manifest that the gentlemen of Ireland never thought of a radical cure, from overlooking the real cause of the disease, which in fact lay in themselves and not in the wretches they doomed to the gallows.'[54]

Young was supported in the thrust of his conclusions by the Lord Lieutenant himself. The Earl of Halifax reported to London that the Whiteboy rising was 'the blind effect of a rabble destitute of employment and wretched in their circumstances'. Before leaving his post in 1762, Halifax scolded the grandees of Munster and south Leinster when he pointed out that 'the mere execution of the laws, without the example of those who execute them, must always be defective'.[55]

Ultimately, it was not the many repressive actions taken by the government that led to the demise of the Whiteboys of the 1760s (there was a significant sequel in the 1780s and numerous imitations). If it was the extreme moistness of Irish weather that spawned the movement, it was conditions at the other end of the meteorological scale that brought their race to a conclusion. In 1766, a major drought hit the country. So widespread and serious was the lack of rainfall that, once again, famine threatened. The river Shannon, exploited by members of the hurling fraternity in the harsh winter of 1740–41, came close to drying up. The hay crop was ravaged, and while supplies of wheat were adequate, the staple crops of potato and oats were devastated. Whatever about its unusual origins, the picture was a familiar one and would frequently recur in a precarious economy so dependent on agriculture. Food prices rose to a point where they were unaffordable to all but the most comfortably off. As with the ruinous famine of 1741, the government banned grain exports, an interesting contrast with the Great Famine of the mid-nineteenth century. As if drought and crop failure were insufficient punishment, a smallpox outbreak coincided with the threatened famine. In the face of such an emergency, the Whiteboy threat withered.

But a Rubicon had been crossed. Blood had been spilled on both sides. The Whiteboys themselves would return, and when the threat they posed finally receded, they would be supplanted by a legion of surrogates. The many issues raised during their first eruption into Irish rural life would recur. One by one, those specific conflicts would be resolved, peaceably or otherwise. But the slight tremor triggered by the Whiteboys of the south-east of Ireland in 1762 would be followed by a succession of aftershocks that would culminate, in 1798, in an earthquake the magnitude of which *na buachaillí bána*, with their local grievances and limited objectives, could never have envisaged.

4

'Paddy is easily persuaded to partake of this amusement':[1] the Oakboys, Steelboys, Rightboys, Defenders and Peep O'Day Boys

'Oakboyism died only to assume other names and
functions in later years.'[2]

(Michael Davitt, *The Fall of Feudalism in Ireland*, 1904)

Belfast, 23 December 1770

There was no Christmas spirit in evidence at Belfast's North Gate. An angry mob of over a thousand men was on its way to the nearby barracks. Armed with everything from pistols to pitchforks, they had but a single object. One of their own, David Douglas, was being held in that barracks. He faced jail or transportation for the crime of maiming a farm animal. The mob that had gathered at Templepatrick Meeting House, ten miles north-west of the city, and had marched en masse to the outskirts of Belfast, was intent on securing his release, and not by bailing him out. If Douglas didn't walk free, they would burn down the entire town.

A small detachment of this unwavering force of enraged Antrim men had broken off from the main group and was heading for the house of the 'convicted' interloper, Waddell Cunningham, a wealthy Belfast merchant who lived in Hercules Lane.* Cunningham, who would require the strength of that hero

* Located on the present site of Royal Avenue.

of Greek mythology if he was to make it through the night, was *persona non grata* to the assembled farmers and labourers. Their gripe with the shipowner was that he had met the rental price demanded by the Uptons of Templepatrick for a farm, and a good man had been thrown off his holding by the new landlord, Clotworthy Upton, the future Baron Templetown.

Cunningham, who wouldn't know a cow from a bison, had taken away a real farmer's home. Now he was about to lose his own. Fire would shortly consume the building, once the arsonists had dealt with the entreaties of a foolhardy concerned citizen. His name was Dr Alexander Halliday and he was pleading with the rioters not to torch Cunningham's house. The doctor would shortly become their prisoner and would be put to good use.

Rather than storm the barracks and risk losing dozens of men to the well-armed soldiers inside, the leaders of the mob decided that if Halliday was courageous enough to risk the wrath of the claque at Cunningham's residence, he was resourceful enough to venture into the barracks and attempt to secure the release of Douglas on behalf of the rioters. The protesting doctor was duly despatched towards the well-guarded building. As he approached, the gate of the barracks opened. If the watching crowd thought that this was done to admit their reluctant emissary, they were profoundly mistaken. Instead of a parley, a line of soldiers stepped forward and fired a volley into the crowd. Five men died and nine more were wounded. After such an act of blatant treachery, it would be well-nigh impossible to dissuade the angry mob from torching the city.

Despite this setback, the 'respectable physician'[3] Dr Halliday played a central role in calming the situation, vitiating the mob's thirst for revenge and allowing the demonstrators to retire with their prize. All of which was too late to rescue the home of Waddell Cunningham. The well-appointed building was already on fire, threatening every other residence on Hercules Street and, indeed, depending on the direction of the freezing wind, much of the city of Belfast. The military garrison watched as the fire took hold and the protestors blocked all attempts to put out the flames. Eventually, in the early hours of Christmas Eve, the mob received the seasonal gift they had come for. In a desperate bid to save the city from the fate of London in 1666, the prisoner was released.

For much of the population of Belfast, that was their introduction to the 'Hearts of Steel'.

'I sware to be loyall ...'[4]

What's in a name? In the case of Irish agrarian secret societies, more than one might expect. There is a tendency to conflate the various groups that were active in the eighty years leading up to the brutal line of demarcation imposed by the Great Famine. They are often labelled in generic terms such as Whiteboys or Ribbonmen.

Therefore, Whiteboy = Rightboy = Oakboy = Steelboy. This equation assumes that the aims and methods of the assorted 'Boys' were practically identical. While a 'shared consciousness found concrete expression in the grievances of agrarian rebels and the remedies they demanded'[5] and while there were marked similarities in their pursuit of those remedies, there were also significant differences. The rebellions in Ulster of the Hearts of Oak and Hearts of Steel, for example, were to conventional warfare what the campaign of the Whiteboys was to its guerrilla equivalent. The Oakboys and Steelboys actually fought occasional pitched daylight skirmishes and did not rely as much on the anonymity of disguise and the sanctuary of dusk as did other, more furtive, groups. The Whiteboys, although they did stage a number of public appearances and overt displays of strength, were a more nocturnal faction.

Furthermore, the issue that first sparked the rebellion of the Whiteboys in south Leinster and east Munster – the enclosure of common land – was not a motivating factor in the Ulster insurgencies of the Hearts of Oak and the Hearts of Steel. The imposition of the tithe provoked the Rightboy revolt, but it was the exploitation of the levy by the much-loathed tithe farmers, rather than the existence of the tax itself, that motivated the Whiteboy conspiracy. In Ulster, the same grievance prompted the Oakboys to rebel, whereas the tithe was an item of relative indifference to the Hearts of Steel a few years later. Some organisations were dominated by landless labourers dependent on conacre for their survival, while others were tacitly supported by landlords with an eye to the main chance. So while the peasants might have been revolting, they were taking matters into their own hands in a multiplicity of divergent causes.

If the emergence of the Whiteboys 'blooded' late eighteenth-century militant agrarianism, then their contemporaries and immediate successors, according to Roy Foster, 'helped identify rural violence as part of the popular tradition'.[6] Or, as a contemporary observer put it more colloquially, 'Paddy is easily persuaded to partake of this amusement'.[7]

Somewhat illogically, although the preponderance of these foundational agrarian subversives were small tenant farmers, they did not necessarily manifest an antipathy towards the very existence of landlordism. In fact, 'direct challenges to the fundamentals of the tenurial system were uncommon'.[8] That would come much later, after the lower-hanging fruit had been plucked. Deference was too engrained to permit over-ambitious objectives. Climbing a drumlin was feasible; trying to scale an Alpine peak was, as yet, beyond comprehension. Besides which, the drumlin was in one's back yard, accessible and exasperating. In addition, in the eighteenth century, the prospect of being hanged for even the most banal of crimes against property – in England at that time illegal tree-felling, stealing a rabbit or blackening your face at night were capital offences – was a major disincentive to the targeting of your betters. Especially when they were also members of the local magistracy and might well pass judgement on your belligerent excursions.

However, although the resistance of groups like the Rightboys, the Oakboys and the Steelboys was not always directed against landlordism per se, through purposeful violence, a surprising element of theatricality and an impressive campaign of epistolary intimidation (bar the often execrable spelling and punctuation evident in threatening letters),* they established a template heavily drawn upon by later societies whose principal objective was very clearly the extirpation of landlordism. Whatever the individual members of the Whiteboys, Rightboys, Oakboys and Steelboys might think or feel about their landlord, or landlords in general, they were not yet ready to take on the monumental task of bucking the ascendancy, its constabulary and its army. The peasant might dream of an environment free of titled or wealthy landowners, 'but the possibility of heaven on earth normally seemed remote, and agrarian rebellion usually flowed from mundane desires for limited economic gain'.[9]

The Whiteboy revolt established a pattern that, consciously or otherwise, was often mimicked by its many descendant combinations. Revolts tended to begin on a small scale, provoked by a single proximate issue and restricted in scope by the initial lack of concerted and co-ordinated activism. Then, as the revolt scaled up and spread from barony to barony, supplementary issues were introduced. These occasionally supplanted the original grievance in importance. While tithes, rack-renting, evictions, wage rates, food prices, 'duty day' obligations, hearth and cess taxes, and even excessive payments to Roman Catholic priests (the 'greedy priests'[10] of eighteenth-century poetry) often featured somewhere on the agendas of the secret societies of the eighteenth and early nineteenth centuries, the emphasis on each issue differed, depending on location or chronology. Issues overlapped and vied for prominence. The nature of the marquee grievances was generally a function of time and place.

The Oakboys and the Steelboys, for example, with a sizeable Presbyterian element, were obviously not required to contribute to the upkeep of Catholic priests, but objected to the obligation to subsidise the incomes of the clergy of the Established Church.

---

* The author of a recent work on the subject, Donal McCracken (*You Will Dye at Midnight: Victorian Threatening Letters*), has described the style of the Irish political poison-pen letter as combining 'pomposity, sweet reason and moral rectitude in staccato, pseudo-legal and blood-curdling English' (*Irish Times*, 5 January 2022).

The tithe, however, was generally only a major bone of contention during periods of agricultural recession, when it became a far more onerous imposition, especially in Munster and parts of Leinster, where it was levied on the staple food of the poor: the potato crop. The rise of the Rightboys in Munster can more easily be understood in the context of the anomaly that the tithe was not levied against potatoes in Ulster, Connacht and certain parts of Leinster.

The point being that we should be conscious of nuance. Although most of these agrarian guerrilla forces liked to operate in the hours of darkness, it would be unwise to pay no heed whatever to the distinct elements of light and shade where their activities in the late eighteenth and early nineteenth centuries are concerned.

The Hearts of Oak

Almost contemporaneous with the Whiteboy revolt in Munster, the Hearts of Oak/Oakboys – 'a disturbance among the Protestant peasants of the north'[11] – emerged in Ulster. As with the southern rebellion, the issue that sparked the Oakboy insurgency was localised and the list of grievances became more textured as the insurrectionary contagion spread and the scope of the rebellion widened. The immediate provocation was the obligation to supply labour for the upkeep of local roads, and to the local county-based cess tax also levied for the same purpose. The added injustice of umpteen variations in the cess tax in different localities in the same county merely exacerbated the problem.

In *A Philosophical Survey of the South of Ireland*, published in 1777, an odd book written in the fictitious persona of an English visitor, the Tyrone clergyman the Rev. Thomas Campbell, an associate of Samuel Johnson and James Boswell, described the genesis of the uprising:

The highways in Ireland were formerly made and repaired by the labour of the housekeepers. He who had a horse, was obliged to work six days in the year, himself and horse: he who had none, was to give six days' labour. It had long been complained that the poor alone were compelled to work; that the rich had been exempted; that instead of mending the public roads, the sweat of their brows had been wasted on private roads, useful only to the overseers.[12]

Campbell's reference to 'overseers' can be taken as a euphemism for the landlords who were the main beneficiaries of the practice. As a man of the cloth substantially dependent on the patronage and/or tithes of the aristocracy, he opted for discretion when it came to the *cui bono* issue of who benefited from the road construction projects. However, such circumspection was not a characteristic of the Oakboys, who fervently believed that their labour and taxes were being used by local landowners for 'building useless bridges' and roads in the vicinity of their own estates and even, on occasions, within their demesnes.

The obligation to provide labour for the upkeep or development of Ulster's roads and bridges dated from legislation passed during the reign of James I, when the plantation of the province was in full spate. From 1710 onwards, county grand juries (the equivalent of today's county councils but with a more aristocratic mien) were entitled to levy a cess or local tax for the construction of new roads. Already set at an unacceptable level, the cess was increased in Armagh in 1763, to the annoyance of the local linen weavers. Two years before, just as the Whiteboy movement was emerging in Munster, a group of weavers and farmers, styling themselves 'Hearts of Oak', had torn down toll gates on turnpike roads. Unlike the Welsh 'Rebecca'* rioters of the 1840s, however, the Oakboys, as they became known, did not don women's clothing while going about their business. Their main concession to display was the wearing of oaken twigs in their hats, though

---

* Rebecca, a maternal figure of biblical origins appropriate for a non-conformist society, is the Welsh equivalent of the imaginary Queen Sive of the Whiteboys. The Rebecca rioters, mostly aggrieved (male) farmers for whom the toll gates were a convenient target, in a thoroughly postmodern gesture, wore dresses as a form of disguise and called themselves *Merched Beca* ('The Daughters of Rebecca').

'their demonstrations were spectacular and carnivalesque'.[13]

In 1763, 'compulsory labour and a burdensome cess brought social tensions to the surface'[14] and the Oakboy movement revived in Armagh before spreading to Monaghan, Cavan, Tyrone, Fermanagh and Derry. In the main, the movement consisted of labourers and small farmers who refused to have anything further to do with fulfilling their legal obligation to work ('duty days') on what they called 'job roads'. The rebellion spread rapidly. 'From parishes it flew to baronies, and from baronies to counties, till at length the greater part of the province was engaged.'[15]

In the *Memoirs of the Political and Private Life of James Caulfield, Earl of Charlemont* by Francis Hardy, published in 1810, a decade after the death of that aristocratic ally of Grattan and Flood in the 'Patriot Parliament', Hardy described the advent of the Oakboys. Lord Charlemont was *Custos Rotulorum* in Armagh at the time of the uprising, the equivalent of a nineteenth-century Lord Lieutenant of the county. According to Hardy, the Oakboys, at their zenith, numbered no more than 500 active members, including some 'farmers of respectable property', although other accounts of Oakboy gatherings cite assemblies of up to 20,000. In his memoir of Charlemont, Hardy contrasted the conduct of the Oakboy campaign with that of the Munster Whiteboys:

> It is to be observed, that though they talked much, though they insulted several gentlemen, erected gallows, and menaced ineffable perdition to all their enemies, no violent cruelty was exercised, as Lord Charlemont said, nor was a single life lost, or any person maimed, in the county of Armagh; a species of conduct totally opposite to that of the southern insurgents, but which his Lordship ascribed, not to any diversity of religion, but to the oppression under which the unfortunate creatures in the south laboured. 'A rebellion of slaves (continued he) is always more bloody than an insurrection of freemen.'[16]

Another obvious contrast between the two contemporaneous movements was religious affiliation. The Oakboys, though not exclusively so, were predominantly Protestant loyalists who 'swore men to be true to the King and the Hearts of Oak'.[17]

As an adjunct to the question of 'job road' obligations came the issue of tithes. This was not just a bone of contention for Catholics. Presbyterians were apt to 'look upon the clergy of the established church with sovereign contempt'.[18] Excessive rent levels were later stirred into the mix, though the latter issue was folded in only lightly. This broadening of the grievance base had the effect of adding supporters to their cause.

However, the Oakboys also had less subtle methods of attracting followers. Those who politely declined the opportunity to join their ranks were, according to James Donnelly Jr, 'immediately taken and made to ride a mile upon a stick, and they are heartily ducked'. This often had the desired effect of artificially boosting the victim's enthusiasm for engagement with the society.

The Oakboys appear to have been quite systematic in their operations. In the pursuit of their tithe reform agenda, for example, they paid visits, designed to intimidate, 'to the resident gentlemen and Anglican clergy of the district'.[19] Later, as they became more audacious, in a deviation that amplified their growing influence, they summoned the local notables before large gatherings of their supporters instead. Many of those unwilling to be paraded in front of their tenants or parishioners were forced to flee. Some sought the sanctuary of the walled city of Derry. A threatening missive, sent to the burghers of that city, insisting that the clerical refugees be handed over to the justice of the Oakboys, reveals something of the religious composition of the movement, because the heavily Presbyterian Hearts of Oak was an equal opportunities offender when it came to antipathy towards the Established Church and the Church of Rome. The letter read: 'It is with astonishment we find your mayor has not obeyed our orders to him, which were to turn out of the once loyal city of Londonderry (which our forefathers so bravely defended against a most hellish, damned set of papists, with the poltroon James at their head) those high-flying clergy, I mean those who call themselves high churchmen.'

The brief flowering of the Hearts of Oak was also attended by a strong sense of the theatrical. Fiddlers and pipers were as important at Oakboy demonstrations as podium speakers or pitchforks. When the Rev. Theodorus Martin and his wife were abducted near Cookstown, Co. Tyrone in July 1763, while travelling in their chaise to a dinner engagement, the rector was forced to accede to the tithe demands of the protestors. The couple were then taken to the main street of the town, where they were met by a second group of Oakboys 'with two fiddlers playing before them the tune called "Hearts of Oak" and several pair of colours flying … They gave us a loud cheer and then fired off several shots behind and about the chaise.'[20] At which point the clergyman and his anxious spouse were sent on their way unmolested.

Although the Oakboys appear to have relied far more on colourful threats than actual physical violence, the official response to the insurrection was decidedly military in nature. This was initially problematic because, owing to the moral certainty on the part of the government of the loyalty and quiescence of Protestant-dominated Ulster, there was little or no military presence in the region. Army units were summoned from the three other provinces to deal with the Oakboy threat. This had the desired effect, the Oakboys generally returning quietly to private life when faced with dragoons and well-armed regiments of infantry. An additional incentive, other than the sight of so many red coats, was a government proclamation in August 1763 granting amnesty to all those prepared to retire peacefully from the fray. The quelling of the Oakboy revolt took a mere five or six weeks, though the movement did, on occasions throughout the 1760s, bubble back into life. Attempts by the authorities to make an example of a number of the leaders of the movement met the staunch refusal of Ulster juries to convict. Only a single capital conviction (for treason) was secured by the Crown in Derry against an Oakboy leader named McDill who became the sole Oakboy 'martyr'. Had the authorities not opted to try and hang their Oakboy prisoners for treason, they might have fared better. Juries were reluctant to convict the leadership of what had often been a politic and merely mischievous insurgency when they knew a negative verdict would lead to the gallows.

However, the insurrection of the Hearts of Oak had not been entirely fruitless. The offensive Road Act that had given rise to the emergence of the insurgency in the first place was repealed in the next parliamentary session and replaced by a more equitable tax levied for the future repair of roads.

'The Hearts of Steel'

More dramatic and sustained was the later revolt of the organisation styling itself the Hearts of Steel. Perhaps, in apportioning themselves such a metallic name they were sending out a subliminal message that they were made of sterner material than the carbon-based Oakboys. So it proved.

Although the issues that gave rise to the founding of the Steelboys were not inherently religious, the movement itself was somewhat more sectarian in nature than the Oakboys. The Steelboy base was in the east of the province, in the overwhelmingly Protestant counties of Antrim and Down. Although both movements had much in common, they were also quite distinct in their tactics, objectives and impact. The Oakboy rebellion was short-lived, lasting little more than a month, while the Hearts of Steel remained in existence for almost three years.

In philosophical terms, as that *über*-chronicler of Irish agrarian radical movements James Donnelly Jr has observed, though both groups sought changes in the imposition of local taxation, the Steelboys, unlike the Hearts of Oak, seldom raised the issue of tithes. Conversely, the 'bread and butter' issue of the Hearts of Steel – high rents and evictions – did not figure so highly on the wish list of the Oakboys.

The Steelboy unrest, like most of its predecessors, began as a single-issue rebellion, a reaction to the imposition of 'fines' for the renewal of leases on the estate of Lord Donegall in Co. Antrim. The 90,000 acres of the Donegall estate in Ulster (he also owned 11,000 acres in Wexford and most of the Inishowen

peninsula in Co. Donegal) included the growing city of Belfast
and stretched almost from Lisburn to Larne. Donegall – a
descendant (and namesake) of Sir Arthur Chichester, Lord
Deputy of Ireland in the early years of the Ulster plantation
– while prepared to re-let farms at the former rent, insisted
on a premium or 'fine' from any tenant who wanted to sign a
new lease, what is known as 'hello money' in modern parlance.
Resentment at this imposition was exacerbated by the knowledge
that the funds thus raised were going to the development of the
self-indulgent landlord's Fisherwick Park estate in Staffordshire.
Donegall had commissioned the celebrated landscape architect
Lancelot 'Capability' Brown to design a Palladian house and
sumptuous gardens and somebody had to pay for both.* Anyone
who could not afford to pay the 'fine' when their lease fell in
was to be evicted and replaced with a tenant prepared to support
Donegall's English vanity project. Either that or the land would
be used for cattle grazing by the landlord himself. As the *Public
Journal* newspaper noted at the time: 'Those fertile fields, which
produced bread for their inhabitants, were converted into
pasturage, and the country, once populous, wore, and still wears,
the face of depopulation and misery.'[21]

Another factor in the resulting chaos was, allegedly, an
avaricious agent who added a premium of his own to the fines
levied by Donegall. Once again, it was domesticated animals that
bore the brunt of the early Steelboy hostilities, as a spate of cattle-
maiming heralded the beginning of the campaign. The unrest,
which began in the winter of 1769–70, quickly spread from Antrim
to Derry, Tyrone and Down and, as the Steelboys discovered their
own power and supplemented their agenda, Ulster ascendancy
figures, as well as farmers deemed to be overcharging for their
products, were forced onto the defensive. Many of the former had
their homes burned, as was the case with the luckless Waddell

* Ironically, within a generation, the house had been stripped and
demolished, and the park reverted to nature when both became too expensive
to maintain. The house was sold to pay Donegall's extravagant debts after his
death in 1799.

Cunningham. His crime had been to outbid the previous owner of an expired lease for Donegall land that was retained by the Upton family of Templepatrick. Arthur Upton, one of the wealthiest middlemen in Ulster, was merely engaging in what was, in his world at least, the unexceptionable practice of passing on to his undertenants the hefty 'fine' that he had agreed to pay Donegall to secure an extension of his lease. However, when Arthur Upton and his successor Clotworthy Upton 'canted' (see below) some of the farms of his under-tenants by advertising the availability at auction of new twenty-one-year leases in the *Belfast Newsletter* in July 1768, they greatly upset tenants who were now in fear of eviction if they did not agree to the Upton terms. In so doing, the Uptons became the midwives to one of the most zealous and destructive agrarian secret societies of the eighteenth century.

As the Steelboys got into their stride after a slow start – antipathy towards the Uptons was, after all, a localised phenomenon – other items began to clog the agenda. The issue of excessive rents was always close to the top of their inventory of grievances. Arson was the standard penalty for the crime of refusing to let out land at twelve shillings an acre, considered by the Steelboys to be a fair rent. Over the previous two decades, some rents on better Ulster land had almost doubled and were edging ever closer to a tariff of £1 an acre. The Steelboys also sought to become price makers rather than price takers when it came to the sale and purchase of basic products like potatoes and grain. They forced farmers and millers to sell at rates they themselves dictated.

One determined opponent of the Steelboys was Sir Richard Johnston, who had inherited Gilford Castle and estate in 1758. His family motto was *Nunquam non paratus* ('Never unprepared'), and Johnston certainly lived up to that maxim in 1772 when, as a Co. Down magistrate, he threw himself into the fight against the secret society. A capable vigilantist, he assembled an informal local militia of friends, neighbours and fellow landowners (it numbered around fifty guns) to protect landlord property and rid the western part of the county, near the Armagh border, of the threat posed by the Steelboys. One of the most prominent members of Johnston's militia was a Presbyterian clergyman from the nearby village of Donaghcloney, the Rev. Samuel Morrell.

On 6 March 1772, Johnston and his vigilante group achieved their apotheosis in the so-called 'Battle of Gilford', when a force of between one and two thousand Steelboys demonstrated their antagonism towards the magistrate and his allies by attacking Gilford Castle. The prelude to the battle was a raid led by Johnston, in which four leading members of the Hearts of Steel organisation were captured. This sparked a retaliatory attack by a well-disciplined local Steelboy force reinforced by recruits from Lurgan and Portadown. The former contingent was led by one of the most celebrated leaders of the Steelboys, the former soldier Richard Savage. The Portadown force was led by one William ('Billy') Redmond. The leaders of the Steelboy force pledged in advance of the attack to 'quarter' Johnston's body and to affix the four severed parts to the corners of Gilford Castle. They would fall short of their objective, but only just.

When the Steelboys arrived, they were opposed by only twenty-three defenders of Gilford Castle, equipped with ten bullets each. So, even if the lower estimate of the numbers of the assault force is correct and every single round found its target, that would barely have accounted for a quarter of the Steelboys. After a determined assault, the attackers succeeded in breaching the demesne wall of the castle and setting fire to a number of outbuildings while maintaining a constant fusillade to cover their onslaught.

> The fire was returned from the house and three … of their men killed, upon which Mr Morrell a dissenting minister, neighbour to Mr Johnston, desirous to prevent further bloodshed, drew up a window in order to speak out to them, but was saluted by four musket balls in his head and breast. He fell dead out of the windows.[22]

Such was the lack of esteem in which Samuel Morrell was held that the attackers continued to fire into his already bloodied corpse. Johnston managed to make his escape by leaping over a wall, diving into the river Bann and swimming to the opposite shore. When he returned with a military force the following day his home had been ransacked and partially burned, and there was little left of the wine in his cellar.

For weeks afterwards Johnston, with military assistance, went in search of the ringleaders of the Down Steelboys. Nine, including Billy Redmond, were captured and sent for trial to Dublin, where a jury acquitted them all. Johnston, instead of seeking financial compensation – his losses were estimated at over £2,000 – looked for some gesture of recognition from the government for his resistance to the Steelboys. He was duly elevated to the baronetcy, his previous status having been that of a mere knight.

As was often the case with any outbreak of violent resistance in Ireland, the success of the Steelboys at the Battle of Gilford contained within it the seeds of ultimate defeat. The authorities could not ignore such an outrageous attack on the property of one of the leading antagonists of the uprising. The response was swift and ferocious.

The appearance of the Steelboys in 1770 coincided with the first in a sequence of bad harvests that continued for the next four years. This, allied to a glut of product on the linen market and a temporary collapse of that trade in 1772–3, brought hard times to Ulster. One of the unforeseen consequences of this economic depression in the province may well have been American independence! As Isaac Butt observed, quoting from Gordon's *History of Ireland*, doubtless with an element of glee: 'So great and wide was the discontent, that many thousands of Protestants emigrated from these parts of Ulster to the American settlements, where they appeared in arms against the British Government, and contributed powerfully, by their zeal and valour, to the separation of the American Colonies from the Empire of Great Britain.'[23]

It was meteorological conditions that, once again, tipped the balance in favour of radical and violent action. Temperatures in the early 1770s were often unseasonably cold, and precipitation was extreme even for Ireland, except when rain was needed to ensure a decent crop. The winter of 1771–2 was particularly severe, with extensive falls of snow. With incomes dropping, many farmers found themselves unable to pay rent and tithes while continuing to feed their families. The Steelboys' Proclamation of March 1772 reflects this. It began: 'Betwixt landlord and rectors, the very marrow is screwed out of our bones … they have reduced us to such a deplorable state by such grievous oppressions that the poor is [*sic*] turned black in the face, and the skin parched on their back.'[24]

Were it not for the capacity to import food from abroad, as the Earl of Abercorn's agent, James Hamilton, put it, 'we must have famished'. In the twelve months to the end of March 1770, Ireland imported over 33,000 tons of wheat, flour, barley and malt. The figure for the previous year had been a modest 2,400 tons. A rise in food prices was one of the principal motivating factors behind membership of the Hearts of Steel. To make matters even worse, the winter of 1769–70 also brought a fodder crisis, with hundreds of cattle starving to death. Is it any wonder, given the variegated nature of the subsistence crisis, that the Hearts of Steel drew broad support from across the community? The ranks of the movement, dominated by weavers and small farmers, were also swelled by a cohort of labourers and even some prosperous tenant farmers. Only the aristocracy remained entirely aloof, though some members of the Ulster gentry proved to be surprisingly neutral, whether out of sympathy or intimidation. Crucially, the leadership, and even the 'other ranks' of the organisation, included a number of men with military *nous*, experience and discipline. This was evident in the ability of William Redmond to gather his Portadown contingent in military formation and then march them home, deliberately foregoing the generous supplies of wine that were discovered in the vanquished Richard Johnston's cellar after the conclusion of the Battle of Gilford.

Unlike the Ribbon or Ribbon/Fenian organisations of the late nineteenth century, with whom they shared an antipathy towards excessive rents and evictions, the Steelboys, by and large, held back from outright murder. Even in the wake of the Battle of Gilford, the defenders – other than the deceased Samuel Morrell and the fugitive Richard Johnston – were released after a brief period of imprisonment. Steelboy killings were in low single figures, and even some murders ascribed to the organisation may not have been committed by any of its members. The Hearts of Steel tended to target the property of their antagonists – houses, outhouses, crops and animals. Their favoured, and more accessible, targets were not landlords, but tenants who had taken evicted farms, often by outbidding the previous occupant in a canting process. This practice involved the advertising of a lease that was about to fall in, and inviting written bids for the farm from interested parties. In what was already becoming a pattern and would develop into a template, transgressive tenants would be warned by threatening letter, usually despatched from the desk of 'Captain Justice' or 'Captain Firebrand'. If the threat was not taken seriously, the new tenant often found his house burning around him.

Arthur Young visited Antrim and Down shortly after peace was restored and the Steelboys had become just another evocative name in the history of Irish agrarian unrest. At a meeting with Samuel Waring, High Sheriff of Co. Down, in 1776, Young questioned Waring about the uprising of the Steelboys. The High Sheriff ascribed some of the blame for the insurrection to the relatively mild punishments meted out to the Oakboys the decade previously: 'The rising of the Steel-boys was owing to … the increase of rents, and complaints of general oppression; but Mr Waring remarked that the pardons which were granted to the Oak-boys a few years before were principally the cause of those new disturbances.'[25]

The rebellion of the Steelboys was met with equal doses of ferocity and leniency, though, in the case of the latter, the clemency shown was entirely unintentional. A number of the movement's leaders and foot-soldiers were identified, captured and hanged. More, however, benefited from partisan juries. At a series of trials in Carrickfergus a year after the dramatic events in Belfast described above, a number of Steelboys were put on trial for their lives. Faced with the prospect of condemning the accused to death, either (a) the sympathetic Protestant juries acquitted their radical co-religionists, (b) the jurymen acquitted because they feared the consequences for themselves if they did not do so, or (c) both of the above.

Either way, the failure of the Crown to secure convictions led to a March 1772 Act of Parliament allowing the authorities to indict and try Steelboys outside the jurisdiction in which they had been apprehended and charged. For many, this meant being sent to Dublin for trial. In a crucial test case in August 1772, however, the authorities fared no better in the capital city, where Protestant juries, although unlikely to face Steelboy intimidation, still took a dim view of the legislation and adopted a sympathetic approach to the 'crimes' of nine accused men. The specially assembled jury took less than twenty minutes to agree to set the prisoners free. Among those acquitted were Billy Redmond and one of the alleged killers of Dr Samuel Morrell at Gilford. The 'obnoxious act of parliament', deemed by opponents of the legislation to be unconstitutional, was repealed in December 1773. Ironically, the repeal of the law and the return of suspected Steelboys for trial in Ulster resulted in more convictions and a number of executions.

The Steelboy uprising lasted for the better part of three years, waxing and waning in accordance with the degree of military repression visited upon its ranks. According to Arthur Young, 'it was in reality owing to the impudence and levelling spirit of the Dissenters'.[26] Though largely Presbyterian ('The Roman Catholics were the most quiet,' said Young) and not overtly sectarian, the Steelboys were, nonetheless, 'potential agen[ts] of denominational strife'.[27] This was primarily because some of their early resentment was aimed at wealthy Catholic farmers who displaced Protestant tenants unwilling to pay higher rents.

After the Battle of Gilford, the authorities in Dublin began to take the Steelboy revolt more seriously. Ten infantry companies and five cavalry squadrons were sent north within days. By the end of March 1772, the local military commander, General Gisborne, could call on five regiments to quell the uprising. They did so with considerable brutality. Gisborne's military, however, did not have things entirely its own way. The Steelboys refused to melt obligingly back into the countryside and wait to be rounded up. In a couple of instances, large forces of the insurgents took on much smaller detachments of regular soldiers but tended to come off worse even in these numerically lopsided encounters. However, in most instances, Steelboy discretion proved the better part of Steelboy valour. By early April 1772, near Gilford for example, the newspaper *Finn's Leinster Journal* reported that 'there was scarce a man to be seen now ... but red coats, the rest are all fled', while nearby Lurgan 'was entirely thinned, unless of old men and young women'.[28] Maintenance of a low profile in the face of military oppression, or an urgent need to emigrate, would probably account for much of the dearth of young visible males. As far as General Gisborne was concerned, it was a clear case of 'good riddance to bad rubbish' in a part of the country that was already overpopulated. He wrote to the Lord Lieutenant, Lord Townsend, 'I never saw a country so thickly inhabited. And do suspect it to be absolutely insufficient to support them. And if that be so, some swarms must go off, and none can be so well spared as the leaders in these repeated insurrections.'[29]

In the military campaign that was brought to bear in order to suppress the movement, some Steelboys (probably no more than twenty)[30] were killed in skirmishes and a small number were hanged. Many chose to emigrate to North America to escape punishment, among them David Douglas, the prisoner freed by the Christmastide 1772 Steelboy invasion of Belfast, and Richard Savage, leader of the Lurgan Steelboys at the Battle of Gilford. Some refugees were reported to have drowned while attempting to escape to Scotland by boat. Some were even issued with pardons by the not entirely unsympathetic Lord Townsend in November 1772, although fifty-eight named individuals, all still at large and viewed as leaders of the conspiracy, were specifically excluded from this amnesty. The viceroy, in offering the qualified pardon, balanced his sanctions against the Steelboys by also castigating Ulster landlords for charging excessive rents at a time of greatly straitened personal circumstances for many tenants.

The Steelboys, because of their radicalism and their Protestantism, are often seen as the precursors of two very different organisations, the Society of United Irishmen and the Orange Order, though the Defenders and the Peep O'Day Boys (covered shortly) have better claims to that accolade. Given that the Steelboys often expressed their loyalty to the king – even, bizarrely, in threatening letters to rack-renting or canting landlords – they were probably closer to the Loyal Orange Institution than to the United Irishmen of Wolfe Tone. Roy Foster sees them as having attempted, with their desire for fair rents and their wish to regulate food prices, to create a 'moral economy'.[31] Their rebellion succeeded in rattling the establishment, and their activities against transgressive tenants made evictions far less attractive or profitable for the landed element of that establishment. They, along with the Oakboys, in the words of their most engaged scribe, James Donnelly Jr, 'fashioned a collective popular consciousness of oppression and instilled a code of behaviour on which the middle-class leaders of the northern United Irishmen were to draw with considerable success in the 1790s'.[32]

Although the teeth had been pulled from the Steelboy movement by the end of 1772, and even though many of its former adherents found themselves fighting against the legitimacy of King George III on American battlefields, the movement did not entirely disappear. Some of 'the unforgiven' singled out for perdition in Townsend's amnesty of November 1772 became privateers and took to banditry, ironically emulating the Roman Catholic woodkernes and raparees of the seventeenth century. Others kept alive the tradition of violent resistance to agrarian authority on a more piecemeal basis through the traditional device of the threatening letter and/or the nocturnal visit with lighted sods of turf.

The laws of Captain Right: the Rightboy revolt, 1786–8

'Sorry I am to add, that, not satisfied with the present extortion, some landlords have been so base as to instigate the insurgents to rob the clergy of their tithes, not in order to alleviate the distress of the tenantry, but that they might add the clergy's share to the cruel rack rents already paid.'[33]

(Attorney General John FitzGibbon, January 1787 speech to the Irish House of Commons)

'A new power has risen in the land, a visionary monarch, a Captain Right, who seems to have more real strength than the legislature ever had.'[34]

(Denis Browne MP, addressing the Irish House of Commons in 1787)

The movement, beginning in 1785, of the group calling itself the Rightboys can be seen as an extension of Whiteboy violence but with the financial demands of the Established Church more prominent than was the case with their precursors. What provoked the transition from 'white' to 'right'? The name, apparently first used in December 1785, had become general by early 1786 and was derived from 'the rebels' conviction of the legitimacy of their aims and methods'.[35]

With each decade of agrarian unrest that passed, and especially in periods of agricultural depression, the issue of tithes became increasingly contentious, until the campaign against the tax reached its climax in the 1830s during the Tithe War. The levels of antagonism towards the levy were often a function of changing patterns in Irish agriculture. Irish land use was in a state of constant flux, the primacy of pasture or tillage often being dictated by shifts in the British market. The 1759 relaxation of the seventeenth-century ban on the export of Irish beef, lamb and butter to Britain had led to an upsurge in pastoral farming. The country's grain and vegetable production during this period, greatly reduced in acreage, was largely for home consumption only. Gradually, however, 'Britain's swelling food requirements became the main driving force behind the extension of the area devoted to corn in Ireland'.[36] This led to a major renewal of grain production, the agricultural activity that attracted the tithe tax. What this meant was, in the words of Isaac Butt, that 'the exemption of the pasture lands of the rich threw the clergyman more for his living upon the potato gardens of the poor'.[37] However, as the wealthier farmers themselves began to revert to tillage to supply a burgeoning British market, resentment against the payment of a tax which benefited the clergy of the country's third largest religion (and a distant third at that) intensified. Worse bitterness was engendered, however, by the levying of tithes in some parts of the country on the potato crops produced on the conacre patches of impoverished cottiers (potatoes were not subject to the levy in Ulster, or indeed in Connacht), and on the turf cut in bogs, where subsistence farmers had turbary rights.

In early 1787, the incumbent attorney general, John FitzGibbon, briefed the Irish House of Commons on the origins and spread of the Rightboys: 'The people assembled in a mass house, and there took an oath to obey the laws of Captain Right, and to starve the clergy. They then proceeded to the next parishes on the following Sunday, and there swore the people in the same manner.' However, according to FitzGibbon, an element of mission creep then set in and the objectives of the Rightboys, after they had spread throughout Munster, became more ambitious. These included interference in the regulation of the Church of Ireland itself (the appointment of parish clerks and even curates) and calls for the allocation of Protestant church buildings for the use of the Roman Catholic Church. Soon their demands included the regulation of land prices and rates of pay for agricultural labourers.

The range of punishments employed by the Rightboys, and described by FitzGibbon, did not appear to have greatly evolved since the days of the Whiteboys.

> If anyone did resist ... in the middle of the night he was dragged from his bed, and buried alive in a grave filled with thorns: or he was sat naked on horseback, and tied to a saddle covered with thorns: in addition to this perhaps his ears were sawed off.[38]

As with the outbreak of Whiteboy violence during the previous decade, there was an element of landlord collusion in the opposition to tithes. According to Thomas Newenham: 'Rising with the value of the crop, they were considered as having the effect of discouraging exertions on the part of the farmers; and ultimately that of injuring the landlords, or at least preventing them from deriving the full benefit from their land.' As a consequence, 'several Protestant country gentlemen ... inspired the peasantry to resist the payment of tithes'.[39] Attorney General FitzGibbon had alluded to this deal with the devil in his January 1787 speech to the House of Commons. After excoriating the 'relentless landlords' of Munster for grinding their tenants into poverty (quite a concession from an aristocratic member of the Irish parliament), he accused many members of the Munster gentry of self-interested cynicism in their encouragement of the Rightboy campaign against tithes. Their object, he averred, was not to remove an unjust burden from the shoulders of their tenants, but to capitalise on a successful conclusion of the campaign by grabbing the tithe money for themselves in the form of increased rents. Or, as Isaac Butt put it more acridly, 'the tithe owners and the landlords were rival claimants for the privilege of fleecing the people'.[40]

The first appearance of this new movement came via a series of intimidatory notices in and around the town of Mallow, Co. Cork, in August 1785, warning farmers not to remit their tithe payments or they would suffer the consequences. When two compliant farmers suffered damage to their property, the die was cast. Threatening notices began to appear elsewhere in the county. By the spring of 1786, the conspiracy had spread to north Kerry. There, in an area around the towns of Castleisland and Tralee, Rightboys, summoned by the sounding of horns, commandeered horses and set fire to the grain stores of unco-operative farmers.

One of the characteristics of the Rightboy revolt, which it shared with other Irish radical movements, was the raid on the 'big house'. These were generally carried out not solely for intimidatory purposes – though that was an ancillary benefit – but in search of weapons and ammunition. One of the most infamous of these took place as the Rightboy insurgency spread to Limerick, where a group of around 300 members of the secret society raided the Palatine settlement between Askeaton and Rathkeale and stole a number of weapons from the descendants of the seventeenth-century German Protestant refugees.

By the middle of 1786, the Rightboys had also established themselves in the traditional Whiteboy strongholds of Kilkenny and Tipperary. So their sphere of influence – if intimidation of tithe proctors equates to 'influence' – was already far wider than that of their predecessors of the 1760s and the 1770s. The spread of the organisation was aided by a number of blatant daytime recruitment marches 'from one parish already evangelised to another not yet converted'.[41] By the summer of that year they had also established their *modus operandi*. Large numbers of their supporters, numbering in the low hundreds, would gather openly at Sunday masses and demand that parishioners swear an oath to adhere to the Rightboy rescript and to a price-list for the maximum amount payable, not just in tithes to Protestant clergy but also in dues to their own priests.

Among the other grievances that gave rise to the emergence of the Rightboys was a frequent provision in leases for 'duty days', which in the case of more substantial farmers might also involve supplying horses for the use of the landlord. In Maria Edgeworth's *Castle Rackrent*, Sir Murtagh Rackrent, according to the narrator (the family steward Thady Quirk), was a past master at extracting this due from his tenants.

> ... when a man vexed him, why the finest day he could pitch on, when the cratur [*sic*] was getting in his own harvest, or thatching his cabin, Sir Murtagh made it a principle to call upon him and his horse: so he taught 'em all, as he said, to know the law of landlord and tenant.[42]

And, according to Isaac Butt, Sir Murtagh's brand of magisterial contempt was far from being entirely fictional: 'The result naturally was, that the landlord demanded this labour exactly at the time when it was most wanted – that is, at the very time when it was most required on the tenant's own farm.' Even worse, tenants 'were often compelled to exceed the stipulated number of days. Some miserably low remuneration, more in the nature of a gratuity than of wages, was given them for this extended labour.'[43] Obviously, little had changed in twenty years. One of the grievances of the earlier Whiteboy movement was that tenants were compelled to work for their landlords for five pence a day.

A broad agenda ensured that the Rightboys of the 1780s attracted a wider range of support than their predecessors. The focus of the Whiteboys on enclosure, conacre rents and the tithe on potatoes limited their appeal to those most affected by those issues, namely landless labourers and small farmers. Reflecting later intra-tenant struggles between the Caravats and Shanavests in the early nineteenth century, larger farmers, and graziers in particular – especially those who employed 'outsiders' or 'strangers' instead of local labour – were as much the enemy of the Whiteboy conspiracy as were landlords. The agenda of the Rightboys, however, managed to span rural social divisions. Their influence, in some instances, extended all the way to the gentry, with occasional examples of aristocratic complicity, as well as instances of that great Irish ocular idiosyncrasy, the blind eye being turned. Examples of the former included, strange to relate, the sister of John FitzGibbon himself, Arabella Jefferyes, and Sir John Colthurst of Ardrum, the bitterly anti-clerical owner of a large estate near Mallow. Both were members of a local organisation known as the Farmers' Club, established with the clear, if unstated, intention of abolishing tithes.

An ally of the outspoken Church of Ireland Bishop Woodward of Cloyne, the barrister and former MP Dominick Trant – a 'resolute defender of the established church'[44] – published a pamphlet in 1787 on the Rightboy insurgency, pithily entitled *Considerations on the present disturbances in the province of Munster, their causes, extent, probable consequences, and remedies*, in which he alleged that there was an element of aristocratic 'command and control' of the conspiracy. One individual in particular, he claimed, had clearly demonstrated 'a love of plunder, and an innate and habitual passion for anarchy and tumult'.[45] However, Trant declined to name this anarchist. The pugnacious John Colthurst, an experienced duellist, safe in the knowledge that the near-sighted Trant had no history of face-to-face combat, decided that the reference applied to him and issued a challenge. Colthurst, who was believed to be one of the best shots in the country, appeared to be unconcerned that he was potentially about to do away with the brother-in-law of

Attorney General FitzGibbon, a man with ties of consanguinity to both sides of the controversy.

After two false starts, caused by the intervention of Dublin city law officers, Trant and Colthurst finally met on 14 February 1787, in Bray, Co. Wicklow. Despite the last-minute nature of the encounter, it appears to have drawn an audience of around four hundred onlookers. They watched as the two men each fired three times and missed, clearly belying Colthurst's reputation for coolness and accuracy. At this point the seconds intervened and sought an apology from Trant. This was not forthcoming. Colthurst, fatefully, called for new pistols. In the final exchange of shots, he managed to wound his adversary but was himself shot in the chest and later died of his wounds. When Trant was tried for murder, he was, constructively, acquitted when a verdict of 'manslaughter in self-defence' was entered. Indicative of the prevailing attitude amongst the aristocracy to the practice of duelling was the reaction of the attorney general himself to his brother-in-law's near-death experience. John FitzGibbon, apparently, had previously harboured no high opinion of Dominick Trant, his relative by marriage. His slaying of the troublesome Colthurst, however, raised him to new heights in the estimation of the country's chief law officer.[46]

In Tipperary, a landlord and *poitín* maker, Samuel Middleton, was one of the leaders of a band of Rightboys until he was apprehended while administering the society's oath to a number of new recruits in 1786. Middleton, rather than face jail or a flogging, then switched sides and later enhanced his reputation as an unscrupulous character by attempting to abduct an heiress with a view to marriage. The involvement of comfortable farmers was also a feature of the movement, although some of this was undoubtedly involuntary. When tenurial issues inevitably crept onto the Rightboy agenda, aristocratic enthusiasm waned.

These issues included opposition to the practice of canting. As the Rightboys' efforts to secure concessions from individual (and often isolated) clergymen began to bear fruit, they were emboldened to move against evicting landlords as well. Their principal demand concerned the concept of the 'three-year waste law'. In an effort to discourage 'land jobbers',* landlords who evicted tenants were expected to suffer a financial penalty by leaving farms untenanted for three years. In the context of subsequent tenurial conflicts, the Rightboy pursuit of obnoxious landlords and land jobbers verged on the unexceptionable. Threats were issued, houses were torched, beatings were administered, some offenders were forced to ride naked on horses with saddles of briars, others were buried up to their necks in pits of thorny furze bushes, but, in comparison with future land campaigns, the penalties for 'canting' were relatively mild and the incidence of such punishments was infrequent.

Where opposition to 'Rightboy law' was more general, the society was capable of a cohesive and concerted response. This extended all the way to potentially crippling blockades. In the case of communal opposition in Thomastown, Co. Kilkenny, for example, the Rightboys asserted their authority by cutting off turf supplies to the village. In the case of opposition from the much more imposing city of Cork, they threatened to starve the city into submission.

It was an unprecedented level of anti-clericalism in the ranks of the Rightboys that prodded prominent members of the Roman Catholic hierarchy into action. The bishop of Ossory, Dr Troy, who had previously condemned the activities of the local Whiteboys, had ample reason to double down on his denunciation of agrarian agitation when his own clergy came under attack for overcharging for their services. Also playing some part in Troy's strident opposition, however, was the knowledge that the relaxation of the anti-Catholic Penal Laws was not irreversible. The authorities might well use rural outrages – a number of ears had already been brutally severed from the heads of their owners and put on display – as a pretext for backsliding into religious repression. As well as excoriating the impudence of the Rightboys from the pulpit – warning that anyone who had taken an oath had committed a mortal sin and 'will sin still more heinously by

---

* An eighteenth-century term that was to morph into the more visceral 'land grabber' in the nineteenth century.

observing it'[47] – Dr Troy also adopted a more strategic approach by closing churches in his diocese on Sundays in order to deter after-mass gatherings. However, according to Michael Davitt, '"Captain Right" was not frightened by the pulpit thunderbolts of the time. His bands visited the presbyteries alike of parson and priest, and made them pay dear for their confederacy with the common enemy of the people, the Dublin Castle of the period.'[48]

One response to Roman Catholic hierarchical denunciations was the transfer of the violent attentions of the Rightboys – previously confined to Church of Ireland clergy – to the priests of their own faith. 'Their chapels were nailed up, their pastors abused and forced from their parishes, and no distinction made in the paroxysm of popular frenzy,' wrote Cornewall Lewis.[49] In Cork, where Dr Matthew McKenna, the irascible Catholic bishop of Cloyne, had supported Troy's message, this refusal to be cowed by priest or prelate took a surprising – and for the Catholic hierarchy, disturbing – turn. Rightboys abandoned their own churches and paraded publicly, with their families in tow, to the nearest Protestant equivalent. It took a meeting of Munster prelates, and timely concessions on priestly dues, to end this unparalleled revolt.

We can never be entirely certain whether the levels of support claimed by organisations like the Rightboys were real or illusory. When required, the Rightboys could command the attendance of large numbers of people at their assemblies and administer hundreds of oaths to their followers. However, the extent to which this was dictated by fellow-feeling, convenience or intimidation is moot. There is little doubt that many who showed up at gatherings at the behest of the Rightboys did so because they feared the consequences of defiance. In his pastoral letter of denunciation, Bishop Troy acknowledged, for example, that many of those who had taken oaths had done so under duress.

Whether the Rightboys benefited from an outpouring of popular support for their objectives and methods, or simply terrified the populations of six southern counties into tame acquiescence – or more likely a combination of the two – they certainly had a knack for bending people to their will. It was well-nigh impossible to get witnesses to testify against members of the organisation, even if they themselves had been subjected to atrocious ill treatment. In an extreme example of this withdrawal of assent, the virulently anti-Catholic high sheriff of Co. Waterford, Richard Musgrave, a future and highly subjective chronicler of the 1798 Rebellion, failed to persuade any of his underlings to administer punishment to a convicted Rightboy. According to an exchange of correspondence between Dublin Castle and the Home Office in London, '[He] could not procure a person to execute the sentence of the law on one of those miscreants who was condemned to be whipped at Carrick-on-Suir, though he offered a large sum of money for that purpose. He was therefore under the necessity of performing that duty himself, in the face on an enraged mob.'[50] Musgrave, later Sir Richard, who was exceptionally enthusiastic about the reformative powers of the whipping post,[51] brought much of that same spirit to the writing of his magnum opus, *Memoirs of the Different Rebellions in Ireland* in 1801, in which he excoriated Roman Catholics and Presbyterian rebels of 1798 with almost equal intensity and exulted in the defeat of the United Irishmen.

The Rightboys were effective in their parallel campaigns of terrorising clergy and the intimidation of tenant farmers. In the former instance, many individual clerics were obliged, for their own safety, to make concessions on the amount of tithe money due to them. In the latter instance, farmers were cajoled or threatened to withhold tithe payments, and the level of contributions declined drastically. In the case of the Church of Ireland diocese of Cloyne, Bishop Woodward informed the most powerful politician in the Irish House of Commons, the speaker, Thomas Conolly, that tithe revenues had declined from £6,000 per annum to a paltry £2,200.

Obviously, it is impossible to separate Irish agrarian agitation from the violence that inevitably accompanied it. However, where the Rightboys were concerned, the level of homicides for which members of the movement were directly responsible was low in comparison to most other secret societies of the eighteenth and nineteenth centuries. As with the Oakboys and Steelboys, animals and buildings suffered the worst punishments meted out by Rightboy 'courts'. Crimes against property were more common than crimes against the person, and where the latter was concerned there was a strong ritualistic element. Their particular calling card was the removal of the ears of someone who consistently defied them, and the purpose of most Rightboy punishments was display and humiliation. Visibility was almost as important as the inflicting of pain. Transgressors had to be seen to be suitably chastised. Hence the frequent use of a white horse named after, with conscious irony, the late Lord Protector himself. 'Cromwell' – employed in the execution of numerous Rightboy punishments – was so called because his saddle, according to *Finn's Leinster Journal* of 19 July 1786, was 'stuck with sharp-pointed nails for the punishment of the disobedient'. The precise link between the late Lord Protector and this particular form of torture is unclear. The use of a white horse was intended to supplement, with emotional torture, the physical anguish induced by the nails. The animal was held to symbolise the abandonment of one's natural allies. This concept was based on the *piseog* (legend) that the hapless King James II had fled from his defeat at the Boyne in 1690 and abandoned his Irish allies while on the back of a white horse, this *piseog* being in direct contradistinction to the equally mythical tradition that the fearless and efficacious King Billy rode a steed of similar hue into the same battle.

While a small number of killings, certainly fewer than a dozen, can be laid at the door of the Rightboys, only two of these were premeditated. One took place in 1787, when a Cork farmer, Denis Twomey, who had disobeyed the society in a dispute over tithes, was shot dead while transporting potatoes.

Far more vicious, however, was the killing in December 1786 of the substantial Tipperary farmer John Dunn. Dunn defied the Rightboys in January of that year and, as his punishment, both his ears were cropped, and part of his cheek was ripped off. These were then 'gibbeted' on a nearby pump for the better part of a week. Rather than submit to the coercion of the secret society, Dunn proposed to give evidence against the men who had assaulted him. To ensure that he was not in a position to do so, the Rightboys struck on 17 December. Dunn was viciously attacked in his own home, where he was decapitated with an axe or a billhook. His widow was then forced to view her husband's severed head before the killers withdrew. It was the single worst atrocity carried out by the Rightboys, and by the spring of 1787 two members of the society, John Heirk and Paul Kirwan, were publicly hanged for their part in the murder before an estimated crowd of 20,000. Four more capital convictions followed in the case.

The initial government response to the insurgency was tepid. This was not helped by the reluctance of Irish parliamentarians – members, it should be recalled, of an exclusively Protestant body – to support legislation designed to protect the clergy of the Established Church. The intervention of local militia organisations and aristocratic vigilante groups also had little impact on the insurgency. In addition, the leading lights of the Munster gentry were largely inert in the face of what they perceived as a threat to interests other than their own. However, as the anti-tithe campaign gained traction and the agenda of the Rightboys broadened, they posed a threat to landowners as well as ministers of the Established Church. Consequently, Dublin Castle and the gentry of the affected areas (the ones who were not themselves actually in league with the Rightboys) began to take more interest in suppressing the agitation.

To quell the revolt, in August 1786, Major General Lord Luttrell was given command of 2,000 troops, but the general and his troops saw precious little action. Luttrell's progress through the bailiwick of the Rightboys had some positive effect in that the level of illegal activity declined in regions where a show of military force was made. Luttrell also engaged in some 'velvet glove' activities. Acting on his own authority, he implemented a number of ad hoc tithe reforms. The government also stirred itself sufficiently in 1787 to pass legislation beefing up the magistracy and annulling all tithe agreements made under duress by nervy clergymen. Also, in a specifically Irish-oriented Riot Act, all the stock-in-trade activities of the Rightboys (digging graves, raiding for weapons, erecting mock gallows) were declared to be punishable by overseas transportation – the establishment of the Botany Bay colony in Australia was still a year off, and

America was out of bounds, but there were other options. Even the nocturnal gallops of the iconic 'Cromwell' were to cease if his handlers did not wish to end their days in West Africa.

In comparison with the punishments inflicted on the agrarian infantrymen of previous and subsequent agitations, the Rightboys got off lightly. According to James Donnelly Jr, although it is impossible to be precise because of the destruction of court records, ninety-three individuals were found guilty of Rightboy offences at sittings of assize courts between the spring of 1786 and the summer of 1788. Of that number, nineteen were sentenced to death. Only one unfortunate, Henry Sidley, was sentenced to transportation,* for the heinous crime of forcing a 'Cork gentleman' to sign a document endorsing the laws of 'Captain Right'. The remaining seventy-three were either fined, sentenced to be whipped (two of those had the particular privilege of being flogged in person by the energetic Sir Richard Musgrave) or despatched to prison for short terms. Indicative of the leniency of the sentences was the fate of Michael Bohan, who had attempted and failed to murder the Tipperary magistrate the Rev. Patrick Hare in October 1786. Hare had ordered troops to fire into a crowd of Rightboys attempting to reach the town of Cashel in August 1786. Four men had been killed and, as a consequence, Hare was a marked man. Had Bohan's pistol not misfired, he might well have succeeded in killing the much-loathed official. At a time when men were hanged for burglary or theft, Bohan's attempted murder drew merely a fine and a year in prison.

While the paucity of convictions can, in part, be accounted for by the intimidation of witnesses and by the organisational precautions often taken by the secret society to ensure that assailants were not known to their targets, as well as by official leniency, the fate of the Rightboys was in stark contrast to the officially sanctioned slaughter that followed the, admittedly, much greater and more menacing insurrection of the United Irishman a dozen years later.

---

* Although six of those sentenced to death were spared the gallows and were among the first residents of Botany Bay.

The very real prospect of falling victim in the field to a redcoat bullet (thirty-five Rightboys were killed in this fashion); the increasing threat of incarceration or worse; political promises of the redress of grievances (which did not eventuate); and the siphoning off of the aristocratic and large farmer cohort of the movement ultimately led to the gelding of the Rightboy revolt. However, one outcome of their advent was that, by their very presence, and arising out of fears of a resurgence of Whiteboyism, they 'prevented the type of wholesale eviction which took place in Scotland in the last half of the eighteenth century'.[52]

The Battle of the Diamond, 1795

'Real Irish cudgels must be root-growing, either oak, black-thorn or crab-tree ... they should not be too long – three feet and two inches is an accommodating length. They must be naturally top-heavy, and have around the end that is to make acquaintance with the cranium, three or four natural lumps.'[53]

(William Carleton, 'The Battle of the Factions', from *Traits and Stories of the Irish Peasantry*, 1830)

Two Ulster factions, the Peep O'Day Boys and the Defenders, are often identified erroneously as agrarian secret societies. While there was undoubtedly an agrarian element associated with their emergence, they were, especially in the case of the former, little more than sectarian alliances. The Peep O'Day Boys earned their name from a series of dawn vigilante-type raids on the homes of Roman Catholic families in Armagh, avowedly in a public-spirited search for illegal arms. The Defenders, as the name suggests, emerged in opposition to this targeting of Catholic householders who happened to be commercial rivals to many Peep O'Day Boys in the thriving linen trade.

In the late eighteenth century, Armagh was a fascinating outlier. It was the most populous county in Ireland, despite being the twenty-seventh in size and harbouring no major centres of habitation within its borders (even today the combined inhabitants of Lurgan and Portadown number around 50,000). This strangely out-of-kilter population was entirely due to its successful cottage-based linen industry, the income from which allowed tenants to survive on holdings that were so small that cottiers outside the county would have found it difficult to survive on them. The county was also divided fairly clearly and evenly along sectarian lines. The northern part of Armagh was almost entirely Protestant, the southern section largely Catholic.

The Munster Whiteboy and Rightboy disturbances did not go unnoticed in this divided county. To members of the wider Protestant community (Church of Ireland members as well as Presbyterians), they served as confirmation that Papist conspirators would not rest until the Protestant and Dissenter population of Ireland had been uprooted. The Peep O'Day Boys were, in part at least, a response to the perception of the Munster turbulence as being sectarian, rather than primarily agrarian in nature: they were less the philosophical inheritors of the Oakboy/Steelboy tradition than the actual precursors of the Orange Order.

Where the Defenders were concerned, there was, at least according to the findings of a Select Committee of the House of Lords in 1793, a wider Defender agenda not dictated by antagonism towards the Peep O'Day Boys. The committee found that the members of the organisation were 'of the Roman Catholic persuasion; in general, poor, ignorant, labouring men, sworn to secrecy ... they talked of being relieved from hearth-money,* tithes, county-cesses, and of lowering their rents'.[54]

Like their principal antagonists, the Defenders would go on to spawn noteworthy successors of their own in the Ribbonmen, who took their cue from the politics of Defenderism (although the Ribbonmen were not noted for their loyalty to the Crown, a rather surprising element of the Defender oath) but spread far beyond the confines of Ulster. Both organisations also had loose ties to larger bodies, the Volunteers in the case of the Peep O'Day

* Payment made for the revenue-raising Hearth Tax levied on householders.

Boys, and the United Irishmen in the case of the Defenders. The former was instrumental in the establishment of the quasi-independent (and entirely Protestant) 'Grattan's Parliament' in Dublin, which endured from 1782 to 1800: the latter was the French-influenced revolutionary republican group responsible for the 1798 Rebellion.

The depredations of the Peep O'Day Boys led, eventually, to the pivotal 'Battle of the Diamond', which took place near Loughgall, Co. Armagh, on 21 September 1795. This fracas is iconic because of its exalted status in the loyalist mythos. It was, in reality, little more than a glorified faction fight, with religion rather than consanguinity or parochialism at its heart.

Like many faction fights, the 'battle' was a prearranged meeting between the combatants. Failed attempts at mediation between the two sides – the priests who often intervened to prevent faction fights from taking place[55] being less influential in this instance – meant that they began to gather in numbers near the Diamond some days beforehand. As word spread of the planned confrontation, reinforcements arrived from farther and farther afield. A representative number of protagonists on both sides were armed, with the Peep O'Day Boys rumoured to be equipped with Volunteer muskets.

The skirmish ended in the routing of the Defenders. The Peep O'Day Boys claimed to have killed at least thirty members of the Roman Catholic faction, though the real fatalities were more likely to have been in single figures. Of greater significance, however, was the formation, in the aftermath of the battle, of the Orange Order at a meeting in the inn kept by one James Sloan in Loughgall. The subsequent depredations of Peep O'Day Boy supporters in Armagh, where up to 7,000 Catholics were forced to flee the county, were of more immediate consequence locally, but in the longer term the existence and the philosophy of the Orange Order made it virtually impossible to create a united thirty-two-county front in any subsequent agrarian agitation, other than the brief flowering of the Tenant League (qv) in the 1850s.

The Battle of the Diamond was followed three years later by the rebellion of the United Irishmen, an insurrection that combined an element of non-sectarian nationalism (the rising in Antrim was almost exclusively Protestant) with a revisiting of the religious pogroms of the mid-seventeenth century (the Wexford rebels were responsible for two notorious massacres of Protestant civilians). The 1798 rebellion, conducted with significant military assistance from post-revolutionary France, was mercilessly crushed by the forces of the Crown, led to the deaths of up to 50,000 people (mostly rebels and civilians), and ultimately brought about the abolition of the semi-independent Irish parliament in Dublin and the introduction of the Act of Union, thus drawing Ireland definitively into the ambit of the Westminster parliament.

5

The old vest, the cravat and the ribbon:
tenant versus tenant, 1806–16

'Tis wonderful how the characteristic credulity of the lower
orders still continues to be duped by a few contemptible,
depraved, insidious leaders, who are grown hardened,
desperate, and practised in seduction; but pardon is often ill
bestowed upon the desperate.'

(Lord Norbury in his opening address to the
Special Commission for the several counties of
Tipperary, Waterford and Kilkenny, 1811)

Reaghstown, Co. Louth, 29–30 October 1816

It is almost impossible to separate fact from fiction, and, given the
scale of the atrocity, it is hardly necessary. There is one fact that
everyone can agree on. Eight people burned to death at the hands
of a vengeful mob at Wildgoose Lodge that night. The house
in which they perished was a fine stone-built thatched building
perched on a hill. It rested above a flood plain that, during the
winter months, was almost invariably inundated with rainwater
which wrapped itself around the hillock to form a *turlough* (a
temporary lake). This left an exposed ridge as the sole causeway
and access to the dwelling for much of the winter.

Once the subject of controversy, but now resolved beyond
dispute, was the religious persuasion of the family of its owner,
'an industrious man' named Edward Lynch. All were Catholics,

as were the killers, who subjected their victims to one of the most gruesome of all possible deaths, incineration. The surname of the tenant of Wildgoose Lodge was ironic, given the object of the lynch mob – most were his own neighbours – as they approached his house that night.

Lynch (who rented from the local landlord, Townley Patten Filgate) was an arch-transgressor in the eyes of the implacable mob. His treachery and collaboration had led to the deaths of three men. He had been 'tried' *in absentia* (and without his knowledge) and found guilty of the odious crime of identifying and testifying against three of his neighbours for their invasion of his home six months previously. Sentence had been passed – it was not entirely clear by whom – and his accusers were there to deliver the final *coup* of this extra-legal process. Did they give any consideration to the fate of Lynch's servants, or were those unfortunates deemed guilty by association with the informer (a mentality that was a regular feature of Irish agrarian violence)? Did it cross their minds that Lynch's five-month-old grandson was living under the old man's roof? Did they care? After all, that callous off-the-shelf maxim 'nits make lice' was often invoked to validate the massacre of the innocent.

The executioners set fire to the thatch of Wildgoose Lodge, stood guard to ensure that no one managed to escape the burning house, and listened to the screams of their eight victims, the farmer and weaver Edward Lynch, his son Michael, his daughter Bridget Rooney and her husband Thomas, their infant child Peter, and domestic servants Ann Cassidy, Bridget Richards and James Rispin, as they perished in the flames.[1] There would be no one left alive to identify the executioners of the informer Edward Lynch, not even an infant who could never bear witness.

A few stones of the original structure remain to this day, wrapped in bushes and brambles and perhaps even visible to slow-moving traffic on the main Dublin–Derry road. It could pass for a storybook fairy fort, well-marked but stubbornly untouched because of local superstitions about the 'little people'. However, even *in extremis*, incensed at human despoliation or depredation, no sylvan sprite would have been capable of wreaking havoc of the kind that gives Wildgoose Lodge such an evil reputation to this day.

The Caravats and the Shanavests, 1806–11

'Caravats and Shanavests have promulgated the laws, have levied contributions ... nocturnal and barbarous outrage has been let loose, and a paltry banditti, of the lowest description, and insignificant when openly opposed, has inflicted the cruellest torture on the peaceable and unprotected cottager – and shameful to tell, the native chastity of the females is universally violated by licentious brutality.'[2]

(Lord Norbury in his opening address to the Special Commission for the several counties of Tipperary, Waterford and Kilkenny, 1811)

'Down with their yellow profession
And down like the snow it will fall
Like Lucifer cast out of Heaven
So will those Shanavests fall.
The old waistcoat I cannot endure
For they like the Orange reply
The Shanavests wear it for clothing
With hunger they would lay down and die.'[3]

(anti-Shanavest ballad from Co. Tipperary)

The Native American Lakota and Crow. Shakespeare's Montagues and Capulets. Their twentieth-century New York City clones, the Sharks and the Jets. The Masserias and Maranzanos from the 1930s' Mafia wars. The Bloods and the Crips of modern Los Angeles. Sworn enemies, fictional and factual, pledged to kill or maim one another on sight. To that small but representative sample of undying animosity can be added two thoroughly obscure and regularly misunderstood Irish adversaries of the early 1800s, the Caravats and the Shanavests.

In histories of Ireland covering the entire 120 years of the existence of the United Kingdom of Great Britain and Ireland, or of the so-called 'long nineteenth century', the Caravats and the Shanavests often do not merit a mention, or even a footnote. In his 1871 work *History of the Land Tenures and Land Classes of Ireland: With an Account of the Various Secret Agrarian Confederacies*, the nationalist historian George Sigerson does not refer to either group even once. Often, when they do emerge from the end-noted shadows, like terrifying chiaroscuro brigands, they are joined at the hip and treated as if they made common cause in the struggle against landlordism.

They did no such thing.

Granted, neither sect harboured any great love of their 'betters', but their aversion to landlordism was as nothing compared to their mutual antagonism. The Caravats and Shanavests, far from making common cause against a shared enemy, pummelled each other mercilessly. Such was the status of their communal loathing that those historians who did not mistake them for two branches of the 'continuity' Whiteboys generally assumed that they were two of the many feuding Irish factions who would often meet (by arrangement) to do battle and to extend the scope, range and history of vendettas whose origins often baffled even the participants. This was, for example, how Michael Davitt treated of them in his *The Fall of Feudalism in Ireland*, while simultaneously eating his cake too by observing that, far from being mere parochial thugs, they were 'otherwise one in sympathy with the general policy of lawless attacks on the adherents of the landlord garrison'.[4]

That they were mere faction-fighters was also the forgivable assumption made by the song collector Patrick Weston Joyce, an associate of the great musicologist Dr George Petrie, when he came across the fiddle tune 'The old vest and cravat' and included it in his *Ancient Irish Music* collection in 1909. Joyce was aware that the tune had its origins in the battles and skirmishes of two antipathetic groups in Munster and south Leinster a century before. However, he was unaware of the real reasons for their antipathy.

Joyce might have been surprised to learn that, although the rivalry ultimately degenerated into uncomplicated factionalism, the animosity between the two groups was originally based not on clan or parish identity but on class. Irish agrarian secret societies did not always need the divisive figure of the landlord against whom to channel their aggression. They were eminently capable, even where sectarian divisions were not a factor, of trading blows with each other based on their social and economic status.

The stamina of the Whiteboys, who endured into the early years of the nineteenth century, and the ubiquity of faction-fighting during the same period, has tended to obscure the true nature of the conflict between the Caravats and the Shanavests.

The hostility between these two disparate groups appears to fall into three distinct and unequal phases or guises. During the first period, from 1802 to 1806, the Caravats had the field more or less to themselves. To all intents and purposes, they were Tipperary Whiteboys, specifically a subset of that movement known locally as the Moyle Rangers (after a local river). They were a 'primitive syndicalist movement'[5] whose grievances were those of the landless and land poor. Their favoured targets were land jobbers who took farms or conacre from which the sitting tenants were being evicted during an era of high rents based on a wartime agricultural boom. They also sought to regulate food prices and rents, and raise the wages of labourers.

The Shanavests were formed from victims of Caravatism in 1805–6, as a vigilante response to the activities of the latter faction. They recruited from the rural middle classes, i.e. those who had been relentlessly harassed by the Caravats for the previous three or four years. In addition to taking direct action in defence of their confrères, whenever they thought they might stimulate the lackadaisical authorities into a corrective response, they would pass on information about their enemies and save themselves the trouble of retaliation. Karl Marx would undoubtedly have recognised and approved of this embryonic class confrontation between the rural proletariat and the agrarian bourgeoisie in pre-industrial Munster. Marx, however, might have been confused or chagrined by the vestigial bourgeois allegiance of some Shanavests to 'a muffled species of nationalism'[6] and to the radical ideology of the now defunct United Irishmen. The dialectic never quite measured up to the multidimensional 'ground hurling' of Irish agrarian malice in early nineteenth-century Tipperary and Kilkenny.

This more noteworthy middle phase of the Caravat-Shanavest conflict petered out when the state finally woke up and intervened in 1811 to bring the burgeoning war (it had spread to eleven counties by then) to an uneasy conclusion. That, however, was far from the final curtain for the Caravat-Shanavest rivalry. It had certainly re-emerged by the mid-1830s, and can be tracked at least as far as the immediate post-Famine period. However, it was far more localised, confined largely to Co. Tipperary (the 'murder' county)[7] and was, by then, little more than the unreconstructed faction-fighting for which it is often mistaken in its earlier iteration.

The antagonism of these two groups was sanguinary (the number 'killed in action' is impossible to calculate but amounted to low double figures at the very least), but it was also colourful. There was considerable preening and display associated with the rivalry, especially when it came to the garments that gave both factions their names. The word 'Caravat' is derived from the cravat ostentatiously worn by one of the early leaders of that faction, Nicholas Hanley, 'a flamboyant dandy'. The name 'Shanavest' comes from the Irish *sean bhéist* meaning old vest or waistcoat, a garment often seen on Patrick Connors, otherwise known as Paudeen Gar (probably *Paudeen gearr* or sharp Patrick in English). Connors was a well-to-do Tipperary publican, part-time policeman, large farmer and, in his off-duty moments, a 'typical mafia chief'.[8] The legend that surrounds the origins of the feud and the baptism of the factions begins at a hanging.

It appears that the career of the narcissistic quasi-highwayman Nicholas Hanley (or Hanly) as a Moyle Ranger/Whiteboy came to an unfortunate and premature conclusion at the business end of a noose during the winter of 1805–6. This came about after he was convicted of the murder of a kinsman or ally of 'Paudeen Gar' Connors for the crime of taking the farm of a recently evicted tenant. In this instance, it was the state that caught up with Hanley, not the nascent rivals of the Moyle Rangers. Among the attendance at his public execution in Clonmel, sporting a disappointingly shoddy waistcoat, was Paudeen Gar. The factions got their names from a brief and unfriendly interaction between the two men before Hanley's defiant and untimely demise.

> When the executioner was fixing the rope upon the culprit's neck, a voice was raised in the crowd: it was that of an athletic, powerful-looking fellow in tattered garments [Paudeen Gar]. He said, 'I came a long distance today to see the cravat put upon that fellow's neck; it becomes him well and will last him for life.' A friend of the doomed man replied ... 'he would sooner drown himself than appear in public in that old vest you wear'.[9]

Before succumbing to the throttling of the metaphorical cravat, Hanley is said to have defiantly tossed his actual neckerchief to the crowd as if it was a bridal bouquet – presumably Connors made no attempt to retrieve it – giving the survivors of his Whiteboy unit their new name. Connors's faction, willy nilly, was obliged to abandon its own rather prosaic name (they were known simply as Paudeen Gar's Boys) for their much more downbeat title, based on the inadequacy of their leader's waistcoat.

Thus did the deadly rivals become Caravats and Shanavests. The rest is history, interlaced with a modicum of folklore and large dollops of gross exaggeration. While there were some extremely bloody confrontations between the two groups – at which participants often mimicked the sartorial trademarks of their leaders, dead and living – the fact was that most Caravat activity was still bound up with the despatch of threatening letters and the doling out of retribution to land jobbers and individual transgressors, rather than with pitched battles waged against the Shanavests.

Caravats, in addition to their self-appointed role as the Robin Hoods of the rural poor, frequently raided in pursuit of arms. For example, when two members, Andrew Kerwick and Laurence Dwyer, stopped the Cork mail coach on 21 November 1810 at

Grange turn-pike gate in Co. Tipperary, they boasted of the fact that they spurned the purses of the occupants of the carriage and stole only two blunderbusses and two pistols.

After months of unrest across much of Munster, the Whiteboy legislation of 1776 – 'which sleeps upon the statute book until called into activity' – was invoked across seven counties to arrest the slide into anarchy. Under this draconian legislation, even those found guilty of taking part in an illegal assembly could be sentenced to imprisonment, the pillory, flogging or some other form of corporal punishment. Anyone caught posting a hostile notice or delivering a threatening letter was committing a capital felony and was liable to execution. Crucially, under the terms of the Whiteboy Acts, magistrates could summon for questioning anyone they suspected of criminality. If the suspect refused to answer questions, they could be jailed until they decided to co-operate. This alone often had the effect of bringing anarchy to an end in some areas because magistrates could remove the bad actors for as long as they insisted on remaining silent. However, the Whiteboy Act could be invoked only in disturbed areas. Some of the actions that could result in a prison sentence, a flogging, transportation or worse in places like Tipperary, Waterford and Kilkenny were not even deemed to be crimes in more tranquil counties.

In a judicial reckoning in 1811 – a series of special commission[*] trials in Tipperary and Kilkenny – the presiding judge, Lord Norbury, outlined a familiar list of the dominant issues on the Caravat agenda. These included tithes, rents, Roman Catholic priestly dues, labourers' wages and the price of food. In Norbury's view, when it came to evictions, as far as the Caravats were concerned, 'the landlord must keep his old tenant at the old rent – all transfers are forbidden – trade is denounced – there is a maximum established for rent, and a minimum for wages'.

Norbury's sentiments were echoed by the solicitor general,

---

[*] A special commission jury was appointed from a reduced panel of potential jurors and generally consisted of wealthier and therefore more malleable (from a prosecution point of view) high-worth individuals.

Charles Kendal Bushe, in his opening address to the special commission jury in Clonmel on 4 February 1811. He underlined the fact that the particular animosity of the Caravats was reserved for 'land grabbers' and 'informers':

> If the former tenant were a beggar or a knave, he must be continued; no honest or industrious man, however willing to succeed him, and to benefit the property, by his capital or labour, is allowed, upon pain of death, to be a competitor with the old proprietor ... every witness who comes forward in aid of the laws is stigmatized [sic] by the odious appellation of informer, and devoted to vengeance and to slaughter.

Bushe also drew attention to 'parochial antipathies' and the Caravat hostility to the 'stranger', i.e. anyone not from the county having the temerity to seek employment in Tipperary. 'It is not long since unfortunate labourers from Kerry,' the solicitor general observed, 'have been forbidden, upon pain of the most dreadful punishment to offer their labour here.'[10]

The Shanavests – presumably they saw themselves as the 'honest and industrious' types invoked by Bushe in his address to the commission – for their part, were entirely reactionary in both senses of the word. Their activities appear to have been confined to large-scale attacks on companies of Caravats at fairs and on 'pattern' (patron) days,* where hundreds of spectators would assemble to witness the latest expression of the rivalry of these two factions.

And the Shanavests had motives beyond the pecuniary in their drive to end the threat posed by their antagonists. Their faction was not just composed of members of a well-to-do farming class who were being denied the opportunity to expand their holdings. It also included members whose daughters were being kidnapped by their sworn adversaries. In some instances, payment was demanded for the return of those abducted, but the primary purpose of making off with the daughter of a Shanavest was

* Holy days or saints' days.

not to obtain a ransom, but to secure a dowry. Eligible farmers' daughters, once kidnapped, tended to be quickly married off to Caravats or their supporters. Many of these unfortunate female pawns in a cynical male intrigue were raped in order to remove any further prospect of securing a partner in marriage, other than one chosen by her captors. By such brutal means did a man of lower social standing increase his chances of securing a prosperous wife and a hefty dowry.

Why, you might wonder, did the Shanavests take the law into their own hands and attempt to vanquish their tormentors themselves? Why not simply do as their aristocratic 'betters' had consistently done, and demand that the authorities take control of the situation and execute, jail or transport the Caravat ringleaders and their other ranks?

The answer is that the ability of even prosperous Irish tenant farmers to persuade Dublin Castle to defend their interests was questionable. The Castle, reinforced by the attitude of local gentry in areas where the agitation was at its worst, tended to the view that intra-peasant mayhem was not necessarily a threat to the interests of the local aristocracy. A common maxim of the day even suggested that 'while there is a fight at a fair there will never be a rebellion'.[11] What did it matter if members of rival criminal gangs considerably reduced the unmanageable element in the community by taking out their enemies? In addition, the nationalist predilections of many Shanavest members, and the memories of the often gratuitous slaughter of 1798, meant that they were unwilling to unleash the military or (far worse) the yeomanry on their own localities in pursuit of renegades they could just as easily deal with themselves.

The bloody disturbances that marked the Caravat-Shanavest 'war' were initially confined to the Tipperary towns of Clonmel, Cashel and Fethard, before spreading south to Waterford and from there to adjacent counties. In some areas the Caravats made common cause with groups of industrial employees from quarries, collieries and textile works. In many instances, existing Whiteboy/agrarian units were folded up into the 'Caravat conspiracy'. Charismatic local leaders with intimidating nicknames ('Captain

Flogger', 'Captain Cutter') emerged to lead the campaign. The acknowledged local leaders were often as colourful as their aliases. One, John Brian ('Captain Wheeler'), was rumoured to have three wives. His desire for a fourth led to the murder of a family of four, burnt to death in their home so that Brian could dispose of the husband of his most recent inamorata.

From 1806 to 1811 in Co. Tipperary, and during the narrower window of 1807–8 in Co. Waterford, bloody encounters between the two groups were common, leading to these skirmishes being dismissed as mere faction fights. Hundreds could be involved on both sides in these premeditated clashes. The Munster Inspector of Police, Major Richard Willcocks, in his evidence to a House of Commons committee in 1824, testified to the size of the two factions ('I have known them to meet in very large bodies … I have seen an entire fair engaged in it') and to the mutual carnage they were capable of inflicting ('I heard of fourteen being lost in one engagement, in the town of Goolden [*sic*]'). Willcocks was referring to an infamous encounter in the village of Golden, Co. Tipperary, on the river Suir, where up to twenty people are thought to have died in a Caravat-Shanavest fracas. Willcocks explained to the members of the committee how these deaths came about, with a hair-raising account of the weaponry deployed when the two factions collided:

> [They were] mostly armed with short guns of a blunderbuss description, cut down muskets we call them, and pistols; frequently old swords … they go with them concealed under their great coats … Those that have not fire-arms are armed with a sort of stick called a *clogh* alpine, that is a large stick, generally ash, pulled out of the ground [or] a part of the barrel of a musket, or the barrel of a gun, and this is studded all around with nails to make it a most desperate weapon; it would be more fatal, I think, than the blow of a sword.[12]

A detailed insight into the conduct, as opposed to the nature, of the two parties comes in the evidence laid before the Special Commission that heard the trials of a number of Caravats in

Tipperary and Kilkenny in 1811. The Commission was presided over by the infamous 'Hanging Judge' Lord Norbury (John Toler), who had traded blows from the bench with Robert Emmet at the latter's trial for treason in 1803. Norbury had been Irish Chief Justice since 1800 and, according to his entry in the *Dictionary of Irish Biography*, his 'scanty knowledge of the law, his gross partiality, his callousness, and his buffoonery, it was asserted, completely disqualified him for the position'.[13] Alongside Toler on the bench was the new Chief Baron of the Irish Exchequer Court, Standish O'Grady, who, as attorney general in 1803, had been a prosecuting barrister in the case against Emmet. O'Grady's strong Limerick accent, and his generally more benign approach to his fellow man, made him a somewhat less forbidding figure on the commission bench.

Despite their distinct identities and priorities, practically no differentiation was made by the commission prosecutors between the two groups. In fact, although the published account of the proceedings was entitled *A Report of the Trials of the Caravats and Shanavests*, little mention was made of the activities of the latter except in a single case in which a Shanavest, James Slattery, was testifying against a number of Caravats. Did this indicate official awareness that the Shanavests were acting as surrogates for the properly constituted authorities and that the main threat to the establishment came from the Caravats? The only hint of the homicidal mass gatherings at which the two groups settled their differences came in the Slattery case. Readers of the report on the trials would come away with the impression that the Caravats were an arm of the wider Whiteboy movement and that the Shanavests were merely a Tipperary faction that was inexplicably hostile to the Caravat campaign.

The charges in the Slattery case, heard by the commission in Clonmel on 6 February 1811, read as follows: 'John Corcoran, William Crehan, Cornelius Hickey, and Philip Codey, were capitally indicted for an assault on James Slattery, on the 6th of November, 1810, and for firing a loaded gun at him, with intent to kill and murder, &c. and also for unlawfully assuming the name of Caravat, and appearing in arms by night.'

Corcoran, Crehan, Hickey and Codey had the mixed fortune to be defended by the former United Irishman Leonard McNally, barrister, playwright and informer. Despite his avowed nationalist sympathies and lawyerly credentials (he had defended Robert Emmet in 1803), McNally was actually one of the Crown's most notorious espionage assets and had betrayed many secrets of the United Irishmen and of his nationalist clients (including Emmet) to Dublin Castle.

James Slattery's evidence was of returning from the races of Coolmoyne, Co. Tipperary with a group of around twenty men, and of being attacked. He testified that his teeth were knocked out and that Corcoran pointed a gun at him. Corcoran tried to shoot him but the gun misfired. It became clear when the witness was cross-examined by McNally that Slattery was a Shanavest and that he was with a group of members of that organisation – rather than twenty of his close personal friends – when they were attacked by a large mob of Caravats. It also emerged from his evidence that Slattery was the nephew of Paudeen Gar Connors – whom he described, incongruously, as 'a poor old man'. Slattery was either coy or uninformed when questioned about the origins of the Caravat-Shanavest rivalry, claiming, bizarrely, that it was a 'foolish dispute about May balls'. He was better informed, however, about the dispute between his uncle and Nicholas Hanley which ended on a gallows in Clonmel in 1806, and he gave a brief account to the court of the animosity between the two men.

Also giving evidence in the case was the parish priest of Fethard, Fr John Ryan. When asked by the lead prosecuting attorney, Solicitor General Charles Kendal Bushe, if the fights between the two sides were 'confined to the lower orders', Ryan replied, 'I think they are; I am not sure whether any respectable parishioner has joined them.' He went on to insist that both sides were 'equally criminal'.

Bushe, as it transpired, was not able to press home the Crown case against Corcoran, Crehan, Hickey and Codey. To his chagrin, O'Grady noticed a flaw in the capital indictment, and that charge was thrown out. The four men were, however, found guilty of a misdemeanour, viz. 'illegally assuming the name of Caravat and appearing in arms and were sentenced to be whipped on three dates in February, May and July 1811.

It was, in all likelihood, the activities of the Special Commission court in Tipperary and Kilkenny in 1811, allied to an enhanced military presence in Tipperary, Kilkenny and Waterford, that brought an end to this second, and more meaningful, phase of Caravat-Shanvest animosity. Norbury lived up to his reputation in handing down sentences that were certainly sufficiently draconian to discourage all but the more committed participants from pursuing the rivalry. A handful of executions and transportations, as well as the splenetic Norbury's insistence that those jailed locally were 'to be exhibited, naked and disgraceful spectacles, and scourged through the county whose tranquillity they had menaced',[14] signalled to the Caravats and the Shanavests that the authorities were taking their activities more seriously, and that they were now seen as a threat to those above their own humble station.

The belated intervention of Dublin Castle in the 'class war' phase of the Caravat-Shanavest antagonism did not entirely end their hostilities. Confrontations persisted but, in the wake of the 1811 clampdown, they seem to have assumed the more mundane qualities of a factional dispute which spilled into the post-Famine period and centred around the annual Gooseberry fair in Ballingarry in south Tipperary on 23 July each year.

According to local Tipperary lore, it took the arrival of the Fenian movement in the 1860s to bring the Gooseberry Fair brawls to an end. The Fenians, often as much of a social as a political movement in rural Ireland, offered a common enemy (England), a cause (militant nationalism) and an alternative focus (military drilling and training) for the testosterone of the younger male population. The much later impact of the Gaelic Athletic Association (GAA, founded in 1884) in channelling clan and parochial rivalries into the (relatively) harmless sports of football and hurling should not be underestimated either. It would be easy to overlook the GAA's role in persuading young men in rural

Ireland to abandon the *clogh alpine** and the blackthorn in favour of the *camán* and *sliotar*.

The murders at Wildgoose Lodge, 1816

'In a chapel called Stonehouse, not far from Ardee,
For Wildgoose Lodge-bound to proceed,
A blood-thirsty gang did the Baronet see
All plotting a murderous deed.
Full forty assassins in dreadful array,
The number 'gainst Paul that combined,
From an altar erected to GOD took their way,
With the spirit of Hell in their mind.'[15]

(from John Graham, 'Sir Harcourt's vision: an historical poem', 1823)

'He then turned round, and taking the Missal between his hands placed it upon the altar … he exclaimed, in a voice of deep determination, first kissing the book! "By this sacred an' holy book of God, I will perform the action which we have met this night to accomplish, be that what it may; an' this I swear upon God's book, and God's althar!"'

('Wildgoose Lodge', William Carleton, *Traits and Stories of the Irish Peasantry*)

The Co. Louth townland of Reaghstown was located about four miles from Ardee in the middle of an area of good arable and pasture land, dominated by aristocratic landowning families like the Filgates, Fortescues and Fosters. The most prominent local grandee was John Foster, speaker of the Irish House of Commons in 1800 and an arch opponent of the Act of Union. Having chosen the wrong side of history – in the medium term at least – he had

---

* A rather nasty weapon that also saw service as a walking stick.

astutely managed to rehabilitate himself with Dublin Castle in the years that followed the dissolution of the 'Patriot Parliament' and still enjoyed substantial power and influence. North Louth, because of its affiliation to the linen industry, tended, like nearby Armagh, to have smaller farms than would have been feasible for affluent peasants in other parts of the country. The county had shared in the agricultural prosperity of the years of Napoleonic conflict and, like most of the other beneficiaries of the war economy, went into an economic decline after Waterloo. The post-war recession was accentuated by the eruption of Mount Tambora in 1815 and the resultant 'Year Without a Summer' (see Chapter 6).

The number of evictions in the county began to rise and there was a move back to grazing, with a consequent increase in agrarian crime as unemployment among redundant agricultural labourers increased. Amid alarming (and familiar) claims of murderous anti-Protestant conspiracies, and demands from Foster for an armed response from Dublin Castle, Louth was proscribed* in 1816 and the Protestant Yeomanry militia and members of the new Peace Preservation Force were deployed to the county. Such was the level of dissent and violence in different parts of Ireland at the time that a retinue of 25,000 troops was being maintained in the country to supplement the militia and the police, should the need arise.

So the backdrop to the Wildgoose Lodge murders was another Irish agricultural depression, an upsurge in agrarian violence in the previously untroubled county of Louth (peace usually, but not always, being a function of prosperity), the threat of famine and a collapse in linen prices vital to the prosperity of Louth, Armagh and Monaghan.

Add to that toxic mixture the continued rise of a new force in violent agrarianism, the Ribbon society. Although, like its Whiteboy antecedents, the threat of Ribbonism was frequently exaggerated by magistrates and landlords (often one and the same), the fact remains that 100 policemen were killed and 500

* This would, typically, have included more oppressive policing and the suspension of *habeas corpus*.

wounded in clashes with members of Ribbon factions during the twenty years before the Great Famine.

As night follows day, it did not take long for rural agitation to re-emerge in the wake of the 1816 subsistence emergency precipitated by the 'Year Without a Summer'. The new perpetrators of rural outrage, although sharing many attributes with their predecessors, were also quite distinct in many respects. The self-styled Ribbonmen* of the second decade of the nineteenth century, while regularly participating in agrarian atrocity, were something of a new broom. Their very existence was a testament to the political reality that the Defenders and the United Irishmen of 1798 had not all been hanged, drawn, quartered or transported, nor committed suicide to avoid trial. At the very least, some of the spirit of the 1790s remained intact within Ribbonism. Although the 'society' of the Ribbonmen would become almost entirely associated with agrarian crime as the nineteenth century progressed, its origins were more sectarian than agrarian, more urban than rural. The political historian Tom Garvin has made a study of these early oath-bound Ribbon society members and has concluded that 'Ribbonism was nationalist, Catholic communalist, if not sectarian, and vaguely radical in a populist mode, with much millennial admixture'.[16] In the 1830s, George Cornewall Lewis, in distinguishing between the Whiteboys and the Ribbonmen, suggested that in certain instances they merged into one another. However, he also argued that Ribbonism had 'much more of the character of an armed and well-organised association, with religious and political objects than the local and irregular combinations of the south and west'.[17] Invocations of Ribbonism were overused during Robert Peel's long tenure as Irish chief secretary. These were designed 'to stiffen the resolve of those who would otherwise recoil at summary executions and public gibbeting premised on dubious evidence'.[18]

Whether a bona fide Ribbon society was behind the atrocity of Wildgoose Lodge is a moot point. It is equally likely that the

---

* The name may have derived from the wearing of a ribbon around the wrist for the purposes of identification. They were also known as Ribandmen.

killings were carried out by a local gang of 'lawless banditti' with no formal extra-parochial structure. However, since the expression 'Ribbonism' was already replacing 'Whiteboyism' as the generic term for agrarian unrest, the issue is of academic importance only. The notion of a formal Ribbon conspiracy in north Louth in 1816 was largely the creation of nervous landowners who failed (or declined) to appreciate that, although they were clearly the enemy, they were too far behind the front lines to be within the reach of the cottiers and labourers leading the agitation. Softer targets were under much greater threat. The brutal murder in March 1816, for example, of the more accessible Castletown miller, Patrick Thornton, whose skull was fractured and whose eyes were gouged out, 'alarmed the more peaceably minded inhabitants' of the baronies of Dundalk and Ardee and resulted in both areas being 'proclaimed to be in a state of disturbance'.[19] But before that murder, the Lord Lieutenant was already well aware of the concerns of the Louth aristocracy, having been 'memorialised' by 'thirty-seven magistrates assembled in Petty Session in Louth'[20] in November 1815. The county's upper echelons were leaving nothing to chance and invoking a Ribbon conspiracy (with its Defenderist sectarian connotations) was a way of getting the attention of Peel and Dublin Castle.

William Carleton, in his short story 'Wildgoose Lodge', also blamed the entire episode on oath-bound Ribbonmen (he had himself, reputedly, once been a member of the society). However, by 1830, Carleton was intent on producing literary 'faction' that played into the prejudices of his new establishment patrons. In Carleton's first pass at relating the story of Wildgoose Lodge in the *Dublin Literary Gazette*, Edward Lynch became the only Protestant in Reaghstown and environs, and his assailants were sworn Ribbonmen led by a 'Captain', Patrick Devane.

Captain James Anton of the Royal Highlanders was stationed with his unit in the area around the time of the trials of the alleged perpetrators of the atrocity. Although he would have been present there months before the belated arrival of William Carleton, Anton's account of the incident and its aftermath, recorded in his memoir *Retrospect of a Military Life*, was not published until 1841 and appears to have been influenced by Carleton's fictions. Anton's account is as colourful as it is unreliable and added considerably to the mythology of the events of 29–30 October 1816. Just as Carleton blamed the killings at Wildgoose Lodge on the Ribbon society, so did Anton. The latter also claimed that Lynch was a former Ribbonman who had abandoned his erstwhile fellow-conspirators and refused them access to his home for covert meetings.

The idea that both attacks on Lynch (10 April and 29–30 October) and his family were Ribbon-inspired is given some credibility by the arrest of one Bryan Clarke on 7 April 1816, near Wildgoose Lodge. His arrest coincided with the introduction to the area of members of Peel's newly established Peace Preservation Force. Clarke was a 'self-professed Ribbon organiser'[21] and was found with an anti-Orange oath on his person. He was also carrying threatening letters due to be circulated among well-to-do Louth farmers. The local grievances vented in such missives included an increase in conacre rents being charged by these farmers; the expansion of grazing; the consequent denial of conacre to labourers and cottiers; the employment of (cheaper) outside labour; and the taking of evicted farms. Three days after the arrest of Clarke, the first raid on the house of Edward Lynch took place. If Anton was correct, this action was designed to punish a deserter from the cause, and the Ribbonmen behaved accordingly. Before they were repulsed with a pitchfork, they had 'stripped him in the presence of his family, and after flogging him, destroyed his furniture, insulted his wife and cut the yarn in the loom'.[22] Crucially, however, rather than feebly accepting the humiliation and indignity visited upon him and his family, Lynch provided the authorities with enough information to arrest three men, Michael Tiernan, Patrick Stanley and Phillip Conlan, for involvement in the raid. The three were tried, convicted and hanged in Dundalk jail in August 1816.

Irrespective of whether Tiernan, Stanley and Conlan were sworn Ribbonmen or members of an ad hoc local secret society, Edward Lynch was now a prime target for the Reaghstown moonlighters.

Carleton's short story 'Wildgoose Lodge'[23] – the version that appears in *Traits and Stories of the Irish Peasantry* – was accepted for generations as an accurate account of the events of the night of 29–30 October 1816. The tale is narrated by an educated Louth man, named simply as 'Jim', who is summoned to a nocturnal meeting in a local Catholic Church building. This gathering of oath-bound accomplices (Carleton couches it in Masonic terms and Jim refers to 'the secret grip of Ribbonism ... that made the joints of my fingers ache for some minutes afterwards') is in thrall to the Captain, a local schoolmaster who 'acted also on Sunday in the capacity of clerk to the priest'. Much alcohol is consumed, fiery speeches are made, those who have failed to answer the summons are condemned as traitors and an oath is administered swearing all to secrecy. What follows is graphic and profoundly disturbing. In these preliminaries, as well as in the atrocity that follows, the perpetrators are portrayed as verging on the fiendish. The word 'satanic' is used on three occasions.

After dwelling at length on the preliminaries, the events of the 'fatal night' are set in train. In keeping with the first principles of pathetic fallacy, as the mob sets out from the chapel, 'over us was a stormy sky, and around us a darkness'. Accompanied by five of his most trusted acolytes, the Captain sets the Lynch house ablaze. As the flames take hold, a woman appears at a window, beggingfor mercy. In response she is 'transfixed with a bayonet and a pike' and is 'instantly tossed back into the flames'. When this draws an audible gasp of horror from many of the more passive spectators present, an angry Captain (named in a postscript as Patrick Devann) turns on these bystanders and reminds them, in Carleton's distinctive phonetic Hiberno-English, that 'It's no use now you know, if one's to hang, all will hang, so your safest way, you persave, is to lave none of them to tell the story.' Later, a similar fate is suffered by the infant child, presented at a window by his distraught mother. The Captain himself, 'with characteristic atrocity, thrust, with a sharp bayonet, the little innocent, along with the person who endeavoured to rescue it, into the red flames'.

We have no dependable information on what exactly transpired at Wildgoose Lodge on that night. Few, if any, reliable witnesses to those events were produced in court. Carleton himself, in his postscript, claims that 'this tale of terror is, unfortunately, too true', while acknowledging that 'the language of the story is partly

William Carleton

but the facts are pretty closely such as were developed during the trial of the murderers'. He then goes on to claim that 'twenty-five or twenty-eight … were hanged and gibbeted in different parts of the county of Louth' arising out of the killings. He adds that Devane (Devann) was gibbeted outside his own home and that his mother 'could neither go into or out of her cabin without seeing his body swinging from the gibbet'. In fact, there were eighteen men executed for the Wildgoose Lodge murders, and Devane's mother died before he was hanged and gibbeted. Such errors (or artistic licence) did not prevent Carleton's account from becoming the accepted version of the appalling crime that befell the Lynches of Wildgoose Lodge. That this was the case can be seen in the account of James Anton. His narrative echoes that of Carleton in all salient details, though he manages to exaggerate the number of victims of the outrage, claiming thirteen deaths in the inferno.

Although the attack on Wildgoose Lodge had clearly not been targeted at one of their own, the gentry of Co. Louth (Filgates, Fosters and Fortescues *et al.*) nonetheless bared their fangs. Frantic reports from the big houses of an imminent and unspeakable sectarian slaughter by a radical Catholic agrarian conspiracy became a convenient fiction into which Dublin Castle opted to buy. When the tale was retold in the 1830s and 1840s by Carleton and Anton, it retained many of these spurious and expedient elements. In the interim, of course, the Munster Rockite insurrection (see Chapter 6), with its undeniable sectarian aspect, offered some validation for the moral panic in the aftermath of the Wildgoose Lodge murders.

It did not take long for the attack to be attributed to the 'Ribandmen' – the *Freeman's Journal* of 3 November 1816 used the term to ascribe blame for the outrage. At first, there was something of a pervasive *omertà* when it came to identifying the culprits. That, however, began to erode because of a heavy military/police presence occasioned by the investigation, and the fact that the cost of the security operation was a charge on local taxes. Furthermore, with a reward of almost £1,500 on offer, information on the identities of the main protagonists began to trickle in.

Arrests were made and further evidence was amassed from suspects under interrogation. Informers were secured. Their evidence, often dubious and contradictory, was to prove crucial in the arrests, trials and executions of the eighteen men, including Patrick Devane, who paid with their lives for the attack on Wildgoose Lodge. Whether or not they had participated in the multiple murders did not always signify. Under pressure from Foster and other members of the Louth grand jury ('the landlord committee that ruled the county'[24]), Robert Peel turned a blind eye to the many abuses of process of local magistrates (also Louth gentry) as they racked up committals, indictments and convictions using 'unscrupulous and self-serving informers and approvers, fabricated evidence, partisan jurors, the acceptance of contradictory and erroneous witness statements … all deployed to convict and execute innocent as well as guilty men'.[25] The establishment of actual guilt, 'beyond reasonable doubt', was of far less importance than the securing of convictions and, by means of state terror, forestalling a mythical insurrection which the Co. Louth aristocracy chose to believe was imminent.

Jurors – supposedly the peers of those on trial, but in reality of a superior social class – 'were prepared to believe the suspect evidence of vacillating and highly questionable characters and to turn a blind eye to the most glaring evidential contradictions in almost every case'.[26] In one instance, that of the Crown witness Thomas Gubby, 'it was much doubted by the authorities if he had even been present at the murders'.[27] Gubby's 'evidence' was light on detail not already in the public domain and was heavily padded with background information on Ribbonism and Defenderism. Three other 'approvers', Bernard Gilroy, Peter Gollogly and Patrick Murphy, turned state's evidence in order to avoid the long walk to the gallows.

Patrick Devane – arrested while working incognito as a labourer in Dublin's Custom House docks – took responsibility for his own defence but proved ineffectual as an advocate and was convicted. At least he was spared the false hopes of some of his co-accused, who were defended by the Castle spy Leonard McNally. After his conviction, Devane was taken by a long and circuitous route, with as much panoply as possible, from Dundalk, where his trial had taken place, back to Wildgoose Lodge, and was executed there with macabre ceremony on 24 July 1817. According to the *Belfast Newsletter* of 29 July:

> Within the walls of the house a beam was extended between the chimneys to which the culprit ascended by a ladder. He addressed the people around him in an audible voice and said: 'Good people, I die guilty. I forgive my prosecutors, pray for me.' After which he was with some difficulty launched into eternity ...

Devane's remains were then gibbeted and suspended near his home for twenty-one months, until 1819. It was during this ghastly interval that William Carleton encountered the schoolteacher's rotting corpse and discovered the story that would become the basis of one of his best-known works.

Floods prevented the execution of ten more men from taking place at Wildgoose Lodge itself, so they were hanged instead from a scaffold in Reaghstown and their bodies gibbeted in groups of three and four in three local villages. The grisly practice of gibbeting the corpses of executed men was, obviously, designed as a warning to all who might want to follow in their wake in challenging the authorities. The customary fate of a corpse, after the exercise of capital punishment, was dissection in the anatomy room of a school of medicine. Five more of those found guilty were also subsequently hanged at Reaghstown in April 1818. Only one, however, Thomas McCullagh, was gibbeted and hung in chains. The bodies of the other four were taken to Dundalk for dissection. Two more were convicted at the Summer Assizes on 3 July 1818, and hanged in Dundalk. The authorities decided that there had probably been enough gruesome warnings. Their bodies too were sent for dissection.

Edward Lynch was not a landlord. Nor was he a landlord's agent or a bailiff. Like most of those who murdered him and his family, he paid rent to the Filgate family. He was not a member of the aristocratic class that established, and supervised the execution of, the rules in early nineteenth-century Ireland. Neither, however, was he a comfortable fellow-traveller of Whiteboys or Ribbonmen. His fate, in the words of historian Theo Hoppen, 'highlights the existence of a continuum of suspicion and envy along which a place must be found for clashes between rich and poor, comfortable farmers and lesser farmers'.[28] Lynch was a victim of that most run-of-the-mill phenomenon in eighteenth- and nineteenth-century rural Ireland, the ferocity of the antipathy between different classes of peasants. Wildgoose Lodge was not the first instance of highly personalised tenant-on-tenant violence, and it would not be the last. It was also neither the first nor the last occasion on which prominent members of the Ascendancy would culpably misrepresent a tragedy with minimal resonance for their community, in order to exploit minority fears of a recrudescence of the savagery of 1641.

The Church of Ireland rector of Killanny in north Co. Louth was the outspoken unionist pastor Sir Harcourt Lees. His views on the religious convictions of his Roman Catholic neighbours earned him the nickname 'No Popery Lees'. Lees exploited the Wildgoose Lodge attack to reinforce his *idée fixe*, the danger posed by the abhorrent (to him and those of his ilk) campaign for Catholic emancipation. He zealously cultivated the notion that Catholics (Lees called them 'image-worshippers') spent every waking hour plotting more efficient ways of murdering Protestants in their beds. He was a firm believer in an imminent 'Popish rebellion' that would make the Scullabogue massacre of 1798 look like a poetry reading. His fellow cleric, the Fermanagh-born poet John Graham, devoted an entire work to Lees, 'Sir Harcourt's Vision: an historical poem'. Nine stanzas, reeking of religious paranoia, deal with the events of Wildgoose Lodge. They conclude as follows.

Two oaths in this island – no man will dispute,
Exist in this wonderful day;
The one of Rome's bishops to persecute,
And heresy to banish away.
The other of Ribbonmen – dreadful to say,
On a very short notice to rise,
Their innocent Protestant neighbours to slay,
And the sixth great commandment to despise.[29]

Quite what those lines had to do with a vicious attack by Catholic peasants on a Catholic tenant farmer and his family, in a predominantly Catholic county, remains an enigma.

6

Planting 'the tree of liberty': rape, arson, murder, sectarianism and the Rockite insurgency, 1821–4

A contemporary image of the mythical Captain Rock

'I will plant the tree of liberty in as many hearths as
I can depend my life upon.'[1]

(extract from a Rockite oath)

'The strict discipline that he enforced – the strict obedience
that he exacted, and the certain, and often horrible
punishment with which he followed up a breach of either,
rendered him at once the terror of government, and the
master of those over whom his authority extended.'[2]

(narrator's description of a Rockite leader in 'Reminiscences
of a Rockite' in the *Dublin Penny Journal*, 1834)

8 April 1822, Co. Cork Assizes[3]

There was no moonlight over north Cork on the night of 17
February 1822, when the women were attacked. Dusk was
descending as the wagons were stopped on the road to Mallow.
The gloom of that early evening, however, did nothing to help
erase the unbearable images that the victims would never be able to
suppress. Now four of the dozen women who had gone through the
ordeal were being asked to relive that ghastly night in a courthouse.
They had been warned to expect an inquisition from the defence
counsel, a certain Mr O'Connell. He was a snake, they were told,
slippery and insinuating. He would try and ingratiate himself first.
Then he would prise open any minor fissures that appeared in their
testimony. They had better leave no room for doubt.

Despite the fact that the attack occurred at around 6.30 p.m.
on a dark, moonless, mid-February evening, the witnesses all
insisted that it was still bright enough for them to identify their
assailants. You don't forget a face, they maintained, even in the
twilight, while it is leering at you and affronting you, your soldier
husband, your nationality and your religion. One of the witnesses,
Elizabeth Blunt, however, did not help their cause when she
identified as an assailant a man in the body of the court who

had no connection whatever to the case. That raised a smirk on the mobile face of Mr O'Connell and excited whispers from the spectators.

In the dock were three accused, Timothy Connors, Patrick Foley and – in what a cohort of betrayed Fenians might have found ironic four decades later – a man named Pierce Nagle.* The four prosecution witnesses, Anne Tapt, Jane Williams, Elizabeth Blunt and Mary Griffin, were being taken back to the night of 17 February. They had been members of a party of soldiers' wives moving their worldly goods to new quarters on board three wagons. The women had just left the village of Kildorrery, halfway between Mitchelstown and Mallow, when the three cars were stopped in the gloom by a dozen men. Two of the interlopers halted the first car while some of the others approached the wagon on which Englishwoman Anne Tapt was sitting. The women's husbands, members of the 1st Rifle Brigade, were somewhere on the other side of the village, nowhere to be seen and of no possible assistance. As Anne Tapt watched the men approach her car, she clung to her daughter and exchanged a frightened glance with Elizabeth Blunt, who was sitting beside her. This, she knew, was Rockite country. Why else would her husband and his colleagues have been moved into the area, other than to put a stop to the murderous activities of this new threat to the peace of rural Munster? A dozen men out and about after dark on a cold February night were unlikely to be engaged in visiting aged relatives.

Before Anne Tapt knew what was happening, she had been grabbed by one of the men. She claimed in her evidence that it was Timothy Connors. He forced her into a ditch and, along with two of his companions, raped her while Pierce Nagle looked on. As this was happening, Elizabeth Blunt managed to flee across the fields with Tapt's distraught daughter.

While the three men took it in turns to rape Anne Tapt, a Scottish army wife, Jane Williams, was suffering a similar fate at

---

* A different Pierce Nagle betrayed the leading members of the Irish Republican Brotherhood in 1865.

the hands of two of the other men. She identified Nagle as one of her assailants. No explanation was offered as to how he might have been in two places at the same time.

The fourth witness, Mary Griffin, another soldier's wife, identified Patrick Foley as having been present on the night, though she testified that she did not see him molest anyone. She herself was protected from harm by one of the Rockites. He was wearing a white coat and 'putting his foot on the witness's foot, whispered to her, "nobody shall have you"'; however, she was unable to do anything to prevent a man 'with a brown great-coat' from carrying off another of the army wives, Mrs Floree, and was unable to account for the clemency shown to her.

Mary Griffin, the wife of a sergeant in the 1st Rifle Brigade, grew alarmed when she was then approached by a third man and asked to identify any of the women who were the wives of non-commissioned officers. Fearing that their treatment would be even worse than that clearly being meted out already, she 'said there was no[ne]'. She appears to have been taken at her word. Before the Rockites departed, one of their number left a pointed message for the women's husbands. Mary Griffin was to 'let the riflemen know that they were Captain Rock's men'.

The jury did not take long to reach its verdict. Ironically, the only man who had been positively identified as an assailant by Anne Tapt was acquitted. Timothy Connors managed to produce a credible alibi. Nagle and Foley were found guilty and sentenced to death. Nagle asked to be heard by the court and 'declared solemnly before the Almighty that he had neither hand, act, or part in the transaction and was not present at it'. His appeal changed nothing. Connors walked free and the other two men were removed from the courtroom to await execution.

Not for the first time, rape had been used as a weapon in the Rockite war, but never before on such a scale. At least two of the women who had been sexually assaulted, despite the occasionally dubious nature of the evidence they had given, could leave the Assizes feeling that they had been avenged.

Mr O'Connell had not managed to shake them.

The rise of Captain Rock

'When I first went to Knocktopher in the summer of 1821 ... the name of Captain Rock was becoming formidable. The place borders on Tipperary whence came nocturnal parties, scouring the country and alarming the inhabitants on a small scale, while the prelude to much darker scenes was to be traced in the wide circulation of what were called the prophecies of Pastorini.'[4]

(Charlotte Elizabeth Tonna, *Irish Recollections*, 1846)

'Hoskins and Going are nearly one;
Hoskins is going, and Going is gone.'[5]

(anonymous doggerel composed after the murder of Major Richard Going in Limerick, 1821)

'To all farmers in the country around ...
Thank God, harvest over and the grain is secure
So banish those Black Boys away from our door
For he that employs them, he will find them dead
For we will burn them asleep in their bed.'[6]

(threatening letter warning against the continued employment of 'strangers' by local farmers, Ashbourne, Co. Meath, 1835)

Nowhere was the cyclical nature of agricultural prices more clearly illustrated than in the first decades of the nineteenth century. Napoleon Bonaparte's imperial ambitions and military aggression proved highly rewarding for Irish farmers. Food prices were high in Ireland's primary (effectively sole) export market, Britain, for most of the period of the Napoleonic Wars. With the agricultural economy booming between the passage of the Act of Union and the Battle of Waterloo, food production was highly profitable and land was at a premium. This served to reduce the availability of the conacre plots on which labourers and poorer farmers could plant their life-preserving potatoes. Thus, much of the agrarian animosity during the first decade and a half of the nineteenth century involved intra-peasant class conflicts such as the feuding of the Caravats and Shanavests.

After Waterloo, however, that familiar ogre, price deflation, returned to haunt tillage and livestock farmers alike. There was a collapse in values, with oats, barley, beef and pork down 50 per cent between 1813 and 1816. When this was coupled with environmental and public health crises from 1817 to 1819, the threat of falling prices was eclipsed by the reality of famine and disease. The potential catastrophe, because of the identity of the new chief secretary, became something of a rehearsal for the Great Famine of 1845–9.

The crisis, caused by the deflation of the immediate post-war era, was accentuated by an event that took place thousands of miles away. Nature, often such a bitter enemy to the Irish peasant, intervened yet again. The huge eruption of Mount Tambora in 1815 on the remote island of Sumbawa in the Lesser Sunda Islands of the Dutch East Indies may have killed more than 70,000 as it spread volcanic ash into the stratosphere, but its impact was not confined to what would later become modern-day Indonesia. Volcanic dust, belched into the earth's atmosphere, would play merry hell with the world's weather systems for the next year.

The year 1816 became known as the 'Year Without a Summer' in North America and Europe. It was as if a huge and very dirty cotton sheet swaddled the northern hemisphere, blocking the rays of the sun. We can thank the resultant dramatic sunsets for some of the best work of the great landscape painter J. M. W. Turner, but that artistic triumph was of no consolation to the thousands of European farmers unable to grow crops or feed their livestock in the coldest summer for fifty years.

The catastrophic effect of yet another distant volcano on Irish society was aggravated by the unwelcome return of typhus. More than 65,000 people died of typhoid fever in 1815–16. But for the administrative skills of a highly capable Irish chief secretary, the future Tory grandee Robert Peel, things might have been much worse. Appointed Irish chief secretary in 1812 (it was not then a cabinet position), Peel intervened to distribute sufficient famine relief to mitigate the worse effects of the crisis. Peel – unloved by Daniel O'Connell, who, predictably, nicknamed him 'Orange Peel' and once challenged him to a duel – did much to enhance the status of the chief secretaryship. His was a technocratic/bureaucratic presence in an administration that came to adopt a more neutral governmental position in the ongoing animosity between Roman Catholics and the Protestant Ascendancy, but he was never less than a hardline martinet when it came to the suppression of agrarian or political crime.

By the 1820s, Ribbonism had become a handy catch-all label applied to a multiplicity of local and parochial uprisings with rents, evictions, tithes, taxes, falling prices, rising prices and the employment of 'strangers' or *spalpeens*, rather than the hiring of local labour, all continuing to figure as grievances. Threatening letters, cattle houghing, assault, incendiarism* and murder were the preferred remedies. The first official appearance of the term 'Ribbon society' was in reference to sectarian clashes in Co. Donegal in 1810. In Robert Peel, the pioneer Ribbonmen found a worthy adversary. He was chief secretary from 1812 until 1819. Two years into his administration, Peel took a significant step in his efforts to curtail this new outbreak of rural violence. The 1814 Peace Preservation Act, one of the dozens of special security measures introduced by British governments in the first century of the uneasy union, allowed Peel to appoint supplementary stipendiary (paid) magistrates in districts that were experiencing the worst disturbances. This permitted Dublin Castle to bypass the often ineffectual local magistracy, who owed their positions to their gentrified status and were 'inefficient, often corrupt and frequently reluctant to undertake any measures that might jeopardise their election prospects'.[7] It also allowed him to appoint paid, professional police constables to work with these more potent magistrates. That the new police force should rapidly

---

* Arson was a particular favourite of the Rockites, with Protestant churches no longer exempt.

acquire a pejorative nickname was entirely predictable. So from 1814 onwards, militant Irish nationalists, radicals and agrarianists could begin to curse the Peelers with a vengeance.

'Blessed is he that readeth and they that hear the words of this prophecy' (Revelation 1:3)[8]

'It is less dangerous to disobey the law of the state than the law of the insurgent.'[9]

(George Cornewall Lewis, *On Local Disturbances in Ireland*)

'What distance is there between the Sun and Moon?
A square foot and an Irish heart in the full Bloom.'[10]

(extract from the Rockite 'catechism', used to administer an oath to the membership)

The Rockites were very much at home in this new 'ribbon' dispensation. While it would be a mistake to classify them as out-and-out nationalists, they were certainly more political and nationalistic than most of their agrarian precursors. They were also more organised.

And there was no denying the sectarianism of the Rockites. The February 1822 attack on the wagon train of soldiers' wives at Kildorrery highlights not only their misogyny (there are many other examples of their ill-treatment of women) but their visceral aversion to Protestantism. The rape of up to nine women on that night was not intended purely as a warning of Rockite ruthlessness to the incoming soldiers of the 1st Rifle Brigade. It also had a religious significance. Part of the rationale behind such an egregious abuse of societal norms was that the violated women, given that most came from different parts of Britain, were almost bound to be exclusively Protestant.

While the Rockites undoubtedly swam in the Ribbon gene-pool – Thomas Bartlett argues that by 1821, fledgling Ribbonism 'appeared to fuse with the Rockite agitation'[11] – they differed from the often vague politics of the Ribbonmen in a number of respects, primarily in their undisguised sectarianism. One of the slogans of the movement was a sanguinary prediction: 'The bloody Protestant time is expired, and they shall be slaughtered like dogs.'[12] At long last, the faulty analysis and special pleading of some of the eighteenth-century Protestant alarmists was actually coming to pass. This agrarian uprising really did have a distinct sectarian edge.

So why were the Rockites different? What was it about their insurgency that added a murky layer of religious bigotry to the palimpsest of class divisions that had marked previous agrarian rebellions? The sectarian rationale was derived from a millenarian religious tract from the eighteenth century that would probably have long since disappeared from public consciousness but for the insertion by the author of an apocalyptic sell-by date.

In the *General History of the Christian Church from her birth to her Final Triumphant States in Heaven chiefly deduced from the Apocalypse of St John the Apostle, by Signor Pastorini*, published in 1771, the British Roman Catholic bishop Charles Walmesley had predicted the demise of Protestantism. Under the pseudonym of Pastorini – described by Sir Richard Musgrave, not unfairly but with a total lack of irony or personal self-awareness, as 'a sanguinary bigot'[13] – Walmesley, a fully paid-up Catholic ideologue and propagandist, capable of matching any of his Protestant counterparts for visceral chauvinism, claimed that the end of the Anglican religion in the 1820s was one of the more desirable 'revelations' of his biblical analysis. He advanced this stirring thesis with the certainty of the Paiute mystic Wovoka, originator of the 'ghost dance' movement in 1889, promising the eradication of the white man from the ancient tribal grounds of the western Native American. The 'Papist' bigotry of Walmesley's nineteenth-century acolytes was a source of embarrassment to middle- and upper-class Catholics and to the leadership of the burgeoning O'Connellite Catholic Association, whose campaign for emancipation was well underway by the mid-1820s. So much so that there were claims that the many circulating Pastorini texts were part of what would be called today a false flag operation. O'Connell himself insisted that the sectarian pamphlets 'were certainly not printed with the assent of any Catholic' and a speaker at a Catholic Association rally asserted that 'Protestant missionaries were circulating them about the kingdom in cheap pamphlets for sinister purposes'.[14]

Walmesley did allow himself (posthumously – he died in 1797) some wriggle room, timing the extinction of Protestantism at some undetermined date between 1821 and 1825. His book was much read at the time of publication, was translated into Latin, French, German and Italian, and proved unsurprisingly popular among Irish Catholics. It came into its own again a half-century after its original publication as the fateful date of 1821 loomed. That the date passed off without incident – certainly the Anglican faith, bar one or two nervous tremors, remained intact – was of little consequence to most of Pastorini's Irish adherents. The final reckoning would undoubtedly come before 1825. This belief was reflected, as was so much of pre-Famine Irish society, in a William Carleton short story, 'The Poor Scholar'. The potato diggers, Dominick McEvoy and his son Jimmy, are cursing Cromwell in the purest Hiberno-English dialect, and expatiating on their plight at the opening of the story, when Jimmy remarks: 'An', doesn't Pastorini say it? Sure, when Twenty-five comes, we'll have our own agin, the right will overcome the might.'[15]

Jimmy, no doubt emboldened by the approach of the Protestant apocalypse, has a plan to raise his parents out of poverty. He is determined to become a scholar or a priest (*sagart* in Irish, pron. *sogarth*). His mother, with a pragmatic view of the potential rewards of a life devoted to erudition rather than farming, tries to dissuade him, but Dominick intervenes:

Who knows but it was the Almighty put the thoughts of it into his head. Pasthorini [*sic*] says that there will soon be a change, an tis a good skame it'll be to have him a sogarth when the fat livins will be walkin' back to their ould owners.[16]

Carleton, a convert to Protestantism himself, was *au fait* with the desperate strain of magical thinking that permeated Catholic faith in the writings of 'Signor Pastorini'. As, from a far more fundamentalist perspective, was Charlotte Elizabeth Tonna.

Tonna, who published successful novels under the name Charlotte Elizabeth – a flimsy *nom de plume* designed to conceal her literary identity from her grasping and abusive Irish husband – was one of the most prolific and successful writers of the pre-Famine period, despite her acute personal struggles with near blindness and total deafness. Tonna was nothing if not forthright in her pejorative assessments of Catholicism. In a memoir of her time in Ireland, *Irish Recollections* (1847), she opined that 'Popery is only a crafty adaptation of Pagan idolatries to its own scheme'. She did not, however, hold a much higher opinion of the Irish aristocracy. Their behavioural excesses would not have appealed to her puritanical nature and she considered that the failure of the Irish gentry to convert the country's Roman Catholics to Protestantism was a prime example of their fecklessness. One of her novels, *The Rockite*, dealt directly with the insurgency and was written from the perspective of the besieged Protestant population of Munster and south Leinster. Her unhappy marriage to an Irish military officer meant that, unlike other English opponents of the Rockites, she actually had some direct residential experience of what it was like to live in the area of Rockite hegemony in the 1820s.

In *Irish Recollections*, Tonna described the impact of the writings of Charles Walmesley on the Catholic population:

Extracts from this impudently mischievous work were disseminated in every possible form among the Romanists; they were translated into Irish; sent in large numbers to every district to be circulated by careful agents: published in hand bills, exhibited in placards, and sung in doggerel rhyme through the streets. There was no article of their faith more devoutly believed by the besotted people than that in 1825 the Protestants of Ireland and of every other country were, by divine appointment, to be put to death.[17]

The Rockite insurgency was actually a rebellion with numerous issues other than Protestant extirpation at its core, had Tonna chosen to see them. What made it different, however, was an underlying crusading element that the author correctly identified. The Rockites had many grievances unconnected with religion, but they also had a mission, and that was to play their part in the realisation of the visions of Pastorini. Their fervour was accentuated by the sudden enthusiasm on the part of Protestants and Dissenters to nudge lifelong Catholics into religious apostasy. Protestant missionaries were travelling the country seeking converts. This well-resourced proselytism included the distribution of Irish-language bibles and the promise of a good education for Irish Catholic children. The sooner the prophecies of Pastorini came to fruition, the sooner would such heretical activity cease. This injection of religious zeal into the conflict, allied to the economic ruin that already beckoned for many Irish farmers, helped to broaden the social parameters of the Rockite movement. The Rockites were far from being a loose coalition of wretched labourers and small farmers lashing out at agrarian privilege. The threat of economic devastation concentrated the minds of far more substantial farmers and a 'belief in the impending destruction of Protestantism went some way to drawing rural Catholics to the Rockite cause and, moreover, mitigated class conflict'.[18]

Like most of its precursors, the Rockite insurgency started out as a localised agitation with limited objectives, though 'more clandestine, violent and disaffected'[19] than movements like that of the Rightboys. The insurrection might never have got off the ground were it not for a dissolute absentee landlord and an agent viewed in west Limerick as having been sent directly from Hell.

Enter the flamboyant Viscount Courtenay and his human rottweiler, Alexander Hoskins. Courtenay, the only male among the fourteen children of the second Viscount Courtenay, was an unabashedly homosexual aristocrat whose extravagant lifestyle often left him on the verge of bankruptcy. His overarching concern was that his Limerick estates, located near Newcastle

West on the Kerry border, should provide him with enough funds to fob off his creditors and allow him to live the life of a profligate gentleman in Paris, or on his £20,000 yacht in the English Channel. As Courtenay's debts became more and more pressing, he tolerated less and less the moderation of his long-standing agent, Edward Carte. Finally, in 1817, Carte was forced to make way for a younger and more aggressive enforcer, the London lawyer Alexander Hoskins, described by the definitive biographer of Captain Rock, James Donnelly – with laudable restraint – as being prone to 'vindictiveness, duplicity, extreme stubbornness, a taste for cruelty, and a strong preference for physical force over firm but quiet measures'.[20] As it happens, his negative attributes were more than matched by those of his Rockite opponents. The reign of Hoskins coincided with the appointment of trustees to run the affairs of the hapless spendthrift Courtenay.

When Hoskins assumed the management of Courtenay's Irish holdings in 1818, he took residence in an imposing and luxurious three-storey building known as the Castle in Newcastle West, where he assumed many of the airs and graces of his employer, taking on a butler, buying expensive furniture and keeping a stable of foxhunters. It was clear from the outset that Hoskins was not about to assume a low social profile. He adopted the same approach to his actual duties. His first job was to reduce arrears of £60,000 that the indulgent Carte had allowed to build up and which Viscount Courtenay urgently required for the restocking of his wine cellar and funding his losses at the baccarat table. Much of Courtenay's land had been re-leased on terms favourable to the landlord at the height of the Napoleonic boom. Declining prices meant that the agreed rents were no longer viable. This state of affairs did not concern Hoskins in the least. He pressed for the agreed rents against prosperous tenants, middlemen and small farmers alike.

His opponents included a number of wealthy relatives of the former agent. Hoskins decided to make an example of these and proceeded against them with all the rigours of the law. His victimisation of the three – Carte's brother, Robert, his nephew, also named Robert, and a third Robert, Robert Parker, the husband of Carte's niece – began when all three demanded rent abatements. Hoskins had the older Robert Carte arrested and jailed. The family of Robert Carte the younger was served with a latitat, a writ which presupposed that its object had taken flight and was in hiding. Parker was subjected to the worst harassment of the three, in the course of which his wife was delivered of a stillborn child. Even the Dublin Castle undersecretary, William Gregory, was not enamoured of Hoskins, once commenting, 'I believe nothing can be more oppressive than the conduct of Lord Courtenay's agent.'[21]

The agent's aggressive pursuit of the relatives of his popular predecessor did not sit well with other tenants on the estate. Indeed, it was from the land leased by Robert Parker that the activist with the greatest claim to being the prototype for Captain Rock emerged. Patrick Dillane was a blacksmith by trade and was employed by Parker, a middleman with extensive landholdings. Hoskins was noted for his recruitment of 'men of bad character' to carry out his wishes. His opponents too recruited their own private army. Dillane, at the behest of Parker, was involved in a fracas in which a detachment of Hoskins's enforcers was subjected to a barrage of stones. Dillane distinguished himself in the affray and earned the title *Carrigah*, meaning Rock. He later bragged that he had been 'christened' as 'Captain Rock' by a local schoolmaster, with a glass of wine taking the place of the sacerdotal baptismal water.

Of more consequence, however, was Dillane's involvement in the event that can be said to have sparked off the Rockite rebellion. On 27 July 1821, the nineteen-year-old son of Alexander Hoskins, Thomas, was fatally wounded by a group of Parker's supporters. Thomas had been waylaid by a group of men, led by Dillane, who shot him and fractured his skull. They were then reported to have danced and played on a fife for the next hour before leaving the scene, with young Hoskins barely clinging to life. He died a few days later. His assassins had been hired to carry out the murder, as Dillane later revealed in court when he became an 'approver'. His evidence ensured the conviction for murder of four men and his apostasy was a huge blow to the morale of the Rockites.

The engagement of outside agents to carry out killings was a common practice with the Rockites. Public notices offering rewards for the murder of transgressors were often posted as a threat, and the use of assassins who were also 'strangers' made identification of the guilty parties more difficult. One such notice, which also highlights the sectarianism of the Rockites, was posted in Cork, seeking outside help to carry out murders in Limerick: 'We the honourable parliament of Ireland do offer a reward of 50 Pounds to any person or persons that will Kill a protestant General, Justice [of the] peace, or a Member of parliament ... and 20 pounds to any person or person[s] that will Kill a protestant, rich or poor, Big or little.'[22]

Alexander Hoskins himself survived an assassination attempt in December 1820, and, just a month before the murder of Thomas Hoskins, the armed guards protecting the Castle had been called upon to beat off a daring, full-frontal assault on the building. The brutal slaying of his son and his own fortunate escape might well have discouraged his interventionist approach. Instead, they had the opposite effect. Hoskins, courageously or recklessly, continued his vigorous pursuit of defaulters. From then on, the conflict began to intensify. A number of 'drivers' employed by Hoskins to secure distrained cattle and goods were murdered. The consequent loss of the ability to seize and move distrained cattle seriously impaired the agent's crusade. Hoskins was also known to employ a network of local informers. Some of the suspected members of that espionage corps were also killed in the days and months following the murder of Thomas Hoskins.

Then the patience of the trustees of the Courtenay estate snapped.

The anarchy that prevailed around Newcastle West was bad for business, and the rent crusade of Hoskins had become far too personal. The bellicose agent was removed from his position and replaced by a local solicitor, Alfred Furlong. Abatements were back on the table; writs and evictions – except in hopeless cases – were to be suspended. Hoskins did not take kindly to his dismissal, assuming, as an act of vengeance, some of the attributes of a follower of Captain Rock himself. He is alleged, before his departure from Limerick, to have shot every pigeon on the estate, emptied Viscount Courtenay's lake of fish, and used his impressive stable of horses to plough up much of the demesne. He had to be escorted out of the area, for his own safety, by a detachment of dragoons and police. We can only assume that they were protecting him from the tenants, and not from the landlord's trustees.

And that should have been that. Hoskins was gone. Courtenay and his trustees were trying to placate their middlemen and tenants. But the continuing presence of a huge military retinue in Limerick – numbering at least 4,000 – promised otherwise. Hoskins had (and the thought would not have deprived him of sleep) opened a Pandora's box. A few expertly directed rocks had miraculously metamorphosed into the Rockites, a new manifestation of Whiteboyism and/or Ribbonism. Captain Rock was not about to stand down his army just because his acolytes had got the better of an obnoxious agent. There was work to be done. Other agents in Limerick and farther afield began to receive threatening letters, warning them that they would suffer the fate of young Thomas Hoskins if rent abatements were not forthcoming. The prevailing economic crisis ensured that, even with the departure of Hoskins, the fire did not go out. With the collapse of grain prices (oats down more than 40 per cent, wheat and barley down almost 60 per cent between 1818 and 1821 – with similarly catastrophic falls in livestock prices) followed by a disastrous 1821 harvest as a result of torrential August rainfall, economic disaster gave way to yet another subsistence crisis. Ironically, however, while the prospect of famine ensured the growth and multiplication of the Rockites, its actual onset, in 1822, caused a temporary cessation in their more heinous activities.

Even before the ignominious departure of Hoskins, the troops of Captain Rock had successfully struck at one of their primary targets, local policeman Major Richard Going. Going had ensured his own notoriety by his participation in a deadly tithe affray. On

15 August 1821, a large group of men descended on the home of a tithe proctor, John Ivis, near Askeaton. Presumably operating on the basis of solid information rather than blind luck, Going was waiting for them with a small but well-armed constabulary force. Two of the attackers were killed; a third died later. Going then strayed into taboo territory by insisting that the bodies of the two dead assailants be buried immediately in quicklime, rather than being returned to their families. Out of this deliberate provocation grew the local myth that one of the men had been buried alive. Going became a favoured Rockite target and within two months members of the society had taken their revenge. On 14 October, Going was waylaid on the Limerick–Askeaton road. As with Thomas Hoskins, he was shot (five times) and his skull was fractured. Going's brutal death was a major coup for the fledgling Rockite movement. The deed was celebrated by the lighting of fires on hills across north Co. Limerick. The Rockites, shortly thereafter, also accounted for the tithe proctor, John Ivis. [23]

The agitation then spread to neighbouring Tipperary, where the worst atrocity of the revolt took place in November 1821. The house of a prosperous farmer and middleman, Edmund Shea, was raided in a search for arms. However, the raid was also prompted by Shea's reputation for land acquisition and his perceived ill-treatment of his sub-tenants. Because Shea and his six male farm labourers resisted the attempted seizure of weapons, the house and outhouses were torched before the raiders left. This policy of incendiarism, though extreme, rarely proved fatal in the course of a three-year conflict. The attack on the Shea household at Gurtnapisha, near Mullinahone, was a notorious exception. The house fire took hold rapidly, trapping Shea's family and employees. Sixteen people, including five children, died in the conflagration. The attack appears to have been an arms raid that went tragically wrong. Later that year, two men, William and Darby Maher, were hanged for the murders before a large assembly of onlookers near the scene of the crime.

The sectarian element of the new movement rapidly found expression as well, especially in the treatment of the Palatine community in Limerick. Their German Protestant ancestors had been refugees from religious wars in Europe, brought to Ireland in the eighteenth century in what was viewed by many Munster Catholics as a return to the days of the planting and settlement of willing Protestants on Catholic land. The Palatines and their successors were based in a number of enclaves around Askeaton, Adare and Rahkeale in Co. Limerick. The first notable Palatine victim of the Rockites was George Sparling.

Sparling had joined forces with Hoskins on the Courtenay estate in an ill-advised project to create another entirely Protestant 'colony' around Newcastle West. The Rockites, anxious to expedite the teachings of Signor Pastorini and play their part in the extinction of Protestantism before the end of 1821, were not about to countenance the opposite, a new and exclusively Protestant settlement in their midst. Although Sparling fell out spectacularly with Hoskins, who distrained the Palatine's possessions and auctioned them off, his zealous Protestantism placed him in an entirely different category to the agent's other victims.

In this instance, the enemy of my enemy was not my friend. In October 1821, Sparling was shot and killed in the first of a number of attacks on Limerick Palatines, culminating in the April 1823 burning of the Palatine village of Glenosheen, a task that was 'outsourced' to upwards of 100 Cork Rockites. Seven houses in the settlement were burned, to the accompanying cries of 'Protestant Palatine devils'. The Rockite animosity towards Palatines was accentuated by the membership of many adult male members of that community in the hated Protestant militia force, the Yeomanry.

The killing of Thomas Hoskins, the abject defeat of his father and the murders of Sparling and Going were to become calling cards for the new movement. Nothing succeeds like success.

The next phase of the Rockite rebellion went much as had its predecessors. Homes, mostly Protestant, across Limerick and then much of the rest of Munster were raided for arms. Whether this was an attempt to even the odds in skirmishes with the military and constabulary (of which there were many), or merely to intimidate Protestants and Dissenters, is unclear. However, to the small and beleaguered Protestant population of Munster and south Leinster, the motivation behind these constant raids was immaterial. Whether they were being attacked for their weapons or their faith, they still saw themselves as being under siege. They woke 'each morning [to] the sad intimation of a robbery, the torture of a neighbour, the destruction of a house or an unfortunate victim sacrificed to brutality'.[24] Their fears were exacerbated by the apparent impunity with which such crimes were being committed.

Although many alleged Rockites were captured and tried, widespread intimidation of witnesses and an *omertà* worthy of the Sicilian Mafia made convictions difficult, even with impressively 'packed' juries. Even a packed Protestant jury, eager to convict, could not bring in preordained verdicts in the absence of thoroughly intimidated or mysteriously deceased prosecution witnesses. The Crown did manage, however, to hang around 100 Rockites between 1822 and the petering out of their exceptionally fierce campaign in 1824. Six hundred more were transported to Australian penal colonies. Many of the guilty verdicts in these cases were post-Insurrection Act (1822), where Dublin Castle, as it was obliged to do so often in concerted campaigns of land agitation, dispensed with jury trials in favour of trial by magistrate.

Women were directly and specifically targeted by the Rockites. This was somewhat ironic, given that some Rockites, like the Caravats before them, dressed up in female costume while on active duty and passed themselves off as so-called 'Lady Rocks'. Abductions and rapes were common during the insurrection and were used – as in the Caravat-Shanavest turmoil – as a means of intimidation, as well as of personal enrichment.

For example, in March 1822, a group of men entered the house of Richard Goold in Liscarrol, Co. Cork, searching for his sister, the eldest daughter of the Goold family. Unable to locate her, they kidnapped instead her sixteen-year-old sibling Honora. Over a period of weeks, the leader of the Rockite gang, James Brown, repeatedly raped her in an attempt to coerce her into marrying him. When she was finally rescued, she was 'in a most pitiable condition'.[25] Brown himself managed to escape punishment, but altogether eleven people were imprisoned or transported for their involvement in the crime. It was one of many abductions during the Rockite insurgency – what were known at the time as 'left-handed marriages' – where prosperous farmers were punished for their wealth by the deflowering of their daughters and by demands for the payment of dowries to ensure that the rapist would 'do the right thing' and wed a young girl whose marital prospects had been jeopardised or ruined outright.

Of course, Captain Rock and his acolytes had other methods of instilling fear into the hearts of their enemies – of whom there were many – be they Protestant or Catholic. One of the characteristics of the Rockite rebellion was the rise in the incidence of threatening letters. It is extremely doubtful that all emanated from some leading cadre within the movement. The likelihood is that many of the hundreds of letters addressing members of the gentry, Protestant clergy or 'obnoxious' tenants who had defied the Rockite code that were posted, delivered quietly by hand in the dead of night, pinned to trees, gateposts or fences, and in one case even affixed to the horn of a slaughtered cow, were examples of private enterprise. Just as many of the agrarian outrages committed since the rise of the Whiteboys in the 1760s were actually freelance operations dutifully ascribed by victim and malefactor to one or other of the known secret societies in a given area, such was probably the case with many of the ominous letters. They often reflected personal grudges rather than universal crimes against peasant probity. In some instances, these notices, posters or threatening letters were taken very seriously indeed and could presage the arrival of protective military or constabulary units to the home, or at least the home district, of the addressee. In other instances, they were treated as carelessly by the recipients as was their spelling and composition by the authors.

These notices varied in length, literacy and threat level. Some were intended to terrorise individuals; others promised a gory end to entire families. Some were written (or ghost-written) by highly loquacious and literate individuals – travelling schoolmasters have been blamed for many – while others were terse and unschooled. As the Rockite rebellion grew to encompass the levying of tithes, the ubiquitous anonymous letters and notices began to reflect this fact. The Rockites went further than many of their antecedents in actually demanding the abolition of tithes. What better way to bring about the realisation of the millenarian prophecies of Signor Pastorini than to deprive the ministers of the Established Church of their benefices? In some instances threats were made against individuals, in others, the threats were more general. Take, for example, the notice to 'all the parishioners of Killaloe to pay no more Tithes to Proctors, or to any Middleman anymore, or the man that will the following day have his Coffin ... we will rank all of them in the number of Protestants & will pay them off the same day'.[26] Interestingly, although the warning was issued to tithe-payers in Co. Clare, the message was signed by 'Captn Starlight Co. Limerick ... Captn Moonlight Co. Cork this fifteenth day of Novr 1821 – no Protestant admitted'. Signs of an expanding Rockite sphere of influence. The Catholic tenants of Clare were being called upon to do their duty.

This expansion was, however, not merely geographic. One of the characteristics of the Rockite insurgency, and one that it does not share with all its predecessors and successors, was its class composition. Whereas in times of relative plenty, agrarian uprisings tended to be staffed by the rural poor, in periods of economic crisis, where the interests of substantial farmers were equally threatened, agrarian movements were more broadly based. Unlike the Caravat-Shanavest disturbances, where intra-tenant rivalries predominated, there was an unusual diversity of class among the ranks of the Rockites, initially at least. While it would be wrong to suggest that this alliance was monolithic, Captain Rock might just as easily dine on beef from his own fields, washed down by French wine, as on potatoes grown in a conacre patch. Sandwiched between the revolt of the Ribbonmen of 1819–20 and the subsequent campaign of the Terry Alts in Clare in the late 1820s – insurgencies dominated by the landless and the land-poor – the rebellion of the Rockites drew support, if not necessarily its leading activists, from right across the social spectrum, with the obvious 'no Protestant admitted' caveat. Indeed, it was the sectarian element of Rockite activities that helped to bind together, however briefly, these disparate social and economic interest groups. That, and communal opposition to the tithe on the part of the workers of conacre potato land, as well as tillage farmers no longer in a financial position to pay their dues to the clergy of their landlord's church.

After the brief hiatus prompted by the debilitating famine of 1822, the Rockite campaign slowly spiralled upwards again in 1823, albeit hampered by the working of the Insurrection Act, the principal instrument deployed by Dublin Castle to combat the insurgency. During the three years in which it operated, parts or all of nine counties were proscribed. Cork, Kerry and Limerick were subject to martial law in their entirety, as well as parts of Tipperary, Kilkenny and Westmeath. As the insurgency spread northwards and west of the Shannon, Clare, King's County (Offaly) and Kildare were added to the list. A sunset-to-sunrise curfew was imposed in all the proscribed areas, the penalty for contravention being transportation to Australia for seven years, the minimum tariff for any offence under the act. Trial by jury was suspended and almost 4,000 men were arrested and tried. However, the magistrates, now acting as juries in the proscribed areas, were fair-minded enough to acquit most of those who came before them, and just over 500 were convicted.[27]

Most of the proscribed areas were also flooded with police as well as military and militia forces. By 1823, there were almost as many British soldiers in Ireland as were stationed there during the 1919–21 War of Independence – more than 20,000. Most were stationed in Munster, south Leinster and the midlands. They were supplemented in Munster by a militia force of 2,500 members of the Yeomanry, and a Peace Preservation Force constabulary unit of broadly similar proportions. In some instances, skirmishes, and what could even be categorised as pitched battles, took place between Rockite forces of up to a thousand men, and militia, constabulary or military units of similar proportions. There were numerous Crossbarry-style encounters in Munster a century before Tom Barry and his West Cork Flying Column engaged the British Army in their celebrated and successful 1921 rearguard action.

A Tale of two Rocks

'As long as Millions shall kneel down
To ask of Thousands for their own.
While Thousands proudly turn away.
And to the Millions answer "nay"
So long the merry reign shall be
Of Captain Rock and his Family.'[28]

(Captain Rock in Thomas Moore's *Memoirs of Captain Rock*)

'The landlords and great men of Ireland are ruining her and themselves. If ye be one of Rock's lawmakers ... you'll never right the wrongs of the country, by doing worse than those that you call your oppressors.'[29]

(Nolan to 'Captain' Maurice Delany in *The Rockite* by Charlotte Elizabeth Tonna)

To those familiar with the sweet and nostalgic sentiments of Thomas Moore's *Irish Melodies*, his *Memoirs of Captain Rock* will come as a surprise. To those familiar with the Protestant fundamentalism of Charlotte Elizabeth Tonna and her chastening experiences while resident in Ireland in the 1820s, her novel *The Rockite* will come as no surprise whatever.

The former is a wicked satire of British misrule in Ireland in 'hard-edged, almost Swiftian prose',[30] written by an avowed Irish nationalist who was not averse, like his later compatriot George Bernard Shaw, to biting the establishment hand that fed him. Or at least a finger or two.

Charlotte Elizabeth Tonna

The latter is a polemic in narrative form. The one-dimensional characters are deployed to highlight the trauma experienced by the ascendancy class in the most intense, bitter and violent conflict since the rebellion of the United Irishmen. Tonna, a dyed-in-the-wool ideologue and an unapologetic bigot, wrote about the despoliation of the Rockites from personal experience.

Moore's work, which could hardly be more different stylistically and philosophically, 'purports to be a memoir by the Rockite leader, of the history and progress of his family's business of riot and general lawlessness since the coming of the English in the twelfth century'.[31] Moore's novel arose directly out of an 1823 tour of Ireland, where, somewhat ironically, he was accompanied by one of the country's wealthiest landowners, the third Marquess of Lansdowne, descendant of Sir William Petty himself. Moore's original intention in making the return journey to the land of his birth was to add to the already impressive corpus of Irish travel literature. However, what he encountered on his trip, which came at the height of the Rockite insurgency, caused him to abandon the literary Baedeker in favour of a fictional swipe at the British maladministration of what Shaw would later dub 'John Bull's Other Island'. The tour was an eye-opener for 'Ireland's Minstrel'. As a biographer notes, 'protected in his childhood, Moore had never been exposed to the full extent of Irish miseries before, and he was shocked by the poverty he encountered on his travels'.[32]

Moore's friendship with Lansdowne, and with many other London-based Anglo-Irish landowners, led him to fudge the central question at issue in the Rockite campaign – that of unsustainable rents. Instead, he opted for safer ground by having his fictional hero concentrate on the issue of tithes, where 'thirteen-fourteenths of the people are ... taxed for the instruction of the small remaining fraction'.[33] Thus, by targeting the Established Church – the literary equivalent of shooting fish in a barrel – 'Moore managed to steer a course in *Memoirs of Captain Rock* that attacked government policy without alienating his landlord friends'.[34]

Memoirs of Captain Rock, as it turns out, is actually a Baedeker of sorts. At its core is a 300-year journey and a catalogue of English abuse of the Irish population. Moore's hero, Captain Rock, traces his lineage back to the depredations of Henry VIII, then proceeds down through the ages, describing a trail of British maltreatment and exploitation, thus validating his current status as 'chieftain' of an insurgency designed to exact retribution for Ireland's 'monotonous round of agony'.

Moore's narrator, an English clergyman into whose possession Captain Rock's memoir has come, represents a class of Everyman in his attitude to all things Irish. At one time in his life, he acknowledges, nothing would have induced him to visit Ireland: 'Often indeed had I declared – so great was my horror of the country – that "I would just as soon trust my person among those savages of the Andamans, who eat up all newcomers, as among the best bred gentleman of Kerry and Tipperary".'

However, he is prevailed upon to undertake missionary work in the hope of 'raising that unfortunate race from darkness'. His principal qualification is his comprehensive knowledge of people who profess the Catholic religion, based on a six-week sojourn in darkest papist Boulogne! It is clear from the first couple of pages that Moore intends to have as much fun as possible at the expense of this pompous and self-righteous evangelist. His twilight encounter with 'the great Captain Rock' takes place in Tipperary, where the latter, rather improbably, presents him with the manuscript that forms the basis of the book. Equally improbably, the narrator then devours the entire manuscript (more than 370 pages) in a single night. The *Memoir* is a lengthy diatribe and a rehearsal of the ills of Ireland, with Captain Rock as a male Cathleen ní Houlihán bemoaning the treatment meted out by British oppressors since the Tudor period. Only towards the end of the tirade do we get into the early decades of the nineteenth century, and even then the Captain glosses over the excesses of his semi-eponymous supporters in favour of attacking the Established Church and, collaterally, the Orange Order. In the case of the latter, he compares that institution to a pack of dogs.

Captain Rock, however, reserves his most plangent criticism for the alliance of 'incumbent' (the local rector) and 'tithe-farmer' in their mutual harassment of the peasantry:

> ... an Incumbent farms his tithes to some neighbour, who, by a skilful application of that mechanic power called the Screw, increases the receipts sufficiently to afford an income for himself as well as the Pastor. The next incumbent claims as his due the whole amount received by this Tithe-farmer, and in his turn, employs another Professor of the art of Screwing, who contrives, by the same process, to raise the value of the living still higher, and transmits it, thus improved to the Incumbent who follows.

The absence of any detailed commentary on the depredations of the Rockites – the name is barely mentioned in the text – is ascribed by the clergyman/narrator towards the end of the book to 'the great press of political business' on the Captain, which 'left him but little leisure for the indulgence of literary pursuits' and caused him to abandon his polemic shortly after the passage of the Act of Union. There are brief references to the eighteenth-century uprisings of the Whiteboys, Oakboys and Steelboys – the Captain claims his father was a member of all three organisations (also highly unlikely) – and a throwaway allusion to Lord Courtenay and 'various acts of oppression on the estate of an absentee nobleman'.[35]

According to Linda Kelly, one of his biographers, 'if Moore's *Irish Melodies* had helped to create a vague poetic sympathy for Ireland's cause, his Captain Rock – in a scathing, mordantly ironic history of his country's wrongs – demanded justice in more immediate terms'. The reaction to this display of sub-Swiftian *sæva indignatio* on the part of the beloved Irish bard was decidedly mixed. Many British establishment figures were scandalised by the work, whether or not they had actually read it. The *British Review* called Moore a 'popist [*sic*] bigot'. But in Ireland itself the work was greeted ecstatically, with 'poverty-stricken peasants clubbing together with their sixpences and shillings to buy copies'. Even *The Times*, not yet quite the establishment newspaper of the post-Crimean period, lavished praise on the work, observing that 'the love of justice, humanity and liberty, breaks out through every apostrophe of the author, however he may affect to Vale his emotions under sarcasm, levity or scorn'. The first edition of *Memoirs of Captain Rock* sold out on the day of publication and its success prompted leading Whig politician, Lord John Russell, to write to Moore that 'your Captain … has given all the Orangemen the jaundice with spleen and envy'.[36]

Moore succeeded admirably in upsetting those he wanted to provoke, while avoiding the estrangement of his patrons. Tonna's work was more narrative-driven and visceral. While Moore's anger was generated by observations made while enjoying the company of one of the richest landlords in the country, Tonna's vituperation, and inclination towards literary revenge, was directed at precisely the sort of character being lionised by 'Ireland's Minstrel'. By the time Tonna left Ireland to return to her native England, making the opposite journey to that of Moore, she had seen as much of Captain Rock as she ever wanted to see. Her novel, *The Rockite*, is Tonna's conscious riposte to Moore's *Memoirs of Captain Rock*, a book she described as 'incitement to rebellion by the Vatican'.[37]

The Rockite was first published in 1829, and written before the Catholic Emancipation Act, a piece of legislation that was anathema to Tonna. In a new preface to a third edition of the book published in 1836, the author does not mince her words when describing the encroachment of Roman Catholicism upon Protestant privilege: 'The Romish Papal power advanced to a station more commanding than her most sanguine adherents would have dared, or her most conscientious opponents could have endured to believe possible, within so few years.' The first pages of the novel are stronger on authorial diatribe than narrative. Tonna blames the misfortunes of the country not on 'the hostile arm of foreign invasion' but as coming 'from among the children of her soil, those enemies who should drench it in kindred blood'.

In the storyline of *The Rockite* – and unlike *Memoirs of Captain Rock* it actually has a sustained narrative – Maurice Delany is demobilised from a dragoon regiment in the autumn of 1821. He must, with extreme reluctance, part with his horse, Blücher. He accepts an invitation from 'a loitering countryman', Denis McCarthy, to lodge with him. Delany, while grateful to McCarthy, is 'not so deficient in the characteristic sagacity of his kindred, as to give the farmer full credit for disinterested generosity in this proceeding'. Delany, as it transpires, was right to be wary. McCarthy, because of his guest's military experience, attempts to recruit Delany to the Rockite cause. The deal is sealed when McCarthy produces the beloved Blücher and makes a gift of him to Delany.

The former Dragoon quickly comes under the influence of the prophecies of Pastorini and is encouraged to view Protestants as 'locusts' and accept that Irish Catholics are 'neglecting to exterminate them'. Delany, depicted by Tonna as a brainwashed dupe, witnesses the cold-blooded murder of an elderly tithe proctor and becomes involved in a series of Rockite attacks, a couple of which involve kidnapping local women. These operations are described as 'the barbarous exploit of tearing an innocent girl from her home and delivering her up to a heartless ruffian' – lest we harbour any doubts about Tonna's opinion of abduction. Delany is a 'Captain', i.e. leader of a Rockite troop, but the man behind much of the planning and decision-making is actually a shadowy figure and 'tyrannic leader' named O'Rourke. One of the women due to be kidnapped, Julia Butler, is the daughter of a landlord. O'Rourke wants Julia for himself, and Maurice 'in his heart pitied the fair girl for whom such a wooer was destined'.

In the attempted (and ultimately unsuccessful) kidnapping of Julia Butler, Maurice is injured. He makes his escape and encounters an opinionated peasant named Nolan, whose wife is not enamoured of the 'stony-hearted factions' she sees all around her: 'the orange faction, of blood-thirsty heretics: and the Rock faction, that is righting our wrongs by destroying us'.

Nolan becomes a mouthpiece for Tonna's antipathy to the Rockites – not that the writer, much given to authorial asides, actually requires one of her characters to perform this function. Nolan is a transgressor; he has made the ultimate error, displeasing Captain Rock by paying his tithes in the face of the threat of distraint*: 'I thought John Rock wouldn't be so hard on his own poor country man, and fellow Catholics, why should he? So I paid the demand; and sure enough, that night the thatch was a-fire over our heads, and glad we were to save the bare lives of us from the burning flame.'

Ultimately, Maurice Delany, sickened by the brutality of the Rockites, turns on his former comrades and is executed by members of the society at O'Rourke's behest. His death is followed by a scathing valedictory from Tonna: 'To re-establish her destructive empire, the church of Rome has made a mighty effort, and beheld that effort crowned with intoxicating success. She now follows up the advantage gained, and aims avowedly at the utter subversion at all that opposes her unchristian way.' Tonna ends *The Rockite* with a sinister invocation, a virtual call to arms: 'Let us not idly mourn over ills which we possess abundant means of removing.'[38]

Anyone reading *The Rockite* and *Memoirs of Captain Rock* back to back would be forgiven for assuming they were written about two distinct conflicts.

* The seizure of farm produce or implements for subsequent sale at auction to meet the financial obligations of tenants in arrears to their landlords.

After a war comes the accounting. How many lives have been lost or ruined? How many of the original objectives, if any, have been achieved? Who is entitled to claim victory? Has victory been Pyrrhic?

In numerical terms, the Rockites and Dublin Castle played out a draw when it came to fatalities. Almost 100 killings of policemen, middlemen, 'strangers', tithe-farmers, tenant farmers, land jobbers and others who fell foul of Captain Rock were attributed to the Rockites. This was roughly the same as the number of hangings carried out by the authorities in the stricken areas. When the handful of Rockites killed in action is added to the pile of scaffold corpses the authorities accumulated, the Castle inches ahead in the macabre numbers game. However, the 600 Rockites who were transported by the authorities were certainly outweighed by the thousand or so opponents of the movement who were beaten, flogged, carded or burned out of their houses in an orgy of violence unequalled since the 1798 Rebellion, and not witnessed again until the War of Independence was fought, a century later, across much of the same geographical terrain.

Many hypotheses have been advanced to account for the end of the most raucous and menacing of agrarian insurgencies since the emergence of the Whiteboys in the 1760s. One of the less convincing theories is that the necessity for political violence evaporated with the rise of O'Connell's Catholic Association and the renewed impetus of the constitutionalist struggle for Catholic emancipation. This train of thought overemphasises the political nature of the Rockite rebellion. While it did incorporate elements of the militant nationalism of Ribbonism, which in turn hearkened back to the era of the Defenders and the United Irishmen, the Rockite insurgency was still primarily agrarian in nature. The campaign for Catholic relief, while it commanded huge popular support in the regions affected by the Rockite insurgency, was not going to bring about a reduction in rents at a time of economic distress; neither was it going to curtail the activities of evicting landlords; nor would it affect the exasperating payment of tithes. O'Connell was a beneficiary of the insurgency – he was paid handsomely for defending Rockites in court, and the existence of the movement accentuated the implicit threat of violence in his approach to the British government – but his emancipation campaign had little or nothing to do with the end of the Rockite revolt.

The rebellion ended because of a combination of factors. One of these was the determined, if somewhat belated, intervention of the authorities. This was signalled by the passage of the Insurrection Act in 1822; the despatch of a large military force to take on the Rockites 'in the field'; the increased use of the hangman's rope; and the transportation of hundreds of prisoners as a way of discouraging further turpitude. However, we can assume, given the scale of the insurgency as opposed to the magnitude of the response (600 convictions, 100 executions), that many active and enthusiastic Rockite floggers, arsonists, carders* and murderers succeeded in returning to private life after the suppression of the movement without incurring any legal consequences. There was no cataclysmic reckoning, as there had been in the case of the failed 1798 Rebellion. Historian James Donnelly Jr, who has devoted much of his career to the study of radical agrarian movements – an *oeuvre* that includes a monumental work on the Rockite revolt, *Captain Rock: The Irish Agrarian Rebellion of 1821–24* (2009) – ascribes the eclipse of the movement not to repressive government measures, although they clearly played a part, but to improved economic conditions. Predictably, a rise in agricultural prices and a slow ascent from the pit of economic depression hived off from the society many of the wealthier tenant farmers who had thrown in their lot with the Rockites. The movement then proceeded to eat itself alive. Rents and tithes were being paid once again with tolerable regularity. With equal predictability, this led to an increase in the number of attacks by labourers and cottiers on wealthier tenant farmers. According to Donnelly, 'the last phase of the Rockite movement consisted of the levying of contributions and plain acts of thievery by some of the poorest elements of the population against farmers of some substance; the latter now responded in certain districts

* 'Carding' was a punishment meted out by members of agrarian secret societies in which nails were driven through a board, which was then drawn across the back of a victim.

by joining local associations sponsored by police magistrates or landowners and by mounting nocturnal patrols against such depredations.'[39] So to all intents and purposes, the final stage of the Rockite rebellion was practically indistinguishable from the factional Caravat-Shanavest conflict of the early 1800s, where the impoverished and the snug turned on each other.

The murder of the prosperous Kilkenny farmer John Marum certainly fell into this category. However, although his death took place in the waning months of the insurgency (March 1824), he had been the subject of considerable animosity since the outset of the conflict because of the frequency of his land acquisitions. As a brother of the Roman Catholic Bishop of Ossory, and a man known to harbour considerable antagonism towards his Protestant neighbours, Marum was not exactly a prototypical Rockite target. Tonna, however, had no doubt about the involvement of Captain Rock in his murder:

Feeling more regard for his worldly possessions than interest in the cause of his religion, he discouraged the Rockite proceedings. Some great outrages having occurred, he represented to government the disturbed state of the Barony, and induced them to send down a body of 'Peelers' as the police were termed. This he knew to be an unpardonable offence, and therefore never went abroad unarmed; taking care to have it known that he did not.[40]

It is likely that Marum's death, ironically, can be ascribed to a local fear that his wealth and acquisitiveness would lead to his buying out a family of Kilkenny Protestant middlemen who were well-liked. Given his record, it was assumed that he would be far less lenient towards his under-tenants than the incumbents. The murder of Marum, a prominent Roman Catholic land jobber, has often been posited – and was at the time – as proof that the Rockites were an essentially non-sectarian organisation. However, the overwhelming weight of evidence suggests otherwise. One swallow, however well-connected to the Roman Catholic hierarchy, does not a summer make.

How should we view the Rockites? Were they agrarian terrorists, vigilantes or nineteenth-century Robin Hoods pledged to defend the oppressed? Certainly not the last. The legend of Mr Hood does not include any examples of the guerrillas of Sherwood Forest intimidating the poor of medieval Nottingham. The same cannot be said of the Rockites. While they had many genuinely avid supporters, they had no compunction about using violence and intimidation to recruit the hesitant or disinclined. 'Self-interest rather than altruism was at the heart of numerous violent outbreaks,' as the authors of a work on nineteenth-century Ribbonism have asserted. Rural Ireland was changing, modernising and increasingly relying on commercial markets rather than subsistence farming. 'Those left behind by change – the landless labourers or the small farmer – looked with envy at the graziers, middleman, and farmers who benefited.'[41]

While the Rockites (unlike their brethren in the more northern and urban-oriented Ribbon movement) were hardly subject to rule by committee, they did have a more complex organisational structure than their predecessors. Local committees existed, communal decisions were made and, although most operations were small smash-and-grab missions, the Rockites were equally capable of putting several hundred men in the field at any given time, and did so on numerous occasions. Rockites on the run even congregated in the mountainous border region of Cork, Kerry and Limerick and, like an Irish Hole in the Wall Gang or an IRA flying column of a century later, lived off what they could appropriate from their targets and defied police, military or yeomanry to displace them.

It takes a level of planning and preparation, rarely demonstrated by any of their short-lived predecessors, to carry on a three-year conflict that positioned itself somewhere between a guerrilla conflict and a conventional war. The Rockites were capable of launching military operations, in significant numbers, in daylight hours, with relative impunity. Furthermore, they could generally rely on the support of the population of the area in which these actions took place. Arguably, the Rockites exhibited almost as much centralised command and control as the War of Independence IRA, a guerrilla force with a high degree of regional and local autonomy where activism tended to be in direct proportion to the zeal and the capabilities of the local leadership, and where the authority of General Headquarters was in inverse proportion to the distance from Dublin.

Ironically, the principal achievements of the Rockites were either partial, temporary or of no benefit to their more militant members. Alexander Hoskins was vanquished. A number of obnoxious opponents were brutally disposed of. Some landlords, rectors or middlemen were intimidated into accommodation. The passage of the 1823 Tithe Composition Act has also been credited to their murderous campaign. But they clearly failed to secure the abolition of tithes, and the Composition Act (as will be seen in the next chapter) caused as many problems as it solved. However, their influence on the anti-tithe movement, which would grow and prosper in the 1830s, was considerable and undeniable. One of the reasons for its success was the constant threat of a return to Rockite-style violence if major concessions were not forthcoming.

Although they had played a small part in advancing the prophecies of Pastorini by causing an element of Protestant flight, the Established Church was as firmly entrenched in 1825 as it had been in 1821. As were the landed classes, although having borne witness to what the Rockites were capable of, their predilection for ejectment was somewhat inhibited. Rockism, despite the alarming physical threat it posed, could not prevent all evictions. However, widespread clearances of the kind later experienced during the Famine were avoided, in part because Rockite violence stayed the hand of landlords.

Their other achievement, as was so often the case with Irish radical and militant movements, was to grease the wheels for constitutionalists. Just as the excesses of the later Fenian movement influenced the decision of William Gladstone that his mission in government should be 'to pacify Ireland', the activities of the Rockites introduced a convenient underlying threat to O'Connell's crusade for Catholic relief. O'Connell, without having to jettison his oft-avowed pacifism, benefited politically from the murderous efficiency of Captain Rock. Like Parnell after him, he was not required to intone King Louis XV's warning '*après moi, le déluge*' for the British government to realise that some concession to Catholic demands would be required in order to avoid a second act from Captain Rock. This synergy, rarely acknowledged by either side, would become a characteristic of Irish agrarian politics in the nineteenth century. When O'Connell and Charles Stewart Parnell looked over their shoulders to survey their more aggressive supporters, it was to ensure that the hard men were not too close, or too far away.

7

The 'sacred tenth': the Tithe War of the 1830s

'Then the Peelers did fall, without murmur or bawl,
Then their guns and their bayonets were shattered,
How sad was their case, when their eyes, nose and face,
When their lives and their firelocks were battered'.

('The Battle of Carrickshock', anonymous,
set to the tune of 'St Patrick's Day')

Carrickshock, Co. Kilkenny, 14 December 1831[1]

Had a hawk (*seabhac*) been hovering over Carrickshock on 14 December 1831 it would have been witness to a deadly barrage of those other items (*carraig*) that give the town its name. 'Carrickshock' – a few fields away from today's M9 motorway, three kilometres south-west of the village of Knocktopher – translates from the Irish *Carraig Seabhac*, the Hawk's Rock.

The air was filled with rocks and stones that day. According to one fortunate survivor, 'the stones hit each other they were so thick'. Those self-cancelling coincidences of trajectory were not enough to save the lives of a dozen members of an almost forty-strong constabulary force. All were armed with rifles, and were escorting a process-server,* Edmund Butler, to protect him from assault. Butler's job that day, his last on God's earth, was to serve latitats (writs)

---

* An agent employed to serve eviction notices on tenants in arrears or on landowners in default on tithe payments.

on behalf of the Rev. Hans Hamilton of Knocktopher on local defaulters, farmers who decided they had paid all the tithes they were ever going to pay to the local Church of Ireland clergyman. Butler was the first to be felled by a fist-sized stone thrown from the ranks of a crowd of around a thousand angry peasants. It may not have killed him outright, but the sequel certainly did.

The 1820s had not been a good time for law enforcement. A couple of major economic depressions, a crippling subsistence crisis in 1822 and the murderous Rockite rebellion had led to a widespread renewal of agrarian violence. The new constabulary force, established in 1822, had lost a dozen men to rioters and Whiteboyism from 1826 to 1830.* Now they had lost the same number of constables in less than an hour in a blood-soaked boreen in rural south Kilkenny.

Had our observant hawk been flying over the Carrickshock/Hugginstown area at around noon on that day, all would have been calm and undisturbed. The weather was unseasonably mild and bright after two weeks of intense rain. Then, shortly after midday, the rustic peace was rent by the insistent ringing of a church bell. But no one was being summoned to mass in the middle of a working Wednesday. All who heard the chimes knew what was about to happen. Butler, the process-server, and his armed escort had been spotted. The faithful were being summoned for a violent purging, not for a religious service. By the time the small force of police and the process-server with his sheaf of summonses reached (or were inveigled into) a narrow pathway between the nearby villages of Hugginstown and Ballyhale, hundreds of people had gathered to ensure that Butler would not serve a single summons that day. No one, however, could have predicted, or even contemplated, what would happen next. The Carrickshock boreen, a long defile with high stone walls on either side, became the Pass of Thermopylae, with the 'polis' or 'Peelers' as the doomed Spartans.

Edmund Butler was a Kilkenny man, well-known locally for doing the bidding of tithe-owners and landlords. The crowd, which did not take long to turn into an ugly mob, wanted to settle

* It lost five more to the Terry Alts in Bealnavallen, Co. Clare, on 4 April 1831 in an attempted prisoner rescue.

his hash once and for all. The mother of all beatings was to be administered in the hope that the broken bones and bruises would persuade him to change his line of work. As the constabulary contingent, thirty-seven officers under the command of Captain James Gibbons – a veteran of the Napoleonic Wars who had joined the new police force shortly after its foundation – surrounded the process-server in a protective circle, the persistent chant went up from the mob: 'Give us Butler.' Gibbons, who had emerged from the Battle of Waterloo unscathed, was not about to hand over the cowering messenger. However, he and his men were in a classic standoff. They could move neither forwards nor backwards, and attempting to break out into the open fields beyond the constricted boreen was not an option either. The high

Chasing the process-server, Aloysius O'Kelly

stone walls prevented lateral movement and the heights were controlled by the enemy.

The stalemate ended when an enterprising member of the peasant army rushed past the police and made an attempt to remove Butler from the sanctuary of the circle of uniforms. One of the policemen grabbed the process-server and attempted to yank him back into the constabulary's ranks. That was when the first rock, the size of a healthy cooking apple, smashed into Butler's skull and sent him crashing to the ground. The well-aimed projectile was the signal for anarchy to be loosed. Gibbons ordered his men to deploy their rifles and open fire. It was the last order of his short career as a policeman. He had survived the worst the Corsican general could throw at him on the battlefield, but he would succumb to the stones and pitchforks of a thousand frenzied peasants in a Kilkenny *botharín*. Some of his men managed a single volley but had no opportunity to reload before they were tumbling under a hail of rocks and trying to avoid the three-pronged bayonet thrusts of dozens of pitchforks. Out of the original force of thirty-eight men, only eleven managed to emerge unharmed, physically at least. Fourteen others survived, but with severe wounds. The rest of the detachment were left, in the words of one of the many gloating ballads that were penned in the wake of the tragedy, 'weltering in black gore'.[2]

Some of the constabulary bullets found their marks as well. Three members of the mob stoning the policemen also lay dead. The indifferent *seabhac*, still hovering above the mayhem, would have been the only independent observer in a position to confirm or scotch the grisly folklore that after the affray an elderly man, a veteran of the horrors of 1798, strolled across the battlefield finishing off any of the injured and immobile policemen who were still clinging to life.

When Edmund Butler's body was recovered from the lane, his mouth was said to have been stuffed with the processes he had intended to serve on the Carrickshock tithe defaulters that day.

'Set aside the tenth sheaf as an offering to pious purposes'[3]

It was all the fault of Henry VIII and his overactive libido.

The portly Tudor monarch's passion for Anne Boleyn, delicately packaged as his 'desire for a male heir', led to his dispute with Rome; which brought on the establishment of the Anglican church; which, in turn, led to the transfer of the ownership of tithes from Roman Catholic priests and monasteries to the clergy of the reformed church; which, 300 years after horny Henry managed to bed his new queen, ultimately led to the Tithe War. A signal triumph for the law of unintended consequences.

For centuries, the overwhelmingly Catholic population of Ireland, a majority in twenty-eight of the thirty-two counties, was obliged to support financially the clergy of 2,450 Church of Ireland parishes. This was even the case in remote parishes where no viable Protestant congregation existed. The French journalist and traveller Gustave de Beaumont visited Ireland in 1835 with his friend Alexis de Tocqueville, and again with his wife, Clementine de Lafayette, in 1837. In his devastating polemic *Ireland: Social, Political and Religious*, he pointed out that in ninety-eight parishes of the Established Church there was not a single parishioner. 'The services of the church are not dispensed in the ratio of the Protestant population, but a Catholic country is partitioned in reference to the Anglican church.' De Beaumont highlighted just a single example. In 1830, the Church of Ireland diocese of Emly numbered 95,700 inhabitants, of whom 1,200 were members of the Church of Ireland. Nonetheless, the diocese had fifteen churches and thirty-one salaried ministers, all paid for by tithes, less than 10 per cent of which came from their co-religionists.[4]

De Beaumont's 1835 travelling companion, de Tocqueville, the author of the seminal *Democracy in America*, noted that the imposition of tithes was a brake on development and modernisation. 'The farmer has been little disposed to invest in clearing land. Hardly was the land cultivated than the tithe collector and the state tax collector would appear.'[5]

The Tithe War, which began in 1830 and ended in 1833; or which began in 1831 and ended in 1836; or 1838 – there was no convenient treaty to mark its official conclusion – tends to be seen as something of an anomaly. In and of itself, so the theory goes, it was a largely peaceful campaign of passive resistance, interspersed with outbreaks of unimaginable violence.

However, it would be a mistake to overemphasise the tranquil nature of the conflict. The advocates of constitutional action were plentiful but were actively supplemented by the seemingly indispensable violence of Irish rural agitation. While peaceful protest was more common than in previous agrarian insurgencies, Captain Moonlight was constantly lurking in the shadows, awaiting his cue. The Tithe War spawned far more appalling atrocities than was the case in the supposedly more bitter and sanguinary (albeit shorter) Land War of 1879–82. It was a violent, sectarian conflict that – although the anti-tithe forces could claim a version of success – managed to achieve only a largely symbolic outcome, while further exacerbating social and religious divisions in Irish society. However, despite its shortcomings as some sort of Gandhi-esque national movement of passive resistance, it did unite the normally contending tiers of Irish rural society, effect a psychologically important emblematic victory; and offer a template founded on civil disobedience – without an overabundance of civility – for future 'slightly' constitutional agrarian movements. And all this was achieved without any recognisable national leadership cadre.

As we have seen from previous manifestations of agrarian unrest, the tithe was the 'gift' that kept on taking; in financial terms, from almost anyone who planted and cultivated, in political terms, as a wound that was regularly reopened. So why, in the 1830s, did the previously multi-layered conflicts of Whiteboy, Rightboy *et al.* boil down to the single issue that allows us to describe the period of agrarian conflict of the early 1830s as The Tithe War?

The principal reason why all other grievances were set aside, temporarily, in a full-tilt assault on the creature comforts of Church of Ireland clergy was that it had become an issue that almost all the tenant farmers of Munster and south Leinster – grazier, 'snug' tillage farmer (small farmer), cottier and labourer

– urgently needed to prioritise. The graziers were latecomers to the feast. The sowers and reapers had been *in situ* for generations. What made the Established Church/tenant farmer conflict of the 1830s different was a piece of legislation passed in 1823 that might well have had the effect of removing a major injustice. However, like other Irish solutions to Irish problems, it merely made matters worse.

In 1823, the parliament of the still relatively fresh-faced United Kingdom of Great Britain and Ireland passed the Tithe Composition Act. During its passage through the House of Commons, the chief secretary for Ireland, Henry Goulburn, had acknowledged the huge injustice at the centre of the perennial tithe controversy: 'In England the tithes were paid by the middling and higher classes, by those who had a considerable, or at least some, capital employed in agriculture; in Ireland they were paid by the very lowest of the peasantry, and almost by them alone.'[6]

The new legislation had the effect of repealing the cosy arrangement that wealthy graziers had succeeded in establishing for themselves just under a century earlier, when pastureland was removed from the snare of the tithe. After 1735, if you raised cattle or sheep, tithes became someone else's problem. This, among other things, had ensured that livestock and dairy farmers in Ireland had no incentive to make common cause with their fellow rustics in the cattle-houghing, ear-cropping, anti-tithe crusades of the late eighteenth century. The 1823 Tithe Composition Act, in an effort to meet the legitimate grievances of tillage farmers – and Munster conacre potato growers who hardly even merited the description 'farmer' – changed all that. From that point onwards, tithes would be levied on the value of land, rather than merely on the income produced from tillage cultivation. Tithe commissioners would assess the quality of the land and assign a tithe rate per acre. This meant that the annual yield inspection of crops by that much-loathed figure, the tithe proctor, would no longer be necessary. This should have had the effect of reducing tensions. Which indeed it did. For a while.

The reason the 1823 Tithe Composition Act did not become the permanent corrective that it was intended to be was because it allowed a fatal opt-out. 'Composition' – the application of a tax on all land, pasture and tillage – remained voluntary. The failure to introduce an element of compulsion meant that for many tenant farmers, nurturing unrealisable expectations of the new legislation, it was a case of *plus ça change, plus c'est la même chose*. Under the terms of the legislation, the decision on whether to retain the status quo or opt for composition was left up to local Church of Ireland special vestries. These were generally made up of the highest-net-worth individuals in any given parish. Many of those were either graziers themselves or landlords with a vested interest in pastoral farming, i.e. well-fed turkeys with no inclination to vote for Christmas. While some vestries – especially where the aristocracy and lesser gentry profited from tillage – did opt for composition, many chose to leave matters, with all their inherent inequities, exactly as they were. By the middle of February 1824, the Lord Lieutenant had received communications from just over 40 per cent of the 2,450 Church of Ireland parishes in the country. In only 240 parishes out of 1,033 that had aired the matter had the decision gone in favour of composition.[7] Some progress, however, was made in the direction of universal composition in the late 1820s. By 1832, more than 1,500 of the 2,450 parishes had agreed to compound tithes. By then, however, much of the damage caused by the initial reluctance to opt for composition had already been done.

So the clergy of the Church of Ireland – almost half of whom had never darkened the door of a church in the parishes from which they drew their tithe levies – thus acquired, overnight, a wider and more secure financial base. They also, willy-nilly, recruited a whole new segment of the grumbling classes as antagonists. Livestock and dairy farmers in parishes where composition was accepted – and whose great-great-grandfathers had probably been the last members of the family obliged to keep the local reverend in the style to which he was accustomed – were going to be out of pocket. But, in addition to that newly disgruntled constituency, for a sizeable cohort of frustrated and disappointed tillage farmers, as well as the impoverished renters of conacre potato patches in Munster and south Leinster, absolutely nothing had changed.

Tenant farmers who, previously, had grudgingly tolerated the tithe as long as it was regularly adjusted in proportion to their income, now turned their attention towards its extinction.

The Tithe Composition Act, largely a British political response to the ferocity of the Rockite insurgency, therefore, brought one controversy to an end, in theory at least, while introducing a couple more in its place. One of the many things that it did not do was standardise tithe rates in different parts of Ireland. These still varied wildly from region to region. In some areas of the country, before the passage of the act, tithe payments were as high as rents. In other regions, however, the rate was as low as a third of the amount owed to the landlord. There was often very little rhyme or reason for the disparities, other than the negotiating abilities of tenant farmers or clergymen when it came to establishing rates. The 1823 act, in areas where tithes were compounded, often had the effect of simply moving the pieces around the board and creating brand-new anomalies.

Obviously, one reason for post-composition variations was the quality of the land being assessed for the levy. A small Connacht farm bordering on bogland could hardly be afforded a value comparable to the verdant grasslands of the east midlands or south Leinster. Accordingly, the average rate in Leinster, post-composition, was pegged at around two shillings per acre; Munster at one and sixpence; while land in Connacht and Ulster came in at around a shilling an acre. However, within those averages were some stark regional divergences. If you ever find yourself wondering why opposition to tithes during the eponymous 'war' began on the banks of the river Nore – not the first time the peasants of that part of the country had initiated social revolt – it is probably worth bearing in mind that the average tithe valuation in Kilkenny varied from a low of two shillings per acre to a high of almost twice that. The region in which the Tithe War can be said to have begun, around the attractive village of Graiguenamanagh, could boast of a valuation of 96 halfpence, or four shillings, an acre. No greater incentive to rebellion was required.

Neither did the Tithe Composition Act entirely exempt the blatantly impoverished, as was the case with the tithe in Britain.

Nor did it review the crippling liability of conacre potato growers, many of whom lived barely above subsistence levels, or decree that no farmer (other than the seething graziers) would end up paying more in tithes than had been the case in 1822. In short, in an effort to end an obvious injustice, the government managed to incense almost everyone liable for the payment of tithes. The difference in the 1830s to previous eruptions, however, was that no one was interested in half-measures any longer. The challenge for this more broadly based movement was not just to negotiate a reduction in the amounts flowing to the clergy of the Church of Ireland, or to insist on more frequent assessments of land value by tithe commissioners, but to abolish the hated tax once and for all. This time they would not be distracted by other grievances. High rents and the local cess taxes were resented, but, if you were a Catholic or Presbyterian tenant farmer, unlike the tithe, at least you had something to show for each: your land, in the case of rent, and the maintenance of roads and bridges in return for the cess tax.

The new post-composition tithe regime also contained, baked into its metrics, the seeds of an entirely new grievance. What the Tithe Commissioners were doing was assessing a 'year zero' value of a tenant farmer's land. This was based on the potential productivity of that land. Furthermore, the tax on those acres was to be a fixed charge for the next seven years. However, the capacity of the farmer to live up to the year zero valuation on an annual basis was hardly immutable. Farm income could vary from year to year, or it could fluctuate wildly. Between 1820 and 1830, grain prices declined by 25 per cent. Under the old regime, based on a percentage of the value of the crop, the tithe would have plummeted accordingly. But the assigned tithe value of the land on which the grain was grown – as opposed to the actual market value of the land, or of its produce – did not decline. Even though the tillage farmer's income had dipped in tandem with the price he could get for his grain, his tithe liability remained static and constituted a higher percentage of his income in bad times. Now the tillage-farmer had something in common with the grazier. The establishment had chanced on a new regimen by which it could impoverish both. Added to all that was the fact that composition made it easier to assess the annual income of Church of Ireland rectors. Nothing was calculated to be more infuriating for a Catholic tithe payer than to compare his own worth with that of a salaried cleric to whose annual stipend he was unwillingly contributing.

What was equally galling was the frequent presence of a Church of Ireland minister on the local bench. Many clerics of the Established Church, because of their elevated social status, doubled as magistrates. This, in the case of legal disputes over the payment of tithes, theoretically put them in the position of plaintiff and judge. While most, in fact, sensibly recused themselves when such cases came before them, there was still a perception that they exerted an overweening influence on their fellow magistrates.

Alexis de Tocqueville, in his invaluable account of Ireland in the 1830s – partial enough to be an antidote to Arthur Young's narrative of the 1760s – recorded a case that came to his attention at the Galway Assizes in August 1836, of a Church of Ireland minister of Moylough by the name of O'Rourke: 'The revenues of the rector were considerable; his duties few; as minister he levied the tithe, as Justice of the peace he saw to it that it was paid without resistance.' O'Rourke was the son of a former Catholic priest who had converted to Protestantism and had gone on to become a Church of Ireland rector. He was succeeded in that avocation by his son, who, as a consequence of his father's apostasy, 'was especially abhorred by the Catholics who formed the great mass of the surrounding population'. This might have had as much to do with his zeal as a magistrate, where 'he showed himself to be an inflexible and violent persecutor of the poor'. So reviled was O'Rourke that at least two attempts were made to assassinate him.[8] One of his mortal enemies was, however, much more resourceful than a pair of failed killers. A local solicitor by the name of Kilkelly managed to extract a sizeable sum from the Rev. O'Rourke for a number of civil infractions and, in a provocative locational use of irony, began, with the proceeds of the litigation, to build a small Catholic church opposite the rector's residence, where he could not fail to miss the 'pretty little Catholic chapel'

LAND IS ALL THAT MATTERS

that was being built with his own money. De Tocqueville could barely disguise his delight at the subsequent fate of the tithe-happy zealot. The French author happened to catch the epilogue at Galway Assizes when O'Rourke was found to have impregnated a maidservant ('Molly X'). His fate, de Tocqueville opined, would be enforced exile, and the tithe cause would, accordingly, lose one of its most uncompromising stalwarts in that part of the country.

When hundreds of thousands of Irish peasant farmers put their hands into their shallow pockets and handed over a penny a month to an organisation calling itself the Catholic Association, they may have done so because their neighbour was doing likewise, or because they fervently believed in the symbolic importance of the removal of the last measures that prevented them, legally, from becoming the equal of their Protestant countrymen.

However, unless they were barristers anxious to become King's Counsel or lowly civil servants looking to rise through the ranks, there wasn't actually a whole lot in it for them. Granted, they could now become Members of Parliament, assuming they could find themselves a nice 'pocket borough' in the gift of an obliging (and acquisitive) aristocrat. The 1832 Reform Act was still a glint in the eye of Earl Grey, after whom a grateful nation would name a brand of tea as a reward for his role in the evolution of democracy. Of course, these new blue-collar parliamentarians would then be obliged to support themselves in a magnificent city, London, where the cost of an establishment was considerably higher than in Lixnaw, Shercock, Kinawley or wherever it was they hailed from.

In many respects, the achievement of emancipation in 1829, although it did ensure a level of Irish Catholic representation in the Mother of Parliaments, which would prove useful for the anti-tithe movement, was a zero-sum game for the average Irish tenant farmer. A cynic might go so far as to label it a three-card trick. A Catholic Association supporter might well, at long last, have gained a fellow-Catholic as his local Member of Parliament, but he had probably lost his vote in the process. This unfortunate outcome came about as the apparent corollary of Catholic relief, viz. the reduction of the franchise in Ireland with the abolition of the voting rights of tenant farmers whose land value fell below forty shillings – the co-called Forty-Shilling Freeholders.

So while the ultimate success of the campaign for Catholic emancipation might have been inspiring and offered encouragement to further constitutional action for social and economic betterment, Catholic relief, *per se*, was a lot like one of those aristocratic architectural follies that began to appear on landed estates in the eighteenth century. It looked and felt good, but it didn't actually do very much for the average observer.

Could the efficacy of the emancipation campaign be parlayed into a successful move against tithes? Would concerted action, a final push, see the 'sacred tenth' follow the 'parish cess' (already abolished) into oblivion? Unfortunately, one vital ingredient of the triumph of 1829 would be largely absent from this next phase in the perennial struggle with the British establishment and the Irish Protestant Ascendancy. The Liberator – victor of the Clare by-election, advocate supreme, champion of Roman Catholic rights, destroyer of the last of the malevolent Penal Laws – had done enough liberating, for the time being at least. Daniel O'Connell would not be assuming leadership of the movement aimed at the impoverishment of the clergy of the Established Church. He refused to pay his own tithes, insisting that any bailiff who fancied his chances could 'sell the very bed from under him, but he would never consent to pay a single farthing'.[9] He might be prevailed upon to make the odd supportive speech, and did become involved in legislative efforts at reform in the House of Commons, but, while he was perfectly content to see some of his erstwhile supporters assume local leadership roles in this struggle, he had other (parliamentary) fish to fry. After the success of the emancipation crusade, O'Connell was intent on pursuing repeal of the Act of Union, what would later become known as Home Rule. In the 1830s, this largely took the form of an 'indoor policy' of parliamentary procedures (annual failed attempts to introduce remedial legislation) before the 'outdoor policy' of the 1840s (the staging of a series of so-called 'monster meetings') became the preferred, but no more successful, option.

Moreover, given the success of a campaign conducted on constitutional lines (Catholic relief), O'Connell was not anxious to identify himself too closely with a movement that had more than a whiff of Whiteboyism about it. This meant that while The Liberator spurned an active leadership role in what would become a national, albeit loosely organised, mass movement, 'the people prominent on anti-tithe platforms of 1832 were on the emancipation platforms of 1828 … though O'Connell set repeal as the ultimate goal he and his followers were never inhibited from creating as much trouble as possible on any other front and what more suitable one than tithes'.[10]

Hurlers on the ditch: Kilkenny, 1830–3

Any national elite leadership vacuum in the anti-tithe campaign was, however, filled by a number of formidable Roman Catholic clerics. Being named Doyle was not a prerequisite for a prominent role in the anti-tithe agitation, but it appears to have helped. Enter Fr Martin Doyle of Graiguenamanagh and the even more formidable Bishop James Doyle of the diocese of Kildare and Leighlin, or JKL (James of Kildare and Leighlin), as he was better known to his own and adjacent flocks. JKL was the *éminence grise* of Irish Catholicism before the divisive ultra-montanist leadership of Cardinal Paul Cullen (an alumnus of Carlow College) began two decades later.

The involvement of the Roman Catholic clergy was enabled by the capacity of this new anti-tithe movement to remain on the right side of the law – a cadre of highly respectable middle-class Catholics at the helm certainly helped. The role of powerful and influential prelates like JKL and the even more nationalistic Maynooth professor Dr John MacHale – soon to become Archbishop of Tuam (1834) – was given added piquancy by the continued proselytising efforts of clergy of the Anglican church's 'New Reformation' or 'Second Reformation' in Ireland. This was a movement led by conservative evangelicals, known as 'Biblicals' or 'New Reformers', beginning in the 1820s, which sought to convert

Roman Catholics to the Anglican religion. Catholic farmers, gaining no benefit from tithes paid to a complacent, indolent Protestant clergyman was one thing. Of a different order entirely were the activities of these visiting evangelical clerics travelling through the Irish countryside, bible in hand (often an Irish-language version), informing them of the error of their ways.

Although tithes collected in Ireland were making no direct contribution to the activities of these missionaries, their presence had the effect of adding insult to injury. Doyle, and later MacHale, were, from the outset, among the leading Irish Catholic prelates on a war footing with the New Reformation. Doyle, in the manner of an astute football manager, even took to 'marking' the more evangelical of the resident Church of Ireland pastors in his own diocese. Hence the presence of the doughty Fr Martin Doyle in Graiguenamanagh, where he was deputed to 'mark' the fundamentalist Anglican curate, the Rev. Luke McDonald, who had assumed most of the duties of the elderly and ineffectual rector of the parish, the Rev. Alcock.

Bishop Doyle's leadership role in the anti-tithe crusade was entirely moral in nature; he had no organisational involvement in the campaign. However, his support for the movement was of crucial importance. Doyle was, after all, the man who had roundly condemned the prophecies of Pastorini and had instructed his clergy to preach against Walmsley's fallacies, fantasies and half-truths in the mid-1820s. Furthermore, in 1831, he condemned the activities of emerging agrarian secret societies (little more than glorified factions) in his diocese calling themselves the Whitefeet and Blackfeet.* So he could hardly be dismissed as an irredentist, anti-Protestant, Catholic prelate, or an apologist for agrarian anarchy. Doyle's publication of a pamphlet in 1831 in which he threw his considerable intellectual heft behind the

* De Tocqueville referenced a conversation between a priest and a Carlow Whitefeet leader in which the latter observed that 'Emancipation has done nothing for us. Mr. O'Connell and the rich Catholics go to parliament. We are starving just the same' (Larkin (ed.), *Alexis de Tocqueville's Journey in Ireland*, 40).

anti-tithe movement was critical in validating the campaign. 'There are many noble traits in the Irish character,' he wrote, 'but an innate love of justice, and an indomitable hatred of oppression is like a gem upon the front of our nation which no darkness can obscure.' His next line was a memorable and oft-quoted rallying call: 'To this firm quality I trace their hatred of tithe: may it be as lasting as their love of justice.'[11]

It was Fr Martin Doyle, JKL's activist surrogate, who became the proximate cause of the outbreak of the Tithe War in November 1830, when he refused to remit tithes on a forty-acre farm he had rented near Graiguenamanagh (more commonly known as 'Graigue' or 'Graig'). There was an understanding that Catholic priests were not required to pay tithes on any land attached to their presbyteries. However, the Rev. McDonald decided that Doyle's additional forty-acre farm did not fall within the ambit of that long-established custom. The Roman Catholic parish priest thought otherwise, and had the ideal platform to begin a campaign with the far from limited objective of introducing 'measures to prevent the further payment of tithes in the parish'.[12] He was joined in his resistance by his parishioners, who sent petitions to the ailing Rev. Alcock and to his superior, the bishop of the Church of Ireland diocese of Leighlin and Ferns. Not that Doyle's specific case was the sole motivating factor in Graiguenamanagh for the campaign that followed. In 1827, around the time of the final piece of composition legislation, an agreement had been reached with local tithe-payers for the payment of a sum of £1,000 to the Church of Ireland parish. By 1830, it was felt by many Graigue residents that the sum previously agreed was too high and did not reflect the decline in agricultural prices in the interim. A bad harvest in 1829 led to the movement gathering pace the following year.

What the later Land War was to the boycott, the Tithe War was to the sport of hurling. It was under the aegis of Fr Doyle's leadership that the landmark tactic of disguising public anti-tithe meetings as gatherings of hurlers was devised. This was after the authorities banned other forms of public meeting in Kilkenny. The rationale, itself later challenged by Dublin Castle, was that such 'sporting' assemblies were entirely legal. The fact that many of those attending these impromptu 'matches' – taking place on the property of the Rev. Alcock, for example – were also carrying a useful weapon with them (the *camán* itself) was a convenient bonus. Kilkenny, a fanatical hurling county even more than half a century before the founding of the Gaelic Athletic Association, was the logical location for such a transparent ruse. A string of 'hurling matches' followed across the county as the anti-tithe agitation intensified.

When a delegation of hurlers gathered on the front lawn outside the Knocktopher, Co. Kilkenny rectory of the Rev. Hans Hamilton on 27 December 1830, he refused to have any dealings with them. Hamilton had, in the 1820s, at the height of the Rockite insurgency, housed the future novelist and evangelical anti-Catholic proselytiser, Charlotte Elizabeth Tonna, in an effort to protect her from an abusive relationship with her military husband, Captain George Phelan, owner of a Kilkenny estate. Although she had moved to England by the time of the Tithe War, Tonna, in her *Irish Recollections*, published in 1847, offered an account of Hamilton's opening encounter with 'the men who had been first trained to work as Rockites [and] now called themselves Hurlers, from a sport in which the Kilkenny men excel'.[13] Hamilton was summoned to his front door to meet with half-a-dozen men. However, they proved to be but the advance guard of a much larger group of silent, observant and intimidating 'hurlers'. Tonna described Hamilton's shock on being confronted with this show of force: 'He saw this waste ground covered with men, to the number of two or three thousand, armed with the formidable hooked sticks* that they used in hurling, and with shillelaghs loaded with lead, besides concealed firearms, and other dangerous weapons.'[14]

The response of tithe owners (clergymen and tithe farmers) to what became an organised refusal to pay the levy varied from restraint to distraint. Some attempted to come to terms with

---

* The nineteenth-century hurley (*camán*) closely resembled a modern hockey stick.

their defaulters; others began to seize their assets. The latter route offered ample scope for violent resistance. That this did not invariably occur is testimony to a degree of subtlety and finesse among the strategists of this novel agrarian movement. Granted, there was a substantial level of organised and impromptu violence, but in many cases, victims of distraint were dissuaded from reacting violently, in a tactic that has been credited to the Dublin solicitor Patrick Costello. Borrowing from the principles of passive resistance espoused by members of the Quaker faith, farmers were encouraged not to resist the seizure of their assets, usually cattle or sheep. One of the acknowledged leaders of the movement, future MP Patrick Lalor (father of James Fintan Lalor), for example, allowed two dozen sheep to be removed by the tithe proctor's drivers from his farm in Tenakill in Queen's County (Laois). However, in keeping with the new strategy, he subsequently ensured there were no bids for his distrained sheep at an auction in Mountrath in March 1831.

The writer W. R. Le Fanu, brother of the great Irish gothic novelist Sheridan Le Fanu and son of the rector of the parish of Abington, part of which was in Limerick and part in Tipperary, devoted a chapter of his autobiography, *Seventy Years of Irish Life*, to his memories of the Tithe War. In the neighbouring parish of Doon, the Church of Ireland clergyman the Rev. Charles Coote, and the Roman Catholic parish priest, described only as 'Father H—', had been on generally good terms. Unlike the case of Doyle in Graigue, no tithes were ever demanded of the priest for a 'considerable farm' that he owned in the area. However, when, in 1831, the Catholic priest denounced tithes in general and, in particular, the payment of same to Coote, the gloves came off. Coote insisted on his tithe. The priest declined to pay and defied Coote to distrain any of his cattle. The rector obliged the parish priest by seizing a single beast. The priest, sarcastically, wished Coote good fortune in trying to sell the cow at auction. At this point, the dispute reached ludicrous proportions when the Doon rector managed to secure military backing from Dublin Castle to ensure that the sale of the animal went off peacefully. On the day of the auction, four companies of Scottish Highland infantry marched through the village, their piper playing the rousing air 'The Campbells are Coming'. The kilted infantrymen being deemed insufficient to guarantee the cow's change of ownership, there then followed 'a troop of lancers and artillery with two guns'.

Coote might well have justified this over-reaction by pointing out that 'many thousands of the country people were assembled' at the appointed hour of the auction. Certainly, none were there to bid up the price of the controversial animal. It was a situation tailor-made for an ugly clash. Instead, it ended in farce when a local farmer entered a bid well above the beast's value. This hapless tyro was under the misapprehension that the sale would not be valid unless there were three bids for the animal. After there were no further bids, the cow was duly knocked down by a grateful auctioneer to the bewildered, and now considerably out of pocket, farmer. The sum involved covered the priest's unpaid tithe.

Returning to their bivouac, the Scottish soldiers were subjected to a barrage of stones and opened fire on their assailants, wounding one man, before the cavalrymen dispersed the crowd with their swords. 'From that day,' according to Le Fanu, 'Mr. Coote was a marked man.' So, it transpired, were the members of the Le Fanu family, collateral damage in the campaign of vilification of the rector of the neighbouring parish. 'At this time none of us went out alone, and we were always well-armed.' Le Fanu's sister, who assumed, naively as it transpired, that she would be exempt from any form of violence, was attacked when she ventured out without an escort.

Le Fanu himself was assaulted while riding out with a companion. But for the fact that they were armed and on horseback and waved pistols at their would-be assailants, the writer acknowledged that 'I should not have been alive many minutes'. Le Fanu's horse, though fatally wounded by a blow from a spade, managed to survive for long enough to get his young rider safely home. In the course of the attack, Le Fanu sought the assistance of a Catholic priest, who grimly shrugged off the plea 'and passed on'. Had Le Fanu taken a different route, he was later told, 'four armed men lay in wait, in a plantation by the road, to shoot us'.

Le Fanu also observed that the practice of what became known as boycotting in the 1880s was far from a product of that decade: 'Placards were posted all through the neighbourhood ordering that no one should work for Mr. Coote on pain of death.' When half-a-dozen grateful young men whom Coote had saved from transportation (their sentences were based on perjured evidence) tried to defy this local edict by cutting turf for the Doon rector, they were chased from the bog by a hostile crowd. Later, one of the six was assaulted and left for dead by his assailants.[15]

The anti-tithe campaign was already well-established by the summer of 1831 and hardly needed martyrs to augment its vehemence. But it acquired them anyway, at the hands of the largely Protestant and much reviled yeomanry militia force at Newtownbarry, Co. Wexford, on 18 June. While one is often sceptical of the use of the term 'massacre' in the context of Irish civilian history – the killing of more than one person was often so described – the events of Newtownbarry certainly merit that title. The local Anglican rector, the Rev. Alexander McClintock, was a dedicated 'New Reformation' evangelical. Resentment at his particular brand of religiosity the resultant refusal to pay tithes, allied to the failure of the local tenantry to support the anointed candidate of their landlord, Lord Farnham, in the general election of 1832, prompted McClintock to seize the cattle of a number of defaulting farmers. His aggressive pursuit of his tithes was met by passive resistance to distraint, followed by a concerted effort to thwart him by ensuring that there were no bids for the seized livestock at the subsequent auction.

When a number of the beasts enterprisingly managed to escape from their handlers at the time of the abortive sale, their owners attempted to identify and repossess their animals. A detachment of yeomanry, a militia force that had earned the antipathy of the Catholic population for its crude and callous exertions during the rising of 1798, was sent to recover the wandering cattle and was subjected to a fusillade of missiles from their rescuers. The yeomanry responded with a hail of bullets and killed up to eighteen of their antagonists. It was the final curtain for the yeomanry in a policing capacity, and the force was disbanded shortly thereafter.

The Farnham dynasty (the Maxwells) swung into action in the House of Commons and the House of Lords in defence of the killings. Henry Maxwell, the Cavan MP (much of the Farnham land was in that county), justified the actions of the yeomanry by claiming that they had come under fire first and that their response was one of self-defence.[16] Lord Farnham – an arch proselytiser of the 'New Reformation' – went on the offensive in the House of Lords, blaming the affray, and the deaths, on the opposition of Dr James Doyle to the payment of tithes.

A week after the pre-emptive intervention of Henry Maxwell MP came the more considered response of the newly elected Wexford MP, Henry Lambert. He deprecated the use of the yeomanry and took issue with Maxwell's rush to exonerate the force:

> The shouting of a few boys, the alleged apprehension of the rescue of some cattle distrained for tithe, perhaps a few stones thrown, were the pretence for commencing a murderous fire on the people, which was continued in every direction; and it appears that the Yeomanry officers themselves found considerable difficulty in putting a stop, after several discharges of musketry, to this atrocious and indiscriminate massacre.[17]

Events like those at Newtownbarry, and the later killing of twelve unarmed civilians at Rathcormac in Co. Cork, on 18 December 1834, helped to transform what had begun as a negotiation (with individual Church of Ireland ministers for tithe reductions) into an insurrection, the central objective being the outright abolition of the tax. The slaughter of Newtownbarry, however, had done nothing to prepare an Irish public, inured to the deaths of civilians at the hands of the police or military, for the carnage at Carrickshock described earlier in the chapter.

The background to that slaughter was the refusal of the Rev. Hans Hamilton of the Knocktopher union of parishes to agree to a reduction in the tithe. This led to a widespread refusal on the part of farmers in that region of Kilkenny to pay the levy. Hamilton responded by obtaining decrees against the defaulters from the court of exchequer and, through his tithe agent, engaged the services of an unpopular local man, Edmund Butler, to serve the legal documents. Butler's first two days of work as a process-server passed off without incident. It was when he resumed his mission on 14 December, accompanied by a detachment of policemen, that all hell broke loose.

In his novel *The Tithe Proctor*, William Carleton reflected, briefly, on the 'Battle of Carrickshock'. Butler was characterised by Carleton as arrogant, abusive and given to displays of anti-Catholic profanity. As a result, when he 'was within their grasp … they were determined, to a man, "to have the process-server or blood"'.[18] In her memoir, Charlotte Elizabeth Tonna wrote of the impact of the massacre on her friend, the Rev. Hans Hamilton, and his family: 'as soon as possible Dr and Mrs Hamilton, disguised and in a common cart, made their escape to Kilkenny, taking shelter with Lord Ormonde, whence they came to England, forever exiled from their beloved and lovely home'.[19]

Naturally, the response from the Tory and unionist press and politicians to the slaughter of a dozen members of the constabulary was apoplectic. An investigation by Dublin Castle claimed that the assault was premeditated: 'We think there are grounds for believing that the catastrophe of this day was brought about by previous design and effected by dextrous contrivance.'[20] News of the atrocity had not yet reached Westminster by the following day (15 December), when there were, ironically, palliative motions introduced by the chief secretary, Edward Stanley – later three-time prime minister the Earl of Derby – in the Commons and another future prime minister, Lord Melbourne, in the Lords, establishing a select committee 'to inquire whether it may not be possible to … remove the present causes of complaint'.[21]

The accounting for Carrickshock was swift but almost entirely ineffectual. In 1832, Kilkenny was placed under martial law. Eighteen local individuals were charged and brought before the courts for involvement in the carnage, but none was convicted.

Unionists locally blamed the intimidation of jurors for this outcome, and possibly with some justification. But there were other factors that contributed to the failure of the state to 'avenge' the Carrickshock deaths. One of the eleven men sent for trial to the Kilkenny assizes for murder was successfully defended by Daniel O'Connell himself. The Dublin lawyer, Patrick Costello, one of the architects of the policy of passive resistance to distraint, was attorney for a number of the other prisoners. The man believed to have had a leading role in the instigation of the assault on the police, William Keane (or Kane) – a local hedge schoolmaster and 1798 veteran who had apparently advocated that the Rev. Hans Hamilton 'ought to be torn limb from limb' – was never captured and may well have fled to North America. This was despite the offer of a £100 reward for information leading to his capture.[22] Keane had allegedly enticed Captain Gibbons, along with Butler's police escort, into the laneway where so many of them met their end.

The Carrickshock massacre, while largely forgotten today, was clearly embedded in local Kilkenny folk memory. There are dozens of references to the affray in the National Folklore collection. These include verses of a number of triumphalist and often gory songs written in the immediate aftermath of the tragedy, in which there is precious little sympathy for the members of the constabulary force who lost their lives. While hardly admirable, these sentiments are at least understandable in the context of the times.

One of the blood-curdling, gloating ballads was written by Ned Drea from nearby Hugginstown. Drea's nickname was 'Ned of the Hills', which, while it might have been a nod towards his affection for serene highland landscapes, also suggests, as does the tone of his verse, an affiliation with agrarian crime.

The Chapel bells they were kept sounding;
The people heaving in great numbers flocked.
O'er gripes and ditches with speed all bounding
To meet the peelers at Carrickshock.
'Twas then commenced an awful slaughter

For sixteen minutes there [was] nothing but fun.
With their pikes and scythes they gave them no quarter,
But stood the brunt without fife or drums.[23]

Whether it was brought about by the 'fun' at Carrickshock or by the assumption that the end of the tithe regime was nigh, within weeks, courtesy of the inevitable subversive capillary action, the agitation had spread beyond its source. Rapidly, in the case of the rest of Leinster and Munster, then more slowly to Connacht and parts of Ulster. In January 1832, the first Protestant clerical fatality was recorded when the Rev. Irwine Whitty of Golden, Co. Tipperary was murdered close to his home. He was bludgeoned to death for the 'crime' of having brought almost a thousand writs against local defaulters. In October 1832, a second clergyman, the fervently evangelical Rev. George Houston of Feighcullen, Co. Kildare, was murdered. He had been instrumental in the establishment of a Protestant 'colony' in the area and his fundamentalist zeal had led to the local landlord, Sir Gerald Aylmer, evicting Catholic tenants to make way for Houston's new parishioners. Before his assassination, Houston required twenty-four-hour police protection, had his railings decorated with dead rats and, in a dress rehearsal for the boycott of the Land War, was abandoned by all his servants. Matters were even worse from a fiscal perspective. Houston's heavily policed attempts at distraint, and the cost of his permanent armed guard, proved prohibitively expensive and achieved nothing more than the hastening of his death.[24] A few weeks later, in December 1832, the Rev. Charles Ferguson, rector of Timoleague, Co. Cork, was murdered following his attempts in November to collect the tithes to which he was entitled.

The massacre at Carrickshock and the deaths of Ferguson, Whitty and Houston persuaded many Protestant clergyman (such as the clearly intimidated Hans Hamilton of Knocktopher) that it was time to remove themselves and their families from the line of fire. Some fled to the cities; others, like Hamilton, abandoned the country altogether.

The investigation of the Parliamentary Committee of Enquiry into Tithes, established by the government of Earl Grey the day after Carrickshock, ultimately led to the 1832 attempt to legislate away the problem with the so-called Stanley Composition Act. This somewhat sickly remedial effort was named for the Irish chief secretary who, the previous year, had been responsible for one of the most far-reaching pieces of restorative legislation in the tortured history of the Union of Ireland and Great Britain. This was the 1831 Education Act, establishing the Irish primary school system.

Stanley's attempt to legislate the Tithe War out of existence was less enduring. The 1832 composition did introduce some changes designed to redress the grievances of the anti-tithe campaigners. There was a small reduction in levies; composition was to be externally mandated, not privately agreed; and only leaseholders were to pay tithes, not 'tenants at will'. But there was also a decent helping of red meat on the menu from the hawkish Stanley for the supporters of the clergy of the Established Church. There would be no more tolerance of default. The government was firmly on the side of its beleaguered clergymen. The military and police (though not the out-of-favour yeomanry) would be deployed to make sure that everyone paid up on time and with no further argument. A sum of £60,000 was advanced by the government to cover arrears owed to Church of Ireland clergy. The administration of Earl Grey then sought to suppress the anti-tithe movement, and repay itself its own loan, by the collection of arrears through the use of military and constabulary force. With entirely predictable results.

Those given to passive resistance proceeded, where possible, to resist passively. The anarchic moonlighters accentuated the mayhem. Government policy, however, made the former course of action more problematic, the latter more plausible. Passive resistance almost wilted in the face of this stern official resolve.

By the middle of 1833, the country was in uproar – a state of 'suppressed insurrection', according to the *Dublin Evening Post*[5] – with the inheritors of the Whiteboy and Rockite traditions temporarily in the ascendant. With little or no relaxation in the demands of the obdurate tithe-owners, and given the determination of the government to meet resistance with as much force as was deemed necessary, a volatile situation became incendiary – arson also being a favoured tactic of the Whiteboy/Ribbon element. Vandalising Protestant churches ran it a close second.

Meanwhile, with the Whig government implementing Tory-style coercion policies, Daniel O'Connell's 'Repeal project' became the main constitutional political beneficiary, without the necessity for any energetic involvement on his part in the anti-tithe campaign. After the 1832 general election, a cohort of thirty-nine Repeal MPs – including the future Chartist icon Feargus O'Connor and Patrick Lalor of Queen's County – many of whom had been blooded in anti-tithe agitation, replaced sitting Whig MPs in Irish seats.

In an example of what would become standard British government agrarian policy in the nineteenth century – coercion, followed by conciliation, followed by coercion, followed by ... you probably get the idea – in August 1833, the administration attempted to defuse the situation by putting a wedge between the anti-tithe trigger and the clerical flintlock. This took the form of a sop, the Church Temporalities Act, that abolished the payment of church cess, another ecclesiastical tax occasionally levied for the erection or refurbishment of Protestant church buildings. More important, however, was a much more generous allocation of funds to cover the tithe arrears of 1831–3, a sum far in excess of that apportioned by Stanley the previous year. It became known as the 'Church Million Act' because it covered arrears of just over that figure and provided enough funds to enable Protestant clergymen to hold off on latitats, writs, summonses and other hostile actions until at least November 1834. However, the move failed to take into account the ideological purists among the Irish Protestant clergy. Their recalcitrance and resistance to compromise had not been diminished by physical threats. Furthermore, generous as the settlement appeared to be, it covered only about half of the arrears due to Protestant clergymen.

Long before 'Newtownbarry 2.0', when a dozen protestors were killed at Rathcormac, Co. Cork, in December 1834, after a clash with British army infantry and cavalry units – O'Connell commented that the atrocity 'did in point of law amount to murder'[26] – the objectives of the anti-tithe movement, insofar as it was ever a co-ordinated campaign, had changed irrevocably from reformation to abolition. The presence of a Church of Ireland minister, Archdeacon Ryder, a local magistrate, at the Rathcormac affray, doing his distraining in person, was much commented upon in Britain at the time and did little for the tithe cause there. After the killing of three men in April 1834 near Newcastle West, Co. Limerick, in a failed attempt to recover distrained cattle, the *Freeman's Journal*, well on its way to becoming the definitive nineteenth-century voice of Irish constitutional nationalism, sounded the death knell of the tithe: 'There is only one way of tranquilising the country in this respect, and that way is by an honest and utter abolition of tithes – no half-measures will do.'[27]

The newly appointed under-secretary, Thomas Drummond – perhaps the most far-sighted Dublin Castle administrator under the Union – a former employee of the Ordnance Survey with a better than average familiarity with rural Ireland, was responsible for at least one step that reduced tensions. In keeping with his famous dictum that 'property has its duties as well as its rights'; in October 1835, he issued a memorandum to magistrates that ended the provocative and often self-fulfilling practice of ritually protecting operations to recover tithes with a police or a military escort. The thrust of the memo was reinforced by the refusal by Dublin Castle of a number of such requests for assistance after 1835. Irreconcilable clergymen who were dissatisfied with the terms of the Church Million Act might seek to prolong the crisis, but, thenceforth, they would do so without military or constabulary help.

The conflict sporadically blazed back into life from the mid-1830s until the solution implied in the Church Million Act was finally delivered in 1838 with a Tithe Rentcharge (Ireland) Act that ended the conflict. Under the terms of the legislation, tithes were converted to a rental charge of 75 per cent of the prevailing rate in each parish (later reduced to 68 per cent). Responsibility for payment no longer devolved on farmers but was instead transferred from tenant to landlord. The landowner then passed on this additional cost to his tenants. Thus were tithes 'abolished' in what, in reality, amounted to a discounting operation that removed the 'stain' but charged handsomely for the cleaning service. In other words, 'tithe had not been abolished, but it was made invisible'.[28] Both sides had retreated from their stated or implied objectives, and the genius of the 1838 legislation (a victory over the legislative equivalent of repetitive strain injury) was that it allowed them to do so. Whereas the hated tithes were no longer a symbolic and financial affront to Catholic farmers, the clergy of the Established Church still enjoyed the benefits, albeit indirectly, of tenant subvention. In addition, they no longer had to collect their salaries at bayonet point from a seething peasantry. Some landlords, Catholic or Protestant, might well seethe at the imposition, or at the apparent inviolability of Church of Ireland clerical privilege – which still had three decades to run – but they were generally amenable either to logic or, failing that, to the courts.

One permanent casualty of the conflict, however, was any semblance of a cordial relationship between a Catholic peasantry and the clergy of the Church of Ireland. Trust had evaporated on both sides. W. R. Le Fanu put it succinctly and baldly in his 1894 memoir *Seventy Years of Irish Life*: 'In 1831 came the tithe war, and with it our friendly relations with the priests and people ceased.' When the war ended, he observed, 'the old cordial relations with the peasantry never could be quite restored'.[29]

From the point of view of most Church of Ireland clergymen – already embittered by the success of the Catholic Association in 1829, and still recovering from the threat of the Pastorini menace of the mid-1820s – the anti-tithe campaign did more than simply endanger their annual income. It was far more existential a threat than that, striking at an innate sense of entitlement and gesturing towards the slippery slope to a future Roman Catholic Ascendancy. Many feared a return to a 1798 Wexford-style sectarian rebellion and were angry and disillusioned at what they saw as the government's inability or unwillingness to protect them, opting instead for 'inept military repression mixed with erratic concession'.[30]

Samuel Hussey, agent to Lord Kenmare, in his memoir, *The Reminiscences of an Irish Land Agent*, recounted a second-hand anecdote involving the Church of Ireland prelate of the Cork diocese, Archbishop Magee. As a young clergyman, Magee had attended a tithe debate in the House of Commons. As he was leaving, he was assisted in donning his coat by a polite member of the growing radical wing of the Whig party. Magee could not resist a gibe. 'I am very much obliged to you, sir,' he informed the Radical MP acidly, 'for reversing the policy of your friends inside, who are taking the coats off our backs.'[31]

For the tenants, having managed, however unsatisfactorily, finally to jettison the hated tithe, it was an opportunity to sit back and reflect on the struggle just past. Some of the lessons of the fight for emancipation had been learned. Political pressure, civil disobedience and passive resistance might not have entirely superseded agrarian violence, but adopting a constitutional approach had played an important role in the outcome of the Tithe War. Furthermore, although there had been an element of centralised and elite guidance (Doyle was inspirational, Costello seminal and O'Connell not entirely divorced from proceedings), the crusade against tithes had been more of a series of separate and distinct local campaigns.

'If winter comes, can spring be far behind' is the optimistic final line of Shelley's 'Ode to the West Wind'. But, taken out of context, the line can also have sinister connotations. How does it relate to the end of the Tithe War? Because that divisive conflict was 'mere prologue'. As Thomas Bartlett points out in his *Ireland, a History*, the Tithe War was simply a prelude 'to an assault on rent, that other "Protestant tax"'.[32] It did not escape the attention of some observers that the cessation of tithe hostilities left the peasant army at something of a loose end. Their focus might easily return to some of the other unresolved matters that had been at the heart of Whiteboy activities since the 1760s, and they might be tempted to repeat some, or all, of the methods that had brought the Tithe War to stalemate and a psychologically favourable conclusion.

W. R. Le Fanu noted in *Seventy Years of Irish Life* that 'the landlords looked on with indifference, and showed little sympathy with the clergy in their difficulties. My brother used to say: "Never mind, their time will come; rents will be attacked, as tithes are now, with the same machinery, and with like success.'[33]

In 1837, Charlotte Elizabeth Tonna paid a visit to her former Irish home, no doubt astonished that in her absence, thus far at least, the Apocalypse had been deferred. However, she was dismayed at what she found: 'Popery rampant, insolent, overbearing, and evidently calculating on soon possessing the land in undisturbed security: Protestantism depressed, discouraged, menaced, and barely enjoying an uncertain toleration, on the one hand from government, on the other from the mass of the Romish populace.'[34]

Tonna concluded that things could only get worse. From her perspective, that is precisely what happened.

8

Topographica Hibernica #2: *mapping and valuing – the Ordnance Survey and Griffith's Valuation*

'Oh give us if you please, Griffith's Valuation,
That's the word to say, down with Compensation,
That's the rent to pay – Griffith's Valuation.'[1]

(anonymous verse from the 1880s)

WHAT DO IRISH language etymologists John O'Donovan and Eugene O'Curry, folk music collector George Petrie, and Irish under-secretaries Thomas Larcom and Thomas Drummond have in common? They were all, at one time or another, employed by the Ordnance Survey of Ireland.

That such a set of supremely talented individuals, with such a variety of skills, worked together for the same organisation hints at an agreeably subversive cultural influence on cartography that had little to do with the primary function of their employer. The Ordnance Survey involved, after all, the ostensibly soulless (and potentially dangerous) work of mapping the fields, forests, hills, lakes, rivers, mountains, ruins and bogs, as well as the towns and cities of Ireland on a scale of six inches to the mile. While the Ordnance Survey of Ireland (OSI) performed its principal task with undoubted skill and precision, a small number of cultural polymaths among its ranks also managed to tag on a number of valuable supplementary functions that, on the face of it, had scant connection to their job description. A form of poetry – or at least a few hearty ballads – was created out of what could have been mere cartographic prose. The extraordinary collateral influence of the early nineteenth-century OSI is reminiscent of the equally characterless period of motorway building in Celtic Tiger Ireland, where the obligation to employ archaeologists to go over the ground in advance of construction work turned up a number of antiquities that might otherwise have remained undiscovered.

The OSI was established as the Rockite rebellion was beginning to peter out and the Catholic emancipation campaign was finding its voice. It started its work in 1824 as a Board of Ordnance/ Ministry of Defence project. Although the result was a series of maps of considerable intrinsic beauty, the purpose of the enterprise was far more bureaucratic. It was to be a detailed study, along the lines of the work done in the Down Survey, the provocative canvass that had yet to be entirely supplanted even by the 1820s. Using the latest available mapping techniques (the engineers then devised some more of their own), Irish land valuations were to be revised for taxation purposes. An 1824 House of Commons select committee, under the chairmanship of the Irish MP and Limerick landlord Thomas Spring Rice, had found the existing valuation and taxation system to be 'inaccurate, inequitable and corrupt'. The government was advised to proceed with a new survey to overcome 'the obscurity and wants of uniformity of the general system, as well as the inequality incidental to the mode of apportioning these local taxes'.[2] Unlike the Down Survey, however, and a smaller-scale Williamite effort in the 1690s, this project would, avowedly at least, not be adjunct to conquest and colonisation and would, according to Spring Rice, be a 'great national work', a collaborative effort with 'important scientific, practical and political results'.[3]

The representation of the survey as a constructive civil society project was, however, not enhanced by the fact that the engineers carrying out the work were, initially at least, all British Army officers, mostly recruited from the Royal Engineers and the Royal Artillery. This was partly at the insistence of the Lord Lieutenant, Marquess Wellesley, elder brother of the Duke of Wellington – the victor of Waterloo being Master General of the Ordnance at the time. Most of the work was heavily militarised, and civilian input 'served merely as the muscles for the military skeleton'.[4] Only the engraving of maps was entrusted to Irish civilians. Even the grunt work was carried out by three companies of British Army sappers and miners.

The man placed in charge of the operation was the director of the Ordnance Survey in 1824, Colonel Thomas Colby of the Royal Engineers. His task was to map more than 60,000 Irish townlands, as well as 331 baronies* and 32 counties incorporating numerous villages, towns and a small number of municipalities. The decision to create such detailed maps made Ireland the first country in the world, when the project had been completed in 1846, to have its total area mapped on a six-inch scale (1:10,000). The success of the project, apparent before it was completed, led to demands in 1839 from 'scientific and public bodies and by country noblemen and gentlemen'[5] for a similar British 'six-inch' survey. By the time the Famine-beleaguered Assistant Secretary to the Treasury, Sir Charles Edward Trevelyan, testified to a House of Commons select committee in 1846, the decision had been taken to emulate the Irish survey in the rest of the United Kingdom, because, according to the normally bloody-minded and parsimonious Trevelyan, 'it would not be proper to give the inhabitants of one part of the kingdom any advantage which is not possessed, as far as possible, by those of others'.[6] Trevelyan (see Chapter 9) was nothing if not gratingly consistent.

One of Colby's first decisions was to divest himself of the function of valuing the land his cartographers were mapping, a potential minefield in a still turbulent colony. This led to the appointment of Richard Griffith, a geologist, to the position of Commissioner of Valuation and the more delicate task of establishing a base figure on individual farms from which taxes, such as the local cess tax, could be calculated. The mapping of the country by the Ordnance Survey began in 1825 and Griffith's work followed on from 1830 until his retirement in 1868.

---

* Most baronies are named after the largest town included within their boundaries (e.g. Mohill, Co. Leitrim, Athenry, Co. Galway). Others, however, have more exotic origins. Iraghticonnor in Co. Kerry, for example, which means 'Inheritance of the O'Connors', and Magonhy in the same county, which is based on an Irish name meaning 'the plain of the wolf warrior'.

While it is true that the survey, from the outset, 'standardized and anglicized the representation of the Irish landscape',[7] thanks to the perspicacity and tenacity of Colby and the particular genius of one of his passionate English subalterns, Thomas Larcom, the OSI became much more than a mere technical exercise in cartography. In an inspired example of mission creep, Colby, open to originating 'collateral objects',[8] instructed each of his engineers to pay heed to antiquities and local folklore. Adherence to his guidelines often depended on the level of cultural and historical enthusiasm displayed by individual engineers for a process that became known as 'memoir' work.

This latter aspect of the project was boosted in 1828 by the appointment of the twenty-seven-year-old Captain Thomas Larcom as a local director of the survey in Ireland. Larcom, an idealist who fervently believed that 'minor prejudices obstruct the improvement of Ireland, and they can only be removed by diffusion of real knowledge',[9] wanted to go beyond even Colby's template. He drew up a pamphlet entitled *Heads of Inquiry*. Engineers were now expected, in addition to recording landscape and natural features, to document 'ancient and modern historical monuments, towns, public buildings, landed estates, industries, mills, infrastructure and communications'.[10]

Not all of Larcom's engineers were best pleased with such a variety of tasks, many of which fell well outside their comfort zones. One ingrate complained about being despatched 'on a scampering duty to collect names and legends from old women'. In time, and with Larcom's bureaucratic talent for squeezing fiscal blood from administrative stones, funding was made available for civilian assistants to supplement or to take over the work of the engineers in documenting the social, cultural and historical traditions of the areas being mapped.

One of the most perplexing questions faced by the survey – lyrically delineated in Brian Friel's 1980 masterpiece *Translations*[*] – was the issue of place-names. Over centuries of invasion

---

[*] Friel also addresses the military nature of the survey in the play, although this was somewhat less of an issue by 1833, when *Translations* is set.

and conquest (Viking, Norman, Elizabethan, Cromwellian, Williamite), nomenclature had changed frequently. However, this did not mean that 'Old Irish' names had altogether disappeared. Quite the contrary: many were still in use in the 1820s and more lurked hidden in the regional subconscious and were used locally and demotically, even if absent from official documents. Colby wanted to devise a system, in his own words, 'to establish a standard orthography, and for future reference, to identify the several localities with the names by which they had formerly been called'.[11] Decisions on the naming of localities would not, however, fall entirely on the shoulders of the Ordnance Survey engineers themselves, or be unduly influenced by regional grandees. They would also include contributions from local experts or interested parties.

The employment of Gaelic scholars in this process was invaluable. This was, for example, how the orthographer and etymologist John O'Donovan came to work for the survey. Larcom, on his arrival in Dublin, had recruited O'Donovan to teach him Irish. Their pedagogical relationship did not last beyond a few enjoyable breakfast meetings, but Larcom remembered his former tutor when the Irish language lexicographer Edward O'Reilly, the first scholar taken on to address the knotty problem of multiple place-names, died suddenly in April 1830. O'Donovan, much of whose work was initially archive-based, was also allowed to hire his own assistants, and one of the first to be taken on was the antiquarian and music collector George Petrie. In time, both men, and a very small battalion of assistants (including O'Donovan's brother-in-law, the eminent Gaelic academic Eugene O'Curry), would travel the countryside identifying and solving etymological conundrums. Their mission was to realise the goal of Larcom, that 'the different spellings and alias names of every townland [should be] collected from all accessible documents ... to render the name ultimately adopted as nearly as possible consistent with the ancient orthography'.[12] It was not always plain sailing, with O'Donovan sometimes spoiled for choice and occasionally swamped by a superfluity of the 'wee names of stones and splits and holes'[13] collected by his underlings.

It was from this sociological and cultural research that a distinct but related (and short-lived) project emerged. Colby managed to secure funding for Larcom to publish a series of localised memoir books covering the material, over and above the merely cartographical, which had been assembled by his scholars. These memoirs* (the name was derived from the French *aides-mémoires*, as in 'report') embraced 'Natural Features and History; Modern and Ancient Topography; Social and Productive Economy'.[14] The first volume in the series, *Memoir of the city and northwestern liberties of Londonderry, parish of Templemore*, was published in 1837 and quickly sold out its 1,500 copies.

The testimony and anecdote contained in the memoirs was often highly detailed, personalised and idiosyncratic, such as the information that in the parish of Glynn in Co. Antrim, 'John English, 20 years of age, was killed accidentally by the garden wall falling on him' or that in Derry, a local farmer, 'Jacob Johnstone, and a few others have the front of their houses ornamented with a little flower garden', while another tenant would not allow land near a suspected fairy fort to be disturbed.[15]

As it transpired, *Memoir of the city and northwestern liberties of Londonderry, parish of Templemore*, coming in at 350 pages and chronically over-budget at a cost of £1,700[16] – production values were rigorous in the extreme – was the only volume to be published contemporaneously. The prospect of future expenditure on such a scale, on dozens of similar volumes, saw the funding withdrawn in 1840. Collation of material for future editions of the memoir series was largely abandoned before any substantial areas outside of Ulster could be included.† A valued friend and associate of Larcom, the Earl of Dunraven, pointed out to Larcom that the memoir programme might have survived past its debut had the expensively produced first volume dealt with a locality somewhat

---

* The original manuscripts are preserved in fifty boxes in the library of the Royal Irish Academy on Dawson Street in Dublin.
† Parts of counties Cork, Galway, Laois, Leitrim, Longford, Mayo, Meath, Monaghan, Roscommon, Sligo and Tipperary have some documentary coverage.

larger than a mere parish. At a going rate of £1,500 per volume, and with more than 2,000 parishes in the country, the total cost would have come in at over £3 million – ten times the original budget assigned to the entire survey and almost four times the actual cost of mapping the country (see below) over two decades. A volume covering an entire county, for example, might not have had the bean counters quaking in their boots at the potential cost of the rest of the series. The project died a death, despite having a 'friend at court' in Thomas Drummond, former Ordnance Survey engineer and 'lead mathematician' from 1826, who had been promoted to the position of Irish under-secretary in 1835. His death in 1840 was a blow to Larcom and – given Drummond's administrative skills, his sense of justice and his impartiality while in the post – to the country as a whole.

The response of local communities to the arrival of the survey engineers and sappers in their district was a mixture of curiosity at what exactly the redcoats were about – in one locale they were assumed to be scouting advantageous artillery positions – and delight at the prospect of temporary employment. Rates of pay, however, were not excessively generous at six to ten pence a day for ordinary labourers or for the 'chainmen' responsible for taking measurements. By the late 1830s, the numerical dominance of military personnel had evaporated. The OSI had more than 500 civilian employees when its work was completed in the mid-1840s. They outnumbered military staff by a ratio of 4:1.

One of those civilians, James Blewitt of Ballina, Co. Mayo, despite apparently having only a basic 'hedge school' education, saw fit to report an error in one of the logarithms being used by the survey's mathematicians. His calculations, upon examination, were found to be correct. After the survey came to an official end in 1846, motivated, no doubt, by the spectre of famine, Blewitt emigrated to the United States. In January 2021, his descendant, one Joseph Biden, became the 46th president of the USA.[17]

No doubt there was also an element of resentment on the part of some at the presence of a sizeable military unit in their locality. Famously, this later found fictional expression in the unseen but menacing Donnelly twins in *Translations*. However, in order to distance his sappers and engineers as much as possible from any 'stain' or suspicion of being an appendage of law enforcement, Colby insisted that they work in the field unarmed. Neither were they permitted to come to the assistance of local magistrates in need of military muscle.

One of the civilian employees of the survey was a Westmeath man named John Keegan. Taken on in 1836 as a field draughtsman at 1s 2d a day (he was earning 2s 10d a day by October 1839), Keegan, an intelligent and highly opinionated individual, kept a diary of his time with the survey. In this journal, he bellyached about his remuneration and the accommodation provided by his military employers. Lodgings could be in a local barracks, a public house or under canvas in a military camp. Keegan's diary also offers telling insights into the tensions of pre-Famine rural Ireland. He recorded, as an example of the potential hazards of the job, being mistaken for a bailiff. His disdain for landlords and middlemen (he called the latter 'land sharks') was almost matched by his contempt for some of the peasant husbandry he witnessed, where 'a slovenly system of tillage and neglect of proper crop rotation served only to exhaust and impoverish the land'.[18] In 1842, Keegan visited the estate, near Youghal, where the ill-fated Sir Walter Raleigh was said to have planted the first potatoes in Ireland in the sixteenth century (he probably didn't). Keegan made the following ominous note in his diary at the time: 'It is doubtful whether the potatoes were a blessing or a curse. In one respect they were an evil, for the landlords get high rents and the whole produce of the land, except part of the potatoes on which the people are content to starve.'[19]

It would be easy to dismiss the OSI as nothing more than an assertion of colonial domination or an arrogant exercise in imperial one-upmanship. The profusion of British military personnel in the project certainly lends credence to such an argument. The centrality of accurate maps for military dominance of a vassal state cannot be denied either. However, it is worth remembering that two of the army officers with pivotal roles in the survey,

Drummond and Larcom, would go on to become the most capable and fair-minded Irish under-secretaries of the nineteenth century. Furthermore, Larcom's 'memoir' project, though sadly short-lived, was of no cartographic, military or technocratic use whatsoever to a colonial administration. In a satisfying example of bureaucratic sleight of hand, the government was required to foot the bill for what was essentially an exercise in gathering and preserving local culture and folklore.

Most readers will be familiar with the highly entertaining clip from the film *Monty Python's Life of Brian* in which representatives of various sparring factions of Judean anti-imperialism (Popular Front, People's Front *et al.*) argue about 'what have the Romans ever done for us?' before concluding that their oppressors have actually done quite a lot (acqueducts, sanitation, public baths), while remaining in agreement on the only item that unites them, i.e. the desire to see the back of said Romans. Were the Pythons to have plagiarised themselves and scripted a film entitled, for argument's sake, *1916 and All That*, a similar scene involving Irish revolutionaries would certainly have included the country's Ordnance Survey maps in the merit column of British legacy items.

While the basis of the survey, from a British perspective, was hardly altruistic, and while mistakes were made in the translation of place-names from Irish to English,[20] considerable benefits did accrue to the mapped. At the very least, the maps themselves, despite their sternly scientific, mathematical and topographical origin and purpose, are objects of significant aesthetic value. Also, as Larcom observed to the 1846 Commons Select Committee on the Ordnance Survey, their existence was of profound importance in the tabulation of the results of the 1841 census, the last pre-Famine headcount in Ireland:

> Owing to the information obtained from the use of the Ordnance Survey we were able for the first time to enumerate the people within exact boundaries, and to so far extend the operation of the census, that instead of being a mere enumeration of people, it became in fact a social survey.[21]

From beginning to end, from 1825 to 1846, from the Inishowen peninsula to Dursey Island, from Skerries to Clifden, the mapping of natural features and antiquities, the recording of ancient place-names and the production of maps reflecting Irish geography, history and topography, as well as 'memoirs' revealing decades of Irish culture and lore, the OSI cost a total of £860,000, or just over €100 million today. Granted, that was considerably in excess of the £300,000 Colby had originally flagged. Arguably, its militarised character reinforced the British colonial mission in Ireland; it may have made the country slightly easier for an imperial administration to govern. In his account of post-Famine rural adjustment, *The End of Outrage*, Breandán Mac Suibhne refers to it ruefully as 'a decisive step towards conquering the opacity of the Irish countryside'.[22] But, when one studies an Irish Ordnance survey map today – an object of great beauty as well as considerable utility, still genetically linked to the original calculations, measurements and illustrations made in the nineteenth century – it is hard to resist the conclusion that this was one of those rare projects, whether born of altruism or not, that had a multitude of positive unintended consequences, has redounded to the long-term benefit of the colonised and has left us an extraordinary legacy.

'Not slothful in business, fervent in spirit, serving the Lord':* Griffith's Valuation, 1830–68

As already noted, the first item of which Colonel Thomas Colby divested himself when he accepted responsibility in 1824 for the mapping and the valuation of Ireland's thirty-two counties and 21 million acres was the latter, more problematic, element of his brief. Colby passed his valuation portion to Richard Griffith, a forty-three-year-old Dublin-born geologist, in 1827. Griffith had joined the Boundary Department of the Ordnance Survey in

---

* This is the wording of the epitaph on Griffith's grave in Mount Jerome Cemetery in Dublin.

1825 and became Commissioner for Valuation shortly after Colby decided to stick to cartography.[23] He had a brief military career (a year as an officer in the Royal Irish Regiment of Artillery) as well as considerable experience in the assessment and valuation of land. In the early 1800s, for example, Griffith had worked in Scotland, where he learned to value land by assessing the composition of its soils. In 1809, he was asked to conduct an examination into the nature and extent of Irish bogs and the potential to 'improve' them (i.e. to turn them into productive land through reclamation). Three years later, he became a Professor of Geology at the Royal Dublin Society (RDS) and embarked on the task of creating a geological map for Ireland. After his appointment as Commissioner of Valuation, Griffith resigned from the RDS, but he did eventually manage, with considerable assistance, to compile his geological map, which was published in various editions between 1839 and 1855.[24]

By the end of the 1820s, he was more than ready to begin the task that would consume him until he finally retired, in 1868, in his mid-eighties (he died, as *Sir* Richard Griffith, two days after his ninety-fourth birthday). This began with the Townland Valuation of Ireland, commissioned in 1826, which commenced operations in 1830.[25] It was Griffith's work, rather than that of Colby, Drummond and Larcom, that became indelibly associated with one of the least popular prerequisites of any functioning modern society: taxation. However, while Griffith's team of assessors assigned values to land and housing in urban and rural Ireland, it was the local and national administrations which then decided how much revenue to extract on the basis of the calculation of what would be forever known as 'Griffith's Valuation'.

It is important to note at the outset that Griffith and his inspectors – drilled by Griffith himself in detailed and specific instructions on methodology and on the maintenance of consistency and uniformity[26] – were calculating an intrinsic, rather than a market, valuation for the land being assessed. However, the valuers were not permitted to remove themselves entirely from considerations of commerce. In addition to undertaking an examination of soil and subsoil, they were also obliged, under the terms of the Townland Valuation Act, to take cognizance of a scale of agricultural prices also laid down in the legislation and to adjust their valuation accordingly. In their assessments, good tillage or grazing land would be evaluated at a much higher rate than, for example, an adjacent property of similar size that might contain unimproved bogland or be situated on mountainous terrain. Neither was Griffith indicating through his assessments and valuations the scale of the rents that tenants should be paying to their landlords. Many chose to believe otherwise, however, and some mischievously so.

The work of Griffith's Ordnance Survey Boundary department had a treadmill quality about it. Once the entire country had been assessed, it was almost time to start all over again. Appraisals arrived at by the employees of the department listed the name of the occupier of every property, the lessor (landlord), the acreage held, the types of buildings included on the property and the total valuation. Each entry was then cross-referenced in the first series of the Ordnance Survey maps. This cornucopia of statistical information was ultimately published in more than 200 packed volumes with over a million entries arranged townland by townland, barony by barony, county by county. There is no more comprehensive or valuable source for nineteenth-century Irish social and economic history than this enormous collection.

There were three surveys conducted during Griffith's lengthy tenure. The Townland Valuation of Ireland, which began in 1830, was not an unmitigated success. Griffith's insistence on assigning an overall valuation to each of Ireland's 60,000 townlands, rather than to individual holdings, rendered it impractical for use in the assessment of Poor Law liabilities. For this reason, it was criticised in an 1844 report by a House of Commons select committee, which recommended 'that there ought to be only one valuation for all purposes of local taxation in Ireland. That such valuation should distinguish the value of each tenement separately.'[27]

Arising out of the deliberations of that 1844 select committee, the Tenement Valuation of 1846 followed, undertaken to reconcile values assigned by Griffith with a separate survey carried out by a number of Poor Law Boards of Guardians. This was then merged with what was essentially a third project, a survey prompted by the passage of the General Valuation Act in 1852, and continuing for a dozen years, that sought to reassess values in the wake of the devastating Famine. The result is that the critical period of Griffith's survey is generally deemed to have been from 1847 to 1864.

Griffith's hope was to recalibrate every fourteen years thereafter, but this expectation foundered on the rock of administrative parsimony. Ironically, the government's reluctance to spend any significant sums on later assessments meant that much of the post-Famine economic recovery was missed, costing local government potential revenue and detracting from landlord arguments that rents, far from being excessive, were not keeping pace with agricultural prices and tenant profits. It was intensely galling for landlords to have the Land League demand in the early 1880s that rents be based on the Griffith's Valuation, some of which were thirty years old by then. In 1880, the Irish Land Committee, one of the landowner collectives of the 1880s, cleaved staunchly to the line taken by the House of Commons select committee of 1844. This held that 'Mr. Griffith's valuation was not founded upon an estimate of the probable letting value'. In one of a number of polemical pamphlets published during the Land War, the Land Committee demanded querulously 'how then can anyone assert, or pretend to believe, that the Tenement Valuation was intended to be, or ought to be, a basis for rent'.[28]

Once the members of Griffith's team had assessed the value of land (or property in urban settings), this was then used to calculate tax liabilities. So, for example, if a farm was assigned a valuation of £8 with a Poor Law rate per year of around a shilling in the pound, the Poor Law liability on the land would be eight shillings per annum. Half of this sum was owed by the landlord.* In the case of the county cess tax, used to fund local infrastructure, the rate was generally closer to 2 shillings in the pound (meaning a tax payment of just under 16 shillings per annum) with, in this instance, the entire liability accruing to the tenant. Given the

---

* In the case of a valuation below £4, the landlord was obliged to pay the entire Poor Law rate.

impact on tenant farmers (although Griffith's Valuation created a system that was more equitable than heretofore), it is little wonder that Colonel Thomas Colby wanted his redcoats to have nothing to do with the process.

Working for Griffith appears to have been a more remunerative experience than being an employee of Colby. Since Griffith's department 'was both civilian in purpose and operation', wage rates were generally higher. The indefatigable diarist John Keegan noted with some envy that 'Mr Griffith treats the men on the Boundary Department differently; the men have from 5s to 10s per day and do not work a quarter of the time we do'.[29]

Historians of the nineteenth century tend to encounter Griffith's Valuation in the context of levels of rent. The assessments, willy-nilly, became a yardstick by which rents were measured. On the tenant side, from mid-century, there were perennial demands, passionate but unrealistic, that rents should amount to an annual sum no greater than the Griffith's Valuation of a farm. Discussion of what was or was not a fair rent tended to revolve around how far the annual rent deviated from (as in exceeded) the valuation for taxation purposes which Griffith had assigned. For example, in *Landlords and Tenants in Ireland*, the *Times* journalist Finlay Dun frequently referred to rents being charged by landlords and the difference between those payments and Griffith's Valuation. Dun asserted that in his experience typical rents tended in the 1880s to be set at 10–20 per cent above the valuation. His book was written before the Land Courts, established under Gladstone's Land Act of 1881, began to arbitrate rents and offer reductions averaging around 15 to 20 per cent.[30] That outcome was greeted with consternation by most landlords, some – the ones who were clearly charging excessive rents – because consternation was expected of them. Others, however, were more benevolent landlords, like Baron Clanmorris in Mayo, who already had a rent roll well below Griffith. In the case of tenants on his Foxford property, for example, rent was more than 30 per cent below the Boundary Department valuation.[31]

In 1880, at the height of the Land War, with the Land League demanding that rent should coincide with the valuation, Griffith's daughter, Elizabeth Branston Smith, wrote to *The Times* in an attempt to bury once and for all the notion that her father (who had died two years previously) had any sympathy with such a concept. His assessment, she wrote, 'was only relative to a valuation of property to regulate the taxation of Ireland, and not for the purpose of fixing a letting value, and he always said that he had valued the land from 24 to 30 per cent under its letting value'.[32]

The letter, to which little enough attention was paid, was overtaken by history the following year. The Land Commission, through its peripatetic arbitrative Land Courts, brought rents into much closer alignment with Griffith's Valuation than was the case hitherto. Tenants and the Land League took the view that the courts had simply finished the work Griffith had begun, by finally offering a realistic assessment of the rental value of land.

On the landlord side, there were few takers for that line of argument. Levels of rent, the suppliers of land contended, were either at the discretion of a benign landlord or were dictated by the market on the estates of rack-renting landlords. The term 'rack-rent' itself, which, colloquially, came loaded with pejorative connotations, actually referred to the application of an economic

*Sir Richard Griffith (*Illustrated London News*)*

rent dictated by demand for an available property. The reality was, as will be seen in Chapter 11, that rack-renting was relatively uncommon; was, almost axiomatically, a function of tenant farmers eager to secure a property at any cost (a phenomenon that should be all too familiar in twenty-first-century urban Ireland); and the role of the landlord was merely, and not unreasonably, to accept as his tenant the highest bidder on the available property.* The Irish Land Committee, in its first pamphlet, published in 1880 and intended to stamp out any suggestion of a Griffith/rent relativity, gleefully cited examples in Limerick, Cork and Clare of tenants who were content to bid up rents to more than *twice* Griffith's Valuation. That veritable haymaker was then followed up with a neat right hook in which the oracle himself, Sir Richard Griffith, was quoted as advising, as a rule of thumb, that 'if one-third be added [to valuations] the result will give nearly the full rent value of the land *under ordinary proprietors*'[33] (my italics). No comment, however, was appended by the pamphleteer to Griffith's subtle suggestion that not all Irish landowners were 'ordinary proprietors' from whom a degree of moderation might be expected.

As with all such enterprises, the Boundary Department appraisal included a number of anomalies – inevitable in such an ambitious project. *Thom's Irish Almanac* highlighted an inconsistency where: 'The valuation of some of the Southern and Western counties was made during and immediately subsequent to the famine of 1847–8, when agriculture was greatly neglected, the prices of agricultural produce were very low … the result being that in those counties the valuation is considerably too low, unequal, and less than that of lands of similar quality in the province of Ulster, which were more recently valued.'[34]

Two decades later, in 1869, giving evidence before a House of Commons select committee, J. Townsend Trench, who had effectively succeeded his father, William Steuart Trench, as agent to the Marquess of Lansdowne in Kerry, complained that Griffith's

---

* An understanding of the technical meaning of the term, of course, should not obscure the realities of exploitation, 'canting' and arbitrary eviction that were also frequently associated with rack-renting.

Valuation rates were by then severely out of kilter with rents and needed to be revised. He claimed that 'the letting value of the mountainous parts of Kerry is very often from 30 to 50 per cent above Griffith',[35] i.e. the Boundary Department Valuation needed to be revised upwards. Finlay Dun – no warrior champion of the oppressed tenant – pointed out in 1881 that in some upland areas assessments had been too high. This was because, he contended, inspections were carried out in high summer when 'grass, and indeed all crops looked their best'.[36]

Griffith himself can come across as the archetypal absent-minded professor, or certainly an occasionally insensitive man with scant regard for diplomacy. While his grasp of detail was more than sufficient to permit him to see off attacks on his personal and professional character before an 1869 Commons select committee, for example,[37] he is seen to less positive effect on one of his regular business trips to London. While walking down Bond Street in conversation with the distinguished British geologist Adam Sedgwick, Griffith appeared to be so distracted that Sedgwick broke off from a lengthy discourse and upbraided his companion for his inattention. Rather than making an apology and requesting that Sedgwick resume what appears to have amounted to a passionate dissertation, Griffith astonished the eminent geologist by acknowledging that he had not been listening to a word the other was saying, but instead was using their walk as an opportunity to examine nearby shop windows in the hope of buying a hat for his wife. At this point, the deeply offended Sedgwick turned on his heel and left Griffith to the milliners. When the Irish geologist found what he thought he was looking for, he requested a female shop assistant to try on the hat so that he could confirm the wisdom of his choice. He complimented the assistant by telling her that she looked well in the hat and immediately neutralised the encomium by informing her that, of course, his wife would look three times better when *she* wore it. The hat was, we are told, parcelled up without any further conversation on either side.[38]

On the level of public service, Griffith, a scientist possessed of the finest intellect, ranks alongside Drummond and Larcom as a principled, fair-minded Irish administrator with the welfare of the wider community at heart. He championed the reclamation of land as a route out of poverty for the immiserated of rural Ireland. He was also an advocate for the provision of better housing for Irish labourers through a state-sponsored loan scheme. His personal efforts to ameliorate famine conditions fell foul of the libertarianism and providentialism of the Whig government, in power from 1846. In spite of the assertion of his daughter in her letter to *The Times* in 1880 – which was technically true but lacked nuance – Griffith did have hopes that his enterprise would ultimately affect rents and lead to a 'live and let live' accommodation between tenant and landlord.[39] He would, doubtless, have been surprised that his work, implicitly at least, provided the basis for land purchase valuations in the huge transfer of the 'fee simple' of Ireland from 1885 to the 1930s with the creation of a 'peasant proprietary'. He would have been astonished that his 1852 valuations were still in use until 1980 and might have remained so had a group of Wexford farmers not successfully challenged their validity as the basis for tax assessments.[40]

As a historian of the nineteenth century, because of the gold that can be mined from the pages of Griffith's 202 volumes of information on pre-, early- and mid-Victorian Ireland in the *General Valuation of Rateable Property in Ireland*, it is easy to get carried away with admiration for the man and his remarkable taxonomical enterprise. Griffith's Valuation is the gift that giveth in perpetuity, unlike the nineteenth-century census records, which, for various reasons (not all associated with the shelling of the Four Courts in 1922), no longer survive. One can only imagine how pleased the man himself would be that the indispensable statistical information he and his associates assembled so painstakingly – and not without encountering varying degrees of hostility – is today available at the click of a mouse to anyone who wishes to consult it.

III

Activism

9

Emptying the land: the Famine clearances

'The Irish famine of 1846 killed more than 1,000,000 people,
but it killed poor devils only.'[1]

(Karl Marx, *Das Kapital*, 1867)

'Should this root ever become in any part of Europe, like rice
in some rice countries, the common and favourite vegetable
food of the people ... Population would increase, and rents
would rise much beyond what they are at present.'[2]

(Adam Smith on the financial and economic attractions
of the potato, *An Inquiry into the Nature and Causes of the
Wealth of Nations*, 1776)

'See how starvation meets us in the face
But relief is expected from each foreign place
Come sell all your cattle and don't keep a tail
Before that you part with your corn or your meal
Then next try the landlord and see what they'll do
For they know the potatoes are rotten all through
Tell them for your rent that you'll give them good bail
Before that you'll part with your corn or your meal.'

('A New Song on the Rotten Potatoes', 1847)[3]

Strokestown, 2 November 1847

That the musket balls ever found their target in the gathering twilight was the work of either Lady Luck or a gunman with good night vision and the eye of an accomplished sniper. The shot came from 'a ditch or gripe'⁴ near Doorty Bridge, outside the village of Strokestown in Co. Roscommon. Behind the ditch lurked two assassins. Immediately after the first report, the victim, sitting in the driving seat of the carriage, staggered backwards into the arms of the man who should have been holding the reins. Martin Flanagan could see immediately that his master was beyond help. Dr Shanley, also sitting up front, who was now clutching his arm as if he too had been hit, would be of no assistance. Major Denis Mahon was dead.

But the threat was far from over. Another armed man was emerging from cover and the horses had been spooked by the first shot. Shanley, realising the danger despite the searing pain from the ball in his arm, managed to grab the reins and slow down the agitated horses. That, at least, reduced the chances of the two survivors of the attack ending up with their necks broken under an overturned carriage. But it did nothing to eliminate the peril from the second assassin, who was intent on ensuring that there were no witnesses to the crime.

Flanagan watched helplessly as the shadowy figure raised his pistol and pulled the trigger. There was a spark but no explosion. Just a welcome click and a 'flash in the pan'. The gun had misfired. With an indistinct but unmistakable curse, the man lowered his weapon and turned on his heels. He gathered his comrade as he went and both men fled into the thickening gloom before Shanley or Flanagan could identify either of them.

In the forlorn hope that there might still be some life left in the major, the two men urged on the horses for four miles until they reached Strokestown. But their frenzied dash merely brought forward the post-mortem examination performed by Dr Shanley's son, taking the place of his shaken father.

Major Denis Mahon of Strokestown House had been brutally slain. As bonfires were lit by many of his tenants to celebrate the demise of their tormentor, it was time to round up the usual suspects.

'their pig and a manure heap constitute their only property'[5]

'The Almighty, indeed, sent the potato blight, but the English created the Famine.'[6]

(John Mitchel, *The Last Conquest of Ireland (Perhaps)*, 1861)

'The judgement of God sent the calamity to teach the Irish a lesson, that calamity must not be too much mitigated. The real evil with which we have to contend is not the physical evil of the Famine, but the moral evil of the selfish, perverse and turbulent character of the people.'

(Charles Trevelyan, Assistant Secretary to the Treasury, to Lord Monteagle (Thomas Spring Rice), 9 October 1846)

It has always been the longest and most traumatic chapter in the annals of Irish history. Only the depredations of the universally loathed (in Ireland at least) Oliver Cromwell come close to the distressful narratives of *An Gorta Mór*, the Great Famine. It is an oft-told tale of uncaring landlords, a heartless British government, starvation, destitution, disease, coffin ships, cannibalism,[7] the workhouse, building roads that led nowhere, altruism, cynicism, self-sacrifice, at least one landlord who 'got what was coming to him' and a devastated population too crushed to exact revenge on their overlords or do anything other than accept their calamitous fate with an extraordinary degree of lassitude and indifference.

The Irish people shall never forget the Great Famine. Neither shall we allow anyone else to do so. We demand an apology. But then, when we get one (from British Prime Minister Tony Blair in 1997) it is criticised for being 'too little, too late', insincere, rushed[8] and woefully inadequate. The Great Famine is the decisive Irish coup in a historic point-scoring exercise with our nearest neighbour. After all, there is simply no comeback from responsibility for the deaths of almost a million Irish men, women and children. Moral victory is ours every time.

And there is no doubt that *An Gorta Mór* was far from Britain's finest hour. But neither were the domestic atrocities of the Highland clearances, the Peterloo Massacre or the class genocide of the Great War. Nor were imperial adventures like the rape of the Indian subcontinent – the word 'loot' comes from the Hindi word *lut* meaning 'the spoils of war' – the 1876–8 Great Famine of India (5–10 million dead), the Bengal Famine of 1943 (2–4 million dead) or the rapid administrative evacuation of the newly sundered states of India and Pakistan in 1947 (2 million dead and 14 million refugees).

Was Britain directly culpable for almost a million Irish deaths? Did Britain's failures in Ireland from 1845 to 1849 constitute genocide, before the word itself became a neologism towards the end of World War II? The consensus among academic and popular historians is a (qualified) 'No'! The Great Famine was 'something too monstrous and too impersonal to be the mere product of individual ill-will or the fiendish outcome of a well-planned conspiracy', according to the late Professor Kevin B. Nowlan in his 1994 foreword to one of the earliest dispassionate assessments of the period, *The Great Famine* (1956), edited by University College Dublin (UCD) historians R. Dudley Edwards and T. Desmond Williams. Although, Nowlan added pointedly, 'the excessive tenderness of the administration where private property rights were involved may strike us as unreal'.[9]

Britain was not guilty of deliberate mass murder, though writers from John Mitchel (*The Last Conquest of Ireland (Perhaps)*, 1861) to Tim Pat Coogan (*The Famine Plot*, 2012) would beg to differ. But even so-called 'revisionist' historians – used here in dubious contradistinction to that equally evanescent term 'nationalist' historian – do not afford the Whig administration of Sir John Russell a *nolle prosequi* when it comes to the disappearance of almost 2 million Irish people, lost to starvation, disease and emigration between the censuses of 1841 and 1851. Most, while dismissing claims of culpable genocide, still highlight perverse failures, heartless disregard for human suffering and appalling negligence.

The partial failure of the potato crop in 1845 was hardly an exceptional occurrence in Ireland. The report accompanying the 1851 census recorded twenty-four instances of acute crop failure dating back to the second decade of the eighteenth century. None, however – with the possible exception of that of 1740–41, recorded in a previous chapter – was quite as catastrophic as the consistent failures of the potato crop between 1845 and 1848. During those years, the quantity of potatoes produced in Ireland declined from a figure of close to 15 million tons per annum to barely a fifth of that amount (3,077,000) in 1848. In 1847 – 'Black '47', when, ironically, blight largely spared the crop – the yield had been even more dispiriting, with barely 2 million tons of the staple diet of more than 3 million long-suffering members of the Irish population issuing from the country's diseased fields. Some of that precipitous decline was due to a newfound lack of faith in the durability and reliability of the crop, as well as a paucity of seed potatoes. Most, however, was owing to the devastating effect of *Phytophthora infestans*, or potato blight, over the two previous disastrous growing seasons.

While the population of Ireland declined by 19.85 per cent between the taking of the 1841 and 1851 censuses, the inhabitants of the country still accounted for almost 24 per cent of the United Kingdom total.* It was what happened in subsequent years that was distinctive and destructive. That Irish percentage of the UK population fell to 20 per cent in 1861, to 17 per cent in 1871 and by 1881 the Irish numbers had collapsed to 14.8 per cent of the total population of the United Kingdom.[10] As Joseph Lee has pointed out in *The Modernisation of Irish Society, 1848–1918*, 'What was peculiar, therefore, was not the Famine, but the long-term

---

* It is worth noting that at the time of the Act of Union in 1800, Ireland contributed around 33 per cent of the total population of what was about to become the United Kingdom of Great Britain and Ireland. Irish population numbers doubled by 1841 and still comprised 30.7 per cent of the total UK population (8.2 million of 26.7 million) in the census of that year.

response of Irish society to this short-term calamity.'[11] Lee identifies six main factors that contributed to Irish post-Famine demographics (changing rural class structures, the rising age of marriage, declining marriage rates, declining birth rates, static death rates, emigration). The first of these will be explored in more detail in this chapter.

The impact of the crisis has been more than adequately narrated in a number of excellent volumes since the publication in 1956 of the rigorously academic *The Great Famine* under the editorial supervision of Williams and Edwards, and of the influential popular and bestselling history *The Great Hunger: Ireland 1845–1849* by the Welsh-born writer Cecil Woodham-Smith in 1962. The latter was an indictment of British policy in Ireland during *An Gorta Mór*, where the villain was the British civil servant Charles Edward Trevelyan, assistant secretary to the Treasury, the Whitehall bureaucrat with responsibility for alleviating the calamity. While he largely blamed Irish landlords for the disaster, Trevelyan also saw the Famine as an 'effective mechanism for reducing surplus population'. Woodham-Smith's *The Great Hunger* was a 'torrent of muddled thinking', according to the erstwhile 'big beast' of Irish academic historians, F. S. L. Lyons, in *Irish Historical Studies*. Contrariwise, 'all Ireland was a Belsen', according to another Leviathan, the English historian A. J. P. Taylor, in his *New Statesman* review of Woodham Smith's work.[12]*

Subsequent accounts have veered between broad support for Woodham-Smith's thesis and the so-called 'revisionist'† approach, in which some of the received wisdom of generations (e.g. that the continued export of Irish grain during the Famine years led to the deaths of hundreds of thousands) has been challenged by analysis of the available data. The latter approach is exemplified by the

---

* In their 1963 final examinations, history students in University College, Dublin were confronted with the essay topic '*The Great Hunger* is a great novel', which perhaps marks the moment when the so-called revisionist school of Irish history fired on Fort Sumter.

† A description deprecated by this author on the basis that all academic history should be revisionist; otherwise, it is simply a superfluous reiteration of the work of other historians.

work of Professor Mary Daly in *The Famine in Ireland* (Dundalk, 1986), or what economic historian Cormac Ó Gráda characterises as 'the dispassionate sanitised approach to the Great Famine now dominant in Irish scholarship'.[13]

Of more consequence to this volume are the implications for land use and land tenure of the Great Famine period, which we can define as having lasted from the summer of 1845, up to the census of 1851, by which time the worst of the damage had been done and the ever-diligent Victorian statisticians had assembled enough data to lay bare the extent of the devastation.

The background to the catastrophe is explained in economic historian Raymond Crotty's seminal volume *Irish Agricultural Production, its Volume and Structure*, published in 1966. Crotty outlined the changes in Irish agricultural practice during a long boom period from 1760 to 1815 and the subsequent difficulties of adaptation to the slow decline in food prices that began after the Battle of Waterloo and continued until the end of the Great Famine. Decades of eighteenth-century price increases had led to a movement towards tillage, whereas the post-war recession caused a reversion to pasture. This was because growing crops became 'more unprofitable than grass farming'. The economic imperative thereafter was for the consolidation of farms in order to facilitate the work of the graziers. This, in turn, led to the elimination of much conacre, as labourers were surplus to requirements and their one-acre potato patches were required for cattle to graze over. 'As the tenure system conduced to the population explosion of the late eighteenth century, it now worked powerfully towards an implosion in the nineteenth century,' wrote Crotty. The iron laws of economic determinism, however, clashed with Irish demographic realities. Demography, in the medium term at least, won out over the 'dismal science'. What happened was that 'the biological momentum set up by the population explosion of the years before Waterloo' ensured that population numbers continued to rise, from 6.8 million in 1821 to 8.2 million in 1841. It was *Phytophthora infestans* and the consequent subsistence crisis that enabled the ragged transition from tillage to pasture, a shift that would have ramifications for decades to come.[14]

The headline figures from the decade following the first outbreak of blight in 1845 are stark. The more egregious of two prevailing narratives is that of widespread estate clearances. From 1849 to 1854, Irish landlords evicted at least a quarter of a million people[15] – this figure does not include those who were forced to give up holdings 'voluntarily' (one of a number of famine paradoxes) for the dubious sanctuary of the local workhouse. This was as a consequence of a controversial amendment that was introduced by the Irish Tory landlord Sir William Gregory MP as an annex to proposed palliative legislation in 1847 (covered later). Neither does it include those whose emigration was financially subvented by landlords who found it cheaper to pay for passage to the United States or Canada rather than have their tenants remain in the workhouses and continue as a permanent charge on their Poor Law rates.

Of lesser importance, but also of long-term significance, was the impact of the crisis on the owners of Ireland's land in the early Victorian era. Many had surrendered their estates long before the 'Famine Queen' (a frequent, if provably unjust, soubriquet applied to the English monarch) celebrated her silver jubilee in 1862. Almost 15 per cent of Irish land changed hands in the years after the Great Famine as dozens of bankrupt landlords bolted, or were dragged, towards the exits.

That most unwelcome American import, *Phytophthora infestans*, afflicted most of the continent of Europe. However, the only comparable subsistence crisis to that of the Irish Great Famine was experienced in the Highlands of Scotland. The cataclysmic outcome of the onset of blight in Ireland was based upon the absolute dependence of around one third of the Irish population on the potato for sustenance. Average daily intake of potatoes in Ireland was over two kilos per person. In contrast, in France the average daily intake was 165 grams, in the Netherlands around 800 grams and in Belgium 640 grams.[16] As a general rule in Ireland in 1845, the higher one's socio-economic status, the lower one's consumption of potatoes.

Weather conditions in the 'hungry months' of 1845 in Ireland – when the previous year's crop had been exhausted and the current crop was still in the ground – were even wetter than normal, encouraging the spread of the deadly fungus that had arrived unheralded from the Americas. Within months of the first appearance of blight in the late summer of that year, the constabulary was reporting losses of up to a third of the crop nationally. In early December, the *Freeman's Journal* reported that 'one-half of the potato crop has been already lost as human food'.[17] It was of little or no value as animal feed either. Given that up to one-sixth of the annual output had to be retained as seed for the next growing season, this was even more catastrophic an outcome than it at first appears. The Tory administration of Sir Robert Peel reacted quickly to the emerging crisis. Despite the ongoing debate on the retention of the Corn Laws – restrictive tariffs on imported grain, mostly from the USA – Peel, who had a wealth of experience of Irish famines from his own time as Irish chief secretary, used Barings Bank to quietly purchase £100,000 of Indian corn meal in the United States as early as November 1845. The secrecy was dictated by anticipated opposition from self-interested traders, and from the British Tory establishment, opponents of the movement to repeal the Corn Laws and reduce food prices. Using cheap imported grain to alleviate famine in Ireland was the thin end of the wedge for British landed interests who opposed any concessions to the growing clamour for a 'cheap food' regime from mercantile and entrepreneurial interests.

Because of these official relief measures, the work of private charities and the forbearance of *Phytophthora infestans* in only destroying around half of the annual potato crop that year, a major famine was averted in 1845. However, in 1846, the assumption that the spread of blight had merely been a function of excess precipitation resulted in the planting of an equivalent acreage of potatoes to that of 1845. However, the country was to learn to its cost that blight was a recurring phenomenon, aided by summer rainfall, but not beholden to it. It duly recurred and with much greater intensity. The crop failed again, resulting in an average return of around half a ton per acre, less than 10 per cent of the normal output. In no county in Ireland did the average yield exceed one ton per acre. In a letter to the Treasury on 7 August 1846, Fr

Theobald Mathew, the leader of the Temperance movement in Ireland, described what he witnessed on a journey from Munster:

> On the 27th of last month I passed from Cork to Dublin, and this doomed plant bloomed in all the luxuriance of an abundant harvest. Returning on the 3rd I beheld with sorrow one wide waste of putrefying vegetation. In many places the wretched people were seated on the fences of their decaying gardens, wringing their hands and wailing bitterly at the destruction that had left them foodless … the food of a whole nation has perished.[18]

So 1846 marked the true beginning of the Great Famine, the last, and the worst, major subsistence crisis in Ireland.*

Then, in the summer of 1846, there was a further deterioration unrelated to precipitation or the proliferation of blight. The Whigs, under Lord John Russell – himself an owner of Irish land, although hardly an Irish landowner – replaced the slightly more enlightened (from an Irish perspective) administration of Sir Robert Peel in July 1846. This was in the wake of the epochal parliamentary vote to repeal the Corn Laws which sundered the Tory party. The timing of the change of administration was not propitious. As the editor of *The Nation* newspaper, Charles Gavan Duffy, noted forty years later, 'no man has ever appeared at the head of a great party less fit to be entrusted with duties which appealed to the imagination and the heart'.[19]

Sir Charles Wood became Chancellor of the Exchequer in the new Whig administration and the Treasury Under-Secretary, the senior civil servant Charles Edward Trevelyan, was given direct responsibility for dealing with the subsistence crisis in Ireland. They, along with Russell, are the English names most associated with the Famine and with 'the dismantling of Peel's relief measures'.[20] A century after his death, Trevelyan, a

---

* Although, as we have seen, if more accurate and detailed statistical information was available, the 1740–41 famine may well have resulted in a similar or greater level of excess deaths.

Charles Edward Trevelyan

pietistic providentialist, achieved unexpected immortality when he was referenced in the alternative Irish national anthem, 'The Fields of Athenry', composed by Pete St John. This austere Treasury official's apotheosis came in the line, 'for you stole Trevelyan's corn'. St John, a man with a profound knowledge of Irish history, was probably aware that the grain in question was more likely to have been 'Peel's corn', but that phrase clearly didn't scan. The truth of the matter, highlighted by Cecil Woodham-Smith in her monumental *The Great Hunger*, is that there was little 'Trevelyan's corn' (or succour of any other kind) in evidence during the Famine.

Woodham-Smith's dissection of Trevelyan may have been unjust – he was, after all, merely a 'well-meaning but officious civil-servant with Whig sympathies'[21] – and has certainly resulted in Trevelyan acquiring a villainous status in Ireland not far adrift of Oliver Cromwell. However, even a cursory study of some of his pietistic, fundamentalist and determinist writings on the subject of the Famine leave little room for any sustained sympathy for the man. One of the first sentences that stands out in his own self-serving 1848 account of a famine that was still raging at the time, *The Irish Crisis*, comes on the second page when he rolls his eyes, throws his hands in the air and inquires plaintively, 'What hope is there for a nation which lives on potatoes?'[22] While his argument was rational, informed by the structural deficiencies of an economy that was so reliant on a single crop for the physical survival of a third of its population, his timing (he was writing at the height of the crisis) and his tone – 'self-righteous moralising',[23] according to Mary Daly – indicated a distinct lack of sympathy.

Later, Trevelyan restated his aversion to the chronically dependent Irish peasantry by referring to them as a population 'now sunk in indolence and barbarism'. He also put the primary purpose of the 1838 Poor Law, at least as he saw it, into perspective. In his view, the legislation that had introduced the workhouse to Ireland had the benefit of being as inconvenient for the dissolute landed gentry as it was immiserating for the indolent and barbarous peasantry, in that the annual levying of rates and the application of the 'workhouse test' would achieve its ends when 'the landowners and farmers either enable the people to support themselves by honest industry, or dispose of their property to those who can and will perform this indispensable duty'. Although a trenchant champion of property rights, like many English technocrats and politicians, Trevelyan had about as much regard for the more improvident members of the Irish gentry as he had for *spalpeens* and cottiers. Some sense of his priorities can be gauged from his assertion that the 'master evil of the agricultural system of Ireland … is the law of entail'.* Not rack-renting, not rampant subdivision, not under-investment, not the exploitation of small farmers by middlemen, not the annual auctioning of vital conacre land, not the threat of arbitrary eviction, but the

---

* Whereby the owner of an estate is entitled, for the duration of his or her life, to the income produced by the land, but is not permitted to sell or mortgage the estate.

inability of a landowner to cash in his estate because it must be passed on to subsequent generations, and whose situation 'is often pitiable' as a consequence. Here was Trevelyan's panacea. Change the guard ever so slightly and the halcyon days would return. An infusion of fresh Anglo-Saxon blood (and capital) was all that was required. The potential purchaser of an encumbered estate, at least according to the exceptionally trusting Assistant Secretary of the Treasury, 'may safely be assumed to be an improver'. A few years later, his faith would be dented by the outcome of the 1849 legislation (the Encumbered Estates Act) that finally dispensed with his perceived 'master evil' and transferred almost 15 per cent of the land of Ireland to improvers and carpetbaggers alike.

At one point in his lengthy apologia, which first appeared in the *Edinburgh Review* in January 1848, Trevelyan even inverted Thomas Drummond's famously humane maxim and asserted: 'Property has its rights as well as its duties.' At the end of his mercilessly utilitarian analysis, the profoundly evangelical Trevelyan proclaimed that – invoking the Deity as he was wont to do – 'so far as the maladies of Ireland are traceable to political causes, nearly every practicable remedy has been applied. The deep and inveterate root of social evil remained, and this has been laid bare by a direct stroke of an all-wise and all-merciful Providence.'

Trevelyan also offered a memorable account of the supposedly relaxed and privileged life – thanks to their love affair with the potato – of the Irish peasant: 'A fortnight for planting, a week or ten days for digging, and another fortnight for turf-cutting, suffice for his subsistence; and during the rest of the year, he is at leisure to follow his own inclinations.'[24] Given the forty-seven weeks of the year in which the average cottier could enjoy what Trevelyan called the 'evils of leisure', it should come as a surprise that the best European fiction of the mid-nineteenth century was emanating from the Russian aristocracy and not from Irish peasants with so much spare time on their hands.

The Russell administration, unlike that of Peel, in dealing with the Great Famine, became transfixed by its own *laissez-faire* philosophy.* This held that the market would quickly reassert itself and modify the catastrophic consequences of *Phytophthora infestans* without any significant government intervention. The Whigs also took the entirely wrong-headed view that there was more than sufficient indigenous wealth in Ireland to cope with the crisis and that 'Irish property must pay for Irish poverty'. This orthodoxy, which flew in the face of statistical reality and willfully ignored the existence of a United Kingdom of Great Britain and Ireland, was, however, predicated on a (not entirely unreasonable) Whig loathing and suspicion of Irish Tory 'property'. Irish landlords, in the Whig analysis, were sybaritic, slovenly, uninterested in progressive agriculture and ill-equipped to deal with the structural issues that caused recurring Irish subsistence crises. The Whig approach to the ongoing famine conditions was also based on the familiar principle that in every crisis there is opportunity. However understandable the motivation of the Russell administration was in its desire to end perennial Irish subsistence emergencies, the time to consult the manual on the building of a brick house is not when your wooden-framed structure is already burning around you.

A system of public works, initiated by Peel's administration and designed to provide the destitute with some means of support, was continued for a time by the Whigs. At its height, the public works programme employed one in twelve members of the Irish population. However, under the terms of the 1846 Labour Rate Act, the cost was to fall 'entirely on persons possessed of property in the distressed districts'. Wage rates had to be below those obtaining for farm labour in order not to draw workers away from necessary agricultural work. Rates of pay were, typically, less than a shilling a day, and as little as four pence a day in some parts of the country. Since farm labour rates were at or near to subsistence level, almost by definition public works rates were perilously close to dipping below a subsistence wage. John Mitchel, in his *The Last Conquest of Ireland (Perhaps)*, in which he accused the British

---

* However, as Peel was largely supportive of Whig policies during the Famine, he is hardly deserving of a free pass.

government of a conspiracy to depopulate Ireland, referred to these relief schemes as 'contrivances for slaughter ... more fatal, by far, than batteries of grape-shot, chain-shot, shells and rockets'.[25] Furthermore, public works remuneration during the Whig administration was based on piece work (i.e. payment by results). Under the Tories, a daily rate had been paid irrespective of productivity. The Whig imperative to reduce the risk of indolence had a devastating impact on the earnings of the old, infirm and sick who depended on public works but were not as productive as younger, stronger males. Land agent Samuel Hussey, in his memoir, recalled the construction of dozens of 'ghost' roads during the brief period when 'outdoor relief', i.e. public works, was the favoured option of an addled administration: 'when employment could be given, the people were too emaciated and feeble to work. All over Ireland unfinished roads leading half way to places of no consequence are to-day grass-grown memorials of that ghastly effort of State assistance.'[26]

The operation of the system of public works, despite its many flaws, constituted a bureaucratic success for the Whigs. In October 1846, 100,000 'paupers' had been engaged in public works. Less than six months later, in March 1847, those numbers had swollen to 700,000. Interestingly, 20,000 people were employed on public works in one of the rural blackspots, Co. Clare, while only 1,200 people were similarly employed in the entire province of Ulster, testifying to the huge regional imbalances in the impact of the Famine.

But that was as good as it got. Amidst complaints from wealthier farmers that they were finding it difficult to source labour, and because of orthodox liberal economic fears of 'crowding out' farm work and thus interfering with the 'market', the public works were shut down. In March 1847, the Destitute Poor (Ireland) Act introduced the next phase of the Whig rescue operation: soup kitchens. By July of that year, 3 million people were being fed daily in a network of soup kitchens established with considerable bureaucratic rapidity and efficiency. While it was cheaper for the government to provide direct food aid in this fashion than to retain the more expensive public works, and while the soup kitchens (as long as they lasted) kept people alive, they were unpopular with many because of the indignity involved in accepting charity so directly.

However, that became a problem no longer when, in September 1847, the initiative ended and the soup kitchens were closed down. There had been no recurrence of blight in the potato harvest of that year and therefore, the government concluded, there was no need to maintain the programme of direct food aid. This reasoning, however, glossed over the inconvenient statistic that only 280,000 acres of potatoes had been planted in the spring of 1847, barely a tenth of the 2.5 million acres planted each year before 1845. Potatoes were going to fetch a high price and would be in short supply. Nonetheless, the Whigs, in effect, declared 'mission accomplished ... crisis over' and abandoned the crucial palliative measure of the soup kitchens to private charities and religious organisations like the Society of Friends, one of whose members, the future Liberal chief secretary, William E. Forster, was already distinguishing himself in his altruistic efforts.

It was also during this period, after the cessation of governmental involvement in the direct nourishment of a starving population, that accusations of coercive charity, or 'souperism', began to emerge. These have pervaded Irish folklore, with the imagery of charity, in the form of soup, being extended with one hand by Protestant evangelicals, and bibles with the other. This led to long-standing bitterness and suspicion, to the application of hurtful nicknames to the families of those who were deemed to have succumbed – such as 'Batt the Souper' and 'John the Souper'[27] – and to desperation and subsequent regret. One story is told, for example, in Kerry, 'of a poor old man named Langan who lived in the village of Duagh. He was driven to become "a souper" but before he left he visited the Catholic church in Duagh and standing before Our Lady's statue with tears in his eyes he said, "Goodbye, Holy Mary, till the praties grow again."'[28] As with most folklore and received wisdom, the actual truth or otherwise of such allegations of coercive proselytism are largely irrelevant when rumours begin to circulate and the mythology of souperism becomes entrenched.

Other reasons for the ending of government-sponsored soup kitchens were a financial crisis in Britain itself, which caused a run on the Bank of England and a tightening of credit; a bad harvest, which brought subsistence threats to parts of Britain itself; and the Whig *pièce de résistance* in its efforts to address the structural issues that bedevilled Irish governance, the 1847 Irish Poor Law Extension Act.

This legislation, now that the blight appeared to have passed and taken the subsistence crisis with it, would – or so the theory went – permit the Irish Poor Law to do its work and allow the workhouses of the country's 130 Poor Law Unions (maintained by local rates) to deal with the indigent and destitute Irish. 'Irish property', however reluctantly, would pick up the tab for 'Irish poverty' from that point onwards, much to the relief of zealous guardians of the British Exchequer like Sir Charles Wood and Charles Edward Trevelyan. However, this optimistic assumption was laced with the vinegar of an insidious amendment introduced by an Irish Tory Member of Parliament for Dublin, Sir William Gregory, future husband of the yet-to-be-conceived Augusta Gregory, partner of W. B. Yeats in the Abbey Theatre (Sir William was thirty-five years her senior; she was his second wife). Gregory's amendment, whatever its intentions, was a cynical piece of aristocratic social engineering which facilitated the estate clearances that were becoming a feature of the landlord response to the Famine.

The so-called Gregory Clause, inserted by the landlord of the Coole Park estate in Co. Galway,* ensured that anyone applying for admission to a workhouse under the terms of the 1847 act was not eligible for such 'relief' if they farmed more than a quarter of an acre of land, a measure that 'probably only worked to intensify an already-strong tendency towards eviction on the part of Irish landlords faced with crippling rates burdens and a mass of destitute tenants who were heavily in arrears'.[29] It was opposed by only two Irish Members of Parliament, an illustration of how ineffective O'Connell's supporters could be (he himself died in 1847) in fighting for Famine-era remedial measures.

* Inherited from his father in 1847.

For thousands of families, Gregory's amendment presented two stark options. They could either retain their minuscule holding and risk starvation, or they could give up their tiny plot of land in order to access the grim local workhouse with no prospect of ever emerging from that institution and re-entering the economy with a plot of land to maintain them. The provision was relaxed in 1848 to allow the wives and children of smallholders to continue to be admitted to workhouses, but there was to be no relief for farmers determined to retain their land. Although he had a potentially superior claim to fame in that he may have been the model for the fictional Irish politician Phineas Finn in Anthony Trollope's Palliser novels (he and Trollope had been schoolmates), it is for his amendment to the Irish Poor Law Extension Act that Gregory is less than fondly remembered. The 'Gregory Clause' was, in effect, a clearance charter. According to economic historian Cormac Ó Gráda, it was 'directly responsible for thousands of deaths. While some landlords and farmers connived with their tenants at obtaining relief without surrendering possession, more had no compunction about using the Gregory clause as a mechanism for clearing their estates.'[30] Figures for evictions before 1849 are problematic, but between 1839 and 1843, just under 24,000 ejectments were carried out from the 769,000 Irish farms of more than one acre, an average of fewer than 5,000 evictions per annum. Figures climbed between 1845 and 1847 to around 13,000, but then shot up, post-'Gregory clause', between 1848 and 1851, when almost 60,000 families were ejected, an average of 15,000 a year, more than three times the pre-Famine rate.[31]

Not that admission to your neighbourhood workhouse was an inviting prospect. They were designed to be off-putting and unattractive, and that was just the architecture. The prevailing ethos guaranteed that only sheer desperation would prompt an application for admission. Families were immediately separated on entering these grim institutions; inmates were expected to work; the food was barely sufficient to sustain life; and, given the level of overcrowding, the chances of contracting a fatal disease were probably greater than of being similarly infected in the community. By early 1845, 123 workhouses had been built across the 130 Poor Law districts of the country. They accommodated 42,000 people, just 50 per cent of their capacity in a nation racked by poverty: an indication of their unpopularity. By June 1850, around 150 workhouse buildings had been completed. Designed to accommodate fewer than 100,000, they were now housing 264,000 inmates, with many other desperate cases unable to gain access.

To take just one example, the Fermoy workhouse had a capacity of 800. By early 1847, it housed almost 1,400 people (including thirty sick children sharing three beds) and had a morbidity rate of almost 25 per cent. The fact that each Poor Law Union was expected to be self-financing led to huge variations in the quality of the accommodation in each of these institutions. Landlords, who had often encouraged, or at least tolerated, a level of subdivision on their estates in order to increase their potential electoral vote in parliamentary contests, now found themselves in a position where they were obliged to pay the Poor Law rates for all tenants with holdings of less than £4 in value, and half the rates of those with holdings worth more than £4. For many landowners, especially in parts of the country where rents had dried up, that road had only one destination: the bankruptcy court.

Of course, death was not confined to the workhouse. It was ubiquitous. Land agent Samuel Murray Hussey, then based in Bantry, witnessed scenes he described as 'appalling':

> Whole families used to starve in their cabins without their plight being discovered until the stench of their decaying corpses attracted notice ... Very soon all the coffins had been exhausted, and in many places the dead were taken to the graves and dropped in through the hinged bottom of a trap-coffin.[32]

With the potato crop annihilated, the millions who depended on it were obliged to seek whatever assistance was available from government or private sources; enter an unfamiliar cash economy to purchase an alternative (such as oats) which had almost doubled in price; or starve.

George Bingham, 3rd Earl of Lucan

'I'll evict the lot of you': the Famine clearances

'Jerry Sullivan's house and place had about them all the marks and tokens of gradual decline. The thatch on the roof had begun to get black, and in some places was sinking into rotten ridges; the yard was untidy and dirty; the walls and hedges were broken and dismantled; and the gates were lying about, or swinging upon single hinges.'[33]

(William Carleton, *The Black Prophet*, a tale of the Irish Famine, 1846)

'The poor were driven into the town, estates were cleared, and notices to quit were served. If that did not answer, the houses were levelled. Perhaps fifty families were cleared for every three or four kept. The only refuge of those poor creatures then was to go into the town.'[34]

(James O'Connell, speech in Tralee, Co. Kerry)

It is one of life's ironies that the 1st Earl of Lucan, Patrick Sarsfield, Jacobite hero of the Williamite war of 1690–1, is one of the most revered figures in Irish history. The irony lies in the fact that one of his successors to the title, the 3rd Earl of Lucan, is very far from being similarly revered. George Charles Bingham, born in 1800, received an upper-class British 'public' (i.e. private) education (Westminster School, 1812–16). He then began a military career, where 'his severity and pettiness made him deeply unpopular with his officers and men'.[35] His lack of popularity with comrades in uniform, however, was trifling in comparison to the odium in which he was held by his Mayo tenants in the 1840s. That was when he retired from the army, bored beyond his limited capacity for tedium, and took up residence on his family's 60,000-acre estate near Castlebar.

Bingham had little time for either his tenants or their religion of preference, pledging when he took over his estate (after sacking that *rara avis*, an agent who was a 'popular local figure') that he 'would not breed paupers to pay priests'. Unlike others of his ilk, Bingham did not rely on the cover of the Great Famine to rid himself of his unwanted tenants. He began to clear his estate in the early 1840s, earning himself the unenviable but potent nickname 'The Exterminator'. On one occasion, believing their tormentor to be safely in London, a number of his tenants chose a bad moment to burn him in effigy in Castlebar. While the flames consumed the dummy Lucan, cheered on by an approving crowd, the real thing suddenly appeared in their midst on horseback and scattered the crowd with the imprecation, 'I'll evict the lot of you.'[36]

He was as good as his word, ejecting almost 1,000 of his tenants in a determined effort to 'clear' his estate and demolishing over 300 'fourth-class' houses (mud huts or cabins) in the parish of Ballinrobe alone. He also declined to pay his Poor Law rates in full, in order to avoid the necessity of supporting his evicted tenants in the Castlebar workhouse (he was chair of the local Board of Guardians), and then engineered the closure of that establishment. The arrival in Liverpool of 'thousands of persons … from that district' was highlighted in the House of Commons by George Poulett Scrope, MP for Stroud, in February 1847. Scrope alleged that the Castlebar Guardians 'had succeeded either in starving paupers to death, or in driving them to the shores of this country, and thus clearing the district of them'.[37] Lucan, who at the time owed the Westport Board of Guardians £309 and the Castlebar Board £692, was stung into an immediate, if evasive, response. In a classic non-denial in the House of Lords, he failed to refute the allegation that he had defaulted on his Poor Law payments and offered a convoluted explanation for the closure of the Castlebar workhouse at the height of a calamitous subsistence crisis. Criticised by one of his peers, the Scottish laird Viscount Duncan, Lucan observed tartly that he 'was scarcely prepared to be lectured by a Scotchman [sic] on a question relating to the grant of relief. He did not believe that in Scotland there was such a thing as a workhouse.'[38] Here his Lordship was merely being pedantic, as workhouses in Scotland (of which there were seventy at the time) were known locally as 'poorhouses'.

While his former tenants were either deported back to Ireland (a regular occurrence when Irish famine victims threw themselves on the mercy of English Poor Law guardians), managed to secure employment in Liverpool; or used the port as a gateway to the Americas – an unlikely occurrence given their abject poverty; Bingham replaced them with sheep, cattle and prosperous 'ranchers'. Many of these, despite the gibes aimed at Viscount Duncan in the House of Lords, hailed from Scotland, home of the poorhouse. In 1856, Lucan rented out the land around Cloonacastle, near Ballinrobe, to a Scottish grazier named James Simpson. Simpson was still in situ in the 1880s when he told the Richmond Commission* that before the Famine there had been no livestock farms in the area. His land had been released for grazing by Lucan's clearances. He also told the commissioners that many of the evicted tenants were still living locally and 'still pine for the land'.[39] Local newspapers discovered that, of Lucan's

---

* One of a number of parliamentary bodies appointed to investigate Irish land tenure at around that time.

evicted tenants, 478 were in receipt of some form of public relief, 170 had emigrated and 265 were either dead or entirely destitute.[40]

Lucan blithely ignored the whirlwind of abuse that blew in his direction from Mayo, the rest of Ireland and the Houses of Parliament. He was unapologetic and possibly even somewhat bewildered by the vilification to which he was subjected for the 'improvements' made to his estate by the removal of most of its inhabitants. He even went as far as to invoke the Famine as proof that the consolidation of his lands was in the best interest of his tenants. Presumably, he meant the few that still remained on his property. His *Dictionary of Irish Biography* entry notes that 'the execration he received in these years only aggravated his harshness, irascibility, and self-righteousness'.[41]

Lucan's evicted tenants, were they not well beyond humour by then, would have had the last laugh as their former landlord went on to notoriety and ridicule in the Crimean War as the man who ordered the infamous and sanguinary Charge of the Light Brigade at the Battle of Balaclava in October 1854. After the loss of almost 500 members of a brigade commanded by his brother-in-law, Lord Cardigan (the two men cordially loathed each other), Bingham was recalled to England the following January. When he returned, humiliated, to Castlebar, he received an address of welcome from his 'loyal and devoted tenantry', justification for the conclusion that not all loyal addresses to landlords were sincere and heartfelt. Which does not prevent them from occasionally being cited, as proof of tenant contentment, by historians apparently unversed in the Irish capacity for mockery, irony and productive hypocrisy.

Lucan, though boundlessly enthusiastic in the scattering of his tenants, was hardly unique. His is but one of the portraits in the extensive and colourful rogues' gallery of evicting landlords who took advantage of the Great Famine. Many landowners exercised extreme patience with tenants who were unable to pay their rents. Some – like Lord Lismore in Co. Tipperary, who fed the starving in his own residence – went out of their way to alleviate suffering.

Others, however, did not. Elsewhere in Mayo, where three-quarters of the county's farms were valued at under £4 and were, therefore, a charge on the Poor Law rates of their landlords, John Walsh, property owner of Castlehill, Crossmolina, owed his local Board of Guardians (the Ballina Union) £63 18s. Rather than pay up, he chose to evict his Mullet peninsula tenants *en masse* a few days before Christmas 1847, transferring the burden of housing them to his creditor, the self-same Ballina Union. He then demanded the assistance of a company of soldiers as he, his agent, his agent's son and one of his shepherds strutted up and down the peninsula unroofing the houses of his former tenants. When he discovered that some of the dispossessed had crept back into the ruins of their houses and erected lean-tos and makeshift tents under which they continued to live, he instructed his shepherd to destroy this improvised accommodation. Since the Ballina workhouse was already overcrowded, many of his tenants were unable to get access to shelter in the depths of winter and died from exposure to the elements.[42]

Sir Roger Palmer, owner of 90,000 acres of Mayo, carried out wholesale evictions on his estate in July 1848. One newspaper reported that Palmer's 'crowbar invincibles' had destroyed a number of houses in the process and forced tenants to sleep in the open.

> We witnessed the wretched creatures endeavouring to root out the timber of the houses, with the intention of constructing some sort of sheds to screen their children from the heavy rain falling at the time. The pitiless pelting storm has continued ever since, and if they have survived its severity, they must be more than human beings.[43]

Not all Mayo landlords were like Bingham, Palmer and Walsh. Lord Oranmore and Samuel O'Malley, for example, played fast and loose with the Gregory clause in continuing to accommodate their tenants. They formally agreed to tenants surrendering their holdings in order to obtain relief in the local workhouse. However, both men immediately reinstated most of the tenants on their holdings as caretakers, so that they could retain the land. O'Malley was criticised for this benevolence by the imperious

Marquess of Sligo, who, despite his misleading geographical title, owned almost 120,000 acres around Westport. Sligo, a perennial absentee who cleared his own estate of distressed tenants, described himself as feeling 'under the necessity of ejecting or being ejected'.[44] In a letter to fellow Mayo landowner, the MP George Moore, Sligo scolded Moore for failing to evict en masse, insisting that 'you must on reflection feel that the cause you follow is tending to exterminate your tenantry'. 'You will be a second Sir Samuel,' Sligo continued, in a convoluted case of special pleading. 'You are morally bona fide the exterminator … In my heart's belief you and Sir Samuel do more ruin, and injure and persecute and exterminate your tenants than any man in Mayo. You will disagree *in toto* – time will show who saves most of his tenants and most of his rents.'[45] Sligo's priority was clearly the latter, and he might have been in a better position to lecture his peers had he been up to date with his Poor Law taxes. He simply refused to pay the rates and owed £1,648 by 1848.

Estate clearances were far from a west of Ireland monopoly either. They were a countrywide phenomenon and not even Ulster was exempt. Armagh, Antrim and Monaghan had notably high levels of ejectments between 1846 and 1848. Roughly one tenth of the populations of Clare, Kerry and Galway were left on the side of the road. It is hardly surprising that the number of bailiffs increased three-fold during the Famine period.

One of the most infamous clearances took place in Tipperary – the county with the highest level of Famine evictions – in Toomevara. At the time of the Famine, it was a village with around 900 inhabitants. The land in and around the village was owned by the Rev. Massy Dawson of Ballynacourty from the scenic Glen of Aherlow. In May 1848, Dawson appointed a new agent, Richard Ievers Wilson, to supervise the rent collections on his estate. Wilson approached his task with some fervour. Most of Dawson's land was in the hands of middlemen who had a habit of collecting rent from their under-tenants and then failing to pass it on to the agent. Unfortunately for the townspeople of Toomevara, when Wilson sought vacant possession of the land leased to the middlemen, they became collateral damage. On

24 May 1849, a Nenagh-based sub-sheriff, protected by sixty members of the constabulary, arrived in the village to evict the tenants, some of whom had actually handed over their rent money to the middlemen and had receipts to prove it. Between forty and fifty cabins were levelled, and 500 people were dispossessed. To enhance their misery, it began to rain heavily as the clearances progressed. With nowhere to go – the nearest workhouse in Nenagh being already 'filled from floor to ceiling'[46] – those evicted were obliged to build temporary shelters along the walls of the local church and school house. When even those spaces ran out, many were compelled to resort to the only property remaining to them, their family graves in the local cemetery, where, according to the *Tipperary Vindicator*, 'asses cars and turf baskets were also upturned and gave shelter to scores of half-clad wretches'.[47] The local unionist newspaper, the *Nenagh Guardian*, which blamed the middlemen for the clearances, attempted to justify the actions of the Rev. Dawson and his agent by pledging that 'it is Mr. Dawson's intention to repair the houses left standing, and also to improve the whole town by building a better description of buildings in it'. It also exonerated landlord and agent by claiming that the inhabitants of the village of Toomevara were 'vile characters', before concluding that 'the greater portion of the village has been a plague spot on the estate – it was the resort of all evicted tenants from neighbouring estates – in short, it was in part a den of midnight thieves and highway robbers'.[48]

Adding further insult to injury, in February 1850 a number of 'hut tumblers', mostly local men in need of money, were despatched to level the makeshift shelters still occupied by a number of those who had been evicted the previous May. The agent, rather than the landlord, came in for most of the blame for the clearances. At the time of his death, rumours, or wishful thinking, abounded that Wilson's flesh had 'melted away' at the time of his demise and that 'he was a mass of corrupt matter so that he could scarcely be coffined'.[49]

What did the government make of these extensive clearances? They were a necessary evil, according to Trevelyan. In *The Irish Crisis*, he commented on the future of the 'cotter [*sic*] and conacre tenants' and observed that 'the position occupied by these classes is no longer tenable, and it is necessary for them to either become substantial farmers, or to live by the wages of their labour'.[50] Since he offered no road map by which labourers could magically become 'substantial farmers', we must assume that, realistically, they would remain as labourers, but would somehow enter the cash economy rather than continue to rely on conacre and the potato. Trevelyan ignored some of the other options, i.e. to starve, to seek passage on an emigrant ship or to fester in the workhouse. As James Donnelly has commented acidly, 'although a towering mass of human misery lay behind the twin processes of clearance and consolidation, Trevelyan (and many others) could minimise the human tragedy and concentrate on the economic miracle in the making'.[51]

Precisely how many people were evicted during the Famine is impossible to say. Estimates vary from 250,000 to 580,000, with possibly 100,000 families, or around 400,000 people, being cleared from estates at the height of the crisis between 1846 and 1848.[52] Whatever the true figure, for many of those left on the side of the road, unable to gain access to overcrowded workhouses, their eviction was tantamount to a death sentence.

Dropping the pilots: The Encumbered Estates Act (1849)

'The habits of the Irish gentry grew, beyond measure, brutal and reckless ... Their drunkenness, their blasphemy, their ferocious duelling left the squires of England far behind ... Fortunately, their recklessness was sure, in the end, to work, to a certain extent, its own cure; and in the background of their swinish and uproarious drinking-bouts the Encumbered Estates Act rises to our view'.[53]

(Goldwin Smith, *Irish History and Irish Character*, 1862)

If Ireland had a problem with indigent tenants, it was also faced with a plethora of bankrupt landlords. Average rent rolls declined by as much as a third during the Famine, while landlord expenditure on poor relief increased.[54] Something had to give. Like Ernest Hemingway character's explanation of how he arrived at a state of insolvency – 'gradually, then suddenly' – many of the country's landlords had been slowly winding their way toward financial collapse. That process accelerated when the Famine struck. It is reckoned that up to a quarter of the country's landowners experienced financial difficulties after 1846. Most of them had little option but to look on while their debts rose, not all having brought on their predicament by their own improvidence. The Irish gentry, like the British aristocracy from which many had sprung or with whom most identified, took inheritance very seriously indeed. So much so that many landowners had nothing other than a 'life interest' in their estates. What had been passed on to them must be kept intact for future generations. This practice generally had a legal basis, an 'entail' that scuttled the chances of a heavily indebted inheritor selling or mortgaging his estate to pay off his creditors.* An entail rendered land 'inalienable'. This legal instrument had imposed an element of discipline on titled families over the years. Although the Marquess of Donegal might have disagreed with that contention. When he inherited his title in 1844, it came with 30,000 acres of Irish land. Unfortunately, this was accompanied by debts accumulated by his ancestors of £400,000 – fourteen times the annual rent roll. And that was before the impact of the Famine.

So in the context of collapsing land values and debt-ridden ('encumbered') estates, something had to give. The rigidity of the entail, which had already been relaxed somewhat in custom and practice over the years, was finally addressed in 1849 in the legislation framed as the Encumbered Estates Act. The intention was to rid the country of bankrupt landlords, to sell off their land, pay off creditors – which would be of considerable national economic benefit in itself – and to start afresh with well-funded landowners who had sufficient capital to invest in their newly acquired estates. The potential impact on the tenant was ignored and, as Michael Davitt put it, they 'were virtually bought with

---

* Fans of the novels of P. G. Wodehouse will be familiar with the concept.

the land'.[55] It was assumed, capital being in rather short supply in Ireland, that most of the investors who would snap up bankrupt, but nonetheless attractive, Irish estates would be financially sound, diligent and British: a stealthy nineteenth-century version of the seventeenth-century policy of 'plantation'.

However, like many British designs for its stricken neighbour, things did not quite go according to plan. The first estates came on the market in 1850 at knock-down prices. Some 'encumbered' land in Connacht, for example, was on offer at 5 shillings an acre. The estate of Lord Mountcashell (62,000 acres in Cork and Antrim) was bought for £240,000.* Such a sum would, pre-Famine, have implied that the annual rent roll on the estate amounted to between £9,000 and £10,000. It was actually twice that. Mountcashell, not best pleased to be offloading his property at a 50 per cent discount, grumbled disparagingly about the Encumbered Estates Commissioner, Charles Hargreave, who presided over the transfer. Hargreave, small of stature, inhabited unprepossessing office space on the top floor of an old Dublin Georgian house in Henrietta Street. Mountcashell was heard to complain bitterly that losing his estate for half its value was bad enough, 'but to be sold up by a dwarf in a garret was more than he could endure'.[56]

In the colourful phrase of land agent Samuel Hussey, observing all these transactions from the sidelines, 'properties were sold like chairs and tables at a paltry auction'.[57] However, contrary to the hopes and expectations of the likes of Trevelyan, it was mainly Irish mattresses that were raided to purchase such bargains. The fond expectation that a reliable cadre of British agronomists and enlightened capitalists would move in, ready to invest their birthright in the modernisation of Irish agriculture, was never fully realised. Instead, the purchasers tended to be solvent members of the Irish aristocracy (such creatures still existed) or prosperous Irish professionals – entrepreneurs, builders, merchants, solicitors, doctors – whose wealth remained untouched by the Famine, who

---

* This translates at around €400 an acre today. An acre of land in the west of Ireland in 2024 would probably fetch between €8,000 and €12,000.

were capable of identifying a bargain, and whose social aspirations included the ownership of a country estate. Most of these *nouveau riche* owners had no commitment to the sitting tenants and many, learning well from their 'betters', rapidly cleared their estates and took on new tenants, many of whom were graziers willing to pay higher rents.

Typical of this new breed of 'carpetbagger' was one Henry O'Shea, a Limerick solicitor who made a considerable sum of money buying and selling – today it would be called 'flipping' – encumbered estates. Some of the money thus accumulated was later lavished on the mediocre military career of his feckless eldest son, Captain William Henry O'Shea, subsequently the nemesis of Charles Stewart Parnell.

A more typical purchaser, one bent on retaining his newly acquired property, was the Roscommon-born merchant Martin McDonnell, who had made a sizeable sum in a number of retail businesses in Co. Galway and had a lucrative trade in supplying workhouses. McDonnell and his brothers used the 'profits from their successful merchandising businesses to enable them to become extensive landowners'.[58] Martin McDonnell, for example, bought part of the Buoyvanagh estate of the late Lord Fitzgerald and Vesey, near Tuam. Just over 1,500 acres was knocked down to him for £5,850, around fifteen times the annual rent roll of £371. Before the Famine, that same acreage would probably have cost McDonnell at least twenty-five times the annual rental.

Those who arrived late to the feast (in the mid-1850s, when land prices had doubled) had an even greater incentive to rid themselves of insolvent tenants and to monetise their investment as quickly as possible. The Encumbered Estates Act was one of the reasons the levels of eviction remained high in the early 1850s, with almost 50,000 ejectments between 1850 and 1854, including 20,000 in 1850 alone. In 1881, at the height of the Land War, even the *Times* journalist Finlay Dun – who rarely saw a landlord whom he did not venerate – recognised the impact of many of these Estates Court purchases as 'illustrating all the evils of extravagant rents, insecurity of tenure, and ruthless appropriation of tenants' improvements'.[59] Moreover, as might be expected from eager venture capitalists, these *nouveaux rentiers* were unlikely to offer any financial inducement to their tenants to leave the country. There is little or no evidence of assisted emigration arising out of the transfer of property under the 1849 Encumbered Estates Act.

Altogether, around 3,000 landlord holdings were sold through the Estates Courts. Some £20 million changed hands in the course of those sales, the bulk of it coming from Irishmen of means or with access to credit. Samuel Hussey calculated that 85 per cent of 'encumbered' land went to Irish buyers. Most were to disappoint Charles Edward Trevelyan when it came to their priorities. They were far more interested in a quick return on their investments (especially if they had bought late and taken on a mortgage) than in spending even more money 'improving' their estates. One consequence of the 1849 legislation – it would be an exaggeration to describe it as a beneficial effect – was a reduction in the number of absentee landlords by 30 per cent. The generation of *rentiers* who faced the threat of the Land League in the 1880s was of a very different stripe indeed to the landowners of the early 1840s. Far more middle-class, far more Catholic, far more urban and, arguably, even more ruthless when challenged.

'Shovelling out' the tenantry: assisted emigration to the Americas

'From Derry Quay we sailed away on the 23rd of May,
We were boarded by a pleasant crew bound for Amerikay,
Fresh water there we did take on, five thousand gallons or more,
In case we'd run short, going to New York far away from the
    Shamrock shore.'

('Paddy's Green Shamrock Shore', traditional song)

The introduction of the Poor Law to Ireland in 1838, as we have seen, posed something of a dilemma for the landlord who wished to engage in the wholesale eviction of tenants. Aside from the legal expenses that must be incurred in ejecting tenants in arrears, he was now faced with the possibility that his former tenants would seek sanctuary – if cheerless survival can be called that – in the local workhouse. Because they were no longer his tenants, he had no ongoing liability for their Poor Law rates, but somebody would have to pay for this influx. His own rates burden would increase, as would those of his neighbours.

Even before the Famine, a number of landlords, desirous of loosening the grip of middlemen, of 'improving' their own estates, perhaps farming their land themselves or simply ridding themselves of chronically indigent tenants unable to pay their rent, had – reluctantly in many cases – opted to subsidise the removal of their tenants to North America.

The practice of assisted emigration existed before the Great Hunger. John Mitchel, for example, cited a Derry newspaper advertisement inviting Ulster 'gentlemen' to send their 'overstock tenantry' to Canada in 1843.[60] But when the blight struck for a second time in 1846, the incentive for landlords to pay for the passage of tenants to North America increased exponentially. A Kilkenny landlord, Colonel Wandesforde, spent £15,000 ridding himself of 3,000 of his tenants that year. In 1847, there were 5,000 landlord-assisted migrations to Canada alone, around 2,000 from the Irish estate of future British Prime Minister Lord Palmerston, then Foreign Secretary in Russell's government. The arrival in St John, New Brunswick* of a shipload of Palmerston's tenants in November 1847, who had been misled into expecting clothing and money when they landed, drew a rebuke from the St John city council. Its members protested to the British government about the behaviour of one of its senior cabinet members in misleading and mistreating his tenants and in offloading destitute and diseased Irish paupers onto the streets of their city.

Similar numbers were despatched between 1848 and 1850, amid growing doubts as to the entirely voluntary nature of the process, with some landlords 'said to be forcing emigration on their reluctant cottiers'.[61] Only in the 1850s was there a slackening off, and even then, the practice continued at a reduced level.

* Not to be confused with St John's, Newfoundland.

The land agent, William Steuart Trench, became a zealous adherent of assisted emigration as a solution to a range of problems on the estates he managed. He either suggested or initiated schemes on four of the properties under his supervision, including the huge Lansdowne estate in Co. Kerry. His enthusiasm for exporting the problem of tenant penury predated the Famine. When he managed the Shirley estate in Monaghan from 1843 to 1845 – owned by the largely absentee landlord Evelyn John Shirley until his death in 1856 – Trench proposed an emigration scheme to his employer. In the case of the Shirley tenants from Farney, Co. Monaghan, Trench had good cause to wish to see the back of as many of them as possible. In one of his first encounters with the Farney peasantry, Trench had been manhandled and badly beaten by a number of eager tenants who were expecting to be advised of a reduction in their rent. They had been greatly disappointed when Shirley instructed Trench to inform them that no discount was forthcoming. But for the intervention of a local priest, Trench might not have survived the encounter.

As the agent of the Marquess of Lansdowne, in November 1850 Trench travelled to England to meet with 'that most enlightened and liberal statesman' (his obsequious description of his new employer) in order to try to impress some financial realities upon the proprietor of the Kenmare, Co. Kerry estate. Trench pointed out that upwards of 3,000 of Lansdowne's tenants were in receipt of workhouse relief at a cost of £5 a head per annum. The likelihood of either figure declining was remote. Trench informed Lansdowne that after his Poor Law rates had been paid, he could expect no income from his Kerry estate for years to come. The proposition the agent then put to the landlord was that he should offer free passage to the USA to all those receiving relief in the Kenmare workhouse who were chargeable to his estate. Trench, anticipating Lansdowne's queries, had already made an arrangement with an emigration agent and assured the marquess that the costs of passage, 'with a small sum per head for outfit and a few shillings on landing, would not exceed from £13,000 to £14,000, a sum less than it would cost to support them in the workhouse for a single year'.

Lansdowne, seeing the wisdom of the scheme, immediately gave the agent £8,000 to begin the process. When Trench returned to Kenmare, 'the announcement at first was scarcely credited: it was considered by the paupers to be too good news to be true. But when it began to be believed and appreciated, a rush was made to get away at once.' At a rate of 200 a week, the occupants of the Kenmare workhouse were despatched to Cork, and 'in a little more than a year 3,500 paupers had left Kenmare for America'.[62] All departed carefully, Trench claimed, a statement that can be taken with a grain of salt. In 1844, giving evidence to the Devon Commission, a fellow land agent had observed of the phenomenon of assisted emigration that 'there's such a clinging to the country that they would live on anything rather than go'. Perhaps four years of famine had weakened the tenacity of Lansdowne's Kenmare tenants, but one wonders what the result would have been had Trench polled his 'paupers' and asked was their preference for a new life in America or their old life, under improved conditions, in Ireland.

The Sligo landowner, Sir Robert Gore Booth, who sent a number of his own tenants to New Brunswick in 1847 on a 'well-victualled ship' observed that most still preferred 'poverty on their own holdings to prosperity elsewhere'.[63] The ethics of his scheme did not concern Trench. As far as he was concerned, no one was being forced to leave, so he had no qualms. The plan he outlined to Lansdowne was 'cheaper to him, and *better for them*' (his italics). He even insisted that Lansdowne's tenants were 'terrified lest all the money should be exhausted before his or her name could be entered upon the emigration list'.[64]

The relief of Trench and other agents and landlords at having rid themselves of these 'charges' was not matched by the welcome they received in North America, Canada in particular. Morbidity on the notorious Atlantic 'coffin ships' – nowhere near as high as mythology suggests, but still running at around 20 per cent on the less carefully monitored Canadian routes in 1847 – accounted for a representative share of 'assisted' emigrants who were just as likely to perish en route, or after landing, as their 'voluntary' brethren.

The arrival of thousands of 'diseased' Irish immigrants caused panic in Canada – which had already taken more than its fair share of crofters from the Scottish Highland clearances – and the cities of the American east coast. This was the case no matter who had paid for their passage. Canadian concerns were not just for the well-being of Canadians either. There was an outpouring of moral outrage aimed directly at the perceived callousness of the Irish grandees, who were seen to be using their fortunes to transfer their problems 3,000 miles across the Atlantic Ocean. The two Sligo landlords, Robert Gore-Booth and Lord Palmerston, were, for example, eviscerated by the chief emigration officer in St John, New Brunswick, for 'inhuman callousness' in 'shovelling out' their tenants. Gore-Booth did not help his cause when he admitted that he had taken the opportunity to get rid of some 'bad characters' on his estate.

Not unnaturally, the various programmes of assisted emigration also attracted the ire of Irish nationalists. *The Nation* newspaper, staffed by many of the men who would later break with O'Connell and the Repeal movement and stage the abortive Young Ireland rebellion in 1848, regularly condemned the ad hoc programme. The acerbic John Mitchel, editor of the short-lived *United Irishman* – closed down as seditious by Dublin Castle after only sixteen issues – was a scathing critic. In his polemic, *The Last Conquest of Ireland (Perhaps)*, Mitchel – later an enthusiastic supporter of the resumption of the North Atlantic slave trade – denounced assisted emigration as 'part of the plan to clear our island of its own people and confirm England in the peaceable possession of her farm'.[65]

Government financial contributions to assisted emigration were negligible. Some thought had been given to the wisdom of subventing mass emigration with Poor Law Guardian funding. Despite a recommendation from the pre-Famine Devon Commission that such a scheme be underwritten ('Emigration is considered by the committee to be peculiarly applicable as a remedial measure'),* Peel, 'even in the worst moments of 1846

---

* The report of the commission suggested that conditions in rural Ireland would be stabilised by the 'removal of *about* [my italics] one hundred and ninety-two thousand, three hundred and sixty-eight families'. Victorians were not given to rounding up.

273

... maintained that emigration was really irrelevant as a solution of Irish difficulties'. His successor, Lord John Russell, felt that 'there was no use in sending them from starving at Skibbereen to starving at Montreal'.[66]

It should not come as a shock to learn that Trevelyan did not approve of using government resources 'to relieve the mother-country by transferring large masses of people to the Colonies', although, in the spirit of the axiom that 'Irish property should pay for Irish poverty', he conceded that 'those who have purchased or inherited estates in which a redundant population has been permitted or encouraged to grow up, may with propriety assist some of their people to emigrate ... So long as emigration is conducted only at the expense of the proprietor, it is not likely to be carried to an injurious or dangerous extent.'[67]

Between 3 and 4 per cent of emigrants during the 1846–51 period had their passage paid for or assisted by landlords or the exchequer. The estimated figure for assisted emigration is around 30,000 of those who fled the country.

Some of the stratagems used to subsidise emigration where formal assistance had not been secured were, to say the least, imaginative. In Mayo, in what smacks of a very Irish 'nod and a wink' form of collusion, landlords who doubled as magistrates ordered the transportation of felons for a variety of crimes. Both judge and accused, however, were well aware that said crime had been committed with the express intention of attracting just such a sentence. A Westport barrister, Michael Shaughnessy, told a Commons committee that he had personally ordered a number of such transportations because the accused 'had no alternative but starvation or the commission of crime'.[68]

One way or another, Ireland had not heard the last of the hundreds of thousands who emigrated, with or without external financial assistance, to the USA. Emigrants' remittances sent to encourage other family members to make the same journey continued to deplete the Irish population for decades. The Fenian rebellion of 1867 was largely funded by Irish-American money, as was the Land War of 1879–82. In the latter instance, Irish-Americans and their offspring, who had prospered in the

United States since the Famine, must have taken a particular delight in seeing their money being used to discommode the establishment class they blamed for their very presence in America and which had, entirely unintentionally of course, contributed to their good fortune.

For one landlord, however, retribution came long before the birth of the Land League.

Major Denis Mahon

Today, Strokestown House in Co. Roscommon, a Palladian mansion set in magnificent tree-lined grounds, is the location of an extensive archive of estate papers and of Ireland's National Famine Museum. In 1845, it was a heavily encumbered holding in the hands of Major Denis Mahon, who had inherited debts of £30,000 on an estate where overcrowding and subdivision were rampant. Almost 12,000 people were living on 11,000 acres. Strokestown had been badly mismanaged for decades, with around 60 per cent of the de facto tenants not even featuring on the rent-roll, and with £13,000 in arrears owed. Mahon, who was a magistrate and an unreconstructed unionist, had little or no time for nationalist political activism, the Roman Catholic Church, the Repeal movement or recalcitrant tenants and, according to his entry in the *Dictionary of Irish Biography*, 'in traditional backwoods gentry fashion he conflated political protest with agrarian crime and found the origins of both in sectarian conspiracy'.[69] The local agrarian secret society styled itself the Molly Maguires, a name more often associated with Donegal that would come to be tied to the Ancient Order of Hibernians and, when exported, earn even greater notoriety in the Pennsylvania anthracite fields than in Roscommon.

Mahon, to stem the bleeding, appointed the professional land management company (later a banking institution) Guinness and Mahon to run the estate. The agent appointed by the company, John Ross Mahon, may or may not have been Major Denis Mahon's second cousin. The two men were not initially *ad idem*

Major Denis Mahon

when it came to the mechanism for dealing with the crippling debts of the estate. John Ross Mahon, on first visiting Strokestown, identified the obvious problem of the chronic overcrowding and abject poverty of the estate's tenants. 'Of course they were all absolutely starving,' he told the Bessborough Commission in 1881. 'I saw the impossibility, not only of rent being paid, but of the people living.'[70] The new agent's solution was to remove two-thirds of the Strokestown tenants and, at a cost of around £24,000 to his employer, ship them to Canada. Major Denis Mahon baulked at the enormous cost, despite being shown by his agent how maintaining his tenants in the local workhouse would prove to be even more expensive. Instead, Major Mahon proposed (from a safe distance – he was based in England in the winter of 1846–7) the eviction of a number of his more troublesome tenants, suspected of membership of the Molly Maguires.

Major Mahon's attitude towards his tenants was in part at least, informed by his relationship with the Strokestown Roman

Catholic parish priest, the Rev. Michael McDermott. Both men served on the local famine relief committee and were frequently at loggerheads. Their mutual antipathy came to a head in August 1847, when McDermott attacked Mahon at a relief committee meeting for having 'amused himself' over the winter in comfort in London, claiming that he 'had left [his] people starve in the streets and die, without ever looking after them'.[71]

Eventually, Mahon succumbed to his namesake's logic and agreed to fund the passages of 1,400 families to new lives in Canada, with their arrears forgiven. However, the take-up of the scheme locally was not impressive. Only 217 families agreed to Mahon's terms (amounting to just over 800 people). Most of those who declined the offer of assisted emigration (around 3,000 people) were later ejected from their holdings. It is believed that most were dead within a year of their evictions. Some died in the workhouse; others, unable to gain admission there, simply perished on the roads of Roscommon.

However, many of those who opted for passage to Canada hardly fared much better. Mahon engaged four ships to transport his tenants. The *Virginius* departed from Liverpool for St John, New Brunswick in May 1847, and the *Naomi*, the ironically named *Erin's Queen* and the *John Munn* followed with more of Mahon's tenants later that year. In the case of the *Virginius*, 476 Strokestown tenants embarked, some already suffering from fever and dysentery; 158 perished at sea, 19 died while the ship was at anchor and 90 died while in the Canadian quarantine station of Gross Îsle. Describing the condition of the passengers on board the *Virginius* after it docked in New Brunswick, George Mellis Douglas, the local medical superintendent, wrote that 'the few that were able to come on deck were ghastly yellow-looking spectres, unshaven and hollow-cheeked, and, without exception the worst looking passengers I have ever seen'.[72] His description of the horrors of the other Mahon ships was along similar lines. All told, 268 of Mahon's tenants died at sea, while almost as many succumbed to disease after reaching Canada.

Word of the appalling condition in which the first Strokestown emigrants had arrived, and of the number who had not survived the trip, quickly got back to Roscommon. Rumours abounded locally that one of the unseaworthy craft engaged by Mahon had sunk, with all hands. This was untrue, but did little to enhance the landlord's reputation. Mahon defended himself against a wave of attacks in the British and Irish press by claiming to have spent £14,000 of his own money on the human cargo transported by the *Virginius, Naomi, Erin's Queen* and *John Munn*. But there was no gainsaying the stark morbidity figures.

The fatal result of the mounting anger in Strokestown has already been described at the opening of this chapter. On 2 November 1847, Mahon became the first Irish landlord to be assassinated during the Famine as a direct consequence of actions he had taken to mitigate the impact of the crisis on his estate. His death came in the peak year for crime in the 1840s, rising to three times the pre-Famine level. However, the nature of criminal activity had changed radically and was in lock-step with the subsistence crisis. Cattle- and sheep-rustling numbers shot up eleven-fold; robbery and burglary increased by a factor of five. The incidence of rape dropped by more than 60 per cent.[73]

Three men were arrested for Mahon's murder in 1848. One, Michael Gardener, turned 'approver', offered damning evidence against the other two and was himself transported to Australia. On 8 August 1848, Owen Beirne and Patrick Hasty were hanged for the killing of Major Denis Mahon.

While Mahon's death was greeted with bonfires and celebrations in Roscommon, it did little to advance the cause of those arguing for better treatment for Ireland from the Whig administration. Unionist politicians, such as Lord Farnham, used the murder to advance their claims of a Catholic conspiracy to slaughter Irish Protestant landlords. While the Whigs needed no excuse to continue their obsession with the palliative and restorative qualities of the 'market', 'the murder ultimately played a part in the progressive diminution of official Irish relief aid during the period'.[74] The murder of Mahon had the effect of reinforcing voices within government stridently denouncing the incorrigible Irish and calling for even fewer resources to be allocated to the relief of distress.

The work of the 'Great Disposer': the impact of the Famine on land use

'Rejoice and make merry, you'll hunger no more,
John Bull will soon send you all victuals galore,
A French cook* to dress them with boiler and pot,
And a kitchen well-heated to keep the broth hot.'

(*Fermanagh Reporter*, 1 April 1847)

In 1851, the report of the census commissioners contained a tone-deaf reference to the effect that 'we have every reason for thankfulness that years of suffering have been followed by years of prosperity'.[75] This earnest platitude of the commissioners flew in the face of the stark statistical reality of a shocking 19.85 per cent decline in the Irish population over the previous decade. Between 1841 and 1851, the number of people in Ireland dropped from 8,175,124 to 6,552,385. The question of exactly how many people had actually lived on the island of Ireland in the summer of 1845, before the first effects of potato blight were felt, is one that we shall never be able to answer conclusively. Even the bullish 1851 census report suggests that, without famine conditions, the population of Ireland would have amounted to 9,018,779 in 1851, so 'it is important to account ... for the deficiency in the population of nearly two and a half million'.[76] Of the roughly 1.8 million people who simply 'disappeared' between 1845 and 1851 (inclusive), 1,172,758 are recorded as having emigrated – around 400,000 to Britain[77] – so most of the rest must therefore have died of starvation or disease. One of those diseases was the cholera epidemic that struck in 1849 and accounted for 35,089 deaths, or, in the quaint phraseology of the census commissioners, 'for some wise and inscrutable reason, upon which man can only speculate, it seemed good to the Great Disposer of events to mitigate

---

* This is a reference to the London-based French chef Alexis Soyer, who opened a well-publicised soup kitchen in Dublin a few days after the poem appeared.

considerably its fatality'.[78] A roundabout way of saying 'it could have been worse'!

Like most economic or subsistence catastrophes, the impact of the Great Famine was not spread equally. While one-fifth of the Irish population vanished, less than 15 per cent of the country's land changed hands, as bankrupt landlords sold out or used the Encumbered Estates Court to divest themselves of their holdings. Further down the pecking order, more than 200,000 smallholdings, farms of less than fifteen acres, simply disappeared.[79] Almost half of these were holdings of between one and five acres. The social class that suffered the greatest impact was the agricultural proletariat. The Trinity College, Dublin historian David Fitzpatrick has calculated that there were 1.2 million Irish male farm labourers in 1845. That figure had declined to around 900,000 by the time of the 1851 census. Ten years later, there were 700,000 left, a drop of 42 per cent in sixteen years.[80] Because there were now fewer of them, there was an increase in demand for the services of farm labourers, and average wages increased.

However, given the tensions that had often existed in the pre-Famine era between the wealthier members of the Irish peasantry and the restive cohort of agricultural labourers, the decline in the size and influence of the latter social class was bound to change the power dynamic, as well as the political and social imperatives of rural Ireland, in the decades ahead. According to Joseph Lee, 'the class balance swung sharply in favour of farmers, and within the farming community it swung even more sharply in favour of bigger and against smaller farmers'.[81] This, as we shall see, would have unexpected consequences. Among these was the increased politicisation of a tenant farmer class that was no longer overly concerned with the possibility of another Caravat-like onslaught from their 'social inferiors'. Without the danger of being outflanked by the hugely diminished army of labourers, the prosperous farmer was now at liberty to take on his landlord. This meant that 'the large farmers – who constituted a new rural upper middle class – turned to politics as a means of fulfilling their social and economic aspirations'.[82]

For those who survived the 1845–51 period and who were able to remain in Ireland, things undoubtedly improved: 'There was a trickle-down effect to most sectors of the economy.'[83] The loss of so many farmers who did little more than produce enough food for their own families 'cleared the way for the fuller commercialisation of Irish agriculture'.[84] The rural economy became far more market-oriented. Produce from farms was sold for cash rather than consumed by its producers. Average farm sizes grew, thanks to the disappearance of thousands of smallholdings. The number of farms of over fifteen acres increased from 277,000 to 290,000 between 1845 and 1851. The standard of housing improved, with a huge reduction in the numbers of 'fourth-class' dwellings – usually one-roomed mud cabins. According to the 1841 census, one-third of the housing stock in the country was 'fourth class'. This was down to just over 10 per cent in the 1851 census. Personal wealth, at least as reflected in bank savings accounts, increased enormously. These quadrupled in value over a period of thirty years, from £8 million in 1846 to £32.8 million in 1876.[85]

The assumption that the Famine alone led to the sudden end of subdivision and to Irish adherence to the practice of 'impartible inheritance' (where a single child inherited a farm) has been challenged by, among others, economic historian Cormac Ó Gráda. He points out that this process had already begun before the 1840s: 'Even before the Famine, better-off farmers sought to pass the land on to one heir while catering for other siblings through a combination of education and direct financial assistance.'[86] In addition, impartible inheritance was also encouraged by price movements that favoured livestock over crop production. Between 1845 and 1914, the overall acreage under the four main crops (potatoes, oats, wheat and barley) dropped precipitously from 5.6 million to 1.83 million acres, in a country with almost 20 million acres of available land.[87] The sustained decline in the amount of Irish land under tillage was also partly due to an understandable reluctance to plant potatoes. Between the Great Famine and the Great War, the national acreage devoted to the potato crop fell from 2.1 million to 580,000. The apparently inexorable shift from labour-intensive tillage to land-hungry pasture was a further disincentive to subdivide; 'land was subordinated to people before the famine: henceforth people were subordinated to the land,' wrote Joseph Lee.[88] Post-Famine, it was also emigrants' remittances – estimated by Trevelyan himself at £200,000 in the twelve months from April 1846 – and the possibility of refuge in North America with family members who had been first to emigrate, which stopped the destructive practice of subdivision, a practice almost invariably prohibited by landlords after the Famine.

With a much smaller population to support (4.4 million in 1911, almost halved since 1845), a hugely reduced dependence on the potato, a shrunken supply of agricultural labourers and relatively secure markets in Britain for Irish cattle and sheep, the country made the transition from growing crops to rearing livestock. In 1845, potatoes, grain and livestock had each accounted for one third of total output. By the onset of the Great War, cattle and sheep accounted for three-quarters of agricultural production. This transition had an inevitable demographic impact. The stark observation of Joseph Lee neatly encapsulates the new reality: 'The Irish farmer behaved as a rational economic man, and after the wave of famine evictions ebbed, it was he, not the landlord, who drove his children and labourers off the land.'[89]

By 1853, the Great Munster Fair in Limerick was a testament to the changes that had already begun. Farmers and dealers drove their cattle to the fair from the surrounding counties. The growing railway network brought livestock from farther afield. A special platform had to be built in Limerick railway station in order to accommodate them. Buyers came from as far away as London and Liverpool. The Great Munster Fair that year was said to have surpassed even the celebrated October livestock fair in Ballinasloe, Co. Galway.

The middleman, already a dying breed since the end of the eighteenth century, now became an endangered species. Thanks to the long leases (often as much as three lifetimes) regularly handed out to middlemen in the late eighteenth century, many landlords had been unable to sell land, or raise rents, to take advantage of increased land prices in the period before the

Famine. Many generational scores were settled in the 1850s, with landlords refusing abatements to middlemen whose own rent-rolls had collapsed. Some landlords took over tenancies directly themselves, a phenomenon that had long been on the increase. In more instances, the middlemen and their under-tenants were simply replaced with cattle or sheep, a trend that ensured that Ireland today is one of the few countries in the world with more livestock than people, and the only country in the world with a population smaller than that of the 1840s.

The relative paucity of ejectments in nineteenth-century Ireland – especially genuine evictions in which tenants were not re-admitted as caretakers, or reinstated after coming to an arrangement with the landlord – is often cited as proof of the comparatively benign nature of Irish land tenure. However, this cloaks a parallel reality that bathes the Irish aristocracy in a somewhat harsher light. Often, when the Irish peasantry most needed the forbearance of their landlords, it was not forthcoming. The dearth of evictions in times of relative prosperity hardly stands as a testament to the moderation of the country's gentry. Such restraint is explained by the modern axiom, 'if it ain't broke, don't fix it'. Why go to the expense and frustration, except in cases of chronic arrears, of evicting viable tenants? It would be bad for business.

However, times of crisis and economic depression (e.g. the Great Famine and the prolonged economic depression from 1877 to the mid-1890s) brought spikes in eviction rates. When the going got tough, many owners contrived to make it even tougher. For many (not all) Famine landlords, logic dictated 'the necessity of ejecting or being ejected', to reiterate the rubric of Lord Sligo. After the Great Famine, as we shall see, the relationship between landlord and tenant began to change, slowly but radically. Historian Kevin Whelan – not a member of what James Donnelly has called the 'forgive and forget' school of Famine historiography – has a pithy and caustic assessment of the impact of the actions of a number of Irish landlords during the decade from 1845 to 1855. Perhaps he had Charles Edward Trevelyan in mind when he wrote:

The Famine clearances in Ireland should be seen as equivalent in their impact to the enclosure movement in England and the eighteenth-century Highland clearances – all three were assaults on the poor and on alternative cultural formations, carried out by the gentry, backed by the coercive power of the state, and implemented in the name of 'progress'.[90]

In many respects, the often divisive academic debate about responsibility for the Famine is as irrelevant to the 'public square' as are many of the other contested issues relating to the land struggle. Most Irish people since the 1850s have accepted a binary, 'black and white' Famine narrative, albeit one based primarily on folklore and inherited preconceptions.

Russell, Wood and Trevelyan did not lack for support in Britain. The *Illustrated London News*, for example, much praised in Ireland for the Famine reportage of its journalists and artists, had adopted a rather more utilitarian editorial line by 1849 when it came to assessing 'plight and right'. By the end of the 1840s, some British sympathy had evaporated because of O'Connell's thankless Repeal campaign and the 'stab in the back' of the hapless rebellion of the Young Irelanders in 1848. Russell even cited the former when shutting down the soup kitchens.[91] Weighed in the balance, the landlords, in the opinion of the *Illustrated London News*, were now considered to be more worthy of the sympathy of that journal's readers: 'It ... should be remembered that few of them have it in their power to be merciful or generous to their poorer tenantry ... They are themselves engaged in a life and death struggle with their creditors.'[92]

However, as far as John Mitchel and many of his contemporaries were concerned, Russell, Wood, Trevelyan and their enablers were guilty of, at best, a pattern of callous neglect that led to the deaths of hundreds of thousands of Irish people and the permanent banishment of as many more. The untroubled consciences of the British triumvirate most responsible for Irish affairs between 1846 and 1850, when contrasted with the fury of Mitchel and his contemporaries, serves as a metaphor for the parallel lines along which the Irish and British travelled for decades in their mutual relationship. Flawed perceptions, misinformation, blatant atavism and erroneous received wisdom no longer dominate the debates historians conduct among themselves when discussing the intricacies of land tenure, or the 'reason why' of the Great Famine. But, for better or for worse, they certainly drove Irish discourse in the century after that cataclysmic event. For decades, John Mitchel's thesis, neatly summarised in his adage 'The Almighty, indeed, sent the potato blight, but the English created the Famine', dominated Irish memory. Mitchel's philippics may have favoured special pleading over intellectual rigour, but they were 'by far the most widely read works of Irish history in the nineteenth century'.[93] They informed the rebellion of the Fenians in 1867 and even the triumph of Sinn Féin and the IRA in the 1920s. More importantly, from the point of view of this work, their echoes reverberated in 1879 in Mayo in the maelstrom that led to the establishment of the Land League. A simple desire to be avenged, whether or not it was wrong-headed or misplaced, played a minor but significant role in the movement that ultimately ended the ownership of Irish land by an agrarian, largely Anglo-Irish, aristocracy.

Even today, a variation of Mitchel's analysis is never far from the surface, despite the earnest corrective efforts of professional historians during the Famine sesquicentennial commemorative period of the late 1990s and in the years since then. It will probably never totally disappear, no matter how many learned papers and articles urge us to view the actions of Russell, Wood and Trevelyan in the context of the politics and society of the 1840s. According to one of the foremost authorities on the period, the economic historian Cormac Ó Gráda, 'individual memories of the famine, coupled with "collective memory" of the event in later years, influenced the political culture of both Ireland and Irish-America, and indeed still play a role'.[94]

A chastened Tony Blair would probably agree.

10

The Indian summer of the Irish landlord, 1848–78

'Let it not be mistaken. The two great curses of Ireland are
bad landlords and bad agents, and in nineteen cases out of
every twenty, the origin of the crime lies with the Landlord
or Agent, instead of the tenant.'

(William Carleton, author's foreword to
Valentine McClutchy: The Irish Agent)

John George Adair, c.1880

8 April 1861, Derryveagh, Co. Donegal

The sights and sounds were all too familiar. That they had become increasingly rare since the end of the Great Famine merely served to heighten the horror. The paucity of ejectments, and the uniqueness of Derryveagh as a mass clearance, served merely to underline the misery that was to be inflicted. While 200 policemen looked on, the Donegal deputy sheriff Samuel Crookshank and his bailiffs were using crowbars, curses and battering rams to clear out the tenants of John George Adair and demolish the homes of the inhabitants of half-a-dozen townlands in north Donegal. The peaceful starkness of the landscape contrasted with the exertions of the crowbar-wielders as they razed the houses and nullified the identities of people whose families had lived on this land for decades. Their holdings were dismal and unpromising. The soil offered meagre prospects; it was rocky and almost unworkable. Which was why they had never envisaged a day like this. Who would be so eager to possess himself of their desolate holdings that he would summon two companies of policemen and a dozen bailiffs to his cause? As one of the tenants, an elderly man named Owen Ward, vacated his home of many years, he kissed the whitewashed walls of the house and urged the other members of the family to do likewise. Ward, like his neighbours, was shocked at the arbitrary actions of their landlord. 'They owed no rent. They had done no man wrong.'[1]

The *Derry Standard* reported that, 'when dispossessed, the families grouped themselves on the ground, beside the ruins of their late homes, having no place of refuge near. The dumb animals refused to leave the wallsteads, and in some cases were with difficulty rescued from the falling timbers.'[2] Deeply moved by what they witnessed were a number of the police-bystanders, deployed to protect the bailiffs. The melancholy spectacle was reported to have left them in tears. Their emotions were, in part, provoked by the knowledge that their presence had been wholly unnecessary. So stunned were the Derryveagh tenants at what was happening to their homes that they put up not the slightest resistance. A local Poor Law inspector, Robert Hamilton, in a report submitted on the conduct of the ejectments, wrote that he had seen nothing similar since the Famine evictions in Mayo. The authorities, not eager to preside over the recurrence of an event akin to one of the notorious Famine clearances, had subjected the legal process underpinning the Derryveagh evictions to intense scrutiny, but no flaw could be found in Adair's paperwork. He could proceed, and they were obliged to protect the men who had been hired to do his work: 'The Crown could pardon a murderer, but could not prevent an eviction.'[3] Only the intervention of an unlikely act of parliament could have saved Adair's luckless tenants.

It took three days to evict the forty-seven Derryveagh families; 244 men, women and children were left to fend for themselves. The possibility of creeping back into their houses when darkness fell had been effectively eliminated. Most of the sad and dilapidated buildings were now roofless. The 'crowbar brigade' had done its work well: '11,602 acres of virtually barren land [was] cleared of human habitation.'[4]

Their landlord wouldn't hear of any talk about the 'Ulster custom' either. None of the tenants was going to receive a shilling for their supposed 'interest' in their holdings. They could whistle for it. All forty-seven families were to be left on the side of the road, penniless.

'Black Jack' Adair had revenged the murder of his steward. With compound interest.

'The forest of the silver birches': landlords and tenants, 1848–78

'The hamlet clustering on its hill is seen,
A score of petty homesteads, dark and mean;
Poor always, not despairing until now;
Long used, as well as poverty knows how,
With life's oppressive trifles to contend.
This day will bring its history to an end.'

(from 'The Eviction', William Allingham, inspired by the Derryveagh ejectments of 1861)

'And there was peace in the valley' – although this was a concord built on the tragic foundation of 2 million deaths and departures.

A quarter of the population had vanished, as had 200,000 holdings. So between the 1850s and the 1880s, the numbers involved in agriculture declined and farm sizes grew accordingly. Farmers married later in life. The Crimean War brought prosperity and helped see off the Tenant League (covered later). Fewer people were murdered in land-related crime (100 between 1857 and 1878). Eviction rates plummeted compared to the Famine period. The number of ejectments climbed above 1,000 a year only four times between 1854 and 1878, and in two of those years, 1863 (1,552) and 1864 (1,590), the country was in the grip of a serious economic downturn. An average of around 1,000 evictions per annum in the three decades before the Land War was a relatively modest level of disturbance when set against a total of over half a million peasant holdings (c.570,000).

After the traumatic watershed of *An Gorta Mór* – a period of tenant capitulation that often prompted the militants of the late nineteenth century to accuse the Famine generation of lassitude and passivity* – the sectional and regional insurrectionary spirit of 1760–1830 gave way to a less localised, less violent activism, where agrarianism became the fellow traveller of constitutional nationalism, while never entirely abandoning its shadowy Ribbon-Fenian alter ego. Irish radical movements advanced with the ploughshare in one hand and the ballot box in the other. The hougher and the carder, while not entirely redundant, were largely supplanted by the branch secretary, the pragmatic parish priest, the raucous public meeting, the honing of ostracisation to a fine art and the profane subversion of parliamentary procedure. The men in suits were making nuisances of themselves, so that the men in white shirts didn't have to.

Not that the landlord class abandoned its *laager* mentality even with a measurable reduction in agrarian crime. Many still felt themselves to be afloat in a precarious wooden dinghy in

---

* Michael Davitt referred to this apathy as 'the spirit of social disease that crept into the life of Ireland in 1846' (*The Fall of Feudalism in Ireland*, 57).

waters teeming with sharks. Some had hardly moved from the apocalyptic narratives of the 1820s. Strident aristocratic allegations of religious warfare as the basis of land agitation diminished, but did not entirely dissipate.

Was it dangerous to be a landlord, or associated with property ownership, in the decades after the Famine? While there were undoubtedly less perilous avocations (not too many apothecaries were murdered in the course of their professional work), empirical evidence suggests that it was relatively safe to be an agent or a landlord from the 1850s to the 1880s. Nine landlords, a single agent, seven bailiffs and ten estate servants lost their lives to agrarian agitation during that period. Twenty-seven killings over two decades (1857–78) in which around 2,000 people died violently surely qualifies as an acceptable risk-to-reward ratio. 'It was more dangerous to work on the Irish railways, to ride to foxhounds, or to be a member of a European royal house'[5] – in fact, it was far more dangerous being a tenant farmer. In excess of seventy tenants, or members of their families, were murdered during the same period, mostly in disputes with other tenants.

However, while the Irish landowning class, now rather less Protestant than in the days before the passage of the Encumbered Estates Act, was unlikely to be subjected to any form of Pastorini-esque mass slaughter, its ascendancy status was undoubtedly being threatened by the Catholic *nouveax riches*, by a radically altered political *zeitgeist*, and by a subtle change in mindset when it came to land tenure and ownership.

In practical terms, the encumbered estates legislation had only a minimal impact. While one-seventh of the land was now in the hands of the Irish professional and mercantile classes, six-sevenths still belonged to its pre-Famine owners. The act did have the effect of reducing the percentage of absentee landlords, but, in general, succeeded only in replacing them with new landowners busily managing their stores in Athlone and Tralee, or their practices in Dublin and Cork. The act, however, did have an entirely unintended effect. It encouraged the belief among the tenantry that evolution, if not revolution, was possible. Land, it now transpired, could change hands. What if those hands were the calloused digits of the men and women who actually worked the soil? If a Dublin solicitor managed to acquire an entire estate at a knock-down price from a family who had been gifted the land by Cromwell himself, could a tenant farmer not aspire to purchasing his own portion of that estate?

On the surface, however, things appeared to proceed much as normal. God remained in his heaven beaming contentedly on the perpetuation of the Protestant ascendancy and the enduring success of the Anglican hierarchy in maintaining its established status.

John George Adair, Irish born and bred, had an identity problem. He couldn't seem to make up his mind whether he wanted to be a Texas rancher or a Scottish laird. So he compromised and tried to be both. In the 1860s he cleared much of the land he had bought in 1859, in the area around Derryveagh (which translates from Irish as 'the forest of the silver birches' – there were precious few still in evidence when he acquired the land) and imported thousands of blackfaced sheep[6] along with their Scottish shepherds.

In 1877, he entered into an unequal* partnership with one of the legendary figures of the American west, the Texas cowman Charles Goodnight, in a spread that he insisted should bear his initials, the JA Ranch in Palo Duro, Texas. Goodnight took $30,000 of Adair's money to keep himself afloat as the economic depression sparked by the financial 'Panic of '73' began to bite, but his opinion of his 'sleeping partner' was not dissimilar to that of Adair's former Donegal tenants. 'He was an overbearing old son of a gun,' said Goodnight, the man who had first blazed a trail in 1866 for cattle drives from Texas to rail junctions in the Midwest, 'and would have been beat up several times if it hadn't been for me.'[7]

The former career move, however, his desire to emulate a Scottish laird, was of more consequence to Irish tenant farmers than his yearning to be taken seriously as a Texan rancher.

Adair was the wealthy son of a gentleman farmer from Queen's County (Laois) and – it seems hardly credible given his subsequent history – had stood as a 'tenant right' candidate in

---

* Adair retained two-thirds of all the profits from their jointly owned ranch.

the 1852 parliamentary election in Limerick. He was once even described by *The Nation* as 'a cultured young squire'.[8] But since he also happened to be the nephew of the self-regarding *agent extraordinaire* William Steuart Trench, he was unlikely to become a lifelong champion of the oppressed tenant, especially because he shared much of his uncle's arrogance, paranoia and native disdain.

By the 1860s, Adair had deviated from the straight and narrow course of support for tenant right. Having managed to capitalise on the Encumbered Estates Act and acquire a portfolio of land from bankrupt post-Famine estates, he then set about evicting many of his new tenants. Between 1852 and 1857, he spent almost £35,000 on land in Tipperary, Kilkenny and Queen's County, nine lots in total, comprising almost 5,000 acres.

But it is his responsibility for one of the most infamous mass evictions of the period between the Great Famine and the Land War which is his abiding legacy and the principal reason Adair is remembered somewhat more fondly (if at all) in the USA than in his native country. In 1857, he acquired around 30,000 acres in the remote and unpromising but ruggedly beautiful Glenveagh/Derryveagh/Gartan region of north Donegal. He claimed to have been 'so struck … with the charms of the scenery, that he determined to become proprietor of the place'.[9] In 1867, he copper-fastened his aristocratic pretensions by building the magnificent Glenveagh House on the site of his newly acquired property. When he purchased the Donegal land in 1859, he claimed that his desire was to 'open up these remote districts and to elevate and improve the condition of the people'.[10] He must have been made aware, at the time of the transaction, that a previous owner of some of the Donegal land that he was now purchasing, a man named Marshall, had been murdered in 1840 while coming home from church, in front of dozens of witnesses 'who let the murderer walk quietly away'.[11] It did not weigh on his mind at the time, but it would later.

Adair, seldom less than bellicose, shared that characteristic with many of his imported Scottish shepherds. Given the manner in which they had come by their positions, the Scottish crofters were unlikely to have been popular in north Donegal to begin with. However, they seemed to go out of their way to alienate local feeling. According to Trinity College, Dublin historian William Vaughan in his account of the episode, *Sin, Sheep and Scotsmen: John George Adair and the Derryveagh Evictions, 1861*, 'the best that can be said of their moral character was that their faults had the doubtful merit of simplicity: perjury, theft, murder, adultery were at one time or another imputed to them'.[12] Two were murdered, and the second murder victim was one of two of the former crofters who had spent time in Irish prisons between 1861 and 1863.

The Derryveagh evictions were prompted by the killing of Adair's Scottish steward, James Murray, on 13 November 1861. Murray's skull had been fractured by a blow from a large stone. He had managed to get off a single pistol shot before being overpowered by his assailant or, more likely, assailants. Adair believed that his Derryveagh tenants could identify Murray's killers, but instead they were sheltering him (or them). What followed was a vindictive campaign of ejectment, in the course of which 244 men, women and children from forty-seven families were expelled from their holdings. A charitable organisation, the Donegal Relief Committee, ultimately paid for the passage of most of those evicted to Australia. There they were given jobs. In that sense alone Adair had been successful in his stated object, to 'improve the condition of the people'.

Not all of those evicted, however, were fortunate enough to secure passage to Australia. Long before that happened, according to Cork MP Vincent Scully in the House of Commons on 24 June 1861, 'one old man died within a few days from the hardships he had suffered, and two other men had become lunatics'.[13] Scully, in a debate on his motion to, in effect, remove Adair as a local magistrate because of his conduct, challenged the landlord to come up with a shred of proof that his Derryveagh tenants had been harbouring Murray's killers. Seven of Adair's fellow magistrates had already passed a resolution condemning his actions. His landowning neighbours 'seemed to regard him as a deadly combustible, planted in their midst'.[14] Even the prime minister (and Irish landlord), Lord Palmerston, poured cold water over Adair's allegations against his tenants and questioned the landlord's motives. 'A man's mind,' Palmerston told the House of Commons, 'must, indeed, be very much distorted who can fancy it a real justification for sweeping away a whole population that he thought ought to give evidence against a murderer, when probably they know no more about the deed than he did himself.'[15]

Even before the murder of Murray, Adair, in January 1860, had served eviction notices on his tenants. He had failed to follow through with any expulsions, however, by November of the same year. His attitude changed when the constabulary failed to catch Murray's murderer. Adair decided to proceed with the evictions. One-fifth of those evicted were permitted to return as caretakers of their late holdings, but only three families were permanently reinstated. Adair seemed to be convinced that his tenants were all Ribbonmen, a 'lawless, violent, thieving, murderous gang, whose extirpation is a mission which has devolved on him in the interests of "society"'.[16]

Adair was not shy about defending his actions. He had, he insisted, merely done what was required to protect himself against a Ribbon conspiracy. 'What course was left to me?' he wrote. 'I offered to abandon these evictions with pleasure, if government could give me any assurance or guarantee for the safety of myself or my servants.'[17] He claimed that 'upwards of 600' of his sheep had been stolen or killed,* that he was being ostracised locally and that he had been mocked over the murder of Murray by tongue-in-cheek local assertions that 'the fairies came out of the rocks and killed him'.[18] The implication of the defence of his actions was that his Derryveagh tenants had got no more than they deserved.

However, William Vaughan has established that the steward was probably murdered by, or at the behest of, his Scottish lodger, Dugald Rankin. Rankin was alleged to be having an affair with James Murray's wife. This was hinted at by Vincent Scully in the 24 June 1861 Commons debate, when he alleged that Adair

---

* Some had indeed been killed, but by his own shepherds in an effort to secure compensation for criminal damage. Others had fallen victim to inclement weather (HC Deb, 24 June 1861, vol. 163, c. 1495).

had cynically used the Murray killing for his own purposes, in order to clear the Derryveagh tenancies. In the same debate, the MP for Dungarvan, John Maguire, accused an unnamed suspect (Rankin) of being 'extremely intimate with the dead man's wife' and of having worn the dead man's clothes at his funeral.[19]

Journalist and politician Alexander Martin Sullivan spent some time in Donegal when Adair was establishing his vast land portfolio in the county. This amounted to ninety square miles by the time Adair finally pocketed his chequebook. Sullivan visited Derryveagh and formed a favourable impression of the rather cloistered and isolated community around Gartan Lough. He became involved in the effort to find shelter and employment for the evictees in Australia. As they departed for their new lives from Dublin Port, he 'bade these poor people a last adieu'. More than a decade later, he revisited Derryveagh. From the shores of Gartan Lough, he could see the fine castle at Glenveagh that Adair had built for himself: 'My thoughts wandered back to that terrible April morning on Gartan side. In fancy I heard rolling across those hills the widow's wail, the women's parting cry. I thought of the farewell at the graves; of the crowd upon the fore-deck of that steamer.'[20]

Adair died in the USA in 1885. In a final irony, his gothic castle and Donegal estate now belong to, among others, the descendants of some of the families he evicted in April 1861. This is because the entire property was gifted to the Irish state by a subsequent owner, the Philadelphian Henry McIlhenny. Locals like to believe that the outcome was even more poetic, claiming that McIlhenny was descended from one of the evicted families. It would be comforting to think that was true, but, unfortunately, the story, while gratifying, appears to be apocryphal.

If any further illustration was required that not all evicting landlords were lofty Anglo-Irish Protestant grandees, the case of William Scully should clinch the argument. Scully was the son of the Catholic political activist Denys Scully, a precursor and occasional ally of Daniel O'Connell in the early struggle for Catholic emancipation. That William Scully did not die in the religion that his father fought hard to reinvigorate politically was an irascible response to the strident criticism of his own impetuousness and brutality from an enraged member of the Catholic clergy.

By the time of the Famine, Scully had acquired a sizeable estate in Tipperary, where 'he concentrated rigorously on maximising profits, often at the expense of his tenants'.[21] Unlike most of his peers, who were generally stand-offish when it came to personal participation in evictions, Scully liked to lead his bailiffs into the fray. By thus annihilating the traditional *cordon sanitaire* between landlord and tenant on eviction day, he copper-fastened his unpopularity. Scully was found not guilty of shooting two tenants during an 1849 eviction and was later convicted, at the Kilkenny Assizes in 1865, of assaulting a female tenant. He was sentenced to a year in jail.

Paradoxically, however, Scully was also an 'improving' landlord, albeit one with modernising ideas who paid scant heed to the plight or the needs of his tenants. His biographer has written of him that 'in Scully's view the only salvation for Irish agriculture was to improve the fertility of the soil and to produce animals and animal products for the nearby growing urban markets'.[22] This can be read as shorthand for carrying out estate clearances, and the subsequent purchase of a dairy or beef herd that would ruminate across the land formerly occupied by the evictees. 'Modernisation' and 'improvement' could be ugly processes if you happened to be a tenant on land required by a moderniser for his Jerseys or Herefords.

Scully was clearly a devotee of extant land legislation, but only insofar as it certified the primacy of the landlord. In the infamous 'Battle of Ballycohey' (a village located approximately five kilometres from Tipperary town) of August 1868, however, he sought to vary the terms of the law considerably. Under existing statutes, tenants at will could be evicted only after first being given six months' notice. Scully tried to force his Ballycohey tenants to agree instead to an altogether briefer three-week cooling-off period. When they refused, and failed to turn up in Dobbyns' Hotel in Tipperary town to sign new agreements, Scully led his

team of bailiffs to Ballycohey on three separate occasions to serve
notices to evict. His intemperate response was to prove fatal for
one of his bailiffs and one of the members of the accompanying
police force, after the potential evictees twice succeeded in avoiding
the serving of the processes by absenting themselves from their
homes. Determined that his third visit to Ballycohey would not
be entirely wasted, Scully, along with a policeman named Morrow
and two bailiffs named Gorman and Maher, entered the house of
one of the tenants, John Dwyer. Too late they realised that they
had walked into a well-prepared ambush. They were met with
a hail of bullets and Morrow and Gorman were killed instantly.
Scully and Maher were wounded. According to Michael Davitt
and others, the landlord wore chain armour under his coat. This
was a persistent rumour that Scully always strenuously denied. The
allegation, however, was given some credibility by the fact that,
of the half-dozen bullets recovered from Scully's body, none were
taken from his trunk.

No one ever faced trial for the gunfight at Ballycohey. The
acknowledged leader of the local agrarian resistance, one Michael
O'Dwyer, suspected of masterminding the ambush, was reported
to have fled to America. John Dwyer, owner of the house in
which Scully almost met his maker, was not required to keep an
appointment with the hangman either, having been careful to
establish an alibi. He died in his bed in 1903 'having enjoyed wide
celebrity in his native county since 1868'.[23]

At the inquest into the deaths of the policeman and the bailiff,
the coroner's jury commented that 'the conduct of Mr. William
Scully, as regards proceedings towards his tenants at Ballycohey,
is much to be deprecated; and the sooner legislative enactments
be passed to put a stop to any such proceedings, the better for
the peace and welfare of the country'.[24] Thus did the Ballycohey
jury ensure its place in the pantheon of defiant Irish coroner's
court verdicts.

There was precious little support for Scully in Ireland or in
Britain. The 'Battle of Ballycohey' was well-publicised. *The Times*,
although broadly sympathetic to Scully's 'prosecution of his
right[s]', also described him as a 'very rash man' and wondered

how he had been 'able to obtain an escort of policemen to protect him in any high-handed and unreasonable proceedings'.[25] As a result of this press exposure, Scully became the living, breathing role model for the archetypal evil Irish landlord, a trope almost as beloved of the liberal English press as of their Irish nationalist equivalents. One of the luminaries who watched in horror as the events in Ballycohey unfolded was the Liberal Party leader, William Gladstone. Scully's immoderate spleen undoubtedly helped to shape Gladstone's – already jaundiced – view of Irish landlords. Four months after the Ballycohey fracas, Gladstone found himself in a position where he could curb the excesses of proprietors like Scully, when he became prime minister. He began the long process of hobbling the Irish aristocracy and democratising Irish land tenure.

It is probably fitting that Scully went on to make a fortune in the USA. By the end of the nineteenth century, he was the proud owner of 250,000 acres of American land in the rural Midwest. He became an American citizen in 1902 and died a millionaire in 1906. He carried one of the Ballycohey bullets to his grave but at least had the satisfaction of outliving John Dwyer by three years.

Irony recognises no boundaries, so it was entirely fitting that William Scully should be the younger brother of Vincent Scully, the Cork MP who became embroiled in the Derryveagh eviction controversy of 1861 as a harsh critic of John George Adair and his yearning for an uninterrupted view of his Donegal property. Unimpressed by his brother's actions at Ballycohey, Scully senior complained to *The Times* about the consistent use of the name 'Mr. Scully' in their coverage of the incident. He feared that it 'would seem to designate the head of the family'.[26] There was a clear dearth of sibling affection among the sons of Denys Scully.

Shortly after the 'Battle of Ballycohey', the ubiquitous 'Rory of the Hills' made a brief appearance in a ballad in dishonour of Scully. It began as follows.

I met a man on Slievenamon and I asked was Scully dead,
I cannot give you that account but I hear he's bad in bed,

He turned my mother out of doors, but I may meet him still,
I'm the bold Tipperary mountaineer, I'm Rory of the Hill.[27]

Derryveagh was, as we have already seen, something of an aberration. Levels of post-Famine eviction were low, and estate clearances were almost unheard of. Adair, however, was not a solitary rogue landlord in the decades between the Famine and the Land War. The 1878 assassination in Donegal of William Clements, 3rd Earl of Leitrim, was largely a consequence of his general belligerence and of a threat to evict up to twenty families from his Donegal estate. Leitrim's *Dictionary of Irish Biography* entry tells us that 'displays of independence by tenants usually moved him to fury, and he was alleged to have struck tenants on several occasions'.[28]

In 1876, two years before his death, Leitrim had evicted four families for cutting down trees and another six for gathering seaweed or cutting turf, liberties with his property that he particularly abhorred. Although he aroused Catholic anger in 1858 when he took possession of a church located on his estate, Leitrim did not discriminate between Catholic and Presbyterian tenants when it came to ejectments. Like Adair before him, he was almost as unpopular with his fellow Donegal landlords as he was with his tenants. The local gentry believed that the general loathing of Leitrim rubbed off unfairly on them. Neither did he have a good relationship with Dublin Castle. On one occasion, in a gesture of spite towards the Lord Lieutenant, Lord Carlisle, he packed a hotel on his Connemara estate at his own expense to prevent Carlisle from securing a room there. By way of retaliation for this humiliation, Carlisle engineered the dismissal of Clements as a justice of the peace for counties Leitrim and Donegal.

Leitrim's personal reputation was hardly exemplary. He was surrounded by persistent rumours that he was a sexual predator who insisted on exercising *droit de seigneur* over the daughters of his tenants before their marriages. While this may well be little more than malicious *ex post facto* folklore to justify the killing of a titled aristocrat, it was widely believed at the time. According to Michael Davitt, Leitrim was notorious for 'using his power over the tenants for designs against the honour of their daughters' and succumbed 'to the revenge of a farmer's son whose sister had suffered an unforgivable wrong'.[29]

Leitrim was well aware that he was a marked man and generally travelled with an armed escort. On 2 April 1878, however, he must have thought he was sufficiently well protected by the occupants of two carriages travelling in convoy, and by his own two revolvers, to drive from his home at Manorvaughan to nearby Milford. When Leitrim's carriage slowed to ascend a steep hill near Cratlagh wood, two armed men, Michael McElwee and Neil Shiels, were waiting. A fusillade of bullets killed Leitrim's coachman, Charles Buchanan, and mortally wounded John Makim, a court clerk. Despite being peppered with bullets himself, Leitrim managed to escape from the carriage and grapple with his assailants before being despatched by a blow to the head that split the stock of the rifle which finally killed him. The occupants of the second carriage were at least 200 metres away from the scene of the killings and made no attempt to intervene, leading to inevitable allegations of complicity.

Either a generous sprinkling of tenants made the long journey to Dublin or the earl's reputation preceded him to the metropolis, because, at his burial, concerted attempts were made to disrupt the funeral. Members of the public booed and hissed as Leitrim's cortège passed on its way to the Clements family vault in St Michan's Church. An attempt was made to drag his coffin from the carriage that was conveying it. This effort failed when the police intervened. Later, the funeral service was accompanied by a chorus of jibes and catcalls from outside St Michan's.[30]

No one was executed for the murder of Lord Leitrim. Neil Shiels died before he could be brought to trial and McElwee – despite reward offers of up to £10,000 (from Leitrim's heir) to anyone who would come forward with information – was never convicted. He died in 1921. In 1960, a plaque was erected in Fanad, Co. Donegal, celebrating the role of Shiels, McElwee and an associate, Michael Heraghty, in the killing of Leitrim, in ending 'the tyranny of landlordism'.

The failure 'to rise in sterner wrath' and the 'wonderful little hunchback': the Tenant League, James Fintan Lalor and the limits of agrarian activism

'The land question contains, and the legislative question does not contain, the materials from which victory is manufactured, and that, therefore, if we be truly in earnest and determined on success, it is on the former question, and not on the latter, we must take our stand.'[31]

(James Fintan Lalor, letter to *The Irish Felon*, 24 June 1848)

'In the minds of the Irish peasantry, a resistance to landlord oppression is associated with revolt against the British Crown. Rebellion against that Crown is regarded as a movement against the grievances which are connected with the tenure of land.'[32]

(Isaac Butt, *The Irish People and the Irish Land*, 1867)

Its importance has probably been exaggerated almost as much as the estimate of fatalities, but the so-called 'Battle of Dolly's Brae' in Co. Down on 12 July 1849, in which Orange Order marchers attacked Catholic property after they encountered resistance to their annual Twelfth procession, was hardly a promising straw in the wind for prospects of joint north-south tenant right agitation. It hadn't been that long since the Orange Order had emerged from a period of legal suppression, and the killings at Dolly's Brae – probably in single figures,[33] rather than the emotive estimate of forty dead Catholics – prompted renewed restrictions on marching and public demonstrations with the passage of the Party Processions Act of 1850. Yet, *mirabile dictu*, within twelve months of Dolly's Brae, a cogent tenant right organisation was established which included a significant representation of northern Presbyterians making common cause with southern Catholics.

All the more surprising was that the initiative leading to the foundation of the short-lived Tenant League came from two

Roman Catholic priests in Co. Kilkenny. Their resourcefulness marked a radical departure from the 'hugger mugger' secret societies of old, and presaged a form of constitutional agrarianism favouring the enactment of remedial legislation over the houghing of cattle. Davitt called it 'the programme of the Whiteboys and Ribbonmen reduced to moral and constitutional standards and plans of action'.[34]

However, this period of factional collaboration was even briefer than the lifespan of the Tenant League itself. It was also a coalition that did not recur, and the fact that it occurred in the first place, though a notable feather in the organisation's cap, served only to throw into sharp relief the difficulty of shelving sectarian paranoia and religious differences to make common cause in the pursuit of an issue of mutual concern. It is interesting that when one of the founders of the Tenant League, Charles Gavan Duffy, wrote an account of its mayfly lease on life, he entitled it *The League of North and South*. This brief and unlikely alliance of Presbyterian and Catholic tenants was the unique selling point of the Tenant League, as Duffy was well aware.

Charles Gavan Duffy

The origins of the Tenant League, or the Irish Tenant Right League – to give it its more ponderous title – can probably be traced back to the founding of a tenant protection society in 1849, by two Roman Catholic priests, Fr Thomas O'Shea and Fr Matthew O'Keeffe in Callan, Co. Kilkenny, seedbed of so much rural agitation since the middle of the eighteenth century. The object of the society was to defend the interests of the tenants of the Earl of Desart, described by Charles Gavan Duffy as 'an active exterminator' who had cleared more than 400 people from his estate during the Famine. The avowed aims of the society were 'Fair Rents, Tenant Right, and Employment' and the organisation's membership cards even included the serenely subversive axiom of the late Irish under-secretary, Thomas Drummond, that 'property has its duties as well as its rights'. By July 1850, the fledgling Callan society had been joined by twenty similar organisations in Kilkenny and adjoining counties.

What prompted the unlikely Catholic/Presbyterian-north/south alliance was a perceived threat to the 'Ulster Custom'. This convention tacitly recognised, though not in any solemnised form, that Ulster tenants had a financial interest in their holdings and were entitled to benefit from any improvements they had made to their farms. Accordingly, they could sell the 'interest' in their farm if they vacated. This time-honoured model had been challenged by the report of the pre-Famine Devon Commission (1844) as being inimical to the 'just rights of property'[35] (although the commission also suggested a regime of compensation for improvement). The custom had also been given no formal recognition in the framing of the 1849 Encumbered Estates legislation, where 'no conditions favourable to tenants were imposed on the purchasers'.[36] So there was a certain nervousness in the Glens and in 'Drumlin country' that induced northern Protestant (mostly Presbyterian) tenants to put aside their suspicions of Rome and collaborate with a largely Papist organisation founded to address that very issue. Sturdy Presbyterian farmers were determined not to surrender their traditional rights, which, they maintained, had accrued as early as the seventeenth century, when they were required to assist their overlords in repelling the constant threat of 'wolf and woodkerne'.

Their stance was encapsulated in a couplet from a contemporary northern poem:

> And now our rights, but favours none, we're seeking at your
> hands
> We gave our Yeomen services – we'll keep our Yeomen lands.[37]

The Tenant League wanted to achieve for their southern Catholic supporters what their Orange brethren feared they were about to lose.

First onto the field, in 1848, was the Ulster Tenant Right Association, founded by the liberal/unionist journalist James MacKnight, editor of the official organ of the general assembly of the Presbyterian Church, the *Banner of Ulster*, and the radical MP, William Sharman Crawford, a 'benevolent' landlord of 6,000 acres in Co. Down. Crawford, a fully paid-up member of that substantial group of former allies with whom Daniel O'Connell had succeeded in falling out, had, as MP for Dundalk, and later as a radical member for the English constituency of Rochdale, introduced half-a-dozen pieces of legislation to formalise the 'Ulster Custom', the first as early as 1836. They had all met with the same result, a fatal combination of resigned apathy from government and opposition benches and splenetic opposition from the champions of property rights in the House of Commons.

When three Dublin journalist/editors, Charles Gavan Duffy of *The Nation*, John Gray of the *Freeman's Journal* and English-born Frederick Lucas, founder of *The Tablet* – 'chief organ of Catholic opinion in the Empire', a man who enjoyed 'the confidence of the Catholic clergy'[38] – sought to bring together the burgeoning tenant protection societies in the south in a single national body, MacKnight and Crawford were persuaded to become founder members of the new Tenant Right League at a Dublin meeting. This was presided over by MacKnight himself in August 1850. The meeting was attended by more than 300 delegates. According to Duffy, 'it was an authentic Parliament of Ireland … representing the whole nation'. Geographically, perhaps it was, since it included 'reserved stern Covenanters from the north' who sat beside 'priests who had lived through the horrors of a famine which left their churches empty and their grave-yards overflowing'. But it was hardly representative of a population that still included almost a million farm labourers and as many cottiers. The interests of the absent members of the labouring class were dealt with in a pious resolution 'that it be an instruction to the League ... to take into consideration at the earliest possible period the condition of the farm labourers, and to suggest some measure for their permanent protection and improvement'.[39] This vagueness did not carry over into the seminal resolutions of the convention on the subject closest to the members' hearts, 'tenant right', a phrase susceptible of a number of interpretations.

Thus, in a sense, were the '3Fs' born. Although the concepts of 'fair rent, free sale and fixity of tenure' were hardly new, it was the first time in which issues of such signal importance to Irish tenant farmers had been packaged in this way. While the three elements of this agrarian troika are largely self-explanatory ('free sale' being associated with the recognition of a tenant's financial 'interest' in their rented property), the Tenant League did not attempt to address issues of land ownership – two of its most prominent members, Crawford and Mayo MP George Henry Moore, were landlords themselves – or the parlous position of the cottiers and labourers since the Famine. This was a fundamental issue that separated the Tenant League from the Land League of the 1880s. While the latter was, as we shall see, led by a rural bourgeoisie, it did include in its ranks, albeit briefly, a number of poorer peasants and a representative smattering of the landless proletariat. The Tenant League was composed almost entirely of prosperous farmers. A clue to the composition of its membership and its policy priorities can probably be seen in the disappearance of the Callan society's stress on employment from the sloganeering of the Tenant League.

Because within the proximate causes of the formation of the Tenant League lay the seeds of its own self-immolation. It was a misdirected sledgehammer deployed to crack a peanut. Its southern membership 'represented the reaction of the prosperous, market-orientated wheat and barley growers'[40] of Kilkenny and

Tipperary to a temporary fall in prices between 1847 and 1849. The Callan society, founded by Reverends O'Shea and O'Keeffe, was established after an especially bad wheat harvest. Even the *Kilkenny Journal* of 17 November 1849 recognised that the league consisted of 'a class of respectable and sturdy farmers who were possessed of competent means'. The founding of the league was a step towards retaining those means. To Joseph Lee, the composition of the organisation 'doomed the League from the outset'. He points out in *The Modernisation of Irish Society* that less than 5 per cent of the delegates to the inaugural convention of September 1850 came from west of a line drawn from Derry to Cork.[41] Although there were other factors involved in the strangulation of the league by 1854, it was the onset of the Crimean War and the resulting rise in grain prices, leading to the renewal of generous cash-flows into the pockets of Munster/south Leinster tillage farmers, which cooled their ardour for political agitation and transferred their attention once again to the next harvest.

Neither did it take long for the north-south axis to collapse. Crawford sought allies for tenant right issues in the House of Commons. His fellow radicals, led by the great British parliamentarian John Bright, offered support, as did a group of southern Irish MPs, many of whom were members of a loosely affiliated body known as the Catholic Defence Association, better known in Westminster circles as 'the Pope's Brass Band'. This caucus of Catholic MPs had largely come about in opposition to the 1851 Ecclesiastical Titles Act, a piece of legislation introduced to frustrate efforts by the papacy to restore the Roman Catholic diocesan structure in Britain. While this alliance increased the total vote in favour of Crawford's seventh failed attempt to have the 'Ulster Custom' recognised by the House of Commons, it also afforded the Tories and the Orange Order an opportunity to excoriate Crawford for his association with Irish MPs intent on the repeal of both the Union and the anti-papist Ecclesiastical Titles Act. In May 1852 the *Belfast Newsletter* depicted the radical MP as 'the ally of papists and infidel-levelling democrats',[42] thus managing the problematic task of turning the word 'democrat' into a term of abuse. In the 1852 election campaign, his unionist opponents – Crawford was opposed to Repeal but was a federalist/devolutionist – made it their business to ensure that he failed to secure a parliamentary seat in Co. Down. This was achieved with the turbulent assistance of violent mobs who broke up his election meetings.

Presbyterian enthusiasm for the league was also modified by the threat of northern landlords to consign the dangerously chimerical 'Ulster Custom' to agrarian oblivion if their tenants did not vote for Conservative candidates in the general election. Since these were the days before the passage of the Ballot Act of 1872, tenants were obliged to declare their support publicly for the electoral candidate of their choice, a declaration that was likely to be carefully monitored and duly noted in certain quarters. This resulted in the return of only a single candidate in Ulster who was sympathetic to the aims of the Tenant League.

Elsewhere, however, the Tenant League seemed to do well, returning forty-eight members to the new parliament. At least this was how it appeared. That, after all, was the number of Irish MPs who signed up to the principles of the league (support for the 3Fs) and agreed to sit as members of an Independent Irish Party (IIP) pledged to oppose the incumbent government. This, of course, meant spurning all blandishments of political office.

However, the truth was somewhat more predictable. Many of the forty-eight members of the Independent Irish Party were opportunists who had climbed onto the Tenant League bandwagon in order to secure their seats. Their allegiance was less than skin-deep. Others were affiliated to the Catholic Defence Association and were more desirous of securing the repeal of the Ecclesiastical Titles Act – insofar as they were preoccupied with securing anything other than their own advancement and self-interest – than of safeguarding the prosperity of the affluent tillage farmers of the basin of the 'Three Sisters'.*

The first two careerists to renege on their commitments were John Sadleir and William Keogh, whose flaming effigies would feature at public meetings for many years into the future. The former was a

---

* The rivers Barrow, Nore and Suir, draining counties Kilkenny, Tipperary and Waterford.

wealthy banker and financial speculator – inept, as it turned out. The latter, a barrister, was pithily described by Charles Gavan Duffy as 'a man of remarkable ability, and embarrassed by no scruples'.[43]

The 1852 election had left the Irish parliamentarians in the giddy position of holding the balance of power. A confident IIP chose to bring down the Tory government of Lord Derby. Their votes were instrumental in the installation of Lord Aberdeen in Downing Street at the head of a Whig administration. When Sadleir and Keogh, both leading lights in the Catholic Defence Association, accepted positions in Aberdeen's government without extracting the vaguest concession on tenant right in return, Duffy and Lucas cried foul. Oddly, MacKnight declined to join the chorus of vitriol aimed at the two deserters, on the basis that their defection, and the inclusion of two Irish MPs in a British administration, served only to strengthen the Union. Thus ended, definitively, north-south solidarity. The unity of Orange(ish) and Green had been transitory and turned out to be a once-only offer.

Sadleir, 'the Prince of Swindlers', would later be exposed as a charlatan and embezzler in 1856 with the collapse of his Tipperary Bank, followed by his suicide by prussic acid on Hampstead

John Sadleir MP

Heath. His destiny was to figure as the model for the corrupt financier Mr Merdle in *Little Dorrit* by Charles Dickens. Keogh refused to fade away so dramatically. He went on to become an exceptionally disagreeable judge whose longevity, bilious presence on the bench and solidly conservative decisions ensured his success in enraging an entire generation of nationalists. Such was his status as a hate figure that he was protected around the clock by RIC bodyguards. When it was once suggested to him that his protection detail should be doubled in size, he declined the offer, responding acerbically, 'I have the most implicit confidence in the invincible cowardice of my fellow countrymen.'[44]

The IIP was supposed to be a bird flying on two wings: repeal of the Ecclesiastical Titles Act and tenant right. But when British Catholic bishops managed the not terribly arduous task of circumventing the legislation preventing them from associating their dioceses with British place-names, the powerful Archbishop of Dublin, Paul Cullen, pounced. Never enamoured of the IIP to begin with – Duffy unfairly characterised him as 'plain, clumsy, slow of speech, and intellectually narrow and ill-informed'[45] – he now discouraged Catholic priests from maintaining any involvement with the party or the Tenant League. Cullen's disapproval of the likes of Gavan Duffy and the progressive Catholic editor of *The Tablet*, Frederick Lucas (a convert to Catholicism from the Society of Friends), influenced many of the erstwhile members of the Catholic Defence Association to sever their connection with league and party. This hastened the end of the activities of the Tenant League, already doomed by the rise in grain prices during the Crimean War.

Lucas travelled to Rome to seek the pontiff's censure of Cullen's perceived *coup de grâce* and died in 1855 without having secured papal disapprobation of the ultramontanist prelate. Gavan Duffy emigrated to Australia and probably achieved far more politically – including some significant agrarian innovations – in the state of Victoria (where he became state premier) than he would ever have been permitted to achieve in the House of Commons.

In the preface to his 1886 book *The League of North and South*, Duffy takes Parnell's parliamentary lieutenant, Justin McCarthy, to task for damning the Tenant League with too faint praise. Duffy, conscious of the Tenant League's unique selling point, accused the Land League and the Irish Parliamentary party of having 'failed to win the ear of the North'. McCarthy could hardly challenge this assertion, given that Duffy was referring to northern Dissenters – the Presbyterian tenants of Church of Ireland landlords – rather than to the Ulster Catholic voters who returned a number of Irish Parliamentary Party members to the House of Commons in the 1880s. But even Duffy was forced to concede what might well stand as the epitaph of the Tenant League, when he admitted of its more effective successors of the 1880s that 'you taught the people to rise in sterner wrath against their oppressors than the men of 1850 excited'.[46]

Early in 1847, the editors of *The Nation*, Charles Gavan Duffy and John Mitchel, were intrigued by a series of well-written and lucidly argued letters from an unknown correspondent who signed himself James F. Lalor of Tinakill House, Raheen, Queen's County (Laois), but who wished, for the moment at least, to be known by the alias 'Rolla', a clumsy anagram of his surname.[47] These missives argued against continued support for an insipid

James Fintan Lalor, 2007 bicentenary stamp, An Post

Repeal movement and condemned the lack of ambition of the objective itself ('a petty parish question'). The mysterious correspondent complained about the apparent lack of interest of Repealers in the issue of landlordism and advocated an immediate strike against rent rather than the continuation of an arid campaign against the Act of Union. The land struggle, he maintained, was the engine of Irish nationalism, the key that unlocked the door to an Irish exit from the United Kingdom.

Mitchel was impressed by the rhetoric and the ideology of 'Lalor'. Duffy, while admiring the passion and literary guile of this new correspondent, was less certain. He responded personally to Lalor's first letter to *The Nation* by suggesting that 'I can well fancy you bringing an untrained Titanic force into our counsels that would flutter the conventionalities of certain trim and curled gentlemen', but he baulked at the implications of Lalor's programme.[48]

Mitchel's stewardship of the militant *United Irishman* – after his split with Duffy and *The Nation* in December 1847 – was of insufficient duration (his newspaper was suppressed by Dublin Castle after only three months of revolutionary philippics) to exploit the philosophic and the literary skills of this somewhat enigmatic recluse. Instead, Lalor became a regular contributor to *The Irish Felon*, the equally mutinous successor to the *United Irishman*, founded by Mitchel's colleague John Martin. Martin's association with *The Irish Felon* ensured that he quickly followed his friend to Tasmania. Lalor made a significant contribution to Martin's transportation, because his letters to *The Irish Felon* – which take up more than seventy pages of an early volume of his collected writings[49] – were cited in court during the Young Irelander's treason-felony trial. This is hardly surprising, given that one of Lalor's communications had included the following seditious gem: 'We have determined to set about creating, as speedily as possible, a military organisation, of which the *Felon's* office shall be the centre and citadel.'[50]

Lalor, despite an appeal to the chief secretary, was not permitted to take sole responsibility for the content of his published letters. Dublin Castle wanted the leading Young Irelander, Martin, on the boat to Australia, not an obscure (and already ailing) bedroom revolutionary.

Lalor, as it happened, had an interesting dissenting pedigree of his own. He was an acolyte of Bishop James Doyle of Kildare and Leighlin ('JKL') and the son of Patrick Lalor, who, at the height of the tithe controversy, had refused to pay his dues to the Church of Ireland and had the word 'tithe' painted on twenty of his sheep when they were distrained. Patrick Lalor later won a parliamentary seat as a supporter of O'Connell.

James Fintan Lalor himself suffered greatly from ill-health as both a child and an adult and was described admiringly but insensitively by Michael Davitt, in *The Fall of Feudalism in Ireland*, as 'the wonderful little hunchback from the village in Queen's County',[51] adding that 'it was only in the head and heart of a little, deformed gentleman-farmer's son ... that the spirit and fire and purpose of a true Celtic revolutionist were found'. To Davitt, Lalor was a precursor who 'combined the national sentiment with the agrarian interest and passion, and would have rallied the aggressive Whiteboy and Ribbon spirit ... behind a movement that would have given Lord Clarendon[*] a social insurrection, as well as a revolutionary nationalist uprising, to deal with'.[52]

In one of his letters to *The Irish Felon*, Lalor himself had enunciated his dual aims of a lethal (for Dublin Castle) combination of land agitation and nationalist rebellion. He was not a believer in the old Irish nostrum 'those who hunt two hares catch neither'. 'My wish,' he wrote, 'is to combine and cement the two into one ... I want to ally the town and the country. Repeal is the question of the town population; and the tenure question is that of the country peasantry; both combined, taking each in its full extent and efficacy, form the question of Ireland, her question for the battle-day.'[53]

Based on his openly seditious correspondence in *The Irish Felon*, Lalor himself was arrested in July 1848. He served six months in prison before being released on health grounds.

While he was an advocate of passive resistance, he was always

* Lord Lieutenant of Ireland, 1847–52.

open to the possibility that this 'might have to become active resistance'.[54] On his release from jail, Lalor immediately made contact with the remnant of the Young Irelanders who remained at large and began to plot an uprising in which he himself, because of the poor state of his health, was unlikely to be in any position to participate. This initiative led to another abortive Young Ireland raid in Cappoquin, Co. Waterford, in September 1849, which was just as quickly suppressed as the previous iteration of Young Ireland militancy at the Widow McCormack's cottage in Ballingarry, Co. Tipperary, in 1848. Three months after this latest futile gesture, Lalor succumbed to bronchitis and died on 27 December at the age of forty. His attempted coup has since been almost entirely forgotten.

The failure of his revolutionary enterprises belies Lalor's legacy and his influence on the land struggle, if not the fight for legislative independence. He had a profound impact on Davitt, whose Land League slogan, 'the land for the people', borrowed heavily from one of Lalor's most famous dictums: 'The soil of Ireland for the people of Ireland'. Davitt also credits Lalor with giving the American economist and activist Henry George 'the social gospel of land nationalization minus all its pro-rebellious Irish bearings'.[55] In the twentieth century, his marriage of agrarianism and nationalism had a significant impact on Arthur Griffith. And it was his nascent socialism, much admired by Henry George, which exerted a profound influence on the ideas and the writings of James Connolly. On Patrick Pearse's last visit to the National Library of Ireland, in 1916, he was seen to be reading Lalor's fifth and final missive to *The Irish Felon*, 'Clearing Decks'.[56]

Lalor's philosophy is neatly encapsulated in one of his more memorable observations, made in a letter written on 21 June 1848 to *The Irish Felon*. It was the mission statement of a logician, a dreamer perhaps, well ahead of his time:

The principle I state, and mean to stand upon, is this, the entire ownership of Ireland, moral and material, up to the sun and down to the centre, is vested of right in the people of Ireland; that they, and none but they, are the land-owners and law-makers of this island; that all laws are null and void not made by them, and all titles to land invalid not conferred or confirmed by them …[57]

James Fintan Lalor's premature death was far from the end of his family's involvement in political activity and discourse. His brother Richard went on to become a supporter of the Land League and a Parnellite MP from 1880 to 1892. Another brother, Peter, is celebrated in Australia, where he emigrated in 1852, as the leader of the armed uprising of miners in the so-called 'Eureka Stockade' rebellion of 1854 in Ballarat, Victoria, an altogether bloodier and more consequential encounter than the Cappoquin skirmish of 1849. Peter Lalor later went on to become speaker of the Victorian Legislative Assembly in 1880.

Lalor is something of a prophet without honour in his own country. His ideas were taken seriously in his lifetime only by a committed cadre of militant nationalists and agrarianists. There was no place for his instinctive egalitarianism in the Ireland of the post-independence period. However, when it comes to the generation of revolutionary personalities to emerge from the Young Ireland movement (Thomas Davis, John O'Leary, Charles Gavan Duffy *et al.*), he is more than worthy of his place in that pantheon.

From Deasy to the Grand Old Man: land legislation, 1860–71

'According to the general practice in Ireland, the landlord builds neither dwelling-house nor farm offices, nor puts fences, gates, etc., into good order, before he lets his land to the tenant … without which, in England or Scotland, no tenant would be found to rent it.'

(Report of the Devon Commission, 1844)

It will probably come as no surprise to learn that, before 1860, relationships between Irish landlords and their tenant farmers were, in the main, 'based on tenure, not on contract'.[58] What might be more surprising, however, is that under British Common Law there was no power of summary eviction for the non-payment of rent. 'Tenants at will' who worked the land on a year-by-year basis could not just be peremptorily ejected if they simply declined, omitted or were unable to pay their rent. Their landlord was obliged to go to court and engage in an off-putting and tedious legal process to secure an ejectment.

However, despite an Act of Union passed in 1800 which, theoretically, made Ireland a fully fledged member of the United Kingdom of Great Britain and Ireland and, therefore, one would have assumed, subject to every nook and cranny of the Common Law, matters were arranged differently on 'John Bull's Other Island'. In Ireland, a series of Acts of Parliament had been passed with the object of being 'rid of every formality by which the old Common Law delayed and obstructed the forfeiture of the tenant's estate'.[59] English Common Law, as it related to Irish property, was over a period of time neutered and reversed. Sixty separate pieces of land legislation relating to Ireland were, for example, passed during the reign of King George III alone. This was ten times the number of laws deemed necessary for the governance of property in England and Wales over the same period. Some were enacted in the old Irish landlord-dominated parliament in College Green in Dublin; more came from Westminster after the Act of Union.

The so-called 'Irish Ejectment Code' that emerged from this raft of legislation overwhelmingly served the interests of the landlord. In 1816, for example, in the wake of the economic depression that followed the end of the Napoleonic Wars, legislation was passed to facilitate the ejectment of a tenant in arrears who was fortunate enough to have the protection afforded by a lease. An ejectment order could now be secured in a County Court, instead of a superior court, at minimal cost. A major disincentive to eviction – the high cost of legally ejecting a leaseholder – had been swept away.

Which is not to suggest that an epidemic of ejectments immediately followed. To some extent, this legislation rapidly became irrelevant anyway as fewer and fewer landlords were willing to offer leases to their tenants from the 1820s onwards. By 1851, it was necessary to legislate out of existence one of the few disincentives remaining which protected the rights of the much more vulnerable 'tenant at will'. The Civil Bill Court Act of that year made it just as straightforward to eject a struggling tenant at will as a defaulting leaseholder. A visit to the County Court would again suffice. British landlords – still required to incur the cost of a superior court action before they could evict even a yearly tenant – must have looked enviously at the concessions Irish squires seemed to be able to extract from their political masters/allies. However, it should be acknowledged that at least 'the landlord ... could not simply remove the tenant by force'.[60] He was still obliged to take some form of legal action, however inexpensive, before being permitted to eject a tenant. There are even recorded instances of the police protecting tenants against illegal evictions which has not been preceded by the required court processes.

However, as if the law was not already fearlessly on the side of the landlord, a pivotal piece of modifying legislation in 1860 made matters worse, in theory at least, for the tenant, when the 'modernising' Landlord and Tenant Law Amendment Act (Ireland) was introduced. Like 'improvement', the word 'modernising' could have a pejorative connotation in an Irish context if you happened to be a tenant. This legislation was supposed to define the rights and obligations on both sides of the tenurial arrangement but, in its final form, was decidedly one-sided in its implications. The legislation became better known as Deasy's Act, after the Irish attorney general in the Whig administration of Lord Palmerston, Rickard Morgan Deasy, who was responsible for its introduction. In its totality, the act was an effort to bring some order to the chaos of Ireland's copious land legislation. The devil, however, was in the detail. The nub of the act – the last identifiably retrograde Irish land legislation passed by the UK parliament – came in Section 3, in the ominous phrase, 'the relation of landlord and tenant shall be deemed to be founded on the express or implied contract of the parties, and not upon tenure or service'.[61]

In the case of the leaseholder, it was implicit in the new legislation that the tenant acquired contractual rights in a property but no proprietary interest of any kind. The status of the tenant at will, i.e. a tenant without a lease, was covered by the use of the word 'implied'. Although there was no formal written contract with the tenant at will, its existence was to be taken as read. This phraseology was, in part, an attempt to impose a sensible English template on years of higgledy-piggledy Irish land law, as well as on centuries of uniquely Hibernian custom and practice.

Deasy's Act was based on the legal assumption that land was solely and entirely the property of the person in whom the 'fee simple' was vested, i.e. in an Irish context, the landlord. It definitively removed any vestigial feudal notions of land being held in return for service to an overlord and declined to take into account peculiarly Irish practices, such as the 'Ulster Custom'. The tenant was merely an entity who was permitted the use of a specific area of the landowner's holding for a fixed term (or undefined, in the case of a tenant at will) upon payment of an annual rent. There was no hint whatsoever of any recognition of any tenant interest, express or implied. It was a modernising fist breaking a jerry-built pre-modern window.

What Deasy's Act meant, for example, was that if a farm fell into significant arrears, the landlord was entitled to eject a tenant without compensation for improvements made by that tenant. This was the case even if the value of those improvements amounted to a multiple of the rent owed. Furthermore, by serving a 'notice to quit' even where no rent was owed and the tenant was 'in good standing', the landlord could seize the farm (it was, after all, *his* land) and all the improvements effected by the tenant, without paying a penny in reparation. 'The governing principle of the legislation was that whatever attached to the freehold became part of the freehold.'[62] Common law, as well as custom and practice, were shown the door and replaced by the ineluctable certitudes of ownership and contract 'abolishing the surviving customary rights of the Irish peasantry'.[63]

However, as with much Ireland-only Westminster legislation, theory and practice failed to merge seamlessly.

Section 3 of Deasy's Act, while still being 'the foundation of the law of landlord and tenant in Ireland', was found, as recently as 2003, by the Irish Law Reform Commission, to have had little 'impact on the development of Irish landlord and tenant law'.[64] In practical terms, it does not appear to have led to a major upsurge in evictions, other than during a period of economic depression from 1860 to 1863, and even then only 8,000 evictions took place during that entire decade.[65] Subsequent ameliorative legislation, in the form of Gladstone's two land acts of 1870 and 1881, ensured that its influence was mainly symbolic and psychological.

Whatever the reality on the ground, however, it was probably the high point of the 'Indian summer of landlordism in Ireland'[66] and the nadir of tenants' legal rights. 'By 1860 the power of the Irish landlord was at its zenith.'[67] Deasy's Act and the decade that followed were akin to the fairground car cresting the summit of the rollercoaster switchback. There then followed that brief pause where the occupants are permitted half a second to enjoy the view. By the late 1870s, however, the precipitous descent had begun.

Ironically, one of the men who was influential in the formulation of Deasy's Act, the Trinity College, Dublin economist William Neilson Hancock, an adviser to the Palmerston government, experienced a Damascene conversion when he later researched the history of Irish land tenure and discovered the Brehon laws, a tradition far removed from English legal principles and based on collective/clan ownership. Gladstone, in the framing of his flawed but well-meaning 1870 Land Act, benefited from the work of scholars like Hancock in adopting a less Anglocentric approach to his own legislation.

The Fenians intervened between the passage of Deasy's Act in 1860 and the first major piece of cohesive remedial land legislation in 1870. Despite their military ineptitude, they played a critical role in Gladstone's introduction of his 1870 Land Act. It was Fenian violence in Britain, rather than the faltering and abortive efforts of the Irish Republican Brotherhood in Ireland itself, which ultimately persuaded Gladstone that his mission was 'to pacify Ireland'.

THE FENIAN GUY FAWKES.

'*The Fenian Guy Fawkes*', Punch, *December 1867 (John Tenniel)*

The first reform introduced by the new Liberal government hardly involved a prodigious or insurmountable challenge. The enduring boil of the existence of a minority 'established' Church of Ireland was lanced – and the issue of tithes finally laid to rest – by Gladstone in the 1869 Church Disestablishment Act. The Liberal prime minister then addressed himself to what he saw as the major running sore in Hiberno-British relations – the land issue in all its vexing complexities. He sought to tackle head-on, some of the worst anomalies and inflexible legal certainties of Deasy's Act. This was to be achieved by rectifying the palpable injustice inherent in the tenuous status of tenant improvements and restoring elements of custom and practice in the landlord-tenant relationship overlooked or overridden by the 1860 law.

In 1870, the land of Ireland was still owned by around 10,000 landlords. Most of the Irish population of 5.5 million lived outside the major cities. In the census of 1871, Dublin, Belfast, Cork, Limerick and Galway accounted for fewer than 600,000 people. Most of the remaining 5 million were, outside of north-east Ulster, heavily dependent on the land, either as leaseholders, tenants at will, cottiers or farm labourers. Just over 40 per cent of the working population was involved in agriculture (down from 48 per cent in 1851), whereas just under 20 per cent was involved in manufacturing. A further 15 per cent was in domestic service. The number of leases tended to vary according to the size of the holding. Where farms were valued at less than £15, almost 84 per cent of the tenancies were 'at will'. Whereas with farms with a value of more than £100, 75 per cent of the tenants had leases of various durations.[68] Rents were rising, but not rapidly. Between 1848 and 1878, they increased by an average of 20 per cent as against a rise in the value of agricultural output of 50 per cent.

The Famine had clearly revealed the serious need for land reform in Ireland, but the years following that cataclysm produced British administrations unwilling to inject capital into the development of Irish agriculture, or reform the system of Irish landholding to give more rights to tenants. The latter course would have allowed Irish tenants to invest their own capital in developing their holdings without the risk of subsequent eviction and a write-off of their capital, or of enduring the galling experience of having their rents raised because of improvements they had made themselves.

This lack of reform was also predicated on concerns on the part of British landed interests over the potential for 'leakage'. This was the patrician fear that any ameliorative legislation introduced in Ireland would later be applied to Britain by the devious Liberals. The old Whig element within the broader Liberal Party, for example, could only be persuaded to support Irish land measures if they were ring-fenced and applied solely to Ireland. This was difficult to achieve legislatively. It was also paradoxical and illogical in the context of Ireland as an integral part of the United Kingdom.

Were it not for Gladstone's pre-eminent status within his own cabinet, it is doubtful if he would even have achieved the merely incremental progress of his 1870 legislation. He had little support for his reforms from within his cabinet, an august body composed mostly of either *laissez-faire* advocates disinclined to interfere in any relationship between landowner and tenant, or members of the British landowning class unwilling to upset the status quo. He was supported by the president of the Board of Trade, the Quaker radical John Bright (who was keen to see the state support tenants in buying out their land), and by the Irish chief secretary, Chichester Parkinson-Fortescue.

One of the explanations for the retrospectively obvious flaws in Gladstone's 1870 legislation was his need to 'make haste slowly' with a bill that he could force through cabinet. He was fortunate in that there was little love for Irish landlords within the British body politic by the middle of the Victorian era. The activities of the likes of Adair and Scully, although they were only a tiny medieval minority of the Irish landlord class, had seen to that. There was a distinct head of steam building behind the notion that, three years after the Fenian rebellion and the bloody mainland aftermath (the 'Manchester Martyrs' and the Clerkenwell bombing), *Irish* landlords could be sacrificed for the sake of peace in Ireland.

The 1870 Land Act, a demonstrably cautious and conservative piece of legislation, primarily sought to rectify three outstanding issues. It offered tenants compensation for 'disturbance'. This involved an arbitrary eviction where a tenant was 'in good standing' and was to apply irrespective of whether or not the tenant had 'improved' the value of the land. The act also mandated compensation for the tenant's improvements where eviction was based on a tenancy in arrears, i.e. non-payment of rent. Finally, it legalised the 'Ulster Custom' on estates where it was found to have previously existed before the passage of the legislation. In addition to these remedial measures, the legislation also, at the instigation of John Bright, included a clause (the 'Bright clause') that allocated a modest amount of exchequer funding to tenants wishing to buy out their landlords and acquire their own land. The required capital (a maximum of two-thirds of the cost of the farm) would be lent to the tenant and was to be paid back over thirty-five years at the rate of £5 per year for every £100 borrowed.

The flaws did not take long to become apparent. The 1870 act failed to define the 'Ulster Custom', and also left it up to the courts to decide where it applied. This had traditionally guaranteed northern tenants security of tenure as long as their rent was up to date, entitled them to some payment for their interest in a farm from an incoming tenant, and permitted them to assign their interest in a farm to an heir. Naturally, some landlords sought to prove in court that it did not apply to their land and dragged many unwilling tenants into expensive litigation.

Of equal import was the serious deficiency that saw leaseholders being excluded from the bill. The terms of the 1870 legislation applied only to tenants at will. The idea of intervening in any formal contractual relationship between landlord and tenant was a bridge too far for a majority of the cabinet. As a result, many landlords – to circumvent the punitive elements of the legislation – were suddenly eager to persuade tenants to sign leases. Other stop-gap solutions were found by landlords to work around the provisions of the new law. In 1881, the year of Gladstone's 'amending' legislation to his own 1870 Land Act, Finlay Dun referenced something he called 'the Leinster lease'. This was a contractual agreement drawn up by the Duke of Leinster – owner of 73,000 acres of superior south midlands land – with his tenants which, among other provisions, obliged a tenant on quitting the holding 'to make no claim for compensation under any of the clauses or provisions of the Landlord and Tenant (Ireland) Act, 1870'.[69]

The 'compensation for disturbance' clause also turned out to be something of a mirage in that it applied only to tenancies entered into after the passage of the act; no compensation was forthcoming if a tenant had sub-let or subdivided without the landlord's written permission; and there was no solution offered to the conundrum of the logical landlord workaround, i.e. since compensation for disturbance applied only to tenants 'in good standing', a landlord could raise the rent to a point where the tenant fell into arrears, *et voilà*, he could then be evicted without any right to compensation for disturbance – Catch-22 a century before the publication of the celebrated novel. A further nail in the coffin of the 'disturbance' clause was the fact that some of the amounts involved were quite small, and incoming tenants were often willing to pay the compensation themselves in order to persuade the landlord to get rid of the sitting tenant on land they coveted.

The clause relating to compensation for 'improvements' made by the farmer over the course of his tenancy – which was owed by landlords even to a tenant in arrears – was so hedged around with caveats and exceptions that it resembled a country house maze. Even if the evicted tenant was compensated for draining his land, building outhouses and so on, the landlord was allowed to deduct all rent moneys owed from the sum paid in compensation for such improvements. In addition, in a particularly perverse measure, a calculation had to be made of the time during which the tenant had 'enjoyed' the benefits of his own improvements. That could also be deducted from the final sum.

Like the Wandering Minstrel in Gilbert and Sullivan's *The Mikado*, the 1870 Land Act was 'a thing of shreds and patches', though it inspired no 'ballads, songs and snatches'. It was ineffective on almost every level. Even the Bright clause failed to unleash a flood of tenant purchase, as few if any tenants could come up with one-third of the cost price of their holdings and could not, therefore, benefit from the exchequer funding. In the case of the 'Ulster Custom', landlords could simply increase rents and thus devalue the tenant right. As a rule of thumb, every shilling of a rent increase took away a pound from the value of the tenant right.

To Michael Davitt, 'the Land Act of 1870 was ... a concession to what Mr. Gladstone termed "the intensity of Fenianism"'.[70] 'The Act,' according to Joseph Lee, 'was well-intentioned, but neither Gladstone, nor his critics, understood Irish agriculture ... Gladstone's first land Act therefore had no economic, and indeed few social, consequences.'[71] That, understandably, was not how the legislation was viewed in 1870 and thereafter by landlords themselves. Samuel Murray Hussey described Gladstone as 'the most dangerous Englishman of the nineteenth century' and 'the most malevolent imp of mischief that ever ruined any one country'.[72]

Although the 1870 act launched Gladstone on an irreversible course of conciliation, as was so often the case with the remedial land legislation of both Liberal and Tory governments in the late nineteenth century, the velvet glove was tightly drawn over an iron fist. An upsurge in agrarian violence in the midlands over the preceding two years had led to the suspension of *habeas corpus* in Co. Westmeath as well as parts of Meath and King's County (Offaly). This permitted the RIC to arrest and detain without trial anyone they suspected of involvement in Ribbon society activity. The 1871 Protection of Life and Property (Ireland) Act (better known as the Westmeath Act) was one of dozens of pieces of coercion legislation deployed by a similar number of British governments whenever consternation over intensifying rural violence beset the Houses of Parliament in London. Little of the bloodshed in the midlands, however, involved animosity between tenants and their landlords. Instead, it pitched prosperous farmers against labourers, and labourers against 'strangers' who were securing employment in the affected areas. There was also a Luddite element to the tenant-labourer aggression, with some farmers being admonished by threatening notices to abandon the purchase or the hire of mowing machines. This new technology threatened the livelihoods of casual employees. In some instances, machines were damaged and hay that had been saved by machine was burned as a warning.[73]

However, when a landlord, James Fethersonhaugh, fell victim to this upsurge of Ribbon activity in April 1868, and when a copy of an alleged Ribbon oath was found in a Mullingar public house which included the pledge 'I will think it no sin to kill and massacre a Protestant whenever opportunity serves', Gladstone was in no position to resist the resultant moral panic, especially as one of those stirring the pot was his own Lord Lieutenant, Lord Spencer. In anticipation of the passage of the legislation, many of the leaders of the agitation quietly removed themselves from the Irish midlands. In the absence of the more resolute agitators, the trouble quickly subsided. The Westmeath Act, however, remained on the statute books until 1877. By the time a far more punitive successor, the Protection of Person and Property Act, was introduced in 1881, the Westmeath Act would have been ineffective anyway. The Irish midlands was quiescent. Uproar and outrage had moved westwards, and the Land War had begun.

11

From Irishtown to Kilmainham:
the First Land War, 1879–82

CROWNING THE O'CALIBAN.

Punch *magazine, 22 December 1883 (John Tenniel)*

'What the Irish want is the abolition of landlordism, that
every tenant shall own the soil he tills … The Irish don't
want landlordism modified but abolished.'[1]

(James Redpath, *Talks About Ireland*, 1881)

12 February 1881, Artane, Co. Dublin

It was *mano a mano* – a straight contest between the Land Leaguer and the Emergency Man. Andrew Kettle could well afford his rent. He was, after all, a wealthy north Dublin farmer who kept his own horses. However, as a dedicated Land Leaguer, he had chosen not to pay. He had known all along how things would pan out. The sheriff would seize some of his property and auction it off to raise the funds to compensate his landlord, the aristocratic Lord Talbot, owner of Malahide Castle. That was why a large crowd had gathered at Kettle's house in Artane.

Norris Goddard was one of the calmer members of the febrile crowd that day. As far as most of those present were concerned, Goddard was as welcome as the potato blight. He was there to keep Kettle honest and to make sure that Lord Talbot de Malahide got the £40 in rent he was owed.

The nervous auctioneer, aware of the tension, surveyed the crowd warily and began proceedings hesitantly. He was looking for bids on two of Kettle's horses. That, however, was easier said than done. Most of the crowd were supporters of Kettle and the Land League; they had no intention of bidding for either of the two animals. Their presence in large numbers was also intended as an encouragement to any other likely bidders to keep their hands in their pockets.[2]

But Goddard was not to be deterred or intimidated. With a couple of almost imperceptible motions, he undermined the oppressive tactics of the Land League faithful. He opened the bidding on the first animal at £5 and stayed in the race before allowing himself to be outbid by Kettle's brother. Lot #1 fetched £20. The second horse went for £30, again to Kettle's brother, who had been expecting to purchase both animals on his brother's behalf for next to nothing. Instead, the sheriff, after the harassed auctioneer's fee was deducted, would have £40 to hand over to Lord Talbot de Malahide in lieu of rent.

When the bidding concluded, the assembled crowd gave three cheers for the Land League, but the chorus was a hollow one.

The Land War had now been raging for more than twelve months. Norris Goddard had just demonstrated that the league was no longer going to have matters all its own way.

TWO FORCES.

Punch *magazine, 29 October 1881 (John Tenniel)*

The Tale of a great sham?

'Then what was the Land League for? And what were we all supposed to be doing? And how was it that the Land League was still going on? In short, what did it all mean?'

(Anna Parnell, *The Tale of a Great Sham*)

The turbulent conscience of the Land League floundered in the water and drowned in 1911. That is not a metaphor. The tragedy took place off the beach at Ilfracombe on the north Devon coast of England. The victim was Anna Parnell. When she died, she had outlived her celebrated brother by two decades. She had also outlived her usefulness to him by three decades. She had briefly become proxy leader of a cause in which she fervently believed, whose slogans she endorsed (or devised herself), and which, like a recalcitrant horse in one of the many foxhunts her acolytes disrupted, had shrugged her off when she tugged on the reins to alter its direction.

Anna lacked the pragmatism of Charles Stewart Parnell, the sibling who outmanoeuvred and disillusioned her three decades before her untimely death. Her cri de coeur on the very purpose of the Land League, outlined above, is a function of how she was sidelined for the crime of ideological purity. She was airbrushed to such an extent that more than a hundred years elapsed between the abrupt and enforced liquidation of the Ladies Land League and the appearance of her acerbic memoir of that period, *The Tale of a Great Sham* (1986), a full century after it might have made any difference.

There are many answers to the fundamental question Anna Parnell posed, 'Then what was the Land League for?' When she took up the cudgels on behalf of that recently proscribed organisation in October 1881, the answer might have appeared to be simplicity itself. The objective, surely, was the realisation of that suitably all-encompassing goal of 'tenant right'. Though still a rather vague concept, it had, for a couple of years, produced some stirring catch cries: 'Hold the harvest', 'The land for the people', 'Keep a firm grip on your homesteads'. It also united some strange bedfellows, from large farmers like Andrew Kettle to champions of land nationalisation such as the American journalist Henry George and his Irish acolyte Michael Davitt. That was before sectional agendas reasserted themselves, as they have a habit of doing.

Anna Parnell's error was to have been naïve enough to believe the rhetoric of the campaign which, by default, she was briefly allowed to lead. She, for example, assumed that the phrase 'no rent manifesto' actually involved the non-payment of rent. Her brother's cynical support for the document, issued after the October 1881 arrests of the agrarian political leadership, was designed 'to hasten the collapse of the Land League'.[3] Anna's display of good faith, and her perceived extremism, meant that she was trampled in the rush for the appropriate exit by a range of special interests – or disinterest, in the case of her esteemed brother – as the First Land War came to a messy and unsatisfactory conclusion for many of its equally earnest foot soldiers.

It is a struggle known to posterity as a 'war'. It is assigned a specific start date and it even concluded with a 'treaty'. It had its own generals (Parnell and Davitt), NCOs (Matthew Harris, Thomas Brennan *et al.*), able propagandists (James Daly of the *Connaught Telegraph*, William O'Brien of *United Ireland*) and a legion of infantrymen (far too numerous to mention). Its murkier activities offered ample scope for collateral damage in the form of intimidation and assaults. Many of those involved grievous bodily harm not to the perceived enemy – process-servers, 'emergency men', landlords or their agents – but to transgressive neighbours. Whether there were enough violent fatalities during the First Land War (1879–82) – sixty-seven homicides in all – to justify the emotive description 'war' is debatable. However, the more pedantic alternative, the 'Late Victorian Interlude of Irish Agrarian Civil Strife', lacks a certain pithiness, and almost 15,000 evictions in three years (more than the combined total for the previous thirty years) makes the 'Land Scuffle' equally untenable.

In the three decades after the end of the Great Famine, while the Irish countryside had not exactly been quiescent, rates of agrarian crime rarely crept past 500 cases per annum. Many of those crimes did not involve violent assaults against the person or property. Included in the statistics were incidences of intimidation, including vitriolic threatening letters.

The fundamental reason for the decline in agrarian crime between the catastrophe of the Great Famine and the economic depression of the late 1877–82 period was that there were just not that many evictions taking place. The truth was that, for a period of almost thirty years, widespread clearances and even more sporadic individual evictions were few and far between. On most landed estates, 'tenancies from year to year existed for generations and descended from father to son'.[4] Between 1851 and 1880, there were approximately 600,000 Irish tenant farmers working the land owned by around 12,000 landlords. During that thirty-year period there were 53,472 evictions, or just under 1,800 per annum. However, only 41,107 of those ejectments were permanent. In 23 per cent of all cases, the tenant families were later re-admitted to their farms. So the real rate of eviction was 1,370 per annum, around 0.002 per cent of all Irish tenancies.[5]

The great US journalist Henry George had been despatched by the radical nationalist Irish-American editor Patrick Ford to cover the Land War for his New York-based *Irish World* newspaper. George, author of the bestselling economics monograph of the nineteenth century (*Progress and Poverty*) and an advocate of land nationalisation, pointed out that tenurial arrangements in Ireland were no different to those in his own country:

> The Irish land system, which is so much talked of as though it were some peculiarly atrocious system, is essentially the same land system which prevails in all civilized countries, which we of the United States have accepted unquestioningly.[6]

But then many wars, including those of the twenty-first century, are fought for reasons other than those enunciated by the antagonists. The First Land War was no different. We must also be wary of interpreting the Land War as the continuation of separatism by other means. Both poles of Irish separatism, the constitutional and the militant, found some expression in the events of the Land War, but neither account for its vigour or its motivation. The London *Daily News* reporter Bernard Becker, veteran narrator of the Land War, put it succinctly in his book *Disturbed Ireland* (1881) when he noted that:

> Very few in Mayo, and hardly anybody at all in Connemara, seem to take any account of Home Rule, or of any other rule except that of the Land League. The possibility of a

Parliament on College-green* affects the people of the West far less than the remotest chance of securing some share of the land.[7]

'Revolution of rising expectations'

The presumptive opening of the conflict was 20 April 1879, the date of an angry and well-attended rent protest meeting in Irishtown, Co. Mayo, a county that was hardly a revolutionary plum ripe for picking, or a likely prospect to kick-start a tenurial insurrection. In his survey of the agrarian history of the county, *Land and Popular Politics in Ireland*, Donald Jordan has pointed out that over the previous 120 years, agrarian protest movements in Ireland had been largely confined to the more prosperous counties of the east, south and midlands, 'in which the social and economic convulsions associated with the developing market-oriented and cash-based economy had spawned frequent periods of agrarian violence'.[8]

So this was a different kind of agrarian uprising.

The backdrop was one of a profound agricultural crisis: Irish potato production had fallen by almost 75 per cent, blight had reappeared in the south-west of the country, and a series of cold, wet summers meant that the population in parts of the west, already in abject poverty, was edging closer to famine. Economic depression in Britain had also cut off, or at least impaired, the outlet of emigration. In parts of the west of Ireland, famine conditions were avoided only by the efforts of private relief committees and the availability of shopkeeper credit. In an article for the *Freeman's Journal* in August 1879, journalist and future MP William O'Brien outlined the importance of mercantile credit while clearly operating under no illusions as to the motivation of the merchants for continuing to advance further borrowing facilities. The shopkeepers of Mayo, 'having trusted and ventured much, unless they would lose all, they had

* The location of the Irish parliament before the Act of Union of 1801.

to trust and venture more. Had they closed their purse strings, had they abandoned or even greatly abridged their credit system, those who were already their heavy debtors must have been simply starved or beggared.'[9]

The Land War offers some of the more beguiling fables of nineteenth-century Irish history. The mythology – born of that noble imagined past dreamed up in the pages of the Gaelic League's journal *An Claidheamh Soluis* and the Abbey Theatre rehearsal rooms of the National Literary Society, and later reinforced by works of history like John Pomfret's 1930 account *The Struggle for Land in Ireland, 1800–1923* – took it as axiomatic that a dogged and unified tenantry opposed an oppressive and seigneurial landholding elite and, courtesy of inspired leadership and peasant cohesion, routed the forces of feudalism.

While there is a significant seam of truth in the motherlode of myth, the reality is rather less fuzzy and heartening than the legend. The Land War of 1879–82 was 'not a mass uprising of the Irish rural population'.[10] Flawed social memory with little evidential basis, and the exigencies of nation-building in the 1920s and 1930s, led to the creation of a binary construct, entirely lacking in nuance, when it came to the issue of Irish land tenure. As that guru of agrarian revisionism, the economic historian Barbara Lewis Solow, elegantly put it, 'The eventual triumph of Irish separatism depended on many complex factors, and in the long struggle, stories of eviction and rack-renting were pressed into service as economic myths. As economic myths they did yeoman service.'[11]

Leadership there certainly was. The wily Charles Stewart Parnell, the dogged ex-Fenian Michael Davitt, the dour but unswerving John Dillon, and the campaigning journalist William O'Brien led an inspiring officer corps prepared to take personal and political risks in the cause of agrarian reform. There was also forthright co-operation and solidarity among the rank-and-file membership of the Land League, for a while at least. Without extensive collaboration, voluntary or enforced, the political and economic strategy that became known as 'boycotting' – so-called because a Mayo priest realised that his congregation could not get their tongues around the word 'ostracisation' and named the practice after its most celebrated victim – would have been nullified.

But the proposition that a resolute, united Irish peasantry marched in lockstep to vanquish the cloistered and privileged occupants of the 'big house' is as erroneous as it is alluring. One eminent Irish historian, R. V. Comerford, has warned against 'the warm glow of old assumptions about this being a highlight of the ever-onward march of human liberty and progress'.[12] Supporters of the Land League were prone to just as much backbiting, intimidation, insularity, victimisation and intra-organisational anarchy as the membership of any radical socio-political movement before or since. Furthermore, the Land League was not an organisation in which, in any real sense, an empowered peasantry took control of its own destiny. The leadership of the organisation came, predominantly, from a rural merchant caste with a vested interest in targeting the country's landlords, and a bloc of relatively comfortable farmers with a vested interest in protecting their own comforts. For a brief period, the fortunes of small and large farmers, but never their interests, converged, before the elite element made its excuses and bolted, pulling the supports behind them as they departed through the escape tunnel.

Another significant element of the rural population, farm labourers – most of whom had aspirations to possess land of their own – were under-represented in the activist ranks of the Land League. More than half (54 per cent) of the Land League suspects arrested and incarcerated without charge under 1880s coercion legislation were farmers or farmer's sons. That cohort represented only 37 per cent of the male labour force. Labourers made up 28 per cent of the labour force, but only 6 per cent of those interned when *habeas corpus* was suspended in 1881 'to wrest the power to rule large parts of Ireland from the Land League'.[13] Either farm labourers – a dwindling population since the days of the Great Famine – were adept at keeping out of trouble, or they were less than wholehearted when it came to showing solidarity with their 'betters'.[14]

The impoverished tenant farmers of the west and south-west may have made up the rank and file of this agrarian infantry, but it was a more equestrian element that led the campaign. As R. V. Comerford acidly put it, 'there were many hundreds on horseback at the Irishtown meeting'.[15] *The Times* journalist Finlay Dun observed that 'the Land League agitation generally originates with the publicans, small shopkeepers and bankrupt farmers, rather than with the actual land occupiers'.[16]

The era of the Land League, according to Joseph Lee, simply 'crowned the strong farmer as the cock of the country walk'. The Land War pitted rancher and retailer against *rentier*. It was the 'strong farmer' tenants who, along with their temporary allies – from miller to milliner – were the real winners of an agrarian conflict that began long before 1879 and, like the Hundred Years' War, flared into flame from time to time when the protagonists recovered from their exhaustion, or encountered terrain that looked strategically advantageous. However, by the early twentieth century, it was the erstwhile partners of the 1880s who were at each other's throats. The graziers and the small farmers found they had little to unite them any longer when it became clear that the 'Season of the Rancher' was one of the principal consequences of the Land War agitation.

This had always been an unlikely coalition, a function of the declining fortunes of disparate interest groups.

Resources were squeezed during the worldwide economic depression that followed on from one of those periodic financial panics in the US economy. This one was the 'Panic of '73', scion of the 'Panic of '57', parent of the 'Panic of '93'. The Irish tenant farmer, who, by the 1880s, had come to rely on credit advanced by the shopkeepers of the market towns of rural Ireland, was faced with a stark choice: he could use his dwindling resources to pay the rent owed on his landholding, or he could repay his debts to the shopkeepers, who provided him with groceries, seeds, hardware and the occasional luxury 'on tick'. A report in the *Freeman's Journal* in 1879 claimed that Mayo farmers alone owed £200,000 to the county's merchants and shopkeepers.[17] Many farmers were reported to have owed the equivalent of three to five years' rent to shopkeepers – and some as much as ten years' rent. The same newspaper, on 20 August 1881, reported the support of the nationalist prelate, Archbishop Croke of Cashel, for Gladstone's 1881 land legislation. 'I am decidedly of the opinion,' Croke averred, 'that the great bulk of our farming classes, and indeed, *shopkeeping classes*, would be glad to see the present land bill passed' (my italics).

How this all came about has some interesting parallels with more recent Irish financial/economic collapses. The Tory administration of Benjamin Disraeli had appointed the Duke of Richmond and Gordon to chair a commission appointed to examine the efficacy of Gladstone's land legislation of 1870. In evidence to the commission, one of its specialist assistant commissioners, Professor Baldwin, outlined the extent of tenant farmer indebtedness, and how it had come about in the relatively prosperous era since the last subsistence crisis of 1861–2: 'The banks gave money on easy terms to shopkeepers, and then the shopkeepers, as it were, forced a system of credit upon the small farmers ... The people got the goods on easy terms, and, owing to their want of forethought and thrift, they accepted the goods so offered to them; and all of a sudden that has collapsed.'[18]

By taking control of an organisation that validated (and even elevated) the practice of declining to remit biannual rent payments, the shopkeepers who assumed leadership positions in the Land League were simply protecting their own interests. The message, though understated, left no room for ambiguity. The Merchant of Ennis whispered, 'If you can't pay your rent *and* your commercial debts, then refuse to pay rent to Lord [insert name of local aristocrat] until you get an abatement.' What was generally on offer to the landlord was a rental payment in line with Griffith's Valuation. Rents on some estates were at, or even below, Griffith's Valuation, but most were an average of 20 per cent above. The league and its supporters tended to fetishise Griffith's Valuation as an assessment of land values that should be reflected in levels of rent, without acknowledging the inconvenient corollary that since the Griffith survey had begun in 1847, most rents had fallen considerably in real terms when measured against the 50 per cent increase in agricultural prices. It was not until the middle of the 1870s that the upward drift of agricultural prices had been reversed.

This classic 'revolution of rising expectations' – the phrase originated with Alexis de Tocqueville in his *L'Ancien Régime et La Révolution* (1856), and has been endorsed in the context of the Land War in the work of a number of latter-day historians[19] – was no free-for-all blitz on property, merely a highly targeted mugging of the landholding aristocracy, in which 'one class of Irish capitalists waged economic war against another class of Irish capitalists'.[20] Debts owed to banks, merchants or the local 'gombeen man' (moneylender) were exempt from this assault. The country's landlords, previously secure behind their demesne walls – unless their own debts grew to be excessive and the bailiffs came calling, as in the case of Anthony Trollope's fictional MacDermotts of Ballcloran – discovered the truth of the axiom that, when it came to a congress of straitened creditors, 'there is no honour among thieves'. In a twenty-first-century context, what happened could be encapsulated in the anachronistic image of the merchants tossing the landlords under the bus. It was akin to the primacy, witnessed in our very own 'panic of 2010' of 'senior' over 'junior' debt.

The relative flexibility of the system of mercantile debt (which implied the continued extension of credit even when only a percentage of the bills were repaid), in tandem with the need to make future purchases from shopkeepers in a growing cash economy, ultimately triumphed over the absolute inflexibility of the tenurial system. In the latter instance, a large wad of cash was paid over, in full, twice a year – or else. The Land League held out the prospect of pulling the teeth of the 'or else' element of that axiom. It offered the tenant farmer a place of sanctuary – though the roof often leaked – and the prospect of continuing to have his cake, albeit on account, while still eating it.

This was especially true when it came to the 'substantial' farmer. As an alternative to the absolute non-payment of rent – a stratagem generally favoured by the more impoverished tenants, who could not afford to pay anyway – the Land League adopted the policy of 'rent at the point of a bayonet' in order to recruit more affluent tenant farmers, mostly based in prosperous Leinster. This strategy involved tenants holding off payment until the last possible moment. If effective, or so the theory went, this policy would bleed the more impecunious landlords of resources, deny them vital cash flow and involve them in costly litigation. 'The chronic poverty of Irish landlordism was potentially its Achilles heel.'[21] The league undertook to defray any legal costs that might accrue to the tenant in adopting this approach. However, 'the low-risk nature of the strategy was ... objectively in the interests of the more substantial tenantry'[22] and reflected agrarian tactics favoured by large farmer interests.

But the abiding myth bequeathed by the agrarian ferment of the 1880s was the notion that a revolutionary spirit of equality and fraternity motivated and united the Irish peasantry throughout the 1879–82 conflict. The reality was that tensions between large farmers and the social classes beneath them (smallholders, cottiers, labourers) were as frequent and intense as those between landlord and tenant. 'Large farmers and landlords prospered together'[23] and, in tandem with Roman Catholic clergy (continuing their political recovery from the dark days of the Penal Laws), were the stewards of nineteenth-century rural Ireland. By 1861, barely a decade after the end of the Great Famine, 40 per cent of Irish land was held (though not owned) by farmers working 100 acres or more. A new class of livestock-rearing graziers was asserting itself and was beginning to acquire farm land that might otherwise have been available to subsistence farmers or landless labourers. The conflicts caused by these post-Famine acquisitions had long been a source of rural tension and would be exacerbated in the first three decades of the twentieth century. The transitory success of the Land League was, in part at least, due to the creation of a temporary small farmer/grazier coalition. But their interests never quite interlocked, and the alliance was short-lived. However, the *rapprochement* lasted long enough to discomfit the landlords and set in train a series of events that ultimately led to the demise of the Irish landed aristocracy. The tacit landlord policy of 'divide and conquer' deployed along the fault lines of class in rural Ireland, which had served them well for decades, became temporarily redundant. The prosperous graziers and big tillage farmers, who had been in the ascendant in the aftermath of the Great Famine, no longer offered a buffer between the gentry and the lower peasantry. Although this agrarian alliance was short-lived, it set in motion a chain reaction that would end the dominance of landlordism.

The other significant alliance of the period was, of course, that between the clergy of the Roman Catholic Church and the tenant movement. Among the members of the hierarchy, the sterling support of the nationalist Archbishop of Cashel and Emly, Thomas Croke, mitigated the unexpected opposition of his elderly fellow nationalist prelate, Archbishop John MacHale of Tuam – a supporter of the Tenant League of the 1850s – to the first Westport meeting of the Land League attended by Parnell in June 1879. MacHale, then approaching his nineties, warned Parnell in a letter to the *Freeman's Journal* that he would be sharing a platform with members of a 'lawless and occult association' (viz. the Irish Republican Brotherhood, the IRB).[24] The archbishop advised Parnell to stay well away from Westport. Parnell, who at all costs wanted to *avoid* a Fenian takeover of the agrarian movement – this was one of his reasons for accepting the invitation to speak – took up MacHale's misguided gauntlet and carried it all the way on the train to Westport, where he duly addressed the meeting.

The premier 'Castle Bishop' of the period, the Cardinal Archbishop of Dublin, Edward McCabe, was the most prominent prelate of the 1880s who voiced opposition to the activities of the league. But his grace reserved his most splenetic invective for the membership of the Ladies Land League. He particularly deprecated the appearance of women on public platforms and condemned their presence at public meetings. 'Like Mary,' he once wrote, invoking no less an authority than the Blessed Virgin herself, 'their place is [in] the seclusion of the home.' In a pastoral letter to the priests of his archdiocese in 1881, the misogynistic prelate instructed his clergy to have no truck with women who 'forget the modesty of their sex'.[25]

For every McCabe, however, there were dozens of parish priests and curates who actively participated in Land League activities, assumed executive positions in local branches and negotiated with landlords and agents for rent abatements. As Michael Davitt observed, in places where the clergy did not come forward to assume leadership positions, the vacuum was instead often filled by local Fenians.[26] The mirror image of McCabe was the 'Land League priest', Eugene Sheehy of Kilmallock, Co. Limerick, who in 1884 became a founder member of the Gaelic Athletic Association. Brother of the radical Parnellite MP David Sheehy and uncle of the feminist and suffragist Hanna Sheehy-Skeffington, Fr Sheehy was also involved in the early education of Eamon de Valera. He served five months in prison in 1881 for his Land League activities. Unlike other clerics who supped with the IRB with a lengthy spoon, Sheehy made little secret of his affiliation to the ideals of that organisation and indeed may well have been an active member. On his release from Kilmainham Gaol at the end of September 1881, the treasurer of the Land League and alleged motive force behind the murderous Invincibles, Patrick Egan, sent Sheehy a telegram 'congratulating him upon his release, and hoping he may long be spared to help in the holy war against Saxon rule'.[27] There was, after all, much of the *jihad* about the agrarian agitation of the 1880s.

The 'holy war' status of the conflict was encouraged by William O'Brien's often blood-curdling Land League-owned newspaper, *United Ireland*. On its debut on 13 August 1881, alongside unhelpful advertisements for 'Cheap emigration to Canada' and a report of a man's arm being eaten by a cob horse in Maynooth, *United Ireland* introduced to its readership villains like 'Buckshot' Forster (chief secretary William E. Forster) and promised to be 'a Weekly National Monster Meeting'. It carried a piece in that first edition entitled 'Who Are the Landlords?', which travelled all the way back in time to historic land confiscations, starting with the invasions of Henry II and Strongbow.

The newspaper also reprinted a hair-raising editorial from Jeremiah O'Donovan Rossa's fiery New York-based *United Irishman*, copies of which were regularly confiscated by the RIC and the Dublin Metropolitan Police. The piece was labelled 'A Warning to Landlords' by the doughty Rossa, who would back up his incessant threats a few years later with a dynamite campaign aimed at targets in Britain. His message to the nation's landowners was stark: 'a record will be kept of every landlord who exercises the power of eviction in Ireland, and for every such death sentence executed on a tenant a death sentence will be recorded by the Irish race against the murderer's house and the Irish race all the world over will give encouragement to the avenging angel.'[28]

Rossa never troubled himself with nuance when it came to the art of sedition. Given the level of evictions during the Land War (*c*.15,000), however, there was an inadequate supply of landlords (*c*.10,000) to satisfy the 'avenging angel'.

'The eyes and ears of Dublin Castle'

Assessing the Land League era is not helped by the fact that agrarian issues also became identified with the struggle for legislative independence. Tenants tended to be nationalist. Landlords, almost without exception (Parnell was an obvious one), were unionist. Furthermore, the latter were found guilty, in the court of public opinion, of being anything but passively aggressive opponents of Irish legislative independence. They were regularly accused, in the classic nationalist cliché, of being the 'eyes and ears of Dublin Castle'. *Ipso facto*, an agrarian assault on the landlord class was an integral part of the wider struggle for devolution. This trope failed to take into account the reality that 'land hunger' occasionally ran directly counter to the objectives of that political struggle (see Chapter 17).

The binary construct of issues of land tenure (homogenous and saintly tenants versus grasping and diabolical landlords) was a convenient *ex post facto* paradigm fashioned by the twentieth-century propagandists of Irish separatism and exceptionalism. It was a by-product of 'nationalist populism' and 'an interpretation more in sympathy with the new nation than with the realities of the past'.[29] It lionised the efficacy and nobility of the Irish tenant and encouraged an overly benign belief in his capacity for sustained agrarian radicalism and *esprit de corps*.

The truth was rather more prosaic and predictable. An alternative view of the 1879–82 Land War is of a period of pervasive anomie, of a civil conflict that often pitched the impoverished against the merely impecunious, bent the highly stratified social structures of rural Ireland beyond breaking point, facilitated the rise of petty tyrants and unleashed fratricidal violence, the scars of which had still not healed a generation later when the struggle was no longer against the so-called 'eyes and ears of Dublin Castle', but against the Castle itself.

Bailiffs use a battering ram at an eviction – from the Lawrence Collection, National Library of Ireland

The emergency men and the end of deference

However, amidst all the menacing intra-peasant mayhem, the mythology of the Land War often stacks up quite well. It certainly signalled an acceleration in the demise of forelock-tugging deference. The practice of social ostracisation – which was actually a tried and tested phenomenon of some antiquity in Irish landlord-tenant relations – came into its own during the Land War, notably in the case of the man whose surname would become the most enduring neologism of the period, Captain Charles Boycott, the English-born agent of Lord Erne based in the Lough Mask area of Co. Mayo.

Captain Charles Boycott as depicted by Spy in Vanity Fair

And what of the landlord response to the emerging crisis? Initially, their approach was patchwork in nature. Some landlords offered reductions in light of the prevailing economic conditions. Others did likewise, but only to avoid potential bankruptcy in the absence of a rent roll. Many resorted to eviction as a form of warning, often re-admitting tenants as caretakers or allowing them to resume their holdings on payment of arrears. A small number adopted a Cromwellian stance and evicted mercilessly.

It wasn't until January 1881 that some sort of syndicated approach was adopted by the country's landlords with the formation of the Property Defence Association (PDA), sometimes known as the Emergency Committee or the Orange Emergency Committee. This landlord support group, constructively amounting to a small private army, remained in existence until 1919. The PDA was funded by contributions from landlords to a central fund, as well as donations from concerned aristocrats in Britain anxious to assist their separated brethren. The 'chief organizer of the landlord faction'[30] was Norris Goddard, the PDA's energetic chief field officer. In the estimation of the formidable Resident Magistrate (RM), Clifford Lloyd – hardly an objective source – 'no man in Ireland went through more danger or performed his duty more conscientiously to his employers … Like the little petrel, he was to be found wherever the storm raged most furiously'.[31]

Clifford Lloyd

Goddard was assisted by paid recruits who became known as 'emergency men'. This pooling of landlord resources was followed by the establishment of a similar enterprise, the Land Corporation, the following year, or, as *United Ireland* described it, 'Mr Art McMurough Kavanagh's Gunpowder Plot'.[32] The primary purpose of the Land Corporation was to remove one of the major obstacles to eviction by purchasing boycotted holdings from landlords. The corporation had its origins in 1882 in the sumptuous surroundings of Dublin's Shelbourne Hotel. The six founders, who included Art MacMurrough Kavanagh and the Marquess of Headfort, were a self-selecting oligarchy, all of whom were members of London's Carlton Club, physical and spiritual home of the Tory Party.

Kavanagh, owner of Borris Castle in County Carlow and its accompanying estate, appropriately for a nationalist *bête noire*, was descended from Dermot MacMurrough, the twelfth-century King of Leinster responsible for the introduction of the Normans to Ireland. The symbolism was irresistible for the nationalist and agrarian propagandists of *United Ireland*, who obliged the insouciant Kavanagh by goading him mercilessly in the pages of the journal.

Kavanagh was an extraordinary individual who overcame the handicap of being born with arms and legs barely six inches long. He certainly refused to allow his disabilities to prevent his enjoyment of those traditional aristocratic pursuits involving the killing of animals, edible or otherwise. A specially devised saddle allowed him to ride to hounds. In his memoir, *The Reminiscences of an Irish Land Agent*, the equally redoubtable Samuel M. Hussey recalled of the baron of Borris: 'On one occasion the saddle turned under him, and the horse trotted back to the stable-yard, with his master hanging under him, his hair sweeping the ground, bleeding profusely; he merely cursed the groom with emphatic volubility, had himself more safely readjusted, and then rode out once more.'[33]

At the age of eighteen, Kavanagh had been banished from Carlow by his mother when he was found to be having affairs with a number of young women on the Borris estate. MP for Carlow from 1868, as a Justice of the Peace he would often hear cases under an oak tree in the courtyard of Borris Castle accompanied by his pet bear, Bessy. When attending the House of Commons, Kavanagh sailed to London on his schooner, the *Lady Eva*, moored the vessel outside the Houses of Parliament and gained access to the Palace of Westminster via an entrance adjoining the river Thames. His manservant carried him into the chamber, placed him on the Tory benches and awaited his master's pleasure. The schooner journeys became unnecessary when Kavanagh lost his seat in the general election of 1880.

Once the Land League faced concerted, rather than piecemeal, landlord opposition, it did not take long for Norris Goddard and his emergency men to make their presence felt. Legally, landlords had two options when it came to dealing with tenants in arrears. They could go to court and seek an ejectment order for the non-payment of rent, or they could sue their tenant for debt. In the former instance the sheriff seized the land, and the tenant had six months to pay arrears of rent and his landlord's legal costs. If he obliged, a court decree would restore him to his holding. By the end of September 1881, evictions were at around 2,000 a month from an average of just under 600 for the first quarter of the year.

In the case of an action for debt – and in the early 1870s, the ratio of ejectment orders to the utilisation of the debt process was 1:50 (one possible explanation for the paucity of evictions) – the sheriff seized land, effects and livestock and brought the latter to auction. If the tenant didn't pay his rent and landlord costs immediately, he surrendered all rights to his farm. His effects and livestock were then sold to defray his financial obligations to his landlord. For the landlord, the major disadvantage of the latter course of action was the risk, incurred frequently during the Land War, that the auction of his defaulting tenant's effects would be boycotted and no money could be had. This was where the emergency men came into their own from early 1881. Goddard and the employees of the PDA began to intervene in auctions – as in the case of Andrew Kettle (mentioned previously) – and bid for both the tenants' interest in properties and distrained livestock and effects, while local Land League members 'looked on and hooted with displeasure' as their cattle were led away.[34]

The first PDA breakthrough came at an auction in Dungarvan, Co. Waterford, of the distrained property of a relatively prosperous tenant named Walsh. The well-resourced emergency men secured Walsh's livestock with successful bids, much to the chagrin of the farmer and the local Land League leadership. The vexation of the latter increased exponentially a short time later. Walsh complained that his support for the activities of the league had cost him £400. When John Dillon himself handed him a compensatory cheque for £150, he used the money to settle up with his landlord and recover his farm, thereby causing much consternation and soul-searching among the burghers of the local Land League.

The experience of Walsh was not unique. Under advisement from the PDA, landlords began to take action against the wealthiest of their tenants, the ones who could well afford to pay their rents or arrears and who had the most to lose. In Cork, for example, between March and September 1881 there were ninety livestock sales provoked by actions for debt taken by the landlords of the county and supported by the PDA. This policy of making an example of their most solvent and affluent tenants was employed 'as the method of bringing the whole estate ... to heel'.[35]

Like much else in the Land War, after a period of trial and error, this policy proved to be not as ingenious as it first appeared. The emergency men were, after all, bidding with landlord money taken from the coffers of the PDA. They might make a profit by selling on distrained cattle, but when it came to the sale of the 'interest' in the evicted tenant's farm, it was a zero-sum game. The emergency men were depleting landlord resources even though no rent would be forthcoming for any of the farms that were bought until a new tenant had been secured. Such an eventuality was highly problematic. Anyone who took an evicted farm during the Land War risked far more than instant opprobrium; they risked death or grievous bodily harm. The activities of the emergency men, who travelled the country participating in these auctions, could never be a long-term project. It was a financial foot race, a question of whose resources or willpower would run out first, those of the league (largely funded from the United States) or the PDA.

But in the early days of PDA activity, such were the inroads being made by the emergency men that John Dillon felt constrained to address the issue in March 1881. He acknowledged that the activities of the PDA were having a greater impact on the Land League campaign than the government coercion legislation designed for that purpose (the Protection of Person and Property (Ireland) Act 1881). But he went on to claim in a speech in Thurles that 'they [the tenants] must remember that each sale costs the landlords a lot of money, and the landlords have less money than the league has, and the people, if they kept up the fight, could wear out the emergency committee before they wore the league out'.[36] Both sides were involved in a paper chase, a game of hare and hounds with shredded banknotes as the scent.

At the end of June 1881, the Land League had more than £30,000 in its bank accounts. Between October 1881 and May 1882, however, with its coffers regularly being replenished from America, the league would disburse a hefty £70,000 in supporting prisoners and evicted tenants. The league's finances were not helped by the establishment of a number of bogus branches that were formed with the sole intention of getting access to the organisation's relief funds. These 'branches' provided no income, while draining the league's resources.

Cosy notions of tenant solidarity and partnership were not enhanced when IPP MP Tim Healy proposed, at a Land League executive meeting in 1881, that it was time for the 'charity' cases being financially assisted by the organisation to throw themselves at the mercy of the Poor Law Guardians and apply for relief. Healy's rationale was that those who were in chronic arrears should no longer be the responsibility of the league, because their participation in a strike against rent had little or nothing to do with a principled stand against landlordism, but was simply based on their inability to pay their rent in the first place. Why should the Land League carry them, the nationalist MP argued, when local ratepayers, many of whom were landlords, could foot the bill instead? According to Healy's logic – the measure was opposed by, among others, James Daly and Anna Parnell – the only tenants

347

who should be receiving financial support from the league were those who were actually in a position to pay their rent but were endangering their tenancies by refusing to do so. These were, in the main, substantial farmers.

By the end of 1881, the financial pressure on the league was becoming unbearable. As agitation turned to anarchy, more and more revenue was being expended on the defence and support of the acolytes of Captain Moonlight and Rory of the Hills, in court and in prison. It became increasingly apparent to the more affluent cohort of Land League supporters that the deficits being faced by the league might lead to the withdrawal of funds from the organisation that were keeping many of them afloat. Furthermore, the power of the boycott, the only real guarantee that they would be in a position to reclaim their still vacant farms if they were actually evicted, was being neutralised by an increasingly determined breed of 'land grabbers', who were prepared to shrug off ostracisation within their local communities. A growing number of farmers were prepared to risk social opprobrium, as long as it came in a package with a decent-sized parcel of land attached, at an acceptable rent. With the more militant activists being committed to prison in greater numbers, the retributive agents of physical intimidation were also in shorter supply.

The great Land Court race

It was only when the Duke of Richmond's findings regarding the failure of the 1870 Land Act were confirmed by the subsequent Liberal government's own Bessborough Commission that Gladstone moved to give full legal effect to the '3 Fs' in his 1881 Land Act, embark on a mission to pacify the Land League and effectively concede the principle of 'dual ownership' of Irish land. The 1881 land legislation had some impact on the levels of civil strife that had plagued Ireland since 1879, mainly through the establishment of the Land Commission and its official rent arbitration system (Land Courts). But the legislation was burdened with design flaws. These included an unwillingness to tackle the issues of farmers in arrears (there was no access to the Land Courts unless your rent was fully paid up) and, once again, tenants with leases.

Because it failed to offer a definitive solution, Gladstone's bill was opposed by the league, by Parnell and by the bulk of Irish parliamentarians, as an inadequate instrument for the resolution of landlord-tenant issues. The 'war' dragged on as the Land League issued instructions to its members that the arbitrative Land Courts were to be treated as one would a repast with the Devil himself. A long spoon was to be deployed. Tenants should wait until the league itself had brought a number of test cases before the arbitration courts to see if they were functioning equitably, or if they were just another Machiavellian Liberal/landlord ruse.

However, the effect of the introduction of a judicial system of rent arbitration on the Irish farming community was akin to the impact on the adult male population of the United States of the announcement in 1848 by James W. Marshall that he had discovered gold at Sutter's Mill in northern California. The word 'stampede' is not inappropriate to describe the rush of tenants to the courts to have their rent arbitrated. One of the victims of this inevitable onslaught was Land League solidarity and credibility.

Just as unwise as the instruction to 'hang fire' on the new Land Courts was the issuing of the 'No Rent Manifesto' on 18 October 1881.[37] This came in the wake of the arrest of the Land League leadership and scores of activists as well as the banning of the league itself. The *Freeman's Journal*, *The Nation* and the highly respected nationalist prelate, Archbishop Croke of Cashel, were among the opponents of a nationwide rent strike.

Even for some of the erstwhile regional luminaries of the Land League, the choice was stark. You could adhere to the stirring 'No Rent Manifesto' and thus risk eviction and/or the sale of your assets. You would be doing this, not in the hope of securing a better offer from the landlord himself, but in support of a political gesture designed to procure the release of the Land League leadership. Alternatively, you could pay what you owed the landlord, have your rent arbitrated and suppress your natural but not overwhelming concern about the imprisonment without trial of the men whose leadership had contributed hugely to the establishment of the courts in the first place. When it quickly became clear that the Land Courts were offering average discounts of 15–20 per cent, most tenants took a deep breath, held their noses and travelled the lower road. Some might have done so with red faces, but an abatement was an abatement.

To the more substantial farmers, a positive outcome in the Land Court promised a return to the era of rising expectations. To the chronically insolvent, it was of little or no use. Even a 20 per cent reduction of their rental tariff was of minimal assistance. There came a parting of the ways. Substantial tenants cashed in their chips and hurried to arbitration, leaving small farmers, cottiers and labourers to fend for themselves, albeit with some determined assistance from the formidable Anna Parnell and the Ladies Land League.

The work of the organisation led by Parnell's radical sibling – itself proscribed in early 1882 – included the provision of more than 200 wooden huts to be used to house evicted tenants. These were prefabricated, measured about twenty feet in length and had galvanised tin roofs. They could be erected quickly and dismantled with ease for use elsewhere in the event of an evicted tenant being re-admitted by his landlord, or abandoning the land altogether and seeking a livelihood elsewhere, probably in Liverpool or Boston.

The suspicion of the authorities, not entirely groundless, was that the huts had less to do with charitable care for the evicted than with monitoring the activities of new tenants who had taken over the farms of the families who had been ejected.[38]

However, when it came to a genuine choice – and not all tenants had such a choice – between a Ladies Land League hut or a hearing in front of one of Mr Gladstone's obliging commissioners in a Land Court, it took a loyal league zealot to opt for the galvanised roof. Hundreds of apparently true-blue apparatchiks proved to be sky-blue at best. As the edifice created by the league began to crumble, the tenant movement divided into two irreconcilable camps. The legion of the contented pocketed their rental discounts and paid off landlord *and* grocer. The *sans culottes* seethed and gave expression to their resentment at this turn of events by boosting the RIC statistics for agrarian 'outrages'. Meanwhile, the man who had predicted the hegemony of Captain Moonlight, should he be jailed, sat in his rather comfortable accommodation in Kilmainham Gaol, dreamed of pastures new and waited for opportunity to knock and to unlock his cell door. It was later alleged by A. M. Sullivan, owner of *The Nation* newspaper, that Parnell had only appended his signature to the ill-starred 'No Rent Manifesto' because he was morally certain that it would provoke the proscription of the Land League.[39] This was undoubtedly 'a consummation devoutly to be wished' by the organisation's titular leader, because his primary focus had already shifted from the land issue to that of a more concerted push for Home Rule.

The treaty

The concordat that emerged from Kilmainham in May 1882, and was ferried between Parnell and Gladstone by the ambitious and duplicitous William Henry O'Shea MP, got the Irish leader and the British prime minister off their respective hooks while bringing down on Parnell's head the criticism of elements of his previously loyal (but never unquestioning) support.

To Irish radicals, the foot-soldiers who bought into the Land League slogan 'the land for the people', the Kilmainham accord 'was a Parnellite surrender rather than a bargain'.[40] While there was a Gladstonian promise of new legislation to give tenants in arrears access to the Land Courts, the British prime minister still demurred when it came to any interference between two contracting parties. There was little or nothing in this 'virtual' treaty for leaseholders. The disappointment and anger of many of Parnell's supporters with the agreement was somewhat mitigated by the resignation of the unpopular chief secretary, William E. Forster, who was unable to stomach what he perceived as the concessions made to violent agrarianism. If 'Buckshot' Forster was 'agin' the pact, this line of reasoning went, it must have something going for it.

For his part, Parnell agreed to do his utmost to end agrarian violence, a promise that came dangerously close to an admission that he could turn off that bloodied tap whenever he chose to do so. His willingness to come to an agreement with Gladstone was governed by his perception that the 'No Rent Manifesto' had failed; that his advice to tenants to await test cases in the Land Courts had not been heeded; and that agrarian violence was assuming a momentum of its own that would soon become uncontrollable.

With the Land League consigned to history since its proscription in October 1881, Parnell moved quickly to shut down his sister Anna's radical substitute, the Ladies Land League, and, without sentiment, brought down the curtain on the First Land War. His direction of travel now turned ninety degrees. The hope of at least a hearing on Home Rule from the Liberal prime minister, and the voices of opposition from within his own following, were both stifled by the brutal murders of the chief secretary for Ireland, Lord Frederick Cavendish, and the under-secretary, Thomas H. Burke, in Phoenix Park on 6 May 1882, days after Parnell's letter to Gladstone had secured his release from Kilmainham. Parnell turned out to be an unintended beneficiary of the savagery of the Invincibles.

In his memoir of the Land League era, *The Fall of Feudalism in Ireland*, Michael Davitt observed that the agreement with Gladstone had placed Parnell in a tricky position *vis-à-vis* his own political support. To Davitt, the Kilmainham accord was 'a virtual surrender of the movement to its enemies ... The Phoenix Park murders saved Mr. Parnell from the perils which lurked in the terms of the compact, while both events snatched from the Land League the guerdon of triumph.'[41]

Parnell the pragmatist had gone as far as he was prepared to go in fomenting social upheaval. 'The high hopes for political and social revolution of some of the Land League's founders had not been achieved,'[42] according to Paul Bew. That, however, posed no philosophical difficulties for Parnell. He now sought a measure of reciprocation for his leadership of the land struggle from his erstwhile agrarian supporters, in the achievement of his fundamental devolutionary political aims. It was payback time.

The first stirrings of peasant proprietorship

The fact that the Land League boasted a leadership that was prepared to do jail time, along with the thousand-odd foot soldiers incarcerated between March 1881 and July 1882, played a significant role in the impact of the organisation. Their incarceration, though not unduly onerous (they were allowed to wear their own clothes, furnish their cells and bring in their own food), added some much-needed fuel to the fire of the agrarian rebellion. Their absence from the field also removed a possible moderating influence on the acolytes of Captain Moonlight, a significant contributory factor to the rural mayhem of the winter of 1881–2.

If it achieved nothing else – and its achievements were considerable despite only having taken a modest enough £1.4 million off Irish rents[43] – the Land League certainly softened up landlords for the approaching era of tenant acquisition. Ironically, it was the tenants who proved reluctant at first to enter the promised land of peasant proprietary. At the time of the founding of the Land League in 1879, it was seen in conservative agrarian circles as an unduly radical step, one more associated with neo-Fenian objectives than with the less ambitious 'fixity of tenure' demands of league precursors such as the moderate Central Tenants Defence Association led by Andrew Kettle.[44] While there was a delayed reaction, one of the consequences of the First Land War was a dawning realisation on the part of both landlord and tenant that it was high time to end a relationship that had endured for centuries. The question was, how was this to come about?

The economic downturn that began in the 1870s and, arguably, endured until the first decade of the twentieth century played a substantial role. This declining market – though there were some interludes of rising prices – inured landlords to the prospect of the continuation of falling incomes from tenants now unwilling to pay historic rents. The advent and persistence of the 'Long Depression' persuaded them that 'land purchase offered the prospect of exchanging land for money'.[45]

By the time Gavrilo Princip changed the world in Sarajevo in 1914 – conclusively ending the agricultural 'bear' market – three-quarters of Irish occupiers had, through loans from the British government, put enough money in the pockets of the Irish aristocracy to persuade them to divest themselves of millions of acres of Irish land. Just as the aggression of the Land League had concentrated the mind of William Gladstone on his 1881 legislation, so did Tory antipathy to a repeat performance stimulate the drive towards tenant ownership of Irish land. That, and the expectation that a raft of enabling land purchase legislation would subvert rural Irish adherence to Home Rule.

In short, the success of the Land League campaign, insofar as it was successful in briefly unifying a heterogenous Irish tenantry, was based on that old saw, 'the enemy of my enemy is my friend'. There was a temporary convergence of the economic interests of a number of habitually antagonistic groups. The tectonic plates of the traditional alliances and interests in rural Ireland shifted. The resulting tremor was brief but dramatic, and its consequences took some time to assert themselves. The Land War marked the beginning of the end of incrementalism and accommodation. The seismic shock heralded a 'changing of the guard' as the old guard was ultimately replaced by a new urban-rural, middle-class nexus.

There is, of course, another possible interpretation of that word 'guard'. The new dispensation was an alliance that was determined to protect and guard its own interests. The graziers wanted to lock down their holdings; the shopkeepers and tradesmen wanted to secure the payment of their debts. Tagging along behind both was a rural peasantry who wanted rent reductions and tenure guarantees, who provided much of the muscle and who, like the firebrand Anna Parnell, outlived their usefulness. The priorities of the real leadership of the agrarian movement of the Land War ensured that it was not some fuzzy, idealistic crusade in support of Wolfe Tone's 'men of no property'.

A cadre of relatively comfortable farmers and equally prosperous tradesmen defended their gains and pressed forward with their campaign for economic and social dominance. They harnessed their own potency, augmented it with the raw power of peasant activism and began the process of ridding themselves of the irritating and over-prolonged regime of landlord hegemony.

When viewed dispassionately, the story of the Land War is of how small farmers, and their Fenian allies, were exploited by a new elite to shake the money tree and topple the aristocracy from the uppermost branches.

12

'Tenant on tenant' violence in the 1880s

'A true revolutionary movement in Ireland should, in
my opinion, partake of both a constitutional and an
illegal character. It should be both an open and a secret
organisation using the constitution for its own purposes, but
also taking advantage of its secret combination.'[1]

(Charles Stewart Parnell, in an interview with journalist
Albert Chester Ives of the *New York Herald*, 1880)

The Maamtrasna murder trials at Green Street courthouse
*(*New York Times*)*

17 November 1882, Green Street Courthouse, Dublin

Maolra Seoighe sat impassively throughout his trial. This had less to do with his personal conviction that, since he was innocent of the crimes of which he was accused, the jury would naturally find him 'not guilty', than with the fact that he spoke almost no English.

His court-appointed interpreter, an Irish-speaking RIC constable named Evans, was providing him with a sketchy account of proceedings. The accused man had very little sense of what was going on around him. He knew the jury was considering his case. He did not need to speak English to be aware of that. When they returned after six minutes to deliver their verdict, he must have felt optimistic. It hadn't taken them long to see through the lies of the prosecution witnesses and acknowledge his innocence. He had taken no part in the brutal murders of his five Joyce cousins in Maamtrasna. He had been tucked up in bed when the Joyces were shot (the males) or bludgeoned to death (the females), for who knew what reason. Seoighe watched, uncomprehendingly, as the foreman of the jury delivered the verdict. When Evans turned to him, ashen-faced, and told him in Irish that he had been found guilty of murder, the prisoner almost fainted. He clutched the railing of the dock to support himself. Looking towards the heavens, for God himself to witness his truth, he began to speak *as Gaeilge*. The *Freeman's Journal* court reporter recorded what happened next:

> ... looking upwards with a fervent expression and attitude of invocation, [he] spoke in Irish. The interpreter rendered it as follows – 'He leaves it to God and the virgin above his head. He had no dealing with it, no more than the person who was never born, nor had he against anyone else. For the last twenty years he had done no harm, and if he had, might he never go to heaven. He was as clear of this as the child yet to be born.'[2]

Before Maolra Seoighe (Myles Joyce) was hanged in Galway jail, the two men destined to die with him, Patrick Joyce and

Patrick Casey, admitted their involvement in the horrific crime at Maamtrasna and exonerated Seoighe. He had not been a member of the seven-man gang who slaughtered the Joyces in their tiny cabin. The Lord Lieutenant, Earl Spencer, now had the power of life or death over a seemingly innocent man. He could, on the basis of this convincing new evidence, quash the sentence of Myles Joyce. Instead, he ordered the execution to proceed.

Maolra Seoighe, according to those who witnessed his execution, died an appalling death. To the last he continued to loudly declare his innocence. He might have saved his breath. The executioner, William Marwood, had no sympathy, and no Irish. Neither did he perform his duties in an exemplary manner:

> The rope caught in the wretched man's arm, and for some seconds it was seen being jerked and tugged in the writhing of his last agony. The grim hangman cast an angry glance into the pit, and then, hissing an obscene oath at the struggling victim, sat on the beam, and kicked him into eternity.[3]

In 2018, the Irish state, which had played no part in the judicial murder of Maolra Seoighe, awarded him a posthumous pardon. A specially commissioned 2017 report from UCD Law professor Niamh Howlin described the verdict in his case as 'unfair by the standards of criminal justice at the time' and concluded that 'the witness evidence against him was of doubtful reliability'.[4]

A succession of Irish informers, approvers, false witnesses and corrupt lawyers conspired to end Myles Joyce's life. The crime of which he was accused was of a piece with the petty jealousies, feuds, infighting and callous perjury that led to his fatal appointment with William Marwood.

Joyce was as much a victim of the gruesome 'tenant-on-tenant' violence of the 1880s as any of the farmers, herders or labourers murdered by their neighbours.

The 'other' Land Wars, 1879–90

'Mob law has here ruled. [The Land League] has persecuted farmers and others who have not obeyed its orders ... I have it on good authority that the farmers will hail deliverance from this yoke.'[5]

(Special Resident Magistrate Clifford Lloyd to Under-Secretary Thomas H. Burke on agrarian intimidation in Co. Limerick, 16 October 1881)

'Sir Denis Fitzpatrick and his daughter were making a tour of the Kerry fjords some years ago, and the lady asked a boatman on Caragh Lake, what would happen to a tenant who took an evicted farm. The reply was: "I don't think he'd do it again, Miss, leastways it's in the next world alone he'd have the chance of making such a fool of himself."'[6]

(Samuel Murray Hussey, *The Reminiscences of an Irish Land Agent*)

There might well have been two distinct and separate commissions of inquiry, both commencing on 17 September 1888, their terms of reference and their judges coinciding.

The '*Times* Commission' – as it was known in Ireland – placed the 'newspaper of record', aka 'The Thunderer', in the dock, and observers were forced to endure months of barren grievance testimony from a succession of Irish peasants before getting to the core of the proceedings, viz. the complete vindication of Charles Stewart Parnell.

On the other hand, the 'Parnell Commission' – as it was more commonly known in Britain, particularly in Conservative circles – chose to postpone the presentation of its case against Parnell in favour of a litany of violence, intimidation, sedition, incitement and thuggery that *The Times* claimed had been unleashed by the Land League, and its enablers in the IPP, during (and after) the Land War of 1879–82. Like the choice of the 'American Civil War', as opposed to the 'War Between the States', or 'Derry' as against

Images from The Times *Commission – including
William Henry O'Shea giving evidence (top left)*

'Londonderry', the nomenclature (*Times* or Parnell) chosen to describe the Special Commission, presided over by Justices Hannen, Day and Smith, betrayed one's political allegiance.

For the record, the tribunal's actual title was 'The Special Commission to inquire into and report upon the charges and allegations made against certain members of Parliament and other persons in the course of the proceedings in an action entitled *O'Donnell versus Walter and another*'. It is not hard to see why an abbreviation – whichever one was selected – was appropriate.

This three-judge tribunal was expected to establish the authenticity (or otherwise) of the infamous *Times* facsimile letter of 18 April 1887, and of a variety of related correspondence that allegedly linked Parnell to the activities of the lethal Invincibles and tied the leadership of his party to a violent conspiracy to end landlordism and subvert the Union.

The Times, in early 1887, had devoted a series of disparaging articles, entitled 'Parnellism and Crime', to undermining the legitimacy of Parnell and his supporters by alleging that leading members of the IPP were morally responsible for many of the murders and assaults carried out during the Land War. This was in spite of data offered to the House of Commons in January 1881 by Thomas Sexton MP demonstrating that in the sixteen counties where Land League meetings had been held since its inception, 'the average of crime was less than in the counties where there had been no meetings'.[7]

The 'gotcha' moment for *The Times* came with the publication of a letter on 18 April 1887, apparently signed by Parnell himself, praising the Invincibles for the murder of under-secretary Thomas H. Burke, in Phoenix Park in May 1882. This apparent *coup de grâce*, however, would rebound on the newspaper with the evisceration of Richard Pigott, the man who had 'acquired' the letters on their behalf. His ritual judicial slaughter came about when Pigott himself was exposed as the forger of the documents in late February 1888. That aspect of the proceedings, however, although by far the more colourful and dramatic, does not fall within the scope of this volume.*

What is of greater interest here is what one involuntary observer, the reporter John MacDonald of the London *Daily News*, described dismissively as 'a dismal monotone of cruelty and crime ... the *viva voce* history of a people, one of the dreariest, saddest histories in the world'.[8] For weeks, between the opening of the evidentiary phase of the proceedings (late October 1888) and the demolition of Pigott, *The Times* (as de facto prosecutors) presented a doleful parade of murder, abuse and mistreatment in rural Ireland from witnesses who had, by their own accounts, fallen foul of Ribbon-Fenianism, 'moonlighters', vindictive Land League

---

* The author has written about the cross-examination of Pigott by Sir Charles Russell at the Commission, and the Maamtrasna murders and trials, in the volume *Conspiracy: Irish Political Trials* (2009), published by the Royal Irish Academy.

'court' decisions, rural warrior chieftains or sectional feuds. Some of the avowed victims were exposed under cross-examination as charlatans tempted by the inducements of *The Times* to tell the presiding judges what the newspaper wanted the Commission to hear.[*] Others, while giving evidence, slyly recanted statements made in Ireland which had so excited the representatives of *The Times* that the newspaper stumped up for a trip to London for witnesses they expected to make the commissioners blanch.

Many of the witnesses who crossed the Irish Sea, however, were credible and compelling. Their hair-raising evidence contributed to a deeply unflattering picture of Ireland. While Irish peasant society was never quite as Dante-esque as *The Times* attested, it certainly qualified as, at the very least, the Fourth or Fifth Circle of Hell (Greed and Wrath).

Late Victorian Irish rural society fell far short of the idyllic. Its vices were as numerous as its virtues, despite the prevailing mythos of a noble and beleaguered Irish peasantry, whose occasional forays into violent behaviour were morally justified on the basis of the iniquitous tenurial system against which they struggled. The argument in favour of tactics that amounted to civil disobedience was that, when political redress was impossible, an oppressed peasantry had limited options in prosecuting its cause. Which was fine as far as it went. However, it fell far short of validating the anarchy that gripped the country in the latter half of the first Land War.

The truth was that were many in rural Ireland in the 1880s – just as there had been in similar periods of disturbance throughout the nineteenth century – who had little interest in collective remedial action, unless it could be turned to their advantage. The Land Wars of the 1880s were often used as camouflage for the settling of scores, the achievement of petty power, the intimidation and brutalising of neighbours, and even the acquisition of land. The Irish countryside could be a 'fatal environment', one just as savage as that described

---

[*] The evidence produced here is of witnesses whose testimony either went unchallenged by counsel for the Parnellites or was not shaken under cross-examination.

by Richard Slotkin in his eponymous masterpiece on gun violence in the American west during the nineteenth century.[9]

The two extremes of the weaponry of the Land War – the legitimate boycott and the illicit handgun – were often employed indiscriminately. Both could be used to intimidate (in the case of the former) or maim and murder (in the case of the latter) at the behest of 'village tyrants'.[10] These parochial warlords burrowed their way into leadership roles in the wider agrarian movement and pursued agendas that often had little or nothing to do with the objectives of the Land League, or even of the more extreme Ribbon/Fenian movement. Questionable and vindictive decisions arrived at by the league's increasingly influential 'courts' – little more than local branch meetings to which 'offenders' were summoned – could be used as a fig leaf by vested interests to conceal self-serving objectives. Long-standing vendettas were pursued; land was channelled towards favoured candidates; a *pax barbarica* was maintained under cover of edicts promulgated by muscular elements who often assumed de facto control of their village or townland. On occasions, the hard men even fell out amongst themselves. A Galway witness before the Special Commission, Michael Hoarty – 'a singularly intelligent witness', according to John MacDonald of the *Daily News*, who covered every day of the Commission's proceedings – testified that he was simultaneously a member of the IRB and of the Irish National League. That dual status did not prevent a number of 'moonlighters' from firing into his house, one of whom was later caught with a National League membership ticket about his person.[11]

Between 1880 and 1882, there were 50 agrarian murders, 148 attempted murders (classified as 'firing at the person'), 776 cases of arson and 325 incidents of 'firing into dwelling houses'. On top of that, 300 cattle were killed or maimed and 5,536 threatening letters or notices were penned and distributed.[12] The RIC took it upon itself to establish 235 protection posts for persons perceived to be under threat.[13] In his opening address to the Special Commission, the attorney general, Sir Richard Webster, acting for *The Times*, characterised this violence as part of a strategy to rid the country of its 'English garrison of landlords' and as a prelude to a bloody campaign for legislative independence:

> The way in which this conspiracy worked and was intended to work was, if necessary, by the commission of crimes which would injure both the landlord and the tenant, which in 99 cases out of 100 injured the tenant and did not injure the landlord, in order to drive the 'English garrison' – the Irish landlords – from any possession in the soil of Ireland.[14]

Webster's analysis of the strategy of the Land League was, of course, largely special pleading made in support of his brief. *The Times* required him to establish the existence of a subversive conspiracy. However, in suggesting that the turmoil unleashed in the Irish countryside during the Land War injured the tenant rather than the landlord in 99 per cent of cases, Webster was not far wrong. While he was exaggerating the scope of the Land League campaign on behalf of his client, he managed to identify correctly the real victims of the unleashing of 'Captain Moonlight' during the Land War: ordinary tenant farmers.

Webster's job was to link the Land League or its successor, the Irish National League, into as many as possible of the hundreds of agrarian crimes brought to the attention of the Special Commission. This he largely failed to do. Many of the newspaper's own witnesses, farmers who had been the victims of exemplary violence, declined to oblige Webster and point the finger of blame at the league. Anarchic elements in lawless counties did not require even the proverbial 'nod and a wink' from the officers of the local Land League branch to wage war. Many attacks went far beyond what even the most militant members of the Land League leadership would have countenanced. Some had little or nothing to do with the proverbial 'Land League law' and were simply brutal assaults carried out by elements who 'availed of the climate of uncertainty to pursue old wrongs'.[15] It was a phenomenon that we shall encounter again in barely modified form during the 1919–21 War of Independence.

Although the Land League leadership at national and local level, and its supporters in the press, ritually condemned murder and battery, there were understandable doubts as to the sincerity of many of those denunciations. Many ordinary Land League members, and even some of the leadership cadre with enduring ties to Fenianism and Ribbonism, surreptitiously believed that, to paraphrase an infamous axiom, 'the only good grabber was a dead grabber'. And some of the dead, or the maimed, must have known the risk they ran in taking up farms from which the previous tenants had been evicted. The murder of 'land grabbers' (the expression had quietly replaced the pejorative 'land jobbers' as the nineteenth century progressed) was hardly unique to the 1880s, but the punishment was more frequent and more permanent than in previous conflicts.

Hundreds of other victims, however, can have had little inkling that their transgressions (continuing to work for a 'grabber', paying rent to their landlord, refusing to accept the rulings of Land League courts) were either capital offences or merited the beatings, maiming or incendiary attacks that were administered by the self-appointed enforcers.

Galwayman Peter Dempsey, for example, could have been in no doubt as to the potential fate that lay in store for him when he took over the farm of one Martin Bermingham, on the estate of Lord Dunsandle near Loughrea, Co. Galway. Bermingham had been evicted for non-payment of rent. The Bermingham farm had originally been taken by a local man, Murty Hynes. Hynes's life was threatened and he thought better of his decision. At a public Land League meeting near Craughwell on 18 September 1880, attended by 4,000 supporters, Hynes mounted the platform and agreed to surrender the farm. The gesture earned him the cheers of the crowd. The land then lay vacant for another three months – a league tactic designed to put financial pressure on the landlord – until Dempsey upended the strategy by taking the farm. The new tenant was warned by the local RIC District Inspector, Dominick Barry, to accept a round-the-clock police guard. Dempsey, foolhardy or naïve, declined Barry's offer, insisting that – according to the policeman's evidence before the

Special Commission – 'he was amongst his friends, and he did not apprehend any injury'. He was proven wrong on both counts.

Dempsey may well have had some (silent) supporters in the area, but they were of little use to him on 29 May 1881, when he was shot dead, in full view of his two young daughters, on his way to mass.[16] Only close friends had the courage to attend his funeral. Dempsey's widow heard people singing in celebration outside her house on the night of her husband's murder and was aware that bonfires were lit to acclaim his death. She remained in situ, under a permanent police guard, finding it almost impossible to get anyone to work for her. After four years, she abandoned Loughrea entirely.

However, what expectation would another tenant of Lord Dunsandle, James Connors, have had when he took some bogland that had been vacated by a local 'bog-ranger' named Keogh? He had given up the bog because of his reluctance to 'take care of the wildfowl', a condition of occupancy imposed by the landlord. Connors assumed Keogh's turbary rights and immediately found himself being boycotted. He was subjected to abuse in the streets of Loughrea and had difficulty purchasing food for his family. Provisions had to be bought for the family by the local RIC and delivered to the Connors house at night.

Then, on 11 May 1881, barely a fortnight after agreeing to rent the bogland, Connors and his wife, Julia, set out to travel fifteen miles by horse and cart to the funeral of the man's father. The couple were barely a mile from home when they came under fire, and James Connors was shot dead. His wife recognised her husband's murderers, who made no attempt to disguise themselves. Only a handful of neighbours attended Connors's wake, and his widow continued to experience difficulty in purchasing food for her family even after her husband's death. Her cause was not helped by the fact that she had given evidence against two men, John Ryan and Patrick Keogh, who were tried for her husband's murder. Although she identified them as the killers, both men were acquitted.

Could John Doloughty, a sixty-year-old agricultural labourer with seven children, murdered in Co. Clare on 9 July 1881, have anticipated his fate? Doloughty's 'crime' did not even loosely measure up to the iniquities of Peter Dempsey. He had no land of his own. He was merely a lowly herder working for a Clare farmer, James Lynch. It was Lynch who had taken a farm from which a family named Hynes had been evicted. Doloughty had remained loyal to Lynch despite threats of boycotting and a nocturnal visit the previous October from three armed and masked men. During this 'moonlighting' escapade, his life had been threatened and shots were fired at him. His loyalty to the 'land grabber' Lynch would ultimately cost John Doloughty his life.[17]

Even further down the transgressional pecking order were those who defied the 'No Rent Manifesto' and handed over rent (often a sum already reduced by the Land Courts) to their landlords. These included Kerry farmer Jeremiah O'Sullivan, whose house was attacked in December 1880 and who was informed (via a semi-literate threatening letter) that if he had the temerity to pay his rent again he would be shot. His fellow tenants had petitioned their landlord for a reduction and some clearly took umbrage at O'Sullivan's defection. Ironically, although he had broken ranks, O'Sullivan had actually paid his landlord less than his fellow tenants were willing to concede.

An elderly (and almost completely deaf) Cork man named Jeremiah Buckley was not as fortunate as O'Sullivan. He had his ears cut off for paying his rent in October 1880. In giving evidence to the Special Commission, Buckley displayed a certain gallows humour about his misfortune. Asked about the scissors that had been used to lop off his ears, he replied 'with a smile and a nod … "I don't think that they were good."'

Both those outcomes, however, paled beside the fates of Michael Mahony and Michael Moroney. The former, in October 1881, was shot dead for the crime of paying his rent against the wishes of his neighbours.[18] The latter was a tenant of Thomas Brown of Newgrove, Co. Clare. When he defied the 'No Rent Manifesto' in December 1881 and paid his rent to Brown's agent, Charles Perry, Moroney too was murdered.

Then there were the cases presented by *The Times* to the three commissioners as proof positive of a Land League criminal conspiracy. These cases, once the evidence was subjected to scrutiny, emerged as having no relevance whatever to the Land War. Most were connected to inter- or intra-family feuds and jealousies.

One of these involved the murder of Cornelius Hickey near Castleisland, Co. Kerry – a particular Land War blackspot – in June 1882. While *The Times* maintained that Hickey had been murdered as a 'land grabber', the questions posed to his widow, Mary Hickey, by Parnellite counsel, Sir Charles Russell, point towards a long-running dispute between Cornelius Hickey and his brothers-in-law, Mary Hickey's siblings. The animosity first cost him his leg – amputated after a gun attack – and then his life, as he died some days after the amputation. Hickey refused to identify his attackers to the RIC.[19] Before claiming that Hickey was a victim of a malevolent Land League decree, *The Times* would have done well to consult the land agent Samuel Murray Hussey, no friend of the league, who was unequivocal in his autobiography that Hickey, 'a humble man, but one enjoying apparently the confidence and respect of all his neighbours', was the victim of 'private hostility, one of those motives that always take advantage of a state of disturbance in order to gratify private ends'.[20]

Even the leading Land Leaguer Timothy Harrington, editor of the *Kerry Sentinel* and future secretary of the Irish National League, became concerned at the dubious nature of some of the cases being taken up by local branches. He pointed out that, as the Land War progressed, there was considerable slippage in the definition of 'land grabbing'. Harrington cited an example of his own, where he had been asked to pursue a case of alleged 'land grabbing' dating back fifteen years. He could see clearly that Land League branch officers in Kerry were abusing their newly acquired power. Despite some blatant conflicts of interest, they were using their influence to sway a number of 'court' actions brought before local branches. In the case of one evicted tenant, Edward Ferris, his brother-in-law, John Talbot, a Tralee shopkeeper and Land League committee member, pushed through a league 'court' decision ordering the new occupants of Ferris's former holding to vacate. This was despite their insistence that Ferris had given their tenancy his blessing after his eviction, and was now second guessing his prior approval. It was apparent that 'leading members of local branches were using the power of the league to further personal and family gain'.[21] In one instance, Harrington warned the Tralee Land League branch that it faced dissolution if it continued to hear cases outside its legitimate remit. Through the editorial pages of his newspaper, the *Kerry Sentinel*, Harrington also warned the Ardfert Land League branch 'to be very careful in the selection of the cases presented to them for consideration at the meetings of the League ... cases which it was absurd to entertain, and in which it would be impossible to do any good, were being brought forward constantly'.[22]

While the First Land War effectively ended in 1882 with the 'Kilmainham Treaty' and the passage of the Arrears Act, the killing did not stop. One of the most controversial atrocities of the mid-1880s, which was especially counter-productive for the Irish National League and was covered extensively in evidence to the Commission, was the killing in November 1885 of John Curtin, a prosperous dairy farmer of 160 acres at Castle Farm near Fieries, situated halfway between Tralee and Killarney. On the night of 13 November, in a raid on his farmhouse, Curtin shot dead one of the raiders, Timothy Sullivan, and was himself killed in the altercation. What the precise purpose of the five raiders was remains a mystery. They may have been attempting to steal weapons (the Curtins had at least two guns), or they may have had some personal issue with Curtin. It is clear from the evidential subtext, revealed in testimony to the Special Commission, that the raid had little or nothing to do with 'Land League law'. The dairy farmer himself was vice-president of the local Irish National League (INL) branch in nearby Fieries (not far from Farranfore). His two sons, George and Daniel, were members of the same INL branch. Curtin was taking the lead in tenant negotiations on a rent abatement from Lord Kenmare at the time of his murder.

Curtin had been the victim of a previous attempted raid, avowedly also a search for weapons. In 1881, at the height of the Land War, a group of men demanding guns had attempted to gain entry to the Curtin house. Curtin spoke to them from an upstairs window and threatened to shoot the first man who tried to enter his home. He was then quizzed about his affiliation to the Land League (he was not a member at that time) and his payment of rent (he had remitted the full amount to Lord Kenmare's agent). The intervention of Curtin's wife, who offered the raiders a 'rusty old gun' to secure their withdrawal, brought the confrontation to a peaceful end.

As with numerous murky personalised disagreements that ended in similar tragedies, the private (some sort of localised dispute or vendetta) became public in the Curtin case. The lives of the Curtin family rapidly disintegrated when, despite John Curtin's Irish National League affiliation, the death of the young raider, Timothy Sullivan, carried more weight with the local power brokers. These included the parish priest, a Fr O'Connor, whose only public statement on the matter offered sympathy to the mother of Timothy Sullivan and did not mention Curtin. O'Connor's curate, however, a Fr Murphy, did condemn the killing of Curtin in the strongest possible terms at mass on the Sunday after the raid. Ominously, however, from the point of view of the family, a large number of parishioners walked out of the church as Murphy was speaking. Shortly afterwards, the Curtins found themselves the subject of a boycott. This went to extremes when the RIC was forced to intervene to prevent the family being attacked while attending mass. The crowd vented its anger on the pew that the Curtins normally occupied in the local church, which was smashed to pieces. When an attempt was made to replace it, the carpenter employed to do the job was badly beaten. Most of the Curtins' workmen were persuaded, or intimidated, into abandoning the family. The Curtins were hooted at when they ventured out in public. Spiteful ballads were penned about John Curtin and were posted publicly. The family's situation worsened after two men named Casey and Daly, both farmers' sons, were tried and sentenced to fourteen years' penal servitude for their involvement in Curtin's murder.[23] The four younger Curtins – Lizzie, Norah, Daniel and George – gave evidence at the trial. Thereafter, the family was followed by loud taunts of 'murderers' and 'informers'.

Although it was no Maamtrasna, the Curtin case created a stir in Ireland and in Britain. It did little for the reputation of the INL, which, having created the sword of the boycott, was now, willy-nilly, taxed by the Tory press with every instance of ostracisation, whatever its origins or its intent. Michael Davitt travelled to Fieries in an apparent attempt to resolve the controversy, but he did the INL's cause few favours by visiting the family of Timothy Sullivan while shunning the Curtins. The episode is not recorded in his part-*apologia*, part-history, *The Fall of Feudalism in Ireland*. In her evidence to the Special Commission, Lizzie Curtin insisted that their situation deteriorated still further in the wake of Davitt's visit.

Even the intervention of a clearly embarrassed Alfred Webb, the Quaker treasurer of the INL, to bring the boycott to an end had little effect. A letter from Webb – who visited the area and, unlike Davitt, spent time with the Curtins – to local INL branches was forthright:

> I spent last Sunday with the family. I will never forget my experiences. Were I now to relate them they might be used as arguments for coercion ... It is the duty of all nationalists openly, unequivocally and effectually to stand by the family ... What makes me more determined not to keep silence is the shameful and horrible calumnies afloat in Dublin concerning the Curtin family.[24]

Before circulating the letter, Webb had also called a meeting in the grounds of the local church and berated the members of the Fieries community for their apparently groundless use of the boycott. If a senior league official could not shame those behind the ill-treatment of the Curtins into suspending their campaign, there were clearly darker and more sinister forces at work than a fatal act of self-defence on the part of the late John Curtin. In her survey of the period, and of the proceedings of the Special Commission, Queen's University, Belfast historian Margaret O'Callaghan summed up the Curtin episode thus: 'What this demonstrates is that offences for which Irish nationalist politicians were held to be answerable encompassed every private vendetta of a peasant society.'[25]

Getting to the heart of the Curtin controversy, almost 140 years on, is an impossible task. However, a tentative parsing of the available facts is possible. Any notion of the direct involvement of the Fieries INL branch in the initial raid and the subsequent boycott can be safely dismissed. Curtin's son George did so emphatically in his evidence to the Special Commission, and Curtin's daughter Lizzie refused to entertain the possibility in her own evidence. Which is not to say that individual members of the INL, or former members of the old Land League, might not have been involved in the killing or the subsequent abuse of the Curtin family.

There was undoubtedly additional animosity created by the trials of Casey and Daly, but that tended only to exacerbate the situation. The boycott predated the indictment of the two men. When asked at the Special Commission if the RIC had received any local assistance in their investigation into the Curtin murder, Sergeant Francis Meehan replied tersely, 'None whatever.'

The date of the atrocity is significant also. By 1885, the Land League had been defunct for almost four years, and the temporary alliance that bound 'snug' farmer to cottier and labourer in the early days of the Land War had been consigned to history. It is apparent, like so many of the killings recorded in this volume, that there was a class element involved in the second raid at least. The Curtins rented a 160-acre dairy farm in fertile mid-Kerry. They were wealthy enough to source most of their food supplies from Cork (more than fifty miles distant) rather than doing so locally, or even relying on traders in Tralee or Killarney, ten miles distant in either direction. They employed four male and five female servants. The family was also prominent enough locally to have its own dedicated pew directly beneath the altar rails of the local church. Curtin's involvement in the INL, a very different beast from the Land League of 1879–82, was no guarantee of immunity from violence. The INL was not a grass-roots 'bread and butter' organisation like the early Land League. Curtin's local executive position was more likely to have been based on his social status than his militancy. Much had changed since the heady days of the Land League. In 1881, a grazier with 160 acres might well have been an officer, NCO or in the 'other ranks' in the trenches of the Land War. By 1885, however, he would be more likely to feature in the crosshairs of the weapons of local Ribbon societies in Kerry and elsewhere. With the passage of the Ashbourne Act of 1885, the first faint strains of the overture to the grand opera of peasant ownership were detectable. John Curtin might not have been a landlord, but he was already climbing the ladder and might well have decided to pull it up after him when he finally benefited from tenant purchase. Such sentiments were more than enough, as in times past, for Curtin to become a target of envious or obstreperous neighbours.

The fact that the family interest in the farm was auctioned in February 1887, and that there were no bidders, is also indicative. The Curtins' interest in the farm was later sold privately at one-quarter of its value to one Jeremiah McMahon, secretary of the local INL branch and a man suspected by the RIC of involvement in agrarian crime.[26] It is unlikely that this was the ultimate outcome the 1885 raiders had in mind, but at some point, as the screws tightened on the Curtin family (who ended the boycott by leaving the area in April 1887), the discounted sale of the interest in their farm must have become a lively possibility, and an excellent financial reason for certain people to maintain a specious boycott.

Some of the killings described here subsequently led to almost inevitable miscarriages of justice when cases came to trial. The Crown sought to bring killers to book as expeditiously as possible, and Her Majesty's Crown solicitors were often less than scrupulous. Francis Hynes was tried and convicted for the murder of John Doloughty by a 'packed' Special Commission jury in Dublin. The Special Commission was a creation of the 1881 Protection of Person and Property Act. This element of the 1881 Liberal coercion legislation allowed an accused suspect to be tried in Dublin, far removed from the threat of local jury partiality, tampering or intimidation. The members of the Special Commission jury were also unlikely to be peers of the accused because they were drawn from a small cohort of high-net-worth Dublin ratepayers. The most favourably regarded prosecution counsel of the period was one who was adept at 'packing' a Special Commission jury with the 'twelve good men and true' (and all were men) who were most likely to convict whomever it was that the Crown solicitors' office chose to offer up as the accused. The most talented exponent of this art in the 1880s was the barrister Peter O'Brien, who would go on to become the 1st Baron O'Brien, Lord Chief Justice of Ireland, from 1889 to 1913. To *United Ireland*, and to his own intense amusement, however, he would always be plain old 'Peter the Packer'.

The case of Francis Hynes was heard by a 'runaway jury', most of whose urban, upper-middle-class members had gleefully escaped the attentions of their minders the night before reaching their verdict. Relieved of the pressure of being captains of industry and business, albeit with the life of a potentially innocent man in their hands, their bibulous evening ended in a series of drunken skirmishes along the corridors of the Imperial Hotel on Sackville Street. These were witnessed and reported on by *United Ireland* editor William O'Brien. His account, published the following day in the *Freeman's Journal*, cost the proprietor of that newspaper, Edmund Dwyer Gray, six weeks in prison for printing a seditious libel. Truth was no defence in such cases.

The jury's decision, arrived at on the morning after their revels, cost Francis Hynes his life.

It is not the function of this volume to assess the merits of the *Times* case against the leadership of the Irish National League for complicity in agrarian violence. While the newspaper was humiliated in its prosecution of Parnell himself – in the specific instance of the letters forged by Richard Pigott – it would be naïve to assume that none of Parnell's colleagues had dabbled in incitement to violence, either indirectly, through inflammatory speeches, or less obliquely by the covert encouragement of punitive actions against those who had contravened 'Land League law'. That was certainly the opinion of the three Special Commission judges in their final report, when they found that 'the respondents did enter into a conspiracy by a system of coercion and intimidation to promote an agrarian agitation against the payment of agricultural rents, for the purpose of impoverishing and expelling from the country the Irish landlords ... with the intention by its means to bring about the absolute independence of Ireland as a separate nation'.[27] In reality, the principal finding of Justices Hannen, Day and Smith amounted to little more than a statement of the blindlingly obvious. While nationalists might claim that the violence of the Land War had been grievance-led, impulsive and unplanned, there was a tacit consensus that it was only through a decidedly unspontaneous level of orchestration of violent agrarianism that the agitation had been politically effective.

However, by attempting to overwhelm the commissioners with hundreds of instances of alleged Irish Parliamentary Party complicity in agrarian outrage, the prosecutors often chose their examples unwisely. Just as they had been foolhardy in placing their faith in a broken reed such as Richard Pigott – a near bankrupt former newspaper editor and part-time pornographer – the *Times* frequently presented case studies uncontaminated with the aroma of 'Land League law'. What emerged, quite unintentionally, from much of the *Times*'s evidence, thanks to astute and well-informed cross-examination, was a plethora of violent incidents that were carried out by 'privateers' without reference to either the Land League or even to local Ribbon/Fenian elements. Occasionally masquerading as members of retributive secret societies, but just as often not bothering to do so, these groups or individuals simply took advantage of the general chaos to initiate feuds, advance their claims to land held by others, discomfit graziers and substantial farmers, and generally play the game of 'beggar thy neighbour'.

Michael Davitt's assessment of the realpolitik of rural Ireland in the 1880s is revealing, perhaps more so than he intended. In describing the functioning of the league in rural communities, he wrote, 'the "branch" became the committee of public safety for the locality'. Given the French revolutionary experience associated with the Parisian Committee of Public Safety under the leadership of the merciless Maximilien Robespierre, it was an unfortunate choice of words. Davitt wrote in *The Fall of Feudalism in Ireland* that:

> The local branches of the league in Ireland were now the centres of active operations in the carrying-out of the policy of what can be called aggressive moral force ... In some instances the open organization was completely under the control of the extremists of the district, and while the general work of the league was carried out on its merits, the branch was used as a shield for the ulterior ends of the more advanced movement. This generally happened where the clergy were unfriendly towards the agitation, or when, as frequently occurred, the local moderate leaders would be inclined to use the league for personal or trade purposes.[28]

Thus did Davitt, while recognising the widespread infiltration of ordinary IRB members in the form of Ribbon/Fenian involvement, also tacitly acknowledge the role of 'privateers' in at least some of the agrarian violence of the 1880s.

'Keen, cunning and audacious ...':[29] the murders at Maamtrasna

> 'Myles Joyce is as innocent as the child unborn of the crime of murder of the Joyce family.'[30]
>
> ('Dying declaration'/*ex post facto* confession of Patrick Joyce before his execution for his role in the Maamtrasna murders)

The Maamtrasna murders of August 1882 offer us a supercharged version of intra-peasant rancour. Not only was a family almost wiped out, but a second extended family became collateral damage as a consequence of opportunistic treachery. The pettiness, homicidal malice and malevolent envy that often plagued rural

Maolra Seoighe (Myles Joyce)
This image is reproduced courtesy of the National Library of Ireland
[ALB40 /36]

Ireland was never more clearly illustrated than in the case of the tragic Joyce family of Maamtrasna, Co. Galway, five of whom were brutally murdered by their neighbours in August 1882 for who knows precisely what 'crime'. There is little or no evidence of Land League or Ribbon/Fenian involvement. All the indications point towards a personal grudge being acted out in the most horrendously vindictive fashion.

The issue between John Joyce and his killers may have been as serious as information allegedly supplied by a member of the Joyce family to the RIC on the murderers of two bailiffs of Lord Ardilaun (the Huddys). Their bodies had been dumped in Lough Mask in January 1882. However, it was just as likely to have been as trivial a matter as differences over the grazing of sheep on common hillside land; accusations of the persistent theft of the sheep of his neighbours by John Joyce; an aggrieved lover rejected by the daughter of the house; or even a threat by Joyce to take legal proceedings against the owners of cattle trespassing on his land.[31]

Add to that the prosecution of a local feud that prompted members of another family of Joyces (known locally as the 'Maolras') to come forward and implicate four of their cousins, also Joyces (known locally as the 'Seáns'), in the murders, and sedimentary layers of antipathy are laid bare.

So appalling was this sanguinary outlier of the Land War that the 'landlord press' eagerly exploited the event. The unionist *Dublin Evening Mail* of 21 August 1882 wrote in an editorial: 'The massacre of the Joyces in Galway will stand out as an imperishable monument to the diabolical genius which called the Land League into existence.'[32] The *Weekly Irish Times* of 26 August 1882 invoked the American west in its condemnation of the atrocity: 'This massacre, even in the blood-stained region where it occurred, stands unequalled in all that can excite emotions of horror and indignation, and probably has never been paralleled, save when in past ages on the border states of America a midnight Indian raid converted a peaceful homestead into a shambles wreaking with blood.'[33]

The moral certainty, however, that Maamtrasna was a product of local tensions unconnected to the wider agrarian conflict and had nothing whatever to with landlord-tenant relations meant that the atrocity hardly featured in evidence before the Special Commission. The atrocity might have been grist to the mill of the *Daily Express* and the *Irish Times* but the killers could not be shoehorned into the bloated *Times* Chamber of Horrors. That newspaper produced no witnesses who were prepared to ascribe the killings to the Land League and, in fact, the only speculation as to the motivation for the Maamtrasna murders came from a late witness, produced by Michael Davitt on 5 July 1889, the barrister John Louden. He was one of the motive forces behind the pivotal Irishtown, Co. Mayo meeting of April 1879, and an early Land League leader. In his striking testimony, he referred to a shadowy organisation that he called the 'Herds League' and which he blamed for a number of Mayo murders (including those of the Huddys and the Joyces). Louden also made the sensational claim that the mysterious 'Herds League' was in the pay of an RIC Head Constable named Whelehan, and that its members were employed as *agents provocateurs*.[34] Quite why a state-sponsored murder squad would have been involved in the slaughter of a humble family in rural Mayo, Louden did not explain.*

When it came to miscarriages of justice, the most blatantly tainted verdict of the 1880s was, of course, not the Hynes case, but the death sentence handed down on Maolra Seoighe (Myles Joyce). Joyce, his two brothers and a nephew were falsely and maliciously accused by his antagonistic cousins of the murder of the ill-fated Maamtrasna Joyces.[35] Just as petty jealousies and tensions had led to the murders of John Joyce and his family on 17 August 1882, so did conflict between the 'Maolras' and the 'Seáns' – a feud whose origins have never been entirely clear – lead to perjury, false arrest, a miscarriage of justice, death and lengthy periods of imprisonment. While the 'Maolras' had indeed witnessed some of the comings and goings that culminated in the Maamtrasna murders, and correctly identified at least two of the killers, Patrick Joyce and Patrick Casey, they had chosen to perjure themselves by adding the names of the four 'Seáns' – their sworn enemies – to the list of the men they claimed to have seen out and about on the night of the murders. Their hope was to bring their feud to an end by having the Crown despatch their adversaries. Their strategy worked only in the tragic case of Myles Joyce. His two brothers and his nephew were browbeaten into pleading guilty to having been accessories in a crime with which they had no connection, in order to save themselves from the gallows. The three Joyces served twenty years in jail before being released, two of them as elderly men.

The Special Commission cost *The Times* upwards of £200,000 and almost bankrupted the newspaper. The £5,000 settlement

---

* Whelehan, an RIC Head Constable, was not in a position to contradict Louden because he had been killed in 1887. According to Louden, Whelehan's death took place during one of his 'got up jobs'. In its issue of 15 October 1887, *United Ireland* also claimed to have evidence that Whelehan (alias 'Gerald Whelan') had been involved in covert operations for the RIC as far back as 1875.

reached with Parnell was a drop in the ocean compared with the costs wished upon *The Times* by the Salisbury government when the newspaper was forced to fund what was only a moderately successful attempt to blacken the reputation of constitutional Irish nationalism. The reputational damage to the peasantry of rural Ireland might have been far greater had the testimony of the victims of agrarian violence not been presented as an unrelenting dirge by newspapers (other than *The Times*) whose correspondents were waiting with unconcealed resentment for the 'dismal monotone of cruelty and crime'[36] to end, and for the allegations against Parnell to be belatedly addressed. They had come for fireworks, not tedium. Their boredom made it easier for nationalists to ignore some of the more embarrassing Special Commission testimony.

The parade of human misery presented by *The Times* was often dismissed after the event as mere misdirection – a desperate delaying gambit by a prosecution increasingly reluctant to buttress its false accusations against the Irish leader. However, whether or not the newspaper established a prima facie case of violent conspiracy against the Land League and, by extension, the representatives of the Irish Parliamentary Party, the sheer weight of evidence (once the charlatans are deleted) cannot simply be ignored.

In its efforts to unmask the depravity of the league (and the parallel Tory push to expose Ireland as a violent society unworthy of self-government), *The Times* backed a substantial number of losers. However, in so doing, the newspaper still, albeit unintentionally, performed a useful service. Much of the testimony contained in the nine lengthy books of evidence, while it often does little to support the thesis that *The Times* outlined in the 'Parnellism and Crime' articles, offers insights into the dominance of class, kin and factional acrimony in rural Ireland. Whatever the offences of John Joyce, John Curtin and Jeremiah Hickey, they were either deemed serious enough by local tribunes for the three men to pay with their lives, or the prevailing chaos provided convenient cover for personal grievances to become capital offences.

13

'A tumult of passion': the Plan of Campaign

'Dissoluteness, subscriptions to the Land League, and
borrowing money at the banks, have in five years reduced
the tenantry to the verge of bankruptcy, and headed by
Parnell they again come to their landlords and demand
large reductions. And this will occur again and again until
the landlords are ruined and the tenants become sole
proprietors of their holdings.'[1]

(George Moore, *Parnell and His Island*, 1887)

The nine-minute eggs, the uncrowned king and the 'Plan'

The agrarian struggle of 1879–82 was not the end of the Land
Wars. What it did portend, however, was a further quickening in
the slow demise of submissiveness and a profound interrogation
of the stifling role played by landlords in a market-oriented
economy. In addition to a decline in peasant genuflection,
galling but tolerable, landlords also had to weather a crisis of
falling expectations when it came to the lure of their 'product'.
Aristocrats with farms to rent had heretofore been inoculated
against a flaccid market for their land. Excess demand had
enabled them to evict without any real fear of financial
consequences. That there would always be prospective tenants
was the prevailing rationale. Many of these would be more than
willing to pay a higher rent than the previous tenant. What was
achieved, by default, by the seemingly interminable economic

depression of the 1880s and 1890s, and by the aggressive and collaborative nature of the Land League campaign, was a subtle shift in the balance of agrarian power. The widespread fall in farm incomes, allied to the vehemence of the Land League campaign against land grabbers, made it more likely that evicted farms would remain vacant and of no assistance to a hard-up landlord. So, on a purely economic level, a new logic prevailed. If Farmer A was unable to make sufficient profit from a piece of land, what made Farmer B so certain that he could do better when prospects were so far from rosy? Stir in the presence of the Land League, augmented by the threats of the Ribbonmen/ Fenians, and this made the acquisition of a holding recently vacated by an evicted tenant a trebly unattractive proposition. It added up to a temporary, albeit artificial, decline in the demand for farm land.

The rules of the game had changed. In 1886, William Gladstone, a convert to Irish self-government, introduced a flawed and ultimately unsuccessful Home Rule Bill that was defeated by a united Conservative Party, and the rump of a divided Liberal Party. While the Tories, under the Marquess of Salisbury, regained power shortly thereafter, the issue of devolution for Ireland now had 'elephant in the room' status. If, in the future, the Liberal Party required Irish support in order to govern, the beast would inevitably become the centre of attention. But the Tories, although unyieldingly antagonistic to Home Rule, couldn't ignore the animal entirely. They would, in the cliché of the day, spend much of their time in office attempting to dispatch it with kindness by introducing a raft of measures far more progressive than would normally be associated with a Conservative government.

The period immediately before the First Land War (1879–82) was one of agricultural depression and appalling weather. Both combined to ensure that rents were beyond the capacity of many tenants to pay – or, at least, the capacity to pay their landlords and their other creditors at the same time. By 1886, after a brief respite, amplified by the positive decisions coming from the Land Courts (positive from the tenant's point of view at least), 1877 returned with a vengeance. The crippling economic recession of the 1870s was proving to be more cyclonic than cyclical, continuing to hover like an obstinate barometric depression. And indeed the weather too was beginning to emulate the pattern of the 1877–9 deluge. Two years of climate-induced crop failure, allied to a return of plummeting prices, was the unavoidable prelude to a resurgence of defaults, evictions and 'outrages'. Four years after waving an unsentimental farewell to the First Land War, Irish landlords and tenants found themselves facing into an unwelcome sequel. The Second Land War (1886–90) masqueraded as the so-called 'Plan of Campaign', a form of self-financing 'No Rent Manifesto'. The Plan, however, was rather more managerially astute, and was generally executed with more discrimination than its battering ram of a predecessor.

If you were just keeping raw scores, the Plan of Campaign appears on the surface to have been an almost undiluted success. Of the 116 estates on which it was put into operation,* mostly in Munster and Connacht, only in fifteen cases was it the tenants who capitulated.[2] Such undercooked statistics, however, can be a little deceptive. The Plan of Campaign often provoked a more concerted response from landlords than had the First Land War. It also permitted the insouciant Arthur Balfour to unleash his predatory instincts.

The chief secretary whose reign encompassed most of the duration of the Plan was not an enthusiastic soul-searcher. Unlike his Liberal counterparts of the First Land War, who often agonised over their own flouting of civil liberties, the Tory response to the agrarian agitation of the latter half of the 1880s, with Balfour at the helm, was conducted with the minimum of breast-beating angst. Balfour's 1887 coercion legislation was responsible for dozens of arrests and jailings. The proactive chief secretary also attempted to stiffen the resolve of landlords by corralling them into collaborative combinations, but he was a better jailer than

---

* Various figures have been advanced for the actual number of estates affected. Davitt put it at 84; others have claimed as many as 203. One of the reasons for the disparity is that some landlords immediately came to terms when even the possibility of the introduction of the Plan was mooted.

he was a shepherd. One of his more imaginative plans was a concerted nationwide eviction-fest aimed at the tenant leadership on major Plan estates. His rationale was that the removal of the soiled sticking plaster in one swift movement was far less painful than adopting the incremental approach. His scheme foundered over a lack of resolve on the part of a number of landlords who committed to it, and then chickened out.

When it comes to the apparent high success rate of the insurgents in the Second Land War, it is also worth bearing in mind that, in many instances, the de facto military council of the Irish National League (William O'Brien, John Dillon, Timothy Harrington) who prosecuted the Plan, chose their opponents wisely. A lot of potentially easy marks were included in the list of estates where the Plan was enacted. Landowners known to be in dire financial straits, and where an extended period without a rent roll could conceivably result in bankruptcy, were favoured targets. However, the organisers, perhaps unwisely, also took on opponents who were far from insolvent. They opted, often with an eye to creative propaganda, to try their luck with a number of landlords who could only be characterised as 'nine-minute eggs'.[*] These were uncompromising grandees with well-earned reputations for rack-renting and bloody-mindedness. All the better if they were egregious absentees. O'Brien, Dillon and Harrington found their poster boy in Hubert George de Burgh Canning, the 2nd Marquess of Clanricarde, an unloved misanthropic millionaire with 1,900 Galway tenants who produced for him an annual rental income of £25,000 (worth around €3 million today) from a Portumna estate of more than 50,000 acres.

Clanricarde was almost a parody of the archetypal pantomime villain. Grandson of the late British prime minister George Canning, he was loathed almost as much by his brethren in the British establishment as he was by his Irish tenants. He visited his Galway estate only once in his lifetime, not even bothering to attend his mother's funeral there in 1876. Despite his great wealth, he was rumoured to bring sandwiches to his London club and eat

* With thanks to P. G. Wodehouse for this neat encapsulation of pugnacity.

Clanricarde, as depicted by Spy in Vanity Fair

them on the sly rather than pay for a meal in that establishment's dining room. He bought and hoarded fine art without any great appreciation for the aesthetic significance of what he was purchasing. Lord Darlington's immortal definition of the cynic in Oscar Wilde's *Lady Windermere's Fan*, one who 'knows the price of everything and the value of nothing', could have been coined to describe Clanricarde.

During the First Land War, the life of his agent, John Henry Blake, had been threatened. With a complete lack of self-awareness, or any consciousness of irony, Clanricarde (like Lord Derby before him) had observed that he would not be intimidated by any threat to his employees. In 1882, Blake and his driver, Thady Ruane, were both murdered on the way to mass in Loughrea. Clanricarde, known locally as Lord Clanrackrent, rapidly and without sentiment acquired a new agent, Francis Joyce. *United Ireland's* assessment of Clanricarde, even taking its obvious lack of balance into consideration, was pithily apposite: a 'miserly little millionaire in London [who] has never done a hand's turn for the miserable wretches from whom his vast revenue is wrung'.[3] This was accurate enough, except that even £25,000 a year must have meant relatively little to someone possessed of such vast wealth.* Which makes the tenacity with which he clung to this revenue, in the face of prodigious vilification and overwhelming peer pressure, all the more surprising. Even the government decision to withdraw police protection for his 1888 evictions failed to break his resolve.

Politically, the first half of 1886 was taken up with the introduction and defeat, by thirty votes, of William Gladstone's gift to the party that kept him in power, the First Home Rule Bill. Although, simultaneously, Irish farmers were giving vent to their newfound grievances, demands for rent abatements were flooding in and agrarian crime was on the rise, especially in Kerry, where 'moonlighting' was becoming thoroughly professionalised; this was not a good time to rock the boat by distracting from the thrust towards Irish self-government. The necessity for moderation, however, ended altogether with the defeat of Parnell and Gladstone's Home Rule project. The magisterial Marquess of Salisbury was now prime minister, and he was as partial to Irish devolution as to the amputation of a limb. This boat could be rocked with impunity.

While Parnell, after the 'Kilmainham Treaty', might have largely abandoned the agrarian struggle in preference for a serious drive towards Home Rule, his interest in the public sphere dissipated almost entirely with the seismic June 1886 defeat. Never in robust good health[†] and demoralised by the setback to his constitutional ambitions, he settled into a quasi-hermetic existence with Katharine O'Shea at their Eltham home. To the vacuum created by the defeat of Home Rule and the fall of Gladstone's government in the subsequent general election was

---

* At the time of his death, Clanricarde's estate amounted to the equivalent of almost half a billion euros today.

† He suffered from an ailment described by Parnell himself as a kidney complaint and by other observers as the degenerative ailment Bright's disease (Alfred Robbins, *Parnell: The Last Five Years* (London, 1926), 197–8).

now added a further lacuna, the absence of a dominant figure at the head of the Irish Parliamentary Party and the National League. This cavernous gap was quickly filled by a return to the *status quo ante bellum*, the revival of recidivist agrarianism.

Parnell haughtily disapproved of this development – although there must have been a certain gratification in seeing the aristocratic Irish confederates of the slayers of the Home Rule project having their pockets picked – but there was little he could do about it in the face of the combined brio of two of his closest allies and the secretary of the Irish National League. He managed to persuade Davitt to keep his distance from the project on the basis of its 'tactical unwisdom'. He complained that O'Brien and Dillon had not 'communicated to him their intention to open up in this way the agrarian conflict again'. He also decried the potential danger the Plan posed to the Home Rule crusade.

To have actively opposed the Plan of Campaign, however – other than through expressions of icy indifference – would have necessitated a level of political engagement of which Parnell was not capable in the months after the rejection of Home Rule. He would have been compelled to fill the vacuum himself, and he had little to offer at the time. One of his final gestures, before his lengthy hibernation, had been the introduction of remedial legislation, which, if passed, would have obviated the necessity for further popular agitation. His Tenant Relief Bill was designed to reopen the Land Courts to tenants whose rents were now fixed for more than a decade, and to admit leaseholders to the terms of the 1881 Land Act.

It was the failure of the party leader's private member's legislation that was one of the proximate causes for the launching of the Plan of Campaign. Dillon had warned the House of Commons that the rejection of Parnell's measures would result in a 'tumult of passion' being released in Ireland. He didn't add that he could be quite certain of that, because he intended to release it. The Tory response to the growing economic crisis was to take refuge in the prayer of the prevaricator ('Dear Lord, give me the strength never to put off until tomorrow what I can postpone until the day after') and appoint a commission of enquiry. This was chaired by the former Liberal Lord Lieutenant, Lord Cowper. When it finally reported, it gave considerable comfort to those calling for further rent abatements. The report conceded that, 'The fall in the price of produce of all kinds, and in all parts of the country, has much impaired the ability of the farmer to pay the full rent.'[4]

In the debate on Parnell's bill, the former Liberal MP most loathed by Irish party members for his Home Rule apostasy, Joseph Chamberlain, spoke knowledgeably and reasonably about the impact of the fall in prices. 'If the judicial rents were fixed upon the basis of former prices,' he pointed out to the House of Commons, 'and at that time they were fair, then they must necessarily be unfair now.'[5] He then endeared himself still further to the IPP by flying in the face of the logic of his own contribution and voting against the measure.

Neither was there any need for the Plan's advocates to give further consideration to the exigencies of British party politics. The occasional nihilism of the Plan of Campaign could be an embarrassment to Gladstone's party, but the prospect of disconcerting the Liberals while they were in opposition was not especially daunting for the O'Brien-Dillon-Harrington nexus. In fact, there was limited adverse Liberal reaction. Gladstone viewed the Plan with a certain jaundiced resignation and described it as 'the child of the present administration'[6] created by the government's refusal to accept Parnell's Tenant Relief Bill. A number of his own MPs, mostly on the radical wing of the party (Henry Labouchère, C. A. V. Conybeare and G. J. Shaw Lefevre, for example) were exceptionally supportive of the Plan and regularly appeared in person to observe and condemn wholesale evictions.

On the other hand, the potential for irritating the Tories was especially alluring.[7] Nothing seemed to appeal more, to William O'Brien in particular, than to *épater les bourgeois*, as long as the bourgeoisie in question sat on the Conservative party front benches. He suggested, in a 24 July 1886 *United Ireland* editorial, that, what he called the conciliatory Conservative policy of 'Paddy go-easy' would be short-lived. Like Dillon, he could make the statement with some confidence, because he was determined to guarantee its transience.

'A Plan of Campaign: A Memo for the Country'

The context for the introduction of the Plan was not just a meltdown in farm prices and incomes, but the fact that, temporarily at least, the issue of tenant purchase was in bad odour. In 1886, Gladstone intended to accompany his 1886 Home Rule legislation with a tenant relief measure incorporating a significant 'buyout' element. This was a form of atonement for far less ambitious proposals put forward in his own 1870 and 1881 Land Acts. The Tory caretaker government of Salisbury had shown the way with a more full-blooded approach in the land purchase legislation of the 1885 Ashbourne Act. As with these previous baby steps towards peasant proprietorship, it was the exchequer that would foot the bill if the 1886 measure were to pass through parliament. This was an exchequer on which the Irish inhabitants of the United Kingdom had as much claim as their British counterparts. But the opposition of a significant cohort of parliamentarians to the Home Rule legislation, and not just those on the radical wing of the Liberal Party, had been predicated on the land purchase legislation that was to follow. A number of MPs chose to be outraged at the prospect of the payment of millions of pounds from the *British* exchequer to Irish landlords in order to persuade them to part with their estates to undeserving (by definition) Irish tenants. William O'Brien made a wry note, in *United Ireland* on 17 July 1886, of the irony of one consequence of landlord opposition to Home Rule: 'The landlords have helped their friends to break down the golden bridge that was generously provided for their retreat ... They have themselves to thank if they have now to pass through the bitter waters of tribulation. The liberal offer they have refused can never be repeated.'

United Ireland itself became midwife to the Plan of Campaign. In its pages, on 23 October 1886, a few weeks before the November 'gale day' on which rent was due, an unsigned article (written by the secretary of the Irish National League, the Kerry journalist and politician Timothy Harrington) outlined a radical template in the renewed struggle for rent abatements. Forswearing ambiguous slogans like 'the land for the people', the approach was to be more collectivist and managerial and would exploit 'a skill begotten of experience', i.e. lessons learned during the First Land War.

'A Plan of Campaign: A Memo for the Country' proposed that a group of tenants on chosen estates would jointly seek an abatement from their landlord. If this was refused, their rent, minus the proposed reduction, would be lodged in an 'Estate Fund' bank account. If this combination/agitation resulted in tenants being evicted, the fund would be used to support them. Crucially, the secretary of the Irish National League also made a perilous promise that, in the event of the fund running out, the tenants would continue to be supported from the resources of the Irish National League itself. This was a blank cheque that came back to haunt Harrington, William O'Brien and John Dillon, the men on whom the burden of leadership fell. It almost went without saying that if anyone took up the land of an evicted Plan tenant, they would be subject to a boycott. A similar fate awaited any of the subscribing tenants who resiled from the Plan and made their own arrangements with the landlord.

The article went on to warn the *United Ireland* readership against disruptive landlord ploys. These included the dissemination of false information about Plan participants secretly agreeing to come to terms with landlords, or misinterpreting visits by agents to the houses of striking tenants. Participating tenants most in danger of eviction were warned to sell all their livestock in advance in order to avoid distraint proceedings. In an editorial in his newspaper, William O'Brien, who, of course, had wielded considerable influence on the composition of the document, commented: 'It is simple, it is lawful, and given thorough earnestness on the part of the tenantry to begin with, it is irresistible.' He then went on to offer further nourishment to Harrington's hostage to fortune by assuring his readers that, in the event of tenant funds drying up, 'the National League would guarantee grants of the same amount during the continuance of the struggle'.

Given the increasingly dire economic conditions, the Plan spread rapidly on what O'Brien described as 'estates where the people were driven to the last pitch of desperation'.[8] By early December 1886, the *Freeman's Journal* was able to announce that

'The Plan of Campaign advances rapidly'.[9] In most instances, the Plan initiatives were locally inspired, but there are numerous examples of nationalist politicians like William Redmond and O'Brien shovelling the coal themselves if some locomotives were slow to start.

While O'Brien may have genuinely believed the cleverly structured Plan to be lawful, by early 1887 it was being treated by the civil authorities as an 'unlawful and criminal conspiracy'. However, in its early weeks, the Plan went, to all intents and purposes, unchallenged by an administration caught unawares and unwilling to provoke yet another 'war'. In a January 1887 memo, the incumbent chief secretary, Michael Hicks Beach, described the Plan as 'an effort by concerted action on the part of one class to deprive another class of rights to which the latter class is by law entitled',[10] a matter-of-fact and bloodless assessment with which even John Dillon might have agreed. The chief secretary's guarded response was based on a legal opinion from the attorney general, Hugh Holmes, regarding the taking of Plan 'rents' on the Cork estate of Charles William Talbot-Ponsonby. The Crown's leading law officer told the local RIC divisional commissioner, Captain Plunkett, that 'I do not see how any action can be taken by the executive'.[11]

This inertia did not last far beyond an intensification in the rhetoric of the Plan leadership, Dillon in particular, in the early months of the campaign. Dublin Castle made note of speeches being made at mass gatherings around the country. Hicks Beach explained in a memo to the cabinet that 'at first Mr. Dillon seemed to be alone in taking it up, and his early speeches were moderate and harmless'.[12] But on 21 November, Dillon gave the administration its first opening, an opportunity to put the legality of the Plan to the test in a superior court. He 'made a very violent speech' and, simultaneously, 'there was sufficient evidence available to support an indictment for conspiracy against both him and Mr. O'Brien'.[13]

A Queen's Bench ruling on 14 December 1886 described Dillon as a person of 'evil fame' and held that the Plan was a 'criminal conspiracy'.[14] He was given twelve days to find £2,000 or go to prison for six months. He would spend much of the next three years in and out of jail – as would O'Brien – for making equally seditious speeches, and for his continued propagation of a 'criminal conspiracy'. In truth, Dillon's flamethrower rhetoric was difficult for the Castle to ignore.

One of the prerequisites for the success of the Plan was tenant solidarity, just as had been the case in the First Land War. This was jeopardised by tenants who, overtly or covertly, came to terms with their landlords. Reprisals were swift in the case of individuals who resiled from the compact made by the adherents of the Plan. Warnings on the Clanricarde estate in Galway often took the form of attacks on animals, rather than human beings. In June 1889, James Kennedy, who was believed to have paid his rent, had three of his cattle mutilated. John White, also a Clanricarde tenant, came to a rental arrangement in September 1889. Three of his bullocks were killed when it became known that he had settled. On the estate of Lord Kenmare in Kerry, however, warnings came in more unequivocal fashion. In March 1889, Humphrey Moynihan, a Kenmare estate tenant, abandoned

William O'Brien MP, editor of
United Ireland *and champion of the Plan of Campaign*

the Plan by paying his rent. Days later, 'as he and his family were sitting at supper the window was smashed and the barrels of several guns were thrust through. A number of shots were fired.'[15] The family escaped injury but a horse stabled in a corner of the kitchen (who was presumably indoors in expectation of an attack) was wounded. A few months later, in July 1889, Giles Cooper, another Kenmare tenant who paid his rent in defiance of Plan strictures, was attacked when a single shot was fired through the door of his house. No member of the family was injured.

In many instances, such warnings proved effective. On the estate of Arthur Smith Barry in Tipperary, according to a confidential Dublin Castle memo, 'to save their property from sale by the Sheriff, ten of the tenants paid the amount due'. They were immediately subject to a boycott that threatened to ruin their businesses. Caught between the devil and a deep, unattractively hued sea, they sought to claw their way back into the good offices of the Plan organisers: 'they eventually humbly besought the forgiveness of the conspirators, and begged to be allowed to rejoin the combination, paying a heavy fine as a punishment for their honesty and promising not again to pay their rents.'[16]

Dillon's speeches, without specifically identifying individuals, still often targeted potential apostates and clearly tipped over into sedition. In Herbertstown, Co. Limerick in April 1888, for example, he raided the military codebook for his rhetoric: 'I have always said that going into this struggle is very like going into battle, and in a battle when a man turns his tail his officer will shoot him in the head.'[17]

Having located their 'smoking gun', courtesy of the Queen's Bench ruling of 14 December, the Castle struck forcibly at the leadership cadre of the Plan in Loughrea, Co. Galway on 16 December 1886. Dillon, Matt Harris and David Sheehy, all IPP MPs and O'Brien – without a constituency after narrowly losing his Tyrone seat in the July election – were arrested for collecting Plan 'rents' from tenants on Clanricarde's estate.[18] O'Brien described the move as 'Sir M. Hicks Beach's first whiff of grapeshot'.[19] Because it was deemed unlikely that the state would secure a conviction in Galway – Hicks Beach told the cabinet in a January 1887 memo that it was 'hopeless with the present jury system to prosecute successfully crime of this kind in the counties in which agrarian agitation most prevails'[20] – the Loughrea prosecution was rapidly abandoned and became, in effect, a state show trial for conspiracy in Dublin. A number of other alleged conspirators were added to the docket. The situation was a win-win for the Castle. A Dublin jury might conceivably convict the 'traversers'. If it didn't, then the government could point to the ineffectuality of ordinary legal procedures and introduce stringent coercion measures in their place.

On 24 February 1887, the jury disagreed on its verdict, the Crown abandoned the prosecution and a new Crimes Act beckoned. Whatever that might bring in the future, Hicks Beach also outlined a current strategy. 'Those who advocate [the Plan] by speech or writing,' he noted, 'may be prosecuted for sedition, or for inciting others to join in a criminal combination.'[21]

His successor needed no encouragement to deliver on that implied threat.

Enter the Old Etonian Arthur James Balfour, so named for his godfather, the Duke of Wellington himself. The Plan of Campaign was about to be subject to a will of steel with an exceptionally low boredom threshold.

'Mr Golfour' tees off

On 7 March 1887, Michael Hicks Beach cited serious illness (failing eyesight) as the reason for his departure from the Irish Office, that 'sorry nursing-farm for damaged reputations'.[22] Irish nationalists nodded sagely. Yet another chief secretary had bitten the dust, debilitated and broken by the toxic miasma of the infamous 'Irish Question'. They then rubbed their hands in glee when his replacement was announced. Arthur Balfour, the new chief secretary, was a nephew of the prime minister, Robert Gascoyne Cecil, Marquess of Salisbury. His prior cabinet appointment, as Scottish secretary, had given rise to the phrase 'Bob's your uncle' and a mistaken belief that his relationship to the less than avuncular Salisbury was his sole qualification for high office. Based on initial impressions, he certainly had the appearance of being merely a lofty and languid scion of privilege. But first impressions are often erroneous. Before he became a well-established political heavyweight, Balfour's capabilities were frequently underestimated, as *United Ireland* did in an editorial on 12 March 1887, less than a week after his appointment. The newspaper described him as 'a delicate lily of the aristocracy'. Aristocratic he certainly was, but there was nothing florid or delicate about the new chief secretary. The ultra-partisan Parnellite journal continued sardonically: 'He is a rickety and lackadaisical young man whom one could better imagine dining off the contemplation of a sunflower than tackling a problem in statesmanship which foiled Cromwell and broke Mr. Forster's stubborn heart.'[23]

Noting Balfour's 'aristocratic languor', the *Freeman's Journal* was cynically in agreement with *United Ireland*'s evaluation of this new occupant of the hardship posting that was the Irish Office: 'This young gentleman has three qualifications for the post. He is the nephew of Lord Salisbury; he has no reputation for statesmanship to injure; and he knows nothing of Ireland.'[24]

Balfour's devotion to the sport of golf (which earned him the nickname 'Mr Golfour' in *United Ireland*) and his authorship of a work entitled *A defence of philosophic doubt*, burnished the unrealistically foppish image the *Freeman's Journal* and *United Ireland* were intent on creating for him. There was an implied assumption in these assessments that Balfour's health, mental and physical, would quickly be undermined by the rigours of the Irish Office, just as had that of a number of his recent predecessors, most notably Hicks Beach and George Otto Trevelyan. Even the card-carrying Liberal journal the *Pall Mall Gazette* worried for Balfour's future. While condemning the appointment as blatant nepotism, the newspaper wailed that it was 'nepotism not of the patronizing but of the murderous order',[25] implying that Salisbury was trying to rid himself permanently of an irksome family member.

As it transpired, Balfour, informed by his handling of crofter revolts in the Scottish highlands, was a considerably more robust adversary than *United Ireland* and many other nationalist antagonists had bargained for. Despite his apparent interest in the subject, 'philosophic doubt' was not something that ever appeared to plague the Right Honourable Arthur James Balfour himself.

Coincidentally, on the same day that Balfour assumed office (7 March 1887), *The Times* published, to an impressive display of public lethargy, the first of a series of articles entitled 'Parnellism and Crime'. Before *The Times* series concluded, the apathy had dissipated and Balfour would have cause to train the cannons of the 'Thunderer' against the Plan, the Irish National League and the IPP. On 18 April, the newspaper published what purported to be a facsimile of a letter signed by Parnell which advertised his approval of the murder of Thomas H. Burke by the Invincibles in Dublin's Phoenix Park on 6 May 1882. The article caused a political earthquake, despite the repeated claims of Parnell that the letter was a clumsy forgery. A fraud it most certainly was, as the later admission of the forger, the Dublin journalist Richard Pigott, would prove. Inexpert it was not. Pigott managed a

Arthur Balfour

very credible pass at imitating Parnell's familiar and distinctive signature. Until, however, conclusive evidence to the contrary was secured, Parnell was guilty until proven innocent in the court of British public opinion.

Balfour fully intended to operate a 'carrot and stick' policy in Ireland, but he shared Uncle Robert's view that the baton should come first. The stick made an early appearance with the introduction of a new Crimes Bill (the Criminal Law Amendment Bill). Some measures in particular invoked a sense of *déjà vu*. Jury trials were to be replaced by decisions made in courts of summary jurisdiction (petty sessions, assizes) by two RMs. The Plan and the National League were, essentially, criminalised in certain 'proclaimed' (i.e. martial law) districts of the country. Public meetings could be banned and freedom of expression in Irish newspapers was heavily circumscribed. However, unlike the two punitive Liberal coercion acts of the 1880s, Balfour's Crimes Bill, when it became law, had no 'sunset clause'. It was intended as a piece of permanent legislation.

Duly inaugurating a new era of 'carrot and stick' politics (which would subsequently morph into a conciliation phase of 'killing Home Rule with kindness'), Balfour later pleased no one in particular with the introduction of his Land Law (Ireland) Bill. This finally enabled leaseholders to repair to the Land Courts (if that was their wont) to have their rents fixed by an independent arbitrator. However, by way of propitiating his natural constituency, Balfour also made it cheaper and simpler for landlords to evict, with the 'eviction made easy clause', as it came to be known. Landowners were no longer obliged to employ a hard-necked process-server to hand over, in person, notices to quit and risk the physical consequences. These could henceforward be sent by registered mail at minimal cost and no physical peril.

From Bruff to 'New Tipperary'

The Plan of Campaign agitation began on the O'Grady estate in Bruff, Co. Limerick in early November 1886, moved quickly to take in the Earl of Clanricarde's tenants and then spread countrywide, with the principal cockpits being Woodford in Co. Galway and the estates of Ponsonby in Cork, Lord Dillon in Mayo and Lansdowne in Queen's County. However, less than one per cent of all Irish landed estates were ever included in the Plan's portfolio. Most Irish MPs offered their support, though some, like Dillon, Harris and Sheehy, were far more active than others, the diffident element being conscious of their party leader's disapproval of this militant renewal of land agitation. Michael Davitt, although sympathetic, was somewhat lukewarm about the project. Davitt, 'nobbled' by Parnell on his return from the USA in 1887 and, convinced to remain aloof, was already moving towards the principle of land nationalisation anyway. Rent abatement was a mere quarter measure.

However, Davitt's advocacy was passionate in comparison with the hostility of Parnell, who was annoyed at not having been consulted before the launch of the project. The party leader took his time before publicly opposing the Plan,* and his disengagement from politics during his exile in Eltham had diminished his influence anyway, but his clear opposition from the outset cast a shadow over the campaign.

In a last-ditch attempt to stymie the entire project, Parnell summoned O'Brien to a meeting in London in early December 1886. It took place in bizarre circumstances reminiscent of a Cold War pre-dawn spy swap. The two men met near Greenwich Observatory on a murky morning, with visibility reduced to such a degree that O'Brien could barely even discern the 'ugly carcass' of the observatory itself. He groped about in the smog for a while, in danger of plunging into an icy river Thames. Then, from out of the mist,

> I suddenly came upon Parnell's figure emerging from the gloom in a guise so strange and with a face so ghastly that the effect could scarcely have been more startling if it was his ghost I had met wandering in the eternal shades … the

* On 8 May 1888, he made a speech in opposition to the plan at the Liberal Eighty Club.

unearthly, half-extinguished eyes flickering mournfully out of their deep caverns, the complexion of dead clay, the overgrown fair beard, and the locks rolling down behind, almost to the shoulders. It was the apparition of a poet plunged in some divine anguish, or a mad scientist mourning over the fate of some forlorn invention.[26]

After this inauspicious beginning, matters failed to improve. O'Brien's account, written in 1920, points towards an amiable chat between old friends with an eventual meeting of minds and a Parnell who was 'manifestly relieved'. Alternative versions – those of Katharine O'Shea and senior Liberal Party *apparatchik* John Morley, for example – suggest otherwise. They both claim that Parnell remained irked and hostile. O'Brien argued to his Chief that the Plan of Campaign was merely the continuation of Parnell's own 1886 Tenant Relief Bill by other means. Among other concerns expressed by the ailing party leader (these included the fear that Dillon had already antagonised the Liberals with some of his inflammatory speeches), Parnell was anxious to avoid an open-ended drain on National League funds. O'Brien, interestingly, assured his leader that the Plan 'was only devised as an expedient for one winter'.[27] Katharine O'Shea's account of Parnell's response to the meeting suggests that the party leader still thoroughly disapproved of the Plan, despite his favourite lieutenant's attempt to justify it: 'I shall let O'Brien run it by himself,' he told her.[28] 'I shall allow O'Brien to run it into the ground' may well have been his intended meaning.

There was no better example of O'Brien's ability to overreach than the saga of 'New Tipperary', inscribed in 1889, just as the Plan appeared to be devoid of purpose or direction. It was, according to Michael Davitt, 'a big blunder. The Tipperary fight was a grave mistake'.[29] It was also a costly mistake, with the final bill coming in at over £40,000.

Arthur Smith Barry, the antagonist in this case, was a landlord who adopted a leadership role in combating the Plan. A leading member of the Irish Unionist Alliance with an Irish rent roll approaching £30,000 per annum and an additional 5,000 acres in

Cheshire, he viewed the Plan as 'communistic'. He led a syndicate of landowners – dubbed by *United Ireland* the 'Eviction Syndicate' when its existence emerged – who purchased the Ponsonby estate in 1889, when it looked as if a capitulation in Youghal to the Plan was on the cards. With the encouragement of Balfour, who did not want the Plan to succeed on one of its marquee estates, the Smith Barry syndicate fought back. As evictions on the Ponsonby estate began to climb, Smith Barry's Tipperary tenants engaged in a syndicalist gambit of their own. They organised what was, in essence, a sympathetic rent strike. This forced Smith Barry to engage on two fronts simultaneously. The Tipperary landlord, however, was equal to the task and dug in his heels. His riposte included the eviction of a number of sympathetic tenants from their business properties in Tipperary town. The highly imaginative, but ultimately doomed, tenant response to the trader ejectment was the establishment of an alternative town on its outskirts, dubbed 'New Tipperary' – 'two rows of wooden houses, twenty-six in number with two small rooms on the ground floor and three still smaller ones above'.[30] This undertaking turned out to be more mirage than oasis. The Tipperary strike, encouraged by O'Brien, who staked much of his radical reputation on its success, succeeded only in draining vital funds from the league's coffers, and it ultimately collapsed. This did little for O'Brien's status as a tactician. An antagonistic pamphlet published in 1890 by a group calling itself the Liberal Union of Ireland (whose position, despite the name, was similar to that adopted in similar publications by the better-known unionist pressure group, the Irish Loyal and Patriotic Union) was not far from the truth when it observed: 'That prosperous tradesmen who have no grievances whatever should give up flourishing businesses and fine houses which they themselves have built, and for which they pay only a nominal rent, is sheer insanity, and this brilliant idea seems to have originated in the fertile brain of Mr. William O'Brien, MP.'[31]

O'Brien, who significantly underplayed his leading role in the 'New Tipperary' debacle in his memoirs ('I was a mere marvelling looker-on in Galway jail') and ascribed 'credit' for the scheme to the Irish party MPs T. P. Gill and William Redmond, saw it as an

entirely new departure in the agrarian struggle. The Smith Barry
tenants were not, technically, even part of the Plan of Campaign.
Their stand had little or nothing to do with personal economic
grievances. Smith Barry was a relatively generous landlord,
but one who was now launched on a class-based crusade. The
opposition of his tenants was as much an engagement in a wider
battle as was Smith Barry's own leadership of the syndicate that
aimed to preserve the Ponsonby estate for privilege and posterity.
The 'inconceivable disinterestedness' of the New Tipperary
project marked it out as more of a philosophical engagement
with landlordism, though it was far from what O'Brien held, with
customary hyperbole, to have been the battlefield on which 'Irish
landlordism fought its last ferocious battle'.[32]

The editor and the viceroy

While the Plan found an ideal antagonist in Clanricarde – a
plaster villain whose misanthropic tendencies cast the campaign
in a soft light even in England – not so cut and dried was the
conflict with Henry Charles Petty-Fitzmaurice, the 5th Marquess
of Lansdowne. A contributory factor in taking on this particular
opponent was likely to have been his impeccable establishment
credentials, albeit as a Liberal rather than a Tory grandee.
Although mostly associated with the county of Kerry, where
the bulk of his land was (a significant portion remains in the
hands of the family there to this day), Lansdowne, who at the
time was the Governor General of Canada, also had an estate on
more fertile land in Queen's County (Laois). While the relatively
impoverished tenants of Lansdowne's Kerry estates remained
aloof from the Plan, those on the far more prosperous Lansdowne
estate of Luggacurren, midway between Abbeyleix and Athy, who
were not unduly distressed, demanded abatements that were
refused by Lansdowne and his agent, J. Townsend Trench, son of
William Steuart Trench.

William O'Brien, despite evidence that some of the evicted
tenants could well afford the rents demanded of them, seemed

to take the Luggacurren fight personally. His interactions with Lansdowne and Trench are more redolent of social revolution and the ultimate appropriation of landlord property than of the application of economic pressure designed to achieve a more short-term victory for the Luggacurren tenants. He made a number of scathing and inflammatory speeches about the Queen's County conflict, including one at Maryborough (Portlaoise), which Trench alleged 'was nothing less than an incentive to murder Lord Lansdowne and me'.[33] O'Brien went so far as to take the fight all the way to Canada, the Lansdowne 'palace gates'. He travelled, in an attempt at landlord-shaming, with one of the wealthier Laois tenants, Denis Kilbride. Although O'Brien claims in one of his autobiographies to have viewed this incursion as a case of 'roses, roses, all the way',[34] the reality was rather different. His welcome from the membership of the Canadian Orange Order was resourcefully hostile. There were attempts on his life and, despite his claim to the contrary, the hearts and minds of the Canadian people were not alienated from their aristocratic Governor General. While the object of the journey had not been

Henry Charles Petty-Fitzmaurice, the 5th Marquess of Lansdowne

to win either the heart or the mind of Lansdowne himself, the controversy surrounding O'Brien's Canadian crusade merely increased the landowner's determination to defeat the aims of the Plan. And within months came an endorsement of his stance from the Salisbury administration, when he was appointed Viceroy of India, the real jewel in the imperialist administrative crown.

Despite his feigned satisfaction regarding the Canadian junket, the experience may have softened the cough of O'Brien when it came to the Luggacurren dispute. Shortly after his return to Ireland, he made a speech there in late July 1887 which bore little resemblance to some of his previous fire and brimstone sermons. The lusty English poet and political activist Wilfrid Scawen Blunt, who had added the Plan to his list of causes, commented in his account of that period, on the unwelcome moderation of the address. It 'seemed rather disappointing to the audience, who preferred the violent but incoherent address of their curates'.[35]

O'Brien, however, had recovered much of his aplomb and belligerence by early August and abandoned moderation in two speeches at Mitchelstown, Co. Cork. He knowingly talked his way into a prison cell with his unalloyed vituperation and a threat to make any further evictions 'a dear and expensive job for the government and for Dublin Castle'.[36] On 23 September, he was sentenced to three months in jail. Incarcerated along with him in Cork, and later Tullamore, prisons was a local activist and substantial farmer (he farmed a 200-acre property a mile outside Mitchelstown) named John Mandeville, who was originally given a two-month sentence. Both men, in a gesture that would become extremely familiar, refused to wear prison clothing or perform menial prison duties. Mandeville, as a consequence, was subjected to a punishing prison regime designed to break his will. Instead, it broke his large muscular frame. By December 1887, Mandeville had lost three stone in weight and his eyesight was failing. Within seven months of his release, he was dead. A coroner's inquest linked his death to his treatment while incarcerated.

The birth of 'Bloody Balfour'

Events at Mitchelstown, Co. Cork in September 1887 ensured that the effete 'Mr. Golfour' rapidly metamorphosed into 'Bloody Balfour'.

A major public demonstration in support of O'Brien and Mandeville on 9 September, the day of their arraignment (neither man was present) before a petty sessions court, was attended by a crowd estimated at 5,000. The protest was to be addressed by John Dillon. Before the speeches commenced, a contingent of the RIC entered the main square in the town with a government notetaker and attempted to install him on the platform. The crowd demurred and the RIC force withdrew, but returned shortly thereafter with reinforcements. When they began to use bayonets and rifle butts to carve a passage back to the platform, they were met with fists and stones. Heavily outnumbered, the RIC force retreated again to the local barracks, which overlooked the square. There is little difference in the accounts of what had happened up to that point. Major discrepancies, however, surround the sequel. On the RIC side, the narrative emerged of an all-out attack on the barracks. Then, in defence of a colleague being viciously assaulted on the steps of the building, a number of constables opened fire from an upstairs window to disperse the rioters. On the nationalist side, the narrative was of a peaceable crowd being fired on by undisciplined and unnerved RIC men. The next undisputed fact is that three men, John Shinnick, John Casey and Michael Lonergan, died as a result of the fusillade, one on the spot, two more within the week from their wounds. The tragedy was witnessed not just by John Dillon but by the wealthy radical Liberal MP Henry Labouchère. He was unequivocal in his condemnation of the local RIC operation, and scathing about the role of the officials in charge: 'They are responsible for the deaths which took place. They by their bungling and bullying created the disturbance, and if every man had his deserts they would be sentenced to a lengthy term of imprisonment.'[37]

The so-called Mitchelstown Massacre begat the slogan 'Remember Mitchelstown'. This was coined not by a rabid nationalist orator in full cry but by the Grand Old Man himself. William Gladstone was first to invoke the memory of the Mitchelstown killings in those precise terms. According to his biographer, John Morley, the episode, and the manner in which it was later brushed off in the House of Commons by Balfour, 'set Mr. Gladstone on fire'.[38]

Loose ends

The high-water mark of the Plan was its first full year, 1887. That was a period of instant success on a number of estates. Thereafter, the negative influence of Parnell's opposition, the efficacy of the Crimes Act, the muscularity of Balfour's response, increased landlord solidarity (syndicates like that led by Smith Barry emerged on five additional 'test' estates), the frequent imprisonments of O'Brien and Dillon and the financial drain of ongoing rent strikes – despite the formation of a Tenant's Defence Association that raised more than £60,000 in its first year – asserted themselves to weaken the project. The Plan also became a victim of the 1890 Parnellite split after the catastrophic O'Shea divorce case. It is, for example, to this period of mutual loathing that O'Brien ultimately ascribed the failure of the New Tipperary project.

All that and Rome too! 'The Pope came to the rescue,' John Morley tartly observed in his biography of William Gladstone. The former Liberal chief secretary and Gladstonian confidante was referring to the intervention of Pope Leo XIII in the Plan of Campaign at the behest of the Tory government. 'They beat the Orange drum in Ulster with one hand,' wrote Morley, 'with the other they stealthily twitched the sleeve of Monsignor Persico.'[39] Persico was the Pope's envoy to Ireland, despatched by the Holy See to investigate whether or not the Plan was contrary to Catholic law. He arrived in July 1887 and spent six months consulting with members of the Irish Roman Catholic hierarchy, most of whom – Archbishops Croke of Cashel and Walsh of Dublin in particular – were in favour of the Plan and offered no discouragement to the clergy of their parishes in leading or supporting the agitation.

The result, however, of the British intervention in Rome was a papal rescript in April 1888 condemning the Plan and decrying the practice of boycotting. It was, in effect, a 'cease and desist' order to Irish Catholic clergy and was reinforced in June when it was followed by the papal encyclical *Saepe Nos*, addressed to the Irish bishops. In this, Leo XIII warned Irish Catholics to take part in no activities forbidden by the Divine Law. To their credit, most members of the Irish Roman Catholic clergy ignored a partisan encyclical that bore more of the hallmarks of British diplomatic pressure and papal authoritarianism than it did of rigorous objectivity. The Irish clerical reaction to the condemnation of the Plan belied the prediction Parnell made to O'Brien at their spectral Greenwich meeting. He told the *United Ireland* editor: 'Yes, the Irish priests, individually, are splendid fellows, but in a semi-revolutionary movement like ours a time comes sooner or later when a priest has to choose between Rome and Ireland, and he will always choose Rome.'[40]

Rome had, predictably, shied away from support for social revolution (the Vatican was still three years away from the spirit of the progressive encyclical *Rerum Novarum*). Irish priests, however, were more tolerant of political dissent, for the moment at least.

Endgame?

One of the apparent strengths of the Plan can also be seen as a weakness. For pragmatic reasons to do with the allocation of resources and lessons learned about the consequences of an incarcerated leadership cadre, the organisers were selective about which landlords to tangle with. In an interview with *United Ireland*, Harrington had emphasised that scarce National League funds were only going to be made available for winnable fights. He observed that 'It is a great mistake on the part of the rural branches of the National League to recommend for support to us what may be termed cases of pure poverty. They drain away the funds of the organisation, and beyond giving a certain amount of encouragement to local branches of the League, I do not think they are of much practical effect in settling the land question.'[41]

There would be no sentimental rushes of blood to the head when it came to identifying the battles to pursue.

However, this strategy allowed the opponents of the Plan to marshal their resources as well. Back in February 1882, at the height of the First Land War, there was an interesting exchange in the House of Commons between Henry Chaplin, the Tory MP and future cabinet minister, and the Irish chief secretary, the luckless William E. Forster. Chaplin had enquired of Forster whether it was the case that the government intended to withdraw 'the protection of the police from the caretakers placed in vacant farms in Ireland by the Property Defence Association'.

Although the question had been submitted without prior notice, Forster replied anyway. He pointed out that the PDA request had been for two or more policemen to accompany each caretaker in order to guard against evicted tenants repossessing themselves of their houses and land. This, Forster pointed out, was impractical, since it would have required a police force of 50–100,000 constables. He then went further and stretched credulity, as politicians often do when they indulge in special pleading. There was, he said, no need for police protection 'on the spot', as constables would quickly be available if called upon: 'We believe it will be more effectual for the whole purpose in view of maintaining law and order to have a good system of patrolling.'[42] Which would have offered little solace to the beleaguered caretakers – the emergency men of the Orange Emergency Committee and the Property Defence Association – or to their employers.

Fast forward to the era of the Plan and, because of the more episodic nature of evictions and clearances in the late 1880s, the RIC was in a position to deploy hundreds of constables to keep the peace at mass ejectments, often accompanied by military backup, and could afford to leave eight to ten constables, commanded by a sergeant, to protect the landlord's caretakers.[43]

It is not possible to apportion an end date to the Plan of Campaign. On some estates, it ended before it began; on others it continued well into the 1890s, with evicted tenants still living in wooden huts erected by Plan organisers. While many of Smith Barry's tenants had already capitulated by 1891, some did not return to their properties until 1896. Michael Davitt charted expenditures of over £230,000 on Plan-related activities from 1887 to 1893, with an additional £29,000 'distributed to evicted tenants' from National League resources over the following ten years. So some evicted Plan tenants were still being maintained from political funds up to the passage of the 1903 Wyndham Land Purchase Act.

Was it all worth the 80 per cent success rate, the eviction of 7,000 people, the jailing of a further 5,000, National League expenditure of more than a quarter of a million pounds and government security expenses of more than £115,000? A quarter of that sum went to support the execrable Clanricarde. It certainly continued the production line of nationalist 'martyrs' (there were more than twenty Plan-related deaths, Mandeville's being the most high-profile) and propaganda victories. It was easy to ignore the reality that Dillon and O'Brien had promised universal success – and in doing so alienated their leader – but had failed to deliver. From a unionist point of view, the rearguard action against the Plan also signposted a potential route to survival for the landlord class: unity through syndication. However, the potential of that route was never fully explored. In addition, it introduced a new and adroit player to the bear pit of Irish political conflict. Arthur Balfour made a number of mistakes (putting his faith in spiritless landlords was just one) during his tenure as chief secretary, but he learned many lessons as well. He would prove to be a resourceful and dangerous pupil.

14

'The peasant will not tire first':
the Bodyke evictions, June 1887

'Bodyke bore a very evil reputation, many murders had
taken place in its vicinity, and a short time before there had
been a skirmish with fire-arms near the village between the
constabulary and the people.'[1]

(Colonel Alfred E. Turner, *Sixty Years of a Soldier's Life*, 1912)

Margaret McNamara and her sons before the arrival of the bailiffs
This image is reproduced courtesy of the National Library of Ireland
[EB_2662]

Bodyke, Co. Clare, 27 May 1887

The old lady poses defiantly in the window of the whitewashed thatched cottage. A dozen supporters, including two priests, also stare into the camera. The older of the two clerics is seated and sports an elegant top hat. Standing beside him is a grizzled old man in threadbare clothes wearing a 'topper' that has seen better decades. The entrance to the cottage and the two windows not occupied by the determined eighty-year-old widow, Margaret McNamara, have been blockaded with the heavy trunks of recently felled trees. Everything is in readiness for the approach of the 450-strong force of constabulary and soldiers, which will be heavily outnumbered when the tolling of chapel bells and the blowing of horns summons a hostile crowd numbering close to 5,000. When the time comes for the police and military to dislodge the defiant widow, her three sons and two daughters from their home and their nineteen-acre holding, the McNamaras will not lack for support.

The setting for this ominous tableau was a 'pleasant little village with a score or two of houses and half a dozen shops'.[2] Bodyke in Co. Clare was almost impossible to find on any map. It was also small enough to lack a resident priest. The inhabitants were obliged to attend mass in nearby Toomgraney, in the other half of the parish. But, as the visiting *Pall Mall Gazette* correspondent Henry Norman wryly commented, 'it is blessed with a police barracks'. The presence of the paramilitary *gendarmerie* in such an apparently insignificant hamlet was entirely necessary, according to the newly appointed divisional magistrate, Colonel Alfred E. Turner. Turner had seen service in India twice and had survived the Gordon debacle in the Sudan, so he was not easily intimidated. But even such a grizzled warrior was uneasy about this apparently inconsequential village, whose 'evil reputation' had spread beyond Co. Clare. Henry Norman was told by a Limerick jarvey that it was more than his livelihood was worth to convey him to Bodyke 'if you're anything to do with the sheriff'.

This turbulent recent past was now mere prologue. Norman, a plethora of fellow journalists, Michael Davitt, the Quaker philanthropist James Hack Tuke, five Home Rule MPs and upwards of a dozen priests were not present in Co. Clare merely to enjoy the spectacle of Bodyke's abundant local 'blossom'd furze, unprofitably gay'.³ They were there because of the presence of two magistrates (Colonels Turner and Miller), the county sub-sheriff James McMahon, 300 members of the RIC and 150 members of the Royal Welsh Fusiliers – imported from Fermoy barracks – all of whom were about the business of the local landlord, Colonel John O'Callaghan. A spectacle was in store that would be either affectingly poignant or unnervingly violent – or both. There were rumours that at least one of the houses to be targeted by the bailiffs had been mined.

The Bodyke evictions were about to begin.

Clare, 1880

Colonel John O'Callaghan, scion of an ancient Cork family, impolitely moved by Cromwell to Clare in the mid-seventeenth century, was the owner of almost 5,000 acres of land in his native county, which supported around 100 tenants. He and his family lived in some splendour in Maryfort House in Tulla in the south-eastern part of Clare, not far from the river Shannon. The O'Callaghan ancestral home was a fine three-storey, five-bay residence over a high basement with splendid south-facing views across adjacent terraces and distant parkland. According to the *Pall Mall Gazette* journalist Henry Norman, who would not have been particularly well-disposed towards the chatelaine of Maryfort, the building 'might have been transplanted straight from the most aristocratic West-end square of London'. O'Callaghan had inherited the estate from his father in 1849.

In 1879, O'Callaghan, 'a soldierly-looking man of sixty, with iron-grey hair and a moustache',⁵ managed his own estates and, by and large, dealt fairly with his tenants. The main strike against him was that, in common with hundreds of his ilk in the period after the Famine, he had cleared his estates of the most indigent of his tenants. By 1881, O'Callaghan was approaching the heights

of landlord infamy previously attained by Hubert de Burgh-
Canning, Marquess of Clanricarde. What happened between
1879 and 1881 to alter the perception of O'Callaghan so radically
in the eyes of both his tenants and outside observers, and to invite
so much public obloquy?

The rot began to set in when the increasingly immiserated
tenants on his estate rejected the offer of a small rent abatement
in late 1879. When O'Callaghan refused to countenance a more
generous reduction, he was subjected by the Land League to a
boycott. He also suffered a degree of personal humiliation when
his appearance in the village of Tulla was greeted with catcalls
and the slinging of mud. It was early in the Land War, a time
when even a boycotted landlord could still contemplate moving
around freely. That privilege would be one of the first to disappear
when the Land League campaign intensified. In the case of
O'Callaghan himself, by the summer of 1881, he had turned Fort
Anne, the house of his late brother-in-law (Major Westropp),
into an improvised police barracks where eight to ten RIC men
were stationed as a protection detail for the O'Callaghan estate.

Evictions began on the estate in the summer of 1880, one
of the first victims being a two-month-old infant. While
O'Callaghan was not the only landlord who obdurately refused
to meet the demands and/or respond to the difficulties of his
tenants, he was certainly out of step with some of his fellow
Clare landowners in adamantly refusing to come to terms
before being obliged to do so by the Land Court. His East
Clare neighbours, the Vandeleurs (Ralahine) and the Moloneys
(Kiltannon), offered abatements to their tenants of 15–20 per
cent in 1879, before coming under any severe pressure from the
Land League agitation. Major F. N. Westropp of Tulla remitted
six months' rent at around the same time.[6]

A Land League meeting in Scariff on 20 November 1880, well
attended by members of the Clare clergy, passed a motion to the
effect that 'we in future decline to pay exorbitant rents which
have tended to expatriate our population, and call upon all tenant
farmers to pay no more rent than Griffith's Valuation and to refuse
to take land rendered vacant for non-payment of a just rent'.[7] In

the case of the O'Callaghan estate, rents had already outstripped the Griffith valuation by more than 80 per cent, so this demand amounted to a declaration of war with O'Callaghan.

The following month, O'Callaghan took up the gauntlet thrown down at Scariff in a Christmas Eve letter to the *Clare Journal*, a newspaper which had once categorised the Land League as an agent of 'social terrorism and imprudent intimidation'.[8] O'Callaghan blamed the discontent amongst his tenants not on rack-rents or the imminent threat of eviction, but on the activities of 'stump orators and agitators' and the 'vile, dishonest, lawless doctrines' of the Land League. He went on to demand 'firm government' and insist that 'it is utter madness for any government, either Liberal or Conservative, to think that they can rule Ireland by conciliation'. He then concluded in a tone of plaintive protest, as 'one of those "Boycotted" landlords, left as I am with Mrs. O'Callaghan running the post daily, a distance of three Irish miles, armed with a revolver and express rifle. I have to remain at home to take charge of the estate, with two domestics.'[9]

What followed was the first 'Battle of Bodyke'. On 1 June 1881, O'Callaghan himself, armed with twenty-six eviction writs and accompanied by an RM (O'Hara), a process-server named Alloway and 150 members of the RIC, made for Bodyke. As the cavalcade approached the hamlet, the church bell pealed to alert the villagers. The bell ringer also managed to annoy the inhabitants of two beehives, who played a conspicuous role in proceedings, mostly at the expense of the mounts of a half-dozen RIC constables.

The most colourful first-hand account of what followed came from the Bodyke/Toomgraney parish priest, Fr Peter Murphy, who attempted to interpose himself, with limited success, between the constabulary and a large group of supporters from the surrounding countryside. They had responded to the peal of the church bells and were armed with pitchforks, clubs and sticks. For a couple of hours, from 10.30 a.m. to 12.30 p.m., the stand-off was peaceful. At which point the RIC mounted police were ordered to charge the crowd. This assault resulted in head injuries to a local farmer, John Moloney (he died the following day). Thereafter, the gloves were off, and when the RIC moved against the house of Edmund Malone, who was being served with the first writ, they came under rifle fire from an adjacent hill. Some of the shots were directed at the RM's car, on which Fr Murphy was seated. 'They whistled close by us,' Murphy recalled. 'Immediately some other shots were discharged from the heights on the left, which were directed towards the police, who immediately returned fire, and scattered all around the hill, firing at the point from which the shots came.'[10]

Murphy also claimed to have seen the police themselves, having reached the spot where the shots had been coming from and found no one, open fire from the hill on the unarmed crowd below. 'I saw many of the people's hats with bullet holes,' he told Jesse Craigen, a representative of the Democratic Federation, a British organisation supportive of the Land League campaign; he had travelled to Clare as an observer. The *Irish Times* reporter described what occurred as 'petty warfare of the guerrilla type'.[11]

What happened next demonstrated a level of ruthless resourcefulness on the part of the RIC. The police, having given chase to a group of men they suspected of being responsible for the gunshots, caught up with at least sixteen of them. All were unarmed when they were apprehended. Acting on a presumption of guilt, the RIC constables seized and handcuffed the unsuccessful fugitives to one another. They were then used as human shields as the constabulary and the process-server moved warily around the village and served the writs.

Before the bell finally sounded for the end of Round One, however, there was an entertaining if rather bizarre postscript to the first Bodyke skirmish. This came in the form of the submission made by counsel on behalf of O'Callaghan when the issue of rent arbitration on the Clare estates came before the Court of the Irish Land Commission. The brief submitted on O'Callaghan's behalf was a triumph of casuistry, hyperbole, melodrama and pathos. It was entirely predictable that the landlord would be presented to the Land Court as a model of fairness, more sinned against than sinning. However, this apologia ventured well beyond the borders of credulity. The Land Court must have wondered who was this almost saintly paragon, plagued by importuning tenants inclined to 'sloth and extravagance' who were castigated as 'wolves on the track of the Russian traveller'. Tenants who, furthermore, had enjoyed two consecutive bounteous harvests and who 'desired their farms for nothing'. O'Callaghan's opening offer to the Land Court was not a modest reduction but a forthright and breathtaking demand for an increase in the rent from a tribunal that had been handing down abatements of up to 50 per cent in the most egregious cases, and averaging close to 20 per cent across the board.[12] The commissioners may well have been impressed by the highly combative rhetoric, but they were not swayed by the arguments. The Land Court reduced rents on the O'Callaghan estate by a whopping 35 per cent.

'Is the game worth the candle?' – Bodyke, 1887

The return of the spectre of agricultural depression meant that by 1886 many of O'Callaghan's tenants were unable to pay even the arbitrated rents that their landlord in 1882 had querulously claimed would reduce him to penury. By 1887, the Bodyke tenants had formed a 'combination' under the auspices of the Plan of Campaign, had lodged the rental amount they were willing to pay with local MP Joseph Cox and were ready to resist any attempt to dislodge them. O'Callaghan was equally intransigent. His rationale was that, while a number of tenants were 'broken men' to whom he was prepared to forgive up to half of their arrears, others in a position to pay were hiding behind the misery of their less fortunate neighbours and, therefore, he was not willing to grant an 'all-round' reduction as demanded by the 'combination'.[13]

The hurried response of the Tory government of Lord Salisbury to the violence that attended the introduction of the Plan of Campaign in the especially troublesome south-west corner of Ireland was to despatch the formidable Major General Sir Redvers Buller to take command of all civil and military forces in Kerry and Clare as a 'special commissioner'. Buller was a square-jawed, Victoria Cross-winning veteran of colonial conflicts against Boers, Zulus, Egyptians and Sudanese. His appointment was, predictably, not welcomed by Irish nationalists. He was perceived as a bellicose martinet who had a 'short way' with natives and whose purpose in taking up his new post was to crush the Plan. However, the major general, while professionally unsympathetic to agrarian agitation, and eager to suppress the Irish National League, was personally dismissive of the kind of obdurate landlords targeted by the Plan. A short while after his appointment, having got his feet under the desk and having formed his own views, he wrote to Michael Hicks Beach, the Tory chief secretary at the time, in the following scathing terms:

> For 120 years British bayonets have backed up landlords in extracting excessive rents, and have supported them in grossly neglecting their tenantry. What is the result of these 120 years? – the tenants have combined against the injustice and persecutions; and where are the landlords? Nowhere. Bankrupt in money, in political, and in moral power.[14]

Buller concluded with the cri de coeur of the conflicted policeman: 'is the game worth the candle?' The Salisbury government, married to notions of the inviolability of contract, and beset on all sides by a vocal patrician element within its own ranks, clearly believed that it was.

In regard to the specifics of O'Callaghan's conduct of his business affairs, Buller and the equally combative Turner were less than sympathetic. In his memoir, *Sixty Years of a Soldier's Life*, Turner recollected of the Bodyke section of O'Callaghan's estate that 'Sir Redvers Buller and myself had satisfied ourselves that the rents demanded were much too high, and that the tenants could not pay them'. Buller, he recalled, agreed to intervene on behalf of O'Callaghan only 'under the sanction and at the wish of Sir Michael Hicks-Beach'.

In September 1886, O'Callaghan had rejected an offer from the tenants of £907 in lieu of a (disputed) total of £2,100 in arrears owed by fifty-seven tenants – £300 of this sum was to come from a donation offered by the philanthropist James Hack Tuke. In the spring of 1887, Buller and Turner brought tenants and landlord together in an attempt to arrive at a mutually satisfactory settlement, but both sides remained implacable and on a war footing.[15] Once official intervention failed, the stage was set for the sequel to the violent scenes of 1881.

It is likely, however, that not all the Bodyke tenants were intent on defying their landlord. A few days after the lengthy eviction campaign ended, Hosford, O'Callaghan's Limerick-based agent and partner in the firm of Delmege and Hosford, wrote a long letter to the *Irish Times*. He offered a detailed account of the failed negotiations from the landlord's perspective and claimed that O'Callaghan had been prepared to come to terms with most of the tenants. He blamed the breakdown on 'the mischievous interference of outsiders, as well as the terror in the minds of the tenants at the idea of daring to disobey the orders of the National League'.[16]

What Hosford was getting at was an earlier claim that a number of Bodyke tenants had covertly settled with the landlord, and that the National League, suspecting this, had attempted to smoke out the faithless by demanding that all tenants produce notices from the office of Delmege and Hosford demanding payment of rent. This edict, Hosford claimed, had led to a minor deluge of frantic appeals by the compromised tenants for 'a circular demanding rent as if they had not paid, so as to prevent them [from] being boycotted or perhaps shot'. Some demanded that they be served with ejectment papers despite having paid their rent, while others went even further and forged ejectment orders 'so as to save themselves'. It is possible that Hosford was being mischievous himself, but his allegation has the ring of truth about it.

Even before the settlement efforts broke down, O'Callagahan, predictably, found that his status as a boycotted landlord was restored, as was his well-armed RIC bodyguard. This he would occasionally shrug off, almost defying the local Ribbonmen to risk an attempt on his life. He may even have believed the local *piseog* (superstition) that clung to him. 'Sure, your Honour, the two eyes of the Colonel are not the same colour,' Turner was told by a local man, 'and the bullet that can kill such a man cannot be made by hand of man.'

Buller did not like O'Callaghan, informing Hicks Beach that, in his opinion, the Clare landlord was a 'driveller'.[17] Turner himself, described as 'the kindly and able magistrate in charge of the district'[18] in James Hack Tuke's memoir,* was of the view that O'Callaghan was one of a minority of tone-deaf landlords out of step with the impending change of key in landlord/tenant relations. In the wonderfully indiscreet memoir of the RIC officer Samuel Waters, both Buller and Turner are assailed as being 'much too liberal in their ideas for the times'.[19]

The spate of Bodyke evictions that began in late May 1887 – along with the Woodford sequel on the property of the Earl of Clanricarde – had a profound influence on the campaign for agrarian reform. Because the Plan was more limited and methodical than the almost formless chaos of the Land War, each of its set pieces assumed a special significance, was extensively reported and was subjected to intense commentary. However, although Bodyke, Woodford and the creation of New Tipperary were primarily concerned with the 'bread and butter' matters of sustainable rents and security of tenure, there was also a sense in which such fundamental issues now had only a transient centrality. The proximity of the Land War and the Plan of Campaign had overstretched tenant patience and the tolerance of the wider public for the oligarchic proprietorship model of the Irish system of landholding. The political successes of the Land War, and the logic of a Conservative Party 'conciliation' policy in the wake of the failure of the first Home Rule Bill, suggested that even the Tory government had come around to the view that the continuation of the landlord/tenant system was unconscionable. The tentative experiment in land purchase of the 1885 'Ashbourne' Act – the first piece of legislation entirely devoted to the notion of peasant proprietorship – did not come

---

* *United Ireland* would have wholeheartedly disagreed, accusing Turner in 1888 of 'truculent tyranny'.

out of the blue. That it was a piece of Tory legislation, albeit an opportunistic attempt to 'purchase' House of Commons support of the Irish Party, was also significant.

The escalation of agrarian tensions since the latest economic downturn, and the involvement of some of the more radical elements of the Liberal Party – freed from the shackles of government – gave added cachet to the second 'Battle of Bodyke'.

While never a 'pseudo-event/media event', as defined by Daniel Boorstin (i.e. contrived merely to attract attention), it was certainly eviction as spectacle. Representatives of the local, national, English and European press were on hand for much of the prolonged episode, as was a small contingent of political figures, including Michael Davitt. They were there to pass judgement on the former element of the policy of 'kicks and halfpence',[20] which Davitt ascribed to a Conservative administration that had ominously promised 'twenty years of resolute government' for Ireland when coming to power.

Also heavily implicated, in a partial reprise of his role in the 1881 melée, was the local parish priest, Fr Peter Murphy, acting in concert with his curate, Fr Hannan* (a cleric described by Alfred Turner as 'a magnificent specimen of a young Irish priest'). In 1881, Murphy had been more of an honest broker, pledged to avoid violence. In 1887, his involvement, while retaining the same priority, took on more of a proprietorial aspect. He and Hannan acted as negotiators with O'Callaghan's representatives, but Murphy still maintained a level of independence from the Plan, and from the Bodyke combination, which allowed Turner to describe him as someone 'with whom I was on friendly terms'. That relationship must have become strained on both sides during the fortnight of evictions, but their meeting on the first day of the Bodyke campaign began with the priest complaining to the magistrate about 'how his house had been invaded by English visitors, who had, he supposed, come to Bodyke expecting to find a hotel. They completely filled his house, he said, and sure he had not a corner left for himself.' The 'English visitors' were three

* Sometimes spelled as 'Hannen' or 'Hannon'.

Liberal MPs, S. D. Waddy, Joseph Pease and the total abstinence champion Sir Wilfrid Lawson, two of whom (Pease and Lawson) were also accompanied by their wives. Murphy's highly qualified welcome for these observers could only have been surpassed by the annoyance of his housekeeper.

The roles of pantomime villains of the piece were taken by O'Callaghan (who, unlike the 1881 staging, absented himself from proceedings), his agent, Hosford – blamed in some quarters for egging on O'Callaghan, though it is doubtful if the landlord required any such fodder – the hapless Clare sub-sheriff James McMahon and his imperious colleague, fellow sub-sheriff Edward Croker, as well as Colonel Turner.

There was, as will become apparent, a pattern to the resistance of the tenants as, one by one, they were picked off, often after their houses were pounded and battered into partial oblivion. That pattern tended to include the brazen and illicit re-occupation of their damaged homes. O'Callaghan's inevitable victory over his recalcitrant tenants – peasants who were ill-equipped to withstand a military force of more than 300 armed men – was partial, hollow and costly.

The first port of call of the bailiffs, police and military was the assault on the house of the Widow McNamara on 27 May 1887. It was to be an inauspicious beginning for the task force. A large and sullen crowd surrounding the house obeyed Fr Murphy's injunction against violent resistance but still banded together to deny access to the bailiffs who were designated to secure the removal of the family. Turner ordered a baton charge, but shortly after this commenced, the county sub-sheriff, McMahon, suffered an apparent epileptic fit, much to the amusement and satisfaction of the catcalling onlookers. Hostilities were immediately suspended while the stricken sheriff was removed from the field of battle.

But this was only a temporary cessation. On 2 June, the eviction task force returned in numbers. The *Pall Mall Gazette* correspondent, Henry Norman, firmly nailing his colours to the mast, offered this atmospheric description of the progress of the RIC and the 2nd Royal Welsh Fusiliers towards Bodyke: 'ludicrous it was to see all this display of the tactics and precautions of glorious war in so inglorious a task as marching upon a perfectly peaceful people for the martial purpose of pulling about their ears the poor cabins they had built for themselves'.[21]

It was little wonder that Norman's reports, which continued in this vein, were unfavourably received in Westminster. The *Pall Mall Gazette* correspondent was upbraided for his coverage by Edward King Harman, parliamentary under-secretary for Ireland in the House of Commons. Harman sniffed haughtily that 'the statements in the *Pall Mall Gazette* are very highly coloured, greatly exaggerated, and generally inaccurate'.[22]

The unfortunate McMahon resigned his position as sub-sheriff for health reasons and was replaced by a preening but resolute colleague, Edward William Croker, who was given to wearing an ostentatious tweed sports jacket, shooting helmet and leggings, while sporting a silk handkerchief. Croker was now in charge of the bailiffs, recruited, according to the exceptionally partial Henry Norman, from the north of Ireland, and whose 'hangdog, villainous faces one would expect to find upon men who are tempted to high pay into the very meanest and most degrading work, except that of bawd, on God's earth'. To demonstrate that they meant business, in case the presence of crowbars might have been misinterpreted, each had a revolver 'strapped ostentatiously round his waist'.

Upon the resumption of the evictions on 2 June, the bailiffs wasted little time in renewing the abandoned assault on the cottage of the Widow McNamara, still protected by the stocky wooden *chevaux de frise* protruding from the doors and windows.

Once again, crowbars and sledgehammers were used against the wall of the house, throwing up a 'blinding cloud of dust'. Soon a small, waist-high hole was created. However, before the bailiffs could enter, their newly fashioned opening was filled by 'three sturdy young fellows, two fine-looking young women, with the pleasant old face of the eighty-year[-old] widow surrounded by its white frilled cap, in the background'. The body language of each of the five McNamara children stated emphatically '*j'y suis, j'y reste*'. Croker urged on the bailiffs – or the 'fourteen cowardly gaol-birds', as Norman characterised them – but they hung back, wary of what awaited them inside the cottage. Croker then 'swore under his breath' (though the fact that the distant Norman heard him suggests that he made little effort to stifle his curses) and demanded of the RIC District Inspector that he send in his men instead. Davitt and the English MPs interposed themselves between the police and the cottage, Davitt pointing out ineffectually that the members of the constabulary were there in support of the bailiffs, who were legally obliged to attempt an entry first. He might as well have been King Lear railing against the storm. He and his allies were pushed aside and three strapping RIC men tried to effect an entry. As Norman described it, 'The men and women inside fought like tigers to push them back and for a moment all was a confused scuffle. The excitement was at its intensest, and one expected every instant to see the flash of firearms from the inside. Then the constables got inside, and the crowbarmen entered in their wake.'

Even then, the skirmish was far from over. The McNamaras refused to leave their home, the two girls tossing the wrecking crew's crowbars back through the hole they had just been used to create. Davitt himself then managed to get inside the cottage and, speaking in Irish, which he, probably correctly, assumed would not be understood by the sheriff, bailiffs or policemen, suggested that the Widow McNamara should lie down on her bed and compel the forces of law and order to carry her out of the building. The old lady obliged and a lengthy stalemate followed, during which the widow was advised by one of the priests in attendance to 'let Croker carry you out on his back'.

Eventually, the stand-off ended and the family members were escorted from the building amid cries of 'Three cheers for the Plan of Campaign' from one of the daughters of Margaret McNamara.

The postscript had an inevitability about it. With 'catlike tread' worthy of a Gilbert and Sullivan light opera, the McNamaras stole upon their foes later that day and reoccupied their home. By nightfall, smoke was drifting from the chimney.

The campaign resumed the following day. Croker's prime target was the house of an elderly tenant, Michael Hussey. An unknown number of activists waited inside Hussey's cottage while three men sat atop his roof. One of them, like a military spotter, relayed reports of the movements of the RIC and Welsh Fusiliers to the indoor defenders via the chimney. The emergency men approached the building warily, uncertain what to expect, but assuming the defenders of Castle Hussey were not going to give up without a fight. At first, the emergency men were met with boiling water poured on top of them by Hussey's daughter Maggie. Croker's face was badly scalded by a direct hit, his skin peeling off and leaving a wound that must have scarred the man for life. Colonel Turner's response was to call up the fusiliers and order them to train their rifles on the house. Only when Fr Murphy pleaded with the magistrate not to open fire on the occupants of the house did Turner relent and order the soldiers to withdraw.

In his own memoir, Turner described what happened next. Either Hussey himself or one of his allies had clearly learned an interesting lesson from the first display of Bodyke resistance in 1881. The Husseys, heeding Parnell's famous advice, were keeping not just a firm but an ingenious grip on their homestead. When Croker's platoon entered the house, with suspicious ease, its members were attacked by the inhabitants of a strategically placed beehive. Unfortunately for the defenders, this display of tactical nous backfired badly. Instead of going for the 'hated minions of the law' (Turner's own description of the force nominally under his command), 'Seeing a light through a chimney or hole in the roof, the whole swarm flew up to and through this and settled promptly in myriads on the boys who were astride the roof.' One of the defenders was badly stung and required treatment and, according to Turner, 'our prompt sending for our own doctor to treat the enemy who had been hurling missiles at us, seemed to the people like the touch of Nature which makes us wondrous kind, and made them think that we were agents only compelled to carry out duties which were hateful to us'.[23] Bear in mind that Turner wrote his memoir a quarter of a century after the events described. His spectacles were rose-tinted. He was being hopelessly unrealistic if he believed that the large group protesting the evictions would ever ascribe altruism to the members of the task force.

If the population of Bodyke and its hinterland had actually put such a positive complexion on the withdrawal of Turner's force, they would have been rapidly disabused of any notion that this armistice was anything but temporary. On 6 June, Turner was back with defensive shields, in the form of umbrellas, to protect his troops against boiling water and other indignities. They might also have proved useful against the incessant rain that day, conditions that did not discourage hundreds of people from continuing to offer support to the Bodyke tenants.

Either Croker's injuries at the hands of Maggie Hussey or the quality and ferocity of the resistance prompted the sheriff to reappraise his strategy. Instead of opting to assault another well-defended property, he chose to go where his presence would not be expected. He marched his forces through the village and descended on the houses of a number of unprepared tenants three miles away, in the direction of Broadford. Their first destination was the ten-acre farm of Thomas Lyddy. Caught unawares, Lyddy was prepared to defend his holding with a pitchfork until Michael Davitt persuaded him to surrender his weapon. He and his family then submitted quietly to the eviction, but by nightfall had reinstated themselves in their cottage. Exactly the same scenario was played out in the case of Lyddy's neighbour, a man named Moloney.

One of the more memorable set pieces of a campaign that, in aggregate, aspired to the condition of grand opera came on 10 June, almost a fortnight after the marathon operation had begun. This particular tune was a soprano quartet, sung by the indomitable O'Halloran sisters.

Buried in the Lawrence Collection is a photograph of four teenage girls taken against the backdrop of a whitewashed wall, possibly the gable end of their house. The sun is in their eyes. They are the O'Halloran sisters. Three are markedly similar in appearance, two even have the look of identical twins. The fourth girl, probably the youngest, sixteen-year-old Sarah, is chalk to the cheese of her three more moon-faced and heavy-set sisters. She is staring at the camera sceptically, with the beginnings of a wry smile about her face. Henry Norman described her as having 'laughing

The O'Halloran sisters
This image is reproduced courtesy of the National Library of Ireland
[EB_2664]

blue eyes and a smile like concentrated sunshine'. The four girls
are well-dressed, look well-nourished and gaze confidently into
the lens. It is hard to disagree with Norman's assessment that they
'did not present at all the appearance of an ordinary Irish peasant
family, but rather that of a well-to-do household of the English
lower middle class'.[24]

The Special Correspondent of the *Freeman's Journal*, taking his
cue from the Rev. Matthew Kenny of Scariff, a witness to the
day's action, characterised the O'Halloran family home, behind
an ancient rath (a circular earthwork) known as the Hill of Kilnoe,
as 'the dwelling which is to be henceforth known in Irish history
under the title ... O'Halloran's Fort'.[25] It was an imposing two-
storey stone structure set among hedgerows, 'a most charming
landscape ... at once impressive and harmonious'. There was
little charm and harmony in evidence at Kilnoe on 10 June 1887,
although, depending on which side you supported in the 'Fight for

Halloran's [*sic*] Fort'[26] (Henry Norman's designation), 'impressive' would certainly have been the *mot juste*.

O'Halloran, aged around sixty at the time of the evictions, was, unlike many of the previous victims of the emergency men, a substantial farmer. He had made significant improvements to his land and dwelling and felt that he was being penalised for the enhancement in the value of his property with increased rent demands from a landlord who had not invested a penny of his own in its development.

The 'fort' had certainly been sufficiently fortified to merit the title. All but one of its doors and windows had been blocked with tree stumps and thorny bushes. As a precaution against damage or distraint, most of the furniture had been taken away and hidden in a nearby hedge.

Turner approached the house diffidently. As the crowbars began their percussive assault downstairs, two of the O'Halloran girls, by means of two specially prepared portholes in the wall of their first-floor redoubt, merrily began to pour scalding water on the heads of the bailiffs, much to the approval of the supportive crowd being kept at a distance from the field of battle. The bailiffs withdrew, as did the two girls. The O'Hallorans were first to return, armed with two more pans of water, which they made clear they would empty on the heads of anyone who approached the house with a crowbar. At this point, Turner, fatigued by days of vitriol (metaphorical and allegedly literal) or provoked by the apparent glee of the two girls, who were reported to have been 'laughing merrily' – overreacted and called up the riflemen. The girls were warned that if they rained any more boiled water on the heads of the bailiffs, they would be shot. They chose to ignore the threat and continued to pour water, and worse – copious amounts of urine were also deployed by the members of the O'Halloran clan – on the heads of the crowbar wielders.

The *United Ireland* caricaturist J. D. Reigh, though not present in Bodyke himself, captured well the essence of the scene in his weekly cartoon, while apportioning scant credit to the defensive capabilities of the O'Halloran sisters. In a coloured drawing full of incidental Breughel-esque detail, a red-coated Welsh Fusilier aims his rifle at an upstairs opening in the gable end of the O'Halloran house. From there, a young man pours boiling water onto the heads of a number of disconcerted bailiffs below. Around the corner, his brother is in the act of successfully detaching two RIC constables from a ladder and sending them flailing to the ground twelve feet below. In another detail, a tall, moustached RIC man is seen leading three impossibly young girls away from the house, the smallest of whom appears to be in distress.[27] The O'Halloran girls reportedly caused considerable anguish, but there is no evidence that they fell victim to that emotion themselves.

The final outcome of the siege was a smattering of injured policemen, at least one blood-stained O'Halloran (male) and the surrender of the family, brokered by Fr Hannan, whose timely intervention prevented the defenestration of an RIC man who had been unwise enough to allow himself to be captured by the two young men. Three of the O'Halloran girls were then marched off between two files of constables before Turner ordered their release. They subsequently appeared in court and were each sentenced to a month's hard labour.

And that was part of the pattern of the punishment for the Bodyke resistance: the women of the village figured as prominently in the subsequent arraignments as did their menfolk. For example, at the Ennis petty sessions on 18 June, four of those arrested in Bodyke were either punished or sent for trial at the next assizes. Three were women, the sisters Ann and Bridget McNamara and their cousin Johanna Kennedy.[28]

At one of the daily public meetings in Bodyke – between speakers the crowd was entertained by local bands – Davitt drew attention to the role played by the women of the village in the defence of their homes and explicitly criticised the men for their relative inactivity.[29] In addition to the exploits already described, one woman tried unsuccessfully to impale a bailiff with a salmon gaff; three young girls used boiling hot porridge as a weapon; another girl, thinking laterally and literally rather than figuratively, met Turner with vitriol.[30] Other weapons employed by the women included dung, sticks and bottles, as well as more conventional projectiles such as stones. One woman, a Mrs Murphy, shoved her child in the face of the O'Callaghan estate's agent, exclaiming 'Hosford, did ye ever get a child, ye cruel murderer!'

Even the younger female children played their parts. On 14 June, a small girl, seeing the advancing column of police and military, raced to the nearest well and stirred up its muddy base to render it undrinkable. When she was upbraided by a stick-waving Colonel Miller – the local RM – threatened with a 'licking' and ordered to 'get away you little witch', she coolly continued to stir up sediment and was then joined defiantly in this display of civil disobedience by her sister.[31]

The behaviour of the women of Bodyke, and particularly their spicy language, may even have had an impact on the delicate feelings of some constabulary members. While travelling between Tralee and Cork, the American journalist William Henry Hurlbert got into conversation with a gentleman who was on his way back from assessing some property in Castleisland, Co. Kerry. The latter was clearly aghast at the tactics of the women of Bodyke in defence of their homes and visited his horror vicariously on the helmets of the RIC. 'This same gentleman,' quoth Hurlbert, 'said that at the Bodyke evictions, of which so much has been heard, the girls and women swarmed about the police using language so revoltingly obscene that the policemen blushed – such language, he said, as was never heard from decent Irishwomen in the days of his youth.' Hurlbert was a willing listener who did not question his fellow traveller too closely, or at all, on the provenance of his information.

An acknowledgement that it was the women of Bodyke who had played the primary role in the resistance to the evictions came also in an interestingly gendered editorial comment from the liberal *London Daily News* on 9 June:

> We cannot afford to hold a little army in reserve to operate against every handful of old women gathered together in disaffection on the hillside. Yet, under the existing system, we shall have to do it, for the peasant will not tire first. She is by temperament one of the most tenacious of human beings

in a course of passive resistance. The soldiery will probably be the first to yield to the strain.

In his assessment of the Bodyke evictions, twenty-five years after the event, Turner expressed a soldierly admiration for his opponents: 'I never saw anything to compare with the obstinacy and courage of despair with which the Bodyke tenantry defended their hearths and homes.'[32]

There were probably no winners in Bodyke. The tenants, although most simply re-occupied their homes after the task force had departed, suffered much damage to their property, and those who provided the most determined resistance ended up with jail terms of between one and three months' duration.

O'Callaghan certainly did not triumph. While there may have been some sympathy for his plight among the other landowners of Co. Clare and beyond, and vocal support from the membership of the PDA – though even the Unionist MP for Tyrone, T. W. Russell, described O'Callaghan as 'all that was worst in the Irish landlord'[33] – he would have been far better off financially had he settled with his tenants for the sum of £907, the deal he was offered back in September 1886. The thirty-odd evictions he secured were reported to have cost him somewhere in the region of £5,000. In the subsequent agreement, arrived at in February 1888, O'Callaghan was offered a payment of £1,255, which he was obliged to accept. The settlement allowed the Bodyke tenants back onto their farms (which, in reality, most of them had never abandoned) and, as well as the arrears foregone, cost O'Callaghan another £200 in lawyers' fees. Turner acknowledged that the entire exercise had been 'futile and fruitless' for the landlord.

There were other major losers to whose losses O'Callaghan was midwife. The RIC emerged from the episode with further reputational damage, having, in the words of John Dillon in the House of Commons, behaved like 'so many bullies trying to intimidate and frighten the people' and who were effectively employed as bailiffs rather than operating only in their support.[34] The Press Association described the behaviour of the members of the force at Bodyke to have been 'entirely unwarranted'.[35]

The major loser, however, was 'property' itself. The Bodyke evictions on their own might not have been sufficiently out of the ordinary to have shifted the meltwater point of the slowly moving glacier that stood as an apt metaphor for Irish landlord-tenant relations. But taken in conjunction with Woodford and other egregious examples of landlord privilege, tyranny or blind indifference during the Plan of Campaign, it helped to accelerate the process of change. In just two months, April and May 1887, there were almost 5,000 evictions in Ireland, albeit more than half of those evicted were re-admitted to their holdings as caretakers.[36] Was this interminable conflict to be allowed to continue ad nauseam? The 1881 Land Act, the 'Kilmainham Treaty', the Arrears Act, were just the most recent palliative remedies that had failed to alleviate the symptoms. Periods of respite from land agitation were getting shorter and more infrequent. Ultimately, one or other of the sides would weary of the conflict. Time would tell if the assessment of the *Daily News*, that 'the peasant will not tire first', would prove to be correct.

The acceptance in the House of Commons by the newly appointed chief secretary for Ireland, Arthur Balfour, that 'Colonel O'Callaghan has acted harshly towards his tenants – let us grant that he used his legal rights in a most inhuman manner' was something of a milestone for an administration generally more fixated on agrarian outrage than on the comportment of the less wholesome members of the landholding class. Even Balfour's corollary, that the government was nonetheless obliged to come to the assistance of the likes of O'Callaghan 'firmly, if not cheerfully', added fuel to the arguments of voices already being raised in favour of an end to landlordism and a rapid move towards peasant proprietorship, thus rendering unnecessary further expensive and politically damaging police and military interventions in agrarian matters.

Despite adverse commentary on Bodyke in conservative British newspapers like *The Times* and the *Daily Express*, there was an implicit acceptance among liberals (with both a small and a capital 'L') that the days of the landlord were numbered in Ireland and that the practice of holding onto extensive estates and letting land to those who obviously would be better off in possession of the fee simple themselves was antediluvian. Although Henry Norman's coverage of the Bodyke evictions for the *Pall Mall Gazette* had rankled with the Tory establishment – Balfour had observed of him in his laconic manner that 'the fact of his [Norman] holding a certain opinion is no ground why it should be entertained by anybody else'[37] – it had helped to cut through any residual lassitude and indifference on the part of the British public and had worsened the already bad odour in which Irish landlords were, by now, commonly held in Britain. This burgeoning hostility increased in direct proportion to the general awareness of the cost of the Bodyke evictions to the taxpayer, the final bill coming to over £1,000[38] – a paltry sum when compared with O'Callaghan's losses, but one that, it was dawning on more members of the wider British public, could be eliminated entirely with the removal of the Irish landlord class.

IV

Reclamation

15

The 'closing down' sale

'Down with the Church, down with the landlords, down
with the agents, down with everything, say I, that stands in
the way of our own green land coming back to us again.'
'What wonderful grand fun we'll have fightin' among
ourselves when it does come!' said a thick-set Herculean
fellow at the lower end of the table.
'Well now, I often thought of that!' replied his neighbour
in a whisper. 'It'll be bloody work then in airnest, as sure as
you and I live to see it. Anything that has happened up to
this will be only a joke to what will happen then.'[1]

(William Steuart Trench, *Realities of Irish Life*, 1868)

'I need scarcely say that the creation of peasant proprietors,
as far as it goes, is a displacement of the landed gentry.'[2]

(Isaac Butt, *The Irish People and the Irish Land*, 1867)

1 February 1900, meeting of the MPs of the National Federation, National League and People's Rights Association

John Dillon's feigned generosity had exploded in his face. He had agreed to a member of the rump Parnellite faction becoming leader of the reunited party, hoping for a subaltern figure to be chosen whom he could then quickly supplant. Instead, John Redmond, a politician of substance, had been selected as the Westminster figurehead of this new umbrella body, the United Irish League. The blanched products of the Parnellite split, the National Federation, National League and People's Rights Association, all 'practically bankrupt, without policy, programme or money'[3] (according to the grizzled Land War activist Andrew Kettle), were now footnotes. The perennially erratic Tim Healy would quickly untether himself and reincarnate as a gadfly one-man political party, but Dillon could not indulge himself in such crass displays of egotism. He was going to have to play second fiddle to Redmond.

Rewind to 1891.

William O'Brien was jaded and in failing health after five years of intermittent incarceration. He was also terminally disillusioned by the recrimination of the Parnellite Split. Normally content in the role of Horatio, he had been obliged to turn on his Hamlet. With a heavy heart, he opposed the retention of Parnell as party leader and, shortly thereafter, made what was supposed to be his final exit from the cesspit of Irish politics. He retired to live in a modest dwelling ('Mallow Cottage' on Clew Bay) near Westport, with his new wife, Sophie Raffalovich, the wealthy daughter of one of the Tsar of Russia's bankers. O'Brien was going to spend the rest of his life admiring the nearby Croagh Patrick, musing on the piratic life of the Mayo adventurer Grace O'Malley (Granuaile) from her base on the nearby Clare Island,* cultivating his roses, and enjoying 'an almost perfect sense of retirement from the world'.[4] The heady pleasure of connubial bliss would be a soothing alternative to the collective bile of the previous eighteen months.

---

* One of O'Brien's self-appointed tasks was the completion of a novel on Grace O'Malley entitled *A Queen of Men*.

Even the premature death of Parnell in October 1891 had done nothing to staunch the bloodletting brought on by the O'Shea divorce and the refusal of the party leader to go gently into political oblivion. With volatile firebrands like Timothy Healy poking the ashes to see if another spark could be ignited, there was little hope of the sides reconciling. The Tories were sitting back, observing the self-inflicted slaughter with smug satisfaction and doing what any sensible person would do when a rival is intent on hanging himself: continue to feed out the rope. O'Brien wanted none of it. His time had passed.

Until 1898 at any rate, when he re-entered the lists on a white charger named the United Irish League. In the words of Kettle, 'the flint and steel accidentally came together and the spark was fanned into a flame'.[5]

Granuaile's former haven of Clare Island had a lot to do with O'Brien's change of heart. The island in the mouth of Clew Bay covered 4,000 acres farmed by ninety-five families. In the early 1890s, shortly after the O'Briens moved into Mallow Cottage, the Clare Islanders were subjected to the regime of a new owner, a 'land jobber' who had acquired the fee simple to the island and 'who so harassed his tenants that the historic and beautiful island was a constant scene of turmoil arising out of bailiff and police expeditions in gunboats to serve writs or carry out ejectments'.[6] O'Brien persuaded the newly established Congested Districts Board (covered later) 'to make Clare Island its first experiment' by purchasing the land and offering it to the tenants. O'Brien and the Roman Catholic Archbishop of Tuam agreed to guarantee the islanders' repayments for a seven-year period. O'Brien could have relied on the wealth of his wife to stave off bankruptcy in the event of a default, but, as he recorded, 'to the immortal credit of the islanders the guarantee never cost us a farthing'.[7]

Chaperoning the Clare Islanders towards economic sustainability was one of the factors that forced O'Brien to acknowledge that the life of a historical fiction-writing hermit was not in his tea leaves. Much had changed since his crusading career as a radical reporter (*Freeman's Journal*), militant editor (*United Ireland*), and committed activist (the Plan of Campaign). Excessive rents were less contentious in the late 1890s than the fundamental structural revolution that had been transforming Irish agriculture since the Famine. This was the increasing dominance of the wealthy grazier class, the 'new landlords' or the new 'grabbers'.

The pejorative designation 'land grabber' was undergoing a subtle metamorphosis in the west of Ireland. It was now being applied to graziers – many of whom were not even farmers themselves – who were renting fields acquired at auction. The lease offered to the highest bidder by landlords was for no more than eleven months. Thus did merchants, professionals and cattlemen acquire herds, and landlords circumvent some of the punitive provisions of the land acts. The cattle were generally sold on before the expiration of the eleven-month term.

Where cattle now grazed, tillage farms had maintained any number of small farmers in the past. Land poverty was the virus that was plaguing O'Brien's adopted home county of Mayo. O'Brien found it impossible to bury himself in literary projects and ignore the predicament of many of his neighbours. Instead, calling on his experience at the highest levels of the Land League and the Plan of Campaign, he – almost single-handedly it seemed at times – sought to give structure to the recrudescence of agrarian agitation in the west of Ireland with an entirely new organisation, one that would mimic those of his campaigning past but would, insofar as possible, remain within the law.

Fast forward to 1898.

A wave of patriotism was engendered by the centenary of the rebellion of the United Irishmen. Set that against the redundancy of the country's three nationalist political tribes (Dillonites, Redmondites, Healyites) and stir in the threat of yet another subsistence crisis in the west of Ireland, observed at close quarters by O'Brien himself. The result was the rapid rise of a new agrarian force with O'Brien at the helm, the United Irish League (UIL), founded (and funded) by the former *United Ireland* editor in January 1898. At first, this new pretender went unremarked upon among Irish MPs and operatives at Westminster. Rapidly, however, with some help from an enthusiastic Michael Davitt, the UIL graduated from minor irritant to 'coming storm', to 'force to be reckoned with', before reaching a numerical tipping point where it threatened to render the three warring factions of the old Parliamentary Party redundant. A merger was negotiated as an alternative to a hostile takeover and the UIL, which began as a lineal descendant of the Land League, metamorphosed into the child of the Irish National League. 'In face of the hostility of the heads of all the sections,' wrote O'Brien in his final memoir, *Evening Memories*, the UIL, 'healed, by a process little short of a miracle, the festering wound of the Split.'[8]

Fortunately, O'Brien also managed to finish *A Queen of Men, Grace O'Malley* before climbing back into the political ring. From 1898 onwards, he would be creating history. There was to be no time for any more historical fiction.

Land purchase – from swaddling clothes to faltering steps, 1848–96

'I grieve to say that my experience of the Celt leads me to believe that Providence has not endowed him with sufficient energy to do more than eat potatoes that are put into his mouth.'[9]

(Lord Lieutenant, the Earl of Zetland, to Arthur Balfour, 27 October 1890)

In 1884, as had been the case for the better part of two and a half centuries, barely 3 per cent of Irish land was tenant-owned. By 1909, that figure had risen to 46 per cent. What happened over the intervening quarter-century to bring about the transfer of the fee simple of so much Irish real estate? Why did Irish landlords voluntarily hand over their estates (at a price) to their tenants in the twenty-five years between the passage of the Purchase of Land (Ireland) Act of 1885 (the Ashbourne Act) and the Land Act of 1909 (Birrell's Land Purchase Act)?

As it happens, this wholesale transfer did not occur at a steady rate. It was rather like a slow bicycle race where the rules change as the participants approach the finish line and they are instructed to sprint for all they are worth. From 1885 to 1902, the pace was stately, that of a corpulent gentleman progressing uphill. Around 70,000 tenant farmers took advantage of increasingly radical Tory legislation to rid themselves of their landlords.

From 1903 onwards, however, the dripping tap began to gush as hundreds of thousands of Irish tenant farmers put the 'proprietor' into 'peasant proprietorship'. The aggression (passive and otherwise) of the Land Wars of the 1880s and 1890s had undoubtedly predisposed many landlords to sell up. Few, however, actually did so. The 'push' factor of potential violence was insufficient on its own to persuade landowners to part with their estates. They were not, in the main, directly in the line of fire. Many may have quietly harboured the sentiment actually articulated by the Earl of Clanricarde, when he refused to be intimidated by injuries done to his agent or bailiffs. It was the 'pull' factor that decided the issue, the appealing prospect of a sizeable cash dividend in return for divesting themselves, in some cases at least, of refractory tenants; threatening letters; armed escorts; and the need to be constantly alert. Landlords finally put the 'purchase' into 'land purchase' when a colonial administration they had learned to distrust began offering sums of money with sufficient digits to the left of the decimal point to enable them to move on.

In modern parlance, it was a relatively simple case of 'show me the money'. The Tory administration of Arthur Balfour did just that, and the rush to the exits began.

If the tempo of land purchase was stately between 1885 and 1903, the pace of tenant acquisition between the passage of the 1869 Church Disestablishment Act and the 1881 Land Act was positively glacial.

In 1869, Gladstone's first effort at political reform in Ireland, the Church Disestablishment Act, divested the Church of Ireland of its land holdings and offered terms to its tenants to purchase. Church lands were transferred to the Church Temporalities Commission and sold off. Those who were *in situ* on the land already could borrow 75 per cent of the purchase price at an interest rate of 4 per cent. Six thousand of the 8,400 Church of Ireland tenants opted to do so, an indication in itself of an appetite for land purchase. The rest became the tenants of new landlords.

Almost as an afterthought, at the instigation of the radical MP John Bright, Gladstone's first Land Act (1870) included a further provision for tenant acquisition. The price was high, because the few tenants opting to purchase paid twenty-five years' rent for the privilege of owner/occupation. The government advanced two-thirds of the purchase price, repayable at 5 per cent over thirty-five years. In essence, the annuities, which generally amounted to more than the annual rent, had to be repaid within a single generation. The take-up on this less than generous offer (inferior to the deal availed of by the tenants of the Church of Ireland the previous year) was a dismal 873 tenants. Tenant purchase then lay dormant for a decade.

When Gladstone attempted to bring the Land War to an end with his 1881 legislation, he included a land purchase clause in his new statute. The terms and conditions were barely more attractive than those of 1870. The newly created Land Commission was permitted to advance 75 per cent of the purchase price to any tenant able to come to an arrangement with his landlord. This was repayable on the same terms as the 1870 provisions (5 per cent over thirty-five years). This element of the 1881 legislation was another dismal failure. The take-up, at 731 purchases, was even lower than the unenthusiastic response of 1870. Few tenants were in sufficient funds to raise the 25 per cent needed to draw down the full government loan.

The first serious attempt to introduce a credible land purchase regime, in 1885, was a consequence of an activity very familiar in modern Ireland: 'auction politics'. The Liberal government of William Gladstone had lost a seemingly unimportant Commons vote and chosen, for tactical reasons, to resign from office. That should have led to an immediate general election. However, after the passage of electoral reform legislation in 1884, a major constituency revision was underway, rendering an election impossible for a period of six months. As a consequence, from the summer of

1885 until the end of November, the UK was governed by a Tory caretaker administration under the Marquess of Salisbury. With the Tories and the Liberals evenly matched, the eighty-plus seats likely to fall to the Parnellites in Ireland suddenly became mightily significant. Hence the preparation by the Irish Lord Chancellor, Lord Ashbourne (Irish attorney general from 1877 to 1880 as Edward Gibson) of land purchase legislation that, it was hoped, would entice Parnell to throw his support behind the Tories in the November/December election. This the Irish party leader duly did, but for reasons extraneous to this narrative.*

Ashbourne's legislation took account of the reasons underlying the miserable failure of the faltering attempts at land purchase of Gladstone's two Liberal administrations. The entire purchase price of holdings would be advanced by the government. This would be repaid at an interest rate of 4 per cent over forty-nine years, ensuring that the burden would, in most cases, be shared across two generations of tenants. The main drawback of Ashbourne's vastly improved template was the meagre amount of money allocated to the scheme. A mere £5 million would be dispensed on a first-come-first-served basis. The entire sum was drawn down within three years and, with the Tories back in power under Salisbury in 1888, was topped up with another, equally inadequate, £5 million. More than 25,400 tenants were enabled to purchase their holdings and 942,600 acres changed hands at an average price of 17.5 'years purchase' (i.e. of annual rental payments). While this was obvious progress, and pointed the way for later Tory schemes, it was still a drop in the ocean. By 1890, around 5 per cent of Irish land was owned by a 'yeoman' farming class.

Enter Arthur J. Balfour, prime ministerial nephew, Irish chief secretary and point man for Uncle Robert's policy of 'killing Home Rule with kindness' – albeit a kindness tempered with regular infusions of coercion whenever the natives became restless.

---

* Parnell entered into negotiations with the caretaker Lord Lieutenant, Lord Carnarvon, and was hopeful of Tory support for a measure of Home Rule. This failed to materialise.

In 1891, with the supplementary Ashbourne Act funds from 1888 having been exhausted, Balfour introduced his own land purchase legislation. This was predicated on the distribution of a much more generous sum of £33 million and otherwise adhered to the terms and conditions of the 1885 act. However, it was modified by a suspicious Treasury to such an extent – hedged with fiscal safeguards and caveats – that it was a bureaucratic nightmare. Potential beneficiaries shied away. It was left to one of Balfour's successors, his younger brother Gerald (chief secretary from 1895 to 1900), to rectify the inadequacies of his elder sibling's efforts with his own legislation in 1896. This dispensed with many of the Pooterish Treasury disincentives and also empowered the Land Court to sell 1,500 bankrupt estates, for which no other purchasers had been found, to their tenants. Gerald Balfour's measure even received the imprimatur of Michael Davitt, who wrote that it 'was another gain for the movement which had the abolition of the whole landlord system as a primary purpose', although it was 'bristling ... with legal technicalities'.[10] Under the 1891 and 1896 acts, a further 47,000 tenants purchased their holdings. To the, doubtless, delight of the Treasury, this cost the exchequer only £13 million, less than half the proposed amount.

Of rather more significance, however, was another item of agrarian reform Arthur Balfour introduced in 1891. This was the future prime minister's attempt to deal with the fundamental issue – arguably of more importance than facilitating the purchase of their farms by relatively prosperous tenants – of the hundreds of thousands of small uneconomic holdings (generally ten acres or less in size), worked by small farmers, cottiers and labourers, which were simply not economically viable.

The establishment of the Congested Districts Board (CDB) – a quasi-independent body – was Balfour's acknowledgment that, in the words of historian Pauric Travers, 'land purchase was not the complete panacea for Irish agricultural problems that some of its proponents hoped'.[11] Despite the dominant governmental obsession with the hostile interactions of tenant and landlord, there was a reluctant acceptance on the part of the ruling establishment of an alternative reality: that most disturbances of the rural peace were actually violent acts wreaked by tenant upon tenant. At least some of this rancour was based on the class differences inherent in the radical inequities of Irish agrarian life.

Just as the Balfourian marriage of conciliation and coercion was aimed at reducing or eradicating tenant/landlord hostilities, the establishment of the CDB was designed to eliminate this more common and mundane form of agrarian violence by alleviating intra-tenant economic disparities. The initiative was later supplemented by the establishment, in 1899, during the administration of Gerald Balfour, of the Department of Agriculture and Technical Instruction. This was partly due to pressure from the agricultural crusader Sir Horace Plunkett and the so-called 'Recess committee' report of 1896: a semi-official body chaired by the founder of the agricultural co-operative movement.

Congested districts, mostly situated along the west coast from Donegal to West Cork,* were defined as areas with a rateable valuation of less than thirty shillings. This amounted to one sixth of the area of the country and almost 10 per cent of the population. The functions of the new board were all-encompassing. Untenanted land was to be purchased and redistributed; infrastructural development (the building of roads, bridges and piers in particular) was to be prioritised. Where feasible, efforts were to be made to attract industries to the 'congested' regions. The fishing industry was to be subvented and developed. The board was also made responsible for agricultural education and was to assist in the process of internal migration and emigration. In the case of the latter 'hot potato', the board ultimately declined to become involved and contented itself with moving tenants from the congested west to untenanted land elsewhere in the country.

By the time of Augustine Birrell's tenure as chief secretary (1907–16), the board's budget amounted to more than £200,000

---

* The original 'congested districts' were Donegal, Leitrim, Sligo, Mayo, Roscommon, Galway and West Cork. Over time, parts of Clare and Kerry were added, and the congested districts covered one-third of the land mass of the country.

per annum (the equivalent of almost £30 million today). All told, in addition to much valuable infrastructural and development work, the Congested Districts Board, up to the time of its abolition in 1923 by the Irish Free State, was responsible for the transfer of land on almost a thousand estates (937), amounting to 2,265,000 acres, at a cost just shy of £10 million (around £1.5 billion today). Crucially, from 1909, the board was given the power to acquire land compulsorily and redistribute it to small farmers and the landless.[12] Although it was far from the ultimate solution to the ills of the western seaboard, and although it did not forestall the founding of the United Irish League in 1898, William O'Brien heartily approved of its establishment. He was conscious that 'the Board's main function lay in providing what ... was now the obvious and only real solution to the problems of the West: the purchase of grazing lands to which tenants could be transferred'. O'Brien's approval extended as far as an unexpected encomium. In April 1894, he wrote of his former sworn adversary that 'Mr. Balfour has unlearned a good many of his blunders of his hot youth in Ireland. Perhaps some of us have unlearned some of our first impressions about him.'[13]

Balfour more than earned O'Brien's plaudits. His insistence that, to be credible and accepted, the CDB would have to be positioned at arm's length from Dublin Castle – and with a long arm – did not go down well with the bureaucratic cadre of that establishment. However, the political carapace that served Balfour well during the Plan of Campaign was more than capable of repelling anguished bureaucrats.

After Balfour moved on to greater things, the CDB frequently fell foul of the Treasury. The board's expenditures often tipped into the red, and the counting of beans was not one of its strong points. This was a regular bone of contention in Whitehall. The Treasury's ongoing disapproval was aggravated by the fact that the board had been given rights to borrow, on its own authority, the finance for capital projects. At one point, the fractious relationship between funder and funded was so strained that the board took the former to court. The case did not end until it reached the House of Lords.[14]

George Wyndham

'The most fortunate financial treaty ever obtained for Ireland':[15] the Wyndham Land Purchase Act, 1903

'The Wyndham Act would have been far more beneficial, if the Government had given the tenant a free grant of some of the purchase money, and insisted on his finding some more of it himself, whereby would have been created a deeper interest in his land than is now inspired in his breast by the mere transference of his lease from his old landlord to the Government.'[16]

(Samuel Hussey, *The Reminiscences of an Irish Land Agent*, 1904)

He was a distant relative of that most romantic of Irish revolutionary figures, Lord Edward Fitzgerald – to whom he appears to have borne a physical resemblance – and would become the author of a book on seventeenth-century French poetry. He had started his political career in Ireland, as private secretary to Arthur Balfour. Now he was a Tory Irish chief secretary himself, making good use of his 'suave manners'[17] and broadly hinting at his covert support for Home Rule in order to charm the natives. At some point, he was bound to become prime minister,* though many of his colleagues saw him as a 'dandified lightweight' and he was prone to bouts of severe depression followed by periods of furious activity.[18] In pursuit of his lofty ambitions, George Wyndham had a signature piece of legislation to pass, a statute that would become 'the most far-reaching reform of the Irish land problem by any British government under the Act of Union'.[19] It would bring about the final 'abolition of landlordism' and rid Ireland of the 'most accursed institution planted there by England'.[20]

On assuming the role of chief secretary returned to office – still led by the venerable Marquess of Salisbury – were returned to office, Wyndham, like the month of March, had 'come in like a lion'. Elements of the 1887 Crimes Act of his former mentor, Arthur Balfour, were revived in response to a renewed campaign of agrarian agitation, including extensive boycotting, by the United Irish League. After the agricultural depression of the mid-1890s, which had prompted the establishment of the league, the first phase of Wyndham's tenure, beginning in November 1900, had seen a further deterioration in economic conditions. Inevitably, agrarian crime increased. Predictably, Dublin Castle responded as before, with punitive coercion measures.

But, as it transpired, Wyndham's mind was set on higher things, albeit for pragmatic rather than altruistic reasons. One of his primary aims appears to have been to improve the Irish peasant gene pool. In a memorandum to cabinet in 1902, he characterised the inhabitants of the congested districts as 'obscene reptiles' who urgently needed to become 'part of the Aryan race'.[21] Enter, or rather re-enter, Wilfrid Scawen Blunt, poet and noted English Hibernophile whose personal relationship with Wyndham had

---

* Wyndham's tacit personal support (he denied any official knowledge) for a devolutionary scheme devised in 1904 by his under-secretary, Sir Anthony McDonnell, infuriated unionists and led to his resignation in March 1905. While he remained in politics, he never again held ministerial office. He died suddenly in 1913, yet another 'lost prime minister'.

survived incarceration in Ireland during the Plan of Campaign. Before Blunt's deviation into Irish land politics, the two men – Blunt in his fifties and Wyndham in his twenties – had bonded when the future Irish chief secretary was an enthusiastic member of the Crabbet Club. This was 'a self-consciously frivolous male mutual admiration society, whose activities included reciting verses in praise of sin and playing nude tennis matches at Blunt's country residence', according to Patrick Maume, author of Wyndham's entry in the *Dictionary of Irish Biography*.[22] Other distinguished members of this nineteenth-century Bullingdon Club were Lord Alfred Douglas (Wyndham's cousin) and his lover, Oscar Wilde.

Blunt, because of the credibility he had earned by his jail term in 1888, had the ear of the leadership of the Irish Party and was frequently pressed into service as a go-between when the chief secretary wanted an insight into John Redmond's thinking. Wyndham informed the poet and diarist in 1902 that his revival of coercion was merely an elaborate performance – an iron glove sheathing a velvet fist. Blunt confided to his diary on 4 February 1902 that Wyndham was 'far more in sympathy with the Nationalists than with the Castle party which he despises for its sycophancy, or the Ulster Protestants whom he dislikes for their sour bigotry ... I gather from him that he was obliged to threaten resignation rather than go in for a policy of extreme coercion, which has always failed and will fail again.'[23]

Wyndham told Blunt that his half-hearted revival of Balfour's penal coercion policies – cartoons in nationalist journals depicted an angry ghost of Lord Edward Fitzgerald admonishing his descendant for this infamy – was an essential feint. It would enable the passage of remedial land legislation that would otherwise moulder in Cabinet. It was, according to the chief secretary, 'the price he had had to pay for obtaining a free hand from his colleagues in the Cabinet ... and the support of the *Times* could only be bought by coercion'.[24]

The land purchase legislation Wyndham produced, though an inevitably flawed compromise, was nonetheless monumental in its import. If Gladstone's late nineteenth-century land legislation marked the beginning of the end of landlordism in Ireland, the

1903 Wyndham Land Purchase Act flagged, to borrow from Winston Churchill's 1942 Mansion House speech, 'the end of the beginning'. Wyndham himself vaguely saw the statute that bore his name as an overture to some limited form of Home Rule. In reality, in its strengthening of Ireland's *kulak* class – the 'snug' farmers – it was a prelude, though not necessarily a major contribution, to full legislative independence in 1922. Indeed, it can be seen as the apotheosis of the Tory strategy for governing Ireland: the last successful piece of progressive legislation introduced by a Conservative administration (out of office as a single party government from 1906 until the achievement of Irish independence).

However, although there were vehement denials that the new framework was in any way a 'concession to anarchy', it would be foolish to underestimate the part played in the legislation by the relentless pressure to which the government was subjected by the UIL at grass-roots level, where 'agrarian agitation played a decisive role in persuading the government to introduce a new Land Act'. Just as Parnell was aware that ameliorative legislation was in preparation in 1881 and urged his supporters into action to extract attractive concessions, William O'Brien emphasised the need for his own agrarian militia to make a nuisance of itself in order to push the Tories in the direction of a decisive land purchase scheme that would sweep away the various ersatz versions in place since 1885. As in the winter of 1880–1, the principal weapon was the boycott, deployed, in the words of John Dillon, 'to make it hot for the graziers and grabbers'.[25] This potent UIL agitation was both prologue and backdrop to the subsequent land purchase legislation.

Gladstone's 1881 act, in creating the Land Courts and Land Commission, had included a provision for rent realignments every fifteen years.[*] Although the next formal adjustment was not

---

[*] An element of the legislation vigorously opposed by Parnell as having the potential to be a source of ongoing animosity between tenant and landlord 'and keep classes in Ireland divided so that we may thus be prevented from utilising our united strength for the purposes of recovering our lost rights of legislating for ourselves' (William O'Brien, *Recollections*, 330–31).

due until 1911, the first, in 1896 – to the consternation of landlords – had reduced rents by an average of more than 20 per cent. This was on a par with the initial Land Court reductions in 1881–2. The prospect of a similar rental discount in 1911 was too appalling for many marginal landlords to contemplate, and there was a sense in which the writing was on the wall for landowners. So there was an appetite for some form of compromise that would quicken the pace of tenant purchase. What the influential Earl of Dunraven dubbed 'a certain vague, half unconscious movement of public opinion towards a different solution of the problem than a "fight to the finish"'.[26]

The gap between what landlords wanted for their holdings and what tenants were prepared to pay for theirs was still too wide. Wyndham was open to filling that breach with enhanced government funding. All he had to do was persuade a reluctant Cabinet that it was worth throwing more than £100 million at Ireland in order to bring a final end to the tedious firefighting constantly required in countering agrarian unrest. The rise of the United Irish League – although its agitation was directed as much at the break-up of grazing farms as it was at excessive rents and evictions – ironically gave Wyndham a useful argument when it came to making his case.

Just as the most subtle of movements, or a sudden thaw, can cause an avalanche, so did an easily ignored contribution to the 'Letters to the Editor' sections of the Dublin daily newspapers on 3 September 1902 bring about an agrarian revolution. It was an unlikely intervention that came in the form of a despatch from a little-known landlord, Captain John Shawe-Taylor of Ardrahan in Co. Galway. His main claim to fame was that he was a nephew of Lady Augusta Gregory. Shawe-Taylor suggested – and he was not the first to do so – that the solution to the perennial problem of Irish agrarian unrest was a conference of the representatives of landlords and tenants dedicated to ending '200 years of land war'. He then proceeded to name the eight men he would ideally like to see sitting around the negotiating table. His wish-list included, among others, those inveterate antagonists Arthur Smith Barry (now Lord Barrymore) and William O'Brien, both veterans of the sodden trenches of 'New Tipperary'.[27] Many readers contemplating Shawe-Taylor's initiative over their boiled egg, toast and coffee – if they even noticed the letter – probably concluded that the correspondent would be as well off placing four cats and four dogs in a large sack and awaiting the outcome.

Fortunately, the letter was brought to the attention of the chief secretary, and within days Wyndham had amplified the Shawe-Taylor proposal. 'No government can settle the Irish land question,' he wrote. 'It must be settled by the parties interested.'[28] Wyndham's intervention ensured that an unlikely diplomatic *démarche* from an improbable source suddenly became airborne. One of the other imponderables helping the initiative was support for the proposal from a now more emollient William O'Brien. The new Irish Party leader, John Redmond (another of the names on Shawe-Taylor's list), acknowledged that, 'But for William O'Brien there would have been no Land Conference and no Land Purchase act'.[29]

Although the same could not be said of the Scottish-born and highly independent unionist MP for south Tyrone, Thomas Wallace Russell, he still became something of a Sharman Crawford figure in the delivery of a peasant proprietary. For the first time since the Tenant League of the 1850s, thanks largely to his efforts, Presbyterian tenant farmers in Ulster found themselves on the same side of an argument as the largely Catholic and exceptionally nationalistic supporters of the UIL, although William O'Brien's description of Russell as one of the 'bigots of south Tyrone'[30] was unlikely to have endeared the motive force behind the UIL to this potential and influential unionist ally. The perennially uncharitable Tim Healy once referred to Russell – 'a vehement opponent of the Licensed trade' – as being 'devoid of the geniality and humour of his race, he sported a bilious face and splenetic manners'.[31]

Russell's vocal advocacy of compulsory land purchase did not endear him to many of his more conservative unionist colleagues either, especially when he began to run candidates against sitting unionist MPs with insufficient affection for land purchase of any kind, voluntary or compulsory. An early and ominous success for Russell came in early 1902, when the independent unionist candidate he sponsored, James Woods, narrowly defeated (by 147 votes) the official unionist candidate, Colonel R. F. Wallace, in a by-election in East Down. 'Russellism' (an 'insidious internal threat'[32]) became a dirty word among some mainstream Ulster unionists, who falsely implied, or overtly asserted, that the man himself was a latter-day Lundy prepared to sell the pass on the Union as contentedly as he would force out the country's landlords. Russell, despite making common cause on agrarian issues with the nationalist enemy (the UIL, for example, offered Woods its support in East Down), did so in a context where the issue of Home Rule (temporarily laid to rest by the failure of Gladstone's second Home Rule bill in 1893) was largely irrelevant. Privately, Russell acknowledged that compulsory acquisition of estates was not within the bounds of practical politics. However, his energetic Ulster Farmers' and Labourers' Union campaign was designed to force the government to introduce a viable measure of voluntary purchase.

Compulsory acquisition was also favoured by the UIL. In addition to ensuring that all Irish farmers would be offered the opportunity to purchase the land they worked, a mandatory regime effectively guaranteed a lower purchase price. The demand for compulsory purchase united the UIL and T. W. Russell's supporters. Landlords, on the other hand, could see where compulsory purchase would lead. As well as reducing the sale value of their land, many had no desire to sell their entire estates and some were determined not to sell at all. Balfour's government (he became prime minister in July 1902), not unexpectedly, sided with the landlords.

When the original landlord selections of Shawe-Taylor declined to participate in the proposed colloquium – Smith Barry provocatively described the very idea of a conference as 'capitulating to the enemy' – their places were taken by four willing aristocrats led by Lord Dunraven (the conference is often named after him) and Lord Mayo. O'Brien, Redmond, Russell and Timothy Harrington led for the tenants. Proceedings, which began in mid-December 1902, were exceptionally business-like for an Irish talking shop. In a matter of weeks, proposals were advanced to government.* The most noteworthy of these concerned the transfer of property from landlord to tenant, 'the substitution,' wrote Dunraven, 'of an occupying proprietary in lieu of a system of dual ownership'.[33] The conference recommended that the gap between what the landlord demanded for a holding and what his tenant was prepared to pay should be made up from government funds. Previous negative experiences with interest-bearing stocks as a form of payment to the sellers meant that these transactions were to be cash only. However, given that the loans were to be repaid by tenants over a period of time, the funding was raised by exchequer borrowing rather than taxation. This was in the form of an issue of Guaranteed Land Stock at 2¾ per cent per annum. This course of action would have negative repercussions in the years ahead.

In formulating a new land purchase bill, Wyndham wanted to ensure that selling up was an attractive proposition. Landlords were to be given a 12 per cent bonus, over and above the price agreed with their tenants, to expedite their (entirely voluntary) removal. Negotiations would also take place estate by estate, rather than undergoing the potentially more fraught and tedious process of landlords hammering out agreements with individual tenants. To persuade landlords to remain in the country, they were to be entitled to sell their demesne lands to the Estates Commissioners appointed to supervise the entire process. They could then lease back their houses and contiguous demesne lands on the same annuity terms as their tenants. Some were thus able to replace crippling mortgages with the 'easy terms' available to the tenants. Landlords were also allowed to retain, where they already existed (with certain limitations), 'any right of hunting, shooting, fishing, and taking game'.[34]

* Dunraven claims in his autobiography that one of the reasons for making haste was that Dillon and Davitt were out of the country (in the USA) at the time and the stimulus to come to as rapid an agreement as possible was their imminent return and the necessity to present both of those influential land warriors with a *fait accompli* (Earl of Dunraven, *Past Times and Pastimes*, Volume 2 (London, 1922), 11).

Wyndham was also conscious that the entire package had to appeal to the tenant, so the annuity that was applied to the purchase was to be reduced from 4 per cent to 3.25 per cent and the period of repayment was definitively extended to two generations, with the annuities to continue for 68½ years. Of equal importance, from O'Brien's point of view at least, was the provision that untenanted lands could be bought up and passed on to recently evicted tenants – described by Dunraven as 'the wounded soldiers of the Land War'[35] – or to the 'land poor', in order to create viable holdings. Gladstone's 1881 act was also invoked when his creation, the Land Commission, was permitted to acquire estates for redistribution.

Wyndham experienced considerable difficulty in forcing his proposals through Cabinet. Colonial secretary Joseph Chamberlain and the 'Liberal Unionist' rump which had adhered to the Tory party after the failure of Gladstone's 1886 Home Rule legislation were opposed. It took Balfour's support to carry the measure. Given the arduous internal struggle for acceptance of the purchase programme, the chief secretary was chagrined at the response to his bill of a number of prominent Irish nationalists. O'Brien's support was assured from the outset. A national convention of the UIL also approved the thrust of the bill, subject to a number of amendments. Redmond described the legislation in the Commons as 'the greatest effort yet made to settle the Irish land question',[36] kept up a non-stop political dialogue with Wyndham in London and managed also to secure the support of a majority of the Irish Party MPs.

However, three vital antagonists were opposed to Wyndham's panacea: Dillon, Davitt and Thomas Sexton. Sexton – once a leading Irish party MP, now increasingly at odds with his former colleagues – had at his disposal the editorial columns of the *Freeman's Journal*, of whose board he was chairman. All three of these hugely influential figures made their opposition to the legislation public, though Dillon agreed to abide by the decision of his party to support the bill. All three were united in their view that the deal was drastically overgenerous to the exiting landlords, whom Dillon preferred to see 'driven out of

Ireland'[37] rather than permitted to leave with their silver spoons intact.

Beyond that very basic point of agreement, the three men parted company when it came to the supplementary reasons for their opposition. Sexton's auxiliary motives were, perhaps, the most ignoble, derived largely from personal pique. He had become an embittered and marginalised figure since his quixotic decision to resign as an MP in 1896. He was increasingly alienated from his former colleagues, and he wielded the *Freeman's Journal* like a longsword, cutting down to size the 'tall poppies' of the Irish Party. He was also personally aggrieved because O'Brien had reneged on a promise to consult him.[38] 'For this,' wrote Tim Healy caustically, 'he will never be forgiven.'[39] The *Journal* was a consistent critic of the scheme, demanding that the price tenants pay for their holdings be set at around two-thirds of the sums agreed by the Land Conference.

Dillon had travelled quite a distance since his enthusiastic endorsement of the Plan of Campaign, with all its potential to endanger the IPP/Liberal alliance and Parnell's drive for Home Rule. As noted by Wilfrid Scawen Blunt in his 1903 diary, Dillon had now developed a thoroughly utilitarian streak when it came to land issues, believing that 'the land trouble is a weapon in Nationalist hands, and that to settle it finally would be to risk Home Rule'.[40] Dillon saw Wyndham as a Greek Trojan War commander and his purchase bill as an outsized wooden horse. His fears cannot have been allayed by T. W. Russell's assertions on public platforms in Ulster that 'compulsory purchase would dilute any movement for Home Rule'.[41]

Davitt, still a staunch acolyte of the socialist economics of Henry George, had an abiding and lonely faith in the efficacy of land nationalisation. He was of the view that the impetus on the part of the tenants' representatives for coming to terms with the landlords was largely a function of a failure of nerve. They 'took fright, and went into the land conference', according to Davitt, because the leadership of the UIL faced a return to the dock, and a potential four-figure damages award, after the Roscommon landlord Lord de Freyne began a legal action against them for a boycotting campaign of which he was the victim. De Freyne had refused to sell his land to the CDB after that body purchased the neighbouring 90,000-acre estate of Lord Dillon. Disturbances on de Freyne's lands began when his tenants became aware that annuities payable by tenants to the CDB on the Dillon estate were markedly lower than de Freyne's rents.

One of Davitt's beefs, which might have resonated with O'Brien, given his own intimate knowledge of the real grievances of labourers and small farmers in the west of Ireland, was the missed opportunity of coming to grips with the fundamental issue of extensive grazier lands. 'No clause was inserted,' he wrote, 'to encourage tillage industry by means that would make the buying of grazing lands conditional upon the compulsory allocation of some percentage of such soil by the purchasers to the employment of labour.'[42]

However, the thesis Davitt advanced publicly, as he beheld the remote prospect of land nationalisation crumble in the face of tenant/landlord eagerness to divide the cake being baked by Wyndham, was that the price being paid to the landlords was simply too high: 'The terms secured for the owners in the joint agreement represented the reconquest by Lord Dunraven [of] almost all that the land movement and the land acts had won during the preceding twenty years.'[43]

Despite the obligatory displays of parliamentary brinkmanship on all sides, once Chamberlain 'made up his mind to a glum silence'[44] and Redmond had secured at least some of his cherished amendments, the bill became law in August 1903. It was an immediate success with the Irish peasantry, akin to the race to the Land Courts in 1881. Samuel Hussey, whose memoir, *The Reminiscences of an Irish Land Agent*, was published the year after the passage of the Wyndham act, reckoned that tenants who bought out their landlord and paid their annuities were getting a discount of 20 per cent on their rent, which had been the intention all along. Of course, the legislation sounded the death knell of the land agent. They took 3 per cent of the value of their landlord's transactions into an unpredictable retirement.[45]

Hussey under escort

While the stampede to cash in and cash out was instant and prolonged, the 1903 Land Purchase Act soon became a victim of bureaucratic infighting. It was almost beaten to death by a Treasury that blanched at the scale of the financial transfers implied in the legislation. The Whitehall mandarins ensured that the funds made available for the purchase of the estates of the willing were restricted to £5 million a year. At that rate, it would take more than twenty years for the allocated sum to be spent. Applications continued to pour in despite this restriction and by 1908, while £28 million had been advanced, bids to the value of £56 million were still outstanding.

By 1909, almost half the land mass of Ireland was yet to be transferred. The Tories were no longer in power and another major complication threatened to bring Wyndham's house of cards tumbling down. The market value of the £33 million in Guaranteed Stock, issued in 1903 to fund Wyndham's signature scheme, had significantly depreciated. To continue with the 1903 arrangements might potentially involve a loss of £8 million to the Treasury. In 1909, Asquith's Liberal government, with Augustine Birrell as chief secretary, altered the terms of the land purchase legislation to bypass some of the financial obligations incurred by its predecessors. He was, by implication, siding with the Dillonite analysis of Wyndham's legislation 'that landlords were being grossly overpaid for their tenanted estates'.[46] One of the key elements of Birrell's template was that payment to landlords was to be no longer in cash but in the form of government stock paying 3 per cent per annum. This constituted an immediate disincentive to landlords to part with their estates. In addition, the landlord 'bonus' was reduced in most cases, no longer a guaranteed sum but one paid on a graduated scale, depending on the value the landlord secured from the tenants for his land. The greater the number of 'years purchase' received, the smaller the landlord bonus, an inverse ratio arrangement that originally had been envisaged back in 1903 and had then been revised.

Land War veteran Andrew Kettle, however, identified no particular bounty for the tenant in Birrell's legislation. 'The Birrell Land Act of 1909,' he wrote, 'was not put forward in the interests of the tenants, nor in any Irish interest, but was merely for the relief of the British Treasury.'[47] Tenants were required

Augustine Birrell

to pay an additional annual 0.25 per cent on their annuities, for example. However, these demerits were, to some extent at least, mitigated by the fact that the new bill offered additional assistance to the CDB, introduced an element of compulsory purchase and provided land for labourers.

The 1903 and 1909 legislation took a wrecking ball to the concept of dual ownership. All told, 256,000 farms were purchased by their tenants at a cost to the exchequer (recoverable from the purchasers) of £82 million. The peak years were 1906–8, when almost 100,000 holdings changed hands.[48] The entire process came grinding to a halt shortly after the assassination of Archduke Franz Ferdinand and Duchess Sophie at Sarajevo in 1914. When it resumed, after independence and partition, landlords (north and south) would be compelled to sell by the governments of the Irish Free State and of Northern Ireland. By the time the traditional European warring parties resumed hostilities in 1939, 'landlords in Ireland were a memory'.[49]

The ultimate legacy of half a century of land purchase was the transfer of just over 122,000 holdings and 2,715,000 acres in what would become Northern Ireland (90 per cent of its agricultural land) and 350,000 holdings comprising almost 12 million acres, in what became the Irish Free State. In the latter case, 3 million acres (around 100,000 holdings) remained to be dealt with by the incoming Cosgrave Cumann na nGaedheal government of the 1920s.

And so the contented Irish peasant, now primed to become an owner-occupier of his holding, wandered off into the sunlit uplands and lived happily ever after. In the words of the habitually cynical Tim Healy, 'the act undid the confiscations of James I, Cromwell and William III'.[50] However, since there are three chapters remaining in this narrative, readers will already have concluded that such an idyllic vision is utterly fallacious. Andrew Kettle ruefully described the Wyndham settlement as 'a one-sided transaction which has not stopped the decay of the country'.[51]

As the acerbic historian of the Irish land struggle Barbara Solow tartly put it in her revisionist assessment of the entire corpus of late nineteenth-century land legislation, 'it is ironic to view land purchase as a solution to anything ... Thirty years of land tenure legislation, and in the west there were still tenants living as they had in 1870, huddled in a hovel, clothed in rags, on a diet of potatoes, with the great hope of meat once a year, at Christmas.' Solow was critiquing what she viewed as a perverse obsession with rent reductions – a solution to a set of complex land issues that 'prevented [landlords] from investing in Irish land'[52] – as well as the failure of imagination that led to a rolling cycle of agricultural depressions, and a solution predicated on the simplistic removal of the Irish *junker* class instead of the injection of levels of capital that might have led to sustainable economic development in rural Ireland. Did the process of 'peasant proprietorship' ask the wrong questions? Was it the case that 'the land settlement was in fact the settlement of the land tenure question only'?[53]

That hardened opponent of the land purchase programme, John Dillon, acknowledged to Wilfrid Scawen Blunt in 1910 that 'Wyndham's land bill has had the effect of changing the whole character of the peasantry. Instead of being careless, idle and improvident, they have become like the French peasantry, industrial and economical.'[54] Dillon, however, was ignoring the bigger picture. The Wyndham wave had lifted a number of boats, but in so doing had inundated the leakier vessels so they were not fit for purpose or 'purchase'.

While the Wyndham and Birrell acts of 1903 and 1909 'confirmed the decline of landlord power'[55] and made a decisive dent in the dominance of the gentry in the Irish tenurial system, they failed to become 'the final solution to the land question',[56] because that was not the ultimate purpose of the legislation. The sickness at the centre of Irish rural life was endemic poverty. Land purchase did precious little to address that issue. Its primary intention – certainly in the Tory iteration – was to end, once and for all, the toxic tenant/landlord conflict by offering a dignified exit to a largely redundant (and increasingly strapped) Irish ascendancy, and to transfer economic power from that aristocracy to a powerful *kulak* class. After that happened, it would be up to the *kulaks* to shift for themselves and to keep the peace.

The exercise of power in local government had already been handed over by the gentry to the bourgeoisie with the creation of county councils in 1898. This final grand gesture, a major extension of the Tory pacification policy, would, it was hoped, create a new cohort of grateful and conservative – and possibly even Conservative – owner-occupiers with a pecuniary interest in suppressing resistance to the status quo. It was also expected, as Dillon feared, to undermine nationalist demands for a potent devolved government. The rationale was simple: peasant proprietorship would 'make the peasant more conservative than the Conservatives'.[57]

What the Wyndham act did achieve was to raise naïve expectations of an unprecedented transfer of land from the wealthy to the impoverished. It was the same sort of unrealistic anticipation that had surrounded the Catholic Relief Act of 1829. While the 1903 legislation was infinitely more beneficial in numerical terms than Catholic emancipation, it also left hundreds of thousands in limbo. While small farmers might be able to purchase their own farm, they were still unable to buy additional land to ensure economic viability. The voracious graziers made certain of that, acquiring acres of tillage and turning it into pasture. Likewise, labourers found themselves still on the sidelines, with the added burden that, as pastoral farming expanded, their job opportunities shrank. The 'Saxon landlord' may have been replaced by the 'Celtic peasant' (the words of Michael Davitt), but for much of the population of rural Ireland – the landless, and the farmer with less than ten acres – the controlled flight of the symbolic object of their resentment had achieved little or nothing. The new Irish rural elite did not have titles or homes in Mayfair. They had herds of cattle and bank accounts large enough to ensure that they could continue indefinitely bidding up the price of the eleven-month land on offer from the earls and marquesses who remained *in situ*, or on any newly purchased holdings being 'flipped' by their owners.

Although it was seismic in its impact, one of the consequences of the Wyndham/Birrell legislation was merely to set the scene for the next major agrarian conflict. That engagement would see the landlords watching from the sidelines as they either sold up or offered pretexts for refusing to do so. The Ranch War, while not exactly a return to the days of Caravat and Shanavest hostility, pitched grazier against labourer and cottier.

The era of landlord versus tenant was coming to an end.

16

'Use the hazel': the Ranch War, 1906–9

'A Policeman's Lament'

'I am sorry to say the times have changed …
For many an Irish Peeler,
But now the people claim their rights,
Too long have been denied them,
Their patience met with scant reward,
The land must be divided,
From north to south, from east to west,
The cries from all the branches,
Is "Drive the bullocks off the land
And then split up the ranches."'[1]

(extract from a ballad composed by James Smith of
Faughalstown, Co. Westmeath in 1906–7)

9 February 1909, the 'Baton Convention'

Joseph Devlin had promised to 'give O'Brien his Waterloo',[2] and
the Grand Master of the Ancient Order of Hibernians (AOH)
was being as good as his word. This gathering would be a straight
faction fight between Belfast and Cork. The 'Mollies' from
Ulster had come armed to the teeth, and in numbers that would
overpower any Munster resistance.

The instructions to the AOH 'stewards' guarding the doors –
and allegedly being paid an honorarium of ten shillings apiece for

their services – were clear. O'Brien's supporters were to be kept out of the Mansion House and beaten up if necessary in order to ensure that they did not gain entry. Devlin's Hibernian goons had arrived by special train from Belfast, had paraded in military formation to Dawson Street and were now guarding the entrances to the venue hosting this national convention of the UIL. Inside the building, their confreres were armed with batons and bludgeons 'fastened to their wrists with thongs of leather',[3] which had been issued for the occasion at the behest of Grand Master Devlin. The 'Special Constables'[4] of the 'Mollies', however, were not alone in spoiling for a fight. Equally hostile were the cattle drivers from the midlands, who had arrived bearing their own weapons of choice – hazel sticks – also with the intention of routing the O'Brienites.

If any of the Corkmen managed to get past the Hibernian Praetorian guard, plan B would come into effect. None of O'Brien's supporters, and certainly not the man himself, was to be allowed a hearing. This convention would be carefully stage-managed and the 3,000 UIL delegates – which included a number of priests – would be shepherded towards approval of chief secretary Birrell's new land bill. The motion to rubber-stamp the curtailment of the funding for further land purchase – lest the burden fall on Irish ratepayers if the distribution of largesse was to continue at its current pace – would be debated and then accepted by acclamation by the well-primed delegates. The alternative, the delegates were to be assured, would bankrupt the country.

John Redmond rose and spoke in favour of the motion to support the corrective Liberal government legislation. He was listened to in a respectful silence broken only by occasional bursts of eager applause. The reception afforded the principal opponent of the bill, William O'Brien, was in sharp contrast. According to *The Times* of 10 February 1909, 'when he began to speak there was a violent manifestation of hostility'. The *Irish Independent*, whose editorial line, in contrast to that of the rival *Freeman's Journal*, was one of opposition to the Liberal proposals, wrote that 'an organised attempt was made by a band of rowdies and Ribbonmen imported from Belfast and armed with bludgeons, to prevent Mr. O'Brien … from being heard at the Convention'.

When O'Brien attempted to speak, some of the audience members broke into pre-arranged 'obscene choruses'. These were spiteful anti-Semitic taunts aimed at his wife, Sophie.[5] Alongside these racist chants, 'whistles were blown, feet were stamped, floor and seats were whacked with sticks'.[6] It was clear that O'Brien's point of view – with which the delegates were already familiar – was not going to be allowed an airing. O'Brien valiantly attempted to make himself heard, refusing to surrender the floor for almost an hour. He had faced down howling Orange demonstrations on Ulster election platforms in the 1880s, and now he was being forced to endure the bellowed insults of members of his own political party and of the organisation he had created in 1898. 'It was the melodious accent of Belfast that reigned,' wrote O'Brien in 1910, 'wherever a delegate was to be hit on the head or a speaker guillotined.' When the Cork MP Eugene Crean, a supporter of O'Brien, rose to appeal for silence and a fair hearing, he was immediately pounced upon 'by a group of brawny Belfast "Mollies" and dragged back by main force'. A red-faced Devlin loudly demanded that his henchmen 'throw the fellow out'. When a number of other O'Brien supporters on the platform party attempted to intervene, another Cork MP, D. D. Sheehan, was struck in the face. North Cork parliamentarian James Gilhooly, a veteran of the Fenian Rising of 1867, was, according to O'Brien's account, then assaulted by a baton-swinging 'Mollie' and advised that 'I'll slaughter you if you say another word'.[7]

Not even W. S. Gilbert and his half-Irish collaborator, Arthur Sullivan, could have done justice to the scene. Sheehan, many years after he had recovered from the injuries and indignities to which he was subjected, wrote that 'it would be quite a comedy of Irish topsy-turvydom were it not, in fact, such a disastrous tragedy'.[8]

In the framing and the aftermath of the Wyndham concessions of 1903, O'Brien had often invoked the principles of 'conference, conciliation and consent' above those of the 'confrontation' to which he had often adhered in the past. He had reached out to unionists, such as T. W. Russell, in an attempted revival of Gavan

Duffy's 'League of North and South'. Now he was to pay the price for that *rapprochement* with loyalism, and for his tweaking of the noses of Redmond, Dillon and the rising force in the Irish party, Joseph Devlin. The West Belfast MP and 'Officer Commanding' the Molly Maguires – the newly assertive northern-based, virulently Catholic, Ancient Order of Hibernians, a startling and aggressive manifestation of 'Catholic-Orangeism'[9] – was secretary of, and power-broker within, the UIL. While there was undoubtedly a 'conference' on 9 February 1909 in Dublin's Mansion House, there was no 'conciliation' whatsoever, and the 'consent' did not include O'Brien and his Cork-based support. The overwhelming decision of the convention was to apply the brakes to exchequer expenditures on land purchase, under the Liberal threat of crippling fiscal implications for Ireland itself.

As far as the vanquished O'Brien was concerned, this effectively put an end to the process that he, Dunraven and Wyndham had initiated in 1903.

'The degenerate offspring of an effete landlordism': the Ranch War, 1906–9

'Fences I note are being made
On holdings both big and small;
Oh! the Lord knows I'm afraid
There won't be land for us all.'[10]

(a verse of a Ranch War ballad 'Back to the Land', as recited
to the Irish Folklore Commission by Roscommon farmer
Patrick Dayer)

The Wyndham act had been a roaring success. Tenants, in droves, were acquiring their land and becoming masters of their own fate. Peasant proprietorship was the logical and final solution to the Sisyphean Irish land question.

It took only a couple of years, however, before wisdom prevailed and disillusionment set in. Land purchase was an attractive but only partial resolution of a sore that continued to run. Ownership of your own land was undoubtedly a boon, provided it was decent land and the acreage was sufficiently extensive to cater to the needs of a farming family. In many instances, this was not the case, and 'small tenants became all too aware of the inadequacy of their meagre holdings and turned their attention to land redistribution'.[11] Owner-occupied holdings of dubious viability – albeit now being worked at an average 20 per cent discount on the twice-yearly rental payments – were just as unsustainable as they had been before the intervention of Wyndham. With landlords (rather optimistically) seen as increasingly irrelevant, attention shifted to the large grazier farms, active participants in a market economy from which smallholders were locked out and which provided little or no employment to landless labourers. Thus, a perverse consequence of Wyndham's act was 'the stimulation its acceptance of land redistribution as a means of relieving congestion … was giving to anti-grazier agitation across the country'.[12]

Be careful what you wish for.

The Ranch War is sometimes referred to as the Third Land War. The conflict had little in common with the struggles of the 1880s, although it was an indirect descendant. In reality, it more truly marked the definitive end of the unlikely alliance that propelled the agitation driving the First Land War of 1879–82.

The fact is that, in order to wage a ranch war, there is a palpable need for the presence of ranches. These proliferated throughout the country in the early years of the twentieth century, after the sustained post-Famine shift from tillage to pasture, especially in north Munster, the midlands/north Leinster and east Connacht. But they were especially abundant in the north midlands, where a goodly percentage of the bovine population of the country took up temporary residence, was fattened on the rich grasslands of Meath and Westmeath, was then exported – generally 'on the hoof', before violently meeting their end in an English abattoir and finding their way to the dining rooms of those who could afford to eat prime beef.

The county of Meath certainly had no shortage of productive land. Simply owning even a modest farm in the rolling plains of the Royal County (so-called because of the presence of *Tara na Rí*, home of the ancient Irish High Kings) almost invariably represented a victory in the lottery of life. First, however, you had to acquire that farm, and therein lay the difficulty.

For a start, there was the problem of the nature of agricultural activity in Meath. It was, by the second decade of the twentieth century, overwhelmingly pastoral. Potatoes and other root crops were cultivated by 'the little people' of the county, the relatively small number of local subsistence farmers. Prosperous Meath farmers did not grow vegetables; they fattened livestock. In 1911, the three Irish Poor Law Unions with the greatest proportion of their agricultural land given over to grass were the Meath unions of Dunshaughlin (80.6 per cent), Navan (71.4 per cent) and Kells (70.4 per cent). A fourth Meath union, Trim, had dropped out of the top five only recently (in 1901).[13] In the words of Irish-Argentine travel writer William Bulfin in his *Rambles in Eirinn* – a work based on a bicycle ride through the country in 1902–3 – Meath was a 'fertile desert ... from which man had banished himself and into which he had sent the beasts to take his place'.[14]

Bulfin's description is echoed in the analysis of the German economist Moritz Bonn, a long-time Irish resident. In his 1906 volume *Modern Ireland and Her Agrarian Problem*, he wrote:

> Many parts of the country, especially in the Counties Kildare, Meath and Dublin, are nothing but grassy deserts ... There is scarcely a human being to be seen, for the cattle graze without a herdsman in the hedged-in fields ... Hundreds and thousands of ruined cottages are scattered about, dwellings in which human beings formerly dwelt. It is these wide 'grazing ranches' which have made Ireland into a land of great silence.[15]

Consolidation of midlands farms had begun in the decade immediately after the Famine, with more than a thousand evictions taking place between 1851 and 1861. North Meath MP

Patrick White reckoned that population density in the county was around one person for every ten acres, and for every human being there were ten bullocks. Fellow nationalist MP John Nugent, addressing a Meath county convention of the AOH, reckoned that one-fifth of the acreage of Meath was let under the 'eleven month' system and, if given over to tillage, would have been capable of supporting almost five thousand families, or around twenty-five thousand people.[16] So the county's wealthy graziers, in addition to their other 'crimes', were catalysts for depopulation.

Meath – as well as neighbouring Westmeath, and much of east Connacht – belonged to the 'rancher'. There were around 130 affluent graziers at the turn of the century who farmed thousands of acres of Meath land. They lived in sequestered grandeur: 'the physical isolation of their homes may have reflected their isolation in the community, or in the case of non-resident graziers their absence … They were for many identified with the landlords, to whom they were a godsend.'[17] The reason these graziers ('props of the landlord system'[18]) were a 'godsend' to the early twentieth-century relics of the aristocracy was because their tenancies obligingly protected landlords from the malign attentions of the Land Commission and the compulsory purchase clauses built into the legislation introduced by Irish Chief Secretary Augustine Birrell in 1909, while simultaneously negating the terms of the tenant-oriented 1881 Gladstone Land Act because of the duration of the contract between them.

Rural folklore had never relinquished the image of the Mephistophelian landlord, but by the second decade of the twentieth century he had been joined by his equally satanic enabler, the grazier or rancher, the latter being all the more loathsome a creature because of his enhanced local visibility and non-patrician status. The landlord no longer stood alone; there were 'intervening levels of exploitation represented by the graziers'.[19] To the rancher, land was merely an input. 'Unlike the tenant farmer, the rancher generally lacked any sense of ancestral or customary ties to the land, and his economic behaviour was less constrained by the traditions of rural society.'[20]

This was reflected in the landlord/grazier adherence to the

'eleven month' system. To circumvent the dual ownership features of nineteenth-century Gladstonian legislation, landlords would auction parcels of land on these short-term leases. They had often obtained a truer market value for their untenanted acres when the bidding concluded. Farms rented via longer leases were not as lucrative and were subject to the provisions of a raft of inhibiting land acts passed since 1881. Under the terms of these auction contracts, the renter was obliged to vacate the rented land after eleven months. In practice, most graziers would vacate and then roll over the contract by agreeing to resume their tenancy – after an interval of one month – on similar terms. They were not even, in reality, often obliged to vacate, because the fallow month, in November or December, fell outside the normal grazing season, when the renting grazier was likely to have disposed of the cattle or sheep being fattened on his ranch.

This system permitted the grazier to vary his land usage depending on the state of the livestock trade. He could easily opt in and opt out of his avocation according to how the market fluctuated; his capital was not committed to the same degree as that of the tillage farmer; and his cattle or sheep were far more profitable (per acre) than the potatoes, oats, barley, turnips or leeks of the neighbouring peasant. While the tillage farmer could reckon on costs of between £17 and £23 an acre (one of his main inputs being labour) the grazing equivalent was between £4 and £8 an acre.[21]

'Eleven month' rentals also allowed professional or business people to dip their toes in the livestock market without the necessity of assuming responsibility for anything as awkward and messy as an actual home farm. They were referred to by one contemporary observer as 'Irish Kulaks'[22] or 'grass grabbers',[23] and by more recent commentators as 'shopkeeper-graziers'[24] who 'exercised almost as powerful an influence over tenants as did many landlords'.[25] Their frequent stranglehold on the allocation of credit in rural Ireland – many had a lucrative sideline as moneylenders or 'gombeen men' – often conferred 'an immunity of sorts' upon their activities. The nationalist politician and journalist Stephen Gwynn, on vacation in Connemara in 1908, observed that most of the local graziers were shopkeepers who took up 'land for stock farming in a country where hardly any cottier or tillage farmer has a holding fit to live on'.[26]

For the small farmer, one actually committed to working the soil rather than operating as a cattle 'jobber', the 'eleven month' system had the effect of shutting him out of the market for land. He could not compete with the short-term rental rates the dealer or the dilettante were prepared to pay when parcels of land came up for auction. The *Midland Tribune*, based in King's County (Offaly), was scathing when it came to the societal impact of the 'eleven month' system. '[It] ruined families, decimated [*sic*] homesteads, retarded agricultural progress, filled the emigrant's ship and populated the workhouses.'[27] But the *Midland Tribune*, in common with many provincial newspapers, made its own unique contribution to the problem. On the page facing that excoriating editorial, the newspaper ran three advertisements for the auctioning of grazing lands on 'eleven month' terms.

What of the timing of the Ranch War, this new insurrection against perceived privilege? It is no coincidence that the agitation in north Munster, much of Connacht and the Leinster midlands began less than three years after the passage of the Wyndham Land Purchase Act of 1903. By 1906, the initial spurt of enthusiasm for a peasant proprietary had been followed by a more realistic apprehension that 'there was little point in giving tenants the land if the size and fertility of their farms were insufficient to provide a secure and reasonable livelihood'.[28] Viability was not guaranteed despite the almost uniform 20 per cent discount on rent that came with the move to annuity payments. Tenant purchase, to be allowed to work, was going to have to be followed by some form of land redistribution. This meant that, while the typhoon was passing over the heads of the landlords, the graziers were in the eye of the storm.

The response of the landless and the small subsistence farmers was to opt for direct action. This often took the form of 'cattle driving': the enforced (and usually nocturnal) removal of a grazier's livestock. It was slightly more humane than the 'cattle houghing' of the Land War, in which livestock were deliberately maimed, although that barbarous practice continued as well.

Driving would often be accompanied by damage to property (especially gates), reminiscent of the anti-enclosure 'levelling' activities of the eighteenth century. Gates were often not simply removed but put beyond use, as in the case of the cattle drivers of Behey, Co. Donegal. There, in 1908, when 'an outsider' was allocated a portion of an estate divided by the Congested Districts Board, his cattle were quietly removed from his land, along with his gates. The cattle were driven elsewhere, and the gates 'lie buried in Behey Lough', according to local folklore sources.[29]

While cattle driving became the punishment *du jour* of the opponents of pasture, it was not the only weapon in their armoury. The boycott, while not as ubiquitous as it had been in the 1880s, was still a useful artillery piece. Between December 1905 and February 1909, the incidence of boycotting increased by over 400 per cent (from 174 to 889). Cases of agrarian crime (rising from 234 in 1906 to 576 in 1908) included a variety of more serious offences.[30] As the Trinity College, Dublin law professor H. Brougham Leech noted in 1912, although cattle driving was, in effect, the new boycotting, 'it is not to be assumed that other measures of terrorism and destruction were neglected. Arson, the burning of hayricks, firing into dwelling houses, spiking meadows, the mutilation of horses and cows, the destruction of turf, the damaging of machinery, and various other forms of lawless violence began to increase and multiply.'[31]

The grazier Henry Persse of Woodville in Co. Galway, victim of a highly effective boycott, was located in the netherworld between landlord and tenant. Persse, a former officer with the Indian police, had come into a convenient legacy, enabling him to take out a lengthy lease on a substantial Galway property. He, according to a largely tongue-in-cheek *New York Times* article of March 1908, had 'been thrilling fashionable audiences in Tory drawing rooms with a tale of his alleged sufferings'. Persse gave the *Times* its headline when he described himself to the newspaper's reporter, with considerable hyperbole, as 'the most persecuted man in Ireland' (the interview took place in the secure surroundings of the drawing room of the Duchess of St Albans in London). The violence to which Persse was subjected, however, seems to have escalated no further than 'a stone thrown through a fanlight in Woodville House and a great deal of subsequent shooting on the part of Persse and his servants', leading the *Times* reporter to observe that 'his posing as a martyr has caused laughter in many quarters'. Persse, yet to experience the delights of cattle driving, nonetheless railed against the boycotters:

> They want the land themselves. Till they get it, it shall be boycotted. It shall be made so useless that nobody will take it, and after a certain time the holder will consent to sell to the Land Commission ... I have come to England to bring these facts before the public and to arouse sympathy with those who are suffering like myself. If I cannot succeed, I may as well die.[32]

A refinement of the boycott, one familiar from aborted Land War asset sales, was also employed as a weapon against 'eleven month' auctions. In December 1908, for example, the *Meath Chronicle* reported that an 'eleven month' letting that was due to take place had mysteriously fallen through. An auctioneer had arrived in the village of Kilmainhamwood by train, from Enfield in the south of the county. He was there to bring down the gavel on the transaction and to transfer a large plot of land to the highest-bidding local grazier. Before he could do so, however, he was intercepted and forcibly informed that he was not welcome in the area. He took the information to heart and the next train back to Enfield. No sale took place.[33] It was, on occasions, only the equally forcible intervention of the RIC which ensured that such auctions went ahead.

The RIC also took a dim view of the practice of cattle driving and challenged the drivers on the rare occasions they received inside information that permitted them to do so. One such instance resulted in tragedy and was memorialised in a field near Riverstown, Co. Sligo. There, according to local folklore, a young man, John Stenson, was shot dead when challenged by the RIC in October 1908, as he and a number of his neighbours removed cattle from a farm in the townland of Ardcumber.[34]

Leading the cattle driving movement from Westminster was that scourge of the grazier, the highly idiosyncratic nationalist

MP Laurence Ginnell from Westmeath – 'the man who refused to take off his hat in the House of Commons'.[35] Son of a farm labourer from Delvin, failed barrister, founding secretary of the UIL, Ginnell was elected as an Irish Parliamentary Party MP in 1906, but never quite managed to settle into the life of amenable lobby fodder. He first came to the attention of the House of Commons with a series of pointed questions on the 1907 theft of the Irish 'Crown Jewels' from Dublin Castle. The tone of his queries suggested that he might have some inkling as to the identity of the thieves, and that they (and the jewels) were to be found nestling in the arms of the British establishment. Ginnell, 'the most tempestuous of ... stormy petrels', was frequently ejected from the chamber of the House of Commons for a variety of misdemeanours, was popularly and facetiously known as 'the member for Ireland' and often cut a lonely figure on the Commons benches, all the more so when he became an advocate for women's suffrage. He was one of the few Irish MPs – William Redmond was another unexpected and honourable exception – to do so.

Laurence Ginnell

Ginnell's enthusiastic support for the cattle drivers of the Irish midlands, and his frequent appearances on public platforms to give expression to this support – some of the platforms being located close to the ranches of particularly obnoxious graziers – was enough on its own to warrant confrontation with the Irish Party leadership. However, he added fuel to the fire in 1909, when he demanded to see his party's financial accounts. Access was denied, and Ginnell and the IPP parted company. He then sat as an independent nationalist until 1918, when he made a timely leap into the arms of Sinn Féin and became a member of the first Dáil after the Republican landslide in the December election of that year.

Ginnell was abetted in his campaign by John FitzGibbon, a Roscommon councillor, and John Hayden, editor of the *Westmeath Examiner*, as well as by the aforementioned South Meath MP, David Sheehy. All four men addressed a number of anti-grazier meetings in Connacht and north Leinster between 1906 and 1909. Ginnell was no stranger to the inside of a prison cell, and his first period of incarceration began in December 1907. He was committed to jail for incitement to cattle driving. He remained in prison for four months until his release on the grounds of ill-health. His imprisonment seems to have done little to inhibit his enthusiasm for mayhem. Two years later, he was, once again, charged with incitement. Ironically, the punitive repercussions for Ginnell of his vocal support for the drivers were often worse than for those actively involved in the driving of cattle. Few of them were ever apprehended and faced jury trials. Most of those arrested were dealt with by magistrates, and the victims generally overcame the trauma of having their animals relocated by claiming financial compensation from local authorities. In 1907, a mere ten cases of cattle driving came before Irish juries, and one conviction was secured. In 1908, a single case had been tried and a conviction obtained, while in 1909, Birrell informed the House of Commons that, 'No case of the kind was tried before a jury'.[36]

Although the intensity of the Ranch War declined after 1909, the practice of driving continued up to and beyond the onset of the

Great War in August 1914. In November of that year, for example, members of the RIC were obliged to draw their weapons to disperse an estimated crowd of up to 1,000 people (accompanied by a band) who fully intended, if permitted to do so, to drive cattle off the estate of Lord Digby near Geashill in King's County. Two years later, in July 1916, up to 1,000 British soldiers – no doubt peeved to be missing the Somme offensive – with the aid of 100 RIC constables, had to be deployed on the Galway/Roscommon border to prevent further drives, after seventeen RIC men were wounded in an altercation as they attempted to return driven livestock to the land of a local grazier.

The slogan favoured by the cattle drivers, and Ginnell's watchword, 'the land for the people, and the bullock for the road', was an ironic variant of the famous battle cry of the Land League, 'the land for the people'. Another popular slogan at the time was 'use the hazel', the sturdy branch of a hazel tree being the instrument most commonly adopted by cattle drovers and cattle drivers alike for the licit and illicit movement of beasts.[37]

Given the agrarian background (via the UIL) of the re-united Irish Party, one might have expected that the hierarchy of the Irish nationalist movement would be critical of graziers. However, while individual members of the UIL (Ginnell, Sheehy *et al.*) did fulminate against grazing, 'the role of the United Irish League in the ranch war fell short of complete commitment and full-scale involvement'.[38] By 1902, the UIL had been shorn of much of its foundational agrarian radicalism. Lip service to the campaign was certainly forthcoming, but Laurence Ginnell became convinced that graziers were themselves joining the UIL 'in order that they may more effectively neutralise it from within'[39] and were making substantial financial contributions to the organisation.

Assigning dates to the Ranch War is problematic. Most historians opt for the 1906–9 period, when cattle driving was at its height. The first public meeting where it was a discernible issue was on 14 October at the Downs in Westmeath, a demonstration, according to the *Irish Times* of 15 October 1906, of 'all who wish to smash and finish ranching and land monopoly and to recover the land for the people'. It was at that 'inaugural' meeting that Ginnell channelled Parnell's famous Ennis speech of 1880, in advocating the tactic that was to characterise 'his' land war: 'If the graziers found their ranches empty some fine morning and after six or eight weeks found their cattle not all together, but some in Connacht, some in Munster, and some among the Wicklow Mountains, and some in the Glens of Antrim … the ranchers would lose their taste for the people's land.'[40]

Between 1907 and 1909, the RIC recorded 1,271 cases of driving and a further 2,000 cases of boycotting. Over that period, 200–300 people were under police protection. However, the end of the agitation was far from uniform. In some parts of the country, it did not lose steam until the end of 1910. One of the factors that contributed to the resolution of the grazier issue was a report in 1909 of the Royal Commission on Congestion in Ireland, chaired by Lord Dudley, which recommended additional powers for the CDB in the compulsory purchase of untenanted lands in the country's 'congested' districts. Crucially, the board's bailiwick was also doubled in size to include almost one-third of the country. An added incentive to end the turmoil was the cost to ratepayers of grazier compensation for the ill-treatment or disappearance of their animals and for enhanced security measures on some grazier lands. One of the responses of the graziers to the threat of having their cattle forcibly relocated had been to further identify themselves with the aristocracy by the recruitment of vigilante 'emergency men' to guard their cattle.

The great imponderable, however – the 'unknown known' – was the extent of the impact of agrarian crime and boycotting on the decisions of graziers to divest themselves of at least some of their extensive holdings. This intimidation, without doubt, accounted for at least some of the concessions that brought the conflict to a gradual end. After enduring boycotts, ranchers were often more amenable to handing over some or all of their holdings to the CDB or the Estates Commissioners for redistribution among their less well-off and highly persuasive neighbours.

Ireland being Ireland, in addition to legitimate anger at the economic impact of the grazier on rural communities, there was an accompanying undercurrent in the Ranch War campaign of what sociologists might dub status anxiety. Ranchers, after all, were not members of the gentry. They were, in the eyes of their social and economic inferiors, simply cattle jobbers with airs, jumped-up peasants getting above themselves. While this begrudgery was accentuated by the post-1903 exodus of the aristocracy, and their replacement at the apex of the societal pyramid by wealth rather than breeding, it existed well before the Wyndham act began to effect social as well as economic change. William Bulfin, with the dispassionate eye of the caustic observer, ridiculed the pretensions and aspirations of many of the social climbers within the grazier class in his *Rambles in Eirinn*. He singled out, for example, a novel tendency on the part of ranchers to shrug off traditional Irish names for their children in preference to calling their daughters 'Louise and Charlotte, and Caroline and Alexandria', instead of Niamh, Rose, Mary and Anne. Similarly, at least according to Bulfin, he encountered far more Clarences and Algernons among the juvenile male graziers than could possibly be permitted to go unsatirised. The young men of this obtrusive new species were sent 'to prepare for the "awmy" or the "baw" and then sent after the hounds – so that they might all the more surely and rapidly ride to the dogs. It lived above its means did this bullockdom of Ireland, and it made beggared snobs of its Algernons and powerless goddesses of its Charlottes.'[41]

Inevitably, the ridicule heaped by their social 'inferiors' on these aspirational 'degenerate offspring of an effete landlordism'[42] were not always compensated for by the warmth of the welcome afforded them by those 'relics of auld dacency' who remained *in situ* behind their demesne walls as the Great War (unbeknownst to one and all) approached. The Irish rural *nouveaux riches* were about as welcome in the drawing rooms of the aristocracy as was the upwardly mobile Mr Collins in Jane Austen's Bennett household in that magisterial primer on petty snobbery, *Pride and Prejudice*. To the peasant, the grazier was the voracious shark; to the predatory landlord, he was that annoying but serviceable pilot fish.

The parting of the waters (with apologies to Thomas Moore)

While there were genuine policy differences between John Dillon and William O'Brien through much of the first decade of the twentieth century – Michael Davitt had died in 1906 and Redmond was doing his best not to be dragged back into the agrarian bearpit – their heightened personal mistrust and mutual aversion was also a factor in dictating the direction of Irish agrarian politics.

From 1904, with Wyndham's purchase scheme already proving highly popular and effective, O'Brien turned his attention to one of the great running sores of rural Ireland, the plight of the agricultural labourer. Back in the 1880s, Parnell had attempted to alleviate the hardships faced by landless labourers with the introduction of private member's legislation that provided for the building of cottages and the provision of half-acre allotments of land. Because the administration of the legislation fell to the Poor Law Guardians, and the financial burden upon local ratepayers, Parnell's programme was honoured more in the breach than in the observance. A burgeoning 'Land and Labour' movement was one of the victims of the 1891 Parnellite Split, and it wasn't until the establishment of the Irish Land and Labour Association (ILLA), under the guidance of two Munster MPs, James J. O'Shee and Daniel Desmond Sheehan, that labourers began to find their voice. Sheehan was a rarity in Irish political life, an anti-clerical 'socialist Home Ruler', whose outsider status was accentuated by his association with William O'Brien, and who was 'critical of the social conservatism of the UIL as regards land redistribution'.[43]

The Congested Districts Board legislation was of some benefit to landless agricultural workers, but it was the passing of the Local Government Act in 1898 that, literally, enfranchised them and allowed the labouring classes to flex their political muscles. When O'Brien was persuaded to assist their cause after the passage of the Wyndham act – in which they received little comfort – he sought to achieve the amelioration of the conditions of the agricultural worker by following the consensus/conference route once again. This prompted an alarmed response from a paranoid Dillon, who detected the scent of a new conspiracy against the influence of the Irish Party. Despite the benign neglect of the leadership of the IPP in taking up the cause of agricultural labourers, a series of public meetings on the issue allowed the ILLA, with Sheehan and O'Shee to the fore, to put pressure on the new Liberal chief secretary, James Bryce (Birrell's predecessor), to introduce legislation that would have more teeth than the Parnell-inspired statute from the 1880s.

It was the divisive politics of the UIL/IPP, almost inevitably, that caused an analogous split at the top of the ILLA. This fissure was a reflection of the rivalry of O'Brien and Dillon. Sheehan (an O'Brienite) and O'Shee (a Dillonite) went their separate ways, the latter accusing Sheehan of creating a 'Donnybrook Fair'* within the ILLA. Two rival labourer bodies emerged from the conflict, and 'the bickering between both rural labour organisations overshadowed the introduction of the new labourers' bill'. [44] Bryce's ameliorative legislation, nonetheless, found favour with the separate organisations, both of which, naturally enough, claimed credit for this coup. They were not the only ones to do so. According to O'Brien's account, the entire matter was settled by a brief conversation on his part with the pragmatic Irish under-secretary, Sir Anthony MacDonnell. O'Brien indicated to the country's leading bureaucrat that a viable scheme for labourers' cottages and allotments would cost a mere £4 million. The under-secretary replied laconically, 'the thing ought to be done and I think can be'.[45] Unsurprisingly, O'Brien's antagonists within the IPP, of whom there were many, entirely discounted the UIL founder's claims. They credited lobbying by Redmond for the remedial legislation introduced by Bryce in 1906.

A draughtman's oversight in the wording of the 1903 Land Purchase Act meant that, technically, Irish ratepayers could be made liable for a portion (around £1 million a year) of the large sums being expended in fulfilment of Wyndham's recipe for

---

* The annual Donnybrook Fair, held in the eponymous Dublin suburb, began in the thirteenth century and continued until the 1850s, when its history of excessive brawling and riotous behaviour proved too much for the respectable denizens of south Dublin.

rural peace. The demands on the UK exchequer had proven to be well in excess of the sums anticipated in the early years of the scheme. Under the terms of Birrell's 1909 Land Bill – legislation designed to slow down the gallop of 'purchase' – the threat to the UK exchequer, and consequently, to Irish rate payers, would abate. Dillon leaped onto the battlements, supported Birrell's legislation and claimed that, unless the 1903 Land Purchase Act – which he had opposed from the outset – was drastically amended, the result would be that 'a crushing burden will be imposed upon the ratepayers of Ireland for the next 68½ years'. O'Brien, for his part, dismissed Dillon's warnings as a 'flimsy and ... imaginary terror'.[46]

Matters came to a head when a National Convention (mentioned previously) was summoned to debate the Land Bill of 1909. O'Brien, in his opposition to Birrell's legislation, was supported by many of the leading Irish unionist figures, and landlords, with whom he had thrashed out the agreement that culminated in Wyndham's 1903 legislation. Their view was that Liberal tinkering (reduction of the landlord 'bonus' and an increase in annuity rates to tenants) would threaten the entire basis of the *entente cordiale* of 1903. This was not a popular position among most nationalists, who, with the Liberals back in power, could smell the sweet scent of Home Rule. Joseph Devlin's AOH detected an additional whiff of treachery: rapprochement and compromise with the Orange foe on the part of O'Brien. The former *United Ireland* editor, hero of the Plan of Campaign, was now perceived by the 'Mollies'* to be in cahoots with Tories, landlords and the Orange Order. His welcome at the National Convention reflected this perception.

The result of the National Convention was a foregone conclusion. The organisation of the conclave had been 'entrusted to a new power which had arisen in Ireland – the Ancient

---

* The original Hibernians (an early nineteenth-century Ulster-based Catholic secret society) 'used to meet in a shebeen owned by a woman named Molly Maguire' (Michael MacDonagh, *The Life of William O'Brien*, 181). Hence the colourful nickname also applied to other secret agrarian societies and later to the syndicalist Irish-American secret organisation in the anthracite mines of Pennsylvania in the late nineteenth century.

Order of Hibernians'.[47] The masonic mien of the AOH – which implicitly flattered its toxic rival, the Orange Order, by aping some of its sectarian rituals – was encouraged by Devlin. The Belfast ringmaster and AOH Grand Master was the lurking power behind whatever thrones Dillon and Redmond had managed to fashion for themselves. To William O'Brien, Devlin was a worthy adversary, a talented organiser and a public speaker blessed with admirable rhetorical gifts, but one whose eloquence consisted of 'pouring a deluge of words over a desert of ideas'.[48]

The chaotic scenes at the 1909 national UIL convention may have been spontaneous, or may have arisen, as D. D. Sheehan alleged, by 'secret and subsidised arrangement',[49] but the result, a conference vote to approve IPP support for the passage of Birrell's act, 'killed Land Purchase stone dead outside the congested districts', according to O'Brien.

The final outcome of the 'Baton Convention' was a further split within Irish constitutional nationalism and agrarianism. O'Brien wanted nothing more to do with a party in which the pietistic Catholic Belfast 'machine boss' Joseph Devlin and the 'Mollies' had acquired so much influence. His establishment of a (rapidly defunct) newspaper, named the *Cork Accent*, derived from his antipathy towards many of those who had poured Belfast-accented bile – 'a cast-iron dialect as irresponsive as a *chevaux de frise*' – upon him at the Mansion House colloquy.[50] To O'Brien, the outcome of the convention was 'attacking the basis of the Land Conference spirit of 1902–3'.[51] His ultimate solution was to lead a cadre of Munster MPs – mostly from his native Cork – out of the party to form the avowedly non-sectarian All For Ireland League, a party unmarried to the IPP's 'uncritical adherence to an alliance with a British Liberal party that had put Irish home rule low on its agenda when not dependent on Irish parliamentary votes' but 'not taken seriously by contemporaries, and largely ignored by historians'.[52]

From that point in his career, O'Brien, one of the great champions of the Irish tenant farmer, but a figure not sufficiently in thrall to the all-consuming divisive nature of the Irish nationalist politics of the early twentieth century, became marginalised.

Much of what he had warned against would quickly come to pass, the partition of the country in 1920 being the realisation of his greatest fear. He had hoped to obviate such an eventuality by maintaining some commonality in the approach to the resolution of agrarian issues and by asserting a confluence of interests with some of the more enlightened members of the Irish aristocracy, as well as some of the more approachable elements within Irish unionism. The obduracy of others and, it must be acknowledged, his own 'propensity ... to equivocate'[53] ensured that he fell short in that battle.

O'Brien and his supporters argued, with some justification, that the decision of the United Irish League to mandate IPP support for Birrell's legislation, while it might have been in keeping with the spirit of the Liberal alliance, applied the brakes to land purchase and left more than 100,000 Irish farmers in a tenurial limbo finally resolved only by the compulsory purchase measures of the government of the Irish Free State, beginning in 1923.

It is ironic that one of the insults hurled at O'Brien in the Mansion House on 9 February 1909, while his supporters were being batoned and beaten inside and outside the venue, was to label him a 'conciliationist'.[54] That the agrarian movement, at least as exemplified by the increasingly complacent and irrelevant IPP, could adopt the word conciliationist as a term of abuse suggested that it was time for the more high-minded O'Brien to make as dignified an exit as possible.

17

The Fourth Land War: land seizures during the War of Independence

'Suddenly finding themselves in possession of their own land
... after a struggle of many generations, they are like men
who have come upon a fortune and are in dread that some
neighbour should hear of it and cast an envious eye on it.'[1]

(Robert Lynd, *Home Life in Ireland*, 1909)

The field in Cormeen, Co. Meath in which Mark Clinton was murdered

10 May 1920, Cloggagh, Co. Meath

Mark Clinton well knew that the approach of the five men boded ill. They were not coming to discuss crop rotation. As they traversed the four-acre field he had a decision to make. Fight or flight? Neither option looked especially attractive. He could see, even at a distance of a hundred yards, that at least one of the men was armed. Presumably, the gunman could run too, and he didn't have to catch up with Clinton to bring down his target.

As far as defensive weapons went, all Clinton had to hand were two plough horses and a few stones. His brother Peter had been lucky the day before; the unseen gunmen had nicked him but he had managed to escape before they could finish him off. The Clintons had been warned not to go near the field, but they had made a promise to their cousins, the Smiths. Despite what had happened to his brother, Mark Clinton was determined to honour their side of the agreement. Still, he should have expected something like this. He should have brought a gun with him – he was in the IRA; he knew how to use one. Rational arguments weren't going to work against the Black Hand Gang.

Clinton stood his ground and the men were on top of him quickly. That was when he noticed that a second member of the group was armed. Bang! The first of the two Clinton plough horses fell dead. Bang! The second collapsed in a heap without a whimper.

'Go on, Billy,' one of the men muttered. Bang!

Mark Clinton bled to death in his father's arms. At the inquest into the young IRA volunteer's killing, Joe Clinton insisted that his son had refused to name the five men who had conspired to end his life. Given the subsequent rapid, focused and brutal IRA response to the murder of one of their own – a killing that could not be ascribed to the Crown forces – few people gave that story much credence.

Mark Clinton knew exactly who had killed him, and he had enough time to pass that information on to his father before he bled to death.

'The last land war'

Lurking in the prospectus for the 1919 Dáil Loan – designed to fund the IRA campaign and the administrative encroachments of the new Sinn Féin 'government' – was a provision inserted to entice the impoverished of rural Ireland to contribute to the end of British hegemony. 'Why You should Subscribe', the poster declared. If the reader managed to reach item 8 before an RIC constable removed the offending poster from wall or telegraph pole, a clear incentive was on offer. This was the establishment of something called the Land Mortgage Bank, which promised to acquire and split up the country's ranches and untenanted land. The passage of the Wyndham and Birrell acts in 1903 and 1909, as well as the cattle driving of the Ranch War and beyond, had failed to transform the grazier – or indeed the landlord – into an endangered species. The poster implied that the increasingly ubiquitous grazier was one of the institutions that Sinn Féin was aiming to sweep away when the people of Ireland entered the nirvana of enlightened republican government.

When the shooting began in earnest in 1920, however, in some parts of the country a desperate and determined legion of the landless and land-deprived decided not to wait for the final triumph of the IRA and the Land Mortgage Bank. They may have been men of little faith, unsentimental sceptics who calculated the odds of a successful outcome of the revolutionary war, and decided to shift for themselves. They had confidence in their capacity to exploit the turmoil descending on Ireland in 1919 – which would degenerate into chaos in 1920. This, they reckoned, would offer a convenient cover for their own efforts 'to acquire and split up the ranches and untenanted land' without the imprimatur of the awe-inspiring Land Mortgage Bank.

Sinn Féin was about to get a bellyful of the new 'land-grabbing'. This time, the 'grabbers' would include many of the party's own supporters. It is one of the great ironies of Irish agrarian history that a successful revolutionary movement might well have been scuttled in advance by what 'was arguably the most troublesome land question of all', provision for the agrarian proletariat.[2]

The prevailing narrative of the Anglo-Irish War is of the glorious victory of a small, courageous and dedicated rebel band against almost insurmountable odds. While this is certainly not inaccurate, the romance of the official version tends to overwhelm a parallel narrative that there was, in some areas at least, almost as much inglorious activity. This was centred on the old problem of land tenure and was connected to the War of Independence by ties of opportunism and convenience. The background to this parallel conflict – this 'other war' – was the termination, c.1909–10, of the Ranch War. The Third Land War faded to black without any fundamental resolution of the issues that had sparked the conflict in the first place. When a new land purchase bill, promised by chief secretary Augustine Birrell for 1913, failed to materialise, veteran cattle drivers dusted off their hazel sticks and reverted to the policy of 'the bullock for the road'. While tillage did make something of a comeback during the 'Great War', this was due, in part at least, to emergency Defence of the Realm Act legislation, which sensibly mandated that as long as the conflict continued, a percentage of farm land must be allocated to the cultivation of crops.

This coincided with the induced coma of the land purchase process. During World War I, the only land of any importance to the British government was the pock-marked terrain of Flanders, Picardy and Gallipoli, available for purchase with the lives of hundreds of thousands of men. With the bulk of the available financial reserves of the UK – supplemented by a crippling tranche of borrowed resources – being sunk into the trenches of the Western Front, there was a severe scarcity of funds left to facilitate Irish farmers in buying out their landlords. That revolutionary programme of peasant proprietary was imprisoned in its own private limbo. Even where redistribution continued, based on historic purchases by the CDB, there was tension and dissatisfaction. When the transfer was mooted of impoverished small Connemara farmers ('congests') to other parts of Galway, where there was 'plenty of good land', it was made clear that they would not be welcome and that the land should be reserved for local claimants. Where estates had been purchased and land reallocated, 'jealousy [was] rife', according to one RIC report. Between 1913 and 1919, seven of the ten members of a local Grazing Land Committee established to divide up farms and estates in Galway were wounded in gun attacks by disgruntled peasants.

One of the responses to this hiatus in tenant purchase, and the perception of unfairness in land distribution, was that frustrated labourers and small farmers staged a number of 'land grabs' and reinstated the Ranch War practice of cattle driving.

This renewal of anti-grazier activity was largely at the instigation of Sinn Féin. In the wake of the sweep conducted by the Crown forces after the failure of the 1916 Rising, more than 3,000 activists – most with little or no involvement in the IRB conspiracy that led to the Easter rebellion – had been incarcerated. From late 1916 into the summer of 1917, these activists had been released from *Ollscoileanna na Reabhlóide* (universities of revolution) such as Frongoch in north Wales. A number of these newly radicalised activists, with a reprise of the Easter Rising unlikely, decided to demonstrate their capacity for turpitude in other ways. The anti-grazier movement was one of the beneficiaries and, as a result, 'the men of substance had cause for anxiety'.[3]

The *éminence grise* of the cattle drivers, the fiery Laurence Ginnell – a man not given to ironic detachment – took the lead in this new agitation, but de Valera himself also endorsed the campaign in a speech in his Clare constituency in February 1918. He called on Sinn Féin clubs nationally 'to divide the land evenly'.[4] However, the hungry winter of 1917–18, a season of chronic food shortages, had as much influence on this renewed agrarian agitation as motivational speeches from Ginnell or de Valera. Grazing land was commandeered all over the country, but especially in Connacht and north Leinster, by large and determined groups of men. The difference between this insurrection and others, however, was that many of the expropriators marched on the untenanted acres in military formation, carried the tricolour aloft as they did so, and adorned the graziers' cattle with the brand 'SF' as they removed them. Some of this land was then allocated to small farmers, landless labourers or farmers' sons not due to inherit. Some was even 'sovietised' in the Bolshevik spirit of the post-1917 period. The land of a Clare landowner, H. V. McNamara, for example, amounting to around 1,000 acres, was seized and held in common by a collective of thirty-seven farmers and fishermen, in an arrangement often characterised as a rural soviet.[5]

Not all labourers were expressing their dissatisfaction with the status quo by means of cattle driving. Some, in fact, were doing precisely the opposite. In Kildare and Meath in the summer of 1919, striking agricultural labourers, members of the Irish Transport and General Workers Union (ITGWU), blockaded the transport of livestock and prevented farmers who refused to come to terms with them from moving their animals. Farm-worker wage strikes were taking place simultaneously in Laois, Galway, Limerick, Cork, Kerry, Tipperary, Wexford and Louth. An RIC report on the Meath and Kildare blockades testified to the efficiency (and qualified passivity) of the picketers: 'the fairs at Navan and Trim were complete failures, farmers being afraid to send their stock, and the roads to Dublin were picketed to prevent cattle being sent to the Dublin Market. Several prosecutions are pending but on the whole there was little disorder.'[6]

Between 1914 and 1918, there were more than 500 instances of cattle driving and almost 1,000 crimes classified by the RIC as 'agrarian outrages'.[7] The scale of rural 'congestion' was still excessive. Of 570,000 holdings in Ireland, 227,000 were less than ten acres in size, *ipso facto* unsustainable. The Land Commission defined 65 per cent of agricultural holdings in each county as 'uneconomic', i.e. with a rateable valuation of below £10. A minimum of 20 acres (of decent land) was deemed necessary for a holding to qualify as sustainable.

While individual members of the UIL continued to support agitation for land redistribution, the IPP/UIL preoccupation with safeguarding Home Rule meant that the party was pulling in opposite directions simultaneously. Support for cattle driving did nothing to enhance the cause of devolution. The Galway MP William O'Malley, for example, while believing that 'cattle driving is the only solution of the grass-farm problem in

Connemara', urged his constituents to abstain from the practice, because 'it is being done to the disadvantage of our cause'.[8] His fellow MP William Duffy advised aggrieved labourers, small farmers and second/third/fourth sons that redress would follow the installation of a devolved government.

Not all, however, were prepared to take their chances with Redmondite pie in the Home Rule sky.

The popular expression of this Great War land hunger was exemplified not just by the resumption of cattle driving but by ad hoc local committees bent on acquiring and redistributing land. The prospect of the landless or land-deprived ever improving their lot had receded still further during the Great War. Food prices had increased, making farming more profitable and pushing up the cost of land. Just as the Land League of the 1880s had been an alliance of interests – and one that failed to cohere for any appreciable length of time – so was Sinn Féin itself, in the words of Peter Hart, a coalition 'of landed and landless, propertied and unpropertied, farmers and agricultural labourers, shopkeepers and shop assistants'.[9] Many of Sinn Féin's rural activists, who emerged from the Ribbon tradition, saw no contradiction in pursuing incongruous political and social goals simultaneously. Therefore, 'the new Sinn Féin ideas were incorporated into the republican and anti-grazier ideology of the secret society'.[10] It was this element that took the lead in the disturbances of the 1918–20 period, where the seizure of land would often be reinforced by the erection of claim-staking flags bearing the legend 'Occupied by order of the Irish Republic'. In one instance, sheep driven from the fields of an Anglo-Irish landowner were daubed in the green, white and orange of the tricolour.[11] The identification of Sinn Féin with the agitation allowed the merely criminal elements involved to conceal their activities behind highly visible expressions of republican loyalty.

Sinn Féin judge, barrister and future post-independence land commissioner Kevin O'Shiel called it the 'last land war'. We can assume he intended this appellation as shorthand for 'the last Irish land war within the confines of empire', or something equally unwieldy. Otherwise, the description is a misnomer, because there was plenty of conflict left over for the early years of the Irish Free State.

Sinn Féin support for land seizures and other forms of direct action stood the party in good stead when it came to the pivotal December 1918 election and its democratic scuttling of the Irish Parliamentary Party. While elements within the IPP (Meath MP David Sheehy, for example) had thrown their weight behind the anti-grazier campaign from the outset, the party of Redmond was, by 1918, more closely identified with the drover than the driver.

In parallel with impromptu (and illicit) land appropriation, groups like the Back to the Land movement functioned on a more legitimate basis. This organisation, which was strongest in the midlands, sought to purchase estates, divide the land into modest but viable parcels, and distribute farms to landless labourers or other aspiring agriculturalists. Back to the Land was supported, in theory at least, by bodies like the Ancient Order of Hibernians and the United Irish League, as well as elements of the trade union movement. Indeed, at times, branches of Back to the Land found it difficult to resist absorption into the UIL, for the Irish Parliamentary Party's parent body, still an organisational behemoth, practised what the late David Fitzpatrick, in his magisterial study of Co. Clare, *Politics and Irish Life, 1913–1921*, referred to as 'the techniques of the party vampire'.[12]

Back to the Land – whose reassuring emblem was that of a farmer behind his plough – often had the resources to purchase or make offers, independent of the official Estates/Land Commissioners or the CDB, on entire estates or large farms.[13] It appears that enterprising (or prudent) bank managers were often willing to fund such transactions. Whether or not the cash offers always represented fair market value was a moot point, but if the alternative was a period of prolonged agitation, which Back to the Land was well capable of arranging – spiced with occasional violent interludes, in which it would always deny any involvement – the option of selling up, even at an obvious discount, might be preferable for the landowner.

The Back to the Land movement achieved considerable traction in realising the ambitions of would-be farmers and landless labourers. Around the town of Oldcastle, Co. Meath alone, by the end of 1919, more than 3,000 acres of 'estate' land had been divided among 170 families by the local organisers of the movement. In March 1921, in its most significant coup in the midlands, the 1,400-acre McRory estate, also in Co. Meath, was purchased and divided among eighty families. The sale of the Fitzherbert family's Proudstown estate, part of which was later used for the creation of Navan Racecourse, was not allowed to proceed until 400 acres had been purchased for redistribution by Back to the Land. The Fitzherberts were left in no doubt about the ability of the organisation to prevent the sale of their property going through. In 1917, Back to the Land had sought, unsuccessfully, to acquire the entire estate. In late September of that year, with North Meath IPP MP Patrick White in attendance, an auction had proceeded for the sale of Proudstown at which, *mirabile dictu*, there was not a single bid.

All of which wartime activity was mere prologue to the virtual anarchy of 1920, a state of affairs that was not entirely due to the serious intensification of the struggle between the IRA and the Crown forces that year. There was another, lesser conflict being fought at the same time as the 'Squad' and the IRA active service units were taking on the British Army, the Black and Tans and the Auxiliaries.[14] As the Anglo-Irish War increased in intensity in that year, so too did this 'other war' – this 'Last Land War' – an elemental struggle pitching the landless and the land-hungry against graziers and landowners unwilling to divest themselves of their properties. This was generally fought in areas of the country that failed to generate any notable success against the Crown forces during the Anglo-Irish War. Indeed, it is safe to assume that the prosecution of this parallel 'war' made a substantial contribution to that lack of republican revolutionary activity.

This conflict was, once again, dictated by the virtual cessation in land purchase, by bad weather in the spring of 1920, and by the lack of emigration during the war years. Although migration had already begun to resume by 1920, the escalation of the Anglo-Irish War and 'the weakening of the state's coercive capacities' led to a renewal of the rural agitation that Sinn Féin had encouraged in the months before the decisive 1918 general election. The resurgence of land seizures and cattle driving was often based on the assumption 'that Sinn Féin endorsed agrarian agitation as a legitimate strand of the struggle for political independence'.[15] By the summer of 1920, that was no longer axiomatic. The expropriation was also aided and abetted by the enforced closure of dozens of rural RIC barracks as the IRA campaign intensified.

On 3 March 1920 came a tragic and deadly throwback to the epochal Land Conference of 1903, when the brother of John Shawe-Taylor, Frank Shawe-Taylor – a land agent and former High Sheriff of County Galway – found himself in the limelight for all the wrong reasons. Shawe-Taylor was murdered near Athenry in the early hours of that morning. He was on his way to Galway when his progress was halted by an ass and cart drawn across the road a short distance from his home, Moorpark. It was a well-planned ambush involving up to eight assailants. When the car stopped and his chauffeur went to investigate, Shawe-Taylor was fired on from both sides of the road simultaneously and was killed instantly. His chauffeur, James Barrett, was wounded in the attack. According to the *Tuam Herald* of 6 March, the suspected motive was Shawe-Taylor's refusal to part with a tract of land on which he was exercising grazing rights. No one was ever charged with his murder. Within a short period, his death was followed by the killing of a north Galway rancher and three herdsmen, one of whom was brutally beaten to death for ignoring threats to leave a grazier's employment. In the words of an RIC Chief Inspector in Galway, 'the greed for land is in the bones of the people and induces treacherous and cruel crimes'.[16] After the murder of Shawe-Taylor, the prevailing refrain of the threatening letters routinely despatched to unpopular graziers assured them that they risked sharing the former High Sheriff's fate if they failed to part with their land.[17]

The attackers of Godfrey Hardy in Co. Clare, although they spared his life, went a step further than Shawe-Taylor's killers.

Hardy, a Crusheen landowner, was badly beaten by a group of up to twenty men, who demanded that he immediately sign over his farm. Hardy refused and was then blindfolded. He was held at gunpoint but still declined to transfer his property under duress. When his sister attempted to intervene, she was forced to retreat after she was fired on by her brother's attackers. Hardy was bold enough to resist the threats of his assailants and survive the encounter, but his family was subsequently boycotted and a number of his employees had shots fired into their homes.

As incidences of the seizure of the land of graziers, rather than simply their cattle, increased, a number of disputes began to make their way into the newly established Sinn Féin/Dáil court system. This was a highly effective parallel structure established in all the traditional legal circuits, mimicking and ultimately superseding the petty sessions and assizes of the colonial administration. Ironically, when Sinn Féin-appointed judges were obliged to adjudicate in cases of violent or coercive land appropriations, their decisions generally went in favour of the plaintiff/proprietor. This did not go down well with the defendants, many of whom were local Sinn Féin activists.

The young barrister Cahir Davitt, son of the Land League founder, was a prominent Dáil court judge who travelled the country and found himself presiding over a number of cases of land appropriation. In his lengthy Bureau of Military History witness statement, Davitt cited one particularly informative case. This involved two Midleton, Co. Cork families whom he named as O'Sullivan and McCarthy. The former (a brother and two sisters) owned a farm, from which the latter's family (represented by an IRA volunteer recently returned from the USA) had been evicted in one of the many late nineteenth-century land conflicts. Davitt was told by the solicitor for the plaintiffs that, not long after the return of McCarthy, the O'Sullivans began to receive threatening letters instructing them to hand over their farm to McCarthy or take the consequences. After the male member of the O'Sullivan family was shot and wounded, they reluctantly agreed to sign over their land to this descendant of the former occupants. This followed the intervention of a local priest – his role throughout was exceptionally dubious – who advised the O'Sullivans'that it was in their best interests to cave in to the threats.

When the Dáil courts were established, the O'Sullivans decided to try their luck. They issued proceedings, claiming that they had been coerced into parting with their farm. Davitt, on hearing the evidence, found in their favour. His verdict, he recalled, was met with vocal disapproval among the spectators in the improvised courtroom. The priest, who had counselled the O'Sullivans to surrender their farm, rose and objected to the verdict, advising Davitt that it 'would not conduce to the peace of the parish'. While Davitt was waving away this intervention, one of the O'Sullivan sisters was physically assaulted by an onlooker. Davitt instructed the 'Republican police' (members of a local IRA unit) standing guard at the back of the court to intervene. Ignoring his commands, they remained impassive, like a line of Roman statues, arms folded, staring eloquently into the middle distance. As Davitt was adjourning the court proceedings, he could clearly hear 'muttered observations casting doubts upon my paternity'. These must have sounded ironic, in the circumstances, to the son of the 'Father of the Land League'. Davitt, a realist, assumed that there was little or no chance that his directive would ever be executed. And so it proved. Clearly indicating that the clerical collar often held more sway than a judicial decree, the intrusive priest brokered his own 'agreement'. The McCarthys 'were left in undisputed possession of their ancestral acres' and the O'Sullivans were obliged to accept an alternative holding.[18]

A small number of IRA recruits, as in the case of the Davitt/'O'Sullivan' dispute, may even have signed up as volunteers in the hope of using their enhanced status, or their newly acquired weapons, to reverse prior evictions; to seize properties themselves; or to assist in the fomenting of the sort of chaos that would facilitate their illicit acquisition of land. East Clare O/C Michael Brennan recorded how he exploited agrarian frustrations and animosities 'to get those fellows into the Volunteers',[19] though he later came to regret this decision and railed against any tolerance by the IRA of parallel agrarian agitation.[20]

The Black Hand Gang

As attested in the Bureau of Military History witness statements of a number of IRA volunteers, the O/C of the Meath Brigade (later O/C of the 1st Eastern Division), Seán Boylan, had his hands full, not just with the local Black and Tans, a detachment of the South Wales Borderers and an Auxiliary force based in the town of Trim, but with a small and aggressive *ad hoc* militia force which, although it included some IRA volunteers, was doing little or nothing to advance the cause of the Irish Republic in his bailiwick. [21] The Cormeen gang, so-called because of the location of its core support around the north-west Meath village of Cormeen – or, to give this cadre of smallholders and labourers its more melodramatic name, the Black Hand Gang – had decided to embrace the spirit of the 1903 Wyndham act, despite the hiatus in funding and the slowing of land purchase to a mere dribble. However, rather than wait for the British government to resume the journey to a peasant proprietary, the Black Hand Gang chose to kickstart the process by creating some of their own facts on the ground in the north-west corner of Co. Meath. This involved threatening, shooting and even using explosives in a concerted drive to force farmers off their land. This would then be redistributed among the membership of this *ad hoc* secret society. [22]

Matters came to head, however, when the gang moved to acquire a sizeable field (*c.*four acres) near the village of Cormeen owned by Philip Smith. Smith, whose prosperous family had farmed in the area for generations, was also the owner of land in nearby Kilmainhamwood, where he now lived. Citing a historic Land War-era eviction as validation, the Cormeen gang announced its decision to annex the field. Smith approached his cousins, the family of Joseph Clinton of the nearby townland of Cloggagh, to seek their assistance in warding off the attentions of the Cormeen gang. Clinton was allowed the use of the land at a peppercorn rent (around one-third of the commercial value) and on 9 May 1920, his son, Peter, entered the field with two plough horses, in effect to stake the family claim. He was fired on by members of the Black Hand Gang and slightly wounded but escaped with his life.

Rather than back down in the face of this threat, another of the young Clintons, twenty-three-year-old IRA volunteer Mark, re-entered the field with the two ill-fated plough horses on 10 May, with fatal consequences.

The dozen or so members of the Cormeen gang were mistaken if they believed that Seán Boylan would ignore the murder of an IRA volunteer, particularly one whose brother, Patrick Clinton, was the Meath IRA brigade intelligence officer and a neighbour of Boylan in Dunboyne. The vague IRA affiliations of some members of the Black Hand Gang did not protect them from Boylan's systematic retribution.

With little difficulty, the membership of the Cormeen gang was identified by Boylan's investigators. Almost all were rounded up in a single night in early June 1920. Nine members of the gang were tried by an IRA court and sentenced to periods in exile of between three and fifteen years. The only quarry who avoided being abducted in the June swoop was the man identified by Boylan as the killer of Clinton, William Gordon. An RAF veteran, Gordon, a young Presbyterian of farming stock, lived near the town of Baileborough in the neighbouring county of Cavan. Based – it is highly probable – on inside information about Boylan's proposed June swoop on the membership of the gang, the RIC detained Gordon before the IRA could 'arrest' him as a murderer. He was charged not with murder but with possession of an illegal weapon, and was remanded to Mountjoy prison. His tenure there had an aura of protective custody rather than incarceration and, when he was returned to Navan for trial, he was rapidly acquitted.

At which point he would have been well advised to get as far away from Co. Meath as he possibly could. Instead, Gordon went drinking with two local RIC constables. Boylan, who had travelled to Navan in the hope of apprehending the elusive Gordon, was advised that his quarry had not immediately headed for the local railway station after his acquittal. He ordered the Navan IRA to search every public house in the town. Gordon was located in the Flathouse bar, close, but not close enough, to Navan railway station. He was taken by Boylan himself, at gun point, to a waiting car and driven to Dunboyne.

Gordon was then tried by an IRA military court and found guilty of murder. When Boylan sought sanction to have his prisoner executed, the Dáil cabinet demurred. Countess Markievicz and the only Presbyterian member of the cabinet, Ernest Blythe, were among those opposed to an execution. Boylan was instructed by Michael Collins, a good friend and fellow IRB member, to put Gordon on trial again. A second hearing took place and the original sentence was confirmed. In early August 1920, William Gordon became the only IRA prisoner of the War of Independence to be executed for murder, and the only prisoner to face a firing squad for his involvement in an agrarian crime.

In his autobiographical work *There Will Be Another Day*, the Donegal-born socialist republican writer and activist Peadar O'Donnell has an interesting take on Sinn Féin policy towards the land seizures of the War of Independence. O'Donnell had little time for the Sinn Féin courts, seeing them as an attempt to suppress class antagonism, with a strong bias towards the defence of the rights of property owners, including landlords. He ordered the men in his Donegal IRA unit to stop co-operating with the courts. O'Donnell was of the view that many IRA members later had cause to regret their involvement in actions taken to enforce Dáil court judgments.[23] However, there is no such self-recrimination in evidence in the Bureau of Military History Witness Statements of Meath War of Independence veterans where the Cormeen seizures were concerned, even in the case of prominent republicans who, like O'Donnell, chose the anti-Treaty side in the Civil War.

Mark Clinton, however, was not the only young activist to be murdered during the War of Independence arising out of an agrarian dispute. Up to very recently, one of the youngest victims of the conflict, fifteen-year-old Fianna Éireann member Francis Murphy from Glann, near Ennistymon, Co. Clare, was assumed to have been a victim of the Crown forces. He was shot and killed while sitting in his home on the night of 14 August 1919. The verdict of the coroner's jury at his inquest was that 'Francis Murphy was wilfully murdered ... by a bullet fired by members of the British Army which caused his immediate death'. The allegation, not uncommon in inquest verdicts before the suppression of coroner's courts in late 1920, was based on the evidence of a witness named Patrick Connole, who told the coroner's jury that he had seen three men in British Army uniform close to the Murphy house at the time of the killing. Connole, however, turned out to have been a less than reliable witness. In March 1920, he was arrested for plotting to kill his former employer, a manager in the West Clare Railway (of Percy French 'Are Ye Right There Michael' fame).

Under interrogation, Connole admitted that he had lied at the Francis Murphy inquest. His testimony had been a quid pro quo arrangement with the young boy's actual killers. In return, they had agreed to help Connole murder his former employer. An alternative explanation for the killing of Francis Murphy – from the RIC – had been raised at the inquest but rejected by the jury in favour of the explanation they preferred to hear. This latter version of events claimed that the boy's father, John Murphy, was the victim of a local agrarian boycott, having taken the side of an unpopular local figure, Michael Neylon, in a land dispute. Neylon and his supporters had already been the target of a number of assaults and assassination attempts dating back to 1913. The shooting into the house had been intended only as a warning.

The RIC report was supported by a British Army investigation. It appears that, notwithstanding the inquest verdict, it was well known locally that the British Army had played no part in the killing of Francis Murphy. When Arthur Griffith, Minister for Home Affairs, published a pamphlet in 1920 entitled *Murders by Crown Forces*, the name of Francis Murphy was not included in the list of victims, although Griffith had been notified directly of the killing in 1919.[24]

The Last Land War

'[This was] a revival of ancient and unwarrantable claims, gross intimidation, cattle-driving, fence-levelling and an "ugly rush" for land. The mind of the people was being diverted from the struggle for freedom into a class war and there was even the possibility that the IRA, itself composed largely of farmer's sons, might be affected.'[25]

('The Land agitation: A grave danger', *The Irish Bulletin*, August 1921).

In 1920, the RIC was a beleaguered force. Its members were under violent attack from the IRA and the rank and file were resigning in their hundreds, but they were also faced with another major threat. It was becoming clear that the renewal of agrarian agitation had begun to intensify since its resurgence in 1918. This new menace was only exacerbated by the abandonment by the force of many small police stations embedded in rural communities and the retrenchment of the RIC into larger urban centres. In 1920, the constabulary recorded the highest incidence of agrarian crime since 1882. Before it died down, the agitation would engulf sixteen counties.

Ironically, the RIC were not the only guardians of the law who were concerned at this phenomenon. Sinn Féin was also conscious of the threat. The steps they took to counter this new and unexpected hazard were often of a piece with their conduct of the ongoing war against the Crown forces, but were clearly out of character with the Sinn Féin of 1917–18. Indeed, the republican response can even be seen as an authoritarian statement of intent, arguably the first stirrings of a counter-revolution even before the one still in hand had been brought to fruition. As the great socialist-republican figure Peadar O'Donnell once caustically observed, 'The Free State was in existence long before the name was adopted.'[26]

In the spring of 1920, another prominent Dáil court judge, Kevin O'Shiel, was summoned to the office of a harried Arthur Griffith. Griffith and the Sinn Féin cabinet were being forced to confront the reality of thousands of farmers being held at bay by landlords who refused to sell out to their tenants. At least until the price was right. Three million acres remained to be transferred, the UK government was ignoring the agrarian frustration and the Dáil was in no position to help, so the peasants were doing it for themselves and the IRA could hardly seek to restore order by intervening on behalf of the graziers. Although as early as 1 May 1920, the official Volunteer periodical, *An t-Óglach*, noted that the 'Irish Republican Army has found it necessary to take drastic steps for the enforcement of law and order' in cases of 'land-greed' in Kerry.[27]

This anarchy, Griffith told O'Shiel, who had already presided over dozens of land arbitration cases by the summer of 1920, had to stop. In O'Shiel's words, 'Griffith … made it very clear to me that he took the gravest possible view of the outbreak and was definitely of the opinion that if it was not speedily and effectively dealt with it might engulf the great Sinn Féin movement … [and] the very Dáil itself.'

An enhanced role for the Dáil courts in land arbitration disputes was the way forward, the cabinet had concluded. This process would have O'Shiel, Cahir Davitt and other Sinn Féin judges, such as Conor Maguire, at the apex. While land distribution was still at the heart of Sinn Féin policy, it could not be conducted in a haphazard, chaotic and violent fashion. In anticipation of unpopular coercive land court settlements, the cabinet approved the establishment of a Land Settlement Commission (LSC) to offer protection to beleaguered landowners such as the Marquess of Lansdowne,* who bemoaned the fact that landowners were experiencing 'the gradual but unrelenting confiscation of their property'.[28] The LSC managed to re-allocate/restore 50,000 acres of land between 1 May 1920 and 31 December 1920. Sinn Féin courts could also, where a landowner was willing, purchase land for redistribution. It was even said that landlords preferred to sell to Sinn Féin because, unlike the CDB, the republicans 'paid in cash'.[29]

Of course, when it came to opportunism – and an almost permanent state of war, of one kind or another, from 1914 to 1923 provided plenty of opportunities – it was not simply a case of the dispossessed taking the fields of the wealthy. There were many noteworthy examples of that familiar Irish shape-shifter, 'the

---

* His Kerry mansion, Dereen House, was burned to the ground during the Civil War.

chancer'. These malevolent sprites, strangers to altruism, swelled the ranks of the 'drivers' and 'grabbers' (the word had suddenly shed its pejorative connotations for much of the rural population) and concealed themselves behind the activism of the genuine agrarian *sans culottes*.

In his comprehensive and highly entertaining Bureau of Military History witness statement, Kevin O'Shiel underscored the legitimacy of Griffith's fears and offered illustrations of the blatant buccaneering in evidence in that wave of expropriation.

O'Shiel, on an exploratory visit to Roscommon, reported that most of the ranches in the county 'had been cleared of stock, and roads and lanes all over the county, were choked with wandering and half-starved beasts'.[30] In his detailed statement to the Bureau of Military History, and a series of revealing articles for the *Irish Times* in the 1960s, O'Shiel cited two cases in the west of Ireland, both of which serve to induce a modicum of cynicism about some of the seizures.

The first case involved an *ad hoc* society in the village of Creggs, Co. Roscommon, where, in 1891, persistent rainfall during a public meeting had contributed to the demise of Charles Stewart Parnell. The cattle drivers of Creggs had an exceptionally low tolerance threshold for rancher resistance. When one local grazier had the effrontery to return his driven cattle to the fields from which they had been waylaid, 'he was stripped naked and beaten through the fair of Creggs'.[31] When the War of Independence began, the drivers of Creggs decided that it would be an opportune moment to graduate from the relocation of cattle to the outright commandeering of ranches. A highly enthusiastic and proactive local 'Land Committee' rapidly assembled a portfolio of around 4,000 acres. Unlike the more orthodox methodology of Back to the Land, this impressive acreage was acquired without the expenditure of any actual cash. Physical threats undoubtedly accounted for at least some of the expropriations. O'Shiel, at an inquiry into some of the Creggs acquisitions, was presented with what was claimed to be a 'properly executed indenture' (a deed transferring ownership) by a defendant's solicitor. The attorney, representing a coterie of unabashed expropriators, loudly insisted to the Sinn Féin judge that 'We are not confiscators'. Swayed, in spite of himself, O'Shiel sought the input of the plaintiff's attorney. His intervention was decisive. 'My client had but to glance at that precious deed,' the lawyer told O'Shiel, 'to see that it involved the surrender to these so-called purchasers of a substantial proportion of his property for an absurdly trivial price. He naturally declined to sign, whereupon two of these brigands, standing on either side of him, drew revolvers and presented them at his head, whilst others began to dig a grave on the lawn in front of him.'[32] His client duly signed. O'Shiel, still a champion of the rule of law, despite the mayhem in evidence all around him, restored the plaintiff to his holding.

Although O'Shiel described the leaders of the Creggs Land Committee as 'Commissars', he ascribed to them a range of comings and goings that would have hardly met with the approval of any self-respecting soviet. The members of the committee rewarded themselves for their honest exertions by excursions to the annual Galway races. There they accommodated themselves in one of the city's better hotels 'and dined and wined well, the wine need I say, being the finest champagne and plenty of it too', according to the incredulous judge.[33]

Armed with the imprimatur of Arthur Griffith himself to stamp out such abuses, O'Shiel demanded to see the 'accounts' of the Creggs Land Committee. When he was refused access to the documents, he amply demonstrated the determination of the Dáil to be less than tolerant towards expropriation. From Co. Clare he imported a short-tempered IRA gunman, Eamon Casey, who threatened to shoot one of the members of the Land Committee if the accounts were not produced. That seemed to do the trick, and O'Shiel reported drily that 'in due course the Creggs Land Committee was wound up and its ill-gotten lands restored to their rightful owners'.

The uniqueness of these Dáil arbitration courts is underscored by such outcomes. Amid the prevailing chaos, they were often beacons of rationality and fairness, at least as far as incumbent landowners were concerned. Many difficult and controversial decisions were made by judges like O'Shiel, Davitt and Maguire, based on evidence and natural justice rather than political expediency. The restoration of seized land to prosperous graziers and unionist landlords was distinctly un-Bolshevik and was understandably resented by the unsuccessful defendants. When a Protestant grandee had his land restored by a Dáil court, there was an obvious danger that disappointed peasants would turn against Sinn Féin and might even, in their anger, risk offering information to the Crown forces in retaliation, despite the likely consequences should their actions be discovered.

In May 1920, O'Shiel was in Kilmaine, Co. Mayo, where he was called upon to adjudicate in a case involving the seizure of a couple of comparatively small holdings belonging to two plaintiffs named Hyland and Murphy. As far back as February 1918, Sinn Féin, still, at the time in anti-grazier mode, had deprecated actions being taken against 'land occupied by relatively small farmers'.[34] The victimisation of Hyland and Murphy, hardly a pair of affluent ranchers, smacked of opportunistic piracy. O'Shiel decided in favour of the plaintiffs and ordered the defendants to vacate the land. As with Cahir Davitt's McCarthy vs O'Sullivan case, the new occupants simply refused to comply and, implicitly defied O'Shiel to enforce his own verdict. The ramifications of this case, however, signposted a reassessment in Sinn Féin thinking. It demonstrated the cabinet's reluctance to continue even the appearance of tolerance of illegal land seizures. According to University of Galway historian Tony Varley, 'It was made clear to persons intent on using intimidation for selfish gain in private land wars that their claims to land would be rejected forthwith.'[35] Griffith intervened personally in the case and obliged a reluctant Minister for Defence, Cathal Brugha – who resented IRA volunteers being used as policemen – to take action. This resulted in the 'arrest' of the illicit occupiers of the Hyland/Murphy lands and their removal to an island in Lough Corrib. There they remained until they agreed to vacate the land. With the official intervention of the IRA and the removal of the recalcitrant 'grabbers' to one of that organisation's infamous 'unknown destinations', a clear message had been sent to those behind the campaign of land appropriation.

In addition to the obvious political threat posed by these seizures – if nothing else, they were a blatant distraction from the military campaign for independence in many of the less 'active' counties – there was another overweening incentive for Sinn Féin to bring the commandeering of grazing land under control.

The Mollies were back in the game.

Gallingly for Sinn Féin, in some parts of the country the tables were being turned on the party by their old nationalist antagonists. In one of the many ironies of Irish agrarian history, those implacable tribal enemies, Sinn Féin and the AOH, found themselves, in essence, switching sides. By the middle of 1920, Sinn Féin had been at the head of a self-declared government for eighteen months. It had become a quasi 'establishment' party. The AOH, licking its wounds after the electoral humiliation of the IPP in 1918, was now, in effect, the rebel nationalist faction. Illicit land seizures, some of which were being provoked by AOH members, had become a major headache for the Dáil administration. From Roscommon, once again, where IRA activity was scant, and the seizure of grazing land a much more popular pastime, a concerned Sinn Féin supporter, Graham Sennett, wrote to the Dáil cabinet's Minister for Agriculture, Art O'Connor, on 20 May 1920, outlining the involvement of the AOH in local land appropriation. His report bore the unambiguous title 'Regarding cattle drivers, marauders, terrorists and hooligans'. If the worm had not already turned, it was certainly in the act of changing its perspective. 'The most vile hooligans that did the dirty work against us in the general election,' Sennett wrote, 'are marching with the tricolour to commandeer lands.'[36]

Sadly, the English language has no word for the level of irony involved in a Sinn Féin functionary berating erstwhile supporters of the (not quite extinct) Irish Parliamentary Party for provoking land seizures. Sennett's letter was despatched on the day of the murder of Mark Clinton, who had acted as a bodyguard for Arthur Griffith against AOH attacks in the East Cavan by-election of 1918. It reinforced the message that the Mollies were intent on causing just as much trouble as private agrarian militias. The time for constructive ambiguity was over. The cabinet took a firm decision to put out the bushfires of agrarian revolt once and for all. Pre-existing disputes could be left to the Dáil courts, but a more explicit message had to be sent to the rural adventurers that they would have nothing to gain from future 'confiscations'.

On 19 June 1920 came legislative confirmation of the new 'get tough' position on land appropriation. A Dáil decree sought to clamp down on the practice. It dismissed the standard justification for seizures, that of a prior claim to 'evicted' farms stretching back to the Land War and beyond. Such assertions were 'of old date, and while many of them may be well-founded, others seem to be of a frivolous nature and are put forward in the hope of intimidating the present occupiers'.

Accordingly, the Dáil proclaimed: 'That the present time, when the Irish people are locked in a life-and-death struggle with their traditional enemy, is ill-chosen for stirring up strife amongst our fellow-countrymen; and that all energies must be directed towards the clearing out – not the occupiers of this or that piece of land – but the foreign invader of our country.'[37]

While the agitation did not dissipate entirely – the ubiquitous threatening letter was still a consequence-free alternative to outright piracy – the Dáil had laid down a marker. The move, although understandably unpopular in many quarters, actually served to enhance the growing credibility of the shadow Sinn Féin administration. The (almost) timely response ensured that the Dáil cabinet was 'lauded for possessing sufficient legitimacy, autonomy and capacity to bring the 1920 agitation to a halt'.[38]

Big house burnings, 1920–3

According to the undisputed expert in this field, Terence Dooley, a total of 275 country houses belonging to the Irish gentry were burned between January 1920 and December 1923 – 76 during the War of Independence and 199 during the shorter but more incendiarist Civil War.[39] This represented about 10 per cent of the total number of 'big houses' nestling behind their demesne walls around the country. Much of the destruction of these venerable buildings during the Anglo-Irish War was for military reasons, to prevent their use as barracks, or in retaliation for attacks on nationalist property by the Crown forces. However, Dooley, as well as a number of other historians who have researched incendiarism on a local level, acknowledges that agrarian issues could also play a role in, for example, the choice of precisely which big house was to be burnt in the event of a reprisal. In the case of the destruction of Castle Cooke in Co. Cork, for example, the 'extensive agricultural operations' of the estate owner, Captain William Cooke-Collis, 'inspired covetousness among local farmers'.[40] It was incidents like these that prompted the late David Fitzpatrick to describe some IRA actions in Clare as 'thinly disguised land seizures'.[41] Tom Barry, in *Guerrilla Days in Ireland* (not the most reliable narrative of the Anglo-Irish War), wrote of the IRA in West Cork encouraging landless men to seize untenanted land. However, Barry then intervened to prevent the arbitrary reassignment of the appropriated land. Instead, it was sold off and the proceeds were retained 'in trust'. After the Truce was declared in July 1921, Barry insisted that he was 'at present awaiting instructions as to where to send the money'. Given Barry's anti-Treaty military

Moore Hall, Co. Mayo – burned during the Civil War

activities in the Civil War, it is likely that he subsequently put the funds to some use.

Dooley also cites the case of the Ballywalter demesne and the burning of Warren's Court, both in Co. Cork, as having somewhat tenuous connections to the IRA campaign.

In Ballywalter, the mansion of the Welsted family was burned to the ground, leading to the final departure from Ireland of the Welsteds themselves. Thereafter, locals frustrated all attempts to sell the estate on the open market. Their tacit expropriation of the land was crowned with success in 1925, when the Land Commission bought the estate for just under half its 1921 market value of around £26,000 and distributed the land thus acquired. Dooley poses similar questions in relation to the alleged IRA burning of Warren's Court near Kilmurry, Co. Cork, whose owner, Robert Warren, claimed, implausibly, that his estate was being used by the IRA 'as the pasture ground for cattle commandeered by them in the locality'. While some IRA volunteers were undoubtedly the heirs of the cattle drivers and may even have participated in such actions themselves, there is no record of IRA units maintaining beef herds to raise money for the purchase of arms or to feed members of Flying Columns in the field. An advisedly sceptical Dooley asks, 'were those who attacked Warren's Court and its surroundings actually republicans or were they simply locals operating a social rather than a political mandate of their own?'[42] The apparent justification for the burning of Warren's Court was that it was about to be occupied and garrisoned by British troops. While this had been mooted, the commandeering of the house was vehemently opposed by its proprietor, Lady Warren, widow of the last male owner of the property, Sir Augustus Warren. Questions also surround the destruction of the house of Lord Castlemayne in Co. Westmeath in July 1921, given 'the recent involvement of the local IRA leader in land disputes'.[43] If the motive was more agrarian than political, then the arson attack paid off handsomely. In 1924, Castlemayne sold his estate to the Land Commission. The land was then apportioned to local farmers.

In some instances, it is hard to fathom the motivation for some of the burnings.* The long-standing refusal, as Dooley points out, to allow historians full access to Land Commission files makes it impossible to verify the anecdotal evidence of cases such as Ballywalter and Warren's Court.

'Local jealousy and petty spite': the murders of Jane and Bernard O'Reilly

What do you do when you are prevented by your own side from taking the property of an 'undeserving' landowner? Since the Dáil edict of June 1920, the option of simply 'grabbing' the land had become potentially unprofitable. So do you seethe in frustration and content yourself with bad-mouthing your nemesis? Or do you come up with an imaginative, and potentially deadly, alternative course of action? If you adopt the latter course, how far would you be prepared to go to achieve your objectives? In the case of the killers of Jane O'Reilly of Derrylangan, Athboy, Co. Meath, the answer was 'as far as was necessary, and beyond'.

To many the burning of the big house, whether the motive was selfless or entirely self-interested, was seen as a form of just retribution. The Cromwellian confiscators were being paid back in kind. Such sentiments, despite their lack of historical validity, were passionately held.

However, the sheer savagery apparent in such acts as the burning of Kilmorna House near Listowel, Co. Kerry, in 1921, and the murder of its occupant – former Ulster King of Arms, the distinguished genealogist Sir Arthur Vicars – for alleged collaboration with Crown forces, was far from unique. Neither was agrarian avarice confined to assaults on the property of the great and good. In fact, as the murder of Jane O'Reilly and

---

* Incendiarism of a motivationally suspicious nature continued during the Civil War, when more than twice as many Anglo-Irish houses were burned in a ten-month period as in the two and a half years of the War of Independence.

her young son will illustrate, there was more than one way to, constructively, exact a full measure of revenge for the crime of being just a touch too well off in rural Ireland.

In the summer of 1921, a former member of the Dublin Metropolitan Police, John Farrell, by then working as a thatcher, disappeared. He lived near Athboy, Co. Meath, in a small labourer's cottage. When he had failed to turn up after a number of weeks, there were inevitable rumours locally, given his past employment, that Farrell was a police informer that had been 'dealt with' by the Meath IRA. There is no independent evidence that this was the case.

Accompanying the rumours of Farrell's killing by the IRA were other, contradictory, accounts. These narratives suggested that Farrell had not been shot for spying, but for reasons that had nothing to do with the IRA campaign. 'The Thatcher', according to this version of events, was a single man occupying accommodation that was 'required' by others. He was, in other words, murdered for his house. However, the story of John Farrell is actually the prologue to one of the worst but least-remembered civilian atrocities of the Anglo-Irish War. Farrell, on the day he was murdered, had been attending a funeral. The woman and child being buried that day were the victims of a small-minded avarice that led to an agrarian double-killing out of kilter with even the worst barbarities of a frequently barbarous conflict.

Farrell was last seen alive after the funeral of Jane O'Reilly and her four-year old son. Both had died in a house fire in Derrylangan.

Jane O'Reilly was born Jane Madden in Swords, Co. Dublin, in 1879. In 1915, when employed as principal of the Rathcairn national school, between the Meath towns of Athboy and Trim – where she had worked for more than ten years – she married Bernard O'Reilly, a farmer from Derrylangan, at the relatively late age, for an Irish woman of that era, of thirty-six. Bernard O'Reilly, previously a shop assistant working in the large county town of Navan, had inherited a forty-nine-acre holding in Derrylangan from his late uncle. Jane O'Reilly was a popular and familiar figure in the area, but not, it appears, with all her neighbours. With her income from teaching and that of her husband from farming, the couple and their child, born in 1917 and called Bernard after his father, were in a position to hire a resident female servant to assist with the domestic chores in their modest thatched cottage. This was described in one newspaper report as 'a tastefully kept farmer's dwelling of the old picturesque type'.[44]

The *Meath Chronicle* of 18 June 1921 described in some detail the tragic accident that had befallen the O'Reilly family in the small hours of the morning of 14 June. At around 5 a.m., Jane O'Reilly awoke to 'the smell of burning and the crackling of timber'. Rousing her husband, she then raced to warn the couple's servant, who immediately made her escape through one of the few unbarred windows in the house. When Jane returned to the bedroom she shared with her husband and their four-year-old son, however, 'the house was then in a mass of flame, the thatched roof burning with alarming rapidity, and the timber of the dwelling in like manner burning like matchwood'. Just as Jane O'Reilly reached her sleeping child, one of the roof timbers gave way and trapped her and her son, 'pinning both in the burning debris'. Her distraught husband could do nothing to save his wife and child, 'although he made desperate efforts to do so', was badly burned in the process and then watched helplessly as his small family disappeared under the fiery remnants of the collapsing roof. It was noon that day before the two bodies, both unrecognisable, were recovered from the wreckage of the 'low commodious thatched dwelling'.

The first news reports of the tragedy ascribed the fire to 'one of those disastrous accidents, which are so inexplicable but not unique'. This is precisely what some of the O'Reillys' neighbours would have wanted the world to believe. The *Chronicle* report concluded with a short account of the funeral from Athboy Church on 16 June to the Hill of Ward Cemetery, 'the mother and child being placed in the one grave'. Among the mourners, on the last day of his own life, was John 'the Thatcher' Farrell. It is highly probable, given the conventions of rural Ireland, that the congregation also included the murderers of Jane and

Bernard O'Reilly, because the tragedy had not been an accident. At the end of the *Chronicle* account was a dramatic addendum, a curt communiqué from Dublin Castle. This read: 'At 5.00 a.m. yesterday the house of Bernard O'Reilly, Derrylangan, Athboy, Co. Meath, was maliciously set on fire and destroyed. His wife and son, aged four years, were unable to escape from the house and were both burned to death.'

The statement from the authorities might have been dismissed as Dublin Castle propaganda, a blatant and typical attempt to pin a tragic accident on the Athboy IRA. The *Meath Chronicle* had three days to digest the communiqué but still carried it, without comment, only at the very end of their lengthy report on the fire. However, it did not take long for the narrative to change. It soon became common knowledge that the O'Reillys had not been victims of a tragic accident.

Since late 1920 – owing to some controversial jury verdicts implicating everyone from named RIC officers to Lloyd George in a number of reprisal killings – Dublin Castle had abandoned coroner's inquests. They were replaced by military 'courts of inquiry' conducted *in camera*. The inquiry into the deaths of Jane and Bernard O'Reilly quickly confirmed the allegation contained in the Dublin Castle communiqué. Both victims of the Derrylangan fire had died of 'shock from burns, wilful murder'.[45]

What followed, as the deaths were subjected to further investigation, was a narrative of 'the emanations of local jealousy and petty spite'. At the preliminary inquiry into the malicious damage compensation claim of Bernard O'Reilly in July 1921, his counsel stated baldly that 'there were some people in the district who objected to a person with a farm marrying a school teacher, or who thought that they would like to see someone else in the school and threatening letters were sent to the Parish Priest and to the lady herself. These letters purported to come from the Irish Republican Army.'[46]

In October, at the Trim Quarter Sessions, in the next presentation of Bernard O'Reilly's compensation claim, the contents of the threatening letter sent to the local parish priest, Fr Matthew O'Farrell, were read in open court.

I. R. Army ... Dear Father O'Farrell,

Unless there be some changes in Rathcairn school the shed of same will be burned in broad daylight; her husband is also warned. Are you aware there is trouble in it for the past twelve months? Her house will be burned also; we get information about her; we must stop her tongue at school. You will have to see after this before further trouble sets in.

From I. R. Army.

A letter of similar nature, with identical handwriting, that had been sent to the O'Reilly family was incinerated in the house fire.

There is not a shred of evidence – from witness statements, RIC files or Brigade Activity Reports – that the IRA was connected with the campaign against Jane O'Reilly in any way. Meath O/C Seán Boylan would never have countenanced an arson attack on the home of a national school principal and a farmer, even if one or both had been suspected of supplying information to the Crown forces, which they most certainly were not. At the Meath compensation hearings in July 1921, where Bernard O'Reilly lodged a claim for £10,000 for the destruction of his house and the murder of his wife and child (he received compensation of £2,500), his counsel informed the tribunal that his client had satisfied himself that the IRA had no involvement in the atrocity. Four years after the killing of his wife and child, O'Reilly underscored his belief that there had been no paramilitary connection to the arsonists who had deprived him of his family when he stood as a republican candidate in the local elections of 1925.[47]

The letter-writing campaign had ended with the threat to burn the O'Reilly home, but it had a prologue of its own. The O'Reilly family had been looking after two children, a niece and nephew sent from England by their mother, a Mrs Fogarty. Sometime before the arson attack, Fogarty had been sent a letter from Derrylangan outlining the alleged neglect that her children were being forced to endure by their uncle and aunt. The letter, rather less literate than the one received by the parish priest – it was largely devoid of the former's oversupply of semi-colons, or indeed of punctuation of any kind – informed Mrs Fogarty that her children were 'wandering through the fields this three days … afeard to go home to the brute they have no cloths on them to keep them warm … she is always persecutin them. This is true as heaven. Do not listen to her lies take them home if possible. A Neighbour.'[48]

The upshot of this 'poison pen' letter was that their mother removed the Fogarty children from Derrylangan and returned them to England.

At the same compensation hearing – as close to a formal inquest as was possible at the time – a local RIC sergeant, James Feely, gave it as his opinion that 'it was from the vicinity of Mrs. Reilly's [sic] place that the perpetrators of the outrage came … there was a certain amount of jealousy about this lady teaching school as she was a farmer's wife and could live without it' – the 'it' in question being her salary of more than £200 per annum. Feely chose not to elaborate on the allegation and no charges were ever brought against anyone for the crime. However, a lot more RIC evidence, pointing in a specific direction, had emerged during the private military court of inquiry, which took place a month after the killing of the O'Reillys. At that hearing, the local RIC District Inspector, a man named Egan, claimed that the fire had been set 'at the instigation of, or with the connivance of Mrs. Doyle and possibly her husband'.[49] Local lore suggests that although the redistribution of the inherited acres of Bernard O'Reilly might have been the ultimate objective, it was the relative wealth of the couple which antagonised their neighbours to the point of arson and murder.

While the deaths of Jane and Bernard O'Reilly Junior were unconnected with the Anglo-Irish War, and were not a direct expression of the agrarian violence of the early 1920s, the arson attack was, nonetheless, emblematic of the almost routine nature of agrarian and political crime by 1921. Distinctions of class were a feature of Irish society: 'tuppence halfpenny looked down on tuppence'. The inevitable corollary was that 'tuppence' often resented the wealth and status of 'tuppence halfpenny'. The anarchy of the early 1920s permitted those so inclined to indulge that resentment.

The tenth commandment advises us that 'thou shalt not covet thy neighbour's goods'. Festering envies and petty jealousies in an unpoliced society – by the spring of 1920, the RIC had withdrawn to a few large towns in each Irish county – offered ample opportunity to go beyond merely coveting, and to actually seize 'thy neighbour's goods'. Twenty years of cattle driving had inured parts of the country to such an environment. Half a decade of land seizures had driven home the message that if thy neighbour had a mite too many goods on his hands, then it was permissible to take appropriative action. While the attack on the home of the O'Reillys in June 1921 did not involve the removal of any of Bernard O'Reilly's cattle, or the seizure of any of his land, nonetheless he was a jumped-up shop assistant who had fallen on his feet and inherited a property that might otherwise have been acquired by Back to the Land, or the Estates Commissioners, and divided amongst the neighbours of his late uncle. To add insult to injury, his wife was bringing an additional £200 a year into their household. Who had ordained that the O'Reillys alone were entitled to this good fortune? One or other of them must, in justice, be prepared to make a financial sacrifice. It was all part and parcel of a chaotic mindset and a twisted logic. It was an extreme variation of what historian Tom Garvin has characterised as 'status resentment',[50] a perverse outlook on life that made it acceptable to threaten, to maim or to seize the property of one's neighbours.

It was the mentality that killed the blameless teacher Jane O'Reilly and her innocent four-year-old son.

V

Redistribution

18

'One more cow, one more sow, one more acre under the plough': land and the Irish Free State

'Any man caught looting or destroying property
should be shot at sight.'[1]

(Michael Collins to the Director of Intelligence, 10 August 1922)

'When a man seizes land in Ireland now he is not seizing
it from the landlord, he is really seizing it from his equally
deserving neighbour.'[2]

(Patrick J. Hogan, Minister for Agriculture,
Dáil Éireann, 5 January 1923)

'He is in conflict with the individuals from whom he acquires
the land, he is in conflict with the small farmers for whom
he is working and who are competing to benefit therefrom
… He is in conflict with lawyers and auctioneers in the
acquisition and pricing of land. His professional expertise is
constantly tested in public as a professional witness under
oath in the courts. He is in conflict with politicians seeking
favours for their supporters.'[3]

(retired Irish Land Commission inspector Martin Brennan
on the working life of a Land Commission inspector)

25 April 1938, the end of the affair

In the end it cost only £10 million. Cheap at half the price.

It could have been much more. Up to £90 million more, according to some pessimists. It was less costly, when adjusted for inflation, than the Louisiana Purchase of 1803, albeit measured in millions of acres rather than of square miles.

First the landlords. Then the Governor General. Now the annuities.

The 1937 constitution had unstitched most of the enveloping cloak of 'dominion status', but now, after some tough negotiation, the Anglo-Irish Trade War (aka the 'Economic War') was over. The treaty ports were coming back, and the much-loathed annuities, payable to the UK government in settlement of the loans made to Irish farmers under the terms of the nineteenth- and twentieth-century land purchase acts, would come to an end after a final payment of £10 million from de Valera's government.

There were critics of this concession, of course – diehards who believed that the land had been stolen by the Tudors, Stuarts and Cromwell in the first place. But de Valera, Seán Lemass and James Ryan, the members of the Irish delegation, were unfazed. There was no point in negotiation without compromise, and de Valera had been happy to abandon his claim for the reimbursement of the £30 million that Irish tenant farmers had already paid out in annuities. A grand total of £40 million to get rid of the landlords was a good deal. The critics would soon get bored and become aggrieved about something else. In the Ireland of the 1930s, they were spoiled for choice.

Back home, the beleaguered farming community, devastated by the six-year trade war, breathed a collective sigh of relief. At last they could recover their losses and develop their holdings with the spare cash that would otherwise have been going to the UK exchequer. The burden of paying out annuities was at an end.

Well ... perhaps not.

The end of annuity payments was to be another classic example of 'Catholic Emancipation Syndrome', i.e. a ground-breaking achievement that breaks precious little ground for its supposed beneficiaries. De Valera had other plans for the annuity money. He was already channelling the *Confessions* of St Augustine of Hippo: 'Please God, make me virtuous, but not just yet.' The £3 million a year that accrued from the annuity funds would still be extracted from the owner/occupiers and would be put to good use elsewhere in a cash-strapped Ireland.

Brother versus brother

'The general condition of affairs makes it quite clear that the land war is coming ... The "land for the people" is almost as respectable an objective as the "Republic" and would make a much wider appeal. Moreover, almost as many abuses could be perpetrated under one pretext as the other.' [4]

('Seizures of land', a memo to the Free State executive council from Patrick Hogan, Minister for Agriculture, 22 December 1922)

The Civil War was at an end, and victory – so went the republican narrative – had gone to a reactionary cabal that was scarcely more acceptable than the imperialists they had replaced. Indeed, the Cumann na nGaedheal government, led by the taciturn W. T. Cosgrave, flanked by the energetic and reactionary Home Affairs minister Kevin O'Higgins, lacked even the redeeming urbanity of many of the members of the departing colonial administration. And they failed to compensate for a deficiency in charisma with a programme that sparkled with any innovative or progressive ideas.

The disillusionment of the members of the military force that the Free State government had insisted on styling pejoratively as 'Irregulars' was shared by the legion of the landless and the land-deprived. When it came to the dispossessed 'congests', Dublin Castle had devoted years to the alternation of repression and conciliation. The new regime was unlikely to be much different, except with a golden harp, rather than a crown, inhabiting the space between the carrot and the stick.

The Civil War cabinet of 'conservative revolutionaries' (Kevin O'Higgins's famous phrase) took power with an already well-developed and jaundiced attitude towards the expropriative and redistributive activities of the new agrarian agitators. These had continued during the period of the Truce (July–December 1921) and added their own grace notes to the soundtrack of the Civil War (June 1922–May 1923). The national reign of terror continued – albeit with radical changes to the plot and the cast of characters – and, so, opportunity beckoned. There was 'brass' to be found in the 'muck' of civil conflict, at least as far as the more enterprising buccaneers were concerned. Their acquisitive instincts were, once again, being encouraged by an entity calling itself Sinn Féin, but this was now a party shorn of all those who recognised the validity of the assurance of Michael Collins that the Anglo-Irish Treaty, signed on 6 December 1921, offered 'the freedom to achieve freedom'.

Republicans like Liam Mellowes and Peadar O'Donnell, who did not subscribe to the incrementalism of Collins, Griffith and Cosgrave, saw political profit in the resumption of agrarian unrest. The latest revolt of the 'congests' was 'a means of mobilising anti-government support'. The inevitable corollary, however, was that the Cumann na nGaedheal administration chose to interpret rural agitation as a specific and direct attack on the legitimacy and authority of the new government – which, of course, it often was. 'Thus,' in the words of legal historian Heather Laird, 'a connection was made between land seizures and anti-Treaty "irregularism" and a corresponding link formed between the defence of private property rights and the defence of the fledgling state.'[5]

On 1 May 1922, with the country on the verge of civil war, the anti-Treaty IRA Army Council had instructed local O/Cs to commandeer certain properties, including all Congested Districts Board land, the estates of absentee landlords and most of the holdings belonging to landowners who had neglected to dispose of their property under the British government land purchase schemes. IRA commandants were instructed to hold the land 'in trust for the Irish people'.[6] While the move was a genuine expression of a principle espoused by many (but not all) anti-Treaty republicans, it was also a blatant bid by militant opponents of the Treaty for the support of the 'congests' (a category not confined by any means to the traditional western stomping ground of the CDB). It certainly had more appeal to the small farmers of the west of Ireland than did the 'steady as she goes' policy of a new Free State government, whose agrarian interventions at times seemed to stretch no further than the collection of land purchase annuities from the farmers fortunate enough to have bought out their landlords, so that these annuities could then be remitted to the British government.

The nation's new governors had been ready – while in their 1920–21 'preparatory phase' – to use revolutionary law to quell the 1920 agitation. They would hardly baulk at the suppression of rampant civil disobedience being supported by members of an insurgency intent upon the destruction of the Irish Free State. By the time that fledging polity was formally established on 6 December 1922, agrarian anarchy posed as many headaches for the Cumann na nGaedheal administration as the waning military efficacy of the anti-Treaty forces. The illicit occupation of grazier properties and landlord-owned estates was continuing, and was now accompanied by rent strikes – a number of which were being conducted against the payment of annuities. The new unarmed police force, An Garda Síochána ('Guardians of the Peace'), established in 1922, was often obliged to summon units of the National Army to assist its members in arresting the illicit occupiers of seized land.

This security deficiency was referred to by the Minister for Agriculture in a seminal memorandum to government on 22 December 1922. Patrick Hogan – 'party polemicist and technocratic legislator'[7] – had been here before. 'I know these signs from my own experience,' he wrote of the worsening state of affairs. This new campaign, he insisted, based on 'letters which have been captured', was well-organised; was 'directed as much against comparatively small farmers as against large landowners'; and 'the general condition of affairs makes it quite clear that the land war is coming'. Hogan, a politician with 'his finger very firmly on the rural pulse',[8] urged the Free State cabinet/executive council to get to grips with this new outbreak of violence, which had already involved gun attacks. He was adamant that the campaign was not susceptible to a conventional policing solution: 'it is quite impossible to deal with the question under the Ministry of Home Affairs as criminal matter. The English tried it here for 20 or 30 years. I saw these measures in operation myself and they were utter failures.'

Hogan's prayers were answered. He got what he was clearly angling for in the shape of the rural equivalent of the sinister enforcers of Oriel House,* the Special Infantry Corps (SIC). This was a concept at which even the crustiest Dublin Castle apparatchik would probably have baulked. It was one of the many ironies of the neophyte Irish Free State that measures that would have been politically unpalatable to a twentieth-century colonial government were deemed acceptable by a hard-pressed foundational nationalist administration. The SIC was established with the twin intentions of crushing agrarian crime and tightening the fetters on militant labour/trade union activity. It thus combined some of the less salubrious features of both the newly disbanded RIC – in its Land War and Plan of Campaign iterations – and the still extant Dublin Metropolitan Police in its handling of the 1913 Lockout.

The SIC was also in a position to kill two birds with a single stone. Some of the labour disputes of the Civil War period were actually occurring in rural Ireland. Many farmers, experiencing falling prices in their principal British markets, were attempting to coerce their labourers into accepting lower wages. This was being resisted by the labourers' representative organisation, the Irish Transport and General Workers Union (ITGWU), at least a third of whose members were employed in agriculture by 1919.[9] A lockout of agricultural labourers in Kilmacthomas, Co. Waterford from May to November 1923 – they had refused to accept the lower pay and longer hours demanded by the Waterford Farmers

---

* Based in Westland Row in Dublin, this was a building housing elements of National Army Intelligence and the Criminal Investigation Department, whose operatives were often accused of participation in the extra-judicial killings of a number of Dublin-based republican activists during the Civil War.

Association[*] – resulted in the Free State government putting the county under martial law and importing the SIC to deal with the strikers. The SIC was instructed to 'use your own discretion re. action to be taken. Use no half measures. Make an example of the place.'[10] An obedient SIC was alleged to have burned the cottages of a number of the striking labourers, in a compelling alternative to conciliation. Local farmers formed a vigilante group, some of whose members were thought to have been responsible for arson attacks and assaults of their own on the strikers. The farm labourers retaliated with attacks on the holdings of their employers, on members of the SIC and on the Free State Army, units of which were deployed to police the dispute. The lockout, not unlike its 1913 urban equivalent in Dublin, ended when the ITGWU ran out of funds to support the labourers and they were 'left at the mercy of the farmers'.

The verdict of the Minister for Home Affairs, Kevin O'Higgins – a martinet with the tenderness of an unpolished diamond – on the entirety of the SIC experiment was that the SIC 'did effective if "rough and ready" work stamping out agrarian anarchy and other serious abuses existing and arising at that time'.[11] Since O'Higgins was not much given to euphemism, we can probably take the word 'stamping' at face value. His view of the expropriators was as clear-cut as his analysis of the SIC's impact – those who were commandeering land were guilty of 'greed, lust, drunkenness and irresponsibility under a political banner … it is not a war properly so-called [but] organised sabotage and [the] disintegration of the social fabric'. If O'Higgins had actually found any specific evidence of lust and drunkenness, he did not share this with his cabinet colleagues.

The absolute commitment of O'Higgins and his colleagues to the retention of the property rights of the grazier and landlord class did not augur well for the social radicalism of the new Free

---

[*] A reduction of eight shillings a week, bringing their pay down to a princely £1 10s a week. 'As much as the industry can stand', according to the farmers' leader, Sir John Keane (Diarmaid Ferriter, *Between Two Hells: The Irish Civil War* (London, 2021), 111).

State government. It would not be entirely cynical to suggest that, in referring to the creators of the Irish Free State as 'conservative revolutionaries', O'Higgins misrepresented the agenda of what was, in many respects, a counter-revolution.

O'Higgins also tacitly supported the *cri de coeur* of his good friend Hogan (both were themselves from 'comfortable' farming backgrounds) demanding that responsibility for dealing with the campaign of agrarian seizures should not be handed over to the Department of Home Affairs, the bailiwick of O'Higgins himself. 'The army must act as armed police as well as military,' he told fellow members of the executive council, in order to 'vindicate the idea of law and ordered government'.[12]

The SIC, when it came into existence in January 1923 – it was affiliated to the Free State Army – was a sizeable force, numbering up to 4,000 men and commanded by Easter Rising veteran Patrick Dalton. While in its size it was a substantial rural militia, it was by no means an elite group. A number of its members were castoffs – pro-Treaty IRA veterans who had failed to make a successful transition into the more disciplined and conventional Irish Free State Army. Some of the SIC officers had also seen service with the Dublin Guard in Kerry during the Civil War. This was a unit with a brutal reputation, and one that is indelibly associated with a number of vicious extra-judicial killings in that county.

Neither did the SIC always draw plaudits in its own areas of operation. For example, the National Army Intelligence section (some of whose operatives were based in Oriel House), reported in the summer of 1923 that the SIC was 'having a very bad effect on the civil population in most districts where it is stationed' and that it was staffed by men of 'low morals'.[13] This assessment was somewhat paradoxical in the context of the charges of 'greed, lust, drunkenness and irresponsibility' laid by Kevin O'Higgins at the door of their antagonists. SIC personnel were often not especially enamoured of their 'terms and conditions'. Captain Higgins of no. 1 Company based at Renmore barracks in Galway, for example, wrote to a friend that 'Connemara is the most desolate place I was ever in, and if the Bolshies wanted to ambush us they needn't fire a shot, all they have to do is roll big boulders down on top of us in the road'.[14] His reference to Bolshevism offers an interesting insight into the perceptions of senior members of the SIC of the politics of their adversaries.

The largely agrarian nature of the work of no. 1 Company is clear from the unit's operational diary from a single week in March 1923:

20 March.	Issued warnings against trespass by stock on land near Tuam.
21 March.	Supervised an eviction at Corrandulla.
23 March.	Collected £7 due to the Land Settlement Commission.
26 March.	Made arrests in connection with land trouble in Gort.
27 March.	Executed a decree for eviction at Killimor.[15]

National Army Intelligence found it difficult to extract coherent statistics from the administratively slapdash SIC on the numbers of those arrested by the force who had been brought before the courts. This dearth of data, allied to the assessment of O'Higgins of the Free State's rural militia as 'rough and ready', suggests that the SIC settled a number of cases out of court by administering its own punishments. Weighed against the horrors of the Civil War in Kerry, the dispensing of a few beatings might seem inconsequential, but they led, inevitably, to resentment against the SIC among many of the landless and small farmers who crossed their path. This, in turn, translated into lingering disaffection with the new Irish Free State in general.

The short-lived SIC (January–December 1923) was, officially at least, responsible for 371 arrests, 173 of which were for a variety of agrarian crimes (land seizures, cattle maiming, trespass). They also cleared dozens of trespassers from occupied land. Some of those arrested were quickly released on signing declarations guaranteeing to keep the peace; others who were charged with more serious offences – in one instance, a case of attempted murder of a Mayo landowner – were detained indefinitely. Livestock left grazing on commandeered land was often sequestered and sold as a supplementary punishment. More than 1,500 cattle were confiscated in this fashion. Many of the SIC's arrests were made under Civil War emergency legislation, which ironically mirrored the many nineteenth-century coercion acts of the British government.

In the case of the members of the collective that seized the McNamara land in Clare (Chapter 17), they were finally removed in December 1923. Either the SIC was not sufficiently heavy-handed (unlikely, because they seized the stock of the collective) or the members of this 'Clare soviet' were prepared to risk jail or injury to retain their commandeered land, because the radicalised farmers and fishermen retook the estate and had to be ejected yet again in May 1924. Their determination to defy the Free State government meant that they were subsequently debarred from benefiting from any future land redistribution schemes. This had been insisted upon by O'Higgins in the debate on the 1923 land bill, when he demanded that those who 'press their claims by their own violence and their own illegalities be placed definitely outside the benefits of this bill'.[16]

The SIC was one of the first units to be disbanded, as part of the general military demobilisation, before the end of 1923. Its continued service was deemed unnecessary with the full deployment of the new Garda Síochána force into rural Ireland and, more significantly, with the passage of the 1923 Land Act by a Free State administration anxious to resume a programme of land purchase in order to pre-empt further agrarian violence.

The Cosgrave government was giving itself an early opportunity to set out its own stall in attacking the fundamental causes of the agrarian unrest and demonstrating that it was going to be something more than a mere conduit for British land purchase annuities.

The changing of the guard: Cumann na nGaedheal, Fianna Fáil and land purchase

'... it is our policy to complete land purchase; it is our policy to make every tenant in the Saorstát the owner of his holding. It is our policy to make every holding in the

Saorstát economic. It is our policy to buy up the congested areas and to buy up the ranch lands outside the congested areas. We can do that. We can do it quickly, and, in spite of the difficulties, it can be done, and it must be done, and we can do it quickly.'[17]

(Patrick J. Hogan, Dáil Éireann, 5 January 1923)

In Aesop's fable of 'The North Wind and the Sun', a bet is placed as to who can force a traveller to remove his coat. The wind, confident in its coercive power, brews up a storm, but with no success. The traveller merely pulls his coat more tightly about himself and struggles onwards. The sun, however, succeeds in parting man and garment by gently increasing the temperature. The moral of the story requires no explication.

Applied to Irish land tenure and the drive to rid the country of the landlord class, the 'North Wind' is represented by generations of rural 'outrage'. The more subtle approach of the 'Sun' is represented by programmes such as the 1903 Wyndham Land Act.

The parable, however, is found wanting in the case of land purchase. The warming rays of the sun managed to persuade the traveller (in this case the landlord) to remove his coat rather than to relinquish it entirely. By the time of the distinctly shaky establishment of the Irish Free State, almost 80 per cent of the occupiers of Irish land had also become owners. However, around two and a half million acres remained in the hands of obdurate landlords unwilling, despite the warming rays of the sun, to hand over their coats altogether.[18] More than 100,000 tenants still waited in frustration to acquire their holdings. More than 3 million acres had yet to be accounted for.[19]

So, to torture the metaphor still further, the government of the new Irish Free State adopted a 'third way'. It stood in the middle of the road, accosted the traveller, and, at gunpoint, ordered him to hand over his coat. As a methodology, it lacked the subtlety of the sun in the fable, but within a generation it had brought about the removal of an aristocratic class that had, according to William O'Brien, descended from 'the throat-cutting and psalm-singing'

Cromwellians. O'Brien, and other propagandists like him, had prepared the way for the final exit of the landlords by the constant 'othering' of the Irish gentry – 'the Irish nation was re-imagined so as to exclude them',[20] according to historian R. V. Comerford – and by the almost formulaic invocation of the Cromwellian confiscations. As Terence Dooley has noted, there were numerous other plantations and re-settlements, but Cromwell 'had assumed mythical proportions of a barbaric nature' and placing the Lord Protector front and centre 'gave land acquisition a moral force that easily justified the compulsory acquisition of lands and the payment for them in virtually worthless bonds'.[21]

Did the Minister protest too much in the presentation of his new land purchase legislation? The 1923 Land Act was introduced with much ballyhoo, as a Free State remedy that would transform all remaining tenant farmers into peasant proprietors and stop at source the flood of illegal expropriation that the SIC would soon be stamping out in its own inimitable fashion. After the SIC stick would come the land act carrot. The new Free State government was attempting to kill mob rule with kindness.

The Minister for Agriculture was emphatic when introducing the legislation. 'The tenant … is entitled to cheap land,' he observed, before assuring his listeners – many of whom must have known better – that 'we can do it quickly'. Was he trying to convince the Dáil or himself? Some of his party colleagues predicted that the legislation would bring an 'end of the agrarian revolution' and 'dispose of the last remnant of landlordism', interventions that proved to be wildly overoptimistic. In an ill-advised hostage to fortune, W. T. Cosgrave himself guaranteed the house that 'the public peace is assured by the passing of this bill'.[22]

The bill did not appear to lack for ambition. Owners of untenanted farms – defined as properties that were either vacant or let under a contract of less than a year in duration,[23] so 'eleven month' land was considered to be untenanted – could be compelled to sell. This acreage was, in the main, still in the hands of landlords, which implied a paucity of sympathy for those on the cusp of dispossession. The British government had given itself limited powers to acquire some 'eleven month' land compulsorily in Birrell's 1909 legislation. Hogan's legislation greatly extended that entitlement. All untenanted land in congested districts was included in the ambit of the legislation, as was land required elsewhere for the relief of congestion.[24] Parallel legislation reconstituted the Land Commission and incorporated into its remit the functions of the Congested Districts Board. At first glance, it was a popular and vote-winning completion of the process of peasant proprietorship, a 'social engineering project of historic magnitude'.[25]

A hint of what might lie in store, however, loitered in the wings during the debate on 5 January 1923. Agrarian idealists, or populists eager to leap onto any bandwagon being driven in the general direction of political power, tended to avoid the awkward conundrum of viability when it came to the business of purchase and redistribution. It was self-evident by the 1920s that any tract of land smaller than 20 acres (or with a rateable valuation of less than £10) was not going to provide a secure future for a family. Now in office, faced with the realities and responsibilities of power, Cumann na nGaedheal and their pragmatic agriculture minister – cut from similar cloth to the hard-headed O'Higgins – understood this. 'Land purchase,' Hogan proclaimed, 'must be an economic proposition.' At the time he made his Dáil remarks, upwards of 300,000 people were reckoned to be living on unsustainable holdings. A decade later, in his criticism of Fianna Fáil's first essay into land purchase legislation, Hogan would sarcastically laud its populist tone as 'good politics' while condemning its attempt to legislate for the acquisition of holdings by the landless as 'rotten economics and rotten national administration'.[26] For their part the Fianna Fáil party that emerged from the second major split in Sinn Féin in 1926, characterised Cumann na nGaedheal agrarian policy, in a striking inversion of the watchword of the Ranch War, as 'the land for the bullock and the man for the road'.[27]

Hogan was a realist when it came to the prospects of the Free State providing land for hundreds of thousands of farm labourers who were 'at present prepared to exercise their claims with gun and torch', he informed W. T. Cosgrave in 1924. A Land Commission survey had put the remaining untenanted land that was actually suitable for redistribution (as opposed to land as yet unpurchased by its occupants) at around 1 million acres. Little enough of that was in the west of Ireland, where most of the 'congests' were situated. Sorting out *that* problem would require the removal of many impoverished farmers to hotly contested 'vacant' land east of the Shannon.

Hogan also had another difficulty. His priority was maintaining and enhancing the lucrative Irish live cattle trade into the British market, despite Sinn Féin condemnation of this policy as an extension of the country's 'economic bondage' and dependence on Britain.[28] His favourite slogan was the inherently self-contradictory 'one more cow, one more sow, one more acre under the plough'. In formulating his legislation, he made a conscious choice to downgrade the claims of the landless in favour of existing tenants with at least some prospect of achieving economic viability. Ultimately, according to Diarmaid Ferriter, farm workers reluctantly accepted this unpalatable reality 'with labourers' representatives concentrating instead on wages and conditions rather than the pursuit of the unrealisable goal of land ownership',[29] a decision that would bring them into regular conflict with the shock troops of the Special Infantry Corps.

If the 1923 Land Act was a genuine attempt by the Free State government to pick up the land purchase process where it had been left off at the outset of the Great War, then raw figures alone underscore the failure of Cosgrave's administration to approach the levels of success of the original Wyndham act. Comparisons with the 1903–14 period are, of course, odious. Most of the low-hanging fruit had already been plucked. Arising out of the 1903 legislation – significantly amended in 1909 – more than 316,000 holdings changed hands before the world war brought the programme to an untimely end. Some 3 per cent of the householders of rural Ireland owned their own land in 1870; that figure had risen to 64 per cent by 1916. Before the European war machines ground into action, more than 11 million acres had been transferred from landlord to tenant. After independence, the revamped Land Commission produced meagre results. The inadequacy of resources was only a partial excuse. The dearth of exchequer funding affected the Land

Commission's bureaucracy alone. The purchase of the residue of landlord estates was financed not from taxation but by the issuing of Land Bonds bearing a rate of interest of 4½ per cent and underwritten, in 1925, by the departed British administration. Finding the means to purchase landed estates or untenanted property was not the problem – although the complexity of the legislation rendered it vulnerable to 'an organised band of landlords with their expert [legal] advisers'[30] looking for ways to circumvent the process. The issue was what to do with the land once it had been acquired. But while the bureaucratic shortcomings of an inadequately resourced Land Commission did have an impact on redistribution, the tepid results of the programme had as much to do with a failure of will. This was a first cousin to the realisation that there simply was not enough available land to satisfy demand. Hogan himself, by 1925, recognised that, while there were around 120,000 'congests' clamouring for land, the Land Commission would only be in a position to acquire 1.2 million acres. If taken to its illogical conclusion, that would equate to an entirely uneconomic 8.5 acres each.

Other realities were also at play. Ireland in the 1920s was home to far more beef cattle than people (it still is). A direct challenge to the nation's graziers, involving the confiscation of rancher land and its re-allocation to small-scale tillage farmers, had no great appeal to Cumann na nGaedheal legislators or to the party's more influential supporters, many of whom happened to be graziers themselves. The government baulked at undermining the worth of the golden bullock. Dismantling landlordism had its appeal, but the government was 'not prepared to take similar action against big commercial farmers, including graziers'.[31] In a parliament bereft of anti-Treaty representatives – de Valera's Sinn Féin was boycotting the Dáil – there was little stomach for radical action. This chimed well with Cumann na nGaedheal's conservative 'counter-revolutionary' instincts.

In 1923, the year of the passage of the first Irish Free State Land Act, 'there were an estimated 114,000 unpurchased tenancies remaining in the Free State'.[32] Between 1923 and 1932, 330,000 acres were acquired by the Land Commission and distributed to

17,000 families. This represented less than a quarter of the available acreage, and barely 15 per cent of the unresolved tenancies. This relative failure, over the course of a decade, to complete the programme of peasant proprietorship was just one of the many factors that led to the defeat of the free-trade-oriented Cumann na nGaedheal in the general election of 1932, and the uneasy transfer of power to a protectionist Fianna Fáil government led by Eamon de Valera.

Another factor was the growing antagonism towards the continued payment of land annuities to the British government, fostered by, among others, that political *rara avis*, a Donegal communist. Peadar O'Donnell – anti-Treaty IRA stalwart and founder, in 1919, of the 'soviet' behind a successful strike at Monaghan County Asylum – had turned his attention, after the Civil War, back to the issue of land ownership. O'Donnell 'viewed annuities as akin to the payment of tribute and therefore a remnant of British colonialism in Ireland'.[33] The collection of annuities had lagged during the War of Independence and the Civil War, and there is no doubt that many tenant farmers lived in hope that either the payments would be abandoned altogether, or arrears would be written off. O'Donnell, through the pages of *An Phoblacht*, the Sinn Féin/IRA newspaper, founded in 1925, highlighted the issue, especially in his native county of Donegal, where the renewed collection of arrears began after the conclusion, in 1926, of the Ultimate Financial Settlement between the Irish Free State and British governments. This obliged the Free State administration to collect the annuities from Irish tenant farmers and remit the payments to the British exchequer. Court decrees for the confiscation of properties in lieu of payment were also being served on farmers in default – wherever any bailiffs could be found to serve them. A number of Donegal bailiffs had chosen to resign rather than become involved in the process of distraint of the properties of those who refused to continue the payment of what O'Donnell liked to call 'rent'. Towards the end of the annuities agitation, the political vehicle used by O'Donnell and like-minded individuals for the prosecution of this renewal of activist agrarianism was the socialistic Saor Éire, established in 1931 and suppressed by the Free State government in the same year.[34]

After the publication in November 1926 of the financial arrangements agreed between the Free State and Britain (the Ultimate Financial Settlement), the continued payment of annuities became a national issue. It was quickly identified by the newly established Fianna Fáil party as a potential vote-winner. O'Donnell's vague pipe-dream of the iniquity of this continued payment of 'tribute' being parlayed into some sort of utopian agrarian/communist revolution, with the IRA in the lead, was waylaid by the distinctly anti-socialist de Valera's adoption of the issue. It was Fianna Fáil (created after the pragmatic de Valera's split with Sinn Féin over its abstentionist policy), not Saor Éire or any other fringe socialist/republican organisation, that became the main beneficiary of the six years of agitation against the continued payment of annuities between 1926 and 1932.

The 1932 general election result led to a new Fianna Fáil administration, one claiming to have the agrarian interests of the 'small man' at heart. The much reviled 'Minister for Grass', Patrick Hogan – the victim of constant attacks accusing him of a desire to turn Ireland into 'one big grazing ranch'[35] – handed over his portfolio to James Ryan, who retained it for the next fifteen years.

If the 1923–32 Cumann na nGaedheal record of land redistribution was disappointing – and hedged around with allegations of an inherent bias towards grazier interests – what of the efforts of Fianna Fáil, opponents of large-scale commercial agriculture and self-proclaimed champions of the dispossessed (Wolfe Tone's 'men of no property') between 1932 and 1939? Under the indicative slogan 'Speed the plough', and the rather more vituperative 'Get Cosgrave out', Fianna Fáil – 'a constructive alternative to communism', according to one of its senior figures, future Taoiseach Seán Lemass – went to the country in the 1932 general election on a pledge of increasing the acreage of tillage and taking some giant steps in the direction of agricultural self-sufficiency. De Valera promised that Irish farmers would be encouraged – and subsidised if necessary – to meet the country's requirements for the staple crops of wheat, oats and barley. This, Fianna Fáil assured rural voters, would increase the earnings of agricultural workers and small farmers by over £3 million per annum, coincidentally the amount still being remitted each year in land annuities.

And it worked. As an electoral ploy at least. Fianna Fáil emerged from the election as the largest party and were able to govern with Labour Party support. 'Great were the expectations of the small farmers; the time seemed ripe for a "new departure".'[36]

The 'Soldiers of Destiny'* – 'a complex coalition of traditionalists, modernisers, visionaries, conservatives, radicals, cranks and optimists',[37] according to Diarmaid Ferriter – after retaining power in a January 1933 general election, were quick to publish their own land legislation under the aegis of former Civil War IRA chief of staff Frank Aiken. Aiken's pass at land redistribution went further than Hogan's and was duly condemned by the Cumann na nGaedheal opposition as 'undiluted communism'.

The power of the Land Commission to appropriate tenant-purchased land was greatly enhanced. Ancillary clauses of Aiken's legislation made it apparent that 'the target of these provisions was clearly extensive non-residential graziers and those letting land to them'. Fianna Fáil was in pursuit of the 'new landlords' who were buying up land previously acquired by tenant farmers under British land purchase programmes. The harassment of the ranchers continued with fresh land legislation in 1936, accentuating the party's more radical approach to redistribution than that of its predecessors, and de Valera's prioritisation of the production of grains and other tillage products in a drive towards agricultural self-sufficiency.

Further legislation in 1939 prompted Fine Gael† charges that Fianna Fáil redistribution policies had endowed the Land Commission with an inordinate amount of authority; 'the powers

---

* The commonly accepted translation of 'Fianna Fáil'.
† Cumann na nGaedheal became Fine Gael in September 1933 after merging with two smaller parties.

are tantamount to confiscation',[38] chided one opposition TD. The Co. Meath rancher Cornelius Garvin would have agreed. He grazed his livestock over 250 acres in Teltown, near Kells. Between 1917 and 1975, farms of over 200 acres declined by 25 per cent,[*] while farms of over thirty acres increased by a similar percentage. Under Fianna Fáil, the commissioners were breaking up large pasture farms, especially if they were non-residential and provided little local employment. An augury might be the arrival of a Land Commission inspector to run the rule over standards of husbandry and land use on a farm. In 1936, the Land Commission clearly decided that Garvin was neglecting or failing to work his land properly – the commission itself defined the parameters of 'neglect' and often did so quite autocratically – and acquired 101 acres of his holding. The commissioners made a return visit in 1959 and took a further eighty-eight acres, leaving Garvin to graze his cattle over a greatly reduced sixty-one acres.[39] What price fixity of tenure, he might well have grumbled. James Dillon, a future Fine Gael leader, once accused the commission of being 'an infinitely worse landlord than Clanricarde ever was'.[40]

But a radical approach is just that; a methodology or prevailing philosophy; an agenda; a preferred modus operandi. As it transpired, the actual performance of de Valera's government was hardly an unmitigated triumph. Cosgrave's administration managed to acquire 330,000 acres of untenanted land over a nine-year period (for an average of c.37,000 acres per annum). Between its first accession to power in February 1932 (with Labour Party support)[†] and March 1940, Fianna Fáil acquired a total of 435,067 acres (an average of 53,000 acres per annum). After a promising start between 1934 and 1936, with the purchase of more than 200,000 acres, Fianna Fáil's acquisition policy hit the brick wall of economic, social and political reality. The Land Commission did

---

[*] In the Connacht grazing areas, farms in this category declined by 70 per cent over the same period.

[†] A snap general election in 1933 led to Fianna Fáil gains but still left de Valera shy of an overall majority. However, with a number of subsequent by-election wins, the party was able to govern without Labour support.

not have the administrative capacity to cope with the demands placed on it by a government that wanted to distinguish itself from its predecessor as rapidly as possible, and inevitable legal challenges to compulsory purchases slowed progress, but there was also a realisation in government – with Seán Lemass as the leading pragmatist – that cattle exports, *faute de mieux*, were the backbone of the Irish economy and acquiring large swathes of grazier land to create more uneconomic tillage-based holdings might, in the words of Patrick Hogan, be 'good politics', but not 'good economics'. Political historian Tom Garvin has written that de Valera had made a 'wager on the weak' that had clear electoral benefits in 1932. However, ultimately, the taoiseach lost that bet when faced with the task of reversing the Cromwellian plantation by relocating the descendants of the dispossessed onto land east of the Shannon. Garvin goes on: 'the large commercial farmers survived because de Valera realised that, despite his own sentimental anti-modernism, he could scarcely forego the productive power of what commercialised agriculture had in the parlous circumstances of the time … this economic importance made the sector's enemies stay their hand.'[41]

By the end of the 1930s, the Land Commission had essentially done its job within the congested districts. Any further large-scale redistribution was going to have to come from the compulsory acquisition of grazier farms in Leinster and elsewhere. In effect, it was a form of legalised land seizure. The truth, seldom publicly acknowledged by the leadership of either of the former Civil War opponents, was that the 'heaven' of universal and absolute land redistribution was unattainable. Some would make it past the pearly gates, but hundreds of thousands would remain in purgatory. The Land Commission was receiving 20–25,000 letters a year during the 1930s, from aspirants in a state of grace, pleading for salvation. Such a demand could never be satisfied on a small and finite land mass bounded by the Irish Sea and the Atlantic Ocean and the land border with Northern Ireland.

The effective arbiter, when it came to both acquisition and redistribution, was the Land Commission inspector. Inspectors were despatched to interrogate all prospective candidates for land within a mile of a newly available property. All potential allottees were interviewed, their needs and their resources were evaluated, and recommendations were made to the commissioners by the omnipotent inspector. In the course of their work, the inspectors were privy to the sort of backbiting and invective unique to rural Ireland. Farmers, with skin in the game, had not a good word to say about their neighbours. One commissioner wrote that 'when the inspector is going his rounds at this work he inevitably hears the whole truth, for the competition for land is so keen that each applicant will see to it that his neighbour will not get away with his particular story'.[42]

Even where peasant dreams were fulfilled, the outcome could be almost as disappointing as the status quo. Redistributed farms tended to be small. Rather than carve out workable holdings for a limited number of applicants, the Land Commission, under social and political pressure, adopted the practice of allocating land in 'a fair and reasonable manner amongst as many ... smallholders as is practicable'.[43] Which meant that redistributed farms were generally between twenty and twenty-five acres in size. By failing to come to grips with issues of efficiency and viability, the Land Commission succeeded in retarding the modernisation of Irish agriculture. In attempting to please everyone, they pleased very few.

Disappointment with the politics of land purchase in an independent Ireland, however, went well beyond the inadequacy of the amounts of land acquired for redistribution. If acquisition was problematic, re-allocation was a more immediate *casus belli*. 'Allegations that political interference was widespread, and that it deprived the Land Commission of much of its autonomy, were common.'[44] Anecdotally, pressure was regularly brought to bear on the Minister for Lands, and on the land commissioners, when it came to the disposal of available properties. Although the commission was given full operational independence in 1933, Cumann na nGaedheal/Fine Gael allegations of Fianna Fáil beneficence towards its own supporters were loud and frequent, echoing similar Fianna Fáil accusations against Cumann na nGaedheal during the years of the Cosgrave administration. Fianna Fáil cumainn (local party clubs) were regularly accused, for example, of malevolently pressurising the commissioners to select for acquisition capacious grazier properties belonging to prominent Fine Gael supporters. Even where politicians were unable to influence the decisions of commissioners and inspectors, they were anxious that their constituents should believe that they had. Calculations by Terence Dooley based on an analysis of Dáil debates from 1923 to 1939 indicate that of 5,300 land-related questions asked by TDs during that period, 75 per cent related to the acquisition or division of land in their constituency.[45]

There was also ongoing resistance to the introduction of 'strangers', i.e. the internal migration of farmers from the former 'congested' kingdom of the CDB to land east or south of the Shannon. Even the doyen of the 'cattle drive', Laurence Ginnell, had, in the throes of the Ranch War, been concerned 'at the prospect of western migrants being "planted" in the rich lands of Meath at the expense of local claimants'.[46]

Which is precisely what happened when culture and economics became entangled.

'No more migrants': the failure to lift the 'curse of Cromwell'

'We must help them to help themselves ... they must not be forever the paupers of the nation.'[47]

(Gearóid O'Sullivan TD, Dáil Éireann, 2 May 1928)

Was it the case that at some point in the 1920s the issues of land distribution, and the revival of the Irish language, would inevitably clash, or coalesce? Whether it was or not, that is exactly what occurred. Was it inevitable that this engagement should promote a visceral anger, and tap into a deep well of racism and bigotry? Whether it was or not, that is exactly what occurred.

Given the Conradh na Gaeilge (Gaelic League) background of much of the leadership (as well as the rank and file) of the Irish revolutionary generation, the stabilisation and retention of the Irish language, and its ultimate replacement of English as the country's lingua franca, was an oft-stated ideal. To what extent it was ever seen as a realistic objective was an entirely different matter. Even the most committed Gaelgeóirí would probably have accepted a linguistic scenario whereby Ireland became Wales, albeit without the princely trappings.

However, although deference – often no more than skin deep – to the Irish language 'as an essential ingredient of Irish nationality'[48] was a sine qua non for Free State politicians, stabilisation of the numbers of Irish speakers was the primary concern in the years after independence, rather than any crusade to create a *pobal fíor-Ghaelach* (a truly Irish-speaking population). While Conradh na Gaeilge had been notably successful in re-acquainting urban Ireland with spoken Irish from the early 1900s, the position of native Irish speakers in the rural Gaelic heartlands of the west of Ireland was parlous. By the time of independence, there were few pockets of Irish speakers outside the ambit of the Congested Districts Board. Migration from the western seaboard, where, astonishingly, near-famine conditions prevailed again in 1922, was rife. A Department of Local Government report that year noted that 'a most painful feature is that the native-speaking population has suffered from economic pressure to an altogether disproportionate extent'.[49] While you did not have to be practically destitute to be a native Irish speaker in the new Ireland, it certainly helped.

Some of the population movement from the western Gaeltacht regions involved the internal migration of 'congests' to Ireland's cities, large towns or more prosperous rural locales, where some sort of employment might be available. Most, however, meant permanent emigration to the UK or the USA, of the type described in works like *Rotha Mór an tSaoil* ('The Great Wheel of Life', also known as *The Hard Road to Klondike*) by Donegal writer Mící Mac Gabhann* (Michael Smith) and *Dialann Deoraí* ('Diary of an Exile') by Dónall MacAmhlaigh (Daniel McAuley).

---

* Mac Gabhann actually made enough money in the USA to enable him to return, later in life, to his native Donegal, where he died in 1948. *Rotha Mór an tSaoil* was published posthumously in 1959, the year before *Dialann Deoraí*.

After independence, it quickly became clear that there was insufficient land along the western seaboard to facilitate redistribution to native Irish speakers and stem the flow of *gaeilgeoirí* from the west, and from the country. The logical alternative was to endeavour to keep these potential emigrants at home, rather than to have them augment the Irish-speaking populations of Liverpool, London, New York and Boston. In order to do so, however, it was imperative that they be allocated viable holdings outside of the region that was formerly the remit of the CDB. And that was going to be hugely problematic.

Even in the 'grazier country' of the Irish midlands, for example, where national public opinion might actually relish the compulsory acquisition of the land of a few of the more obnoxious ranchers, or remaining landlords, there was a more than adequate supply of small farmers and landless ready and willing to step up and move onto any land cleared of cattle. As already noted, even the warrior chief of the drivers himself, Laurence Ginnell, had been wary of the oft-mooted idea of the resettlement of impoverished western *gaeligeoirí* to farms in the Irish midlands. The great tradition of animosity towards the 'stranger' did not just apply to the occasional random travelling *spailpín* seeking temporary agricultural employment outside of his own parish and, *ipso facto*, depriving a native son of a labouring job. The idea of, for example, a cohort of 'congests' being parachuted from Connemara (Galway) or Glenties (Donegal) and transplanted onto Land Commission holdings in the midlands was anathema to a local labourer patiently eyeing a farm in Meath or Westmeath, and waiting to assume ownership. Nonetheless, hundreds of west of Ireland families were transplanted in spite of local antagonism. Between 1937 and 1978, the Land Commission moved 14,500 families from Connacht onto 382,000 acres in the east and the midlands of the country.[50]

The experiments of Rathcairn, Gibbstown and Allenstown in Co. Meath, however, between 1935 and 1940, were of a different order entirely.

The Cumann na nGaedheal government learned early that the solution to a knotty problem was to postpone any decision-making indefinitely, by establishing a commission to delve into the intricacies of the situation and come up with a set of recommendations that could be conveniently ignored, or exuberantly cherry-picked. Thus did *Coimisiún na Gaeltachta* (the Gaeltacht Commission) come about in 1925, under the chairmanship of General Richard Mulcahy, long-time Gaelic Leaguer, former commander of the National Army and a grandee at something of a loose end since his resignation as Minister for Defence after the demobilisation debacle and 'Army mutiny' of 1924.

Mulcahy's commission conducted a series of interviews in existing Gaeltacht areas and reported in August 1926. Central to its recommendations was the advice to the Cosgrave government that the extension of the Gaeltacht beyond its current dwindling area was a matter of urgency. This proposal was integral to the policy of spreading the language, but also had its own subtext. Just as the Gaeltacht was required to expand for the Irish language to be relevant, so did native Irish speakers need to relocate to enable them to thrive economically, and to become proselytisers for the cause of spoken Irish. Were this not to happen, the fate of the native Irish speaker would, according to the commission, be 'one of continued poverty and degradation in his native surroundings ... migratory labour in Britain or elsewhere and government relief; or emigration with the consequent loss to the living language position'.[51]

Predictably, the report was left to gather spider's webs on an administrative shelf, where it would be joined regularly by many more learned reports on the Irish language, and a plethora of other issues, that were required to be put on the long finger. The philosophical enthusiasm for the preservation of the Irish language was always more pronounced than any willingness to engage with the practicalities of such an ambitious project. The Cumann na nGaedheal government baulked at potential relocation costs of £14 million, and even *Gaeilgóir* 'ultra', Finance Minister Ernest Blythe, allowed his innate parsimony to triumph over his championing of the Irish language. Finance said no! Rather than transfer dozens of small farmers to the east of the country, the policy adopted up to 1932 was to relocate western graziers to comparable lands in Leinster and divide up their Connacht ranches among 'congests'.

The commitment of the Fianna Fáil government from 1932 onwards to tackling the issue of western migration, in the spirit of *fiat justitia ruat caelum* ('let justice be done though the heavens fall'), was more genuine than that of its predecessor. Rancorous and often violent local antagonism, exploited for their own political ends by members of opposition parties, principally but not exclusively Fine Gael, ensured that the heavens did fall. Goaded into action by organisations like the leftist 'Muintir na Gaeltachta' ('People of the Gaeltacht') – led by the celebrated Gaelic writer, scholar and leading post-independence republican activist Mairtín Ó Cadhain – de Valera's government went beyond the payment of lip service to the dissemination of the Irish language, clumsily melded land redistribution and the revival of Gaelic, and in the process brought much grief down on its head.

A single case study of the first social experiment in relocation will suffice to expose an almost astonishing level of cruelty and intolerance, and a level of fanaticism that harked back to some of the excesses of the Land War.

In 1935, twenty-eight Connemara families, comprising 182 people, were relocated by the Fianna Fáil government from Co. Galway to land around the Co. Meath village of Rathcairn – then known as 'Rathcarron' and also spelled 'Rathcarne' – located between the towns of Athboy and Trim. This became 'Gaeltacht colony no. 1'.[52] The choice of name was unfortunate and lacked diplomacy and foresight. The newcomers were quickly branded locally as 'colonists', not a comforting or comfortable label in post-independence Ireland. The former agriculture minister, Patrick Hogan, was less than impressed with the government's initiative, and accused Fianna Fáil of 'pandering to the small-farmer and labouring classes in an attempt to secure votes'. Hogan's criticisms, however, were mild in comparison with the bile of local TD Captain Patrick Giles – his rank was a legacy of the Civil War Free State Army. Giles, a former member of the executive council of the proto-fascist Blueshirts, demanded that An Garda Síochána send regular police patrols to protect Rathcairn residents from these new 'fish out of water'. He claimed that the recent arrivals, though now the owners of excellent quality land, were to be found every week in the local labour exchange.[53] At an anti-migrant protest meeting in November 1937, Giles invoked the late Lord Protector himself while wielding a racist dog-whistle, declaring that 'some of the migrants claimed to be the descendants of Meath people driven out by Cromwell, but the majority of them had more foreign blood in their veins ... the migrants brought into Rathcarn [sic] were not much of an asset to Meath'.[54] He further maintained that 'these colonies [will] be English-speaking colonies in five years'.[55]

In the wake of the establishment of 'Gaeltacht colony no. 2', in nearby Gibbstown in 1937, fifty families, many speaking entirely different dialects of Irish, were relocated from Mayo, Kerry, Donegal and Cork.[56] Giles and his two Fine Gael running mates in the general election of 1938, Michael Sweeney and Charles Fagan, took out splenetic advertisements in the *Meath Chronicle* prominently advertising their joint belief that 'Meath wants no more migrants'.[57]

The bilious sentiments of Giles were echoed by the equally venomous Patrick Belton, a renegade Fianna Fáil TD who had defected to Fine Gael in 1933. Belton, a farmer and property developer, accused Fianna Fáil of 'trying to find homes for imbeciles on the land' and alleged that the Connemara migrants, as well as being imbecilic, were exceptionally slothful. He claimed that they slept in until the afternoon and then spent much of their time distilling illicit *poitín*. Strident opposition to the migration policy came also from Meath-based Fianna Fáil party members. At the party's Ard Fheis (convention) in 1937, a NIMBY-ist* Meath delegate suggested that when it came to internal migration, the government 'should try the valleys of Limerick or the plains of Kildare ... they should leave poor old Meath alone'.[58]

Far worse, however, was the treatment meted out to the new migrants by local people in Meath itself, some of whom had themselves been turned down for redistributed land. This extended as far as threats of repercussions, as well as actual violence. This campaign began with the intimidation of Michael Lynam, a

---

* Although the concept was familiar at the time, the acronym for Not In My Back Yard was not.

Land Commission official behind the project, who received death threats from a rejected applicant for land. The migrants' use of the Irish language was ridiculed, and they were advised to stop talking 'gibberish' when overheard in conversation with one another (in at least one instance, according to Mayo migrant Maggie Lynskey, by a Roman Catholic priest in a confessional).[59] Anti-migrant slogans ('No more migrants wanted here', 'This land is not for Connemara people, it is for Meath men') were daubed on their doors. Shots were fired into their homes and one house was burgled. An attempt was made to burn one of the houses being built for the newcomers. Tensions burst into the open with street riots in the town of Athboy.[60]

Eamon Martin, the father of Meath-born novelist Emer Martin, who was brought up in Kilbride, adjacent to the Rathcairn and Gibbstown Gaeltacht areas (thirteen families were relocated to Kilbride from Galway in 1937), recalled to his daughter some of the difficulties the Connemara migrants had on arrival in Meath: 'I remember the Irish speakers trying to come into the local pub for a drink and being run out of the place as soon as they spoke. Sadly, instead of embracing them for what they could teach us, they were looked down on … Some of these new settlers wanted to put their children in the school in Kilbride to learn English rather than keep them stigmatised in their brand new Gaeltacht.'[61]

A bridge-building effort in July 1938, attended by de Valera, while successful in itself, appears to have done little to reduce tensions in the Rathcairn-Gibbstown neighbourhood. Neither did mutual antagonism stop at the Meath border. In *Dialann Deoraí*, Donall MacAmhlaigh wrote about a Meath Gaeltacht* emigrant in England being goaded into a fight over the Rathcairn-Gibbstown resettlement by a fellow Irish exile outside a London dancehall. The ongoing animosity, which lasted into the 1940s and beyond, was not helped by headlines in a regional newspaper,

---

* Technically, Rathcairn and Gibbstown only acquired official Gaeltacht status in 1967. The current population of both villages is just under 2,000 and accounts for around 17 per cent of the total Gaeltacht population of the country.

the 'sensational and inflammatory'[62] *Drogheda Independent* – the *Meath Chronicle* adopted a somewhat more benign approach to the experiment – such as that of 31 August 1946. This read 'Reign of terror in part of Meath' and went on to describe the Connemara migrants as being akin to 'Corsican bandits' and 'red Indians'.

At a ceremony in 2010 to mark the seventy-fifth anniversary of the Rathcairn experiment, it was accepted that tensions had continued in the area until the 1970s. Nonetheless, the Rathcairn-Gibbstown social experiment somehow managed to take root, and in 1967, after a language survey was conducted, the two villages and their hinterland were officially designated as Gaeltacht areas.

Undeterred by the hostility directed at Gaeltacht colonies 1 and 2, in 1940 the government moved twenty-three Irish-speaking families from the area around Clonbur in Co. Galway to Allenstown in Co. Meath, close to Rathcairn and Gibbstown. What happened in Allenstown is succinctly captured in the title of a beautifully produced social history of the area by local resident Martin O'Halloran. *The Lost Gaeltacht* references the 1967 language survey, which noted of Allenstown that 'there has been no recent claim that the language has survived there to an extent that would justify special consideration at this stage'.[63] The settlement was not conferred with Gaeltacht status.

The failed – in purely linguistic terms – Allenstown experiment is something of a metaphor for modern Ireland. A small community weathers adversity, abandons old ways, modernises, takes advantage of educational opportunities, achieves independence and a decent measure of prosperity, and loses its native language.

The 'Economic War', 1932–8

Despite their obvious and, perhaps, inevitable shortcomings – it would take a dozen further pieces of legislation over forty years to get to grips with the issue – both Free State governments between 1922 and 1937 took agriculture and land redistribution seriously, while not necessarily agreeing on how the former could be developed, and the latter achieved. After all, as UCD historian

Paul Rouse articulated in the *Irish Times* in January 2022, 'the social vision that was wrapped around the political revolution was rooted in the construction of a small farming country of prospering rural homesteads',[64] so both parties could hardly do otherwise.

Sadly, prioritisation did not guarantee positive outcomes.

The 1924 Minister and Secretaries Act established not a Department of Agriculture but a Department of *Lands* and Agriculture, finally unmooring 'Technical Instruction' – with which Dublin Castle had coupled agriculture – from its agrarian sibling. If longevity offers any guide to the degree of priority afforded an issue, it is worth pointing out that it took the Irish Free State/Republic of Ireland until 1999 to dispense finally with the Land Commission.* Northern Ireland closed down its own equivalent in 1935. The land acquisition process was not finally completed until the 1980s, at which point almost 2.5 million acres had been distributed at a cost of £287 million. Some 2.34 million acres (947,000 hectares) had passed through the hands of the Land Commission by then, 20 per cent of the total area of agricultural land in the twenty-six counties. The commission finally closed its doors (and effectively sealed off its extensive and invaluable archive) in 1992.

The reality of rural Ireland in the 1920s and 1930s (and into the adjacent decades beyond the remit of this volume) was one of economic stagnation. In fact, mere stagnation, suggestive at least of the maintenance of a sclerotic status quo, would have been preferable to the enormous outflow of humanity, the bulk of whom were from rural Ireland, which ensured that the steady (and then spectacular) population increase following the devastating famine of 1741 was not repeated in the century after the Great Famine of the 1840s. The 1926 census, which registered a population of 2,971,992 in the new Free State – a decline of more than 5 per cent since the 1911 head count – confirmed the essentially rural nature of Irish society. Less than one-third of the population (31 per

---

* Enabling legislation ending its work (the Irish Land Commission Dissolution Act) was passed in 1992 but was not formally enacted (by ministerial order) until 1999.

cent) lived in towns of more than 1,500 people. Ten years later, the urban share was up to 36 per cent. During the decade between 1926 and 1936, the number of people living in rural Ireland had fallen by almost 300,000. The figures for 1946 showed a further decline, with the numbers living in rural Ireland now down to 62 per cent of the total population.

The protectionist economic policies of successive governments, not finally abandoned until the 1960s, played a major part in this decline, ensuring that Ireland is globally unique in having a smaller population today than in the 1840s. However, another of the contributory factors was the parlous demographics of the Irish peasantry. The failure of the Cumann na nGaedheal and Fianna Fáil governments to rise to the (impossible) challenge of providing land for all sent thousands of labourers and uneconomic smallholders to the emigrant boats. Which is not to suggest that the reality would have been all that different had both parties managed to deliver more land for redistribution. Hogan's unpalatable, but nonetheless realistic, assessment of the relative failure of peasant proprietorship to bring economic sustainability in its wake was also a factor in the country's lamentable emigration statistics. As was the dismal failure to industrialise. A grand total of 5,000 new jobs were created in manufacturing between 1926 and 1931. To Cumann na nGaedheal, in the words of historian Diarmaid Ferriter, 'national development was synonymous with agricultural development ... the interests of the farmer and the nation were identical'.[65]

The need to pass on an intact farm to a single member of the inheriting generation accounted for thousands of supernumerary sons and daughters joining those destined to be disappointed by the land purchase programme. Taking 1910 as our base year, by 1939 the total number of agricultural holdings in the twenty-six counties of the new Irish Free State had declined by 19 per cent. Most of those defunct farms were holdings of less than thirty acres. Almost one third (31 per cent) of the country's small farms disappeared over three decades between 1910 and 1940. The only other decline in numbers was a small reduction (14 per cent) in the category of farms of more than 200 acres.[66]

Into that depressed and dilapidated economic climate, further rainfall was introduced with the beginning of the so-called 'Economic War' in 1932. Cumann na nGaedheal had largely functioned in a free-trade – critics would say *laissez-faire* – environment for the duration of its tenure in office. Fianna Fáil was married to protectionism and won two elections, in 1932 and 1933, based on pledges to shelter the developing economy behind tariff walls. Cumann na nGaedheal had used tariffs for raising revenue. Their successors, while grateful for the revenue, had diametrically different motives for erecting new barriers to free trade. However, where there is protection there is retaliation, and not only did de Valera provoke reactive trade tariffs, he also invited economic reprisals from the UK by delivering on a long-standing republican election promise to end the payment of land annuities to the British government.

After independence, remittances were no longer made directly to the UK exchequer by the former tenants. The Free State government became the conduit for these agrarian alimony payments. Cumann na nGaedheal had dutifully remunerated the UK exchequer during its tenure, drawing derision and vilification from Sinn Féin, and later from Fianna Fáil, as it did so. In 1925, Ireland had been relieved of its obligation to pay any further share of the UK public debt after the conclusion of the Ultimate Financial Settlement. In one of his occasional forays into Jesuitical thinking, de Valera argued that land annuities constituted 'public debt'. On this basis, he pledged, in both the general elections of 1927 and 1932, to revoke the payment of annuities.

In 1932, de Valera was required to deliver on his promise. Accordingly, one of the first acts of the new Fianna Fáil government was to pick a fight with a neighbouring state to which Ireland despatched 90 per cent of its exports. He went even further by demanding that the UK government reimburse the £30 million already remitted by Irish tenant farmers in payment of their annuities to the British exchequer. The UK government, in an attempt to extract, in some form or other, what it was due from Ireland, took the logical step of placing a 20 per cent tariff on the live Irish cattle trade. In this fashion, they succeeded in tapping up the country's graziers, albeit indirectly, for their annuities.

The Cumann na nGaedheal opposition threw up its hands in horror at this display of Fianna Fáil disrespect for solemn sovereign agreements. In a Dáil debate, W. T. Cosgrave raided the Irish pantheon and invoked the Land League leadership in his support. He claimed, with a straight face, that the flawless Cumann na nGaedheal record of remission of annuities 'was their vindication of the undertakings and words of Parnell, Redmond, Dillon, Davitt, Healy and the others'.[67] At least one name looks out of place in that roll of honour. One can imagine that Michael Davitt might well have approved of de Valera's defiance of the ultimate phase of a system he described in *The Fall of Feudalism in Ireland* as 'the bastard offspring of force and wrong'.[68]

Thus began a reciprocal trade war in which Irish people were encouraged by their new leaders to invoke the spirit of the great patriotic Dean of St Patrick's Cathedral, Jonathan Swift, and 'burn everything that comes from England except their people and their coal'. The option, however, of Irish householders warming themselves over a British coal fire was quickly removed anyway, when a ban on any such imports was imposed. The option of emigration, in light of the ongoing Great Depression, was also removed for those feeling the pinch of this latest deterioration in Anglo-Irish relations.

The fact that much of the economic hardship consequent on the refusal to remit the land annuities fell on the country's wealthier farmers did not give rise to much lost sleep within the ranks of the Fianna Fáil cabinet. Graziers, hugely reliant on the live export trade to the UK in order to dispose of more than half of their stock each year, were – risibly – encouraged to supply the tiny Irish market with meat. Stories abound from this era of beef farmers returning from rural markets with their stock, having failed to secure an adequate price, only to be forced to agree to half that unacceptable price the following week. Prices fell to such an extent that farmers often slaughtered their cattle rather than bother to bring them to market. The introduction of a 'free beef scheme' by the government in 1934 offered some respite. This was designed to create a price floor for livestock farmers while supplementing the diets of those on unemployment assistance.

Elements within the Fianna Fáil government – not including Finance Minister Sean McEntee – gleefully anticipated that the government-created crisis would provoke a rush back to tillage, and the realisation of de Valera's utopian 'frugal comfort' vision of an agriculturally self-sufficient nation and 'a countryside … bright with cosy homesteads'.* While there was no actual 'Dig for Victory' advertising campaign, there was an assumption that economic necessity would prompt a major change in patterns of land use. However, it would be erroneous to see the 'Economic War' as some sort of conscious experiment in social engineering. That would have required leadership far more devious than even that of which de Valera was capable, although some Cumann na nGaedheal/Fine Gael conspiracy theorists were eager to see Fianna Fáil policy as an effort to bring about a 'peasant agrarian revolution at the expense of export agriculture and the cattle economy' and the 'first step in an Irish anti-Kulak campaign'.[69] A degree of self-sufficiency was achieved, but with the inflexibility of graziers – many of whom were unfamiliar with agricultural practices outside of animal husbandry, and some even lacking that expertise – this had to be brought about with the aid of subsidies for products like wheat, and exercises in price stabilisation. Export bounties and government purchases of cattle saved many livestock exporters – who had little success seeking alternative markets in continental Europe – from ruin.

Despite choking off the annuity payments to the UK, the Irish government continued to collect a reduced sum in annuity payments from Irish farmers. As Joseph Lee acidly observed in his monumental work *Ireland 1912–85, politics and society*, 'this complication was not unduly stressed from Fianna Fáil platforms' during the 1932 general election campaign.[70] This income flow was not retained for future disbursement either – 'Plan of Campaign' style – in the event of an agreement being

* From his famous Radio Éireann broadcast of 17 March 1943.

reached with the government of Ramsay MacDonald. When some distressed graziers, encouraged by the fascistic leader of the new Fine Gael party and Blueshirt *commandante* Eoin O'Duffy, refused to continue making annuity payments to the Fianna Fáil administration – many also declined to remit their property taxes – the government seized animals and sold them, in distraint, on the open market. This return to an atmosphere reminiscent of the Land War had predictable consequences. Sales of distrained livestock were boycotted, purchasers of impounded cattle were targeted and agrarian violence returned to rural Ireland. In Cork, for example, no stranger to armed conflict, there were 197 violent attacks between January 1934 and January 1935.[71]

There was a preliminary attempt at Anglo-Irish détente in 1934 with the so-called 'Coal-Cattle pact' between the antagonists in the Economic War. This, as the name suggests, allowed for some relaxation in tariffs on both commodities and brought about an increase of 24 per cent in Irish live cattle exports to Britain in 1935. This de-escalation of the Economic War represented an element of 'buyer's remorse' from Fianna Fáil, a reluctant acceptance of the centrality of live cattle exports to the UK in the Irish economy.

The 'Coal-Cattle pact' was superseded by a more detailed concordat in April 1938. This was a comprehensive and timely agreement between the two states that allowed joint preferential access to the markets of both. The British prime minister, Neville Chamberlain – although identified with the policy of appeasement of Adolf Hitler – was sufficiently pessimistic about the future of Anglo-German relations to want to ensure the availability of a regular food supply from Ireland. Securing this was more important to Chamberlain than even the retention of the three ports (Cobh, Bearhaven and Lough Swilly) occupied by the British navy since the 1922 Anglo-Irish Treaty. So, with the final ending of the Irish land wars came the parallel capacity to operate a genuine policy of neutrality in the looming European war.

For de Valera, the 1938 Anglo-Irish Treaty, though less offensive than the agreement of the same name signed in his absence in 1922, represented quite a compromise. It was a tacit acknowledgement on his part of the primacy of the markets, an entity dominated, in the Irish context, by the export of live cattle. The concordat was open to criticism as 'a further step along the road towards reintegration into a single market economy with Britain'.[72] The country began to extract itself from that particular set of handcuffs only with the relaxation of Fianna Fáil protectionism by Lemass in the 1960s, and entry into the European Economic Community in 1973.

De Valera did eventually manage to become midwife to a measure of agricultural self-sufficiency in the 1940s, but it took the combined talents of Herr Hitler, Comrade Stalin, Emperor Hirohito, President Roosevelt, Prime Minister Churchill and something akin to a command economy – courtesy of the Emergency Powers Act of 1939 – to bring this about. During 'the Emergency', the country was, by default, required to be self-sufficient in food, so tillage made something of a comeback. But by the outset of World War II, Fianna Fáil had lost some of its small farmer support to a political newcomer, Clann na Talmhan, founded in 1938, angry at the 'losses and humiliations of the Economic War',[73] and eager for a reckoning over land redistribution.

As proof of the axiom that 'what goes around comes around', de Valera was forced to endure the Dáil speeches of one of Clann na Talmhan's founders, Galwayman Michael Donnellan. To make matters worse, Donnellan was a former Sinn Féin and Fianna Fáil member. He liked to keep the chamber informed about the number of passports he was obliged to organise each month. These were for his Galway North constituents, smallholders and farmers' sons, 'the plain people of Ireland',[*] voting with their feet and leaving de Valera's sylvan idyll to its own devices. While Donnellan might have lacked the oratorical flourish and rhetorical bite of a James Dillon[†] – and would be accused by a disillusioned co-founder of his own party (Martin Finnerty) of

---

[*] A phrase coined by writer and critic Seán O'Faoláin in the journal *The Bell* in 1943 but later put to excellent satiric use in the *Irish Times* columns of Myles na Gopaleen/Brian O'Nolan.

[†] Son of John Dillon. A TD from 1937 and leader of Fine Gael from 1959.

himself being a rancher – his polemics were heartfelt and galling for the erstwhile radicals of the Soldiers of Destiny. One of Donnellan's interventions began thus:

> Does the Minister not realise the reason that we have no food in this country today? It is because the people are not placed on the land; uneconomic holders are not given economic holdings ... where there is untenanted land, and where there is a crowd of uneconomic holders living around that untenanted land, it is the duty of the Land Commission to acquire it, to compensate the owner and to divide it amongst the tenants ... when a man begins to talk about land division now he's laughed at. He is told: 'That is what Fianna Fáil told us 20 years ago. They have been 15 years in office and the same thing is happening.'[74]

The land nationaliser in Michael Davitt might have demurred, but the 'Father of the Land League' would have approved.

Conclusion

THE STRUGGLE FOR hegemony over Ireland's land – the Three Hundred Years' War – could conceivably be viewed as something of a giant zero-sum game if we take it that the descendants of those in possession in the 1600s had resumed ownership by the middle of the 1900s. The *aislingi* of the seventeenth- and eighteenth-century Gaelic poets had eventually come to pass.

Of course, such a narrative is all too conveniently circular. It is neat, orderly and tied up with a ribbon of the type used for identification purposes by the eponymous agrarian secret society. But the expression 'zero-sum' does not just apply to the circularity of a conflict, where the *status quo ante bellum* is restored. It also implies a contest and assumes that there are, potentially, winners and losers. In the very broadest sense, the case could be made that the losers of the Three Hundred Years' War were the descendants of those who benefited from the confiscations of the Tudors, Stuarts and Puritans. The winners, therefore, were the heirs of those who had been despatched to the mountains, to the forests, to Connacht, or even to Hell.

Let us, for a moment, however, leave aside the blatant ahistorical contradictions inherent in such a generalisation and simply accept at face value, albeit as one would a fable told to a small child, that the 'Old Irish' had their land stolen, that they waged the Three Hundred Years' War by all means at their disposal, and that they ultimately triumphed and regained their land. The temptation is then to assume that this was a good thing.

It certainly was for some.

In assenting to this beguilingly simplistic version of events, we should, however, not also become victims of another heart-warming fantasy. The final outcome of the Three Hundred Years' War was not the collective triumph of an improvised and united rural militia. In the process of completing the divine circle of repossession, there were casualties other than the heirs of the Tudors, Stuarts and Puritans.

Until a series of exacting professional reassessments starting in the 1950s, 'the benign rhetoric of rural class solidarity'[1] was generally taken as read, as if the Irish peasantry was some sort of undifferentiated entity with common interests who had stormed the citadel in concert. If *Land is All That Matters* has achieved anything, one hopes that it has shamelessly exploited recent scholarship to dispel the myth of a fused and homogenous peasantry overthrowing the evil despotism of landed privilege.

Because it was a revolution and a counter-revolution that went hand in hand, not an integrated peasantry.

The celebrated Land League slogan, 'the land for the people', was only partially realised, and it should probably be reframed as 'the land … for certain people'. In a survey of the sharp end of the conflict in the late nineteenth and early twentieth centuries, Galway University historian Tony Varley concluded that the endgame was characterised by 'the emergence of the "strong farmer" tenants as the main winners from agrarian agitation and land reform'.[2] Amen to that sentiment, and to Joseph Lee's coronation of 'the strong farmer as cock of the country walk'.[3]

Triumph was circumscribed. Victory was compromised. Was any other outcome likely? In mitigation, what was actually achieved managed to avoid the worst of two possible alternative extremes: a continuation of landlord supremacy or the perils of land nationalisation, both potential horror stories. But the *pax agricultura* left a legacy of disappointment and 'what if' speculation. 'The Irish revolution … did not seriously attempt – let alone achieve – a change in the social balance of power.'[4] Ireland did not quickly become Denmark – a modern and prosperous agricultural economy exporting to the world – although this was a Free State aspiration.[5] The 'cakeist' desire to re-apportion the country's land while retaining the dispossessed aristocracy was only partially realised. The utopian promise of land for the landless remained just that, a utopian promise.

But, despite those (often mutually exclusive) deficiencies, to describe the result of the Three Hundred Years' War as a failure would be an equally errant misrepresentation. If it achieved nothing else (and it did), Irish land agitation offered a persuasive template for other agrarian revolutions. 'The Irish formula,' according to American historian Jo Guldi, 'would have a long tail in the twentieth century, when it would provide a multiplicity of observers with answers about how to approach rural poverty throughout the former colonies of the world.'[6] Not even the most revisionist of historians would claim that the lengthy conflict which began with the isolated resistance of seventeenth-century woodkernes, and ended with the £10 million immolation of land annuities, was a dismal letdown. Or that a thorough professional interrogation of the precise nature of that struggle has devalued it in any fashion.

Academic historians are a lot like archaeologists in many ways. They diligently and expertly remove the soil of myth, one spoonful at a time, to reveal the skeletal remains of human history. In doing so, they often shatter firmly held illusions and self-serving fantasies. Comforting fiction gives way to unnerving nonfiction; poetic or romantic traditions are subjected to prosaic analysis. Many would prefer that the ground be left undisturbed, so that endless speculation and special pleading could continue as to the true nature of what was concealed underneath. But those pesky academics come along and ruin everything with their attachment to rigour and the pursuit of truth. Professional historians are compulsive Cassandras; the truth-telling Fools of deluded monarchs on blasted heaths; the indispensable spoilsports of uninformed discourse. Which is not to say that the latter-day scribes have, in subjecting it to such taxing analysis, stripped the traditional Irish tenurial narrative of all its romance and poetry. There is still more than enough legitimate courage, inspiration and sacrifice, alongside the meticulous exposure of cartoon heroes and *anime* villains.

Finally, what of the juxtaposition of the fight for land and the simultaneous fight for sovereignty? It will come as no surprise that this writer is convinced that the work of historians like Samuel Clark, Barbara Solow, James Donnelly, Paul Bew, William Vaughan, Joseph Lee and Terence Dooley have established the primacy of our Three Hundred Years' War 'as the critical development in modern Irish history rather than the allegedly revolutionary events of 1916–23'.[7] Surely it is now accepted that the latter would not have been possible without the former. As we have seen, they complemented each other in a symbiotic relationship that was fundamental when it came to the achievement of legislative independence in 1922. They harmonised seamlessly as long as the land warriors were not being annoying and raucous little siblings to their revolutionary older brothers. At least that is the familial hierarchy assumed by many political historians. The 'national struggle' always takes historiographical precedence over the land conflict. The latter has long been pressed 'into the paralysing straightjacket of nationalist orthodoxy'[8] (Joe Lee's phrase) more than once too often.

Such notions of primacy and precedence were, in part at least, a carry-over from the elitist Fenian orthodoxy of the 1880s (not necessarily shared by the rank-and-file membership) that saw agrarian agitation as a revolutionary Trojan horse, with the agitators in the role of the Greeks. Once the smallholders of Ireland achieved their objectives, so went this purist argument, they would sink back into the soft embrace of reactionary apathy. This militant nationalist wariness of agrarian activism was accentuated during the era of Tory conciliation, of 'killing Home Rule with kindness', that brought major land concessions in response to two worrying Liberal Home Rule bills. However, successive British governments from 1916 to 1920 effected, with admirable thoroughness, the policy of killing Home Rule *without* any discernible kindness, and succeeded in replacing it with a more virulent strain of nationalism. Republicans could easily have set aside their previous coyness when it came to agrarianists, but the dog had already been given a bad name. There was an abiding vestigial suspicion of those who prioritised agrarian activism.

Rural agitation was well worth exploiting, until it wasn't. From the middle of 1920, the separatist struggle took absolute precedence and the rural *sans culottes* were left kicking their heels in the waiting room, staring coldly at the equally redundant champions of labour sequestered there along with them.

When it comes to the relative merits of these complementary/conflicting forces, most of the military iterations of the 'national struggle' – on the grounds of impact or of organisation – are no great advertisements for the perceived precedence of militant nationalism over agrarianism. The farcical 1848 'rebellion' is remembered largely because it was conducted by a charismatic elite of iconic and readily identifiable figures. Militarily, however, was it any more significant than Fintan Lalor's contemporaneous coup attempt with both agrarian and separatist objectives? Was the 1867 Fenian rebellion any more extensive or effective than the insurrections of the eighteenth-century Hearts of Steel, or the nineteenth-century Rockites? Was agrarian agitation merely plugging the gaps between nationalist uprisings, intervals of functional melody between rousing choruses? Or was the reverse actually the case?

Why is James Fintan Lalor not a resident of the Irish pantheon alongside contemporaries such as the equally short-lived Thomas Davis, or the profoundly racist John Mitchel? Why are James Fitzgibbon and D. D. Sheehan not mentioned in the same breath as Arthur Griffith? In part, it must be said, because many land activists, even radicals like Sheehan, are often associated with failed IPP constitutionalism and are lumped in unceremoniously and unjustly with the forgotten men of Irish history. Such are the quirks. Laurence Ginnell jumped ship just in time.

Was the 1903 Wyndham act any less significant a concession than the 1922 Anglo-Irish Treaty? Which of the two made more difference to the lives of Flann O'Brien's 'plain people of Ireland'?

Did the Irish people not lose their land long before they lost their nationhood? The Ireland of the sixteenth century was still an agglomeration of disparate and often warring fiefdoms, rather than a single cohesive national entity. That is one of the things that made it easier to colonise. Alien savagery, economic exploitation and the laments of generations of *filí* (poets) conjured something called 'Ireland' into being. Many of the eighteenth-century members of the ascendancy class had a more sophisticated sense of national separatism than did the descendants of the 'Old Irish'. The latter caught up in time, the former then becoming more focused on defending their privileges.

Tenurial grievances, however, predated any reverence for the emblematic Cathleen ní Houlihán, or the *Sean Bhean Bhocht* (the 'Poor Old Woman'), icons of an Ireland in thrall to its eastern neighbour. They also endangered the successful prosecution of the 'Irish Revolution' during the short and bitter conflict of the Anglo-Irish War.

In early October 2022, the eminent Canadian public intellectual, academic and politician Michael Ignatieff delivered the annual Edmund Burke Lecture in Trinity College, Dublin. In an interview published in the *Irish Times* on the day of the lecture, Ignatieff noted that 'violence has accompanied the creation of your democracy and the question is this: how do modern democratic societies deal with and control this revolutionary legacy?' He clearly had in mind the political violence of the sporadic rebellions of the country's long anti-colonial history. He might, however, just as easily have cited the formative impact of agrarian violence on the creation of our democracy. In contrast, the social historian Jo Guldi clearly had agrarianism in mind when she wrote, in her magisterial *The Long Land War*, that 'Irish violence would stop only when the land was returned to the people'. The word 'land' can easily operate here on two distinct levels. Irish tenurial reform, the result of decades of agitation, was, Guldi adds, 'an aristocrat's truce with an anti-colonial rebellion'.[9] It was, arguably, more efficacious than the actual anti-colonial rebellion. By 1922, 80 per cent of Irish peasants had acquired the 'fee simple' to their own land. The national project had unravelled in a vicious civil conflict.

Furthermore, the Irish revolution, the terror unleashed by the IRA, and the counter-terror endured from the Crown forces, was primarily a rural phenomenon, notwithstanding pivotal events like the 'Squad' killings of Bloody Sunday in November 1920, or the Dublin Brigade's full-frontal assault on the Four Courts in May 1921. Celebrated set-pieces such as those distract from the reality that most of the Crown forces were tied down in communities outside of the major coastal cities of the country. As we have noted, a far higher percentage of the Irish population lived outside of those cities a century ago and felt the impact of the Anglo-Irish War in a far more elemental and direct manner than many of their urban compatriots.

What was it, other than a long history of agrarian 'outrage', that prepared rural Ireland for the two and a half years of this increasingly bitter conflict, followed by a further ten months of the internecine sequel in 1922–3? What prepared IRA volunteers for the targeting and assassination of informers and collaborators? What inured rural communities to the arbitrary retaliation of the Crown forces? What indeed, other than decades of agrarian conflict and violence. None of what was happening in the Anglo-Irish War was especially new for many of those living outside the cities and large towns of the country. The violence may have been more intense and mechanised, but a society accustomed to regular outbreaks of arson, assault and murder, whether it was delivered by men in Crossley tenders or white shirts, by thugs in Tam O'Shanters or 'ruffians' bedecked with ribbons, was immaterial.

Whence came the ruthlessness to target and 'execute', if not from the tradition of violent response to agrarian frustrations that accompanied the political agitation of the Land War, the Plan of Campaign and the Ranch War? Whence came the capacity to withstand overwhelming retaliation on the part of the British state? From a psyche accustomed to sullen resistance to periodic land clearances and to more than a century of coercive legislative response.

And what good did it all do? What quantifiable benefits accrued to rural Ireland from legislative independence that were not already enjoyed?

UCD historian Michael Laffan has written that, 'the Irish revolution … did not seriously attempt – let alone achieve – a change in the social balance of power.' Laffan was referring to the reactionary legacy of the generation of 'conservative revolutionaries' who took power in the 1920s. Rural Ireland had eagerly anticipated, and fought for, the departure of the British administration via the ports of Dublin and Kingstown (Dún Laoghaire). Many of those members of the landed aristocracy who had not already sailed did so once the last brandy had been quaffed at the last Viceregal soirée, and the white-gloved manservants had packed away the silver. But for thousands of eager and impecunious members of the Irish peasantry, the entire transaction made about as much difference as the introduction of Catholic 'relief' had done a century before. The new dispensation, exemplified by the government of Cumann na nGaedheal – after sides were taken in the Civil War – decided that it owed precious little to the 'men of no property', and behaved accordingly. The fact that it enjoyed, and occasionally depended upon, the tacit support of the Farmers' Party – a safe refuge for the 'snug' landowner – tells its own tale. Although taking power with the best of intentions, and with a mandate for change, Fianna Fáil under de Valera were not able to move the dial any great distance either.

It was Darwinism over Marxism, evolution over revolution, with the survival of the fittest still an inescapable reality, try, as the new populists undoubtedly did in the 1930s, to inaugurate radical change. However, we must return to our earlier rubric of qualified success. What was achieved did not measure up to anyone's utopian vision of what was promised. The outcome was imperfect, a new front door secured with baling twine. However, the result is reminiscent of Winston Churchill's take on democracy itself: 'the worst form of government, except for all the others'.

The Three Hundred Years' War produced the worst form of agrarian settlement, except for the possible alternatives.

Abbreviations

Ancient Order of Hibernians (AOH)
Congested Districts Board (CDB)
Gaelic Athletic Association (GAA)
Graduated Landlord Malignity Scale (GLMS)
International Monetary Fund (IMF)
Irish Independent Party (IIP)
Irish Land and Labour Association (ILLA)
Irish National League (INL)
Irish Transport and General Workers Union (ITGWU)
Land Settlement Commission (LSC)
Ordnance Survey of Ireland (OSI)
Property Defence Association (PDA)
Resident Magistrate (RM)
Royal Dublin Society (RDS)
Royal Irish Constabulary (RIC)
Special Infantry Corps (SIC)
Special Resident Magistrate (SRM)
United Irish League (UIL)

Bibliography

Manuscript sources

Irish Military Archives – Bureau of Military History Witness Statements

Seán Boylan, BMH-WS #171
Cahir Davitt, BMH-WS #993
Sean Farrelly, BMH-WS #1734
Séamus Finn, BMH-WS #1060
Patrick O'Reilly, BMH-WS #1650
Kevin O'Shiel, BMH-WS #1770

National Archives of Ireland – Chief Secretary's Papers

CSORP 1881/35119
CSORP 1883/2040

Public Record Office, Kew

Colonial Office (CO) 903/1
TNA, PRO, CAB 37/19, 1887 no. 1
War Office 35/102260023/00029

National Folklore Collection, University College, Dublin

The Schools' Collection
0180, 80
0263, 135
0406, 471
0406, 474
0563, 171

0703, 340
0719, 605
0849, 123
1029, 54

Government publications

A Popular and Complete Edition of the Parnell Commission Report (London, 1890).

Census of Ireland for the year 1851, part V, tables of deaths (1851).

Devon Commission, Minutes of Evidence (1844).

Evidence of the Special Commission to inquire into and report upon the charges and allegations made against certain members of Parliament and other persons in the course of the proceedings in an action entitled O'Donnell versus Walter and another, 11 Volumes (1889).

Instructions by Sir R. Griffith, 1853, to valuators and surveyors in tenement valuation of Ireland; and instructions by Land Commission (Ireland) to Assistant Commissioners, with reference to valuation of agricultural holdings (House of Commons, 1882).

Report and Minutes of Evidence of the House of Commons Select Committee on Ordnance Survey (Ireland), 1846.

Report of the Cowper Commission on the Irish Land Acts (London, 1886).

Report of the Select Committee on Townland Valuation in Ireland, Minutes of Evidence and Appendix and Index, 1844.

Return, by provinces and counties, of cases of evictions which have come to the knowledge of the Constabulary in each year 1849 to 1880 (1881).

Richmond Commission, Minutes of Evidence (1881).

State of Ireland, Minutes of Evidence taken before the Select Committee appointed to inquire into the Disturbances in Ireland in the last session of parliament, 13 May–18 June 1824. (1824).

Other

Dáil debates
House of Commons debates
House of Lords debates

Newspapers

Ireland

Clare Freeman
Clare Independent
Clare Journal
Cork Constitution
Derry Journal
Drogheda Independent
Dublin Daily Express
Dublin Evening Post
Dublin Penny Journal
Freeman's Journal
Irish Felon
Irish Independent
Irish Times
Kerry Sentinel
Meath Chronicle
Midland Tribune
Nenagh Guardian
New York Times
Tipperary Vindicator
United Ireland

Britain

Guardian
Illustrated London News
Manchester Guardian
Pall Mall Gazette
The Times

Memoirs/contemporary works

James Anton, *Retrospect of a Military Life* (Edinburgh, 1841).
Jonah Barrington, *Personal Sketches* (London, 1827).
Bernard Becker, *Disturbed Ireland* (London, 1881).

Isaac Butt, *The Irish Land and the Irish People* (London, 1867).

Thomas Campbell, *A Philosophical Survey of the South of Ireland* (Dublin, 1777).

Jesse Craigen, *Report on a visit to Ireland in the summer of 1881* (Dublin, 1882).

Michael Davitt, *The Fall of Feudalism in Ireland* (London, 1904).

Michael Davitt, *The Times Parnell Commission speech delivered by Michael Davitt in defence of the Land League* (London, 1890).

Gustave de Beaumont, *Ireland: Social, Political and Religious* (London, 1839).

Alexis de Tocqueville, *Journeys to England and Ireland* (New Haven, 1958).

Charles Gavan Duffy, *The League of North and South: an Episode in Irish History, 1850–1854* (London, 1886).

Finlay Dun, *Landlords and Tenants in Ireland* (London, 1881).

Earl of Dunraven, *Past Times and Pastimes* (London, 1922).

Edward Fry, *James Hack Tuke: A Memoir* (London, 1899).

Henry George, *The Irish land question, what it involves and how it can be settled. An appeal to the Land Leagues* (New York, 1881).

William Neilson Hancock, *Report on the Supposed Progressive Decline in Irish Prosperity* (Dublin, 1863).

Timothy Harrington, *The Maamtrasna Massacre* (Dublin, 1884).

Timothy Healy, *Letters and Leaders of my Day, Volume 1* (New York, 1929).

William Henry Hurlbert, *Ireland Under Coercion: The Diary of an American* (London, 1888).

S. M. Hussey, *The Reminiscences of an Irish Land Agent* (London, 1904).

Irish Land Committee, *The Land Question, Ireland: Confiscation or Contract?* (Dublin, 1880).

Irish Land Committee, *The Land Question, Ireland, no. 1, Notes upon the government valuation of land in Ireland, commonly known as 'Griffith's Valuation'* (Dublin, 1880).

Randal Kernan, *A Report of the Trials of the Caravats and Shanavests at the Special Commission for the Several Counties of Tipperary, Waterford and Kilkenny* (Dublin, 1811).

Andrew Kettle, *Material for Victory* (Dublin, 1958).

Thomas A. Larcom, *The history of the survey of Ireland, commonly called the Down survey, A.D. 1655–6* (Dublin, 1851).

W. R. Le Fanu, *Seventy Years of Irish Life* (London, 1894).

Cornewall Lewis, *On Local Disturbances and the Irish Church Question* (London, 1836).

The Liberal Union of Ireland, *The Plan of Campaign: The Smith Barry Estate, Tipperary* (Dublin, 1890).

Clifford Lloyd, *Ireland Under the Land League* (London, 1892).

John MacDonald, *Daily News Diary of the Parnell Commission* (London, 1890).

James McFadden *The Present and the Past of the Agrarian Struggle in Gweedore* (Derry, 1889).

John Mitchel, *The Last Conquest of Ireland (Perhaps)* (London, 1882).

George Moore, *Parnell and His Island* (Dublin, 2004).

John Morley, *The Life of Gladstone* (London, 1908).

Thomas Newenham, *A View of the National, Political and Commercial Circumstances of Ireland* (London, 1809).

Henry Norman, *Bodyke: A Chapter in the History of Irish Landlordism* (London, 1887).

William O'Brien, *Evening Memories* (Dublin, 1920).

William O'Brien, *An Olive Branch in Ireland and Its History* (London, 1910).

Peadar O'Donnell, *There Will Be Another Day* (Dublin, 1963).

Katharine O'Shea, *Charles Stewart Parnell: His Love Story and Political Life* (London, 1914).

James Redpath, *Talks About Ireland* (New York, 1881).

Wilfrid Scawen Blunt, *The Land War in Ireland* (London, 1912).

Wilfrid Scawen Blunt, *My Diaries: Being a Personal Narrative of Events, 1888–1914, Part 2, 1900–1914* (London, 1921).

D. D. Sheehan, *Ireland Since Parnell* (London, 1921).

George Sigerson, *History of the land tenures and land classes of Ireland: with an account of the various secret agrarian confederacies* (London, 1871).

Alexander M. Sullivan, *New Ireland: Political Sketches and Personal Reminiscences* (Glasgow, 1877).

Charlotte Elizabeth Tonna, *Irish Recollections* (Dublin, 2004).

William Steuart Trench, *Realities of Irish Life* (London, 1869).

Charles Edward Trevelyan, *The Irish Crisis* (London, 1848).

Alfred E. Turner, *Sixty Years of a Soldier's Life* (London, 1912).

Edward Wakefield, *An Account of Ireland, Statistical and Political* (London, 1812).

Charles Walmesley, *General History of the Christian Church from her birth to her Final Triumphant States in Heaven chiefly deduced from the Apocalypse of St. John the Apostle, by Signor Pastorini* (New York, 1834).

Patrick White, *Hurlbert Unmasked: an exposure of the thumping English lies of William Henry Hurlbert in his 'Ireland Under Coercion'* (New York, 1890).

Dr Richard Woodward, *Present State of the Church of Ireland* (Dublin, 1808).

Arthur Young, *Tour in Ireland* (London, 1892).

Secondary sources

W. F. Bailey, *The Irish Land Acts: A Short Sketch* (Dublin, 1917).

Stephen Ball (ed.), *A Policeman's Ireland: Recollections of Samuel Walters, RIC* (Cork, 1999).

Jonathan Bardon, *A History of Ulster* (Belfast, 2005).

Thomas Bartlett, *Ireland: A History* (Cambridge, 2010).

Thomas Bartlett (ed.), *The Cambridge History of Ireland, vol. IV* (Cambridge, 2018).

J. C. Beckett, *The Making of Modern Ireland, 1603–1923* (London, 1966).

Paul Bew, *Land and the National Question in Ireland, 1858–82* (New Jersey, 1979).

Paul Bew, *Ancestral Voices in Irish Politics: Judging Dillon and Parnell* (Oxford, 2023).

Moritz Bonn, *Modern Ireland and her Agrarian Problem* (Dublin, 1906).

D. G. Boyce, *Nineteenth Century Ireland, the Search for Stability* (Dublin, 1990).

David N. Buckley, *James Fintan Lalor: Radical* (Cork, 1990).

William Bulfin, *Rambles in Eirinn* (Dublin, 1927).

Helen Burke, *The People and the Poor Law in Nineteenth Century Ireland* (Littlehampton, 1987).

Fergus Campbell, *Land and Revolution: Nationalist Politics in the West of Ireland 1891–1921* (Oxford, 2007).

Fergus Campbell and Tony Varley (eds), *Land Questions in Modern Ireland* (Manchester, 2013).

Samuel Clark and James Donnelly Jr (eds), *Irish Peasants: Violence and Political Unrest 1780–1914* (Wisconsin, 1983).

R. V. Comerford, *The Fenians in Context: Irish Politics and Society, 1848–82* (Dublin, 1998).

R. V. Comerford, *Ireland* (London, 2003).

Peter Connell, *The Land and People of County Meath, 1750–1850* (Dublin, 2004).

Oliver Coogan, *Politics and War in Meath, 1913–1923* (Navan, 2013).

Arlene Crampsie and Francis Ludlow, *Meath: History and Society* (Dublin, 2015).

Raymond Crotty, *Irish Agricultural Production, Its Volume and Structure* (Cork, 1966).

John Crowley, William J. Smyth and Mike Murphy (eds), *Atlas of the Great Irish Famine* (Cork, 2012).

L. M. Cullen, *An Economic History of Ireland Since 1660* (London, 1972).

L. Perry Curtis Jr, *Coercion and Conciliation in Ireland, 1880–1892: A Study in Conservative Unionism* (Princeton, 1963).

L. Perry Curtis Jr, *The Depiction of Eviction in Ireland 1845–1910* (Dublin, 2011).

Mary E. Daly, *The Famine in Ireland* (Dundalk, 1986).

Liam de Paor (ed.), *Milestones in Irish History* (Cork, 1986).

David Dickson, *Arctic Ireland: The Extraordinary Story of the Great Frost and Forgotten Famine of 1740–41* (Belfast, 1997).

David Dickson, *New Foundations: Ireland 1660–1800* (Dublin, 2000).

Dictionary of Irish Biography (Cambridge, 2009).

Myles Dillon (ed.), *Early Irish Society* (Dublin, 1954).

Gillian Doherty, *The Irish Ordnance Survey: History, Culture and Memory* (Dublin, 2004).

James S. Donnelly Jr, *Captain Rock: The Irish Agrarian Rebellion of 1821–1824* (Cork, 2009).

Terence Dooley, *'The land for the people': The Land Question in Independent Ireland* (Dublin, 2004).

Terence Dooley, *The Big Houses and Landed Estates of Ireland: A Research Guide* (Dublin, 2007).

Terence Dooley, *The Murders at Wildgoose Lodge: Agrarian Crime and Punishment in pre-Famine Ireland* (Dublin, 2007).

John Dorney, *The Irish Story*, online blog (www.theirishstory.com).

P. J. Drudy (ed.), *Ireland: Land, Politics and People* (Cambridge, 1982).

Peter Duffy, *The Killing of Major Denis Mahon* (New York, 2007).

Myles Dungan, *How the Irish Won the West* (Dublin, 2006).

Myles Dungan, *The Captain and the King: William O'Shea, Parnell and late Victorian Ireland* (Dublin, 2009).

Myles Dungan, *Four Killings* (London, 2021).

R. Dudley Edwards and T. Desmond Williams (eds), *The Great Famine: Studies in Irish History, 1845–52* (Dublin, 1994).

William L. Feingold, *Revolt of the Tenantry: The Transformation of Local Government in Ireland 1872–1886* (Chicago, 1984).

Diarmaid Ferriter, *The Transformation of Ireland* (London, 2004).

Diarmaid Ferriter, *A Nation and Not a Rabble* (London, 2015).

Diarmaid Ferriter, *Between Two Hells: the Irish Civil War* (London, 2021).

David Fitzpatrick, *Politics and Irish Life, 1913–1921: Provincial Experience of War and Revolution* (Cork, 1999).

L. M. Fogarty, *James Fintan Lalor, Patriot and Political Essayist* (Dublin, 1918).

R. F. Foster, *Modern Ireland, 1600–1972* (London, 1988).

R. F. Foster, *The Irish Story: Telling Tales and Making It Up in Ireland* (London, 2001).

Darragh Gannon and Fearghal McGarry (eds), *Ireland 1922* (Dublin, 2022).

Tom Garvin, *Nationalist Revolutionaries in Ireland, 1858–1928* (Dublin, 2005).

Tom Garvin, *Preventing the Future: Why Was Ireland So Poor for So Long?* (Dublin, 2004).

Patrick Geoghegan, *Liberator: The Life and Death of Daniel O'Connell 1830–1847* (Dublin, 2010).

Stephen Randolph Gibbons, *Captain Rock, Night Errant: The Threatening Letters of Pre-Famine Ireland, 1801–45* (Dublin, 2004).

Alice Stopford Green, *The Making of Ireland and its Undoing, 1200–1600* (London, 1908).

Arthur Gribben (ed.), *The Great Famine and the Irish Diaspora to America* (Amherst, 1999).

Jo Guldi, *The Long Land War: The Global Struggle for Occupancy Rights* (New Haven, 2022)

J. Evitts Haley, *Charles Goodnight: Cowman and Plainsman* (Oklahoma, 1949).

Peter Hart, *The IRA at War* (Oxford, 2003).

Elizabeth R. Hooker, *Readjustments of Agricultural Tenure in Ireland* (Chapel Hill, 1938).

Michael Hopkinson, *The Irish War of Independence* (Montreal, 2004).

K. Theodore Hoppen, *Ireland Since 1800: Conflict and Conformity* (London, 1989).

Kyle Hughes and Donald M. Macraild, *Ribbon Societies in Nineteenth-Century Ireland and its Diaspora* (Liverpool, 2021).

Donald E. Jordan Jr, *Land and Popular Politics in Ireland* (Cambridge, 1994).

P. W. Joyce, *A Smaller Social History of Ancient Ireland* (Dublin, 1906).

William Keaveney, *The Life and Times of Martin McDonnell, Merchant, Landlord and Poor Law Guardian* (Dublin, 2017).

Margaret Kelleher, *The Maamtrasna Murders: Language, Life and Death in Nineteenth Century Ireland* (Dublin, 2018).

James Kelly (ed.), *The Cambridge History of Ireland, Volume III, 1730–1880* (Cambridge, 2018).

James Kelly, *That Damn'd Thing Called Honour: Duelling in Ireland 1570–1860* (Cork, 1995).

John S. Kelly, *The Bodyke Evictions* (Scariff, 1987).

Linda Kelly, *Ireland's Minstrel* (London, 2006).

Michael Laffan, *The Resurrection of Ireland: The Sinn Féin Party, 1916–1923* (Cambridge, 1999).

Emmet Larkin (ed.), *Alexis de Tocqueville's Journey in Ireland, July–August 1835* (Washington, D.C., 1990).

Law Reform Commission, *Consultation Paper on General Law of Landlord and Tenant* (Dublin, 2003).

Joseph Lee, *The Modernisation of Irish Society, 1848–1918* (Dublin, 1989).

H. Brougham Leech, *1848 and 1912: The Continuity of the Irish Revolutionary Movement* (London, 1912).

F. S. L. Lyons, *Ireland Since the Famine* (Glasgow, 1978).

Michael MacDonagh, *The Life of William O'Brien, Irish Nationalist* (London, 1928).

Breandán Mac Suibhne, *The End of Outrage: Post-Famine Adjustment in Rural Ireland* (Oxford, 2017).

Joyce Marlow, *Captain Boycott and the Irish* (London, 1973).

Richard McMahon, *Homicide in Pre-Famine and Famine Ireland* (Liverpool, 2013).

Joel Mokyr, *Why Ireland Starved: A Quantitative and Analytical History of the Irish Economy, 1800–1850* (London 1985).

T. W. Moody and J. C. Beckett (eds), *Ulster Since 1800* (London, 1954).

T. W. Moody and R. A. J. Hawkins (eds), *Florence Arnold-Forster's Irish Journal* (Oxford, 1988).

H. A. L. Morton, *A People's History of England* (London, 1938).

Helen O'Brien, *The Famine Cearance in Toomevara, Co. Tipperary* (Dublin, 2010).

Margaret O'Callaghan, *British High Politics and a Nationalist Ireland* (Cork, 1994).

Cormac Ó Gráda, *The Great Irish Famine* (Cambridge, 1989).

Cormac Ó Gráda, *Ireland before and after the Famine* (Manchester, 1993).

Martin O'Halloran, *The Lost Gaeltacht: the Land Commission Migration – Clonbur, County Galway to Allenstown, County Meath* (Meath, 2020).

Eunan O'Halpin, *Defending Ireland: The Irish State and Its Enemies Since 1922* (Oxford, 1999).

Thomas P. O'Neill (translated by John T. Goulding), *James Fintan Lalor* (Wexford, 1962).

John E. Pomfret, *The Struggle for the Land in Ireland, 1800–1923* (Princeton, 1930).

George Rudé, *Protest and Punishment: The Story of the Social and Political Protestors Transported to Australia, 1788–1868* (Oxford, 1978).

William Sheehan and Maura Cronin (eds), *Riotous Assemblies: Rebels, Riots and Revolts in Ireland* (Cork, 2011).

Homer E. Socolofsky, *Landlord William Scully* (Kansas, 1979).

Barbara Lewis Solow, *The Land Question and the Irish Economy, 1870–1903* (Cambridge, MA, 1971).

Charles Townshend, *Political Violence in Ireland: Government and Resistance since 1848* (Oxford, 1983).

Pauric Travers, *Settlements and Divisions in Ireland, 1870–1922* (Dublin, 1988).

W. E. Vaughan (ed.), *A New History of Ireland, vol.V: Ireland Under the Union 1801–70* (Oxford, 1989).

W. E. Vaughan, *Landlords and Tenants in Mid-Victorian Ireland* (Oxford, 1994).

William Vaughan, *Sin, Sheep and Scotsmen: John George Adair and the Derryveagh Evictions, 1861* (Belfast, 1983).

Jarlath Waldron, *Maamtrasna: The Murders and the Mystery* (Dublin, 1992).

Maurice Walsh, *Bitter Freedom: Ireland in a Revolutionary World* (New York and London, 2015).

Sally Warwick-Haller, *William O'Brien and the Irish Land War* (Dublin, 1990).

T. Desmond Williams (ed.), *Secret Societies in Ireland* (Dublin, 1973).
Cecil Woodham Smith, *The Great Hunger: Ireland 1845–1849* (London, 1991).

PhD theses

Stephen Andrew Ball, *Policing the Land War: Official responses to political protest and agrarian crime in Ireland 1879–91* (PhD thesis, Trinity College, Dublin, 2000).
Patrick Joseph Cosgrove, *The Wyndham Land Act, 1903: The Final Solution to the Irish Land Question?* (PhD thesis, Maynooth University, 2008).
Joan M. Cullen, *Patrick J. Hogan, TD, Minister for Agriculture, 1922–1932: A study of a leading member of the first government of independent Ireland* (PhD thesis, Dublin City University, 1993).
David Gahan, *The land annuities agitation in Ireland 1926–32* (PhD thesis, Maynooth University, 2017).
Donnacha Seán Lucey, *Land and popular politics in County Kerry, 1872–86* (PhD thesis, Maynooth University, 2007).
Adam D. Pole, *Landlord Responses to the Irish Land War, 1879–82* (PhD thesis, Trinity College, Dublin, 2006).
David Patrick Reid, *The Tithe War in Ireland, 1830–1838* (PhD thesis, Trinity College, Dublin, 2013).

Articles

Fergus Campbell, 'Irish Popular Politics and the Making of the Wyndham Land Act, 1901–1903', *The Historical Journal*, vol. 45, no. 4 (Dec. 2002).
Fergus Campbell, 'The Last Land War? Kevin O'Shiel's Memoir of the Irish Revolution (1916–21)', *Archivium Hibernicum*, vol. 57 (2003).
Fergus Campbell, 'The Social Dynamics of Nationalist Politics in the West of Ireland 1898–1918', *Past & Present*, no. 182 (Feb. 2004).
Daniel J. Casey, 'Wildgoose Lodge: the Evidence and the Lore', *Journal of the County Louth Archaeological and Historical Society*, vol. 18, no. 2 (1974).

Gale E. Christianson, 'Secret Societies and Agrarian Violence in Ireland, 1790–1840', *Agricultural History*, vol. 46, no. 3 (July 1972).

L. Perry Curtis Jr, 'Three Oxford Liberals and the Plan of Campaign in Donegal, 1889', *History Ireland*, vol. 19 (May/June 2011).

James S. Donnelly Jr and James J. Donnelly Jr, 'The Rightboy Movement 1785–8', *Studia Hibernica*, no. 17/18 (1977/8).

James S. Donnelly Jr, 'The Whiteboy Movement, 1761–65', *Irish Historical Studies*, vol. 21, no. 81 (Mar. 1978).

James S. Donnelly Jr, 'The Great Famine and its interpreters, old and new', *History Ireland*, Issue 3, Autumn 1993, vol. 1.

James S. Donnelly Jr, 'Hearts of Oak, Hearts of Steel', *Studia Hibernica*, 1981, no. 21 (1981).

Terence Dooley, 'Land and politics in independent Ireland, 1923–48: the case for reappraisal', *Irish Historical Studies*, xxxiv, no. 134 (Nov. 2004).

Michael Drake, 'The Irish Demographic Crisis of 1740–41', *Historical Studies VI* (London, 1968).

Terence M. Dunne, 'Emergence from the Embers: The Meath and Kildare farm labour strike of 1919', 2019, *Saothar: Journal of Irish Labour History* (44).

Terry Dunne, 'Cattle drivers, marauders, terrorists and hooligans', *History Ireland*, vol. 28, no. 4 (July/Aug. 2020).

Steven Engler, Franz Mauelshagen, Jürg Luterbacher, and Johannes Werner, 'The Irish Famine of 1740–1741: Famine Vulnerability and "Climate Migration"', *Climate of the Past*, vol. 9, no. 3 (2013).

Francis Finegan, 'Sir John Howley: 1789–1866', *Irish Quarterly Review*, vol. 40, no. 157 (Mar. 1951).

David Fitzpatrick, 'The Disappearance of the Irish Agricultural Labourer', *Irish Economic and Social History*, VII, 1980.

Fiona Fitzsimons, 'Ordnance Survey Employment Records', *History Ireland*, vol. 27, no. 6 (Nov./Dec. 2019).

Thomas Garvin, 'Defenders, Ribbonmen and others: underground political networks in pre-Famine Ireland' in C. H. E. Philpin (ed.), *Nationalism and Popular Protest in Ireland* (Cambridge, 1987).

Timothy W. Guinnane and Ronald I. Miller, 'Bonds without Bondsmen: Tenant-Right in Nineteenth-Century Ireland', *The Journal of Economic History*, vol. 56, no. 1 (Mar. 1996).

Timothy W. Guinnane and Ronald I. Miller, 'The Limits to Land Reform: The Land Acts in Ireland, 1870–1909', *Economic Development and Cultural Change*, vol. 45, no. 3 (Apr. 1997).

Mary Olive Hussey, 'Sir Richard Griffith: The Man and His Work', *Dublin Historical Record*, vol. 20, no. 2 (Mar. 1965).

David Seth Jones, 'Land reform legislation and security of tenure in Ireland after independence', *Éire-Ireland*, vol. 32 and vol. 33, no. 4, Winter 1997/no. 1–2, Spring/Summer.

Belinda Jupp, 'Ordnance Survey Memoirs of Ireland', *Garden History*, Summer 1994, vol. 22, no. 1.

Shunsuke Katsuta, 'The Rockite Movement in County Cork in the Early 1820s', *Irish Historical Studies*, vol. 33, no. 131 (May 2003).

James Kelly, 'Coping with Crisis: The response to the Famine of 1740–41', *Eighteenth-Century Ireland / Iris an dá chultúr*, vol. 27 (2012).

Thomas R. Kerr, Finbarr McCormick and Aidan O'Sullivan, 'Irish National Strategic Archaeological Research Programme, 2013'; *The Economy of Early Medieval Ireland* (Early Medieval Archaeology Project) Report 7:1 (Dec. 2013).

Anthony Kinsella, 'The Special Infantry Corps', *The Irish Sword*, Winter 1997, no. 82.

Richard Lahert, '*An Maor agus an Meirleach* (The Mayor and the Outlaw): A Postscript to the Carrickshock Affray, 1831', *Decies, Journal of the Old Waterford Society*, Spring 1994, no. 49.

Maria Luddy, 'Abductions in Nineteenth-Century Ireland', *New Hibernia Review*, Summer 2013, vol. 17, no. 2.

James F. Lydon, 'The Braganstown Massacre', *Journal of the County Louth Archaeological and Historical Society*, vol. 19, no. 1 (1977).

F. S. L. Lyons, 'John Dillon and the Plan of Campaign, 1886–90', *Irish Historical Studies*, vol. 14, no. 56 (Sep. 1965).

Patrick S. McWilliams, 'Reactions to the Ordnance Survey: A Window on Prefamine Ireland', *New Hibernia Review*, Spring 2009, vol. 13, no. 1.

Brian Mitchell, 'The Ordnance Survey Memoirs: A Source for Emigration in the 1830s', *History Ireland*, Winter 1996, vol. 4, no. 4.

Patrick O'Donoghue, 'Causes of the opposition to the tithes, 1830–38', *Studia Hibernica*, no. 5 (1965).

Patrick O'Donoghue, 'Opposition to Tithe Payments in 1830–31', *Studia Hibernica*, no. 6 (1966).

John O'Donovan, 'Class, conflict, and the United Irish League in Cork, 1900–1903', *Saothar*, vol. 37 (2012).

Cormac Ó Gráda, 'Ireland's Great Famine: an overview', Centre for Economic Research, Working paper series, WP04/25 (Nov. 2004).

Clare O'Halloran, 'Stories of Subversion: Thomas Moore's "Memoirs of Captain Rock" and Irish Historical Tradition', in *The Irish Review* (Cork), Summer 2014, no. 48.

Réamonn Ó Muiri, 'The Burning of Wildgoose Lodge: A Selection of Documents', *Journal of the County Louth Archaeological and Historical Society*, vol. 21, no. 2 (1986), *Transactions*, Ossory Archaeological Society, vol. 1.

Gary Owens, 'The Carrickshock Incident, 1831: Social Memory and an Irish *cause célèbre*', *Cultural and Social History*, 2004.

Gary Owens, 'A Moral Insurrection: Faction Fighters, Public Demonstrations and the O'Connellite Campaign, 1828', *Irish Historical Studies*, vol. 30, no. 120 (Nov. 1997).

T. F. G. Paterson, 'The Burning of Wildgoose Lodge', *Journal of the County Louth Archaeological Society*, vol. 12, no. 2 (1950).

Angèle Smith, 'Mapped Landscapes: The Politics of Metaphor, Knowledge, and Representation on Nineteenth-Century Irish Ordnance Survey Maps', *Historical Archaeology*, 2007, vol. 41, no. 1, *Between Art & Artifact* (2007).

William Anthony Smyth, 'Sir Richard Griffith's three valuations of Ireland, 1826–1864', *Irish Economic and Social History*, vol. 37 (2010).

Homer E. Socolofsky, 'William Scully: Ireland and America, 1840–1900', *Agricultural History*, vol. 48, no. 1, *Farming in the Midwest, 1840–1900: A Symposium* (Jan. 1974).

Tony Varley 'A Region of Sturdy Smallholders? Western Nationalists and Agrarian Politics during the First World War', *Journal of the Galway Archaeological and Historical Society*, vol. 55 (2003).

Kevin Whelan, 'Clachans: landscape and life in Ireland before and after the Famine' in Patrick J. Duffy and William Nolan (eds), *At the Anvil: Essays in Honour of William J. Smyth* (Dublin, 2012), Chapter 18, 1.

Niall Whelehan, 'Labour and agrarian violence in the Irish midlands, 1850–1870', *Saothar*, vol. 37 (2012).

Fiction

William Carleton, *The Black Prophet, A tale of the Irish Famine* (Belfast, 1847).

William Carleton, *The Poor Scholar, Frank Martin and the Fairies, The Country Dancing Master and other Irish Tales* (London, 1869).

William Carleton, *Traits and Stories of the Irish Peasantry* (First series) (New York, 1877).

William Carleton, 'The Tithe Proctor' in *The Works of William Carleton*, vol. 2 (New York, 1882).

Maria Edgeworth, *Castle Rackrent* (London, 1910).

Francis Ledwidge, 'Lament for Thomas McDonagh', *Complete Poems* (London, 1919).

Margaret Mitchell, *Gone with the Wind* (London, 1957).

Thomas Moore, *Memoirs of Captain Rock* (London, 1854).

Edith Somerville and Martin Ross, *The Irish RM and his Experiences* (London, 1948).

Charlotte Elizabeth Tonna, *The Rockite* (London, 1836).

Anthony Trollope, *The Land Leaguers* (London, 1884).

Acknowledgements

To Neil Belton of Head of Zeus for his confidence that I was equal to the task of completing a project he had secretly nurtured for some time, a single-volume history of the struggle for land in Ireland.

To Karina Maduro of Head of Zeus and Neil Burkey for their patience and understanding as they worked on a volume almost twice the length of even the most wordy publication.

To my agent, that ebullient Welshman Jonathan Williams, for, as always, being my editor of first resort and for reminding me of some of the finer points of punctuation and the correct use of the colon.

To Professors Paul Bew and Terence Dooley for their giant and accommodating shoulders and for their comments, corrections and suggestions. It goes without saying that all remaining errors are my own.

To two equally busy people, Catriona Crowe and Fintan O'Toole, for their much appreciated perusal of the manuscript – tasks undertaken in two unguarded moments on an excursion to the great city of San Francisco for the 2022 Hinterland West festival.

To the writers, researchers and academics (you know who you are) who have opened up the study of the politics of land in Ireland – may your future working lives be improved by access to the Land Commission archives now housed in Port Laoise.

To my wife Nerys for tolerating my *schtick* when she really needed to get back to her own research on the poetry broadcasts of the BBC Third Programme in the 1940s and 1950s.

To the magnificent Doe Library of the University of California, Berkeley (aka 'home from home'), where a gargantuan manuscript was finally hacked into some shape with a few final shards being added.

About the Author

Myles Dungan is a broadcaster and historian. He presents *The History Show* on RTÉ Radio 1 and is an adjunct lecturer and Fulbright scholar in the School of History and Archives, University College Dublin. Dungan has compiled and presented award-winning historical documentaries, and is the author of numerous works on Irish and American history, including *Four Killings: Land Hunger, Murder and a Family in the Irish Revolution.* He holds a PhD from Trinity College Dublin.

Notes

Preface

1. Terence Dooley, '*The Land for the People: The Land Question in Independent Ireland* (Dublin, 2004), 4.
2. *Irish Times*, 9 February 2018.
3. *Irish Times*, 4 August 2021 (report of inquest).
4. *Irish Times*, 28 July 2023.
5. *Irish Times*, 12 July 2022.

Introduction

1. Margaret Mitchell, *Gone with the Wind* (London, 1957), 39.
2. James F. Lydon, 'The Braganstown Massacre', *Journal of the County Louth Archaeological and Historical Society*, vol. 19, no. 1 (1977), 5–16.
3. Barbara L. Solow, 'The Irish land question in a wider context', Fergus Campbell and Tony Varley (eds), *Land Questions in Modern Ireland* (Manchester, 2013) (Kindle edition), 66.
4. Jo Guldi, *The Long Land War: The Global Struggle for Occupancy Rights* (New Haven, Kindle edition, 2022), 28.
5. Gearóid Ó Tuathaigh, 'Irish land questions in the state of the union', Fergus Campbell and Tony Varley (eds) *Land Questions in Modern Ireland*, 5.
6. James S. Donnelly Jr, *Captain Rock: The Irish Agrarian Rebellion of 1821– 1824* (Cork, 2009), 11–12.
7. Donnelly, *Captain Rock*, 15.
8. Paul Bew, *Ancestral Voices in Irish Politics: Judging Dillon and Parnell* (Oxford, 2023), 17.
9. Mitchell, *Gone with the Wind*, 39.
10. Ciarán Moran, 'Do we need a new Land Commission?', *Irish Independent*, 8 August 2023.
11. T. Desmond Williams (ed.), *Secret Societies in Ireland* (Dublin, 1973), 8.

Chapter 1: *Topographica Hibernica*

1. Arthur Young, *Tour in Ireland*, vol. 2 (London, 1892), 1.
2. Young, *Tour in Ireland*, vol. 2, xii.
3. Giraldus Cambrensis, *The Topography of Ireland*, translated by Thomas Forester (Ontario, 2000), 70.
4. Young, *Tour in Ireland*, vol. 2, 5.
5. W. F. Bailey, *The Irish Land Acts: A Short Sketch* (Dublin, 1917), 5.
6. Young, *Tour in Ireland*, vol. 2, 7.
7. Young, *Tour in Ireland*, vol. 2, 8.
8. Young, *Tour in Ireland*, vol. 2, 86.
9. Bailey, *The Irish Land Acts*, 5–6.

Chapter 2: From petty kings to Petty

1. Thomas Davis, *Prose Writings of Thomas Davis* (London, undated), 77.
2. Thomas Bartlett, *Ireland: A History* (Cambridge, 2010), 1–2.
3. Raymond Crotty, *Irish Agricultural Production, its Volume and Structure* (Cork, 1966), 1.
4. P. W. Joyce, *A Smaller Social History of Ancient Ireland* (Dublin, 1906), Chapter 4.
5. Myles Dillon (ed.), *Early Irish Society* (Dublin, 1954), 54.
6. Thomas R. Kerr, Finbarr McCormick and Aidan O'Sullivan, 'Irish National Strategic Archaeological Research Programme, 2013' in *The Economy of Early Medieval Ireland* (Early Medieval Archaeology Project) Report 7:1 December 2013, 8.
7. Kerr, McCormick and O'Sullivan, *The Economy of Early Medieval Ireland*, 8, 9.
8. Alice Stopford Green, *The Making of Ireland and its Undoing, 1200–1600* (London, 1908), x, xi.
9. Stopford Green, *The Making of Ireland and its Undoing*, 107–8, 105.
10. From D. O'Cróinín. 1992. Review of H. Mytum: 'The Origins of Early Christian Ireland', *Linen Hall Review*, 9.2, 23–5, cited in Kerr, McCormick and O'Sullivan, *The Economy of Early Medieval Ireland*, 9.
11. Joyce, *A Smaller Social History of Ancient Ireland*, 86.
12. Bartlett, *Ireland: A History*, 7.
13. Irish Land Committee, *The Land Question, Ireland: Confiscation or Contract?* (Dublin, 1880), 8, 10.
14. Charles Gavan Duffy, *The League of North and South: An Episode in Irish History, 1850–1854* (London, 1886), 26.
15. Crotty, *Irish Agricultural Production*, 2–3.
16. Bartlett, *Ireland: A History*, 104.

17. J. C. Beckett, *The Making of Modern Ireland, 1603–1923* (London, 1966), 83.
18. Thomas A. Larcom, *The history of the survey of Ireland, commonly called the Down survey, A.D. 1655–6* (Dublin, 1851), 120.
19. Larcom, *The history of the survey of Ireland*, 123, 124–5.
20. R. F. Foster, *Modern Ireland, 1600–1972* (London, 1988), 110.
21. Larcom, *The history of the survey of Ireland*, 3.
22. Larcom, *The history of the survey of Ireland*, vii.
23. Beckett, *The Making of Modern Ireland*, 109.
24. Foster, *Modern Ireland*, 110.
25. Terence Dooley, *The big houses and landed estates of Ireland, a research guide* (Dublin, 2007), 15.
26. *Dictionary of Irish Biography*, vol. 8, 85–7.
27. George Sigerson, *History of the land tenures and land classes of Ireland: with an account of the various secret agrarian confederacies* (London, 1871), 118.

Chapter 3: *Na buachaillí bána*

1. James S. Donnelly Jr, 'The Whiteboy Movement, 1761–65', *Irish Historical Studies*, vol. 21, no. 81 (Mar. 1978), 20.
2. Gale E. Christianson, 'Secret Societies and Agrarian Violence in Ireland, 1790–1840', *Agricultural History*, vol. 46, no. 3 (July 1972), 371.
3. Isaac Butt, *The Irish Land and the Irish People* (London, 1867), 73.
4. Maureen Wall in Williams (ed.), *Secret Societies in Ireland*, 16.
5. Wall in Williams (ed.), *Secret Societies in Ireland*, 17.
6. David Dickson, *Arctic Ireland: The Extraordinary Story of the Great Frost and Forgotten Famine of 1740–41* (Belfast, 1997), 62–3.
7. James Kelly, 'Coping with Crisis: The response to the Famine of 1740–41', *Eighteenth-Century Ireland / Iris an dá chultúr*, vol. 27 (2012), 102.
8. L. M. Cullen, *An Economic History of Ireland since 1660* (London, 1972), 68.
9. Michael Drake, 'The Irish Demographic Crisis of 1740–41', *Historical Studies VI* (London, 1968), 103.
10. Steven Engler, Franz Mauelshagen, Jürg Luterbacher, and Johannes Werner, '"The Irish Famine of 1740–1741: Famine Vulnerability and 'Climate Migration'", *Climate of the Past*, 9, no. 3 (2013), 1175.
11. James Kelly, 'Coping with Crisis', 115.
12. David Dickson, *New Foundations: Ireland 1660–1800* (Dublin, 2000), 112.
13. Cullen, *An Economic History of Ireland*, 80.
14. Maria Edgeworth, *Castle Rackrent* (London, 1910), 12.

15. Young, *A Tour in Ireland*, vol. 2, 153.

16. Samuel Clark, 'The importance of agrarian classes: agrarian class structure and collective action in nineteenth-century Ireland,' in P. J. Drudy (ed.), *Ireland: Land, Politics and People* (Cambridge, 1982), 14–21.

17. Young, *A Tour in Ireland*, vol. 1 (London, 1892), 462.

18. R. F. Foster, *Modern Ireland*, 220.

19. Cullen, *Economic History of Ireland*, 79.

20. Cullen, *Economic History of Ireland*, 81.

21. Kevin Whelan, 'Clachans: landscape and life in Ireland before and after the Famine' in Patrick J. Duffy and William Nolan (eds), *At the Anvil: Essays in Honour of William J. Smyth* (Dublin, 2012), Chapter 18, 1.

22. Donald E. Jordan Jr, *Land and Popular Politics in Ireland* (Cambridge, 1994), 54.

23. Evidence of Very Rev. John Patrick Lyons, Dean of Killala – PP of Kilmore Erris – Devon Commission (*Devon Commission, Minutes of Evidence, Pt.II*, PP 1845 (606), xix, 154). Cited in Jordan, *Land and Popular Politics in Ireland*, 55.

24. Edward Wakefield, *An Account of Ireland, Statistical and Political*, vol. 1 (London, 1812), 278.

25. Flaherty, 'A statistical and documentary primer on rundale in Ireland', *Ulster Folklife* (2015), 2–3.

26. Young, *A Tour in Ireland*, vol. 2, 55.

27. Cornewall Lewis, *On Local Disturbances and the Irish Church Question* (London, 1836), 6.

28. Foster, *Modern Ireland*, 222.

29. Butt, *The Irish Land and the Irish People*, 72.

30. James Kelly (ed.), *The Cambridge History of Ireland, Volume III, 1730–1880* (Cambridge, 2018), 5.

31. H. A. L. Morton, *A People's History of England* (London, 1938), 318.

32. Young, *A Tour in Ireland*, vol. 2, 95.

33. Butt, *The Irish Land and the Irish People*, 73.

34. Michael Davitt, *The Fall of Feudalism in Ireland* (London, 1904), 16.

35. Thomas Newenham, *A View of the National, Political and Commercial Circumstances of Ireland* (London, 1809), 129, 140.

36. James S. Donnelly Jr, 'The Whiteboy Movement, 1761–65', *Irish Historical Studies*, vol. 21, no. 81 (Mar. 1978), 38.

37. Donnelly, 'The Whiteboy Movement, 1761–65', 26.

38. Statement of Edward Stack, aged seventy-seven years in 1937/38, University College Dublin, National Folklore Collection UCD, 0405/1/6.

39. Donnelly, 'The Whiteboy Movement, 1761–65', 27.

40. Donnelly, 'The Whiteboy Movement, 1761–65', 27.

41. Lewis, *Local Disturbances*, 6.
42. Lewis, *Local Disturbances*, 11–12.
43. Young, *Tour in Ireland*, vol. 2, 82.
44. Young, *Tour in Ireland*, vol. 1, 82.
45. Lewis, *Local Disturbances*, 14.
46. Young, *Tour in Ireland*, vol. 1, 81.
47. Lewis, *Local Disturbances*, 22.
48. Dr Richard Woodward, *Present State of the Church of Ireland* (Dublin, 1808), 79, 82–5.
49. *Transactions*, Ossory Archaeological Society, vol. 1, 103–7.
50. Young, *Tour in Ireland*, vol. 1, 83.
51. Lewis, *Local Disturbances*, 14.
52. Denis Fahey, 'An Irishman's Diary', *Irish Times*, 28 April 2009.
53. 'An Act to prevent and punish tumultuous risings of persons within this kingdom, and for other purposes therein mentioned', 1775, Irish Statute Book.
54. Young, *Tour in Ireland*, vol. 2, 55.
55. Wall in Williams (ed.), *Secret Societies in Ireland*, 18.

Chapter 4: 'Paddy is easily persuaded to partake of this amusement': the Oakboys, Steelboys, Rightboys, Defenders and Peep O'Day Boys

1. W. Smith to E. B. Littlehales, 15 March 1808, cited in James Kelly (ed.), *The Cambridge History of Ireland, Volume III*, 96.
2. Davitt, *The Fall of Feudalism in Ireland*, 19.
3. Lewis, *Local Disturbances*, 35.
4. Christianson, 'Secret Societies and Agrarian Violence in Ireland, 1790–1840', 376.
5. James S. Donnelly Jr and James J. Donnelly Jr, 'The Rightboy Movement 1785–8', *Studia Hibernica*, 1977/8, no. 17/18, 123.
6. Foster, *Modern Ireland*, 225.
7. W. Smith to E. B. Littlehales, 15 March 1808, HO 100/14ff, 132–6, TNA cited in Thomas Bartlett, 'Ireland during the Revolutionary and Napoleonic Wars' in James Kelly (ed.), *The Cambridge History of Ireland, Volume III*, 96.
8. James S. Donnelly Jr and James J. Donnelly Jr, 'The Rightboy Movement 1785–8', 124.
9. James S. Donnelly Jr and James J. Donnelly Jr, 'The Rightboy Movement 1785–8', 125.
10. Foster, *Modern Ireland*, 207.

11. Lewis, *Local Disturbances*, 33.
12. Thomas Campbell, *A Philosophical Survey of the South of Ireland* (Dublin, 1777), 309.
13. Foster, *Modern Ireland*, 223.
14. Jonathan Bardon, *A History of Ulster* (Belfast, 2005), 206.
15. Campbell, *A Philosophical Survey of the South of Ireland*, 309–10.
16. Lewis, *Local Disturbances*, 33–4.
17. Butt, *The Irish Land and the Irish People*, 77.
18. Wakefield, *An Account of Ireland*, 547.
19. James S. Donnelly Jr, 'Hearts of Oak, Hearts of Steel', *Studia Hibernica*, no. 21 (1981), 8, 9.
20. Donnelly, 'Hearts of Oak, Hearts of Steel', 12.
21. Bardon, *A History of Ulster*, 207.
22. Bardon, *A History of Ulster*, 207.
23. Butt, *The Irish Land and the Irish People*, 79.
24. Bardon, *A History of Ulster*, 208.
25. Young, *Tour in Ireland*, vol. 1, 129.
26. Young, *Tour in Ireland*, vol. 1, 153.
27. David W. Miller, 'The Armagh Troubles, 1784–95' in Samuel Clark and James Donnelly Jr (eds), *Irish Peasants: Violence and Political Unrest 1780–1914* (Wisconsin, 1983), 162.
28. *Finn's Leinster Journal*, 28 March–1 April 1772, cited in Donnelly, 'Hearts of Oak, Hearts of Steel', 64.
29. Donnelly, 'Hearts of Oak, Hearts of Steel', 64.
30. Donnelly, 'Hearts of Oak, Hearts of Steel', 64
31. Foster, *Modern Ireland*, 223.
32. Donnelly, 'Hearts of Oak, Hearts of Steel', 72.
33. Lewis, *Local Disturbances*, 20–22.
34. Lewis, *Local Disturbances*, 101.
35. James S. Donnelly Jr and James J. Donnelly Jr, 'The Rightboy Movement 1785–8', 122.
36. Clark and Donnelly Jr (eds), *Irish Peasants: Violence and Political Unrest*, 30.
37. Butt, *The Irish Land and the Irish People*, 76.
38. Cornewall Lewis, *Local Disturbances*, 20–22.
39. Newenham, *National, Political and Commercial Circumstances of Ireland*, 259.
40. Butt, *The Irish Land and the Irish People*, 77.
41. James S. Donnelly Jr and James J. Donnelly Jr, 'The Rightboy Movement 1785–8', 132.
42. Edgeworth, *Castle Rackrent*, 8.
43. Butt, *The Irish Land and the Irish People*, 75.
44. *Dictionary of Irish Biography*, vol. 9, 447–8.

45. *Considerations on the present disturbances in the province of Munster, their causes, extent, probable consequences, and remedies* (Dublin, 1787), 48–9.
46. James Kelly, *That Damn'd Thing Called Honour: Duelling in Ireland 1570–1860* (Cork, 1995), 145–7.
47. James S. Donnelly Jr and James J. Donnelly Jr, 'The Rightboy Movement 1785–8', 168.
48. Davitt, *The Fall of Feudalism in Ireland*, 24.
49. Lewis, *Local Disturbances*, 31.
50. Lewis, *Local Disturbances*, 254.
51. Jonah Barrington, *Personal Sketches* (London, 1827), 205.
52. Wall in T. Desmond Williams (ed.), *Secret Societies in Ireland*, 24.
53. William Carleton, 'The Battle of the Factions', *Traits and Stories of the Irish Peasantry* (First series) (New York, 1877), 127.
54. Lewis, *Local Disturbances*, 37.
55. Breandán Mac Suibhne, *The End of Outrage: Post-Famine Adjustment in Rural Ireland* (Oxford, 2017), Kindle edition, 34.

Chapter 5: The old vest, the cravat and the ribbon: tenant versus tenant 1806–16

1. Réamonn Ó Muiri, 'The Burning of Wildgoose Lodge: A Selection of Documents', *Journal of the County Louth Archaeological and Historical Society*, vol. 21, no. 2 (1986), 120.
2. Randal Kernan, *A Report of the Trials of the Caravats and Shanavests at the Special Commission for the Several Counties of Tipperary, Waterford and Kilkenny* (Dublin, 1811), 5.
3. National Folklore Collections, the Schools' Collection, vol. 0563, 171.
4. Michael Davitt, *The Fall of Feudalism in Ireland*, 36.
5. Paul E. W. Roberts, 'Caravats and Shanavests: Whiteboyism and Faction Fighting in East Munster, 1802–11' in Clark and Donnelly Jr (eds), *Irish Peasants: Violence and Political Unrest*, 66. The work done by Roberts in his research for this essay was crucial in uncovering the true nature of the Caravat–Shanavest rivalry.
6. K. Theodore Hoppen, *Ireland Since 1800: Conflict and Conformity* (London, 1989), 48.
7. Francis Finegan, 'Sir John Howley: 1789–1866', *Irish Quarterly Review*, vol. 40, no. 157 (Mar. 1951), 104.
8. Roberts, 'Caravats and Shanavests', 70–72.
9. *Liverpool Mercury*, September 1859–May 1860, 'The Tipperary Man to Lord Derby', cited in Finegan, 'Sir John Howley: 1789–1866', 104.
10. Kernan, *A Report of the Trials of the Caravats and Shanavests*, 12, 10.
11. Gary Owens, 'A Moral Insurrection: Faction Fighters, Public

Demonstrations and the O'Connellite Campaign, 1828', *Irish Historical Studies*, vol. 30, no. 120 (Nov. 1997), 525.

12. *State of Ireland, Minutes of Evidence taken before the Select Committee appointed to inquire into the Disturbances in Ireland in the last session of parliament, 13 May –18 June, 1824*, 113–14.
13. *Dictionary of Irish Biography*, vol. 9, 401–3.
14. Kernan, *A Report of the Trials of the Caravats and Shanavests*, 29–33, 69.
15. Terence Dooley, *The Murders at Wildgoose Lodge: Agrarian Crime and Punishment in Pre-Famine Ireland* (Dublin, 2007), 257.
16. Thomas Garvin, 'Defenders, Ribbonmen and others: Underground political networks in pre-Famine Ireland' in C. H. E. Philpin (ed.), *Nationalism and Popular Protest in Ireland* (Cambridge, 1987), 242.
17. Lewis, *Local Disturbances*, 157.
18. Kyle Hughes and Donald M. Macraild, *Ribbon Societies in Nineteenth-Century Ireland and its Diaspora* (Liverpool, 2021), 60.
19. T. F. G. Paterson, 'The Burning of Wildgoose Lodge', *Journal of the County Louth Archaeological Society*, 1950, vol. 12, no. 2 (1950), 159.
20. Daniel J. Casey, 'Wildgoose Lodge: the Evidence and the Lore', *Journal of the County Louth Archaeological and Historical Society*, vol. 18, no. 2 (1974), 141.
21. Hughes and Macraild, *Ribbon Societies in Nineteenth-Century Ireland*, 58.
22. James Anton, *Retrospect of a Military Life* (Edinburgh, 1841), 271.
23. *The Works of William Carleton*, vol. III (New York, 1881), 936–44.
24. Mac Suibhne, *The End of Outrage*, Kindle edition, 27.
25. Hughes and Macraild, *Ribbon Societies in Nineteenth-Century Ireland*, 59.
26. Dooley, *The Murders at Wildgoose Lodge*, 239.
27. Réamonn Ó Muiri, 'The Burning of Wildgoose Lodge', 130.
28. Hoppen, *Ireland Since 1800*, 44.
29. Dooley, *The Murders at Wildgoose Lodge*, 39–41, 257.

Chapter 6: Planting 'the tree of liberty': rape, arson, murder, sectarianism and the Rockite insurgency, 1821–4

1. *Cork Constitution*, 24 March 1823.
2. *The Dublin Penny Journal*, vol. 3, no. 105 (5 July 1834), 2.
3. *Freeman's Journal*, 11 April 1822.
4. Charlotte Elizabeth Tonna, *Irish Recollections* (Dublin, 2004), 33.
5. Stephen Randolph Gibbons, *Captain Rock, Night Errant: The Threatening Letters of Pre-Famine Ireland, 1801–45* (Dublin, 2004), 23.
6. Peter Connell, *The Land and People of County Meath, 1750–1850* (Dublin, 2004), 153.
7. Bartlett, *Ireland, a History*, 250.

8. Charles Walmesley, *General History of the Christian Church from her birth to her Final Triumphant States in Heaven chiefly deduced from the Apocalypse of St. John the Apostle, by Signor Pastorini* (New York, 1834), 1.

9. Lewis, *On local disturbances in Ireland*, 234.

10. Shunsuke Katsuta, 'The Rockite Movement in County Cork in the Early 1820s', *Irish Historical Studies*, May 2003, vol. 33, no. 131, 280.

11. Bartlett, *Ireland, a History*, 248.

12. Bartlett, *Ireland, a History*, 248.

13. Walmesley, *Pastorini* (Editor's Preface), 5.

14. James S. Donnelly Jr, 'Pastorini and Captain Rock: Millenarianism and Sectarianism in the Rockite Movement of 1821–4' in Clark and Donnelly Jr (eds), *Irish Peasants: Violence and Political Unrest*, 109–10.

15. William Carleton, 'The Poor Scholar', *The Poor Scholar, Frank Martin and the Fairies, the Country Dancing Master and Other Irish Tales* (London, 1869), 2.

16. Carleton, 'The Poor Scholar', 7.

17. Tonna, *Irish Recollections*, 11, 33–4.

18. Hughes and Macraild, *Ribbon Societies*, 35.

19. Katsuta, 'The Rockite Movement in County Cork', 287.

20. Donnelly, *Captain Rock*, 31.

21. Donnelly, *Captain Rock*, 26.

22. Katsuta, 'The Rockite Movement in County Cork', 291.

23. *Dublin Evening Post*, 20 October 1821.

24. Thomas Bartlett, 'Ireland during the Revolutionary and Napoleonic Wars' in *The Cambridge History of Ireland, Volume III*, 99.

25. Maria Luddy, 'Abductions in Nineteenth-Century Ireland', *New Hibernia Review*, Summer 2013, vol. 17, no. 2, 17–18.

26. Gibbons, *Captain Rock, Night Errant*, 155.

27. George Rudé, *Protest and Punishment: The Story of the Social and Political Protestors Transported to Australia, 1788–1868* (Oxford, 1978), 77–9.

28. Thomas Moore, *Memoirs of Captain Rock* (London, 1854), 157.

29. Charlotte Elizabeth Tonna, *The Rockite* (London, 1836), 103.

30. Linda Kelly, *Ireland's Minstrel* (London, 2006), 175.

31. Clare O'Halloran, 'Stories of Subversion: Thomas Moore's "Memoirs of Captain Rock" and Irish Historical Tradition', in *The Irish Review* (Cork), Summer 2014, no. 48, 37.

32. Linda Kelly, *Ireland's Minstrel* (London, 2006), 173.

33. Moore, *Memoirs of Captain Rock*, 301.

34. O'Halloran, 'Stories of Subversion', 44.

35. Moore, *Memoirs of Captain Rock*, iii, 233, 309, 307, 154.

36. Kelly, *Ireland's Minstrel*, 174, 176.

37. *Dictionary of Irish Biography*, 419–20.
38. Tonna, *The Rockite*, vol. 27, 93, 99–100, 285.
39. Donnelly, *Captain Rock*, 353.
40. Tonna, *Irish Recollections*, 58–9.
41. Hughes and Macraild, *Ribbon Societies*, 34.

Chapter 7: The 'sacred tenth': the Tithe War of the 1830s

1. Gary Owens, 'The Carrickshock Incident, 1831: Social Memory and an Irish *cause célèbre*', *Cultural and Social History*, 2004; 1:36–64.
2. Gary Owens, 'The Carrickshock Incident', 40–1.
3. Butt, *The Irish People and the Irish Land*, 76.
4. Gustave de Beaumont, *Ireland: Social, Political and Religious* (London, 1839), 368.
5. Emmet Larkin (ed.), *Alexis de Tocqueville's Journey in Ireland, July–August 1835* (Washington D.C., 1990), 64.
6. House of Commons Debate, 16 May 1823, vol. 9, c. 368.
7. Donnelly Jr, *Captain Rock*, 210.
8. Alexis de Tocqueville, *Journeys to England and Ireland* (New Haven, 1958), 183.
9. Patrick Geoghegan, *Liberator: The Life and Death of Daniel O'Connell 1830–1847* (Dublin, 2010), 48.
10. Patrick O'Donoghue, 'Causes of the opposition to the tithes, 1830–38', *Studia Hibernica*, no. 5 (1965), 26.
11. O'Donoghue, 'Opposition to Tithe Payments in 1830–31', *Studia Hibernica*, no. 6 (1966), 76.
12. William Sheehan and Maura Cronin (eds), *Riotous Assemblies: Rebels, Riots and Revolts in Ireland* (Cork, 2011), 84.
13. Tonna, *Irish Recollections*, 169.
14. Tonna, *Irish Recollections*, 169.
15. W. R. Le Fanu, *Seventy Years of Irish Life* (London, 1894), 58–70.
16. House of Commons Debate, 23 June 1831, vol. 4, c. 270.
17. House of Commons Debate, 30 June 1831, vol. 4, c. 553.
18. William Carleton, 'The Tithe Proctor' in *The Works of William Carleton*, vol. 2 (New York, 1882), 471–2.
19. Tonna, *Irish Recollections*, 171.
20. David Patrick Reid, *The Tithe War in Ireland, 1830–1838* (PhD thesis, Trinity College, Dublin, 2013), 89.
21. House of Lords Debate, 15 December 1831, vol. 9, cc. 229–51, House of Commons Debate, 15 December 1831, vol. 9, cc. 259–96.
22. Richard Lahert, '*An Maor agus an Meirleach* (The Mayor and the

Outlaw): A Postscript to the Carrickshock Affray, 1831', *Decies, Journal of the Old Waterford Society*, no. 49, Spring 1994, 45–54.

23. Irish Folklore Collection, the Schools' Collection, vol. 0849, 123.
24. Reid, *The Tithe War in Ireland*, 139.
25. *Dublin Evening Post*, 12 January 1833, cited in Reid, *The Tithe War in Ireland*, 158.
26. Sheehan and Cronin (eds), *Riotous Assemblies*, 93.
27. *Freeman's Journal*, 2 May 1834, cited in Sheehan and Cronin (eds), *Riotous Assemblies*, 90.
28. Thomas Bartlett, *Ireland, a History*, 271.
29. Le Fanu, *Seventy Years of Irish Life*, 58 and 71.
30. Bartlett, *Ireland, a History*, 271.
31. S. M. Hussey, *The Reminiscences of an Irish Land Agent* (London, 1904), 44–5.
32. Bartlett, *Ireland, a History*, 271.
33. Le Fanu, *Seventy Years of Irish Life*, 70.
34. Tonna, *Irish Recollections*, 175.

Chapter 8: *Topographica Hibernica* #2: mapping and valuing – the Ordnance Survey and Griffith's Valuation

1. Mary Olive Hussey, 'Sir Richard Griffith: The Man and His Work', *Dublin Historical Record*, vol. 20, no. 2, 75 (Mar. 1965).
2. Gillian Doherty, *The Irish Ordnance Survey: History, Culture and Memory* (Dublin, 2004), 13.
3. Doherty, *The Irish Ordnance Survey*, 14.
4. Patrick S. McWilliams, 'Reactions to the Ordnance Survey: A Window on Prefamine Ireland', *New Hibernia Review*, Spring 2009, vol. 13, no. 1, 55.
5. Evidence of Charles Edward Trevelyan, *Report and Minutes of Evidence of the House of Commons Select Committee on Ordnance Survey (Ireland), 1846*, 1.
6. *Commons Select Committee on Ordnance Survey (Ireland)*, 3.
7. Angèle Smith, 'Mapped Landscapes: The Politics of Metaphor, Knowledge, and Representation on Nineteenth-Century Irish Ordnance Survey Maps', *Historical Archaeology*, 2007, vol. 41, no. 1, *Between Art & Artifact* (2007), 83.
8. McWilliams, 'Reactions to the Ordnance Survey', 52, 28.
9. Belinda Jupp, 'Ordnance Survey Memoirs of Ireland', *Garden History*, Summer 1994, vol. 22, no. 1, 73.
10. Doherty, *The Irish Ordnance Survey*, 17.
11. Doherty, *The Irish Ordnance Survey*, 18.
12. Doherty, *The Irish Ordnance Survey*, 20.
13. McWilliams, 'Reactions to the Ordnance Survey', 66.

14. Jupp, 'Ordnance Survey Memoirs of Ireland', 72.
15. Jupp, 'Ordnance Survey Memoirs of Ireland', 76.
16. Brian Mitchell, 'The Ordnance Survey Memoirs: A Source for Emigration in the 1830s', *History Ireland*, Winter 1996, vol. 4, no. 4, 13.
17. Fiona Fitzsimons, 'Ordnance Survey Employment Records', *History Ireland*, vol. 27, no. 6 (Nov./Dec. 2019), 31.
18. McWilliams, 'Reactions to the Ordnance Survey', 61.
19. McWilliams, 'Reactions to the Ordnance Survey', 62.
20. Mac Suibhne, *The End of Outrage*, Kindle edition, 38
21. Evidence of Captain Thomas Larcom, *Commons Select Committee on Ordnance Survey (Ireland), 1846*, 13 (96).
22. Mac Suibhne, *The End of Outrage*, Kindle edition, 40.
23. Evidence of Richard Griffith, *Commons Select Committee on Ordnance Survey (Ireland), 1846*, 19 (196).
24. Patrick N. Wyse Jackson, 'Sir Richard John Griffith (1784–1878): A portrait in oils by Stephen Catterson Smith (1806–72)', *Irish Journal of Earth Sciences*, vol. 26, 45 (2008).
25. Irish Land Committee, *The Land Question, Ireland, no. 1, Notes upon the government valuation of land in Ireland, commonly known as 'Griffith's Valuation'* (Dublin, 1880), 4.
26. *Instructions by Sir R. Griffith, 1853, to valuators and surveyors in tenement valuation of Ireland; and instructions by Land Commission (Ireland) to Assistant Commissioners, with reference to valuation of agricultural holdings* (House of Commons, 1882), 3–79.
27. *Report of the Select Committee on Townland Valuation in Ireland, Minutes of Evidence, Appendix and Index*, 1844, iii.
28. Irish Land Committee, *The Land Question, Ireland, no. 1*, 14.
29. McWilliams, 'Reactions to the Ordnance Survey', 60.
30. Dun, *Landlords and Tenants in Ireland*, 53, 55.
31. Donald E. Jordan Jr, *Land and Popular Politics in Ireland* (Cambridge, 1994), 151.
32. *The Times*, 18 November 1880.
33. Irish Land Committee, *The Land Question, Ireland, no. 1, Notes upon the government valuation of land in Ireland, commonly known as 'Griffith's Valuation'* (Dublin, 1880), 19.
34. Irish Land Committee, *The Land Question, Ireland, no. 1*, 17.
35. *House of Commons Select Committee on general valuation: report, proceedings, minutes of evidence, appendix and index*, 160 (4199).
36. Finlay Dun, *Landlords and Tenants in Ireland* (London, 1881), 15.
37. *House of Commons Select Committee on general valuation*, 160 (4199), 184–205.

38. Hussey, 'Sir Richard Griffith: The Man and His Work', 65.

39. William Anthony Smyth, 'Sir Richard Griffith's three valuations of Ireland, 1826–1864', *Irish Economic and Social History*, vol. 37 (2010), 129–31.

40. Smyth, 'Sir Richard Griffith's three valuations of Ireland, 1826–1864', 131.

Chapter 9: Emptying the land: the Famine clearances

1. Karl Marx, *Capital*, i, pt vii, chapter 25. Also cited in Cormac Ó Gráda 'Ireland's Great Famine: An overview', Centre for Economic Research, Working paper series, WP04/25, November 2004, 14.

2. Adam Smith, *An Inquiry into the Nature and Causes of the Wealth of Nations Volume 1* (New York, 1917), 160.

3. https://digitalcollections.tcd.ie/concern/works/x059c860p – accessed 7 July 2022.

4. Peter Duffy, *The Killing of Major Denis Mahon* (New York, 2007), 153.

5. Extract from the Devon Commission report cited in Cecil Woodham Smith, *The Great Hunger: Ireland 1845–1849* (London, 1991), 24.

6. John Mitchel, *The Last Conquest of Ireland (Perhaps)* (London, 1882), 219.

7. In Mayo a starving man was said to have 'extracted the heart and liver … [of] a shipwrecked human body … cast on shore' (*The Times*, 23 May 1849), cited in Cormac Ó Gráda 'Ireland's Great Famine: an overview', Centre for Economic Research, Working paper series, WP04/25, November 2004, 7.

8. *Guardian*, 20 July 2021. 'Tony Blair's "apology" … was hastily written by aides because they could not reach him to approve it, newly released classified documents reveal.'

9. Kevin B. Nowlan in R. Dudley Edwards and T. Desmond Williams (eds), *The Great Famine:Studies in Irish History, 1845–52* (Dublin, 1994), xiii.

10. Office for National Statistics, mid-1851 to mid-2014 Population Estimates for the United Kingdom.

11. Joseph Lee, *The Modernisation of Irish Society, 1848–1918* (Dublin, 1989), 1.

12. James S. Donnelly, 'The Great Famine and its interpreters, old and new', *History Ireland*, issue 3, Autumn 1993, vol. 1.

13. Ó Gráda, *The Great Irish Famine* (Cambridge, 1989), 34fn.

14. Crotty, *Irish Agricultural Production*, 38–9.

15. Cormac Ó Gráda, *The Great Irish Famine*, 56.

16. Cormac Ó Gráda, 'Ireland's Great Famine: an overview', Centre for Economic Research, Working paper series, WP04/25, November 2004, 1.

17. *Freeman's Journal*, 1 December 1845.

18. Charles Edward Trevelyan, *The Irish Crisis* (London, 1848), 39.

19. Charles Gavan Duffy, *The League of North and South*, 6.

20. Helen Burke, *The People and the Poor Law in Nineteenth Century Ireland* (Littlehampton, 1987), 111.
21. Edwards and Williams (eds), *The Great Famine*, 214.
22. Trevelyan, *The Irish Crisis*, 2.
23. Mary. E. Daly, *The Famine in Ireland* (Dundalk, 1986), 114.
24. Trevelyan, *The Irish Crisis*, 5, 33, 163, 26, 31, 162, 201.
25. Mitchel, *The Last Conquest of Ireland (Perhaps)*, 102.
26. Hussey, *The Reminiscences of an Irish Land Agent*, 52.
27. Irish Folklore Collection, the Schools' Collection, vol. 0406, 471.
28. Irish Folklore Collection, the Schools' Collection, vol. 0406, 474.
29. Daly, *The Famine in Ireland*, 95.
30. Cormac Ó Gráda, *Ireland Before and After the Famine* (Manchester, 1993), 124.
31. Daly, *The Famine in Ireland*, 110. Around 13,000 of the evicted families were subsequently re-admitted.
32. Hussey, *The Reminiscences of an Irish Land Agent*, 52–3.
33. William Carleton, *The Black Prophet, a Tale of the Irish Famine* (Belfast, 1847), 33.
34. Butt, *The Irish People and the Irish Land*, 123.
35. *Dictionary of Irish Biography*, vol. 1, 540–1.
36. *Dictionary of Irish Biography*, vol. 1, 540–1.
37. House of Commons Debate, 16 February 1847, vol. 90, c. 23.
38. House of Lords Debate, 16 February 1847, vol. 90, c. 9.
39. Jordan, *Land and Popular Politics in Ireland*, 113.
40. John Crowley, William J. Smyth and Mike Murphy (eds), *Atlas of the Great Irish Famine* (Cork, 2012), 267.
41. *Dictionary of Irish Biography*, vol. 1, 540–1.
42. Jordan, *Land and Popular Politics in Ireland*, 111.
43. *Telegraph*, 14 July 1848, cited in Crowley, Smyth and Murphy (eds), *Atlas of the Great Irish Famine*, 267.
44. Ó Gráda, *Ireland Before and After the Famine*, 130.
45. Jordan, *Land and Popular Politics in Ireland*, 112.
46. Helen O'Brien, *The Famine Clearance in Toomevara, Co. Tipperary* (Dublin, 2010), 33–44, 36.
47. *Tipperary Vindicator*, 26 May 1849, in O'Brien, *The Famine Clearance in Toomevara*, 36.
48. *Nenagh Guardian*, 26 May 1849, in O'Brien, *The Famine Clearance in Toomevara*, 38.
49. Memoirs of Thomas Treacy of Toomevara (1832–1905), in O'Brien, *The Famine Clearance in Toomevara*, 44.
50. Trevelyan, *The Irish Crisis*, 164.

51. Donnelly, 'The Great Famine and its interpreters, old and new', *History Ireland*, issue 3, Autumn 1993, vol. 1.
52. Dr Timothy O'Neill reckons that almost 145,000 families (about 580,000 people) were evicted between 1846 and 1854. The lower estimate is that of Professor Cormac Ó'Gráda in *The Great Irish Famine*.
53. Davitt, *The Fall of Feudalism in Ireland*, 17.
54. Ó Gráda, 'Ireland's Great Famine: An overview', 16.
55. Davitt, *The Fall of Feudalism in Ireland*, 66.
56. J. S. Donnelly Jr, 'Landlords and tenants', in W. E. Vaughan (ed.), *A New History of Ireland, vol. V: Ireland Under the Union 1801–70* (Oxford, 1989), 346.
57. Hussey, *The Reminiscences of an Irish Land Agent*, 70.
58. William Keaveney, *The Life and Times of Martin McDonnell, Merchant, Landlord and Poor Law Guardian* (Dublin, 2017), 109.
59. Dun, *Landlords and Tenants in Ireland*, 8.
60. Mitchel, *The Last Conquest of Ireland (Perhaps)*, 30.
61. Edwards and Williams (eds), *The Great Famine*, 332–4.
62. William Steuart Trench, *Realities of Irish Life* (London, 1869), 73–81, 122–5.
63. Edwards and Williams (eds), *The Great Famine*, 332.
64. Trench, *Realities of Irish Life*, 124, 135.
65. Mitchel, *The Last Conquest of Ireland (Perhaps)*, 141.
66. Edwards and Williams (eds), *The Great Famine*, 342, 343.
67. Trevelyan, *The Irish Crisis*, 148, 149–50.
68. Jordan, *Land and Popular Politics in Ireland*, 110.
69. *Dictionary of Irish Biography*, vol. 6, 295–6.
70. Duffy, *The Killing of Major Denis Mahon*, 85.
71. Duffy, *The Killing of Major Denis Mahon*, 141.
72. Arthur Gribben (ed.), *The Great Famine and the Irish Diaspora to America* (Amherst, 1999), 142.
73. Ó Gráda, 'Ireland's Great Famine: an overview', 5.
74. *Dictionary of Irish Biography*, vol. 6, 295–6.
75. Ó Gráda, *The Great Irish Famine*, 58.
76. *Census of Ireland for the year 1851, part V, tables of deaths*, 245.
77. William Neilson Hancock, *Report on the Supposed Progressive Decline in Irish Prosperity* (Dublin, 1863), 4.
78. *Census of Ireland for the year 1851, part V, tables of deaths*, 251.
79. Ó Gráda, *The Great Irish Famine*, 62.
80. David Fitzpatrick, 'The Disappearance of the Irish Agricultural Labourer', *Irish Economic and Social History*, VII, 1980.
81. Lee, *The Modernisation of Irish Society*, 3.

82. William L. Feingold, *Revolt of the Tenantry: The Transformation of Local Government in Ireland 1872–1886* (Chicago, 1984), 72.

83. Ó Gráda, *The Great Irish Famine*, 58.

84. Jordan, *Land and Popular Politics in Ireland*, 104.

85. Jordan, *Land and Popular Politics in Ireland*, 164.

86. Ó Gráda, *The Great Irish Famine*, 66.

87. Ó Gráda, *The Great Irish Famine*, 64.

88. Lee, *The Modernisation of Irish Society*, 3.

89. Lee, *The Modernisation of Irish Society*, 10.

90. Kevin Whelan, 'Clachans: Landscape and life in Ireland before and after the Famine' in Patrick J. Duffy and William Nolan (eds), *At the Anvil: Essays in Honour of William J. Smyth* (Dublin, 2012), Chapter 18.

91. Joel Mokyr, *Why Ireland starved: A Quantitative and Analytical History of the Irish Economy, 1800–1850* (London, 1985), 291.

92. *Illustrated London News*, 13 October 1849, in Colm Tóibín and Diarmaid Ferriter, *The Irish Famine: A Documentary* (New York, 2002), 144.

93. Bew, *Ancestral Voices*, 47.

94. Ó Gráda, 'Ireland's Great Famine: an overview', 20.

Chapter 10: The Indian summer of the Irish landlord, 1848–78

1. Alexander M. Sullivan, *New Ireland: Political Sketches and Personal Reminiscences* (Glasgow, 1877), 224.

2. Sullivan, *New Ireland*, 228.

3. William Vaughan, *Sin, Sheep and Scotsmen: John George Adair and the Derryveagh Evictions, 1861* (Belfast, 1983), 24.

4. Vaughan, *Sin, Sheep and Scotsmen*, 11.

5. Vaughan, *Sin, Sheep and Scotsmen*, 34.

6. Sullivan, *New Ireland*, 223.

7. J. Evitts Haley, *Charles Goodnight: Cowman and Plainsman* (Oklahoma, 1949), 301.

8. Myles Dungan, *How the Irish Won the West* (Dublin, 2006), 195.

9. Sullivan, *New Ireland*, 219.

10. Vaughan, *Sin, Sheep and Scotsmen*, 14.

11. House of Commons Debate, 24 June 1861, vol. 163, c. 1500.

12. Vaughan, *Sin, Sheep and Scotsmen*, 21.

13. House of Commons Debate, 24 June 1861, vol. 163, c. 1488

14. Sullivan, *New Ireland*, 224.

15. Vaughan, *Sin, Sheep and Scotsmen*, 44.

16. Sullivan, *New Ireland*, 220.

17. Vaughan, *Sin, Sheep and Scotsmen*, 26.

18. House of Commons Debate, 24 June 1861, vol. 163, c. 1489.

19. House of Commons Debate, 24 June 1861, vol. 163, c. 1508.

20. Sullivan, *New Ireland*, 231.

21. *Dictionary of Irish Biography*, vol. 8, 819–20.

22. Homer E. Socolofsky, *Landlord William Scully* (Kansas, 1979), 39.

23. Davitt, *The Fall of Feudalism in Ireland*, 76fn.

24. Homer E. Socolofsky, 'William Scully: Ireland and America, 1840–1900', *Agricultural History*, vol. 48, no. 1, Farming in the Midwest, 1840–1900: A Symposium (Jan. 1974), 165.

25. Socolofsky, *Landlord William Scully*, 58.

26. Socolofsky, *Landlord William Scully*, 60.

27. Socolofsky, *Landlord William Scully*, 61.

28. *Dictionary of Irish Biography*, vol. 2, 579–80.

29. Davitt, *The Fall of Feudalism in Ireland*, 143.

30. *The Times*, 12 April 1878.

31. *The Irish Felon*, 24 June, 1848.

32. Butt, *The Irish People and the Irish Land*, 85.

33. Richard McMahon, *Homicide in Pre-Famine and Famine Ireland* (Liverpool, 2013), 131.

34. Davitt, *The Fall of Feudalism in Ireland*, 69.

35. Brian Kennedy, 'Tenant Right before 1870' in T. W. Moody and J. C. Beckett (eds), *Ulster Since 1800* (London, 1954), 42–3.

36. Duffy, *The League of North and South*, 24.

37. Duffy, *The League of North and South*, 26.

38. Duffy, *The League of North and South*, 31, 106.

39. Duffy, *The League of North and South*, 55.

40. Lee, *The Modernisation of Irish Society*, 39.

41. Lee, *The Modernisation of Irish Society*, 39.

42. *Dictionary of Irish Biography*, vol. 2, 977–9.

43. Duffy, *The League of North and South*, 134.

44. Hussey, *The Reminiscences of an Irish Land Agent*, 130.

45. Duffy, *The League of North and South*, 136.

46. Duffy, *The League of North and South*, vii–viii.

47. Thomas P. O'Neill (translated by John T. Goulding), *James Fintan Lalor* (Wexford, 1962), 61.

48. David N. Buckley, *James Fintan Lalor: Radical* (Cork, 1990), 19.

49. L. M. Fogarty, *James Fintan Lalor, Patriot and Political Essayist* (Dublin, 1918), 52–115.

50. *The Irish Felon*, 1 July 1848.

51. Davitt, *The Fall of Feudalism in Ireland*, 64.

52. Davitt, *The Fall of Feudalism in Ireland*, 57.

53. Fogarty, *James Fintan Lalor, Patriot and Political Essayist*, 60.
54. Charles Townshend, *Political Violence in Ireland: Government and Resistance Since 1848* (Oxford, 1983), 32.
55. Davitt, *The Fall of Feudalism in Ireland*, 64.
56. O'Neill, *James Fintan Lalor*, 122.
57. Fogarty, *James Fintan Lalor, Patriot and Political Essayist*, 60.
58. William Frederick Bailey, *The Irish Land Acts: A Short Sketch of their History and Development* (Dublin, 1917), 12.
59. Bailey, *The Irish Land Acts*, 13.
60. Vaughan, *Landlords and Tenants in Ireland, 1848–1904*, 11.
61. Law Reform Commission, *Consultation Paper on General Law of Landlord and Tenant* (Dublin, 2003), 'Deasy's Act, Section 3' D. 1.10.
62. Bailey, *The Irish Land Acts*, 15.
63. Townshend, *Political Violence in Ireland*, 3.
64. Law Reform Commission, *Consultation Paper on General Law of Landlord and Tenant*, D. 1.11.
65. Timothy W. Guinnane and Ronald I. Miller, 'Bonds without Bondsmen: Tenant-Right in Nineteenth-Century Ireland', *The Journal of Economic History*, vol. 56, no. 1 (Mar. 1996), 118. There were 9,600 evictions but 1,600 tenants were re-admitted.
66. Ó Gráda, *Ireland Before and After the Famine*, 152.
67. John E. Pomfret, *The Struggle for the Land in Ireland, 1800–1923* (Princeton, 1930), 47.
68. Guinnane and Miller, 'Bonds without Bondsmen', 117.
69. Dun, *Landlords and Tenants in Ireland*, 27.
70. Davitt, *The Fall of Feudalism in Ireland*, 76.
71. Lee, *The Modernisation of Irish Society, 1848–1918*, 60–1.
72. Hussey, *The Reminiscences of an Irish Land Agent*, 181.
73. Niall Whelehan, 'Labour and agrarian violence in the Irish midlands, 1850–1870', *Saothar*, vol. 37 (2012), 8.

Chapter 11: From Irishtown to Kilmainham: the First Land War, 1879–82

1. James Redpath, *Talks About Ireland* (New York, 1881), 92.
2. Adam D. Pole, *Landlord Responses to the Irish Land War, 1879–82* (PhD thesis, Trinity College, Dublin, 2006), 126.
3. Bew, *Ancestral Voices*, 78.
4. Barbara Lewis Solow, *The Land Question and the Irish Economy, 1870–1903* (Cambridge, MA, 1971), 52.
5. *Return, by provinces and counties, of cases of evictions which have come to*

the knowledge of the Constabulary in each year 1849 to 1880. P. P. 1881 (c. 185) LXXVII cited in Solow, *The Land Question and the Irish Economy*, 55.

6. Henry George, *The Irish land question, what it involves and how it can be settled. An appeal to the Land Leagues* (New York, 1881), 2.

7. Bernard Becker, *Disturbed Ireland* (London, 1881), 85

8. Jordan, *Land and Popular Politics in Ireland*, 4.

9. *Freeman's Journal*, 25 August 1879.

10. Samuel Clark, 'The Importance of agrarian classes: Agrarian class structure and collective action in nineteenth-century Ireland' in P. J. Drudy (ed.), *Ireland: Land, Politics and People* (Cambridge, 1982), 24.

11. Solow, *The Land Question and the Irish Economy*, 203.

12. R. V. Comerford, *The Fenians in Context: Irish Politics and Society, 1848–82* (Dublin, 1998), 223.

13. Stephen Andrew Ball, *Policing the Land War: Official responses to political protest and agrarian crime in Ireland 1879–91* (PhD thesis, Trinity College, Dublin, 2000), 45.

14. Clark, 'The Importance of agrarian classes', 24.

15. Comerford, *The Fenians in Context*, 231.

16. Dun, *Landlords and Tenants in Ireland*, 71.

17. *Freeman's Journal*, 25 August 1879.

18. Richmond Commission, Minutes of Evidence, part 1, 89.

19. See Samuel Clark, *Social Origins of the Irish Land War* (Princeton, 1979), James Donnelly Jr, *The Land and People of Nineteenth Century Cork: The Rural Economy and the Land Question* (London, 1975) and W. E. Vaughan, *Landlords and Tenants in Mid-Victorian Ireland* (Oxford, 1994).

20. Comerford, *The Fenians in Context*, 234.

21. Paul Bew, *Land and the National Question in Ireland, 1858–82* (New Jersey, 1979), 159.

22. Bew, *Land and the National Question*, 222.

23. Terence Dooley, 'Irish Land Questions, 1879–1923' in Thomas Bartlett (ed.), *The Cambridge History of Ireland, vol. iv* (Cambridge, 2018), 120.

24. *Freeman's Journal*, 7 June 1879.

25. Cardinal Edward McCabe, Pastoral letter to the clergy of the Dublin archdiocese, March 1881.

26. Davitt, *The Fall of Feudalism in Ireland*, 311.

27. *United Ireland*, 8 October 1881.

28. *United Ireland*, 13 August 1881.

29. Dooley, 'Irish Land Questions, 1879–1923', 118.

30. *United Ireland*, 7 October, 1882.

31. Clifford Lloyd, *Ireland Under the Land League* (London, 1892), 120.

32. *United Ireland*, 1 July 1882.
33. Hussey, *Reminiscences*, 153.
34. Bew, *Land and the National Question in Ireland*, 156.
35. Bew, *Land and the National Question in Ireland*, 157.
36. Bew, *Land and the National Question in Ireland*, 157.
37. *United Ireland*, 22 October, 1881.
38. T. W. Moody and R. A. J. Hawkins (eds), *Florence Arnold-Forster's Irish Journal* (Oxford, 1988), 456.
39. Ball, *Policing the Land War*, 31.
40. Bew, *Land and the National Question in Ireland*, 215.
41. Michael Davitt, *The Fall of Feudalism in Ireland* (London, 1904), 362.
42. Bew, *Land and the National Question in Ireland*, 4.
43. Vaughan, *Landlords and Tenants in Ireland*, 37.
44. Bew, *Ancestral Voices*, 44.
45. Vaughan, *Landlords and Tenants in Ireland*, 38.

Chapter 12: 'Tenant on tenant' violence in the 1880s

1. *Evidence of the Special Commission to inquire into and report upon the charges and allegations made against certain members of Parliament and other persons in the course of the proceedings in an action entitled O'Donnell versus Walter and another*, evidence of Albert Chester Ives, vol. 1, 452.
2. *Freeman's Journal*, 20 November 1882.
3. Timothy Harrington, *The Maamtrasna Massacre* (Dublin, 1884), vi.
4. Niamh Howlin, UCD working papers in Law, Criminology and Socio-Legal Studies, Research Paper no. 18/2017.
5. Clifford Lloyd to T. H. Burke, 16 October 1881 NAI, CSORP 1881 35119 (in RP 1882/26088).
6. Hussey, *Reminiscences*, 18.
7. Bew, *Ancestral Voices*, 63.
8. John MacDonald, *Daily News Diary of the Parnell Commission* (London, 1890), 19, 27.
9. Richard Slotkin, *The Fatal Environment: The Myth of the Frontier in the Age of Industrialization, 1800–1890* (Oklahoma, 1985).
10. Ball, *Policing the Land War*, 27.
11. MacDonald, *Daily News Diary of the Parnell Commission*, 30.
12. *Evidence of the Special Commission to inquire into and report upon the charges and allegations made against certain members of Parliament and other persons in the course of the proceedings in an action entitled O'Donnell versus Walter and another*, vol. 1, 176.
13. Bew, *Ancestral Voices*, 43.

14. *Evidence of the Special Commission*, vol. 1, 11.

15. Margaret O'Callaghan, *British High Politics and a Nationalist Ireland* (Cork, 1994), 124.

16. *Evidence of the Special Commission*, Inspector Dominick Barry, Mary Dempsey, Patrick Hughes, vol. 1, 465–71.

17. Myles Dungan, *The Captain and the King: William O'Shea, Parnell and Late Victorian Ireland* (Dublin, 2009), 147.

18. *Evidence of the Special Commission*, Sir Richard Webster, vol. 1, 114 and 120.

19. *Evidence of the Special Commission*, Mary Hickey, Head Constable George Huggins, vol. 2, 206–10.

20. Hussey, *Reminiscences*, 231

21. Donnacha Seán Lucey, *Land and Popular Politics in County Kerry, 1872–86* (PhD thesis, Maynooth University 2007), 82–3.

22. *Kerry Sentinel*, 21 December 1880.

23. *Evidence of the Special Commission*, Lizzie Curtin, George Curtin, Sergeant Francis Meehan, vol. 1, 334–44.

24. *Evidence of the Special Commission*, Lizzie Curtin, vol. 1, 336.

25. O'Callaghan, *British High Politics*, 117–18.

26. *Evidence of the Special Commission*, District Inspector Charles Crance, vol. 2, 194.

27. *A Popular and Complete Edition of the Parnell Commission Report* (London, 1890), 146.

28. Davitt, *The Fall of Feudalism in Ireland*, 311.

29. *Dublin Daily Express*, 20 November 1882, in Margaret Kelleher, *The Maamtrasna Murders: Language, Life and Death in Nineteenth Century Ireland* (Dublin, 2018), 126.

30. Jarlath Waldron, *Maamtrasna, the Murders and the Mystery* (Dublin, 1992), 142–3.

31. Kelleher, *The Maamtrasna Murders*, 73.

32. Cited in Kelleher, *The Maamtrasna Murders*, 72.

33. *Weekly Irish Times*, 26 August 1882, in Kelleher, *The Maamtrasna Murders*, 72.

34. *Evidence of the Special Commission*, John Louden, vol. IX, 554.

35. Waldron, *Maamtrasna*, 40

36. MacDonald, *Daily News Diary*, 19.

Chapter 13: 'A tumult of passion': the Plan of Campaign

1. George Moore, *Parnell and His Island* (Dublin, 2004), 93.

2. Connolly (ed.), *The Oxford Companion to Irish History*, 444.

3. *United Ireland*, 16 October 1886.
4. *Report of the Cowper Commission on the Irish Land Acts* (London, 1886), 16.
5. House of Commons Debate, 26 August 1886, vol. 308, c. 628.
6. *The Times*, 6 July 1888, from a speech made by Gladstone at Hampstead.
7. F. S. L. Lyons, 'John Dillon and the Plan of Campaign, 1886–90', *Irish Historical Studies*, vol. 14, no. 56 (Sep. 1965), 313.
8. William O'Brien, *Evening Memories* (Dublin, 1920), 160.
9. *Freeman's Journal*, 3 December 1886.
10. 13 January 1887, TNA, PRO, CAB 37/19, 1887 no. 1, Memo on Plan of Campaign, 1.
11. *United Ireland*, 4 December 1886.
12. The National Archive (TNA), Public Record Office (PRO), CAB 37/19 1887, no. 1, Memo on Plan of Campaign, 13 January 1887, 3.
13. TNA, PRO, CAB 37/19 1887 no. 1, Memo on Plan of Campaign, 13 January 1887, 3.
14. *Freeman's Journal*, 15 December 1886.
15. Colonial Office (CO) 903/1, 13.
16. CO 903/1, 18.
17. CO 903/1, 12.
18. *Freeman's Journal*, 17 December 1886.
19. O'Brien, *Evening Memories*, 192.
20. TNA, PRO, CAB 37/19, 1887, no. 1, Memo on Plan of Campaign, 13 January 1887, 2.
21. 13 January 1887, TNA, PRO, CAB 37/19, 1887, no. 1, Memo on Plan of Campaign, 1.
22. *United Ireland*, 31 July 1886.
23. *United Ireland*, 12 March 1887.
24. *Freeman's Journal*, 7 March 1887.
25. *Pall Mall Gazette*, 7 March 1887.
26. O'Brien, *Evening Memories*, 177
27. O'Brien, *Evening Memories*, 182.
28. Katharine O'Shea, *Charles Stewart Parnell: His Love Story and Political Life* (London, 1914), 113–14.
29. Davitt, *The Fall of Feudalism in Ireland*, 621.
30. The Liberal Union of Ireland, *The Plan of Campaign: The Smith Barry Estate, Tipperary* (Dublin, 1890), 19.
31. Liberal Union of Ireland, *The Plan of Campaign*, 4.
32. O'Brien, *Evening Memories*, 434, 435, 439.
33. Sally Warwick-Haller, *William O'Brien and the Irish Land War* (Dublin, 1990), 92.
34. O'Brien, *Evening Memories*, 221, 240.

35. Wilfrid Scawen Blunt, *The Land War in Ireland* (London, 1912), 286–7.
36. Warwick-Haller, *William O'Brien and the Irish Land War*, 96.
37. *Evening Star*, 12 November 1887.
38. John Morley, *The Life of Gladstone* (London, 1908), vol. ii, 466.
39. Morley, *The Life of Gladstone*, vol. ii, 468.
40. O'Brien, *Evening Memories*, 181.
41. *United Ireland*, 30 October 1886.
42. House of Commons Debate, 17 February 1882, vol. 266, cc. 983–4.
43. The Woodford Evictions: Report submitted to the Committee of the Property Defence Association at their meeting on Thursday 21 October 1886, 7–10.

Chapter 14: 'The peasant will not tire first': the Bodyke evictions, June 1887

1. Alfred E. Turner, *Sixty Years of a Soldier's Life* (London, 1912), 209.
2. Henry Norman, *Bodyke, A Chapter in the History of Irish Landlordism* (London, 1887), 5.
3. Norman, *Bodyke*, 5–6.
4. Norman, *Bodyke*, 20.
5. Norman, *Bodyke*, 19.
6. Kelly, *The Bodyke Evictions*, 17.
7. *Clare Journal*, 22 November 1880.
8. *Clare Journal*, 8 November 1880.
9. *Clare Journal*, 6 January 1881.
10. Jesse Craigen, *Report on a visit to Ireland in the summer of 1881* (Dublin, 1882), 49–50.
11. *Irish Times*, 3 June 1881.
12. Kelly, *The Bodyke Evictions*, 30–35.
13. *Irish Times*, 3 February 1887.
14. Buller to Beach, 15 November 1886, St Aldwyn MSS, in L. Perry Curtis Jr, *Coercion and Conciliation in Ireland, 1880–1892: A Study in Conservative Unionism* (Princeton, 1963), 155.
15. Turner, *Sixty Years of a Soldier's Life*, 209.
16. *Irish Times*, 21 June 1887.
17. Buller to Beach, 26 January 1887, St Aldwyn MSS, cited in Curtis, *Coercion and Conciliation in Ireland*, 155.
18. Edward Fry, *James Hack Tuke: A Memoir* (London, 1899), 256.
19. Stephen Ball (ed.), *A Policeman's Ireland: Recollections of Samuel Walters, RIC* (Cork, 1999), 61.
20. Davitt, *Fall of Feudalism in Ireland*, 348.

21. Norman, *Bodyke*, 26.
22. *United Ireland*, 18 June 1887.
23. Turner, *Sixty Years of a Soldier's Life*, 213.
24. Norman, *Bodyke*, 55.
25. *Freeman's Journal*, 15 June 1887.
26. Norman, *Bodyke*, 55.
27. *United Ireland*, 18 June 1887.
28. *Irish Times*, 20 June 1887.
29. L. Perry Curtis Jr, *The Depiction of Eviction in Ireland*, 210
30. Turner, *Sixty Years of a Soldier's Life*, 214.
31. *Irish Times*, 15 June 1887.
32. Turner, *Sixty Years of a Soldier's Life*, 214–15.
33. *United Ireland*, 25 June 1887.
34. House of Commons Debate, 29 August 1887, vol. 320, cc. 280–414.
35. *United Ireland*, 25 June 1887.
36. House of Commons Debate, 13 June 1887, vol. 315, c. 1720.
37. House of Commons Debate, 14 July 1887, vol. 317, cc. 796–8.
38. £1,020 4*s* 9*d* to be precise. House of Commons Debate, 28 July 1887, vol. 318, c. 352.

Chapter 15: The 'closing down' sale

1. Trench, *Realities of Irish Life*, 192.
2. Isaac Butt, *The Irish People and the Irish Land*, 260.
3. Andrew Kettle, *Material for Victory* (Dublin, 1958), 104.
4. Warwick-Haller, *William O'Brien and the Irish Land War*, 147.
5. Kettle, *Material for Victory*, 105.
6. Michael MacDonagh, *The Life of William O'Brien, Irish Nationalist* (London, 1928), 148.
7. MacDonagh, *The Life of William O'Brien*, 148.
8. O'Brien, *Evening Memories*, 476.
9. Pauric Travers, *Settlements and Divisions in Ireland, 1870–1922* (Dublin, 1988), 59.
10. Davitt, *The Fall of Feudalism in Ireland*, 683.
11. Travers, *Settlements and Divisions in Ireland*, 57.
12. Timothy W. Guinnane and Ronald I. Miller, 'The Limits to Land Reform: The Land Acts in Ireland, 1870–1909', *Economic Development and Cultural Change*, vol. 45, no. 3 (Apr. 1997), 595–6.
13. Warwick-Haller, *William O'Brien and the Irish Land War*, 152.
14. Travers, *Settlements and Divisions in Ireland*, 58.
15. O'Brien, *Evening Memories*, 483.

16. Hussey, *Reminiscences*, 188.

17. Davitt, *The Fall of Feudalism in Ireland*, 697.

18. *Dictionary of Irish Biography*, vol. 9, 1062–5.

19. Fergus Campbell, 'Irish Popular Politics and the Making of the Wyndham Land Act, 1901–1903', *The Historical Journal*, vol. 45, no. 4 (Dec. 2002), 756.

20. O'Brien, *Evening Memories*, 476.

21. Campbell, 'Irish Popular Politics and the Making of the Wyndham Land Act', 759–60.

22. *Dictionary of Irish Biography*, vol. 9, 1062–5.

23. Wilfrid Scawen Blunt, *My Diaries: Being a Personal Narrative of Events, 1888–1914, Part 2, 1900–1914* (London, 1921), 17, 20.

24. Blunt, *My Diaries*, 31.

25. Campbell, 'Irish Popular Politics and the Making of the Wyndham Land Act', 762.

26. Earl of Dunraven, *Past Times and Pastimes, Volume 2* (London, 1922), 4.

27. *Irish Times*, 3 September 1902.

28. MacDonagh, *The Life of William O'Brien*, 155.

29. MacDonagh, *The Life of William O'Brien*, 155.

30. D. G. Boyce, *Nineteenth Century Ireland: The Search for Stability* (Dublin, 1990), 226.

31. Timothy Healy, *Letters and Leaders of my Day, Volume 1* (New York, 1929), 261.

32. Boyce, *Nineteenth Century Ireland*, 227.

33. Dunraven, *Past Times and Pastimes*, 6, 11, 12.

34. Patrick Joseph Cosgrove, *The Wyndham Land Act, 1903: The Final Solution to the Irish Land Question?* (PhD thesis, Maynooth University, 2008), 120.

35. Dunraven, *Past Times and Pastimes*, 2.

36. Campbell, 'Irish Popular Politics and the Making of the Wyndham Land Act', 755.

37. Blunt, *My Diaries*, 51.

38. *Dictionary of Irish Biography*, vol. 8, 833–5.

39. Healy, *Letters and Leaders of my Day*, 462.

40. Blunt, *My Diaries*, 54.

41. Cosgrove, *The Wyndham Land Act*, 24.

42. Davitt, *The Fall of Feudalism in Ireland*, 707.

43. Davitt, *The Fall of Feudalism in Ireland*, 706.

44. Blunt, *My Diaries*, 55.

45. Hussey, *Reminiscences*, 41.

46. Tony Varley, 'Gaining ground, losing ground: the politics of land reform in twentieth-century Ireland' in Fergus Campbell and Tony Varley (eds), *Land Questions in Modern Ireland* (Manchester, 2013) (Kindle edition), 29.

47. Kettle, *Material for Victory*, 106.
48. Solow, *The Land Question and the Irish Economy*, 193.
49. Guinnane and Miller, 'The Limits to Land Reform', 596.
50. Healy, *Letters and Leaders of my Day*, 461.
51. Kettle, *Material for Victory*, 106.
52. Solow, *The Land Question and the Irish Economy*, 201, 194, 197.
53. Travers, *Settlements and Divisions in Ireland*, 15.
54. Blunt, *My Diaries*, vol. 2, 309.
55. Travers, *Settlements and Divisions in Ireland*, 30.
56. Boyce, *Nineteenth Century Ireland*, 226.
57. Travers, *Settlements and Divisions in Ireland*, 30.

Chapter 16: 'Use the hazel': the Ranch War, 1906–9

1. National Folklore Collection, the Schools Collection, vol. 719, 605.
2. William O'Brien, *An Olive Branch in Ireland and Its History* (London, 1910), 450.
3. O'Brien, *An Olive Branch in Ireland*, 445.
4. D. D. Sheehan, *Ireland Since Parnell* (London, 1921), 213.
5. Warwick-Haller, *William O'Brien and the Irish Land War*, 257.
6. MacDonagh, *The Life of William O'Brien*, 182.
7. O'Brien, *An Olive Branch in Ireland*, 445, 451.
8. Sheehan, *Ireland Since Parnell*, 213.
9. O'Brien, *Evening Memories*, 489.
10. National Folklore Collection, The Schools Collection, vol. 263, 135.
11. David Seth Jones, 'Land reform legislation and security of tenure in Ireland after independence', *Éire-Ireland*, vol. 32 and vol. 33, no. 4, Winter 1997/no. 1–2, Spring/Summer, 116.
12. Tony Varley, 'Gaining ground, losing ground', 30.
13. Jim Gilligan, 'A Lovely Wilderness of Grass: The Graziers of Rural Meath before the Great War' in Arlene Crampsie and Francis Ludlow, *Meath: History and Society* (Dublin, 2015), 605.
14. William Bulfin, *Rambles in Eirinn* (Dublin, 1927), 89.
15. Moritz Bonn, *Modern Ireland and Her Agrarian Problem* (Dublin, 1906), 35–6.
16. Oliver Coogan, *Politics and War in Meath, 1913–1923* (Navan, 2013), 23.
17. Gilligan, 'A Lovely Wilderness of Grass', 624, 628.
18. David Seth Jones, 'The cleavage between graziers and peasants in the land struggle, 1890–1910' in Clark and Donnelly, *Irish peasants, violence and political unrest*, 382.
19. Michael D. Higgins and John P. Gibbons, 'Shopkeeper-graziers and land

agitation in Ireland, 1895–1900' in P. J. Drudy (ed.), *Ireland: Land, Politics and People* (Cambridge, 1982), 93.

20. Jones, 'The cleavage between graziers and peasants', 377–8.

21. Jones, 'The cleavage between graziers and peasants', 3–901.

22. Kevin O'Shiel, Bureau of Military History Witness Statement #1770, 929.

23. Jones, 'The cleavage between graziers and peasants', 381.

24. Higgins and Gibbons, 'Shopkeeper-graziers and land agitation in Ireland, 1895–1900', 93, and David S. Jones, 'The cleavage between graziers and peasants', 379.

25. John O'Donovan, 'Class, conflict, and the United Irish League in Cork, 1900–1903', *Saothar*, vol. 37 (2012), 20.

26. Jones, 'The cleavage between graziers and peasants', 379.

27. *Midland Tribune*, 25 May 1907.

28. Jones, 'The cleavage between graziers and peasants', 387.

29. National Folklore Collection, The Schools Collection, vol. 1029, 54.

30. Jones, 'The cleavage between graziers and peasants', 383.

31. H. Brougham Leech, *1848 and 1912: The Continuity of the Irish Revolutionary Movement* (London, 1912), 78.

32. *New York Times*, 1 March 1908.

33. *Meath Chronicle*, 26 December 1908.

34. National Folklore Collection, the Schools' Collection, vol. 180, 80.

35. Patrick O'Reilly, Bureau of Military History, Witness Statement #1650, 4.

36. HC Deb, 16 March 1910, vol. 15, c. 357.

37. National Folklore Collection, The Schools Collection, vol. 703, 340.

38. Jones, 'The cleavage between graziers and peasants', 385.

39. Fergus Campbell, 'The Social Dynamics of Nationalist Politics in the West of Ireland 1898–1918', *Past & Present*, no. 182 (Feb. 2004), 192.

40. *Irish Times*, 15 October 1906.

41. Bulfin, *Rambles*, 91.

42. Jones, 'The cleavage between graziers and peasants', 405.

43. John O'Donovan, 'Class, conflict, and the United Irish League in Cork, 1900–1903', *Saothar*, 2012, vol. 37 (2012), 20.

44. John O'Donovan, 'Daniel Desmond Sheehan (1873–1948) and the rural labour question in Cork, 1894–1910' in Casey, *Defying the Law of the Land*, 229–30.

45. O'Brien, *An Olive Branch in Ireland*, 393.

46. O'Brien, *An Olive Branch in Ireland*, 435.

47. MacDonagh, *The Life of William O'Brien*, 181.

48. O'Brien, *An Olive Branch in Ireland*, 420.

49. Sheehan, *Ireland Since Parnell*, 214.

50. O'Brien, *An Olive Branch in Ireland*, 448, 446, 445.
51. Warwick-Haller, *William O'Brien and the Irish Land War*, 257.
52. *Dictionary of Irish Biography*, vol. 7, 90–4.
53. *Dictionary of Irish Biography*, vol. 7, 90–4.
54. MacDonagh, *The Life of William O'Brien*, 181.

Chapter 17: The Fourth Land War: land seizures during the War of Independence

1. Robert Lynd, *Home Life in Ireland* (London, 1909), 12, in Diarmaid Ferriter, *The Transformation of Ireland* (London, 2004), 63.
2. Tony Varley 'A Region of Sturdy Smallholders? Western Nationalists and Agrarian Politics during the First World War', *Journal of the Galway Archaeological and Historical Society*, vol. 55 (2003), 129.
3. M. A. G. Ó Tuathaigh, 'The land question, politics and Irish society, 1922–60', in Drudy (ed.), *Ireland: Land, Politics and People*, 169.
4. Fergus Campbell, *Land and Revolution: Nationalist Politics in the West of Ireland 1891–1921* (Oxford, 2007), 241.
5. Heather Laird, 'Patrick Hogan's memorandum on land seizures' in Darragh Gannon and Fearghal McGarry (eds), *Ireland 1922* (Dublin, 2022), 318.
6. Terence M. Dunne, 'Emergence from the Embers: The Meath and Kildare farm labour strike of 1919', 2019, *Saothar: Journal of Irish Labour History* (44), 59, 63.
7. Campbell, 'The Social Dynamics of Nationalist Politics in the West of Ireland', 193.
8. Fergus Campbell, *Land and Revolution: Nationalist Politics in the West of Ireland 1891–1921* (Oxford, 2007), 237.
9. Peter Hart, *The IRA at War* (Oxford, 2003), 17.
10. Fergus Campbell, 'The Social Dynamics of Nationalist Politics in the West of Ireland', 202.
11. Maurice Walsh, *Bitter Freedom: Ireland in a Revolutionary World* (New York and London, 2015), 179.
12. David Fitzpatrick, *Politics and Irish Life, 1913–1921: Provincial Experience of War and Revolution* (Cork, 1999), 101.
13. *Meath Chronicle*, 28 February 1920 (Dyas farm), 20 March 1920 (Liscarton estate).
14. Myles Dungan, *Four Killings* (London, 2021).
15. Tony Varley, 'Land, revolution and counter-revolution in the west', in Crowley, O'Drisceoil, Murphy (eds), *The Atlas of the Irish Revolution*, 495.
16. Fergus Campbell, *Land and Revolution*, 253.

17. Fergus Campbell, 'The Last Land War? Kevin O'Shiel's Memoir of the Irish Revolution (1916–21)', *Archivium Hibernicum*, vol. 57 (2003), 165.

18. Cahir Davitt, Bureau of Military History (BMH) Witness Statement, #993, 85.

19. Terence Dooley, 'The Burning of Irish Country Houses, 1920–21' in Crowley, O'Drisceoil, Murphy (eds) *The Atlas of the Irish Revolution*, 451.

20. Michael Hopkinson, *The Irish War of Independence* (Montreal, 2004), 20.

21. See the statements of Boylan himself, BMH-WS #1715, Sean Farrelly BMH-WS #1734 and Séamus Finn, BMH-WS #1060.

22. Sean Farrelly, BMH-WS #1734, 14.

23. Peadar O'Donnell, *There Will Be Another Day* (Dublin, 1963), 19–20.

24. I am obliged to Padraig Óg Ó Ruairc for this account of the murder of Murphy.

25. *The Irish Bulletin*, 'The Land agitation: a grave danger', August 1921, in Diarmaid Ferriter, *A Nation and Not a Rabble* (London, 2015), 232.

26. Terry Dunne, 'Cattle drivers, marauders, terrorists and hooligans', *History Ireland*, July/August 2020, vol. 28, no. 4, 33.

27. Dunne, 'Cattle drivers, marauders, terrorists and hooligans', 30.

28. Diarmaid Ferriter, *Between Two Hells: The Irish Civil War* (London, 2021), 71.

29. Ferriter, *A Nation and Not a Rabble*, 233.

30. Kevin O'Shiel, 'On the edge of anarchy', *Irish Times*, 23 November 1966.

31. Fergus Campbell, *Land and Revolution*, 251.

32. Kevin O'Shiel, 'No contempt of court', *Irish Times*, 21 November 1966.

33. Kevin O'Shiel, BMH-WS, #1770, 1061.

34. Fergus Campbell, *Land and Revolution*, 241.

35. Tony Varley, 'Land, revolution and counter-revolution in the west', 496.

36. Statement of Kevin O'Shiel, Bureau of Military History Witness Statement #1770, 975.

37. Kevin O'Shiel, BMH-WS #1770, 1010–12.

38. Tony Varley, 'Land, revolution and counter-revolution in the west', 496.

39. Terence Dooley, 'The Burning of Irish Country Houses, 1920–21' in Crowley, O'Drisceoil, Murphy (eds), *The Atlas of the Irish Revolution*, 447–53.

40. Dooley is citing James Donnelly Jr, 'Big House burnings in County Cork', *Eire-Ireland*, vol. 47, no. 3–4, fall/winter 2012, 182.

41. David Fitzpatrick, 'The geography of Irish nationalism, 1910–1921', *Past and Present*, 78 (1978), 119, in Campbell, *Land and Revolution: Nationalist Politics in the West of Ireland 1891–1921*.

42. Dooley, 'The Burning of Irish Country Houses, 1920–21', 452.

43. Terence Dooley, 'Burning down the Big House', *Irish Times*, 2 May 2023.

44. *Meath Chronicle*, 18 June 1921.
45. Deaths registered in the district of Athboy, the union of Trim, in the county of Meath, 1921.
46. *Drogheda Independent*, 30 July 1921.
47. *Meath Chronicle*, 6 June 1925.
48. *Meath Chronicle*, 1 October 1921.
49. Military Court of Inquiry, File #2/50600/88, 13 July 1921, WO35/102260023/00029.
50. Tom Garvin, *Nationalist Revolutionaries in Ireland, 1858–1928* (Dublin, 2005), 90.

Chapter 18: 'One more cow, one more sow, one more acre under the plough': land and the Irish Free State

1. Michael Collins to Director of Intelligence, 10 August 1922, MP, P7/B/4, in Eunan O'Halpin, *Defending Ireland: The Irish State and Its Enemies Since 1922* (Oxford, 1999), 34.
2. Patrick J. Hogan, Dáil debates, vol. 2, c. 607, 5 January 1923.
3. In Ciaran O'Reilly, 'Unveiling the Land Commission', *Irish Independent*, 8 August 2023. It should be noted that Brennan made this statement in 1990 about a career that began in 1952, but his sentiments are applicable to any of the previous three decades.
4. Military Archives, Department of Defence, A. 07869, in Heather Laird, 'Patrick Hogan's memorandum on land seizures "'Agrarian anarchy": Containing the land war', in Darragh Gannon and Fearghal McGarry (eds), *Ireland 1922* (Dublin, 2022), 319.
5. Laird, 'Patrick Hogan's memorandum on land seizures', 318.
6. M. A. G. O'Tuathaigh, 'The land question, politics and Irish society, 1922–60', in Drudy (ed.), *Ireland: Land, Politics and People*, 172.
7. Joan M. Cullen, 'Patrick J. Hogan, TD, Minister for Agriculture, 1922–1932: a study of a leading member of the first government of independent Ireland' (PhD thesis, Dublin City University, 1993), 12.
8. Terence Dooley, 'Land and politics in independent Ireland, 1923–48: The case for reappraisal', *Irish Historical Studies*, xxxiv, no. 134 (Nov. 2004), 177.
9. Terence M. Dunne, 'Emergence from the Embers: The Meath and Kildare farm labour strike of 1919', 2019, *Saothar: Journal of Irish Labour History* (44), 59.
10. Ferriter, *Between Two Hells*, 111.
11. Heather Laird, 'Patrick Hogan's memorandum on land seizures', 321.
12. Memo dated 11 January 1923, submitted to Army Inquiry 1924, UCD Mulcahy Papers P/7/C/21 in 'Rough and ready work: The Special Infantry

Corps', John Dorney, *The Irish Story*, www.theirishstory.com/2015/10/15/rough-and-ready-work-the-special-infantry-corps/#_ednref5 – accessed 17 October 2022. Dorney's blog on the SIC is an excellent and easily accessible account of a largely forgotten unit of the Free State Army.

13. National Army Dublin Command Intelligence Report Numbers 12–16 cw/ops/07/16, in John Dorney, *The Irish Story*.
14. Anthony Kinsella, 'The Special Infantry Corps', *The Irish Sword*, issue 82, Winter 1997, 333–4.
15. Kinsella, 'The Special Infantry Corps', 334–5.
16. Terence Dooley, 'Land and politics in independent Ireland, 1923–48', 180.
17. Patrick J.Hogan, Dáil debates, vol. 2, c. 607, 5 January 1923.
18. L. Perry Curtis Jr, 'Demonising the Irish landlords since the famine' in Casey, *Defying the Law of the Land*, 30.
19. Professor Terence Dooley, 'The 1923 Land Act and its Historical Significance', *Irish Independent*, 9 August 2023.
20. Comerford, *Ireland*, 266.
21. Dooley, *The Land for the People*, 3.
22. Terence Dooley, 'Land and politics in independent Ireland, 1923–48', 180.
23. David Seth Jones, 'Land reform legislation and security of tenure in Ireland after independence', *Éire-Ireland*, vol. 32 and vol. 33, no. 4, Winter 1997/no. 1–2, Spring/Summer, 118.
24. Elizabeth R. Hooker, *Readjustments of Agricultural Tenure in Ireland* (Chapel Hill, 1938), 103.
25. Terence Dooley, 'The 1923 Land Act and its Historical Significance', *Irish Independent*, 9 August 2023.
26. Dooley, *The Land for the People*, 107.
27. Gearóid Ó Tuathaigh, 'Irish Land Questions in the State of the Union', in Fergus Campbell and Tony Varley (eds), *Land Questions in Modern Ireland*, 3.
28. Cullen, 'Patrick J. Hogan, TD, Minister for Agriculture, 1922–1932', 4.
29. Ferriter, *The Transformation of Ireland*, 315.
30. Dooley, *The Land for the People*, 97.
31. Jones, 'Land reform legislation and security of tenure in Ireland after independence', 121.
32. Terence Dooley, 'Land and politics in independent Ireland, 1923–48', 177.
33. David Gahan, *The Land Annuities Agitation in Ireland 1926–32* (PhD thesis, Maynooth University, 2017), 13.
34. F. S. L. Lyons, *Ireland Since the Famine* (Glasgow, 1978), 502.
35. Tony Varley, 'Gaining ground, losing ground', 36.
36. Ó Tuathaigh, The land question, politics and Irish society, 1922', 177 and Tony Varley, 'Gaining ground, losing ground', 183.

37. Ferriter, *The Transformation of Ireland*, 359.
38. Jones, 'Land reform legislation and security of tenure in Ireland after independence', 131, 122, 131.
39. Jones, 'Land reform legislation and security of tenure in Ireland after independence', 139.
40. Terence Dooley, 'Land and politics in independent Ireland, 1923–48', 192.
41. Tom Garvin, *Preventing the Future: Why Was Ireland So Poor for So Long?* (Dublin, 2004), 35.
42. Terence Dooley, 'The Irish Land Commission and its records', *Irish Independent*, 9 August 2023.
43. Terence Dooley, *The Land for the People*, 69–70.
44. Tony Varley, 'Gaining ground, losing ground', 37.
45. Terence Dooley, 'Land and politics in independent Ireland, 1923–48', 186.
46. Tony Varley, 'Gaining ground, losing ground', 32.
47. Deputy Gearóid O'Sullivan, Dáil Éireann, 2 May 1928, vol. 23, no.7.
48. Terence Dooley, '*The Land for the People*', 137.
49. Ferriter, *Between Two Hells*, 70.
50. Terence Dooley, 'The Irish Land Commission and its records', *Irish Independent*, 9 August 2023.
51. *Report of Coimisiún na Gaeltachta* (Dublin 1926), 45, in Dooley, '*The Land for the People*', 138.
52. Martin O'Halloran, *The Lost Gaeltacht: The Land Commission Migration – Clonbur, County Galway to Allenstown, County Meath* (Meath, 2020), 88.
53. Barry Sheppard, 'Rathcairn: Land and language reform in the Irish Free State', *The Irish Story*, www.theirishstory.com/2012/07/13/rath-cairn-land-reform-language-politics-in-the-irish-free-state/#4 – accessed 21 October 2022.
54. *Irish Independent*, 17 November 1938.
55. Dooley, *The Land for the People*, 144.
56. Terence Dooley, 'Migration schemes to County Meath, 1923–48', *Irish Independent*, 8 August 2023, 'The forgotten Gaeltacht: Meath's "colonists" feature in a new film', *Meath Chronicle*, 22 March 2019.
57. *Meath Chronicle*, 18 June 1938.
58. Dooley, *The Land for the People*, 144.
59. 'The forgotten Gaeltacht: Meath's "colonists" feature in a new film', *Meath Chronicle*, 22 March 2019.
60. Terence Dooley, 'Land and politics in independent Ireland, 1923–48', 184.
61. *Irish Independent*, 7 June 2018.
62. Martin O'Halloran, *The Lost Gaeltacht*, 126.
63. Martin O'Halloran, *The Lost Gaeltacht*, 257.
64. *Irish Times*, 1 January 2022.

65. Ferriter, *The Transformation of Ireland*, 314.
66. Ó Tuathaigh, 'The land question, politics and Irish society', 179
67. Dáil debates, vol. 44, cc. 1928–9, 17 November 1932, in Martin O'Donoghue, *The Legacy of the Irish Parliamentary Party in Independent Ireland, 1922–49* (Liverpool, 2019), 146.
68. Davitt, *The Fall of Feudalism in Ireland*, 155.
69. Tony Varley, 'The politics of "holding the balance": Irish farmers' parties and land redistribution in the twentieth century' in Fergus Campbell and Tony Varley, *Land Questions in Modern Ireland* (Manchester, 2013), 245 (Kindle edition).
70. Joseph Lee, *Ireland 1912–85, Politics and Society* (Cambridge, 1989), 178.
71. Ferriter, *Between Two Hells*, 211.
72. Ó Tuathaigh, 'The land question, politics and Irish society', 184.
73. Tony Varley, 'The politics of "holding the balance"', 246.
74. Ó Tuathaigh, 'The land question, politics and Irish society', 186.

Conclusion

1. Ó Tuathaigh, 'The land question, politics and Irish society', 178.
2. Tony Varley, 'Gaining ground, losing ground' (Kindle edition), 26.
3. Joseph Lee, 'The Land War' in Liam de Paor (ed.), *Milestones in Irish History* (Cork, 1986), 115.
4. Michael Laffan, *The Resurrection of Ireland: The Sinn Féin party, 1916–1923* (Cambridge, 1999), 315.
5. Garvin, *Preventing the Future*, 36–7.
6. Guldi, *The Long Land War* (Kindle edition), 40.
7. Campbell and Varley, *Land Questions in Modern Ireland*, Kindle version, location 269.
8. Joseph Lee, 'The Ribbonmen' in Williams (ed.) *Secret Societies in Ireland*, 35.
9. Guldi, *The Long Land War* (Kindle edition), 29–30.

Image Credits

Page 59: © Look and Learn / Bridgeman Images
Page 149: Photo by Kean Collection/Getty Images
Page 154: Mary Evans Picture Library
Page 177: The Picture Art Collection / Alamy Stock Photo
Page 191: Photo by HultonArchive/Illustrated London News/Getty Images
Page 233: Photo by: Photo12/Universal Images Group via Getty Images
Page 249: Photo by: Universal History Archive/Universal Images Group via Getty Images
Page 258: Photo by Universal History Archive/Getty Images
Page 276: akg images/J. Sorges
Page 286: Reprodcued with Panhandle-Plains Historical Museum, Canyon, Texas
Page 302: Antiqua Print Gallery / Alamy Stock Photo
Page 308: The Print Collector / Alamy Stock Photo
Page 310: Boris15 / Shutterstock
Page 319: Photo by The Cartoon Collector/Print Collector/Getty Images
Page 325: Punch Cartoon Library / TopFoto
Page 327: Rogers Fund, 1966 / The Metropolitan Museum of Art
Page 341: History collection 2016 / Alamy Stock Photo
Page 342: Photo by Hulton Archive/Getty Images
Page 343: Look and Learn / Illustrated Papers Collection / Bridgeman Images
Page 356: DEA / BIBLIOTECA AMBROSIANA / Getty Images
Page 360: Look and Learn / Illustrated Papers Collection / Bridgeman Images
Page 377: This image is reproduced courtesy of the National Library of Ireland [ALB40 /36]
Page 385: Look and Learn / Peter Jackson Collection / Bridgeman Images
Page 392: Archive PL / Alamy Stock Photo
Page 396: Photo by Hulton Archive/Getty Images
Page 402: Photo by: Alexander Bassano/Pictures from History/Universal Images Group via Getty Images

Page 409: This image is reproduced courtesy of the National Library of Ireland [EB_2662]

Page 425: This image is reproduced courtesy of the National Library of Ireland [EB_2664]

Page 446: VTR / Alamy Stock Photo

Page 457: DEA / ICAS94 / Contributor

Page 458: Photo by: HUM Images/Universal Images Group via Getty Images

Page 474: Svintage Archive / Alamy Stock Photo

Page 484: Photo: Frank Cogan

Page 507: James Schwabel / Alamy Stock Photo

Index

Page numbers for illustrations are in *italics*.

Peel and 160
replace Whiteboys 74
RIC and 324
violence and 13, 15, 186, 361
Richmond, Charles Gordon-
Lennox, 6th Duke of 335, 348
Rightboys 15, 62, 63, 95–8, 112–25,
126
Riot Act (1787) 62, 123
Riverstown, Co. Sligo 473
Rockites 18, 150, 154, 155–88
Roman Catholic Ascendancy 216
Roman Catholics
forced to flee from Armagh 125,
127
forced to support C of I 84, 193
hierarchical denunciations 120
Land league and 24
'native' 22, 23
Orange order and 301
Presbyterians and 451
Tonna on 164
See also Catholic Church
Roosevelt, Franklin D. 554
'Rory of the Hills' 298–9, 348
Roscommon, County 240–1, 275–6,
502–3, 505
Rossa, Jeremiah O'Donovan 340
Ross, William and James 80
Rouse, Paul 548
Royal Artillery 220
Royal County see Meath, County
Royal Dublin Society (RDS) 229
Royal Engineers 220, 221
Royal Irish Constabulary (RIC)
190–2, 512–14
agrarian agitation 500
attending ejectments 407
Bodyke evictions 411, 413–14, 417,
421–3, 427, 429–30
cattle driving and 473
Curtin family and 370
disbanded 524
evidence data 26, 351
Gordon and 497

informers 377
IRA and 493
Mitchelstown Massacre 404
protection officers 309, 363, 412
Ranch War and 476
Ribbonmen and 324
United Irishman 340
Royal Welsh Fusiliers 411, 421, 423,
427
Ruane, Thady 385
rundale system 19, 70–2
Russell, Sir Charles 361, 368
Russell, Lord John 23, 180, 242, 248,
251–2, 274, 284
Russell, Thomas Wallace (T. W.)
429, 451–3, 455, 465
rustling, livestock 278
Ryan, James 535
Ryan, John 366
Ryan, Fr John 141
Ryder, Archdeacon William 215

Sadleir, John 307–8, 308
St Albans, Beatrix Beauclerk,
Duchess of 472
St John, New Brunswick 270, 273,
277
St John, Pete, 'The Fields of
Athenry' 249
Salisbury, Robert Gascoyne-Cecil,
3rd Marquess of 22, 382, 386,
394–5, 397, 415, 442, 447
Savage, Richard 106, 111
Scariff, Co. Clare 412–13, 425
Scrope, George Poulett 260
Scully, Vincent 293, 298
Scully, William 295–9, 321
secret societies, agrarian 11, 73–4,
95–8, 203, 481
Sedgwick, Adam 235
Sennett, Graham 505
Seoighe, Maolra (Myles Joyce) see
Joyce, Myles (Maolra Seoighe)
separatism, Irish 27, 330, 332, 341,
560, 561

Sullivan, Alexander Martin (A. M.)
295, 351
Sullivan, Arthur 465
Sullivan, Jerry 258
Sullivan, Timothy 369–70, 370
Sweeney, Michael 545
Swift, Jonathan 64, 551

Tablet, The 304, 309
Talbot, James, Lord 326
Talbot, John 368–9
Talbot-Ponsonby, Charles William
391
'Tallaght Races' (1867) 63
Tambora eruption (1815) 144, 159
Tapt, Anne 156, 157
Tasmania 311
Taylor, A. J. P. 244
Taylor, Thomas 54
Templepatrick, Belfast 93–4, 105
'tenant' (definitions) 12–13
tenant farmers 74–6
affluent 337
credit and 24
legislation and 440
Levellers and 82
modest 26, 69–70, 96, 280
numbers 25
rack-renting and 234
tithe payments 197
Tithe War 194
'year zero' value 198
Tenant League 13, 127, 289, 301–10
'tenant on tenant' violence (1880s)
356–80
Tenant Relief Bill (1886) 387–8, 399
Tenant Right Association, Ulster
304
'tenant rights' 13
tenants, landlords and (1848–78)
288–300
Tenement Valuation (1846) 230
Terry Alts 174, 190
Thomastown, Co. Kilkenny 119
Thornton, Patrick 146

'3 Fs' (fair rent, fixity of tenure and
free sale) 13, 305, 348
Three Hundred Years' War 556–63
'Three Sisters' basin 307
Tiernan, Michael 147
Times Commission (1888) 359–80,
360
Times, The 180, 297–8, 361–2, 368,
379–80, 396, 448, 464
Tipperary, County
Adair and 292
anti-Shanavest ballad 131
Ballingarry 142, 313
Ballyporeen 79
Butt on 77
Caravat-Shanavest 'war' 137, 138,
139–42
Cashel 124, 138
Clonmel 85, 89, 138
Drumlummin 80
famine clearances 263–4
Fethard 138
Golden 139
Lord Lismore and 261
martial law 175
'murder' county 134, 139–42, 170
'New Tipperary' 399, 400–1, 418,
451
Rightboys in 122, 124
Scully and 296
Special Commission trials 136,
142
tenant farmers 74–5
Tenant League 306
Toomevara 263–4
Whiteboys in 79, 82, 83, 84, 116,
133
Young Ireland raid 313
Tipperary Vindicator 264
Tithe Composition Act (1823) 187,
195–8
tithe-farmers 78, 79, 84, 95–6, 179, 183
tithe proctor 16, 206
Tithe Rentcharge (Ireland) Act
(1838) 215–16